Cut to the Chaise Lounge

or

I Can't Believe I Swallowed the Remote!

The Best Movie Reviews of

Dennis Littrell

in Categories with Lists, Quizzes and More!

Readers are hereby advised that many of the reviews in this book contain spoilers. This book is primarily about sharing reactions and apprciations and as a way to give readers an idea of what somebody else thought of the films they have viewed.

This is dedicated to the memory of my mother who loved movies, and to the stars, the directors, the bit players, the writers, the camera people, the technicians, the producers, and, yes, the film critics who have enriched our lives with their art.

Table of Contents

Chapter One:

Best Picture Oscar Winners

and

Some Others that Might Have Won

Here are thirty movies worthy of the coveted Oscar for Best Picture. Fifteen of them won, and fifteen did not. See if you can guess which movies won.

Consider yourself a film buff if, off the top of your head, you can get half of them right.

Some of the movies that won are not so well thought of today, and some of the movies that lost are highly regarded, so much so, that if today's Academy voted, the results might be different.

For a bonus, see if you can name the three films on this list that weren't even nominated.

Here are the 30 titles in alphabetical order. Checkmark which ones you think won.

2001: A Space Odyssey (1968)
All About Eve (1950)
American Beauty (1999)
Apocalypse Now (1979)
A Beautiful Mind (2001)
Chicago (2002)
Crash (2004)
Driving Miss Daisy (1989)
Dr. Strangelove, or: How I Learned to Stop Worrying and Love the Bomb (1964)
Elizabeth (1998)
The English Patient (1996)
The Godfather (1972)
The Graduate (1967)
Il Postino (1994)
The Last Picture Show (1971)
Memento (2000)
Million Dollar Baby (2004)
Mister Roberts (1955)
My Fair Lady (1964)
The Pianist (2002)
Platoon (1986)
Roman Holiday (1953)
Schindler's List (1993)
Shakespeare in Love (1998)

A Streetcar Named Desire (1951)
Sunset Boulevard (1950)
The Thin Man (1934)
The Third Man (1949)
Titanic (1997)
The Treasure of the Sierra Madre (1948)

Here are the reviews. The number after the title (1 for horrible through 10 for a great film) is the number of stars I gave the movie. You might want to cross out my number and put in your number. Following each review I reveal whether it was a Best Picture Oscar winner or not, and if not, which picture won, and the nominees.

2001: A Space Odyssey (1968) 10

Still a masterpiece

Regardless of how "bored" some (probably adolescent) viewers may become (forced to maintain their attention span over vast minutes of time on something other than sex, car chases and dripping blood), this is obviously a great movie. At least for the rest of us. Rated in the top 250 at the Internet Movie Database (imdb.com), and the subject of innumerable articles and reviews, Stanley Kubrick's much studied and admired visual, artistic and thematic masterpiece, based on the novel by Arthur C. Clarke, is still—remarkably, after all these years—a mesmerizing motion picture experience even on a television screen.

This is no mean accomplishment when you realize that Kubrick made his film before humans actually walked on the moon in 1969, and furthermore, when you consider how much more we now know about space travel and how much more advanced special effects have become. What I think contemporary movie makers might learn from Kubrick's work is (1) special effects without rhyme or reason may titillate first time viewers and the very young, but quickly grow meaningless; and (2) even in a movie that relies heavily upon special effects and ideas—which *2001: A Space Odyssey* certainly does—it helps a whole lot to have a story to tell.

The story begins in the prehistory and ends in the future. It begins with a pre-human consciousness and ends in mystery. (Note that the last sequence in the movie is labeled in part as being "beyond the infinite"—whatever that metaphysical notion may mean.) Along the way we have a creditable hero (Astronaut Dave Bowman played by Keir Dullea, whom I also recall from *David and Lisa*, 1962) and a very cold and merciless villain (HAL 9000, the computer as megalomaniac—apparently his makers never heard of Issac Asimov's rules for robots!).

Today we know more about pre-humans and more about computers, artificial intelligence and space exploration, and with such knowledge today's movie makers would avoid some of Kubrick's mistakes. For example, the spacecraft was far too roomy (ask the astronauts!). Real space ships must be as small as possible to save fuel and they are incredibly cramped. Also, the year 2001 has come and passed, and we are nowhere near the practical capability of providing artificial gravity in space. And of course computers (or robots) don't have emotions unless such emotions are built or programmed into them.

Yet the visual sense of space and the terrible isolation of being alone in the vast vacuum has never been conveyed so well. Using music synchronized with visual effects laden with meaning for our earth-bound minds and bodies, Kubrick managed to depict the Pythagorean "music of the spheres" in a most splendiferous and awe-inspiring way.

However, the opening sequence with the hairy apes is probably what Kubrick would most like to redo if he had the opportunity. In the first place, the terrain, which is semi-arid, is all wrong. No hairy, long-armed, bent-legged creature would occupy such a landscape. The "foraging" they were supposed to be doing was ludicrous since there was obviously next to nothing to forage. The tapirs (forest-dwelling animals native to South America and Southeast Asia, by the way, and not to the savannas of Africa, which should have been the terrain depicted) were almost comically fat for the ecosystem. And the apes themselves, looking and acting a lot like chimpanzees (no doubt the model that Kubrick used), are in conflict with the fossil record as we know it. Our primordial ancestors, the australopithecines, were upright walking apes and probably not exceedingly hairy since they needed to sweat as they walked and ran over the savannas and grasslands of East Africa.

As for using bones as weapons, yes, there can be little doubt that that is what our ancestors learned to do, followed by using hard wood and stones and then shaped stones. And the idea that a bone tool is a proto-type for all the tools to come is also correct, most saliently in the form of the space ship and HAL.

An interpretation of the ending would necessarily include the idea of time as being something other than we think it is. We see Dave as an astronaut in his thirties, and then as a middle-aged man dining in something like a very expensive Parisian apartment, and then on his death bed, and finally as a soon-to-be-born fetus returning to earth. I think it was wise of Kubrick not to attempt to explain what he clearly points to as unexplainable, as "beyond the infinite."

Perhaps the most haunting image of all, at least for me, is the red and yellow "eye" of the HAL 9000 computer as it coldly viewed the two astronauts talking. Therein was expressed, long before it became fashionable, the coming inexorable conflict between us and our machines, between our culture and our biological nature, between natural and artificial intelligence. Never in the history of cinema has that tension been so concisely conveyed as in that scene and in this movie.

See this for Stanley Kubrick, one of the greatest film makers of all time.

Loser. *Oliver! (1968), starring Ron Moody and directed by Carol Reed, won.*
Also nominated:
Funny Girl (1968)
The Lion in Winter (1968)
Rachel, Rachel (1968)
Romeo and Juliet (1968/I)

*Comment: Today, with almost forty years to think it over, most people would say the Academy made the wrong choice. And the fact that 2001: A Space Odyssey **wasn't even nominated** is surprising. Stanley Kubrick did get nominated as Best Director, but Carol Reed also won that award.*

All about Eve (1950) 10

Classic story; classic performances

When I was a kid I would go to the second-run movie theater virtually every Saturday and watch three features, a cartoon and a newsreel indiscriminately. It was all wonderful to me (although I would hide bashfully behind the seat during the love scenes). I would come out of the theater several hours later (sometimes watching one of the features twice) amazed at what I'd seen and changed forever.

The first adult movie that really held my interest though was *All About Eve*. Such is the power of the all too human story and how directly and clearly it is told from a celebrated script and some sublime direction by Joseph L. Mankiewicz. Bette Davis who was then, by Hollywood standards for actresses, an ancient 41-years-old but not yet halfway through a 58-year movie career, stars as Margo Channing, a New York stage actress feeling very heavily the loss of her splendid youth. Eve Harrington is played with a veiled duplicity by Anne Baxter in a breakout role. I sat with fascination, understanding perfectly how and why she had insinuated herself into Margo's life, and on the edge of my seat to find out what would become of her. Yes, a child may well know of such matters, and it is to the credit of Mankiewicz and everyone involved in the production that a movie could be made that would inform and fire the imagination of a ten-year-old boy while at the same time intrigue and entertain adults. Ah, if only they made "chick flicks" like this today!

Of course, *All About Eve* is more than a chick flick even though the men, Bill Sampson (Gary Merrill) as Margo's beau, and Lloyd Richards (Hugh Marlowe) as a writer (and husband of Margo's best friend, Karen, played by Celest Holm) headed for Hollywood, take a back seat to the main action which is the playing out of the eternal power struggle between (take your pick: they all fit psychologically): youth and age, the daughter and the mother, the bride and the mother-in-law, the upstart and the established talent, the new and the old.

Bette Davis is excellent of course, and the role fits her like a glove. But what transfixed me as a child was the contrast between the wholesome good looks of Anne Baxter and her sneaky treachery. Could someone so pretty be so bad? I may have wondered who I would have preferred for a mother, Davis or Baxter, and perhaps have come away not knowing. For Bette Davis the luster had gone from those famous eyes, and so it was only natural that her character Margo feared the loss of love from men. Even that I understood as a child. And in Baxter, youth would be served and perhaps she could be forgiven the lies because time does not stand still for anyone, especially it does not stand still for a starlet.

Notable in supporting roles are Thelma Ritter and George Sanders, the former as Margo's maid and alter-ego Birdie, the latter as the cynical and barbed theater critic, Addison DeWitt (named perhaps with the 17th/18th century Brit wit and essayist Joseph Addison in mind), who escorts about town none other than a not-so-dumb blonde named Marilyn Monroe in her screen debut. The script, resplendent with some very sharp one-liners, was adapted from the story, "The Wisdom of Eve" (a bit of irony-on-the-square in the title perhaps) by Mary Orr and of course became the Broadway musical *Applause* (not yet a movie). Mankiewicz won Oscars for both his script and his direction, and Sanders won for Best Supporting Actor while the movie itself won for Best Picture over such fine films as *Sunset Boulevard* and *Born Yesterday*. Both Davis and Baxter were nominated for Best Actress but lost out to Judy Holliday in *Born Yesterday*.

Bottom line: one of the great stories of the theater, a classic Hollywood film not to be missed.

Winner.
Also nominated:
Born Yesterday (1950)
Father of the Bride (1950)
King Solomon's Mines (1950)
Sunset Boulevard (1950)

Comment: Tough choice between All About Eve and Sunset Boulevard. Today it would still be a tough choice.

American Beauty (1999) 10

Middle-aged crazy

Lester Burnham (Kevin Spacey) is your usual well-behaved 42-year-old dreg of an American dad until he spots his teenaged daughter's girlfriend, Angela Hayes (Mena Suvari) whose beauty transforms him. Part of the fun of this very funny and enjoyable movie is watching Lester break out of his self-imposed shell and blossom with the rose petals as he tells everybody what he really thinks as though he had nothing to lose.

His daughter Jane is a brooding raven-haired beauty who likes to put on a white-powdered face and red Betty Boop lips to go with her full figure. Thora Birch, who plays Jane, has a face that can mesmerize, and Director Sam Mendes puts her to work mesmerizing us.

Annette Bening, in a comedic tour de force, plays Lester's wife Carolyn, a straitlaced, uptight, worry wart who sells real estate. Next door we have, just moving in, 18-year-old Ricky Fitts, played with sly self-assurance by Wes Bentley, the dope-dealing, Bible-suit wearing, photog son of Marine Corps Colonel Frank Fitts and his mostly catatonic wife. Two houses down there's Jim and Jim, your smiling yuppie fruit loops and all-around neighborhood sweet guys. They are however an embarrassment to Colonel Fitts who is living in the deep, dark corner of a very large denial closet, paranoid to the teeth that his only son has inherited the same shameful desires and will act them out. In an effort to keep Ricky disciplined and on the straight and narrow, the good Colonel practices various forms of child abuse ranging from bare-knuckle beatings to medicated imprisonment.

In other words what we have here is your typical American suburban street. What makes *American Beauty* a great success is a witty script with a deep and beautiful lesson for our age by Alan Ball, superb direction by Sam Mendes and outstanding performances from just about everybody in the cast. Bening is brilliant with her silly finger gestures and her one foot sideways stance, like a fawn just learning to walk, and her squinty little eyes full of merriment, and that raised and then downward pointing index finger of indignant reproof. (But she really needs to keep her pretty shins off the bedposts or at least off the wall.) Mena Suvari is perhaps no more beautiful than any number of other screen darlings, but she has a litany of sexy expressions and poses that inspire delight. Her portrayal of a fast lane teen siren whose talk is bigger than her experience is just perfect. She might be a budding star.

But more than anything this is an uplifting and satisfying tale of an unappreciated, unloved and mostly ignored man who is inspired to transform his life by the beauty of a girl. For many people (and for most women, I would wager) falling in love at first sight with a teenaged girl just because she is beautiful is shallow and beside the point, inappropriate and not fair. But women love men for their power and their strength and their standing in society. Is that fair to those men who have none? Lester's love for Angela was so great that it transcended carnality, but he didn't know that until he began to take off her clothes and then he realized something very beautiful. He could love her without making love to her. If he took advantage of her youth and inexperience, it would cheapen his love for her and possibly destroy it. Maybe some people in the audience felt he wasn't a real man because he stopped, but I tend to feel the opposite. Not that I think there is anything wrong with making love to 18-year-old girls (on the contrary); but if the girl is incapable of experiencing that love, then perhaps it is better to love her from afar without a sexual expression, even at the risk of disappointing her, especially if you're old enough to be her father, and especially if you really do love her. Notice that in the next scene she is bored and for her the magic of sexuality is gone. He might as well *be* her father.

So much of what we are presented through the media is a focus on those males who would only be able to express themselves in some sexually-exploitive manner. So much of what we read insists that this is the only way men are. I'm happy to say that *American Beauty* presents another point of view, and presents it beautifully.

The point made by the surprising ending (and the reason for the presence of the Marine colonel and the two gay guys) is that our contemporary "enlightened" society may recognize the legitimacy of homosexual love, but continues to hypocritically condemn the love of a man for a young girl.

Winner.
Also nominated:
The Cider House Rules (1999)
The Green Mile (1999)
The Insider (1999)
The Sixth Sense (1999)

Comment: American Beauty surprised, but there was no clear choice.

Apocalypse Now (1979) 10

Coppola's phantasmagoric ode to the madness of war

War is a kind of madness. It has its own logic. Kill or be killed. Follow orders, follow the leader. Go crazy. Do horrific things. Become a beast. Do all of this in a steamy jungle amid an alien culture for an unclear purpose in an ineffective way and you've got some idea of what Vietnam was like. Coppola's Vietnam is the Vietnam of a soldier's Thai stick/acid trip. The filming actually took place in the Philippines, but no matter: that's better than Kubrick's excellent Full Metal Jacket which was partially filmed on constructed sets in England of all places.

The jungle is dark and green and deep and unbelievable lush, filled with snakes and tigers, insects that bite and swarm, bats and spiders and little tan men who dig tunnels and can't be seen. You shoot at the jungle, and you shoot and shoot and shoot. And you can imagine the effect it has. Like trying to kill flies with a .357 Magnum. Which is what we tried to do in Vietnam.

Army Capt Ben Willard (Martin Sheen) on R and R in a Saigon hotel, going stir crazy, drinking Martell Cordon Bleu and passing out, gets a knock on the door. He has orders: go up river into Cambodia and terminate an army colonel (Marlon Brando) who has gone AWOL. Oh, and by the way, Colonel Kurtz in his charismatic madness has built his own little unauthorized empire in the jungle, fortified with crazed admirers. You might want to approach with caution.

So this is the plot: a quest to a forbidden land with fantastic adventures along the way providing us with a view of the war from a gunboat. The flares at night, the "purple haze," the tracers flying at the boat, the fog, the black nights, the little things the men do to retain some semblance of sanity, smoke a jay, polish your boots, reread a letter from home.

And then there is the ordinary madness of the war lover personified in Robert Duvall's swashbuckling army colonel who likes to take off his shirt and watch his men surf the waves as all about him bombs are bursting and bullets flying. But he never flinches because to flinch would show weakness and possibly a lack of love for what one is doing. In one of the most memorable lines in all of filmdom, Duvall declares, "I love the smell of napalm in the morning. It smells like victory."

Well, there was no victory. There was only the blood and the bombs, the jungle that could not be beaten back or Agent Orange'd enough, the mud and Charlie, always Charlie hidden somewhere, disguised or invisible and unkillable, like a hydra-headed monster, and dead bodies of your buddies on their way back to the land of the big PXs in body bags. And yet there is always the mission, and so upstream Willard goes. And the more he reads about Col Kurtz the more he admires the man. And then when he gets there, the question arises, how can he penetrate the Colonel's jungle fortress? He has been advised, belatedly, aboard the boat when it was too late to turn back and refuse the mission, that he had a predecessor,

someone else sent to terminate Colonel Kurtz. So Colonel Kurtz will know why you, Capt Willard, are coming to visit.

He calls you a messenger boy. You are put in a bamboo cage. A photojournalist (Dennis Hopper) turned worshipful admirer of the Colonel gives you water, lights a cigarette and puts it in your mouth. Delirious dreams and phantasmagoric nightmares, surreal imaginings and the haunting face of Kurtz and his poetry, quoting T.S. Eliot and Andrew Marvel, flood your mind. You have called an air strike should you not return, and then—was it a dream or was it real?—the head of the soldier who would call the strike is delivered to you on a banana leaf—something like that happened or didn't and maybe you will soon be, or already are, as mad as the Colonel.

Coppola and crew spent two years in the jungle filming this. It is a great epic of mystery and beauty, a fantastic picture of the war, part brutal reality, part imagined enchantment with fascinating characters indelibly spun out by one of the greatest of all film makers. By all means see this for Francis Ford Coppola, one of the few directors who could be considered a genius.

Loser. *Kramer vs. Kramer (1979), starring Dustin Hoffman and Meryl Streep and directed by Robert Benton, won.*
Also nominated:
All That Jazz (1979)
Breaking Away (1979)
Norma Rae (1979)

Comment: Kramer vs. Kramer was a clever and entertaining movie, but Apocalypse Now is the movie that is remembered today and will be remembered in the decades to come.

A Beautiful Mind (2001) 9

Excellent Hollywood version of the man and his madness

This resulted in four well-deserved Academy Awards in 2002: Best Picture for Brian Grazer and the people at Imagine Entertainment, Ron Howard for his direction, Jennifer Connelly for her supporting role, and Akive Goldsman for his script adapted from Sylvia Nasar's biography. It is a beautiful and touching movie, uplifting and full of a lot of things that Hollywood does very well.

Russell Crowe is believable as the arrogant yet vulnerable mathematician John Nash who fell into paranoid schizophrenia while an undergraduate at Princeton University. A philandering and selfish man who is paradoxically almost as lovable as Albert Einstein, Nash can also be humble and exhibit a wry, self-effacing sense of humor. To me he is a great hero, not because of his work in Game Theory for which he was awarded the Nobel Prize in Economics, but because he is one of the very few people ever to conquer, as it were, schizophrenia.

In the outstanding documentary from The American Experience PBS series, "A Brilliant Madness" (2002) Nash explains how he did it: he just stopped listening to the voices. The voices that the paranoid schizophrenic hears are inside his head and they are amazingly persuasive; the delusions are as compelling as monstrous personages come to life, vivid, demanding, in many ways more "real" than the reality we normally experience. So it really was heroic of John Nash to come to grips with his delusions and to mentally shove them aside. The vast majority of paranoid schizophrenics can never do that.

Yet the movie merely resembles his life and his singular experience. Goldsman's script and Howard's direction take the life of John Nash and distill the essence of his triumph while brushing aside many of the unpleasant and non-heroic details. I don't object to this because this movie is clearly aimed at the widest possible audience, and I appreciate the wisdom of that approach. But for those of you interested in a more comprehensive and objective picture of the man I can recommend both the documentary mentioned above and Nasar's biography. I especially found it valuable to view the one-hour documentary because to actually see the man and to hear him speak allowed me to better appreciate the fine performance by Russell Crowe.

I found Jennifer Connelly absolutely mesmerizing as Alicia (not to mention gorgeous). Ed Harris was a hardcore graphic nightmare as the unrelenting Parcher while Paul Bettany was intriguing and clever as Nash's nonexistent buddy. Howard's direction not only got excellent work from everybody, but he was able to bring the pathos and exhilaration of Nash's life to the audience in a very satisfying way emotionally. If you can watch this without shedding a tear or two you may want to check your synaptic connections. Incidentally the makeup work on Crowe and Connelly to allow us the illusion of the passing years was outstanding (and got an Oscar nomination).

The key to the movie and to Howard's vision is the way that the real world and the Nash's delusional world are meshed. It's clear he wanted to compel the audience to share the paranoid schizophrenic experience. While not a paranoid schizophrenic myself I have known people who are, and I have had similar, limited experiences myself under certain, shall we say, circumstances. The sheer terror that can sometimes be felt came through in the car chase scene (yes, Howard managed to get one in) while Nash's obsessive energy was revealed on the walls of the rooms that he had completely covered with pages from magazines that he had frantically searched looking for secret Soviet codes.

Some quibbles: while undergraduates loved beer then as they do now, they did not in 1946 go out for pizza, and if they had they would have called it "pizza pie." There were no pizza parlors and no pizza at the market. If you went to an Italian restaurant you had spaghetti or ravioli, and the pizza that was served was mostly bread with a thin topping of cheese and sauce, nothing like the great thin platters we have today.

New Zealander Russell Crowe's West Virginia accent faded in some scenes only to return strong in another. Incidentally he is not to be confused with Cameron Crowe, who wrote the script for Fast Times at Ridgemont High (1982) and directed such films as Jerry Maguire (1996) and Almost Famous (2000). Russell Crowe has starred in a number of excellent movies including Proof (1991), LA Confidential (1997), The Insider (1999), etc.

Also, no mention in the movie is made of Nash's homosexual experiences nor of his running away to Europe or his desire to renounce his US citizenship. I understand that Howard decided to leave out the homosexual angle because associating homosexuality with schizophrenia would open a can of worms that would detract from the theme of the movie. Also left out was Nash's other paternity with a woman he never married.

Nash is not a saint, but he is a hero, and this beautiful movie is a fine tribute to him and to his accomplishments.

Winner.
Also nominated:
Gosford Park (2001)
In the Bedroom (2001)
The Lord of the Rings: The Fellowship of the Ring (2001)
Moulin Rouge! (2001)

Chicago (2002) 8

Entertainment with an edge

This is a musical in the tradition of musicals that are entertaining and easy to digest, and yet some hours later leave one with some apprehension. Is it really the intent of the story to celebrate getting away with murder? Or is this movie a statement about how murder by women in emotionally trying circumstances can be justified? Or perhaps is this an indictment of the criminal justice system? Or is this just a spicy entertainment?

I'll opt for the latter; however I can tell you that women will find this more agreeable than their spouses. There is a kind of historically revisionist feeling to the sentiments expressed. I seriously doubt that this production, in which murder from jealousy is seemingly justified, would have been produced as a musical comedy before the modern era.

But never mind. What makes Bob Fosse's *Chicago* a hit (and the Academy's Best Picture of 2002) are the beautifully staged and choreographed song and dance numbers, the spiffy direction and neat editing, a lot of leggy flesh along with some fine performances by Queen Latifah, Catherine Zeta-Jones and Renée Zellweger.

In particular I liked Queen Latifah's performance. When she comes on singing "When You're Good to Momma" she just about brings the house down. I also liked her portrayal of the savvy and corrupt Boss Lady on Murderess Row. Zeta-Jones got the Oscar for best Supporting Actress, and she was good, but I think Latifah, who was also nominated, was just as impressive if not more so.

Zellweger, looking almost anorectic compared to the last time I saw her in *Bridget Jones's Diary* (2001)—released only the year before—gives a solid performance in a very demanding role, although to be honest, it appeared that she was doing a lot of lipsyncing. Still one is amazed at how good she and Zeta-Jones were at the old song and dance, not having been previous known for being twinkled-toed.

You might want to see this to compare how it stands up to a long line of filmland musicals, such as Oklahoma, South Pacific, Jesus Christ Superstar, The Phantom of the Opera, etc. Chicago certainly is well within the confines of that venerable traditional, although it is my feeling, that despite the Academy's favor, this is just a notch below the best.

Winner.
Also nominated:
Gangs of New York (2002)
The Hours (2002)
Lord of the Rings: The Two Towers, The (2002)
The Pianist (2002)
Comment: My choice was The Pianist.

Crash (2004) 10

Remarkable take on the clash of cultures in L.A.

Crash was a surprise winner of the Best Picture Oscar for 2006. It's a message movie and the Academy obviously liked the message. The message is that racial intolerance is untenable if you really stop to think about it and see people from some point of view other than your own.

What makes this work is a brilliant conception and adroit direction by John Haggis, a believable script by Haggis and Robert Moresco, and fine film editing by Hughes Winborne. All three won Oscars. They were able to preach, as it were, without preaching. By putting people in positions of racial and ethnic irony, they show us that racial prejudice is absurd. We see events that could happen to anyone regardless of race or ethnicity. We also see that supposed stereotypical behavior that we may hold against another race or ethnic group is sometimes exactly what we do ourselves. The movie points to the truth that everybody is prejudice in one way or another.

The story itself is about several people whose lives accidentally come together ("crash") in the ethnically and racially diverse, sprawling City of the Angels. There are two young black guys who could pass for UCLA students (they think since they're in the Westwood area) who hijack the SUV of an LA politico, Rick Cabot (Brendan Fraser) as he and his wife Jean Cabot (Sandra Bullock) are driving home. There's a double irony here because one of the guys is complaining that people are afraid of them because they're black in a white neighborhood even as they move toward the hijacking! Later we meet the mother of one of the black guys whose brother Graham (Don Cheadle) is an LAPD detective who tells his mother he's bedding a white woman, Ria (Jennifer Esposito) who he thinks is Mexican, oblivious of the fact that her parents are from Puerto Rico and El Salvador!

There's quite a bit of this ironic confusion about race and ethnicity in the movie, the point being that people tend to see others as stereotypes of skin color and language without really being aware of who that person is as an individual. A Persian shopkeeper is thought of as Arab. Hindus are thought to be Muslim. Thais are Chinese. Ignorance is the basis of racial and ethnic prejudice is part of Haggis's message. And he's right.

One of the most beautiful sequences in the movie begins when Shereen (Marina Sirtis) buys some bullets in a gun shop for her father, the Persian shopkeeper. (Pay attention to those bullets!) Later we see Daniel (Michael Pena) talking to his daughter Lara (Ashlyn Sanchez) who is hiding under her bed because she is afraid of the bullets that used to go off in her old neighborhood. Daniel gives her his invisible, impenetrable cloak to wear to protect her, taking it off and putting it around her. Later when the Persian shopkeeper comes hunting Daniel because he thinks Daniel tore up his store, Lara runs to protect her dad who no longer has the impenetrable cloak! I won't tell you want happens. You have got to see the sequence yourself.

Matt Dillon plays a racially prejudice cop who could pass for a young and less sophisticated real life ex-LAPD Det. Mark Fuhrman of O. J. Simpson trial infamy. He is the central character in another interesting sequence beginning with his groping shakedown of a black man's wife.

The stories meld together in a way that reflects how Los Angeles is a cultural melting pot—or is it a salad bowl? The stories that intertwine bring out the underlining preconceptions and prejudices of the people of that salad bowl (or melting pot) in a way that is more effective than a dissertation or documentary might be. Yes, there is some contrivance, but I think it's fair to write that off as poetic license.

Perhaps the most amazing thing about this movie is that although it won the Best Picture Oscar it only cost about $6-million to make. It's one of the most original films I've seen in quite a while and one of the most effective.

Winner.
Also nominated:

Brokeback Mountain (2005)
Capote (2005)
Good Night, and Good Luck. (2005)
Munich (2005)
Comment: Memoirs of a Geisha (2005) might have won had it been nominated. It won for Art Direction and Costume Design.

Driving Miss Daisy (1989) 10

Captivating story skillfully presented

Take an intense and flawless performance by Jessica Tandy (80-years-old when the movie was released in 1989) and a charming and slyly witty performance by Morgan Freeman (closing in on his fifties)—she a rich Jewish lady of the South, high-toned, spoiled, stubborn to a fault, he a black illiterate chauffeur, wise, patient and in need of a job—and we have the basis for a profound character study. What we are studying is both the character of the leads and the character of a way of life passing languidly before our eyes.

Adapted for the screen from his Pulitzer Prize winning stage play by Alfred Uhry and directed by Bruce Beresford, who previously gave us the remarkable Aussie classic, *Breaker Morant* (1980), *Driving Miss Daisy* is one of those films that is a work of art as well as a sociological discovery. Using beautifully constructed scenes carefully observed, Beresford allows us to recall a way of life and a culture that characterized the South during the middle of the last century. Freeman's Hoke Colburn is black; and, as he mumbles, "not all that much has changed" since the days of slavery. He still has to "yes'em" and shuffle his feet and show deference to white folk just to get by. Miss Daisy Werthan herself is rich and very tight with her money. She is also as racially prejudiced as a Dixie sheriff, but blind to her prejudices as she rages against the infirmaries of age.

The movie begins as she loses control of her car and drives it off the road and into a drainage ditch. She is shaken but unharmed. However her driving days are over. Her son Boolie Werthan, played with a fine touch and surprising restraint by comedian Dan Aykroyd, decides to get her a chauffeur. But she will not hear of it. She feels her independence is being threatened, and she doesn't need her son to tell her what to do. She can take care of herself. When Boolie arrives with Hoke, who is clearly black, Miss Daisy declares she will not have that man in her house.

One feels very strongly at this point how compromised the infirm are when they must rely on help from others. Let a stranger into your house and there is no telling where it might end. More that this though, is the underlying idea that dependence on people from a lower social-economic class will in fact have a leveling effect on class distinctions, and this is again something that Miss Daisy (in her ignorance of herself) will not abide.

But Hoke says he has wrestled some hogs in the mud in his time and has yet to let one get away, and he will do what is necessary to secure his position as Miss Daisy's driver. He comes highly recommended, and after listening to him, Boolie has little doubt he got the right man for the job. Miss Daisy of course is having none of it, and indeed she tells him to get out. She refuses to get into the car; she won't let him clean the chandelier or weed her garden. However, he doesn't give up. He takes all of her contrariness with good spirit and a sunny attitude, and then one day as she tries to go shopping on foot, he follows alongside of her in the car, and after some walking she is persuaded to hop in.

On one level this is about racial politics in the South, circa mid- twentieth century, and on another level it is about growing old and coping with life as one grows old. It is about taking care of oneself and getting the most out of life despite the handicap of a declining body. This applies to both Hoke and Miss Daisy. He knows that the physical demands of a chauffeur are more appropriate to his age than some of the physical work he did when younger, and she knows that to live the full social life that she desires, she needs help in getting around. Naturally, as the film progresses they learn from one another. At first they are drawn together by her sharp wit and his appreciation of somebody who can speak the truth with a barb and not mince words. Later they are drawn closer together by their mutual strength of character and the plain fact that she needs a driver and he needs a job. But finally they are drawn together because they become, as she suddenly observes one day, best friends.

This then is a story of love as well—love between two people from different walks of life. The differences are not just those of race and socio-economic status, or of religion and gender, but of world views and personal psychology, hers demanding and exacting, highbrow and imperial, his practical and easy-going, naturistic and democratic.

A tide is turned when her temple is burned to the ground by "the same ones as always" as Hoke informs her, which forces Daisy to realize that her enemies are the same as his. Consequently she attends a speech given by Martin Luther King, Jr. He prefers to wait outside in the car and listen to it on the radio. At once we see the commonality of their understanding, but still the differences of their stations in life remain. The dream and the reality are meshing but slowly, as all things do in the Old South, or, for that matter, most anywhere.

See this above all for the captivating performances by Jessica Tandy and Morgan Freeman, two of the great actors of our time, and for the touching and bittersweet story by Alfred Uhry. Also noteworthy is director Beresford's careful attention to detail and his unobtrusive guidance so that the film flows as sweetly as Tupelo honey on a warm southern day.

Winner.

Also nominated:

Born on the Fourth of July (1989)

Dead Poets Society (1989)

Field of Dreams (1989)

My Left Foot: The Story of Christy Brown (1989)

Dr. Strangelove, or: How I Learned to Stop Worrying and Love the Bomb (1964) 10

Kubrick's Best?

This is the kind of film you can say is "the best ever" and not look like an idiot, a comedy worthy of Voltaire or Cervantes, and a thriller to rival the best Hollywood ever produced. I'm willing to bet this movie will be remembered long after most of the movies of the Twentieth Century have faded to oblivion.

Kubrick's satirical masterpiece was made not long after, and keyed by, the publication of such serious, but absurd academic tomes as Herman Kahn's "On Thermonuclear War" in which the author assured us that nuclear war was not only survivable, but even winnable, and at any rate we could recuperate. Consequently he became one of the focal points of Kubrick's satire, embodied as Dr. Strangelove, the scientist with the arm-jerk Nazi salute and Nazi mentality, played chillingly by Peter Sellers, who also played U.S. president Merkin Muffley and British Air Force Captain Lionel Mandrake. Kubrick and Terry Southern, who wrote the rapier-sharp screen play, proved profoundly prescient when it was discovered some years later that nuclear war really was not winnable because it would usher in a "nuclear winter" that would becloud the entire planet for months or years to come, bringing starvation and death to billions. By making Dr Strangelove a Nazi, Kubrick was looking back, imagining, as we all were in those days, what horrors would have befallen the world had the Nazis gotten the bomb instead of the U.S. Start World War II five years later and we'd probably have Hiroshima in Chicago. Making Dr. Strangelove a Nazi also allowed Kubrick to allude to how the Nazi scientists were incorporated into the Soviet Union's bomb-building arsenal after WW II.

Part of the effectiveness of the movie is how it is dramatically presented. As the Strategic Air Command planes are flying toward the Soviet Union to drop their bombs, the tension is wonderfully emphasized and prolonged by the long, almost languid conversation between a very relaxed Gen. Jack D. Ripper (Sterling Hayden) philosophizing over his cigar on the importance of his precious vital fluids, and a frantic Capt Mandrake politely suggesting that what is going on is madness. This is followed by the out-of-change-for-the-phone soda machine scene with Corporal "Bat" Guano (Keenan Wynn) who is more worried about the possibility of petty theft than the possibility of nuclear war.

Although this film would never have existed without the comedic genius of Terry Southern, major credit for its success must go to the actors, not only to Peter Sellers, who was magnificent, but to Sterling Hayden and George C. Scott who seemed to feed off of one another in a "let's see you top this" flamboyant comedic style. Scott was later to win an academy award for his portrayal of Gen. Patton (Patton 1970), but his work there owed a lot to what he did here as General "Buck" Turgidson. By the way, all these "meaningful" names and most of the hilarious dialogue are the work of Southern, who also penned such sixties classics as Easy Rider (1969), Candy (1968), and The Loved One (1965), the latter from Evelyn Waugh's satirical novel about the funeral industry. Some memorable highlights:

Slim Pickets proving his intimate love for the bomb by riding down on it, like a cowboy breaking a bronco.

Russian Ambassador Sadesky (the name is, yes, an allusion to the Marque de Sade) explains why the Russians built the "doomsday machine," which would blow up the whole world: "We couldn't keep up with [the expense] of the arms race, the space race, the peace race..." (Another prophetic observation, by the way.) "We feared a "doomsday gap" (a take-off on the then current buzz phrase, "missile gap" and of course an absurdity).

The scene at the hotel with Turgidson's girl-friend/secretary in her bikini answering the phone and covering for him as though she is a producer's secretary warding off somebody he doesn't want to talk to. The audience knows the call's about impeding nuclear war, but she must pretend Turgidson is properly indisposed.

Peter Sellers as President Merkin Muffley talking to the Russian premier (Khrushchev) as an enormously patient, kindly father with a drunken son. Incidentally, Muffley's appearance was patterned after Adlai Stevenson, the democratic candidate for president who twice lost to Eisenhower in the fifties. Also note that a merkin is a toupee for the mound of Venus.

Gen. Ripper telling Mandrake how women sensed his power and wanted his vital fluids; and how a significant part of the commie conspiracy was to fluoridate our water and poison us (actually a real concern at the time by some fringe groups).

Second only to Pickens's bronco ride on the bomb as a symbol of the movie is Dr. Strangelove's spastic salute to Hitler...

Finally I have to say that one of the reasons this movie is still vital even though the Soviet Union has disbanded, is that the concern was real. During the Cuban missile crisis in the early sixties, Kennedy and Khrushchev came perilously close to nuclear warfare. Kubrick, Terry Southern and cast are to be commended for showing us the incredible folly of the age of MAD (Mutually Assured Destruction).

Loser. *My Fair Lady (1964), starring Audrey Hepburn and Rex Harrison, and directed by George Cukor, won.*
Also nominated:
Alexis Zorbas (1964)
Becket (1964)
Mary Poppins (1964)

Comment: My Fair Lady is a wonderful movie, but Dr. Strangelove is a great movie. Too bad they were both released in the same year. Becket and Mary Poppins were also outstanding films. Interestingly enough the Beatles film, A Hard Day's Night (1964) was nominated for a solitary award, Best Screenplay Written Directly for the Screen (Alun Owen), but didn't win. 1964 was an excellent year for movies.

Elizabeth (1998) 10

Superb

I wonder if the feminists have discovered this movie and if so, what they think of it. How could they not discover it since it has won a number of awards, including seven Academy Award nominations? Yet, I wonder, because the movie is deeper than might be thought on first blush, and it reverberates, but not with any simplistic sexist answers to the human struggle, but with uncomfortable questions, disturbing allegations.

Allegation number one: a woman can rule and be the equal of a man, but she must suppress her feminine instincts. Uncomfortable question number one: are women as vicious and murderous as our "demonic males"?

What makes *Elizabeth* such a wonderful movie is the uncompromising portrait it presents of a woman in a life or death struggle while in a position of power. Notice that she does NOT become a man, nor take on bogus or pseudo masculine traits to achieve her ends. She remains a woman to the core, yet acts with the kind of aggressive, decisive, brutal intelligence usually assigned to men.

Next question: Is this good to know?

A great work of art should be content to ask the great questions, not presume to answer them.

Cate Blanchett is superb in the title role and wonderfully supported by Geoffrey Rush and Joseph Fiennes. Shekhar Kapur's direction is without a hint of cant or even the slightest pandering to a mass audience, and is psychologically true and without any presumption to moral or spiritual wisdom. There is no preaching or taking sides. The script is a work of scholarship fused with the most compelling dramatic development, climax and resolution. The editing is almost invisible yet we can see that exactly enough was cut away while the essence was preserved;

viz., it is remarkable how we are led to experience the political growth of the young queen and see her take on the attributes of her father, as necessary, and then see her seek refuge in the church and a kind of piety as "the Virgin Queen" in such a short period of elapsed screen time. THAT is film making of the highest quality.

Not enough can be said about the subtle, charming, expansive, vivid and veracious performance of Blanchett, yet Joseph Fiennes is to be commended for achieving success in a difficult and unsympathetic role. Geoffrey Rush's restraint and control in a part that could have easily been overplayed was highly admirable and contributed strongly to the success of the film.

This is not to say that the film is without flaws. The scene where Elizabeth discovers the French duke's homosexuality is unlikely as staged, and her risque behavior with Leicester not in character. Better, I think, would have been to keep him frustrated and allow him only to play at love; however, today's audiences seem to demand coitus always. Leicester's dalliance with one of her ladies was extremely stupid, but in character. The co-incidence of her wearing the acid dress as she betrayed her queen was a delicious if implausible irony. Further it was not made clear how the queen's commands through Walsingham are made viable so that they must be carried out; indeed the under struggle among the ministers was glossed over, although her dismissal of the no longer effective Sir William Cecil was aptly done.

Of course I can presume to answer my queries. I think allegation number one, that a woman as a ruler must abandon her normal sexual drive is true, but the argument is too long for this space. Are women as vicious as men? They don't take the foolish chances that men take, since they can be reproductively rewarded only by staying alive and securing a stable future, whereas men can reproduce prodigiously for a while and then die successfully. But when necessary, women can be as brutal as Genghis Khan, as Elizabeth demonstrates.

Is it good to know that women are also vicious animals, when all the time we would prefer to think of them as fairy tale princesses? Well, something's lost and something's gained in growing up; but, yes, it's important to always keep that in mind when out there in the big world. I might add that it is sobering to realize that women as *reproductive animals* was not even addressed in this film. Therein lies another dimension of femininity that needs exploration...

Loser. *Shakespeare in Love (1989), starring Gwyneth Paltrow and Joseph Fiennes, and directed by John Madden, won.*
Also nominated:
Saving Private Ryan (1998)
The Thin Red Line (1998)
Life Is Beautiful (1997)

Comment: I too preferred Shakespeare in Love. Saving Private Ryan *was the expected winner in some circles. The* Thin Red Line *had no chance, and Robert Benigni's absurdist* Life Is Beautiful *was a bit, shall we say, too absurd for most viewers.*

The English Patient (1996) 9

In some ways superior to the book

This is a beautiful film, reminiscent of something by David Lean, and in some ways superior to the book, which more closely concentrated on Kip, the sapper and Hana, the nurse, whereas the film likes the story of Catherine, the spoiled, and the Count Almasy, the bitter, better.

I think the film is right for a popular audience. But essentially they are similar works done in different genres. By the way, the book disappoints with its phony PC notions about how Kip and some others might have reacted to the atomic bombing of the Japanese cities, the author imagining that Kip would be offended that the bomb was dropped on "brown people" and not on Europeans; but in truth, few at the time really comprehended nor cared about anything other than ending the horror of the worst war in human history. And I would ask the author, would he like to have stormed the island of Japan? It would have been Corregidor and Iwo Jima (average Allied death toll at about 33%) a hundred times over.

Winner.
Also nominated:
Fargo (1996)
Jerry Maguire (1996)
Secrets & Lies (1996)
Shine (1996)

Comment: Far and away the best film that year (IMHO) was Kenneth Branagh's Hamlet *(1996) which won nothing.*

The Godfather (1972) 10

A masterpiece

This is one of the greatest films ever made. Any doubt about that can be dispelled by watching the movie. I missed this when it first came out, and then a curious thing happened. For some reason I thought I had seen the film. One decade and then two went by and I kept hearing what a great film *The Godfather* was. But I was unimpressed because I thought I had seen it.

I don't know what film I had seen, but it wasn't *The Godfather*. Seeing this film for the first time over thirty years after the fact of its production is a startling experience. *The Godfather* is a work of art from first scene to last. There is the most amazing adherence to that fiction which is truer than fact.

I would like to say that I played cards with Mario Puzo who wrote the novel from which the film was adapted and who famously worked with Coppola on the screenplay, but in fact I only played cards with some people who had played cards with Puzo. Ah, such is the effect of celebrity. Puzo became like Coppola something of a legend after this film was produced, and everybody suddenly knew him or played cards with him. Everybody, from the most unsophisticated celluloid fan to the most erudite and jaded critic had walked out of that theater after 171 minutes mesmerized and delighted and emotionally moved by an uncompromising look at not just a Mafia family, but the psychology of families since time immemorial. The truth that we have all lived and experienced was made large on the screen in the form of the Corleones. I can guarantee you that audiences from every culture on the planet would understand the underlying psychology of this movie and take it to some serious extent as their own.

Marlon Brando plays the godfather (the patriarch, of course, or even the warlord if you like) of the past and the present, and then, as must always be the case, comes a new godfather. What is fascinating is who this new godfather is and how he comes to power. The ending of the film is—after so many brilliant scenes and so many psychologically true surprises and so many excursions to Queens and the Bronx and Sicily and Las Vegas (each vignette absolutely integrated into the story of the film)—even more ponderously true and a surprise that sneaks up on us so stealthily that it is not a surprise. And when the credits begin to run after Diana Keaton's tears of realization, we too realize the "message" of the film. It is a message that I think would be understood in the Middle East today (and two thousand years ago as well) as I write this, a message of tribal ways and the rise and fall of warlords and the Machiavellian machinations of the prince who would be king.

But it is Al Pacino's performance as the son of the godfather that in the final analysis steals the show as he goes from the intellectual boy who would be a legitimate American success at the finest colleges, etc. to a man wearing the hat of Al Capone. And Pacino makes us believe every step of the way.

Well, I should not say that it Al Pacino who steals the show. In truth this is Francis Ford Coppola's masterpiece. He would not have the film he has without Al Pacino or Marlon Brandon and certainly not without the novel and script from Mario Puzo, of course; but make no mistake about it. Coppola manicured every scene. He attended to every detail, from the color of the wine to the tires on the cars to the dances and the music to the villas abroad to the sleaze of Las Vegas to the perfect casting of the main characters right down to the extras including both cute and not so cute kids, as indeed life would give us. In some very real sense Coppola lived this movie and it was a part of him, and yet I am stuck by the fact that Puzo invented it.

This is an American classic, an uncompromising work of art that engages, informs and moves the audience—just about any audience—to ask the great questions regarding who we are and what we should do and how we should live. From the wedding to the funeral to the christening to the priest in Latin voice-over as the final vengeance is planned to that final vengeance (that we know will NOT be the final vengeance), we are glued to our seats as the life of human beings (who could very well be us) passes before our transfixed eyes.

Oscars went to Brando as best actor, and to Puzo and Coppola for best screen adaptation. In a rare show of almost universal agreement among movie goers, critics, and the Academy, *The Godfather* won the Oscar as Best Picture in 1972.

Don't miss this as I had for so long, and see it for Coppola who can take his place among the greats of all cinema for this film alone.

Winner.
Also nominated:
Cabaret (1972)
Deliverance (1972)
Sounder (1972)
The Immigrants (1971)
Comment: Easy winner.

The Graduate (1967) 9

Here's to you, Mrs. Robinson

This is one of the defining films of my generation, and of course I saw it when it came out in 1967. Seeing it again after all these years I was struck by both how funny it is and by the brittle, cynical and brilliant performance by Anne Bancroft as Mrs. Robinson. She really is flawless in a part that might easily lend itself to overacting. Instead she is subtle, controlled, focused, and authentic in a way that is both sexy and chilling with just a hint of ironic humor. The maternal manner with which she treats virginal Benjamin Braddock (Dustin Hoffman in a breakout role) emphasizes the creepy, almost incestuous nature of their sterile affair.

Mike Nichols has directed a number of sexual/relationship comedies, including *Carnal Knowledge* (1971), *Who's Afraid of Virginia Woolf?* (1966), Nora Ephron's *Heartburn* (1986) and Carrie Fisher's *Postcards from the Edge* (1990). Nichols's films typically feature talented and charismatic actors and actresses who explore in a deceptively humorous manner the dark side of our human nature. The humor usually has an edgy quality while the taboo elements are somehow resolved into happy endings as in a musical comedy. Nichols likes to work with material from another medium and make it his own. Typically, *The Graduate* is adapted from the novel by Charles Webb. Nichols also likes to feature cutting edge

popular music in the score. What we hear in the background and played over the opening credits is Simon and Garfunkel's "Sounds of Silence." Of course Paul Simon wrote the song "Mrs. Robinson" for this movie, but what I didn't realized until now is his "It's all happening at the zoo" was probably inspired in part by the zoo scene in this film.

Dustin Hoffman's confused and drifting Benjamin, worried about his future and suffocated by his parents' generation, knocked everybody out in those days with his dead-panned, literal delivery of one-liners, some of which were written by Buck Henry, who plays the desk clerk at the rendezvous hotel. I especially loved Ben's answer when his father, enquiring about his Quixotic plan to marry Mrs. Robinson's daughter Elaine (Katharine Ross), asks, "Isn't this a half-baked idea?" In dead seriousness, Benjamin says, "No, sir. It's completely baked."

Memorable is Norman Fell (whom most of us recall from TV's long-running comedy, *Three's Company*) in a small part as the landlord of the Berkeley rooming house. He is of course a past master at dead-panning one-liners; in fact, he is a master at mute dead-panning. One of the funniest bits in the movie is when the camera catches his face as Elaine's father comes out of Ben's room spewing obscenities and insults at Ben.

What we loved about this movie was the youthful point of view; the wonderful chase scene at the end, a Hollywood staple made fresh; the sympathetic character of Benjamin with whom we could readily identify; the cliché-ridden and shallow parents being slyly made fun of; and the sense of getting what we want out of life and doing it our own way. This is a coming-of-ager and a romance and a social satire rolled into one, and a classic Hollywood movie that no aficionado would want to miss.

But see this for Anne Bancroft, a brilliant and perhaps underrated actress in one of her most memorable roles.

Loser. *In the Heat of the Night, starring Sidney Portier and Rod Steiger, and directed by Noman Jewison, won.*
Also nominated:
Bonnie and Clyde (1967)
Doctor Dolittle (1967)
Guess Who's Coming to Dinner (1967)

Comment: Two racially conscious films, In the Heat of the Night and Guess Who's Coming to Dinner, were nominated. The surprise is that they didn't cancel each other out in the voting. Today the movie best remembered is The Graduate.

Il Postino (1994) 10

An ode to friendship, love and poetry

The scene is Italy, circa 1953, a fisherman's village on a small island, Cala di Sotto, presumably in the south.

Internationally acclaimed poet and communist Pablo Neruda and his wife come to the island in exile from Chile. He rents a house on a hill overlooking the ocean. Mario Ruoppolo, son of a fisherman who ironically can't stomach being out on a boat, becomes Neruda's postman. The simple fisherman's son and the great poet strike up a friendship.

The first thing I should say about this poignant and beautiful film is it starts very slowly and you will be tempted to give up on it. Don't! In the tradition of the theater in which the playwright will sometimes make the captive audience squirm a little in boredom (to better set them up for what's to come), Director Michael Radford—an Englishman, by the way—begins slow and then slows down a little. (A German proverb has it that "hunger makes the best cook.") But about one quarter of the way home the story begins to build, and by the time it's over we are in tears.

Massimo Troisi stars as the postman who wants to learn and use the power of poetry to woe the girl he loves. It is a sad irony that he died just as the picture was completed. Veteran French actor Philippe Noiret is suavely brilliant as Neruda, whose receipt of many letters from female fans intrigues Mario and motivates him to learn the master's secret. Maria Grazia Cucinotta, who plays Beatrice Russo, the café owner's daughter who waits tables, does not appear until the movie is almost half over, but she is more than worth the wait! She has eyes as dark as black night and a figure to rival that of Sophia Loren in her prime. It takes Mario ten seconds to fall in love with her. However, Beatrice's mother wants something more than a part time postman for her daughter, a man whose "capital is the fungus between his toes." Thus we have part of our story. But the larger part of the story is the friendship between Neruda and Mario, and how they inspire and learn from one another.

There are a number of brilliantly planned scenes that delight. I especially liked the scene in the church as the priest is saying he cannot accept Neruda as a best man since the man is a godless Communist, when suddenly in the background we see Neruda in suit jacket and tie knelling at the altar as he crosses himself. Very affecting was the scene in which Beatrice sees Neruda upon his return to the island react to Mario's son and hearing his name pronounced, "Pablito," indicating that the boy had been named after him.

This is a film about beauty. I think when we realize the beauty, that's a very good sign. There is a little talk about how poetry works with some excellent examples woven into the script. Ironically, the rather crude mother of Beatrice has some of the best lines, i.e., "One touch and he will have you lying on your back," she advises her daughter. When your mother tells you THAT, I think you can believe she knows what she is talking about! When Mario, who is a natural poet, but a primitive, is asked by Neruda for a way to describe the fisherman's nets, he

replies, "sad." When he is asked to record something about the beauty of his island he spontaneously says, "Beatrice Russo." There is in the background the struggle between the Christian Democrats and the communists in which Mario and Neruda are participants, each in his own way. But this struggle is not emphasized and is in fact given its true devalued place in human affairs. In the words of Mario, who has more important things on his mind, "So what if we beak our chains. What do we do then?"

Loser. *Braveheart (1995), directed by and starring Mel Gibson won.*
Also nominated:
Apollo 13 (1995)
Babe (1995)
Sense and Sensibility(1995)

Comment: Foreign language films are sometimes nominated but they never win.

The Last Picture Show (1971) 10
An American classic

In this nostalgic, atmospheric study of small town life in the fifties as seen a decade later, filmed on location in Wichita Falls and Archer City, Texas (from a novel by the incomparable Larry McMurtry), the force of slow, inevitable change is symbolized in the showing of the last picture at the local movie house. That last picture show, incidentally, is Howard Hawks' celebrated Western, *Red River* (1948) starring John Wayne and Montgomery Clift.

Well, the movie houses came back to life as multiplexes charging eight bucks a pop, but the Western movie died out, and the boys watching that movie went their separate ways into manhood.

Peter Bogdanovich's direction is episodic and leisurely, naturalistic with just a hint of the maudlin. We get a sense of the North Texas prairie wind blowing through a cattle town where there is not a lot to do and a whole lot of time to do it. Hungry women and a sense of drift. Boredom, gray skies and a lot of dust. You could set "Anarene, Texas" down any place in southwestern or midwestern America, circa 1951, and you wouldn't have to change much: a main drag, a Texaco gas station, a café, a feed store, flat lands all around, old pickup trucks and a pool hall, youngsters with a restless yearning to grow up, drinking beer out of brown bottles giggling and elbowing each other in the ribs, and the old boys playing dominoes and telling tales of bygone days.

Robert Surtees's stark, yet romantic black and white cinematography, captures well that bygone era. The wide shot of the bus pulling out, taking Duane off to the Korean War with Sonny watching, standing by the Texaco station with the missing letter in the sign, was a tableau in motion, a moment stopped in our minds.

Cybill Shepherd made her debut here as Jacy Farrow, a bored little rich girl playing at love and sexuality. Part of the restorations in the video not shown in theaters in the early seventies includes some footage of her in the buff after stripping on a diving board (!). She is as shallow as she is pretty, and one of the reasons for seeing this film, although in truth her performance, while engaging, was a little uneven.

The rest of the cast was outstanding, in particular Timothy Bottoms whose Sonny Crawford is warm and forgiving, sweet and innocent. Jeff Bridges's Duane Jackson is two-faced, wild and careless, self-centered and probably going to die in Korea. Ben Johnson and Cloris Leachman deservedly won Oscars as best supporting actors. Leachman was especially good as the lonely 40-year-old wife of the football coach who has an awkward affair with the 18-year-old Sonny, while Johnson played a lovable, crusty guy that the kids looked up to. Sam Bottoms played the retarded Billy with steady, tragic good humor. Ellen Burstyn as Jacy's terminally bored mother, and Eileen Brennan as the wise waitress with a hand on her hip were also very good.

Memorable, but perhaps too obviously insertional, are the medley of country, pop, and rock and roll tunes from the late forties/early fifties jingling out of car radios and 45 record players throughout the film.

Peter Bogdanovich followed this with some hits, including the comedy *What's Up Doc* (1972) with Barbra Streisand, Ryan O'Neal, and Madeline Kahn, and the excellent *Paper Moon* (1973) with Ryan and Tatum O'Neal, but then tailed off. I don't think he ever lived up to the promise of this film, an American classic not to be missed.

Loser. *The French Connection (1971), starring Gene Hackman, and directed by William Friedkin, won.*
Also nominated:
A Clockwork Orange (1971)
Fiddler on the Roof (1971)
Nicholas and Alexandra (1971)

Comment: In addition to The Last Picture Show, *I thought two of the other films nominated, Kubrick's* A Clockwork Orange, *and Jewison's wonderful* Fiddler on the Roof, *were superior to* The French Connection. *Today I think* The French Connection *would finish fourth.*

Memento (2000) 10

Brilliant

I have seen a lot of movies and almost always I know what the director is doing. I know what the actors want to achieve. I know what the aims of the producers are. It's all transparent, but once in a while there is a work of pure genius that makes me think I really don't know anything at all. Memento is such a work.

Looking at the premise of this movie, I recall that it can really happen. Neurologist Oliver Sacks, in his wonderful book, *The Man Who Mistook His Wife for a Hat* (1986), recounts the story of a man who could only hold the memory of the last thirty seconds or so. Leonard's condition in this movie is better. Apparently he can hold in his mind what has happened over the last few minutes. Also he has the ability to follow a kind of learned routine in which he is able to function by continually writing himself notes. In the case recalled by Dr. Sacks, the man could not do that. He could not even remember enough to finish a short conversation.

The idea of taking notes to "remember" is something that some Alzheimer's patients are able to do in the early stages of the disease (which may be where Jonathan Nolan got the idea for his short story on which the film is based.) Sacks recalls such a case in his *An Anthropologist on Mars: Seven Paradoxical Tales (1995)*. The notes act as the man's memory, just as the notes and photos do for Leonard in this movie.

The next question might be, could someone with Leonard's "condition" actually function well enough to get by without being institutionalized or having somebody take care of him on a minute to minute basis? Leonard says, "Habit and routine...conditioning make my life possible." He "remembers" to look in his jacket pocket to see where he is living. Presumably he also does this when he is in his car and has forgotten where he is going and doesn't know where he is. Presumably he has many notes that we don't see him refer to. How does he find his way back to his car after going somewhere? He identifies his car from a photo, but where is it parked? In the scene where he wakes up next to Natalie, he gets up and goes to his jacket and finds her picture so he knows who she is. He also finds a picture of her and Dodd. He somehow "remembers" the significance and writes on the back of her photo, "...she lost someone too. She will help you out of pity." How does he remember these things? Perhaps they are examples of "implicit learning" that "Sammy" was not able to accomplish, what Leonard calls "conditioning." In implicit learning as opposed to "explicit," we learn to do something without knowing we learned it.

Regardless of these questions, this is a brilliantly conceived and plotted thriller, and the acting by the three principals is superb. Guy Pearce, plays Leonard in a most immediate and affecting manner so that we are forced us to identify with him and his predicament. Carrie-Anne Moss, whom you may recall from The Matrix (1999), is mesmerizing with her sexy, mysterious eyes as the hard-edged and haunting Natalie. Joe Pantoliano is first rate as Teddy, the wisecracking, cynical and rather annoying undercover cop.

But what really makes this a stunning movie is the way it is constructed. The scenes are presented in reverse chronological order, so that we know the latest action first, and at the end of the movie find out the earlier action. This seems an extraordinary way to tell a story, but it works. Incidentally, there's a Seinfeld episode told this way, the one where they go to India for a wedding; and to some extent this technique was employed in Quentin Tarantino's *Reservoir Dogs* (1992). What makes it particularly effective here is the material. Leonard, as Teddy points out, is not the same person he was before his wife's death and his injury. For him the arrow of time has lost its meaning. Earlier events are just the same as later ones. Director Christopher Nolan (Jonathan's brother), who also wrote the screenplay, was able to dovetail the action scene by scene as we move backward in time so that what seems true in the beginning becomes different than what is true in the end. And indeed, like Leonard, our experience of the story doesn't depend on time's arrow.

Viewing this the second time (and you may feel a compulsion to do just that) some of the lines that were not funny initially become very funny. The voice-over in the chase scene with Dodd is an example. Leonard finds himself running and he says, "So what am I doing?...I'm chasing him....No, he's chasing me!" Or when Teddy asks about the gun, Leonard says, "Must be his. I don't think they'd let somebody like me carry a gun." Or Teddy's line to Leonard, "I've had more rewarding friendships than this—but I get to keep telling the same jokes."

The key to the powerful psychological "ending" of the film, where we realize what will eventually happen, occurs when Natalie tells Leonard that revenge is useless because he won't remember it. He replies, "It doesn't matter whether I remember or not...." Indeed we see that he really doesn't remember his revenge and that implies that he will... But you really need to see the movie to appreciate the stunning implication.

On another level this is a movie about what makes us human. What would life be like if we lived in an eternal present without reference to the past? We could be easily exploited by those with knowledge of the past, as Leonard is, but there is a deeper question being asked. Does life have any real meaning for a person without memory?

Loser. *A Beautiful Mind (2001), starring Russell Crowe and Jennifer Connelly, and directed by Ron Howard, won. Also nominated:*
Gosford Park (2001)
In the Bedroom (2001)
The Lord of the Rings: The Fellowship of the Ring (2001)
Moulin Rouge! (2001)

*Comment: Memento **was not nominated** although this was the year it was eligible. Memento did receive nominations for Best Screenplay written directly for the screen, and Best Editing, but didn't win anything.*

Million Dollar Baby (2004) 10

A brutally realistic tale not suitable for all viewers

Hilary Swank won her second Best Actress Oscar for her performance as Maggie Fitzgerald, woman boxer, in this outstanding movie directed and produced by Clint Eastwood. Her first was for *Boys Don't Cry* (1999). It's clear she put a lot of work into the part and was outstanding and clearly deserved the award. The movie is one of Clint Eastwood's best. I would not however recommend that everybody see this. The latter part of the movie is brutal and the ending is not pretty.

Morgan Freeman as Eddie "Scrap-Iron" Dupris, a tough-as-nails veteran of 109 fights and owner of only one working eye, narrates part of the action as the jack of all duties at the Hit Pit Gym for boxing hopefuls run by Frankie Dunn (Clint Eastwood). Scrap is addressing somebody. At the end of the film we find out who (but of course I can't say). This is a nice touch that adds some depth to the theme of the movie which is the love that exists (or should) between a father and a daughter.

Clint Eastwood plays the father figure to Swank's irrepressible Maggie, ambitious trailer trash girl with a heart as strong as a bull. Eastwood's Frankie Dunn is a deeply troubled man who is continually writing to his daughter only to have the letters always come back unopened with the words "Return to Sender" on them. Apparently Frankie did something so bad that his daughter will no longer have anything to do with him. I didn't notice that we ever find out what this something was, but it doesn't matter. Frankie's character is such that we forgive him even if his daughter doesn't.

The story starts out like any one of a hundred Hollywood fight movies with the difference being the boxer is a woman. But the story does not end like a "Rocky" contrivance. Instead Eastwood and Paul Higgis, who wrote the heart-wrenching script, opt for a kind of stark realism that will not please some people. There is the sense that this could really happen and is the kind of tragedy that Shakespeare and the Greek dramatists would appreciate.

But the tragedy is not Maggie Fitzgerald's alone. It is also Frankie's. And it is Scrap-Iron's as well. If only Frankie had not trained her. If only Scrap-Iron had gone to Vegas for the title fight and been in her corner. If only Scrap-Iron had not encouraged Maggie. "If only," like so much of life, has no meaning after the fact of what actually happens. Scrap wants to believe that Maggie was the better for having really lived and had a chance at a great personal triumph; and even Maggie herself seems to at least want to believe that. Frankie however is clearly not in agreement.

At the end Frankie, who is a lifelong Catholic who goes to church every Sunday and is looking for the meaning of life, must face a terrible dilemma. Maggie asks him to do something that he cannot do, that goes against his religion. Yet he feels he must do it.

How one interprets the ending—did he do the right thing?—may very well determine whether one likes the film or not. His moral dilemma is very real and I, for one, cannot say what I would have done in his situation, and so for me the horns of the dilemma are very sharp indeed.

I quit watching boxing on TV many ago because of the way the fights excite the blood, since the point of a boxing match is to make the opponent helpless. I don't like feeling like that. This movie, in a way, perhaps accidentally, comes to the same end as many a fight: the winner goes on to another fight, and to an eventual loss, while the loser is made helpless.

Some people might be wondering what the message here is. I'm not sure, but I can tell you this: Shakespeare essentially said there is no message. Life is tale told by an idiot...in the end signifying nothing. And the existentialists will tell you that life has no meaning except for that which we ourselves bestow upon it. I guess Scrap is the existentialist and Frankie the Shakespearean.

And who is Maggie? And who is everywoman and everyman?

Winner.
Also nominated:
The Aviator (2004)
Finding Neverland (2004)
Ray (2004)
Sideways (2004)

Mister Roberts (1955) 10

From tedium to hilarity and nobility

Watching this again many years after I first saw it, I expected to be disappointed. After all, the great films of our youth sometimes turn out to be something less than we had imagined. But *Mister Roberts* does not disappoint. This is one of the gems of the American cinema, a poignant comedy featuring a multitudinously clever and delightful script by Frank Nugent and Joshua Logan from a novel by Thomas Heggen made into a play by Logan and Heggen that ran for many years on Broadway. The movie features sterling performances from Henry Fonda, James Cagney, William Powell and Jack Lemmon. Fonda is particularly brilliant in the kind of role from which legends are made. (He also played the part on Broadway.) You can take all your John Wayne classics and toss them overboard with the Captain's palm tree. Henry Fonda as Lt (j.g.) Doug Roberts, cargo officer of the USS Reluctant, shines forth as the noblest hero of them all. He is a quiet, strong, fair, courageous man in a story sure to mist up your eyes even if you're watching it for the twentieth time.

Jack Lemmon won a supporting Oscar for his performance as Ensign Pulver, a kind of lazy, but slyly resourceful Walter Mitty type who talks a great game but never follows through. James Cagney is the Captain, a sour, resentful man who mercilessly badgers Mister Roberts and grossly neglects the morale of his crew. He is just perfect. The way he bellows "Mister Roberts!" or way he trembles out the line, "Mister...Mister...this time you've gone too far" delights the audience. William Powell, in his last film, plays the ship's wise and ever diplomatic doc with graceful precision.

It is a shame that Henry Fonda, in perhaps his most beloved and certainly one of his finest performances, was not nominated for an Academy Award. I have no idea why. Incidentally, Hollywood legend John Ford directed, but fell ill and Mervyn LeRoy—no slouch himself (e.g., *The Bad Seed*, 1956; *No Time for Sergeants*, 1958, etc.)—finished up.

There are a number of memorable scenes in the film, the kind recalled with delight. My favorite involves the crew, their binoculars and the nurses. I also loved the careful concocting of the "scotch whiskey" by Doc. The weekly letters requesting a transfer, the Hoot Gibson films we (thankfully) never see, the ever worshipful palm tree, Pulver's marbles in a tobacco tin that he shakes in Roberts's face, vowing to prove his manhood by putting them in the captain's overbin, his "firecracker," his "If I could be with you/One hour tonight/To do the things I might/I'm telling you true/I'd be anything but blue," the giddy nurses, and the infamous liberty are other unforgettable bits. But more than anything, what makes this a great movie, are the indelible characters so very true to our experience, and how nicely they meld and contrast.

This is, along with *From Here to Eternity, Das Boot, The Bridge on the River Kwai, The Caine Mutiny, Stalag 17,* and *Twelve O'Clock High,* among my favorite movies to come out of World War II. What sets *Mister Roberts* apart is the humor born of the boredom, frustration, and tedium that most truly characterizes life in the service. In this regard I recall a saying that goes something like this: "War is filled with long stretches of boredom punctuated by moments of absolute terror." The crew of the Reluctant got only the boredom.

Loser. *Marty (1955), starring Ernest Borgnine, and directed by Delbert Mann, won.*
Also nominated:
Love Is a Many-Splendored Thing (1955)
Picnic (1955)
The Rose Tattoo (1955)

Comment: I guess we can say that the Academy missed the boat on this one. Marty was a good movie, but Mister Roberts is a classic.

My Fair Lady (1964) 9

Wonderful, but I missed Julie Andrews

I thought the music was wonderful. I thought Audrey Hepburn was just adorable and so full of energy and grace and just fascinating to watch. Rex Harrison was an absolutely perfect Professor Higgins and never wavered or changed character. My problem (a minor one) is with the ending and with the dubbing.

The story is brilliant of course, taken from George Bernard Shaw's acclaimed play Pygmalion, although materially altered to fit the requirements of a musical comedy. The contrast of the unschooled street urchin Eliza Doolittle and the stuffy, self-possessed confirmed bachelor, a kind of nineteenth century British man of science, wonderfully accomplished in his profession, but blind to himself when it comes to relationships with other people, made for a most interesting match. And the delusive dream of a man forming his own perfect woman (which is the basis of the Pygmalion legend) works so very well with a conceited linguist tutoring a cockney girl. The entire concept is a work of genius with the drunken father and the objectifying Col. Pickering and the very right Mrs. Pierce.

But there are some problems. Freddy is needed of course as another "objectifying" character to make it clear just how desirable Eliza really is and how foolish and blind Professor Higgins is in not seeing this—in theory, of course, because in practice with Audrey Hepburn or Julie Andrews as Eliza, this would seem entirely unnecessary. And indeed without Freddy we do not have the beautiful "On the Street Where You Live." But even with him Prof. Higgins does not see, and indeed even at the resolution of the story, he still does not see, as he asks for his slippers. If this were presented to current London and Broadway audiences it would never play the way it was written. Professor Higgins would need to see the light and he would have to get his own slippers!

The dubbing and the need for it is curious. There is no doubt that Marni Nixon, who did the singing, has a beautiful and commanding voice, and we are the better for having heard her, but why is the dubbing so obvious? It's almost as if Miss Hepburn is saying to the audience: they said it would be better if Miss Nixon sings instead of me because her voice is stronger and so very well trained. And so Hepburn does not completely lip-sync some of the opening words of songs as though to remind us that she is not singing. And the contrast between her delicate voice and then the sudden power of Marni Nixon's is obvious. Beyond this is the question of why Julie Andrews, who has a voice to match that of Miss Nixon, and charisma and charm at least in the same ballpark as Miss Hepburn, wasn't asked to play the part that she knew so very well from her experience on the stage. Still, as another reviewer has so acutely noted, if she had been asked, we would have missed her in Mary Poppins, which

was made the same year. I should also note that Hepburn was 33 or 34 years old when this was made (although she looked almost ten years younger). Nonetheless she was playing the part of "a good girl, I am," whom Pickering identifies in his call to Scotland Yard as being 21 years old.

Curious. But all is forgiven because Audrey Hepburn is just so beautiful, so elegant and so delightful in the part. I especially loved her in the opening scene in her soiled clothes and hat and her sour voice. By the way, I have heard Julie Andrews sing the part, although I never saw her on the stage, and the way she "meow's" Eliza's accent, like a cat's claw on a chalk board, is really amazing. (Get the CD.)

This is one of the best movie musicals ever made, a sheer delight highlighted not only by Rex Harrison and Audrey Hepburn, but by Stanley Holloway as the Liza's lovable rascal father and Wilfrid Hyde-White as the very understanding and very properly British Col. Pickering with opulent direction by the great George Cukor. The sets and production numbers are gorgeous. But see it for Audrey Hepburn, one of the great stars of the silver screen in one of her most memorable roles.

Winner.
Also nominated:
Alexis Zorbas (1964)
Becket (1964)
Dr. Strangelove or: How I Learned to Stop Worrying and Love the Bomb (1964)
Mary Poppins (1964)

The Pianist (2002) 10

Brilliant and ultimately redemptive

It's hard to watch this film and not think of the situation in the Middle East today. What is worse, being stuffed into cattle cars and sent to death camps or being blown up by suicide bombers (or bulldozed by machines of steel)? For me the answer to this strangely relevant question is the former. I know that the old Jewish Defense League that I recall from my college days, whose slogan was something like, "Never Again," would agree and so would most of the population of Israel. I think the terrorist Islamic groups ought to be required to view this film and/or some others like it on what happened to the Jews in Europe during the time of the Nazis so that they might have a better appreciation of why they will never be able to overrun Israel and why the United States continues to support Israel even while questioning some of Sharon's policies.

Director Roman Polanski tells the familiar horror tale, this time with a concentration on the Jews of Warsaw and in particular on the famed pianist Wladyslaw Szpilman. (The screenplay by Ronald Hardwood is based on Szpilman's memoir). Polanski spares us none of the brutality or the sadomasochism that is an inevitable inter-pretation of the events. He has the Jews meekly acqui-esce to the increasingly horrific Nazi demands, and then has them just lie down when told to and accept a bullet through the skull.

(Actually the vast majority of the Jews were not shot, of course, since the bullets were too costly and needed elsewhere. Indeed, as long as I am doing an aside, the stupidity of the Nazis in wasting their resources in geno-cide contributed to their losing the war. Small irony. But of course that was a war they could not win anyway. If by some magic they could have gotten the Jews—especially Jewish physicists—to work for them that would have been their only chance, which once again demonstrates the self-destructive nature of Hitler and his followers.)

Polanski shows us the Jews who collaborated with the Nazis and he even has a Jewish boy in the compound as they await the cattle cars selling candy at inflated prices, and then later a Nazi who talks to his Jewish workers about trading goods and says, rubbing his fingers togeth-er, "That's what you're good at, isn't it?"

It is interesting to compare *The Pianist* with Vittoria De Sica's *The Garden of the Finzi-Continis* (1971), an entirely different sort of film, but one with a similar theme and some similar scenes as the Jews, this time Italian Jews, are loaded into the cattle cars. The experience in these films is always the same for me in at least one respect. I want so much to shout: "Do something! Don't let it hap-pen! Charge them with the sheer mass of your bodies, if nothing else. Better to die fighting than to die like cattle." But of course I was not there. We think we know what we would do, but unless we are confronted with the actual situation, we don't know. And of course we have hind-sight.

At one point, Szpilman and his brother are talking as they eat their thin soup and their bread. The brother tells him that the cattle cars are going to Treblinka but they return empty and that there are no cars containing food that go that way. He concludes, "They are exterminating us."

Polanski's point is that the Nazis were able to actually commit their ghastly mass murders (and the German populace to excuse them) because they had come to be-lieve that Jews were not human and that they were only killing vermin. The Jews had been demonized, which is the first step toward genocide. We declare that our ene-mies are not human, and that allows us to kill them with moral impunity. I had a new thought while I watched this time, thinking: a respect for animals and a belief in ani-mal rights might serve as a moral buffer so that when one group of people hate each other and begin to turn the other into animals, they will still have a step to go before they can begin the mass murders.

It is in the second half when Szpilman goes into hiding that Polanski's film distinguishes itself. Here the focus is entirely on Szpilman and his need to survive. The cine-matography of the Warsaw streets, the apartments he lives in, the snow, the gray buildings, the people below in the streets, the hunger, the music that he hears in his mind but cannot play, the burned-out buildings, and then the scene in which the German officer says, "Play something" and he does. It is here that the film becomes magical and a testament to the best that is in humans. Note that the pianist has become in his beard and his persecution a Christ-like figure who never raised a hand against anyone. He is the Christ who turned the other cheek. And note that it is his ethereal talent as a great musician that saves him. This is Polanski's message and the reason he made the film. The best that is in humans can rise above the brute that is in humans.

See this for Adrien Brody, who gave it everything he had, and then some. His performance will haunt you. Polan-ski's clear, Hollywood-like, almost Spielbergian direction, tells the story a bit too brightly at times, and a bit too simplistically at others, but he has planned well so that in the end we see that he has told it brilliantly. For those who have never actually had the details of the Holocaust acted out for them, this will be quite an eye-opener and a chilling, depressing and deeply disturbing experience. And see it because we need to be reminded of what can happen when we give way to hate and prejudice.

Loser. *Chicago (2002), starring Renée Zellweger and Catherine Zeta-Jones, and directed by Rob Marshall, won. Also nominated:*
Gangs of New York (2002)
The Hours (2002)
The Lord of the Rings: The Two Towers (2002)

Platoon (1986) 8

How a nation lost its innocence

In one sense this can be seen as Oliver Stone's attempt to account for the massacre at My Lai for which Lt. William Calley was famously court-martialed. One recalls a statement made at the time by somebody in close concert with the logic of the Vietnam War: "We had to destroy the village in order to save it." But more inclusively, Oliver Stone's film addresses the question of what war does to us as it focuses on Pvt. Chris Taylor, played by Charlie Sheen, who gave up his student deferment, joined the army and volunteered to fight in Vietnam as his patriotic duty. How the twisted logic of war changes him and cor-rupts him and others in his platoon is the story of the film.

To Oliver Stone's credit it can be said that this movie, first released in 1989, helped to shock a new generation of Americans into understanding just why our involve-ment in Vietnam was a tragic mistake and to warn us not to do anything like that again. The fact that recent military adventures by the US have been limited engagements with limited objectives (instead of the vague and unrestricted policy of stopping the spread of communism, which was the rationale for the war in Vietnam)—engagements that have been carefully orchestrated to avoid becoming mired in the kind of hand-to-hand combat favoring the side defending its own turf as shown in this film, owes something to Stone's vision and to that of other film makers. One also recalls Senator Barry Goldwater R, Arizona) who advocated "winning" the war in Vietnam by "bombing them back into the Stone Age." Stone's film suggests just how impossible that would have been.

Tom Berenger gives a splendid and somewhat horrific performance as Sgt. Barnes, the "War Lover" (the phrase is the title of John Hersey's WWII novel), who kills both friend and foe indiscriminately. Willem DaFoe plays his opposite, Sgt. Elias who is the model of the good soldier. The rest of the cast gives fine support while the script by Stone, partially from personal experience, is full of authentic dialogue and veracious detail. The clash between our civilized nature and our baser instincts is well presented.

It is impossible to fairly compare this to other excellent Vietnam War movies such as *The Deer Hunter* (1978), *Full Metal Jacket* (1987), *Apocalypse Now* (1979), et al., because they are all so different. I do believe that *Platoon* was more of a throwback to World War II movies in the sense that it focused on the dynamics of the soldiers immersed in actual battles with the enemy. Yet on the other hand it falls completely within the Vietnam War genre by looking beyond the battles to address the larger question of why, and the war's consequences. In World War II movies, the why was never in doubt, and the consequences were not an issue.

The theme of this movie has been expressed as the loss of innocence, and that is a fair assessment; but I think it wasn't so much the soldiers themselves that lost their innocence, although many did, but a nation that lost its. We were a different country before Vietnam. We have never been the same since, and we will never be the same again.

Winner.
Also nominated:
Children of a Lesser God (1986)
Hannah and Her Sisters (1986)
The Mission (1986)
A Room with a View (1986)

Roman Holiday (1953) 10

One of the most romantic movies ever made

This was Audrey Hepburn's debut in a starring role. She was 24-years-old and had appeared in two or three other movies but just in bit parts. Here she plays a reigning European princess visiting Rome who would like an escape from her daily regime of official duties, thus the title and theme of the movie, a Roman holiday.

Gregory Peck plays an American newspaper reporter living in the Eternal City. We first see him playing poker with his cronies, and losing. His relative "poverty" and Princess Ann's fabulous wealth and station present a formidable barrier to their ever finding true love and marital happiness. Part of the fun of the script is in seeing how this will play out and how their differences are resolved in the end. I will give you a small hint: very carefully!

The script comes from a story by Dalton Trumbo who is perhaps best known as the author of the anti-war novel, *Johnny Got His Gun.* Trumbo was one of the "Hollywood Ten" who were blacklisted from working in the industry during the excesses of the McCarthy era. He went to Mexico and continued working on film scripts but under assumed names or had his scripts presented by "fronts." In this case Ian McLellan Hunter fronted for Trumbo and won an Academy Award for the story. Later the Academy awarded Trumbo a posthumous Oscar for his work.

Long time Hollywood studio director William Wyler directed the film entirely on location in Rome. He has a formidable list of credits going well back into the silent film era including such outstanding films as *Wuthering Heights* (1939), *The Letter* (1940), *The Little Foxes* (1941), etc. His clear directorial style and his attention to detail work well here. The sets in Rome are charming, especially Peck's bachelor apartment. The bit players, especially Peck's landlord are excellent and the events are dreamy in just the way a romantic meeting in Rome ought to be. Wyler is especially effective in presenting Audrey Hepburn in the most flattering light and getting the audience to identify with her.

Gregory Peck's character should be a bit of an adventurous rake who finds that love is more important than money or fame, but it is impossible for Peck to play a morally compromised character, and so even as he appears to be using Princess Ann for his own ends, his behavior is always correct. I was somewhat amused to notice that at all times Peck appears wearing a tie! Eddie Albert plays Peck's friend, a photographer/artist. It is interesting to note how Hollywood's perception of the paparazzi has changed over the years. Here bloodsucking, intrusive greed does not exist. Instead we have noble self-sacrifice!

I have seen most of Miss Hepburn's movies and I can say that she was never more enchanting than she is here. She is gorgeous and cute at the same time, charming and impish, sweet, regal and very winning. In a sense she started at the top with this film, garnering her only Oscar as Best Actress in 1953; but as her fans know she never came down off that pedestal. Even playing poor Eliza

Doolittle in *My Fair Lady* (1964), there was never any doubt about the quality of her style and character.

This is the most romantic film I have ever seen, perhaps partly because Miss Hepburn is so wonderful, but also because the script in a sense turns the usual woman's romantic fantasy upside down. Instead of the woman finding that the man she is in love with has fabulous wealth and position, it is the other way around!

The ending manages to be realistic yet romantic. There is a hint of something almost spiritual beyond what happens. So convincing are Hepburn and Peck that one can almost believe the story is true; and indeed I am sure that Trumbo lifted the essentials of the plot from some ancient tale.

I have a weakness for movies about unrequited love, or love that goes on forever, or love that is caught at some perfect moment and lives eternally in that moment. *Roman Holiday* is one of those near perfect movies that plays beautifully upon one of these themes.

Loser. *From Here to Eternity (1954) starring Burt Lancaster and Debra Kerr, and directed by Fred Zinneman, won. Also nominated:*
Julius Caesar (1953)
The Robe (1953)
Shane (1953)

Comment: From Here to Eternity, from the novel by James Jones, is an excellent movie, but as the years have gone by, Roman Holiday has surpassed it in popularity.

Schindler's List (1993) 9

Lest we forget...

Steven Spielberg on the holocaust. Naturally the kids are cute even as they are diving into the excrement-filled waters of the latrine to hide from the Nazis... Schindler, played believably by big, handsome Liam Neeson (he was the guy Whoopi Goldberg was panting over at the Oscars last month) is a sweet womanizer who exploits Jewish labor in his factories and then feels guilty about it and ends up saving the lives of eleven hundred. Ben Kingsley plays his accountant with precision and his usual subdued intensity. We have again all the Nazi horror, in some ways worst than ever, and rightly so. Here we see a lot of the random shooting of people. The Nazis just use them for target practice or blow their brains out just to be doing something. The cattle cars are there and the gas ovens and the Nazi psychopaths and all the rest of it, although Spielberg adds some touches like Ralph Fiennes as the Nazi who kept a Jewish woman he was interested in but couldn't love or even rape, but could only beat. And among the guards who are herding the Jews along are a couple who smile at the kids, as though Spielberg is saying, "here is this juxtaposition: the horror of the most

degraded and inhuman acts known to humankind, but look even the monsters think the kids are cute."

We humans ought to have our face rubbed in this at least once a decade. Still I think the actual concentration camp footage seen in, for example, *Sophie's Choice* (1982), to which Spielberg owes something, is as effective as anything could possibly be. When I see those films, shot by the triumphant Allied forces, I am again reminded that just concluded was the most depraved and horrific episode in human history. Nothing we have done was worse than the holocaust, although Stalin's purging of Russian society ranks a clear second. I think the fact that Spielberg filmed the whole thing in black and white and then turned it all to color with the shot of the actual Jews (now middle-aged) that Schindler saved from the Nazis was an unconscious tribute to the power of those grainy, flickering shots of horror, part of the legacy of the twentieth century. Perhaps it was a bit stagy, in the usual Spielberg style; however I have to say showing that one little Jewish girl's red dress (the only bit of color in the movie until the end) was a striking touch: we see her in the red dress when she hides and then when they dig up the bodies we see it again.

Winner.
Also nominated:
The Fugitive (1993)
In the Name of the Father (1993)
The Piano (1993)
The Remains of the Day (1993)

Shakespeare in Love (1998) 10

Hollywood at its best

This is the kind of movie the Academy loves and through its love, rewards.

The script by Stoppard and Norman is erudite and cunning, passionate and playful, filled with witticisms by and about the Bard; and the parallels to Shakespeare and his work, especially the play within a play, *Romeo and Juliet*, and the play to come, *Twelfth Night*, are marvelous and a bit miraculous. The romantic direction by Madden conjures up an Elizabethan England and its London theatre with enough lusty color to delight the poet himself. The acting is wonderful with Gwyneth Paltrow conquering a very demanding and delightful role as Viola/Tom Kent that will beckon and challenge actresses for decades to come. Joseph Fiennes as the young Shakespeare writing his Romeo and Juliet on the fly, fired with the energy from his adulterous love for the lovely Viola, is better than advertised.

Of course what would a Shakespearean play or a great Hollywood movie be without its bit players and supporting roles? Judi Dench as the queen in her Academy Award winning performance gives the impression of somebody doing something marvelously well but with such ease as to look unemployed. (I stole that line from somewhere.)

From the gutter snipe with his rodents to the queen's bad teeth, from Colin Firth's delightfully villainous Lord Wessex to Geoffrey Rush's wise, but bumbling stage manager, from the tavern trollops to the gentry at the ball (in which the sonnet within a play from Romeo and Juliet is once again given life by Fiennes and Paltrow) everything is expertly presented.

This is Hollywood at its best. For all the clunkers and the mass-mindless indulgences that are the usual fare—tinsel town, you are forgiven!

Winner.
Also nominated:
Elizabeth (1998)
Saving Private Ryan (1998)
The Thin Red Line (1998)
Life Is Beautiful (1997)

A Streetcar Named Desire (1951) 10

The other streetcar was named "Cemetery"

"I've always relied on the kindness of strangers," Blanche DuBois tells us near the end of this mesmerizing adaptation of the Tennessee Williams play; but what we have found out is that she has often relied on the warmth of strangers, very often, and now with her looks faded and her charm gone, she has become a sad, neurotic creature desperate for any sort of attention.

Vivian Leigh's portrayal of Tennessee Williams's languished southern rose is one of the most memorable and haunting performances of the American cinema. Seldom in the history of film has there been such excellent casting. Leigh of course won the Academy Award for best actress, but she was not alone. Karl Malden won for best supporting actor and Kim Hunter for best supporting actress. Marlon Brando could easily have won for his raw animal portrayal of Stanley Kowalski. Credit should also go to Elia Kazan for the artful mastery of his direction. In short this is one of the most celebrated movies of all time, a classic, period. But no mistake should be made about where the primary power comes from. It's from Tennessee Williams's Pulitzer Prize winning play, a work of theatrical genius second to none in the history of the American theater. Williams had the gift of understanding and the ability to project the melancholy self-delusion and sexual/social angst of the feminine psyche onto the stage, and to do it with objectivity and compassion. (Cf. Laura in *The Glass Menagerie* and Maggie in *Cat on a Hot Tin Roof*.)

Brando's interpretation of the animalistic Kowalski, typified by his screaming up the stairs, "Stella!" in tight t-shirt and bellowing voice, and his crude way with women, electrified audiences and established him as a star. A string of cinematic successes followed, highlighted by his work in *On the Waterfront* (1954) for which he won an academy award.

I want to add that we are driven by Desire until this silly dance concludes and we arrive at the Cemetery. In a beautifully observed bit of accidental irony, those names—"Desire" and "Cemetery"—are the names of streetcars that ran back and forth on the same line in New Orleans, giving inspiration to Williams's apt and unforgettable title.

Loser. *An American in Paris (1951), starring Gene Kelly and Leslie Caron, and directed by Vincente Minnelli, won.*
Also nominated:
Decision Before Dawn (1951)
A Place in the Sun (1951)
Quo Vadis (1951)

Sunset Boulevard (1950) 10

Among the best ever made

Joe Gillis, a failed writer played with an efficient cynicism by William Holden, blows out a tire escaping the repo man, limps into the driveway of an old Sunset Blvd mansion to hide, and thus enters a decadent world that traps him like a babe in a sticky womb. In this morality-tale, a la Billy Wilder and Charles Brackett, we learn that even an accidental gigolo earns his keep, and then some.

The voice-over and frame are appropriately reminiscent of a Forties' radio show, perhaps "Inner Sanctum" or "The Shadow." The images, from Gloria Swanson's greasy face and spidery fingers, to Eric Von Stroheim's wheezy organ, to the lighted pool with Joe's face down in it, ("This is where you came in") are indelible.

This is a great movie, built on character and story, well-crafted amidst the haunting atmosphere of an "undead" Hollywood. They don't make them like this anymore, truly.

Loser. *All About Eve, starring Bette Davis and Anne Baxter, directed by Joseph L. Mankiewicz, won.*
Also nominated:
Born Yesterday (1950)
Father of the Bride (1950)
King Solomon's Mines (1950)

The Thin Man (1934) 10

One of the classics and a delightful diversion

This, the first Thin Man, is one of the most beloved of the old time movies, and watching it for the first time since I was a child—I'm sure I saw it in the fifties at one of those three features, a cartoon and Movietone for a dime theaters, but remember nothing—it's not hard to see why. The chemistry between William Powell and Myrna Loy (Nick and Nora Charles) is effervescent, bubbly and delicious. It is obvious they are in love and take such joy in each other's company while teasing each other in a most delightful way. You will just love the way Asta, their dog (who is quite a star in this movie himself) covers his eyes in the final scene—such a delicate dog with such delicate feelings! (Actually I understand that all dogs in movies, in those days at least, were females for reasons that might be imagined.)

The movie starts a little slow by modern standards, like a stage play, but becomes increasingly enthralling, until suddenly it is over, and YES, let's do a sequel! And they did, six of them, but, well, sequels may or may not be as good as the original. In this case, I understand they weren't and I'm not surprised. It would be hard to achieve something like The Thin Man again. Everything just fell into place, the plot was agreeable and clever, the lesser characters quirky and intriguing, the direction by W.S. "One Take Woody" Van Dyke smooth and focused, and the twenties going on the thirties (but not really) atmosphere was authentic with the rich holding lavish dinner parties and drinking way too much, especially Nick Charles (Powell) who complained that sleuthing caused him to get behind in his drinking.

The witty dialogue comes first from Dashiell Hammett's novel and then from Albert Hackett who adapted the script. Hackett was just getting warmed up. He wrote his first script in 1931 (something called Up Pops the Devil) and his last for The Father of the Bride Part II in 1995 at the age of 95!—well, he got partial credit for that script which was morphed out of his 1951 script for Father's Little Dividend and the original Father of the Bride (1951).

By the way, I always imagined that "the thin man" was the detective Nick Charles, but actually the thin man is Clyde Wynant, the eccentric inventor played by Edward Ellis who goes missing after the first reel. However, everybody thought the same thing, so in the sequels, the thin man is the detective.

One of the reasons the repartee between Nick and Nora is so great is that it was taken (somewhat) from real life exchanges between Hammett and his longtime live-together girl friend the celebrated playwright, Lillian Hellman.

Anybody with any pretension of knowing Hollywood films has seen this. See it yourself if you haven't. It's a delight and will take you back to a time full of styles so very different from those of today.

Loser. *It Happened One Night (1934), starring Clark Gable and Claudette Colbert, and directed by Frank Capra, understandably won.*
Also nominated:
Eleven other films including The Gay Divorcee (1934), Imitation of Life (1934), etc.

Comment: The long-running format with five nominees occasionally left out a film that might have won, but had the virtue of keeping it simple (and short) for the television show. Starting in 2010 there are ten films nominated for Best Picture.

The Third Man (1949) 10

An atmospheric study in black and white

I'm not one to rave about "glorious black and white" cinematography. Generally speaking, if it was good in black and white, it would be even better in color. However, there are exceptions. Kubrick's *Dr. Strangelove* would not be improved in color, and Orson Welles' *Citizen Kane* would not even work as well in color, partially because of the "Movietone" and front page photography feel that Welles wanted, but also because color would add nothing to the sharp focus on an ultimately empty icon of an entirely black and white medium. And Sir Carol Reed's *The Third Man* is a strongly atmospheric film that clearly is better in black and white. It might be said that if there isn't enough light, it is false to pretend to color. Flowers that bloom at night are usually white.

It's Vienna, in a winter month, just after WWII. The city is still in ruins and rubble, still occupied by Allied troops. There is a forlorn sense of loss and waste hanging in the air like a dark blanket of gloom, and the citizens still suffer from a shortage of consumer goods and basic medicines; a good part of the economy is still driven by the black market. Spring and a colorful rejuvenation seem remote. And so the sharp black and white Oscar-winning cinematography of Robert Krasker, imaginative and deeply evocative of a great city in darkness, was perfect. From the ornate facades of old buildings to the wet catacombs of the sewers to the suddenly illuminated face of a slyly smirking Orson Welles, the camera carries the story driven by the zither theme, played over and over again, sometimes loud and insistent, sometimes soft and yielding, commenting all the while like an ironic jester.

But *The Third Man* is more than brilliant cinematography set to a haunting melody. The well-chosen cast, led by Joseph Cotton as an urban American who writes pulp Westerns, and Alida Valli (who followed this performance with a long career in the Italian cinema) as the misplaced Anna Schmidt, and Trevor Howard as British Major Calloway, and of course Orson Welles as the dark and mysterious Harry Lime, was excellent all around. The script by Graham Greene from his novel of the same name is intelligent and compelling. The editing and direction by Reed paced the story nicely, neither too sharply cut nor too drawn out because this is a film that demands both quick action sequences and moments of mirthless pause for mood and reflection.

This is a great film because almost everything was done right. The result is a work of art that invades and sets up permanent residence in our psyches. I saw this for the first time as a boy many years ago and it remained in my memory as the most mysterious and eerie movie I had ever seen. Seeing it again in the twenty-first century only confirms the experience of that small boy.

This is included in the film noir canon, and indeed it represents itself well there. But *The Third Man* is better understood as a film of stark realism as well as a mystery in the tradition of an older genre that accepts the common standards of human decency as right and correct (as Catholic Graham Greene believed them) and does not give way to amorality or the success of evil. Harry Lime is a man of charm and character, of intelligence and worldly wiles, but he is also a man with a sociopathic personality and a callous disregard for human life other than his own. It is giving away nothing to realize that such a man in Greene's world, in the world of the mystery story—like something from Agatha Christie, perhaps—will not succeed in the end. But what actually does transpire in the end, indelibly marked by the final shot of Anna walking directly in the middle of the road between two matching lines of cold, leafless trees, is from the school of realism, a realism born of nearly a century of intermittent war and recurrent human tragedy for Vienna, for Austria, for most of Europe. There is in this film no compromise with that truth.

See this for Orson Welles, the 25-year-old wunderkind director and star of *Citizen Kane* (1941), here in his early thirties, enjoying the supreme compliment of starring in a film in which are employed, in frank imitation of his work in *Citizen Kane*, some of his original cinematic techniques.

Loser. *All About Eve, starring Bette Davis and Anne Baxter, directed by Joseph L. Mankiewicz, won.*
Also nominated:
Born Yesterday (1950)
Father of the Bride (1950)
King Solomon's Mines (1950)
Sunset Boulevard (1950)

Comment: It's something close to amazing (today) that The Third Man *was **not nominated** for the Best Picture Oscar in 1951, the year it was eligible. However, even if it had been nominated, there was little chance that it would have won, going up against two of the greatest films ever made in* All About Eve *and* Sunset Boulevard. *Carol Reed's direction was nominated but Mankiewicz won that Oscar too.*

Titanic (1998) 8

Grandiose schmaltz skillfully presented

This is much better than word of mouth led me to believe. Of course the script is corny and full of simplistic sentiment and it panders shamelessly to mid-brow sensitivities, and there's no question that the main intent is to jerk mass tears (but we could have guessed that from the

subject). Still the cinematography is wonderful, Kate Winslet is captivating, and the plot clever. This is an old time Hollywood movie made not only to seduce the audience, but the Academy as well. And it succeeds.

Billy Zane is perfectly one-dimensional and completely familiar as the conceited and selfish, immoral heir to a Gilded Age fortune. Kate Winslet as his intended is a ravishing beauty with oomph and a mind of her own. Leonardo DiCaprio as the wily and clever sketch artist who seduces her while twice saving her life comes across curiously as part Huck Finn and part John Boy. His romantic bravado in the freezing water, saying he was so lucky to have won the steamship ticket because it allowed him to meet her, was enough to embarrass even the most hardened Harlequin novelist.

Most of the action before the bow scene was almost painful because just about every line was written so that a ten-year-old could understand what he was supposed to feel about whom. Evil, decadent rich people. Good, clever, hard working poor people. (They even party better.) Cliché followed cliché. But the romantic bow scene was artfully staged, and after that Kate came to life. It was strange to see her in the early scenes. She seemed almost a bad actress, as though the mediocrity of the direction had reduced her. But her part was so big and she had so much to do that her natural talent overcame the early junior high school text and the later schmaltz.

Since the audience knows the ending, Director James Cameron knew he had a fine opportunity for dramatic irony, but his touch was a bit heavy handed, e.g., as they're boarding, a guy says, "We're the luckiest sons of b...s in the world." (Yeah, right.) And since the audience knows eighty-five years of history unknown to the Titanic passengers, we get these further heavy bits of irony: On Picasso: "He won't amount to a thing. Trust me." And, "Freud, who is he? Is he a passenger?" (Check the heads of the mid-brow audience nodding knowingly.)

My sensitivities were most offended, however, when Cameron has the salvage crew smugly celebrate their good fortune before the safe they have hauled up is actually opened. That was the tip off for everybody in the audience to wisely know there would be little of value in the safe. Duh. In real life those guys don't celebrate until the gold is in the hand. Cameron's style is to flatter the audience, make them think they're smart, the usual pandering of a mediocre talent. Cameron even tries his hand at some cheap symbolism, i.e., mommie tells Rose that she must marry this suffocating and insufferable man because they need the money (as she vigorously tightens Rose's confining corset).

All right. Why did the Academy vote this best picture? Simply because it was a popular lavish production squarely in the Hollywood tradition, employing a whole bunch of movie folk, and it was a financial success, just what the industry craves. I should add that everything technical in the film was excellent, and Cameron's dramatic direction was a lot better than his dialogue. Also, because of the exquisite detail, watching the big ship sink was a whole lot of fun.

Winner.
Also nominated:
As Good as It Gets (1997)
The Full Monty (1997)
Good Will Hunting (1997)
L.A. Confidential (1997)

The Treasure of the Sierra Madre (1948) 9

We ain't got no stinkin' badges!

This, one of the funniest lines in cinema, certainly one of the most famous, is actually (as aficionados know) a misquote. What Alfonso Bedoya, who plays "Gold Hat," actually says, when he and his bandito friends are asked for their badges, is "Badges? We ain't got no badges. We don't need no badges. I don't have to show you any stinkin' badges!" I wonder if anybody at the time had any idea how funny this would hit audiences.

John Huston wrote the screenplay (adapting B. Traven's novel) and directed his father, Walter Huston along with Humphrey Bogart, Tim Holt, and Bruce Bennett in this classic from my favorite age of cinema (the late forties/early fifties). Walter Huston won an academy award as Best Supporting Actor in 1948 and John Huston garnered Oscars for his direction and his screenplay. Bogart won nothing, but I have to say he did a great job.

It's easy to think of Humphrey Bogart as always playing Humphrey Bogart as he has done in so many movies, particularly in mysteries and especially as a private eye. But here we see a different Bogart, one who is not entirely sympathetic; indeed as the down and out Fred C. Dobbs he is a bit of a scoundrel and more than a little paranoid. In watching this one realizes that Bogart had a much greater range than he is sometimes given credit for. I also recall him alongside Katharine Hepburn in *The African Queen* (1951) also directed by John Huston, and in *The Caine Mutiny* (1954). In the former he did win an Oscar, and in the latter, as Captain Queeg, he gave perhaps his most unforgettable performance.

This is a tale of greed and the fever that arises when one hunts for gold. Walter Huston plays a crusty old miner named Howard who tries one more time to strike it rich. Dobbs and Bob Curtin (Tim Holt) are seduced by the wily old miner's romantic tales and the three of them go off into the Sierra Madre mountains near Tampico, Mexico to prospect. Naturally they hit pay dirt, but in-between the growing madness of Dobbs and the Mexican bandits, theirs is an uneasy existence. What happens to the gold and to the three men is fascinating to watch, and we sense a timeless human psychology at work. Bob Curtin expresses part of it this way: "You know, the worst ain't so bad when it finally happens. Not half as bad as you figure it'll be before it's happened."

This movie is as good as its reputation, which is considerable, but it's not perfect. Some of it plays a little too simplistically, as when Howard saves the Mexican boy amid the worshipful natives, and some of it is a little silly, as when the bandits mistake gold for sand—not likely! But the almost epic quality of the tale and the felicitous direction as well as many interesting and humorous touches, make this one of the best ever made, and something no true film buff should miss. By the way, the little Mexican boy who sells Dobbs the lottery ticket is a bronzed up Robert Blake.

Loser. *Hamlet (1948) starring Laurence Olivier and Jean Simmons, and directed by Olivier, won.*
Also nominated:
Johnny Belinda (1948)
The Red Shoes (1948)
The Snake Pit (1948)

Comment: It is a shame that it was this Hamlet that the Academy chose to reward. It's not bad, and Olivier is a fine Hamlet. The problem is they cut out a lot. The best Hamlet without question is Kenneth Branagh's from 1996, as mentioned above.

In case you missed it, the three films not nominated were:
2001: A Space Odyssey (1968)
Memento (2000)
The Third Man (1949)

Chapter Two:

Second Guessing the Academy

Here are all the winners and nominees for the years 2010 back to 1945. (Nineteen-forty-five was the first year the nominees were limited to five films. Beginning in 2010 the Academy began allowing ten films to be nominated.)

Circle your choice.

2010 Winner: *The Hurt Locker*
Also nominated: *A Serious Man*
  An Education
  Avatar
  District 9
  Inglourious Basterds
  Precious
  The Blind Side
  Up
  Up in the Air

2009 Winner: *Slumdog Millionaire*
Also nominated: *The Curious Case of Benjamin Button*
  Frost/Nixon
  Milk
  The Reader

2008 Winner: *No Country for Old Men*
Also nominated: *Atonement*
  Juno
  Michael Clayton
  There Will Be Blood

2007 Winner: *The Departed*
Also nominated: *Babel*
  Letters from Iwo Jima
  Little Miss Sunshine
  The Queen

2006 Winner: *Crash*
Also nominated: *Brokeback Mountain*
  Capote
  Good Night, and Good Luck
  Munich

2005 Winner: *Million Dollar Baby*
Also nominated: *The Aviator*
  Finding Neverland
  Ray
  Sideways

2004 Winner: *Lord of the Rings: Return of the King*

Also nominated: *Lost in Translation*
  Master and Commander: The Far Side of the World
  Mystic River
  Seabiscuit

2003 Winner: *Chicago*
Also nominated: *Gangs of New York*
  The Hours
  Lord of the Rings: The Two Towers
  The Pianist

2002 Winner: *A Beautiful Mind*
Also nominated: *Gosford Park*
  In the Bedroom
  Lord of the Rings: The Fellowship of the Ring
  Moulin Rouge

2001 Winner: *Gladiator*
Also nominated: *Chocolat*
  Erin Brockovich
  Traffic (2000)
  Crouching Tiger, Hidden Dragon

2000 Winner: *American Beauty*
Also nominated: *The Cider House Rules*
  The Green Mile
  The Insider
  The Sixth Sense

1999 Winner: *Shakespeare in Love*
Also nominated: *Elizabeth*
  Saving Private Ryan
  The Thin Red Line
  Life Is Beautiful

1998 Winner: *Titanic*
Also nominated: *As Good as It Gets*
  The Full Monty
  Good Will Hunting
  L.A. Confidential

1997 Winner: *The English Patient*
Also nominated: *Fargo*
                 Jerry Maguire
                 Secrets & Lies
                 Shine

1996 Winner: *Braveheart*
Also nominated: *Apollo 13*
                 Babe
                 Il Postino
                 Sense and Sensibility

1995 Winner: *Forrest Gump*
Also nominated: *Four Weddings and a Funeral*
                 Pulp Fiction
                 Quiz Show
                 The Shawshank Redemption

1994 Winner: *Schindler's List*
Also nominated: *The Fugitive*
                 In the Name of the Father
                 The Piano
                 The Remains of the Day

1993 Winner: *Unforgiven*
Also nominated: *The Crying Game*
                 A Few Good Men
                 Howard's End
                 Scent of a Woman

1992 Winner: *The Silence of the Lambs*
Also nominated: *Beauty and the Beast*
                 Bugsy
                 JFK
                 The Prince of Tides

1991 Winner: *Dances with Wolves*
Also nominated: *Awakenings*
                 Ghost
                 The Godfather: Part III
                 Goodfellas

1990 Winner: *Driving Miss Daisy*
Also nominated: *Born on the Fourth of July*
                 Dead Poets Society
                 Field of Dreams
                 My Left Foot: The Story of Christy Brown

1989 Winner: *Rain Man*
Also nominated: *The Accidental Tourist*
                 Dangerous Liaisons
                 Mississippi Burning
                 Working Girl

1988 Winner: *The Last Emperor*
Also nominated: *Broadcast News*
                 Fatal Attraction
                 Hope and Glory

                 Moonstruck

1987 Winner: *Platoon*
Also nominated: *Children of a Lesser God*
                 Hannah and Her Sisters
                 The Mission
                 A Room with a View

1986 Winner: *Out of Africa*
Also nominated: *The Color Purple*
                 Kiss of the Spider Woman
                 Prizzi's Honor
                 Witness

1985 Winner: *Amadeus*
Also nominated: *The Killing Fields*
                 A Passage to India
                 Places in the Heart
                 A Soldier's Story

1984 Winner: *Terms of Endearment*
Also nominated: *The Big Chill*
                 The Dresser
                 The Right Stuff
                 Tender Mercies

1983 Winner: *Gandhi*
Also nominated: *E.T.*
                 Missing
                 Tootsie
                 The Verdict

1982 Winner: *Chariots of Fire*
Also nominated: *Atlantic City*
                 On Golden Pond
                 Raiders of the Lost Ark
                 Reds

1981 Winner: *Ordinary People*
Also nominated: *Coal Miner's Daughter*
                 The Elephant Man
                 Raging Bull
                 Tess

1980 Winner: *Kramer vs. Kramer*
Also nominated: *All That Jazz*
                 Apocalypse Now
                 Breaking Away
                 Norma Rae

1979 Winner: *The Deer Hunter*
Also nominated: *Coming Home*
                 Heaven Can Wait
                 Midnight Express
                 An Unmarried Woman

1978 Winner: *Annie Hall*
Also nominated: *The Goodbye Girl*
                 Julia
                 Star Wars
                 The Turning Point

1977 Winner: *Rocky*
Also nominated: *All the President's Men*
                              Bound for Glory
                              Network
                              Taxi Driver

1976 Winner: *One Flew over the Cuckoo's Nest*
Also nominated: *Barry Lyndon*
                              Dog Day Afternoon
                              Jaws
                              Nashville

1975 Winner: *The Godfather Part II*
Also nominated: *Chinatown*
                              The Conversation
                              Lenny
                              The Towering Inferno

1974 Winner: *The Sting*
Also nominated: *American Graffiti*
                              The Exorcist
                              A Touch of Class
                              Cries and Whispers

1973 Winner: *The Godfather*
Also nominated: *Cabaret*
                              Deliverance
                              Sounder
                              The Emigrants

1972 Winner: *The French Connection*
Also nominated: *A Clockwork Orange*
                              Fiddler on the Roof
                              The Last Picture Show
                              Nicholas and Alexandra

1971 Winner: *Patton*
Also nominated: *Airport*
                              Five Easy Pieces
                              Love Story
                              M*A*S*H

1970 Winner: *Midnight Cowboy*
Also nominated: *Anne of the Thousand Days*
                              Butch Cassidy and the Sundance Kid
                              Hello, Dolly!
                              Z

1969 Winner: *Oliver!*
Also nominated: *Funny Girl*
                              The Lion in Winter
                              Rachel, Rachel
                              Romeo and Juliet

1968 Winner: *In the Heat of the Night*
Also nominated: *Bonnie and Clyde*
                              Doctor Dolittle
                              The Graduate
                              Guess Who's Coming to Dinner

1967 Winner: *A Man for All Seasons*
Also nominated: *Alfie*
                              The Russians Are Coming the Russians Are Coming
                              The Sand Pebbles
                              Who's Afraid of Virginia Woolf?

1966 Winner: *The Sound of Music*
Also nominated: *Darling*
                              Doctor Zhivago
                              Ship of Fools
                              A Thousand Clowns

1965 Winner: *My Fair Lady*
Also nominated: *Alexis Zorbas*
                              Becket
                              Dr. Strangelove
                              Mary Poppins

1964 Winner: *Tom Jones*
Also nominated: *America, America*
                              Cleopatra
                              How the West Was Won
                              Lilies of the Field

1963 Winner: *Lawrence of Arabia*
Also nominated: *The Longest Day*
                              The Music Man
                              Mutiny on the Bounty
                              To Kill a Mockingbird

1962 Winner: *West Side Story*
Also nominated: *Fanny*
                              The Guns of Navarone
                              The Hustler
                              Judgment at Nuremberg

1961 Winner: *The Apartment*
Also nominated: *The Alamo*
                              Elmer Gantry
                              Sons and Lovers
                              The Sundowners

1960 Winner: *Ben-Hur*
Also nominated: *Anatomy of a Murder*
                              The Diary of Anne Frank
                              The Nun's Story
                              Room at the Top

1959 Winner: *Gigi*
Also nominated: *Auntie Mame*
                              Cat on a Hot Tin Roof
                              The Defiant Ones
                              Separate Tables

1958 Winner: *The Bridge on the River Kwai*
Also nominated: *12 Angry Men*
                              Peyton Place
                              Sayonaa

Witness for the Prosecution

1957 Winner: *Around the World in 80 Days*
Also nominated: *Friendly Persuasion*
Giant
The King and I
The Ten Commandments

1956 Winner: *Marty*
Also nominated: *Love Is a Many-Splendored Thing*
Mister Roberts
Picnic
The Rose Tattoo

1955 Winner: *On the Waterfront*
Also nominated: *The Caine Mutiny*
The Country Girl
Seven Brides for Seven Brothers
Three Coins in the Fountain

1954 Winner: *From Here to Eternity*
Also nominated: *Julius Caesar*
The Robe
Roman Holiday
Shane

1953 Winner: *The Greatest Show on Earth*
Also nominated: *High Noon*
Ivanhoe
Moulin Rouge
The Quiet Man

1952 Winner: *An American in Paris*
Also nominated: *Decision Before Dawn*
A Place in the Sun
Quo Vadis
A Streetcar Named Desire

1951 Winner: *All About Eve*

Also nominated: *Born Yesterday*
Father of the Bride
King Solomon's Mines
Sunset Boulevard

1950 Winner: *All the King's Men*
Also nominated: *Battleground*
The Heiress
A Letter to Three Wives
Twelve O'Clock High

1949 Winner: *Hamlet*
Also nominated: *Johnny Belinda*
The Red Shoes
The Snake Pit
The Treasure of the Sierra Madre

1948 Winner: *Gentleman's Agreement*
Also nominated: *The Bishop's Wife*
Crossfire
Great Expectations
Miracle on 34th Street

1947 Winner: *The Best Years of Our Lives*
Also nominated: *The Chronicle History of King Henry the Fifth*
It's a Wonderful Life
The Razor's Edge
The Yearling

1946 Winner: *The Lost Weekend*
Also nominated: *Anchors Aweigh*
The Bells of St. Mary's
Mildred Pierce
Spellbound

1945 Winner: *Going My Way*
Also nominated: *Double Indemnity*
Gaslight
Since You Went Away
Wilson

Chapter Three:

Trashed!

or

I Can't Believe I Watched the Whole Thing:
Ten Very Bad Movies

These are the ten worse films I actually sat through and reviewed. There are hundreds of other films that are just as bad or worse or almost as bad that I did not sit through and did not review. And there are a few films just as bad that I reviewed but for some reason did not trash.

After each review there is a place to indicate your approval or disapproval of my sentiments. Or go to the Website at Amazon.com or IMDb.com and vote and/or comment. (Be kind.)

1

Not to be confused with the first Alien *(1979), directed by Ridley Scott, which is a classic of the sci fi genre.*

Alien Resurrection (1997) 2

I was rooting for the aliens

Just ugly, kind of like a perverse Star Trek for horror fans. The dialogue is particularly bad, one of the worst scripts I've encountered lately. The actors curiously talked like they thought they were making a prison film or perhaps a low-budget Mexican western. B-movie extras would be embarrassed to say some of the lines.

Winona Ryder is horribly miscast and looks and sounds stupid, although her voice is kind of amusing, especially if you like to hear her say "f—-." (I kinda like it.) Sig Weaver is semi-interesting in a bloodless and buff sort of way; but the rest of this dreary, low-brow space shoot 'em up with monsters, is a yawn. If you get off on gross biological freaks in formaldehyde, however, or like to pucker up to T Rex teeth dripping acid, or go for that special feel of flesh being ripped, etc., this might be for you.

Absolutely worst line (but funny as twice-removed accidental humor) is Ron Perlman's comment (after Weaver burns and blows away the grotesque embryos and her own twisted, misshapen clone) "Must be a chick thing."

Banal observation: you'd think after all the years in space, evolving away from mother earth, there would be some advance in degenerate habits; but no, these space terrorists still smoke cigarettes and drink whiskey—and I'M SURE basketball with metal nets will still be played on playgrounds orbiting around Jupiter.

Banal observation number two: with all that fire power, you'd think they'd blow holes in the ship and lose all the air. Alas, no.

There's a special place in hell for people who produce movies like this. In it they are fastened into seats with their eye lids propped open, forced to watch their creations for eternity. I think they should also be forced to talk about how good the movie is and how they've done something just wonderful. And could we hear Winona Ryder tell us once again what a thrill it was working with Sigourney Weaver?

You were right on and I thank you for finally pointing out what a turkey this movie was_____
You were totally unfair and may you reside in that special level of hell in which all the DVDs are blank_____

2

I realize that in the bad old days when the first women were admitted to West Point and similar institutions of higher machismo, the cadets made their lives hellish, but The General's Daughter *goes well beyond what actually happened, and is an insult to West Point done merely to pander to knee jerk loser sentiment in order to make a buck.*

The General's Daughter (1999) 2

Tasteless and stupid

Also offensive, sick and very far removed from reality.

I mean ten West Point cadets sadistically gang rape a co-ed cadet for hours while brutally beating her up, and the Army decides, on a balance of considerations, to just forget it? Huh? And then the general himself, loving father of the girl, tells her to buck up and pretend it didn't happen? What? I mean there are some sociopathic guys at the Point, no doubt, but ten sickies in the same class stupid and sadistic enough to do something like that because they are jealous of her? The Army might well try to cover it up, but they sure as hell would want to know who did it. And it gets worse. The lifestyle that the daughter adopts because of this horror and the insane way she seeks to rid herself of the memory is like something dreamed up by a serial killer screen writer on a bad day. And then, after treating us to this nightmare of degrading misogyny, the authors, looking for a saving grace, run some closing words down the screen telling us that now there are over 200,000 women serving proudly in the military, as though perhaps we ought to be thankful for the events depicted in this film for that fact, or maybe they hoped to create the illusion that those events actually happened!

I'm taking names: the director is Simon West, novel by Nelson DeMille, screenplay by Christopher Bertolini and William Goldman, who, alas, has seen better days. Here's an example of how trite some of the dialogue is. Travola's character is a seasoned veteran who actually fought in Vietnam and now is a warrant officer. He is told by Col. Fowler, another even more seasoned veteran, in dead seriousness that there are three ways to do things, "the right way, the wrong way, and the army way." Wow, that was original probably a hundred years ago, the sort of wisdom usually handed out by drill instructors to Private E-1's during basic training, not something a colonel might say to a warrant officer. Or, here's another. Travolta, recalling how as a raw recruit in Vietnam, he was by chance comforted by the general who asked where he was from, and when he heard from Boston, told him that the Red Sox had won the day before. Orchestral strings soar and the camera pans to the faces of Col. Fowler and Madeleine Stowe to show us they know how uplifting and inspirational that was for the frightened young man.

But don't blame the actors for this travesty. John Travolta, who begins the movie as an undercover sergeant, put a lot of (somewhat stupid) energy into his part, including a funny southern accent, and obviously had a good time. And you can see that James Woods tried hard to infuse some sparkle into the insipid lines and to bring some depth into the shallow and cliché-ridden character he plays. James Cromwell as the general was as ugly as sin and twice as despicable, while Madeleine Stowe looked good enough to ravish. And I thought Leslie Stefanson did a commendable job as the incomprehensible daughter.

Bottom line: a new place in hell has been set aside for the purveyors of this sort of sexploitation thriller We'll call it the Griffin Mill Screening Room (after the Machiavellian producer from The Player (1992)), a place in which the producers, the director and the writers are forced to view their concoction until the evaporation of the last black hole in space or the Big Crunch, whichever comes first.

You were right on..._____
You were totally unfair..._____

3

This is actually a bit of a cult favorite, and so this nasty review got negged by the voters, my son-in-law among them.

Honeymoon in Vegas (1992) 3

Cures insomnia

Sad but good for thirty seconds was Anne Bancroft on her death bed getting her son Nicolas Cage to promise never to marry. This scene is followed by two minutes of running the credits over a cutesy cartoon sequence like something retro from the late fifties or early sixties. *Sure* he's never going to marry, especially when his girlfriend is Sarah Jessica Parker, pretty girl with very rounded tush and gams of steel.

This is a low-brow flick, stupid enough to be campy, or at least that was the idea. Elvis impersonators are always good for a laugh, right? And James Caan as a sleazy Vegas gambler, that's good, huh? And a guy losing his wife in a card game? You gotta love it!

Not. As in NOT funny, NOT clever, NOT interesting and NOT worth watching. I gave up after about fifteen minutes, and I tried, I really did. (Actually, my insomnia was not completely cured. I had a relapse, and I confess: I watched the whole thing!)

You were right on..._____
You were totally unfair..._____

4

Horror is my least favorite genre and I wouldn't have watched this except for the fact that a favorite director, James Mangold, directed. Turns out—to judge from the quality of this movie—he doesn't really like the horror genre either.

Identity (2003) 4

If this were a book it would be psychobabble

This is really a mess. One wonders how such movies get made. James Mangold, who was off to such fine start in his directorial career with the critically acclaimed *Heavy* (1995) and the superior psychodrama *Girl, Interrupted* (1999), and even the slightly offbeat but intriguing *Cop Land* (1997), really loses it here with this bizarro attempt at something like *Psycho* and *David and Lisa* meet Agatha Christie's "Ten Little Indians."

The premise is ridiculous and the resolution just plain silly. Without revealing anything (the denouement of the obtuse plot being perhaps the only thing that might keep the thumb of most intelligent viewers over the age of, say, fourteen, off the stop button), let me say that when it's over you just might feel cheated.

John Cusack stars as an ex-cop, now a chauffeur, who can suture wounds. The scene is the Nevada/California desert during a savage downpour that traps ten (+1) people at an isolated motel where bloody mayhem of the most inexplicable sort ensues as one by one the guests turn up dead. The action consists of wet people screaming and staring with horror at such sights as a dead man with a baseball bat shoved three-quarters of the way down his throat, etc. They insult each other a lot. Prostitutes don't like cops; little guys who never got any, hate prostitutes; and the little boy doesn't really love his mommy, etc. As the coincidences pile up (as the motel proprietor remarked, with the odds against being "trillions to one") we begin to realize that either something supernatural is going on or... You guessed it. It's all a....

But I can't say. We do get a hint of how everything will turn out when Mangold flash-forwards to a group of shrinks and other interested parties who are holding a kind of seance around what seems to be John Cusack's character.

Anyway, even the acting is not that good with the usually very fine Cusack seemingly infected by the deficiencies of the other players, or the stupidities of the script, or the impatient-to-get-it-over-with direction by Mangold. (I don't think the actors wanted too many takes in all that water, and it shows.) At any rate if you want to see a little kid and some mediocre actors overact or a lot of people deadpan the horror their eyes spy while barking at each other or you just like seeing Hollywood players have to make a living while wet, go for it. Otherwise, hit the off button and watch reruns of "That 70's Show."

You were right on..._____
You were totally unfair..._____

5

I also don't care much for serial killer/slasher movies, but there is so much money in making them that some very fine directors and actors have gotten involved. This is actually one of the better efforts.

Copycat (1995) 4

Counterfeit *Silence of the Lambs*

This is an exploitation movie, pure and simple, professionally done. What is being exploited is the public's fear and fascination with psychopathic serial killers. Sigourney Weaver plays a shrink, who is an expert on the species, gone slightly bananas with fear. We have the usual tinkling music to warn us that evil is afoot, the targeted woman alone in her apartment, the investigating cops one step behind, and of course the mad man—or actually mad men: as in *Silence of the Lambs* there are two of them, one in jail and one out.

Why anybody would want to make such a movie is beyond me. Money doesn't really explain it. I think the desire to show others that you can exploit the public better than they can is the motivation.

Holly Hunter plays a homicide detective in a ponytail. She's cute.

You were right on..._____
You were totally unfair..._____

6

One of several movies that exploited the fresh sensuality of a very young Alicia Silverstone. A couple of others besides the well-known and very good Clueless *(1995) are* Scattered Dreams *(1993) and* True Crime *(1995).*

The Crush (1993) 4

A Lolita from hell

This was Alicia Silverstone's debut film after which she went on to star in some Aerosmith videos (what red-blooded American male can ever forget seeing her and Liv Tyler in "Crazy"?) after which she got the lead in *Clueless* (1995).

In *Clueless* of course she was a sweet, adorable and slightly empty-headed Valley Girl. Here she is what might be called a Lolita from hell. Director Alan Shapiro even has her do a Sue Lyon (from Kubrick's 1964 *Lolita*) looking-over-her-sunglasses imitation to start the film. We soon learn that she is 14 "almost 15." (Silverstone was actually 15-years-old during the filming.) She is also rich and very talented, plays a classical piano, knows the scientific names of beetles and wasps, has skipped two grades, etc. The film itself might be dubbed a kind of "Fatal Attraction" for teeny-boppers.

Cary Elwes plays Nick Eliot who is looking for some digs as the film begins. He is a writer who just got a gig with an important, trendy magazine. After nearly bumping into Adrian (Silverstone) with his car, he looks askance and sees a sign advertising a cottage for rent in back of a large house with estate. Turns out this is where Adrian lives with her parents.

Somehow this reminds me of William Holden as the writer Joe Gillis pulling into that driveway on Sunset Boulevard (1950). He should have looked in the other direction! He should have run the other way! When Little Miss Crazy gets a crush, it is a hum-dinger. Maybe Nick should have just surrendered at the start and she would have been bored with him in a couple of months at most. But unfortunately, Nick Eliot is the epitome of the clueless male. He doesn't see the danger until it is too late. He is slightly compromised because he has kissed her, he has wandered about her house when her parents haven't been at home, and worse yet he doesn't have an inkling of the strength of her passion. To be honest I felt a little sorry for her having to deal with all that rejection! I think this would have played more realistically had Adrian's part been given to an ugly little shrew in the making. But then of course the film would not have found any kind of audience.

Well, this is a familiar premise and the kind I like to see worked out and resolved—well, I like to look at Alicia, anyway. Unfortunately Alan Shapiro, who also wrote the script, has the originality of a photocopy machine and just milks the premise while mindlessly escalating the bizarro. Suffice it to say that Little Miss Crazy doesn't take no for an answer and that Nick stupidly behaves in a way that just makes his situation worse. The ending does have the virtue of being nicely ironic while suggesting the hoped-for sequel.

*You were right on...*_____
*You were totally unfair...*_____

7

Something's Gotta Give (2003) 4
Fifty-(or maybe sixty-) something chick flick fantasy

Let's see: Erica Berry (played full out by Diane Keaton in a role to die for—if you're an actress of a certain age) is a successful playwright with a beautiful daughter (Amanda Peet) and at least one very fine bosom buddy (Frances McDormand). Along comes Harry Sanborn (Jack Nicholson, 66) in his PJ's or underwear—I forget which—to be discovered behind the opened door of her refrigerator ("Boy Meets Girl, Cute," as they say in Hollywood). Turns out he is dating her twenty something daughter Marin. Well, gee, what a guy.

However daughter and man about town have not yet consummated their relationship; indeed when they try, Viagra Harry has a heart attack. And now the plot thickens. Enter handsome, dashing, young and very eligible Dr. Julian Mercer (Keanu Reeves) who tells Harry that he

can't go anywhere yet because they need to keep a close watch on his heart. So Erica ends up babysitting him. Ah, yes we can see where this one is going. Playboy of the Western World finally but finally gives up the young stuff, meets the love of his life (Erica), and falls clumsily, but hopelessly in love with her.

For Erica, who hasn't felt a man's touch for lo these many years, it's like electrifying. Ah, but here's the rub. The old bachelor can't comprehend his feelings. After all he has never but never dated anyone over thirty before, and the prospect of COMMITMENT is way scary. So he demurs, shall we say. Meanwhile, the dashing young doctor reveals his romantic and clearly carnal interest in—no, NOT the beautiful young daughter! How prosaic would that be? No, he reveals he has quite a yen for the great playwright herself, and age does not matter in the slightest!

Okay, at this point if I were a woman of any age I would say that my cup doth runneth over. I would also suspect that this Fantasyland is a bit much for belief. But hey, why should the starlets have all the fun?

Anyway, Nancy Meyers's direction of this self-authored fairytale will appeal to its targeted audience no doubt, but don't try to screen this for your boyfriend. He won't survive the first reel.

Incidentally, this flick is not even in the same league as the somewhat similar romantic comedy, *As Good As It Gets* (1997) starring Jack Nicholson and Helen Hunt, which I recommend that you see instead. Jack and Diane give it their best here—and Keaton is very good—but the lame and cloying script defeats their efforts.

*You were right on...*_____
*You were totally unfair...*_____

8

Species (1995) 5
Whatever you do, don't kiss her

Part of this is ripped-off from "Alien" and part of it is a corruption of a very fine sci-fi idea now probably forty-years old. Premise: a message from outside our solar system gives the DNA code for an alien species to grow within a human reproductive cell or embryo. Not able to resist such juicy stuff, scientist Ben Kingsley (as wooden as you'll ever see him) follows the recipe and lo and behold a beautiful monster is reared. And escapes. Of course.

So far so cute. She leaps over fences and crashes through windows and grows from pre-adolescent Michelle Williams to fully ovulating adult Natasha Henstride in days. She has one thing on her mind: reproduction. Anything that gets in her way she kills. She can give a mean tongue kiss that goes out through the back of your head should she feel threatened.

Well, if this is a metaphor for the urgency of the feminine reproductive imperative I think they should have played the Robert Palmer song with the lyric, "She wants to multiple/Are you gonna do it?" in the background.

Anyway, as usual the plot deteriorates into a drawn-out chase scene that Hollywood thinks the mass mind craves along with the usual stupidities. I could watch only because Henstride is sexy enough to forgive a few bad alien genes.

You were right on..._____
You were totally unfair..._____

9

     This is actually a better film than I realized at the time. (I can tell by rereading my review.) It is also something of a cult favorite, a genre that a reviewer cannot trash without getting heavily negged by readers clicking the "not helpful" button. I got negged big time.

Heathers (1989) 5

Rottweilers rule

You know how there used to be half a dozen Jennifers in every high school class? Well, what we have here are three Heathers (last names: Duke, Chandler and McNamara, if anybody cares) who reign as upper crust sosh queens at Westerberg High, home of the Rottweilers. One of the Heather Rottweilers is Shannen Doherty of TV infamy who seems perfectly cast except for the fact that, if she's still in high school, I can play opposite Barbie Doll. *(Note: I had this wrong. As some readers have pointed ed out, Doherty was 18-years-old when this film was made.)*

Trying to work her way into their circle is a one-time study-freak with a talent for forging handwriting named Veronica (would that we had Archie and Jughead as well). I mention her penmanship because it's part of the plot, although why they bothered with the fancy foreshadowing I don't know since most of the story is beside the point anyway.

This is a black comedy that takes off on the usual high school teen angst cliches: suicide, rigid social stratification, dumb jocks, dumb parents, dumb administrators, and even dumber teachers. And there are some very funny bits to be had along the way. Unfortunately playing Veronica is Winona Ryder who, although she is as pretty as pretty can be, even sporting a monocle—yes, somebody must have pointed out to director Michael Lehmann that putting nerd-girl glasses on a pretty girl has been done to death, so he had an Inspiration. Ryder has moments—some of them unintentional—but there is no way she can be seen as a comedic actress. We really needed Rene Zellweger or Reese Witherspoon.

Playing opposite Ryder with some finesse is Christian Slater as J.D. Dean, teen psycho, son of Psycho Dad, who explains that he is blowing up the school "because nobody loves me." What really cracked me up about Christian Slater is that "Columbo" voice he sometimes uses. And what I found funny about Winona Ryder were all those outfits with the cutesy hats and leggings. If only they had let her keep them she might have missed her day in court.

Best bit: the two jocks getting their just deserts and the two cops "investigating" the scene.

So bad it was almost good: Veronica getting her cigarette lit by a dynamite explosion.

Like, this could happen: Veronica and Martha "Dumptruck" Dunnstock doing popcorn and old movies together on prom night.

I want to see her do it again, slowly: the Rottweiler cheerleader doing a twirling handstand.

Bottom line: ignore the implausible and send your parents to bed.

You were right on..._____
You were totally unfair..._____

10

     Not to be confused with David Lynch's Mulholland Drive *(2001).*

Mulholland Falls (1996) 5

Repugnant

This is a particularly vile movie in which virtually all the characters are in that vast hole beneath contempt. It is as though director Lee Tamahori wanted to make the noir-est of film noirs and came up with this degeneracy. Yet, I watched the whole thing, which is something I never do with movies I would rate this low. If it's that bad, why watch it?

Well, perhaps Jennifer Connelly had something to do with it. She did, of course, since she is sexy enough to tempt Gandhi; but I think what really kept me interested was a strong desire to see Nick Nolte's character with his swagger and his bily club and his sharp pointed leather shoes and his fedora and the endless cigarette dangling out of his mouth get his just deserts. I also was intrigued at the sheer depravity of Tamahori's depiction of the L.A. police department circa 1950 and their women who seemed to get off especially well when their men recalled the violence of their day. Note that Jennifer Connelly's character becomes arouses after seeing Nolte beat up her sickie boyfriend and inject a needle into his neck. Indeed, in an early scene Melanie Griffith becomes quite tender with her big strong man as he tells her of some violent deed he had pulled off that day. By the way, Bruce Dern's (uncredited) take on the police commissioner reminds me distinctly of a real life past LA Police Chief whose name temporarily escapes me.

It is also possible I wanted to see John Malkovich's interpretation of a mad nuclear scientist/general, a rendering which doesn't kick in until later in the film. (We do get a peephole view of his technique with Connelly very early on, and he seems quite taken with his work.) I would evaluate Malkovich's cynical, ironic performance as good if this were the first time I had ever seen him. However, while he was slimy and despicable enough to actually make Nolte's character look good in comparison, I was a little disappointed since he seemed more mannerism than substance; and indeed I've seen those mannerisms before. I think the edgy Malkovich style always works better when it is combined with something redeeming as it was in, for example, *Valmont* (1989) and *The Ogre* (1996).

While the LAPD are depicted as thugs, amazingly enough by the end of the film they don't look so bad when compared with the US Military who are out in the desert playing with their atomic toys while using young recruits as radiation guinea pigs, led by a reincarnation of Dr. Strangelove. Incidentally, Tamahori, anxious to get the audience into the hospital ward with all those victims of radiation sickness, doesn't even bother with a reasonable plot device. He just has Nolte and his sidekick spot the unmarked building, demand to know what's inside, and when the military guys say it's off limits, bust heads, go inside, gawk and read a chart. The effect of this scene was to put the head-busting, face-kicking and other brutalities of L.A.'s finest into perspective. What's a little roughhousing with the citizenry compared to inducing radiation disease on army privates?

I had the sense as I stayed with this monstrosity that perhaps future generations will watch this and say, that was how it was in midcentury America. Too bad the LAPD and the US Army can't sue Tamahori for the misrepresentation. Oh, you think I forgot the FBI and how easily they were worked over by the locals...? Considering some recent fine competence by that esteemed branch of government, I will only say maybe Tamahori got something right.

Bottom line: avoid.

You were right on..._____
You were totally unfair..._____

Chapter Four:

Memorable Remakes

or

Deja Vu All Over Again

Let's keep score. Which is better, the original or the latest clone? On a scale of one to ten stars, how do you rate the films? My ratings and a place for your ratings follow each title with a running total at the end of the page.

Murder, My Sweet (1944)

vs.

Farewell, My Lovely (1975)

The main match-up here is Dick Powell (old) versus Robert Mitchum (new) who play Raymond Chandler's Philip Marlowe, Private Eye.

Murder, My Sweet (1944) 8

Film noir in transition

This is based on the novel Farewell, My Lovely by Raymond Chandler. There are many deviations from the text as is usual with Hollywood, although some were necessitated by differences in the art forms. More significant however is the treatment itself which is very different from the way Chandler handled the story. Dick Powell's Philip Marlowe in particular is not nearly as world-weary as he is in the book, and the Los Angeles depicted is not nearly as sleazy as Chandler saw it. Furthermore the ending here with the prospect of a future romance for Marlowe is nothing like the cynicism that Raymond Chandler had in mind. Yet, I understand Chandler liked this film, perhaps because of its popularity.

Comparing this to the remake, Farewell, My Lovely (1975) starring Robert Mitchum as Marlowe and based on the same material, I have to say that this is a more agreeable and entertaining movie, although not nearly as veracious. Both movies really skirt around the racial prejudices of the times. Here in Murder, My Sweet the bar Florian's isn't even a black bar as it was in the novel and in Farewell, My Lovely. There is also no good cop/bad cop angle and nary a hint of police corruption—which is certainly anti-historical since Los Angeles in those days had one of the most corrupt police forces in the country.

But none of this bothered me—partly because I expected it, and partly because the movie stands by itself as an entertaining example of the mystery/murder genre done with an emphasis on a "crime doesn't pay" treatment and an upbeat ending—which is the way Hollywood used to play these things until film noir caught hold in the forties. Although this is a forties film and clearly within the film noir genre, it is best seen, I believe, as an example of a genre in transition.

Claire Trevor plays Helen Grayle, scheming wife of a multimillionaire (and young enough to be his daughter), a woman who freely admits to having affairs as she tries to put the make on Marlowe. No such luck since Marlowe usually prefers his whiskey to his women (at least that is way Chandler wrote the novels). Here too Marlowe seems more interested in Helen's stepdaughter, played by Anne Shirley.

Mike Mazurki, who played the heavy in a score of films around mid-century, plays Moose Malloy, the big, dumb guy who is forever looking for his lost Velma ("cute as lace pants"). Esther Howard has a small part as the alcoholic Jessie Florian, just one scene which she does very well. In the Robert Mitchum film, the part was expanded for Sylvia Miles who got a supporting actress Oscar nomination for her work. As for Anne Shirley, who was known as Dawn O'Day until she played Anne Shirley in the first Anne of Green Gables in 1934, she retired after doing this film and never returned to the screen.

What I think makes Murder, My Sweet (intriguing title, of course, but not really descriptive or accurate) work is the fine direction by Edward Dmytryk (best known for directing the splendid The Caine Mutiny (1954) which starred Humphrey Bogart as the deranged Captain Queeg)—that and the engaging performance by Dick Powell. It's clear that the former song and dance star had a great time playing the tough guy gumshoe. I think he loved the jaunty fedora he wore and the terse tough guy dialogue.

See this for Dick Powell, one of the mainstays of Hollywood during the thirties and forties, a fine actor with charm and a crisp style who made his first splash in the period musicals The Golddiggers of 1933 and The Golddiggers of 1935.

Farewell, My Lovely (1975) 8

Classic gumshoe film noir

The year is 1941 and Joltin' Joe DiMaggio is on a hitting streak, and that is about the only thing in life that world-weary Philip Marlowe takes any pleasure in.

This is a workman-like adaptation of the novel by Raymond Chandler. Dimple-chinned Robert Mitchum at 58, an underrated actor with charisma and star appeal, is unfortunately a bit over the hill as Chandler's hard-nosed, realist gumshoe Philip Marlowe, especially when romancing the babes. Still he does a good job and seems almost made for the part.

The main babe that needs romancing here is Charlotte Rampling who plays Helen Grayle, a scheming, trampy, psychopathic, sexy thing on the make for anything she can get. She's the lovely who goes farewell—well, one of them.

Sylvia Miles got a supporting actress Oscar nomination for her portrayal of Mrs. Florian, one-time show girl turned lush. And Sylvester Stallone, looking almost as young as a choir boy, had a bit part as an anonymous thug. Jack O'Halloran played the very dense and obsessed Moose Malloy with a steady moronic malevolence. John Ireland is the good cop and Harry Dean Stanton the bad one. Kate Murtagh is the madam from hell who likes to throw her considerable weight around.

Comparing this to the original from 1944 entitled "Murder, My Sweet," staring Dick Powell and Claire Trevor, I have to say it is more realistic and edgier, and wonderfully atmospheric, but not as enjoyable, perhaps because Mitchum seems a little dead compared to Powell. But that is entirely the point, as Chandler's intent was to showcase a Philip Marlowe near the end of his tether, a man oppressed with the vileness of life and ready to toss it in.

In either case, the convoluted plot involving the missing "Velma," various Los Angeles dives, dead bodies aplenty, and lots of police and political corruption remains somewhat opaque but still manages to hold our interest.

See this for Robert Mitchum, one of Hollywood's greatest with over a hundred and thirty films to his credit, a man who personified nonchalance on the screen, a guy who felt equally at home in a "B" Western as in a dramatic feature, a man who mesmerized audiences with seeming indifference.

I gave both films eight stars, and even thinking about it again, can't choose between them. Score tied.

Your scores: Old_____ New____

The Postman Always Rings Twice (1946)

vs.

The Postman Always Rings Twice (1981)

Here we've got John Garfield versus Jack Nicholson as the male leads with Lana Turner versus Jessica Lange as the female leads.

The Postman Always Rings Twice (1946) 6

Talky version of Cain's first novel

The best thing about this rather vapid 1946 production of the James M. Cain pulp novel/turned literature is Lana Turner as Cora, but not for her acting, which was ordinary, but because she looked so good. Director Tay Garnett had her in stunning, shapely white dresses, pants and uni's that showed off her figure, complemented by a platinum hairdo that in glorious black and white was so intense it was almost colorful. (People on the set may have needed to wear shades.) After she returns from her

mother's funeral, Garnett has her in the blackest black from a black hat to her black shoes—heels, I should emphasize, since she was almost always in heels in the movie, even returning from the beach or crawling up a canyon in the Santa Monica Mountains, she was in heels.

John Garfield, who plays Frank Chambers as though wandering through the role (which is not entirely inappropriate), is sympathetic and has the kind of raw animal appeal that we would expect to see in Cain's depression-era antihero. But he too was not out to win any acting awards. Cecil Kellaway, who plays Nick (in this case a "Nick Smith," not the Greek immigrant Nick Papadakis from the novel) does the best acting job as he brings a bit of the delusive psychology of an older man with a beautiful young wife to life when he announces that he selling the café and moving to the backwoods of Canada so Cora can take care of him and his invalid sister! This bit of senile daydreaming was not in the novel; indeed a lot of what transpired in this self-conscious, misconstructed flick was not in the novel, including a sappy post-ending in which the title is "explained." I won't go into the explanation except to say it wasn't convincing, but I can understand why they tacked it on since nowhere else (that I know of) is the title explained. Cain's original, and appropriate title was, "Bar-B-Que." See my review of the novel at Amazon.com for some speculation on how they came up with the rather magical title.

A better rendition of the Postman is the 1981 production starring Jack Nicholson and Jessica Lange. It too is no masterpiece, but it is both truer to the novel and less talky. A true to the spirit of the novel adaptation would require a terse, stream-lined directorial style with an emphasis on blind animal passions unconsciously acted out, something novelist Cormac McCarthy might accomplish if he directed film. I think that Christopher Nolan, who directed the strikingly original Memento (2000) could do it.

The Postman Always Rings Twice (1981) 8

Underrated, but still not entirely realized

This remake of the 1946 film which starred Lana Turner and John Garfield is significantly better than its reputation. The script, adapted from James M. Cain's first novel, is by the award-winning playwright David Mamet, while the interesting and focused cinematography is by Sven Nykvist, who did so much exquisite work for Swedish director Ingmar Bergman. An excellent cast is led by Jack Nicholson and Jessica Lange, whose cute animal magnetism is well displayed. Bob Rafelson, who has to his directorial credit the acclaimed Five Easy Pieces (1970) and The King of Marvin Gardens (1972), both also starring Jack Nicholson, captures the raw animal sex that made Cain's novel so appealing (and shocking) to a depression-era readership and brings it up to date. Hollywood movies have gotten more violent and scatological since 1981, but they haven't gotten any sexier. This phenomenon is in part due to fears occasioned by the rise of AIDS encouraged by the usual blue stocking people. Don't see this movie if sex offends you.

Lange is indeed sexy and more closely fits the part of a lower-middle class woman who married an older man, a café owner, for security than the stunning blonde bombshell Lana Turner, who was frankly a little too gorgeous for the part. John Colicos plays the café owner, Nick Papadakis, with clear fidelity to Cain's conception. In the

1946 production, the part was played by Cecil Kellaway, who was decidedly English; indeed they changed the character's name to Smith. Also changed in that production was the name of the lawyer Katz (to Keats). One wonders why. My guess is that in those days they were afraid of offending Greeks, on the one hand, and Jews on the other. Here Katz is played by Michael Lerner who really brings the character to life.

Jack Nicholson's interpretation of Cain's antihero, an ex-con who beat up on the hated railway dicks while chasing any skirt that came his way, the kind of guy who acts out his basic desires in an amoral, animalistic way, was not entirely convincing, perhaps because Nicholson seems a little too sophisticated for the part. Yet, his performance may be the sort better judged by a later generation. I have seen him in so many films that I don't feel I can trust my judgment. My sense is that he's done better work, particularly in the two films mentioned above and also in Chinatown (1974), One Flew Over the Cuckoo's Nest (1975) and such later works as The Shining (1980) and Terms of Endearment (1983).

The problem with bringing Postman successfully to the screen is two-fold. One, the underlying psychology, which so strongly appealed to Cain's depression-era readership, is not merely animalistic. More than that it reflects the economic conflict between the established haves, as represented by the greedy lawyers, the well-heeled insurance companies, the implacable court system and the simple-minded cops, and to a lesser degree by property owner Nick Papadakis himself, and the out of work victims of the depression, the have-nots, represented by Frank and Cora (who had to marry for security). Two—and this is where both cinematic productions failed—the film must be extremely fast-paced, almost exaggeratedly so, to properly capture the spirit and sense of the Cain novel. Frank and Cora are rushing headlong into tragedy and oblivion, and the pace of the film must reflect that. A true to the spirit adaptation would require a terse, stream-lined directorial style with an emphasis on blind passions unconsciously acted out, something novelist Cormac McCarthy might accomplish if he directed film. I think that Christopher Nolan, who directed the strikingly original Memento (2000) could do it.

For me the newer film was the clear winner, 8 to 6.

Your scores: Old_____ New_____

Matches:
    Old School: 0   _____
    Newer film: 1   _____
    Ties: 1   _____

Stars:
    Old School: 14   _____
    Newer film: 16   _____

The Importance of Being Earnest (1952)

vs.

The Importance of Being Earnest (2002)

Judi Dench (new), a justly celebrated actress gets (IMHO) overwhelmed by Dame Edith Evans, also a justly celebrated actress, playing Oscar Wilde's incomparable Lady Bracknell. Blame it (mostly) on the director.

The Importance of Being Earnest (1952) 10

The definitive cinematic production

Oscar Wilde's celebrated masterpiece is a comedy on three levels. First there is the denotative level, one might say, the level in which the bourgeois are entertained *après dîner*. It is on this level that Oscar Wilde follows the great theatrical tradition of comedy from the time of the Greeks through Shakespeare and French farce into the twentieth century to the musical comedy of the London and New York stage. His play on this level is a comedy of manners, pleasant, charming and very clever. The class conscious jokes about the lower orders and the servants are double-edged and add just a touch of squirm to the laughter of the not completely discerning audience. It is on the second level that *The Importance of Being Earnest* becomes one of the greatest plays ever written. On this level, the comedy is a full blown satire of Victorian society, and in particular of its audience. Wilde had the very great pleasure of flattering and making fun of the audience while being applauded for doing so. His subtitle for the play, "A Trivial Comedy for Serious People" is an allusion to these two levels. It is on this second level that Wilde speaks through the voice of Lady Bracknell (and sometimes Algernon), whose ironic and unself-conscious cynicism is so like his own. It is on this level that all the fun is made of the hypocrisy of marriage and its mercenary nature, at least as practiced by the petite bourgeoisie of London town, circa 1895. But there is a third level, a level known of course to the cognoscenti of the time and to modern audiences, but for the most part never dreamed of by the London theater-goers of the day. In this regard I have recently read that "Earnest" was a slang euphemism for being gay, and I suspect this is true. Indeed, I can imagine a whole world of witticism based on being "earnest" and being "Ernest," a world now (perhaps charitably) forgotten. Certainly this knowledge sheds some light on Jack's invention of his invalid friend "Bunbury," whom he finds he must visit to escape unwanted social engagements.

One of the best things about this great play is one can appreciate it on any one of the three levels and find delight on that level alone. One can see Worthy as John Worthy, or as Jack Worthy, or as Ernest Worthy, however one likes. This adaptation, starring the incomparable Dame Edith Evans as Lady Bracknell, and Michael Redgrave (father of Vanessa and Lynn Redgrave) as John Worthy is of course the justly celebrated, clearly definitive screen adaptation. It should be noted, however, that Lady Bracknell is the real star of the show, and when she enters a scene, she steals it. Edith Evans was brilliant and unforgettable and obviously having a wonderful time. Margaret Rutherford is a scream as Miss Prism and Miles Malleson as Chasuble is just, shall I say, darling. I should note that both the male leads were a touch too old for their parts. Redgrave was 42 and Michael Denison, who played Algernon, was 37 when the movie was released in 1952. Yet I think Oscar Wilde would have approved of the casting, probably finding it admirable and fitting that these two men about town would have avoided marriage for so many years. (I won't mention the ages of the actresses.) Joan Greenwood as Gwendolyn achieves just the right amount of flaky innocence and calculated whimsy, while Dorothy Tutin is the very definition of the spoiled, sweet and adorable, man-hunting Cecily Cardew. The direction by Anthony Asquith is unnecessarily directive in the sense that he moved some scenes around, but is essentially without harm.

The best way to appreciate this play, and to pick up all the nuances, and there are nuances aplenty—and jokes upon jokes, sharp social and political observations, and witticisms within prevarications, and lies that are truths and vice-versa—is to view the video, just appreciating it on one level, then read the script, and then view the video again. You're in for a treat.

The Importance of Being Earnest (2002) 5

A misinterpretation

This is an inventive and artful production of Oscar Wilde's play, but I can confidently say that were Oscar Wilde alive today, he would be appalled at the misuse to which his play has been put. Indeed I think I feel the ground rumbling as he rolls over in his grave, and yes he is actually spinning in anguish.

Oliver Parker, who directed and wrote the screen adaptation, simply misinterpreted the play. He focused on the "dashing young bachelors" when the real focus of the play is Lady Bracknell, the absurd and beautifully ironic representation of the Victorian mind who was then and has been for over a hundred years Wilde's singular creation and one of the great characters of English literature. She is supposed to steal every scene she is in and we are to double take every one of her speeches as we feel that she is simultaneous absurd and exactly right. Instead Judi Dench's Lady Bracknell (and I don't blame Dench who is a fine actress) is harsh and stern and literal to the point of being a controlling matriarch when what Wilde had in mind was somebody who was both pompous and almost idiotic yet capable of a penetrating and cynical wisdom (so like the author's). Compared to Dane Edith Evans's brilliant performance in the celebrated cinematic production from 1952, Dench's Lady Bracknell is positively one-dimensional.

The point of Wilde's play was to simultaneously delight and satirize the Victorian audience who came to watch the play. This is the genius of the play: the play-goer might view all of the values of bourgeois society upheld while at the same time they are being made fun of. Not an easy trick, but that is why *The Importance of Being Earnest* is considered one of the greatest plays ever written. This attempt turn it into a light entertainment for today's youthful audiences fails because this play is not a romantic comedy. It is more precisely a satire of a romantic comedy. Its point and Wilde's intent was to make fun of Victorian notions of romance and marrying well and to expose the mercantile nature of that society. It is probably impossible to "translate" the play for the contemporary film viewer since a satire of today's audiences and today's society would require an entirely different set of rapiers.

Parker's additions to the play only amounted to distractions that diluted the essence of the play's incomparable wit. Most of Wilde's witticisms were lost in the glare of Parker's busy work. Recalling Lady Bracknell as a dance hall girl in her youth who became pregnant before being wed was ridiculous and not only added nothing, but misinterpreted her character. Lady Bracknell is not a hypocrite with a compromised past. She is everything she pretends to be and that is the joke. Showing Algernon actually running through the streets to escape creditors or being threatened with debtor's prison was silly and

again missed the point. Algy was "hard up" true and in need of "ready money" but his bills would be paid. Gwendolyn in goggles and cap driving a motor car also added nothing and seemed to place the play some years after the fact.

The big mistake movie directors often make when making a movie from a stage play is to feel compelled to get the play off the stage and out into the streets and countryside. Almost always these attempts are simply distractions. Some of the greatest adaptations—Elia Kazan's *A Streetcar Named Desire* from 1951 comes immediately to mind—played it straight and didn't try anything fancy. Here Parker seems obsessed with "dressing up" the play. What he does is obscure it.

On the positive side the costumes were beautiful and Anna Massy was an indelible Miss Prism. Reese Witherspoon at least looked the part of Cecily and she obviously worked hard. Rupert Everrt had some moments in the beginning that resembled Wilde's Algernon, but he was not able to sustain the impersonation.

My recommendation is that you not bother with this production and instead get the 1952 film starring, in addition to Edith Evans, Michael Redgrave and Margaret Rutherford. It is essentially true to the play as Wilde wrote it, and is a pure delight.

I thought this was a romp for the older film, 10 stars to 5.

Your scores: Old_____ New_____

Matches:

Old School: 1		_____
Newer film: 1		_____
Ties: 1		_____

Stars:

Old School: 24		_____
Newer film: 21		_____

Sabrina (1954)

vs.

Sabrina (1995)

One of the great stars of the silver screen, Audrey Hepburn, goes up against the relatively unknown Julia Ormond. Could there possibly be an upset? The directors are Billy Wilder, one of America's most celebrated, and Sydney Pollack, no slouch himself.

Sabrina (1954) 9

Not to be confused with the teenage witch

You have to be something of a romantic to fully appreciate this remarkable film. It helps a lot to be enchanted

with Audrey Hepburn, as most of us are. Her performance, as the daughter of a chauffeur who gets to choose between two very rich brothers, David and Linus Larrabee (William Holden and Humphrey Bogart), is subtle, slightly mysterious and delightful. Much of the enchantment of her character is based on things implied rather than things said or acted out. We know that her meta-morphous in Paris is guided by the 74-year-old Baron St. Fontanel (Marcel Dalio), whom she meets at cooking school. We can discern that she learned more than how to crack an egg. The transformation of her heart from one brother to the other is revealed primarily in her facial expressions as she measures kisses and the sharp stab of pleasure in the center of her soul. We are kept in limbo about whom she chooses until the very end.

This is a girl's fantasy for grown-ups, and one of the best of its kind. The script, from the play by Samuel A. Taylor, is well-paced and psychologically true in a way that is not immediately obvious. The dialogue, while clearly dated and somewhat pedestrian at times, nonetheless stands up well. The sets are large, very large (director Billy Wilder loved to give us a sense of the vastness of the American corporate empire at mid-century): the Larrabee offices, the garage where Sabrina starts all the cars (I think her father, sleeping overhead really would have awaken instead of just tossing and turning), the family estate with its indoor and outdoor pools and courts. There's some pleasant diversion with old man Larrabee (Walter Hampden) and his huge cigars and olives. (The way Bogie is able to smash the little jar, swoop up the olive and land it in the mouth of the old guy in quick motion was a nice trick that surely wowed them on the set. Did Bogie cut his hand or Hampden swallow some glass?) The servants as Sabrina's cheering section and her father (John Williams) with his very correct class prejudices divert us as well.

As for "old stone face" Bogart being miscast, I don't necessarily agree, but certainly Cary Grant would have been a better match for Miss Hepburn, as we would see in *Charade* (1963). William Holden, on the other hand (in blond coiffeur), seemed completely at ease in a comedic role. Nonetheless, the cynical edge that lent depth to his character in, e.g., *Sunset Boulevard* (1950) and *Stalag 17* (1953), was entirely absent here. I think a scene in which he sardonically justifies his playboy ways might have fleshed him out more.

As for Miss Hepburn, she was entirely involved, subtle, driven, nearly flawless, warm and winning. She is especially gorgeous in black and white. Bogart didn't particularly care for her, I understand, complaining about the many takes in her scenes with him. But she was nearly an ingénue, in her second important film, and he was, in his fifties, the veteran of many, many movies. Somehow they both overcame the lack of chemistry, and in a way, made their relationship "sensible" rather than heated. I think Wilder didn't mind this because he was aiming at something deeper than "happily ever after."

Of course Wilder employs a voice-over, a kind of Wilder signature, almost a joke, because as usual the device is abandoned before long. However it did allow us to hear Hepburn begin the film with the magical words, "Once upon a time..." as she describes the fairyland of her childhood, the Larrabee estate.

See this for Audrey Hepburn, who occasionally played a teenager in film, but was never one.

Sabrina (1995) 9
Cinderella has nothing on her

I was surprised at how good this movie is. A remake of a movie starring Audrey Hepburn, Humphrey Bogart and William Holden, directed by one of the greats of American cinema, Billy Wilder, is not exactly the kind of task for the faint of heart. The fact that Sydney Pollack (*They Shoot Horses Don't They?* (1969), *Tootsie* (1982), *Out of Africa* (1985), etc.) decided to do it must have raised a few eyebrows in Hollywood land.

And let's just say I had preconceptions as I sat down to watch this. No way could this be anything near as good as the original. And for the first twenty minutes or so I was not dissuaded. Julia Ormond, who was given Miss Hepburn's title role, seemed nothing far removed from ordinary; and Greg Kinnear, who played the playboy David Larrabee, seemed a poor imitation of William Holden. Of course Harrison Ford, I told myself, is another story, since he is the embodiment of the fulfillment of the desire of many woman, and a fine, accomplished leading man. He would be, I suspected, the lone bright spot. In the original, Humphrey Bogart, a little past his prime, and in not exactly the best of moods, and not entirely pleased with the relatively inexperienced Audrey Hepburn, played the cool tycoon Linus Larrabee with some distracted forbearance in what many consider one of his lesser performances. Surely Harrison Ford could improve on that.

He did, but what really surprised me was just how diabolically clever the oh, so romantic script by Barbara Benedek and David Rayfiel turned out to be. I mean, Cinderella move over. Sabrina could not have achieved a more glorious existence had she died and gone to heaven. It is hard to imagine a more fulfilling fantasy for a chauffeur's daughter than what transpires here.

Quickly here's the premise of this celluloid fairy tale/romance: Pretty but ordinary Sabrina, born of working class parents, her father the chauffeur of the ultra-rich Larrabees, grows up living above the garage in the palatial Larrabee estate. She watches the lavish parties thrown by the Larrabees from a spot in a tree and falls madly in the kind of puppy love that never goes away with the younger of the Larrabee brothers, David, who is the kind of guy who gives playboys a bad name. When she comes of age, she goes away to Paris (apparently to work for a fashion magazine: in the original Sabrina, she goes to a cooking school in Paris), picks up confidence and a new kind of eye-popping sophistication, comes back and...well, gets noticed.

The basic skeleton of this, the story from the first Sabrina (1954), which is dreamily romantic enough and then some, is greatly augmented here with some very fine psychological touches including developing Sabrina's character beyond the pretty and stylish to something bordering on the wise and heroic. Suffice it to say that we come away feeling she deserves every rainbow's end she gets. I can see Benedek and Rayfiel exclaiming with riotous joy as they are writing the script (trading e-mails perhaps): "They want romance, they want woman's fantasy? They want Sabrina to have a pot of gold and true love everlasting? How about riches beyond counting and the doting attention of the two handsome, very rich brothers? She can take her pick. We've give 'em romance, we'll give 'em dreams come true!" And they do. Not only that, but they keep us guessing about who gets the girl until the last possible moment, and they do that very cleverly.

Of course it helps to have professional direction by Sydney Pollack and a fine cast including Harrison Ford—at his best, by the way—and Julia Ormond, a hard-working and talented actress (I recall her from *Smilla's Sense of Snow*, 1997), who knows how to be cute without fawning, supported by Greg Kinnear, Nancy Marchand, John Wood and Angie Dickinson. I mention Miss Dickinson because, as the mother of a perspective bride about to throw an incredibly lavish wedding, she gets to deliver this "let them eat cake" line: "We thought we'd use recycled paper" (for the wedding invitations).

The script is full of similar witticisms, some verbal, some like eye candy. For example, when Sabrina removes her glasses (the usual Hollywood signal for the adolescent ugly duckling to become a beautiful swan) after gaining sophistication in Paris, she quotes aptly but surprisingly from Gertrude Stein: "America is my country and Paris is my home." (Of course Gertrude Stein never heard of Paris, Texas—but that is another film, and besides, I digress...)

I also liked it when Sabrina is in the arms of her Paris would-be lover who kisses her, and—noticing that she is not as engaged as she might be–observes with perfect decorum, "I'm embarrassed that you're somewhere else."

Memorable was the shot of Harrison Ford momentarily looking jealous and hurt. By the way, he has a number of good lines, and he delivers them well. I especially liked it when he sadly confessed: "I was sent to deal with you. I sent myself."

It is probably better if you haven't seen the original and can experience this on its own merits without the odiousness that sometimes comes with comparisons. Comparing Audrey Hepburn with Julia Ormond is like comparing Grace Kelly with Jennifer Lopez. They really are very different people. And comparing Billy Wilder's 1954 film (from the play by Samuel Taylor) is a little like comparing Lon Chaney's *Phantom of the Opera* with Andrew Lloyd Webber's.

Bottom line: see this for both Harrison Ford who wears the business-first character of the "only surviving heart donor" very well, and for Julia Ormond whose intense and beguiling performance makes us forgive her for not being Audrey Hepburn.

Nine stars apiece, but to be honest (and you can tell from the reviews) I was leaning a little toward the newer film. Match tied; Old School has the lead in stars.

Your scores: Old____ New____

Matches:
    Old School: 1   ____
    Newer film: 1   ____
    Ties: 2   ____
Stars:
    Old School: 33   ____
    Newer film: 30   ____

Dial M for Murder (1954)

vs.

A Perfect Murder (1998)

Grace Kelly versus Gwyneth Paltrow. Ray Milland versus Michael Douglas. Hitchcock versus...Andrew Davis? If I were a bookie, I'd make the former a prohibitive favorite, say ten to one.

Dial M for Murder (1954) 9

Superior Hitchcock with an exquisite Grace Kelly

This is a fine example of the kind of mystery that little old ladies from Pasadena (or Russell Square) adore. Perhaps *Arsenic and Old Lace* (1944) starring Cary Grant might be comparable in its gentile and bloodless ability to glue us to the screen.

This is certainly one of Hitchcock's best, but most of the credit must go to a devilishly clever play written by Frederick Knott from which the movie was adapted. (He also wrote *Wait Until Dark* (1967) starring Audrey Hepburn.) Hitchcock does a good job in not tinkering unnecessarily with the material. He also has the exquisitely beautiful Grace Kelly to play the part of Margot Wendice.

Ray Milland plays, with a kind of high-toned Brit panache, her diabolical husband, Tony Wendice, a one-time tennis star who married mostly for security. John Williams is the prim and proper Chief Inspector Hubbard. He lends to the part a bit of Sherlock Holmesian flair. One especially liked his taking a moment to comb his mustache after the case is solved. Robert Cummings, unfortunately plays Margot's American boyfriend as inventively as a sawhorse. For those of you who might have blinked, Hitchcock makes his traditional appearance in the photo on the wall from Tony Wendice's undergraduate days.

The fulcrum of the plot is the latchkey. It is the clue that (literally) unlocks the mystery. There is a modernized redoing of this movie called *A Perfect Murder* (1998) starring Michael Douglas and Gwyneth Paltrow in which a similar business with latchkeys is employed. I am not very good with clues so it was only after seeing that movie and *Dial M for Murder* for the second time that I finally understood what happened. Follow the latchkey!

Of course I was too distracted by Grace Kelly to fully appreciate such intricacies. I found myself struck with the ironic notion that anyone, even a cuckolded husband, might want to kill Grace Kelly or that a jury might find her guilty of anything! She remains in my psyche America's fairytale princess who quit Hollywood at the height of her popularity after only five years and eleven movies to become a real princess by marrying Prince Rainier of Monaco. Something was lost there, and some-

thing was gained. She was in essence the original Jackie Kennedy Onassis. I think, however, that the old saw about the man who marries for money, earning it, might apply to American princesses as well.

At any rate, Grace Kelly's cool and sublime bearing was on fine display here. Hitchcock cloths her in discreet nightgowns and snug (but certainly not clinging) dresses that show off her delicate figure and her exquisite arms and hint oh so coyly at her subtle sexuality. She was 25-years-old, stunningly beautiful, and in full confidence of her ability as an actress. She had just finished starring opposite James Stewart in another splendid Hitchcock one-room mystery, *Rear Window* (1954), and was about to make *The Country Girl* (1954) with Bing Crosby for which she would win an Oscar for Best Actress.

So see this for Grace Kelly who makes Gwyneth Paltrow (whom I adore) look downright gawky, and for Ray Milland whose urbane scheming seems a layer or two of hell removed from Michael Douglas's evil manipulations.

By the way, the "original theatrical trailer" preceding these Warner Brothers Classic videos is what we used to call the "Coming Attractions"—that is, clips directly from the movie and a promo. You might want to fast forward to the movie itself.

A Perfect Murder (1998) 7

Featuring a two-fisted Gwyneth Paltrow

This quasi-remake of Hitchcock's *Dial M for Murder* (1954)—which was filmed in 3D, by the way—is a rather good thriller in its own right, intelligently done throughout except for a few scenes near the end when Director Andrew Davis and screenwriter Patrick Smith Kelly lose their judgment and opt for a silly knock down, drag out fight.

Michael Douglas plays a quintessential evil kind of guy, evil, ruthless, greedy, two-faced, crafted to excite our loathing ("How's THIS for wet work?"). He is excellent. Gwyneth Paltrow plays his very rich wife who has incredibly poor taste in men. Seems that Gwyneth has become attracted to roles that get her involved with the wrong kind of guys, witness *The Talented Mr. Ripley* (1999) and *Sliding Doors* (1998). But she is also very good, as is Viggo Mortensen who plays the murderous con artist.

The plot is tight and filled with nice twists. The sets are opulent and dripping with money, and neither the direction nor the camera work calls undue attention to itself. But what really makes this fly is the material on which it is based, the devilishly clever play by Frederick Knott, who reigned on Broadway many years ago. I'll bet that Paltrow was persuaded in part to take the role because the same part was played in the Hitchcock movie by the legendary Grace Kelly. Also, another Frederick Knott play made into a movie was *Wait Until Dark* (1967) starring the also legendary Audrey Hepburn. I suspect Paltrow could hardly resist joining such illustrious company, especially when the plot here allows her to take mat-

ters into her own hands, as it were, and give to her two guys considerably more than she gets.

Bottom line: you will be diverted.

Not surprisingly I liked the older film better, 9 to 7.

Your scores: Old_____ New_____

Matches:

Old School: 2		_____
Newer film: 1		_____
Ties: 2		_____

Stars:

Old School: 42		_____
Newer film: 37		_____

Lolita (1962)

vs.

Lolita (1997)

Although both films are adapted with reasonable fidelity from Vladimir Nabokov's novel, the treatments are strikingly different: Kubrick goes for comedy; Lyne opts to emphasize the perversity.

Lolita (1962) 10

One of Kubrick's best

Among Stanley Kubrick's four great cinematic works—the three others: *Dr. Strangelove* (1964), *2001, A Space Odyssey* (1968), and *A Clockwork Orange* (1971)—*Lolita* (1962) is the most uneven, yet in some ways the most brilliant. (I understand that *Barry Lyndon* (1975) is also very good, but I haven't seen it yet.) The casting, from the improbable choice of Peter Sellers as Claire Quilty, to the exactly right choice of Shelley Winters as Charlotte Haze, to the beautiful Sue Lyon as Lolita, to the "old world" James Mason as Humbert Humbert, was inspired. The witty and intensely focused interpretation of Nabokov's black comedic novel was probably as true to Vladimir's spirit as the silver screen could hope to come, and yet the film was clearly and exactly a Stanley Kubrick work of art.

The scene (apparently a Kubrick witticism) in which friends of the dead Charlotte find Humbert in the tub with a scotch and a hand gun, and mistakenly think he is about to blow his brains out from grief when in fact he is in jubilant celebration, is a wonderful variation on Nabokov's text, as is the use of Peter Sellers disguised as a Freudian shrink at the girl's school. However, I thought the Buster Keatonish slapstick improv with the folding cot at the Enchanted Huntress a bit overdone.

Inevitably the recent Adrian Lyne film and Kubrick's must be compared. The photography in the Lyne film was superior, and Lyne more clearly demonstrated the tragic nature of Humbert's all-controlling obsession. Otherwise, Kubrick's Lolita is clearly superior both as entertainment and as cinematic art, mainly because it is free from even a hint of political correctness and passes no judgment. This is essentially a difference in tone and attitude. Lyne's film insists that we appreciate the depraved nature of Humbert's desire and how it ruined Lolita. Kubrick's leads us to believe that Lolita was a tragic figure whose very nature (through no fault of her own, of course) suggests her inevitable corruption, if not by Humbert then by Quilty, or perhaps eventually by our society itself.

But neither film was about the actual relationship depicted in the novel, since no one, given the prudish and hypocritical mentality of the American psyche, and the taboo nature of the material, can ever hope to make a film completely true to Nabokov's vision. Lolita was twelve years old. That is the singular truth that Kubrick and Lyne were not able to show. Much is lost in not understanding that Humbert desired a nymphet, shy of her full sexual development, and not a fifteen-year-old. (Both Sue Lyons and Dominique Swain from Lyne's movie were fifteen years old during the filming.) Nabokov makes it abundantly clear in the novel that it is precisely the delicate, pre-adolescent form of the girl that excites Humbert. One recalls the scene in the novel (not presented in either film) in which the perverted Humbert forces Lolita to sit with him in their vehicle near an elementary school as he watches the children cross the street hoping to spot a nymphet to excite him.

Until such time as people are able to face the broad spectrum of human sexuality without cant and prejudice, and without fear, an authentic version of Nabokov's novel cannot possibly be filmed.

Lolita (1997) 8

Too bad Louis Malle never directed Lolita

The first thing amiss with Adrian Lyne's "Lolita" is that Melanie Griffith is entirely wrong for the part of Charlotte Haze. "The Haze woman" must be UNattractive. Shelly Winters in Kubrick's Lolita (1962) was perfect for the part because she was a woman who had lost her looks. Charlotte must be unattractive as a contrast to Lo (and not just in Humbert's mind); furthermore the references to her as a "fat cow" and Humbert's disinclination to make love to her, do not play well if she's attractive. Melanie Griffith is actually better looking than the young star, Dominique Swain, who plays Lolita. Swain is pretty enough, however, and although not the great beauty that Sue Lyon (who played Lolita in the original) was, she is actually sexier. She does the coquettish muggings better than Sue Lyon did and she is allowed more latitude. Humbert never even kissed Lolita in Kubrick's version!

Nonetheless, the second thing wrong with this interpretation is Swain herself. Although wonderfully directed, she is ironically too old and too well developed with those strong pretty legs. She is hardly a nymphet. She is in fact a fully ovulating female just a shade south of sweet sixteen. (Swain was fifteen when the film was made.) Although she has the diminutive upper body of a preteen, the rest of her is exactly as Humbert would NOT have wanted.

Jeremy Irons does a superior job of making us feel how sad and trapped Humbert is. Frank Langella as the libertine Claire Quilty is excellent and wonderfully cast, but his role is limited. Whereas Peter Sellers played several parts, including the school psychologist, Langella speaks in only two scenes, briefly at the Enchanted Huntress as a spats-wearing past-post Romeo, and then of course in the finale.

Where the Lyne film is clearly superior is in the minutia of the late-forties world of highway America: the country and western stations on the radio, the "Notices" on the back doors of the motels, the movie magazines and comics, the jaw-breakers and the gum under the dashboard, the many mid-drift children's outfits that Swain wears, the vintage motel and gas station signs, etc., etc. Lyne also does a number of nice visuals. The price tag hanging from the dark glasses Humbert is trying on as he desperately tries to see through two windows inside the gas station to what Lolita is doing with whom on the other

side of their station wagon is an example. And then there is that symbolic single cow at the end in the field with Humbert and the station wagon, suggesting a reincarnated Charlotte Haze observing what has befallen Humbert.

Unfortunately Lyne's attention wanders at times. He has Humbert stare at Lolita in the important scene when he first spots her on the lawn much, much too long so that Charlotte could not help but notice his noticing. And in the scene on the front porch, with the three of them together on the swing, Charlotte would have to be blind not to see the sex play between the two. And when Melanie quotes Humbert from his diary calling her "that fat cow" we can see by just looking at her that she is anything but. And the scene with her on his lap while he is trying to read at his desk is totally ineffective since Melanie is quite fetching and most males would be happy to carry her off to bed. Corny and tiresome were Lo's vanilla ice cream and milk mustaches. And we could have been spared the obvious and trite "symbolism" of the bananas and lipstick as Lo rides in the car thinking of Quilty.

But it is entirely right that Lyne makes the motel rooms sorted and cheap. He shows a sign advertising "Children under 14 free" at one of Humbert's choice stopping places, slyly reminding the cognoscente that Nabokov's nymphet should be younger than Shakespeare's Juliet, who was thirteen. (Given the puritanical nature of the American psyche, neither Lyne nor Kubrick was able to make a "true to the book" film.) She becomes a prostitute, effectively speaking, as she negotiates with Humbert over coins for her favors. When Humbert tries to grab her saved-up money for fear she will use it to escape him, she shouts indignantly, "I EARNED that money!"

The really terrible thing about Nabokov's tale that both directors got right is the unrelenting possessiveness of Humbert. That was his undoing of course, and really shows the perverted nature of his love for her. If he had really loved her, he would have stepped aside and let her live a normal life. That's what fathers do. That he loved her as a woman is not as much a tragedy as the jealousy and control. Lolita makes this clear when as the pregnant "Dolly," looking common and matronly in a cheap house with a working-class husband, she sees Humbert for the last time. He begs her to go with him, but she tells him she would almost rather go back to Quilty. Lyne adds a final wound by having Humbert ask her if she can ever forgive him for what he did to her, allowing Lolita to reply (addressing the dog) "Molly, say good-bye to my Dad." "Some Dad!" is Lyne's message.

This interpretation will be more agreeable to some since it re-enforces the idea that teen sexuality is wrong. As usual, we see that nobody cares about the girl. The feminists know she has the sexual power, and they are jealous. They want her off limits so that they have a better currency themselves. This is the political position of the sexual wars, and Lyne has fallen into it. I think we need a French Lolita, as done by somebody like the late Louis

Malle. I don't expect this for another hundred years, however. This film ought to kill the theme for quite a while.

Old school increases its lead by adding 10 stars versus 8.

Your scores: Old_____ New_____

Matches:

Old School: 3		_____
Newer film: 1		_____
Ties: 2		_____

Stars:

Old School: 52		_____
Newer film: 45		_____

Jesus Christ, Superstar (1973)

vs.

Jesus Christ, Superstar (2000)

These are two excellent versions of the Broadway musical. The striking difference is not in the quality of the productions, but in how they appear to the eyes 27 years apart.

Jesus Christ, Superstar (1973) 8

The "groovy" version

I always think of Norman Jewison as the quintessential Hollywood director, a consummate professional with a rather wide range (e.g, *The Cincinnati Kid* (1965), *In the Heat of the Night* (1967), *Fiddler on the Roof* (1971), *Agnes of God* (1985), *Other People's Money* (1991), etc.) a man who has made many successful movies, a man who will do justice to the material in a popular, but not entirely mid-brow fashion. He will attempt nothing fancy, but will go with the reasonable, and he will never stray far from the understanding that the purpose of a movie is to sell tickets and to entertain. He is particularly good at translating stage plays onto the silver screen. Here he is called upon to turn the once controversial Tim Rice/Andrew Lloyd Webber rock opera into a movie. His framing conception is to park a bus load of performers (recalling perhaps a Beatles' Magical Mystery Tour or a Shakespearean troupe) on a barren spot in the Holy Land where they will put on an enthusiastic, low budget production of the play, which is filmed. When they're finished they pack everything back into the bus and drive off. Well, almost everything. Christ, in the form of Ned Neeley, who is perhaps a little too slight, and a little too cute for the part (although no one will ever completely please attempting to play the son of God), is still up on that cross, presumably hanging around for the resurrection that never comes in the staunchly secular Rice/Webber musical. This is Jewison's little statement as he has Yvonne Elliman (Mary Magdalene) and Carl Anderson (Judas) look back.

Seeing this in the year two thousand and one for the first time has certain advantages. One, it doesn't seem such a departure from the traditional London/New York musical, since one has already experienced *Hair*, *Godspell*, *Tommy*, etc. Two, the propriety of playing the crucifixion story to rock music and the controversy of presenting a secular, perhaps sacrilegious Jesus to a mass audience are now moot points. Most Christians, I dare say, now believe *Jesus Christ, Superstar* to be a positive thing for Christianity and even responsible for bringing many people into the fold. Three, one can compare it with the recent film production directed by Gale Edwards and Nick Morris.

That film, starring Glenn Carter as Jesus and Jérôme Pradon as Judas and Renée Castle as Mary Magdalene, with its montage of twentieth century costumes, Judas in a black leather jacket, the Romans in Nazi uniforms, a priest looking like Darth Vader, etc. is snappier, more tightly focused than Jewison's methodically paced compilation. Here, though, we have the groovy feel of threads from the 70s, bell bottoms and exposed chest hairs, along with some very strange head gear for the priests, and soldiers looking like construction workers in pink hard hats. Here we have tanks bizarrely chasing Judas before he is herded among the goats. Here we have a black Judas and an Hawaiian Mary Magdalene, while more recently we have a velvety black Mary Magdalene and a balding European Judas. In both cases we have a blond Jesus dressed all in white often spotlighted in the golden hues of a renaissance painting. While the Edwards production is shot on an elaborately constructed stage, Jewison has the dry rocks and sands of Jerusalem as a backdrop for his scaffolding. Throw in a camel or two and some goats, and there is more of a feel of the Middle East than in the recent film. But does this matter? Is JCS a play about a contemporary Jesus or a modern dress passion play pretending to be about Jesus? Is Jesus a superstar like a rock musician or a superstar like the founder of a religion? Part of the genius of the conception of Rice and Webber is this essential ambiguity. Is he the Son of God, or a historical personage? Most Christians would say he is both. Rice/Webber emphasize that he was a man, like any other.

Musically speaking, and this play is really about the music as much as anything else, both productions are beautiful. The Jewison film is superior in the angelic voice of

Yvonne Elliman and in the power and energy and full range vocals of Carl Anderson's Judas. It suffers from a weak Jesus and some inexplicable guitar riffs and the addition of some music not composed by Webber and Rice. Josh Mostel's libertine King Herod and his mocking "King of the Jews!" is on a par with Rik Mayall who did the mocking as a gay King Herod in the Edwards film. Both could pass for fully degenerate denizens of Sodom and Gomorrah. The pain and agony of the crucifixion is more graphically accomplished here, but Glenn Carter's blood-smeared Jesus is the more tortured.

I could go on making comparisons, some you might agree with and some you might not. But I really think the important thing is that both productions are wonderfully entertaining and engaging—how can one go wrong with such beautiful music and such a compelling story? It's a matter of taste. I had a lot of fun viewing them both.

Jesus Christ, Superstar (2000) 9

A redemptive, but secular Jesus

I saw this before seeing the 1973 Norman Jewison version. This was in fact my first experience with *Jesus Christ, Superstar*, and I must say I was delighted, especially with the acting and the music. Surely this is a different production than that which ran in London and on Broadway since Directors Gale Edwards and Nick Morris use close ups of the actors' faces to great advantage, something not possible on the stage. Lost to the viewer, I suspect, might be the full range of movement and choreography. Not lost is the music of Andrew Lloyd Webber, in particular the title song and the haunting, ironic ballad, "I don't know how to love him." When Mary Magdalene in the person of the velvety Renée Castle breaks into song our spirit is roused and our understanding of one of the ironies of Christianity heightened. The lyric, "He's only a man, and I've had so many men before..." somehow brings to life the enigma that Jesus, God in the flesh, is to all of us.

I recall when JCS was first performed a controversy arose about whether it was sacrilegious. I don't know how that controversy played out, but I can see how some might be offended. (Of course, I was not.) This production does depict a very human Jesus, clad in one scene only in a very scanty loincloth. There is an emphasis on the blood that he shed, wiped from him onto the hands of us all, or, as some have complained, onto the hands of the Jews, who have been getting the bad rap for two thousand years. And there is the question, first of all of making Jesus into a political "superstar." Yet, that too is irony, a dramatic irony that is a truth. He is a superstar in this country and has been for a long time. Whether he is also the son of God is another matter of personal belief.

One does wonder however about some of the costuming. Why are the Romans in Nazi uniforms, recalling an earlier era, and why is Judas in a leather jacket, looking a little like Marlon Brando from *The Wild One* (1954) or perhaps John Travolta from *Grease* (1978)? Perhaps what is suggested is a broader time era, say the entire mid twentieth century.

I found myself comparing this to some other filmed musicals that arose during that same era, the sixties and seventies, *West Side Story*, *Grease*, and *Hair*, musicals that in some sense seemed to break with the pleasant tradition long established with, for example, *Where's Charlie?*, *South Pacific*, *Oklahoma*, etc. In a sense these newer productions seemed out to shock the bourgeoisie as well as to entertain the burghers, to widen the parameters of the London/New York musical comedy tradition and to call on the audience to think. Indeed some imagined that a revolution was in the making. JCS in particular seemed to threaten the religious orthodoxy. In retrospect, however, *Hair* seems more dated than shocking and *West Side Story* and *Grease* totally within the tradition of *My Fair Lady* and *Damn Yankees*. *Jesus Christ, Superstar* now thirty years later also seems totally within that venerable tradition.

Glenn Carter as Jesus was very good. His combination of strength and vulnerability suited well the conception of a Jesus who believed he was sent to earth to die for our sins, a persona half God and half man. True he seemed to lack somewhat in charisma, but in attempting such a part, who wouldn't? Jérôme Pradon as Judas also was excellent in a nicely balanced characterization. When he too laments that he didn't "know how to love him" we know the truth of the very human trap he made for himself (although properly speaking, he was God's instrument). Renée Castle as Mary Magdalene was expressive and sung beautifully; indeed she seemed the very embodiment of a woman in love with a man she cannot possess. However there was something lacking not in her performance, but in the very conception of the part. I felt the need for some rags and dirt and some real destitution. Perhaps Mary Magdalene here is too sanitized, too pretty, too clean and too well behaved to be the real Mary Magdalene.

My only real disappointment with this engrossing and thought-provoking entertainment was in not seeing a glorious resurrection of Jesus. But in retrospect, I realize that would have detracted from the Rice/Webber conception of "a man, like any other man." I think they make a powerful point, because in the deepest religious sense, at least to my mind, we and Christ really are brothers, the immaculate made flesh.

Newer films begin a comeback, 8 to 9 stars.

Your scores: Old_____ New_____

Matches:
    Old School: 3   _____
    Newer film: 2   _____
    Ties: 2

Dangerous Liaisons (1988)

vs.

Valmont (1989)

vs.

Cruel Intentions (1999)

Here we have three films, but I'll just keep score with the first two. The third is actually a modern dress New York City adaptation of the Choderlos de Laclos novel.

Dangerous Liaisons (1988) 9

Sexual decadence before the fall of the guillotine

This is a tale about the *ancien régime* in18th century France before the revolution in which the moral decadence of the privileged classes rivaled that of Sodom and Gomorrah and the ancient Romans. The story comes from a novel by Choderlos de Laclos that was made into a stage play by Christopher Hampton. It is a cynical satire on human sexuality as well as a very subtle examination of sexual hypocrisy and desire, a kind of oh so sophisticated laugh at bourgeois morality that would have delighted Voltaire and Moliere and greatly amused Shakespeare. It is a tale of elaborate lechery and revenge that backfires because it seems that anybody, even the most jagged rake can fall in love, and thereby become the victim.

John Malkovich plays the rake, Vicomte de Valmont, whose sole purpose in life is to seduce women, rob them of their virtue and then move on. Glenn Close plays his back-stabbing confidante and one-time lover, the Marquise de Merteuil. Michelle Pfeiffer plays the coy and virtuous Madame de Tourvel, who is to be Valmont's latest conquest. Uma Thurman is cast as a teenaged ingenue who is betrothed to Merteuil's lover while Keanu Reeves plays her naive music teacher and would-be lover, Chevalier Danceny. Stephen Frears, who has directed such diverse films as *The Grifters* (1990) and *My Beautiful Laundrette* (1985), after a somewhat cryptic start, does an excellent job of bringing the biting cynicism of Laclos and Hampton to the screen.

I know of two other versions of this film, Milos Forman's *Valmont* (1989), starring Colin Firth and Annette Bening, and Roger Vadim's *Dangerous Liaisons* (1960). Regrettably, I haven't seen Vadim's film, but Forman's *Valmont* is excellent. In polite society comparisons are said to be odious. I shall proceed anyway:

John Malkovich vs. Colin Firth. Malkovich is widely recognized as a great actor, but he is clearly miscast in this role, yet he brings a predatory dimension to the part that is in keeping with the overall psychology of the movie. Firth, while not as celebrated for his acting skills as Malkovich, is nonetheless a fine actor, and his charm and playful inventiveness are more in keeping with the character of Valmont, whom women love. Call it even.

Glenn Close vs. Annette Bening. Again Close is considered the more accomplished actor, but Bening is sexier, prettier and considerably more charming. Whether that is a plus as far as the reality of the novel and play are concerned is debatable. For my part I found Bening a lot more fun to watch. Edge to Bening.

Michelle Pfeiffer vs. Meg Tilly. Pfeiffer is a much bigger star and has more experience as an actress. She is beautiful, but Tilly is more passionate. Pfeiffer was nominated for an academy award for best supporting actress for her work here, but did not win. Personally I thought Tilly was more believable and was especially effective in projecting first the repressed passion and then the complete abandonment as she gives herself to Valmont. Pfeiffer's portrayal of Tourvel's coy awakening, with just a hint of duplicity, and then her utter dissolution when he leaves her, was star quality. Edge to Pfeiffer.

Uma Thurman vs. Fairuza Balk. I loved them both. Thurman, of course, is a more statuesque beauty with a polished and controlled acting style, but Balk's wide-eyed innocence was a delight. Call it even.

Keanu Reeves vs. Henry Thomas. Thomas was cute, but almost too juvenile to be believed. Reeves seemed just right for the part. Clear edge to Reeves.

Frears vs. Forman. Frears's direction was more cynical, especially in the duel between Valmont and Merteuil in which their mutual and complementary debauchery is in sharp focus. And his resolution was more clearly defined. Forman's strength was in the delight and playfulness of many of the scenes, especially those relating to the seduction of Tourvel. His direction was more comedic and he allowed a greater development of secondary characters, while Frears concentrated more on the two leads. I give a very small edge to Forman, but would not argue with those preferring Frears.

Bottom line: I liked Forman's movie better, but the voters at IMDb.com preferred Frears's *Dangerous Liaisons*, giving it an average of 7.7 stars out of ten to 6.7 for Valmont.

Some *bon mots*:

Valmont tells Madame de Tourvel as he dumps her, "My love had great difficulty outlasting your virtue. It's beyond my control."

Valmont demands that the Marquise de Merteuil reply to his proposal of a night together, will it be love or war? He says, "A single word is all that is required." Long pause, and then she gives him three, "All right. [Pause.] War."

When Valmont returns from making love to Madame de Tourvel he reveals to Merteuil that for the first time he may be in love. He relates his feelings to her, "I love her. I hate her..." The camera turns to Close, who yawns.

Valmont's aunt while consoling Madame de Tourvel, who has confessed that she is in love with Valmont and can't help herself, says, reflecting the wisdom of all who have been there, "In such matters all advice is useless."

Toward the end, Valmont says, "I have no illusions. I lost them on my travels."

Valmont (1989) 9

Sexual decadence before the time of the guillotine

I liked this better than *Dangerous Liaisons* which came out at about the same time. Of course *Dangerous Liaisons* was very good, and John Malkovich, who played Vicomte de Valmont, is an actor of power, and Glenn Close, who played the Marquise de Merteuil, is highly accomplished, but I preferred the charm of Colin Firth in this film to the brutality of Malkovich, and I thought Annette Bening was just delightful. She played Merteuil with exquisite timing and an ironic witchery and warmth that I shall not soon forget. I preferred her playful, sly wit to Close's cool cynicism.

The story comes from a novel by Choderlos de Laclos set in 18th century France that was made into a stage play by Christopher Hampton. It is a cynical satire on human sexuality as well as a very subtle examination of sexual hypocrisy and desire, a kind of oh so sophisticated laugh at bourgeois morality that would have delighted Voltaire and Moliere and greatly amused Shakespeare. It is a tale of elaborate lechery and revenge that backfires because it seems that anybody, even the most jagged rake can fall in love, and thereby become the victim. The central assumption here is the same as that of the Cavalier poets, name-

ly that marriage kills love. As Merteuil says, "You don't marry your lover."

Meg Tilly played Madame de Tourvel with subtlety and a riveting passion. One of the great sequences in the movie occurs after she has fallen madly in love with Valmont against her will. She stands outside his doorway in the rain for hours looking adoringly and forlornly up at his window. And then she is allowed to enter and receive a cool reception. Valmont says, "Do you want me to lie to you?" and she replies desperately, "Yes," and then it is her passion that overwhelms him, leading to a beautifully ironic twist. Shortly afterward he sees Merteuil, who has become more like a sister than an ex-lover, and says, "I feel awful." She replies, "Are you surprised? [Pause] You are an awful man." Hanging his head he continues, "Do you think a man can change?" "Yes. [Pause] For the worse."

This theme, that it is the beloved who has the power and that once you fall in love you lose all power, is repeated several times in the movie. Valmont pursues women, the harder to get the better, with a relentless and maniacal passion, but once he has them, he immediately loses interest. His making love absentmindedly to Cecile de Volanges (played with wide-eyed innocence and girlish charm by Fairuza Balk) was an incredible irony when we consider what she would cost Gercourt, played with his rather substantial nose in the air by Jeffrey Jones, whom you may recall as the pratfalling principal in *Ferris Bueller's Day Off* (1986).

There is some insidious philosophy here, some sardonic observations on human nature worth mentioning. One is that the man beloved of women gets most of the reproductive tries, and regardless of his rakishness, is still beloved. Another is that duplicity is the accepted, even required, standard of behavior in society, and that when it comes to sex, one must, perforce, always lie.

Milos Forman's direction was invisible and therefore a work of art. The incidental scenes and backdrops depicting the color, squalor and decadence of pre-revolutionary France added just the right amount of atmosphere. The costumes were stunning and much cleaner than they would have been in reality. The elegance and beauty of all the titled people merrily contrasted with the crude ugliness of the common people, rightly reflecting the effete snobbery of the aristocracy before the guillotine fell.

Cruel Intentions (1999) 7

Dangerous Liaisons lite

It's probably better if you haven't seen Stephen Frears's *Dangerous Liaisons* (1989), starring Glenn Close, John Malkovich and Michelle Pfeiffer, or Milos Forman's *Valmont* (1988) with Annette Bening, Colin Firth and Meg Tilly. If you have, Roger Kumble's *Cruel Intentions* (1999), starring Sarah Michelle Gellar, Ryan Phillippe, and Reese

Witherspoon, which is also based on the novel by the Frenchman Choderlos de Laclos, will seem to lack finesse. Kumble wrote his own screenplay as a kind of *Les Liaisons Dangereuses* in modern dress, whereas Frears and Forman relied more heavily upon the stage play by Christopher Hampton, depicting the aristocracy of 18th century France. While the two earlier movies sparkle with wit, insight and a cynicism to chill the fondest heart, Kumble's venture features a more prosaic brand of sexual humor adorned agreeably with young, nubile bodies.

But there is no need to make odious comparisons. Cruel Intentions can stand on its own, and there is plenty to admire, especially Gellar in a role to which she is perfectly suited, and Witherspoon as well. Phillippe is also good, especially when he's being funny, although his unconscious imitation of John Malkovich was a bit obsequious. He delivered some of his lines with the same deadpan expression and intonation. But being as pretty as he is, Phillippe's character is more like Colin Firth's. Selma Blair's narrow-eyed and dotty Cecile was pretty, sexy, and funnier than either Uma Thurman or Fairuza Balk, who played similar roles in the above mentioned movies, respectively.

The scene with the shrink to begin was very agreeable and should have been followed up somehow. We never see Sebastian quite so diabolical later on. Too bad. And seeing a little more of Swoosie Kurtz who played the self-centered, phony and hypocritical Dr. Regina Greenbaum would have enhanced the film.

The idea of making Sebastian and Kathryn step siblings was amusing and spicy, and the inclusion of a raunchy gay footballer was appropriate. Using a black guy as Cecile's harp teacher was kinky good. And being rather

up-front about sex throughout without being overly juvenile was refreshing. The business with Sebastian Valmont's diary of conquests worked well both psychologically and as a plot device.

The main failing with Kumble's movie, aside from the general superficiality, was that Sebastian's "conquest" of Annette was a little too easy, especially with the goody-goody build-up she had been given. Consequently, her falling in love was more like a stumble. There was some physical passion, but nothing like the full-blown emotional passion required. Also I think the ending needed a little work. It seemed that a committee divined it, part of them wanting a "happy" love ending for Reese and Ryan, and the other half wanting to stay somewhat true to the spirit of the original, and so they came to a compromise, as committees will, and we got mishmash.

Incidentally, there is yet a fourth movie version of this tale, *Dangerous Liaisons* (1960), from French director Roger Vadim. I am looking forward to seeing it, if I can find a copy.

The first two films tie, 9-9 with the third getting a 7, which I am not counting.

Your scores: Old_____ New_____

Matches:
   Old School: 3   _____
   Newer film: 2   _____
   Ties: 3   _____
Stars:
   Old School: 69   _____
   Newer film: 63   _____

Open Your Eyes (1997)

vs.

Vanilla Sky (2001)

Since Open Your Eyes *is a Spanish language film, the contest here is between not only an original and a remake but between a foreign film and a domestic one. One thing is clearly even, the beautiful Penélope Cruz appears in both films in the same role.*

Open Your Eyes (1997) 7

Penélope Cruz is splendiferous

This starts out like a love-triangle drama, with César (Eduardo Noriega) the wealthy scion of a restauranteur playing at love with every girl he meets. His latest Nuria (Najwa Nimri) is very aggressive sexually, but other than that of no interest to him. He throws a party, fails to invite her, but she shows up anyway. She knows he's

dumping her but she can't help herself and throws herself at him. He evades her advances, notices Sofia (Penélope Cruz) who has come with his friend to the party, goes over to her and asks her to pretend to be interested in him to protect him from his stalker. (Ah, such technique!) Sofia is amused and interested. And so we have our triangle.

I thought this was an interesting beginning. I expected Nuria to become increasingly obsessive, and for César to fall completely in love with Sofia, who after all is played by the strikingly beautiful and bewitching Penélope Cruz, who by the way, plays a mime at one point and is seen au naturel from the waist up at another. (In case you're interested.) And something like this does indeed happen. But then somewhere around the middle of the film the world of reality and that of César's dreams become indistinguishable. He becomes disfigured in an auto accident. Nuria is dead. Sofia seems to cool toward him, and then to love him. It is unclear what is going on.

Normally at this point I exit. Notions of the supernatural or of virtual reality fusing with reality dreamed up by movie directors to be fed to the movie-going public are usually stupid, confused, juvenile, and entirely unconvincing. However a couple of things kept me around. One, Penélope Cruz. Actually she was enough. But I also wanted to find out how director Alejandro Amenábar would sort this out.

I now understand that I can do that by watching *Vanilla Sky* (2001), the Cameron Crowe remake of this film in which (I am told) the supernatural fusing of virtual reality and reality are made so obvious that even this old guy can figure it out. The fact that Penélope Cruz reprises her role opposite her current flame, Tom Cruise, strikes me as interesting. And Cameron Diaz as the sexually aggressive other seems inviting.

Bottom line: Having to read subtitles causes one to miss some of Penélope Cruz's magic with the camera. On the other hand, one can crunch tortilla chips without fear of being unable to hear the dialogue.

Vanilla Sky (2001) 9

Transcends the original

Here in *Vanilla Sky*, a thoughtful reprise of the Spanish film *Open Your Eyes* (1997), directed by Alejandro Amenabar, we have Tom Cruise, American heart throb and box office buffo paired with his current true love, the amazingly beautiful and very talented Penélope Cruz.

Guess what happens. The public doesn't like him. Even though this is a more finely structured and comprehensible film than *Open Your Eyes* (we'll get to that in moment), Tom Cruise is NOT sympathetic, or at least it takes us until near the end of the film to feel any sympathy for him, and then perhaps what we feel most sympathetic for is the mask that is Tom Cruise in most of the later reels.

I think the problem is that Cruise is miscast. Unlike Eduardo Noriega, who played the same part in the film directed by Alejandro Amenabar, Cruise is too cute and too privileged to elicit our sympathy. We almost feel his character has it coming. After all, he willingly got into the car with his "stalker" (Cameron Diaz) presumably to have a little sexual fun. And this just after spending a Platonic night with Sofia (Penélope Cruz), whom he is now supposed to be in love with. Furthermore—and this may be just a minor point, but a telling one—Cruise's disfigurement was not as gross as was Noriega's. One gets the sense that perhaps Cruise insisted on it being that way.

From another angle, one might ask, is this deja vu all over again? Recall that Cruise was married to Nichole Kidman when he played opposite her in Stanley Kubrick's *Eyes Wide Shut*. Guess what happened. The public didn't like it. Aside from the fact that they didn't understand it, what they didn't like was Tom Cruise. He was NOT sympathetic. One could not identify with his cruising various kinky sexual opportunities as a privileged married doctor.

Having said all that, I still think that this film, directed by the very talented Cameron Crowe, who wrote *Fast Times at Ridgemont High* (1982) and wrote and directed *Almost Famous* (2000), is the better film. Why? Mainly because Crowe demonstrates a better understanding of the underlining theme of the film than did Amenabar. (Of course he had the benefit of Amenabar's film to improve upon.)

What I am getting at is the precarious nature of our brain's experience of reality. On one level, I think that is what the film is really all about. (On another level of course there is a love triangle.) Throw the cryonics mumble jumble out the window and consider that we might, as some people believe, become software. As partial products of our own culture we will (at least in the beginning) experience glitches that will destroy our dreams, just as David Aames's guilty conscience destroyed his lucid dream and made him see a projection of his fear and his guilt instead of seeing his beloved Sofia.

If we do become software, there will be imperfect matches between our biological nature and the artificial neural nets we will fuse with. We will not be freezing ourselves in the future. Instead we will merge with our machines as we live and become part human and part artificial intelligence—something beyond human. This is the glimpse of the future that Cameron Crowe extends to us, a possibility that he saw in the Spanish language film not fully worked out by Amenabar.

Despite his miscasting, I think Tom Cruise gave a spirited performance, and I think only his celebrity and the compromised personality of the character he plays kept some movie goers from fully appreciating his work.

Penélope Cruz is more playful here than she was in *Open Your Eyes* and her role here is somewhat larger. Crowe makes sure she has ample time in front of the camera to mesmerize us, and she does. At some point I realized that she reminded me a little of Audrey Hepburn. Perhaps she has been watching some of Miss Hepburn's films. (I would bet on it.) Regardless, she, whom I first saw in *Belle Epoque* (1992) when she was eighteen, is utterly bewitching.

Also giving an excellent performance is Cameron Diaz as the fatally scorned other woman. She brings a sexy, haunting quality to the part that works well with Cruise's software "experiences." She is not quite as convincing a stalker as was Najwa Nimri in the original, however, and this may be another reason that this film only gets 7.0 out of 10 stars from the voters at IMDb while *Open Your Eyes* gets 7.8.

Usually I prefer the original to the remake, the European film to the Hollywood production, but in this case I think it is *Vanilla Sky* that will be remembered. At any rate, look past Tom Cruise's celebrity and see this for Camer-

on Crowe whose vision of a virtually real future is intriguing and reveals that he did his homework.

New school takes this one, 7-9, tying the match, but Old School is still ahead on stars.

Your scores: Old____ New____

Matches:
	Old School: 3	____
	Newer film: 3	____
	Ties: 3	____

Stars:
	Old School: 76	____
	Newer film: 72	____

Insomnia (1997)

vs.

Insomnia (2002)

As in the last matchup we have a slightly older European film versus a newer American version.

Insomnia (1997) 8

A web of his own making

It has to be appreciated that Detective Jonas Engstrom is from Sweden and not accustomed to the land of the midnight sun of northern Norway, and that the sunlight streaming through his hotel room giving him insomnia is relentlessly there twenty-four hours a day. Thus his judgment is flawed, and when in a fog (literally) he accidentally shots his partner and close friend, his decision to cover it up rather than face the difficulties of owning up is understandable. What follows is a demonstration of the truth of the adage "Oh, what a tangle web we weave when first we practice to deceive" (from Sir Walter Scott).

What is superior about this somewhat familiar plot is both the resolution and the atmosphere. Although this is a realistic cop drama several light years beyond standard US TV fare, and comparable to the best Hollywood efforts, and features a gifted and accomplished actor in the lead role (Stellan Skargard, whom I last saw in the very disturbing *Breaking the Waves* (1996)), it is not completely realized. We are troubled by the decisions that Engstrom makes, particularly in framing an innocent young man, to say nothing of his shooting the dog; and while we understand how he became caught in this trap of his own making, we feel there must be something more than the midnight sun to account for his disintegration. His aborted affair with the hotel clerk Ane (Maria Bonnevie) contributed to the general sense that he was falling apart cognitively and emotionally. But why?

Nonetheless this is a smooth, compelling drama, well-crafted by director Erik Skjoldbjaerg, whose talent is obvious. I am looking forward to his next film, the intriguingly titled, *Prozac Nation* (2000). Gisken Armand as the overseeing detective (and Engstrom's conscience) attracted my eyes as I watched her watching Engstrom. She does a good job in a subtle role. Bjorn Floberg as the writer who occasions the story is sufficiently slimy to arouse our profound distaste and to make us wish that Engstrom would add murder to his other crimes... But does he?

Insomnia (2002) 8

Compelling

This finely wrought remake of the Norwegian film of the same name (1997)—an excellent film by the way—is something close to a thriller masterpiece flawed only by a too-hurried resolution. Christopher Nolan, whose strikingly original *Memento* (2000) is among the best films made in recent years, planned this out very carefully, tying up most of the loose ends without relying on any phony motivation, which we sometimes see in passionate cop dramas. However, the guns blazing at the end was a cheap way out of this psychologically complicated story. Still, I think we can overlook that small fault since the rest of the film is so very well done.

The incomparable Al Pacino gives a mesmerizing performance as Los Angeles police detective Will Dormer who is sent with his partner north to Alaska ostensibly to help in a murder investigation. However we quickly learn that being out of town may help him and his partner avoid an

Internal Affairs investigation to which Dormer may be vulnerable. By the way, "dormir" in French means "to sleep," which is something Dormer does not do for six days, which is very close to the edge of human tolerance. Indeed Dormer's last line in the film is "Just let me sleep."

Pacino is supported by Robin Williams as Walter Finch, a morally-deranged mystery writer who doesn't appear until the film is about half over. He makes up for keeping us waiting with a dramatic performance that will curl your toes. He is even more despicable than Bjorn Floberg was in the Norwegian film. Not only is Robin Williams's appearance subtly altered and his demeanor strange, even his voice is not the same. He is a long way from *Good Morning, Vietnam* (1987) and *Mrs. Doubtfire* (1993), but I think this is, in a more modest way, one of his best performances.

Also featured is Hilary Swank, whom you should see in *Boys Don't Cry* (1999) if you haven't, as Ellie Burr, an ingenue Alaskan detective in awe of the master cop from the big city. Notable in a modest role is Jonathan Jackson as Randy Stetz, a high schooler with a chip on his shoulder. I also liked the brief appearance by Katharine Isabelle, who played the murdered girl's trampy girlfriend.

The key psychological question in both films is why does Will Dormer decide to cover up the accidental shooting? In director Erik Skjoldbjaerg's 1997 film the answer is human nature. That certainly worked, but was not enough for Nolan, and so he gives us Dormer's Internal Affairs problems back in L.A. as further motivation. This works very well for two reasons: One, it is convincing. Recall his spontaneous confession to the hotel clerk (Maura Tierney). And two, the cop problems in Los Angeles are right out of the headlines of recent years. They are real. Nolan even has Ellie find a copy of the Los Angeles *Times* with one of the stories on the front page.

The next psychological question is, is the villain a serial killer in the making? If he is, then Dormer must stop him regardless of his own problems. And therein lies the internal conflict of the film so well projected by Al Pacino. We know that there is something more than the midnight sun to account for Dormer's disintegration. He is a flawed cop. Like some of his real life counterparts in L.A. and elsewhere he took it upon himself, by falsifying evidence, to administer justice to a man he knew was guilty. When he did that, he knew (and this is something he teaches Ellie) that he had lost his integrity as a cop. The temptation to frame somebody we know is guilty of a horrendous crime is very great and many of us would fall into it.

Since I cannot discuss the ending here in any concrete way, let me just say that if Nolan had really taken his time with the ending he might have had Dormer simply murder the villain and face the consequences (or even commit suicide). But I suspect Nolan believed that the heroic character of his star would have been compromised. In Skjoldbjaerg's film the police detective actually shoots the dog to obtain the spent bullet he needs. In Nolan's film the dog is already dead. I think this minor blush of character actually taints Nolan's film to some small degree and leads Nolan down the path to the Hollywood ending to come. But judge for yourself

One final point. A lot can be gotten out of a single camera shot. This is something that Nolan does very well. A case in point is the shot on the plastic evidence bag holding the bullet that Dormer picks up in the lab. Nolan has the camera show us the words on the bag, "chain of custody," and he has the camera linger long enough for us to read them. This nice touch reminds us that THAT very chain of custody is being compromised, another echo of real life criminal investigations from recent years in L.A.

See this for Al Pacino, at his best here, one of the great stars of our era whose ability to command the screen is second to none.

Dead even here, 8 to 8.

Your scores: Old_____ New_____

Matches:
Old School: 3		_____
Newer film: 3		_____
Ties: 4		_____

Stars:
Old School: 84		_____
Newer film: 80		_____

Final score: matches, a tie; stars, slight edge to Old School.

Chapter Five:

Fifty-Three Unconscionable Pans

or

Sorry, I Couldn't Help Myself

Unlike the movies in Chapter Three "Trashed!" which were just plain horrible, some of the movies here are not half bad, but I couldn't help panning them anyway. Indicative of the fun for the viewer is the bare fact that in two of the movies one of the characters met his maker in the arms of Venus, apparently due to a surfeit of sexual excitement. Madonna can do that to you in Body of Evidence *(1993) and so can Sharon Stone in* Basic Instinct *(1992), so be careful.*

As in the "Trashed!" chapter, after each review there is a place to indicate your approval or disapproval of my sentiments—or go to the Website at Amazon.com or IMDb.com and vote and/or comment. (Be kind.)

Presented in alphabetical order.

American Psycho (2000) 6

The original Norman Bates was a pussycat

Relatively speaking, that is.

This is an interesting, if a bit over the top, portrait of a psychopath gone bananas. Presented in white, white, and more white so that the red, red, red of the blood will be all the more contrasting, this approach coincides with the ultra, ultra sophistication of the Harvard and Yale grads working on Wall Street who are so, so very venal and superficial. This is a slasher film that will appeal equally to heartlanders on a date night, and to those blue coasters who need a little extra titillation.

[And then suddenly Bateman takes over my review]:

Yeah, RIGHT. Who cares? Personally, I don't usually watch slasher films, being above that kind of stuff, but this is stylishly done—and I do like style in my blood splattering. Where director Mary Herron screws up is in not realizing that only an idiot sociopath would be so stupid and self-destructive as to so carelessly kill so many people. If there is one thing a sociopath never wants to do is to bring pain upon himself. Don't you think, considering the ending, that Bateman is going to be caught? Huh?

[Resuming control of my review and droning on]:

...although the terms "sociopath" and "psychopath" are often used interchangeably, there is a clear tendency for "psychopath" to be reserved for violent sociopaths. Another reason "psychopath" is correct is because this is a postmodern update of the classic Hitchcock slasher movie *Psycho* (1960) starring...

[Again taking over]:

Shut up. Who cares who it starred? The point here is that this film—we're talking about MY film— is a TOTALLY IN-ACCURATE portrait of a true psycho—I mean sociopath. We don't make ourselves so vulnerable to the Criminal Justice System. We are NOT intent on self-destruction. Believe me if I ever decide to get my jollies by slashing someone up, I will make absolutely sure I can get away with it. Only low IQ psychos like Scott Peterson get caught. And, by the way, what is with this chainsaw business? I mean he tosses it down the stairwell so that it crashes on the floor from how many stories above, and it still works so he can use it on "Christie"? Give me a break.

Oh. You think that it hit her while still running, huh? Ha, ha, ha! Nice shot, dude.

[Again resuming control]:

..notice too that the ending allows for a sequel, yet has all the trappings of an ending. We know that he is going to be caught and yet...

[Coming back out of the screen...]:

We know nothing. The cops are stupid. Nobody will be-

lieve...

[Shoving him back in...]:

...the emphasis on the conspicuous consumption of expensive food and wine, drugs, cigars, the indulgence of any kind of animal pleasure is, on one level a statement about our society—well, Wall Street society—but on another level is part of the usual Hollywood seduction of the audience. This is the fast lane. Wouldn't you like to live in the fast lane for a bit, but of course come back (after they run the credits) to your own way of life? Isn't this the essence of escape? Go to the movies, rent a DVD, kick up your feet and escape for a while, and maybe there will be a catharsis, as the Greek tragedians intended. And when you turn off the set and go to bed you realize that nothing in your life is so extreme and nothing in your life is really that far gone, and yet you have experienced vicariously an extreme emotion, and as a bonus you can feel superior to those Ivy League sickos.

In truth this is a slightly tongue in cheek slasher/serial killer flick. It's a satire of sorts. It is as slick as slick can be, thoroughly engrossing with fine acting from especially Christian Bale who plays Bateman. The direction is as tight as a well-strung banjo, the script nearly hypnotic in its seductive power, the New York ultra-hip sets as eye-widening as seeing the Taj Mahal while the sidebar-like satirical commentary, which (on a third level) parodies the genre, is very funny. Best joke: they're in the restroom of a fancy eating establishment and doing some lines and the guy in the next stall gets a little uptight because they're loud and screams out, "Will you keep it down. I'm trying to do drugs!"

Also funny is how Bateman says what he really thinks and nobody takes him seriously, and how he slips up from time to time and nobody notices.

Incidentally, Reese Witherspoon has a minor part as exactly the kind of clueless woman who might very well marry a psychopath. I liked this touch because I have known a few non-violent sociopaths and I often wondered if their spouses had a clue. Clearly Reese's character did not.

Also excellent in support was Chloe Sevigny as Jean, Bateman's adoring (but also clueless) secretary. The idea here is that women are so bowled over by Bateman's alpha male credentials that they can't see the real person. The only character to really realize who Bateman was (and she ended up listening to that knowledge a little late) was the streetwalker. Well, Jean gets the picture finally as she peruses Bateman's graphic notebook. (By the way, somebody got paid to draw all the stuff in it. I wonder who that was. Was there a mention in the credits, something like, sick psycho doodlings by...?)

Finally: real life irony. The character that Bale played in a movie immediately before this one was Jesus of Nazareth in a TV drama called *Mary, Mother of Jesus* (1999). As Casey Stengel used to say, you could look it up.

You were right on and I thank you for finally pointing out what a dog this movie was_____
You were totally unfair and may you reside in that special level of hell in which all the DVDs are Shopping Channel reruns_____

Austin Powers: International Man of Mystery *(1997) 7*

Seduction, Mike Myers style

This is a James Bond spoof aimed at retro nerds so that we might find an identification in our deprived lives. Hey, in this movie we get to cozy up—in your dreams, retard!—to Elizabeth (drooling all over myself) Hurley. The flick sparkles (if that's the right word) with lame-o jokes and semi-sophisticated satire.

Mike Myers wrote the script and stars as both Austin, the man of mystery (right, like the toe jam smell at the bottom of your closet is a mystery), and the cartoon villain Dr. Evil, who might be Dr. No cleaning his teeth with his pinkie. Speaking of teeth, he has the better teeth of our disjointed duo, speaking of which, notice that Hurley (would that Emma Peel had anything like her figure, but she too was English) doesn't actually soul kiss Austin. I mean, there are not only LIMITS, but contract clauses. I think Hurley was afraid that if she actually swapped tongues with him she would catch some horrid fungus amongus and THAT wouldn't be good for her career. However, check this out: for her next Austin Powers opus, The Spy Who Shagged Me she got $3-million up front.

Look at it this way: if she could make flirty-flirty eyes with Rancid Teeth Man, she could conceivably, in your wildest dreams find YOU attractive, at least as the last man on earth. You and Elizabeth Hurley as the last two humans on earth! Eat your heart out, Sean Connery. Heck, all he had in Dr. No (1962) was Ursula Andress. (Come to recall: yummie, yum, yum.) And you too, Roger Moore. "Bond, James Bond," yourself.

Myers makes himself as disgustingly nerdish as possible, but still the chicks swoon. There's some right-on satire here about the mystery of feminine desire. What DOES a woman want? The nerds never know but James Bond, Harrison Ford and (gulp) Mike Myers don't have to ask.

All right, there is a plot to this Batman-like take off on the sixties become the nineties 007 spy diversion. But it's so familiar that I won't bother with it here. Some of the characters are interesting. There's Alotta Fagina played by Fabiana Udenio recalling Octopussy and Pussy Galore. (Well, she's not interesting, but her name is.) And think about this: Robert Wagner with the eye patch who was once a sophisticated ladies man—for example, The Pink Panther (1964)—is now a bloated old man having to wear extra-large suit coats to hide his pot belly and sagging flesh. Now THAT evens the score for the old nerds who never got the girl, who, by the way, will like this as much as pimple-popping sixteen-year-olds.

Myers knows what he's doing. There's a deep psychological seduction underneath the sixties garb and the nineties toilet humor that makes this strangely satisfying. For my part however I could only bare to watch it all the way to the very, very end in the hope that (PG-13 rating aside) that Hurley would disrobe a little and I could get a glimpse of that exquisite bod. But they teased me, especially in the matrimonial bed scene with the pineapples and the melons and the spice rack—whatta rack! Ha, ha, ha, ha.

Remember as you watch this: it is not as bad as it looks. In fact, once you understand what Mike Myers is doing to your psyche, you might want to see it again.

You were right on..._____
You were totally unfair..._____

Basic Instinct (1992) 6

Near the apex of the sex/slasher genre

We might call this trash, but if we do we'd have to call it very clever trash, the sort of trash one might find dumpster-diving in Beverly Hills.

It stars Michael Douglas (who, by the way, has eclipsed the Hollywood power, if not the screen presence, of his dad, Kirk Douglas) and Sharon Stone who, as usual, finds herself in a part that requires that she take off her clothes and spout hard-edged one-liners: she does both with a certain delight that makes us think she is having a good time.

He's a San Francisco homicide cop named Nick Curran with some questionable shootings hanging over his head, hence his nickname, "Shooter." She's a rich best-selling trash novelist named Catherine Tramell (pen name Catherine Wolfe) who likes kinky sex and other deviancies. It seems that her latest boyfriend (depicted in a blood-splattered opening scene) abruptly, shall we say, met his maker while in the arms of Venus, something predicted in Catherine's latest opus. We are made to believe that she could very well have been that Venus, although of course keeping us in the dark is part of the seduction.

Jeanne Tripplehorn plays Beth Garner, police Internal Affairs shrink who just happens to be Nick's latest main squeeze. It seems that Catherine and Beth had a one-time intimate liaison while undergrads at UC Berkeley. We are led to believe that she too might have done the killings.

So Nick has a choice, whom to believe about who's responsible for all the dead bodies, the blonde Catherine or the brunette Beth? Both seem a little wacko/sexy. He tries them both out, and we see a lot of skin and hear a lot of fast breathing, and are kept on the edge of our whoopee cushions until the very end—and after, actually, as though the purveyors were already counting on the sequel. I am reminded of a lyric from Elvis Costello's "Every day I write the book": "Even in a world where everyone was equal/I'd still own the film rights and be working on the sequel."

In other words, what this film is about is money—money for the producers, director, actors, crew, etc. It's an extreme sexploitation thriller diabolically done with absurd plot twists and plenty of dead bodies and some diverting chase scenes; indeed I suspect that Basic Instinct will be recognized by future film historians as one of the primo examples of the sex/slasher genre, that is, as soft porn with a sick edge.

But wait, why did I watch this? Uh...Sharon Stone amuses me like a comedic actress, but she ain't exactly funny, is she?

Also it's interesting to notice that in these late eighties/early nineties sexploitation flicks it's the women who are the aggressors (I'm thinking also of Single White Female from the same year) while the men play a little tagalong. Michael Douglas is particularly adept at playing the sort of male who seems natural being dominated by Sharon Stone.

Bottom line: mass mind trash, but worth seeing for its ability to define the Hollywood mentality circa 1992.

You were right on..._____
You were totally unfair..._____

Betrayed By Love (1994) 5

Mostly forgettable

Betrayed By Love (don't ya just love these titles?) is a little morality Lifetime "Movie of the Week" pointing out for the umpteenth time that it just doesn't pay for a girl to be too aggressive sexually (she always gets treated as trash) and of course that men are no good, one of the standard Lifetime truths that is, of course, true.

Mare Winningham and Patricia Arquette star. Winningham is excellent. She has charisma and she can act, and her blue collar, non-glamorous image goes well with the commercials. But Patricia Arquette (not to be confused with her sister, Rosanna, whom you may have seen in Desperately Seeking Susan (1985)), is not bad. She plays an unbelievably sensuous poor white trash babe who knows how to surrender. (The sex in these Lifetime MOWs is a little less than explicit, but oh what they love to imply!) I saw her previously in *Ethan Frome* (1992), as Mattie Silver. Here she does the old "on her knees, her arms around his leg" number (so we can imagine what she'll be doing next) and lets him kick her around psychologically.

"Based on actual events."

What I love about "based on actual events" is you can guess how far off they are from the reality of the real story. I could just see the real personality of the woman played by Arquette, a sleazy, desperate bimbo; but of course Patricia Arquette is more like Marilyn Monroe, and you just know the real woman could never be one tenth as attractive; and the married FBI dude she seduces is in real life a sleazy loser himself of course, but in the movie he is a sophisticated handsome sort of guy.

Bottom line: probably not available any more anyway.

You were right on..._____
You were totally unfair..._____

Blame It on Rio (1984) 5

I blame it on the director

Drippy for the most part. One has to blush for Michael Caine who is miscast as a middle aged man who gets seduced by his best friend's daughter while on vacation in Rio de Janeiro. I had the sense that Brazilian Airlines, or whoever, and the Brazilian tourist bureau fronted the funds for this turkey. Perhaps some old boys club as well since this is fantasy wish fulfillment for middle-aged men, pure and simple. This was supposed to be a comedy, a remake of the Claude Berri French film entitled *One Wild Moment* (1978), but the laughs really don't materialize (there are a few chuckles), and anyway you practically have to be French to make this sort of tale work. Either that or play it full out as a farce.

Nonetheless, there must have been some reason I kept watching, since I have no desire to see Michael Caine make a fool of himself (in those huge, ugly glasses with the plastic brown frames), and that reason is Michelle Johnson, who does the seducing. She is very pretty and delightfully sexy and so beguiling that I almost believe her.

But enough about my fantasies. Joseph Bologna plays the girl's father and Caine's best friend in his usual cynical, wise-cracking style, kind of like the low rent Mafia boss/used car salesman persona that he wears so well. Demi Moore has a small part as Caine's daughter, but there is no evidence here to account for her becoming a box office star in the nineties. Valerie Harper plays Caine's wife, who is sick of him and his lack of demonstrativeness and goes on a separate vacation. Caine's superb timing and great concentration as an actor are in

evidence, but somehow he just doesn't quite make it as a poor sap who is torn between lust and propriety.

Stanley Donen (Singing in the Rain (1952), The Pajama Game (1957), Charade (1963), Indiscreet (1958), etc.) directed and was clearly off his best form or past his prime. Or maybe he just wanted to indulge himself an old guy's daydream.

You were right on..._____
You were totally unfair..._____

Bliss (1997) 7

An attempt at sexual honesty

What we have here is a tantra shrink, a psychoanalytic shrink and a women's support group counseling shrink, and together they cure (that's the implication anyway) a woman made frigid, compulsive, obsessive and I forget what else by her father's sexual abuse. This bit of glorification of therapy suffers from the sort of defect usually found in an action/adventure/thriller movie, namely that of simplistic illogic. It seems that what really caused all this harm was the father's mean staff. This is the lie. (A trendy lie, by the way.) However what is really being presented here unbeknown to the authors in an unconscious acting out is the glorification of that staff. This is consistent with shrink psychology since those guys still haven't freed themselves from the Freudian obsession, and it is consistent with the American patriarchy since the one thing so sacred in our society that it cannot be shown publically (except in double X-rated flicks) is the staff erect. Any lesbian can tell you that this kind of psychology is a phony tantalization leading to the lie of "penis envy."

The problem with any attempt at sexual honesty publically expressed is it's really impossible because we are within the sexual system ourselves and subject to its taboos, no matter how we might try to break free. Ironically, this restraint on true expression is felt most keenly by the most highly socialized members of society. Highly educated and over-socialized shrinks typically tend to be blinded more than others (hence society's penchant to make fun of them). And even if they could see the truth, they couldn't express it since they would then be out of business. It is only the crazies and the great artists who can break free of the taboo system to see what's real and to express it. What we have here is unfortunately not the work of a crazy or a great artist, but of highly sensitive, highly socialized members of the human society (those who made the film) trying to make a living. They struggle to break free, but are trapped by the duplicity mechanism of the species, and end up returning something dictated by the society—that is to say, something politically correct.

We can see, however, that the authors of this movie tried to break free and thought they really were on the right track. Ah but, they smelled the possibility of commercial success and in the end conformed to society's prejudices, society's taboos and fed us back the usual sexual BS. The ultra sophisticated tantra shrink, played beautifully and with appropriate sexual duplicity by the talented Terrance Stamp, provides an illustration of what I mean. It is not clear whether he likes his work because of the benefit of what he does for others, or because it affords him the opportunity to put into play his sexual power. Incidentally, the design of his office/lodgings (coincidentally with a view to where the husband (Craig Sheffer) of his sexually-in-need-of-help patient (Sheryl Lee) is working) was perfectly in tune with his character and added significantly to the authentic atmosphere of the film.

I think what we can learn here is the constancy of the veil of illusion that separates us from an authentic view of human sexuality. Our sexuality must be private and not public and as such any public pronouncement must be a lie. It's a hard truth to realize, but something known in the heart of every prude and congressman (although not in their conscious minds). When those with starry-eyed visions of telling it like it really is come close to the holy grail of sexual truth they falter. One might call it the magnetic repulsive nature of sexual knowledge.

Having said all this I applaud the attempt. Incidentally the sex scenes are very sexy and the three stars, Sheffer, Lee and especially Terence Stamp, do an excellent job. Director Lance Young is the one who unfortunately sells out, but he had no choice. As Jesus said about humans in a larger context, he knew not what he did.

You were right on..._____
You were totally unfair..._____

Body of Evidence (1993) 5

Madonna is very sexy in this mediocre thriller

The "Body of Evidence" in the title is Madonna's. It's also the murder weapon, the film's premise being that she murdered her lover by making invigorating love to him, causing the rich old guy to drop dead from excitement. I suppose this could, and actually has, happened. Then again I have an active imagination.

At any rate we could also call this "Madonna on top" or "Madonna in charge" or maybe "She can show you the power you can have from the prone position." One thing about Madonna, other than having no shame (and I admire her for that) is that she can crawl and not feel the slightest bit reduced.

Another thing about Madonna is her unerring sense of how to appeal to her primary audience, namely young girls (now grown women). During the height of her career a few years back Madonna was the woman most admired by teenaged and pre-teenaged girls. (You could look it up,

but just think of the song, "Papa Don't Preach," or her role as the young free-spirit in *Desperately Seeking Susan* (1985).) And you want to know why? Because she was perceived as having it all: fame, fortune, personal freedom, the attention of the males, and, most important, she achieved her success through hard work and a certain audaciousness that suggests courage, the kind of unmitigated self-expression that most of us can only dream about.

She's not especially bad in this mediocre thriller, nor especially good. The script is ridiculous and the treatment without a hint of nuance or subtlety. William Dafoe and Joe Mantegna seemed to be acting on rote and Anne Archer was, alas, a wash. The problem is the movie is so obviously fake that it's like watching bad TV. There's no point other than kinky sex. I'm not sure why Madonna agreed to do this. I can't believe she needed the money, nor can I believe she didn't care about her reputation as a performing artist. I think she was seduced by the "power over men" fantasy of the script. I also think her appearance here exposes her weakness: simply put, she has bad taste because this could not in any way further her career.

On the plus side I saw the unrated version and she was very sexy.

You were right on..._____
You were totally unfair..._____

Borat (2006) 6

Crude and gross but with some telling satire

Although superficially this mockumentary would seem to be a satire of the people of Kazakhstan or the citizens of any country thereabouts, it is really a satire of America the beautiful. Surprise! It makes some good points and there are some laughs. Mostly though I think the average viewer would be grossed out about half the time. But that's okay. For the average movie-goer or DVD watcher, getting grossed out is a lot better than being bored.

Of course you might be bored too. Personally I don't think I could watch the naked mock fight between Borat (Sacha Baron Cohen) and Azamat Bagatov (Ken Davitan) again. I wasn't so much grossed out as made to feel that really I ought to find better ways to waste my time.

Yes, we're bored in America. Our neurons are sated with violence, pornography, and crude, boorish behavior toward our fellows (both real and on TV and in the movies). Which is why, to be successful, people like Sacha Baron Cohen have to turn up the crude volume to get the old laugh-o-meter activated. "A glimpse of stocking used to be looked on as something shocking, now, heaven knows, anything goes."

But should we care? Yes, your preteen sons are going to find out who in the neighborhood has this DVD and they're going to watch it. Will they be scarred for life? Will they "get it"? Will it make them uncouth? Will they watch it more than half a dozen times?

One of the interesting things about this movie is the publicity it got and the controversy it engendered. Kazakhstan initially was greatly offended and protested loudly at this misrepresentation of its people. But then they thought it over and realized that maybe this isn't necessarily such a bad thing. In Hollywood any publicity is good. They probably figured out that what is being made fun of is the average American's provincial attitude toward foreigners. Cohen goes a long way toward proving that with the scene at the rodeo, for example, where his accidentally ironic line, "We support your war of terror!" gets a nice round of applause. And the guy who thinks that somebody with a moustache looks like a Muslim who looks like a terrorist adds a little to the impression that Americans, when they think about foreigners, think superficially.

Actually, they don't do any real thinking. Xenophobia reigns supreme in the heartland—but that would be the heartland of any country. The frequent anti-Semitic shtick throughout was originally aimed at Europeans, I understand, who despite the embarrassment of the Holocaust are apparently as anti-Semitic as ever. But Cohen, who is Jewish, makes fun of the antisemitism of Muslims as well as Westerners. And he makes fun of the uneducated and uncouth as well as the superficially sophisticated—witness the scene at the Magnolia Fine Dining Society.

Some people sued or threatened to sue. Some guys from the University of South Carolina who were caught off guard and drunk, mouthed some stupidities for all of the world to hear. They sued but lost the case, I understand.

Larry Charles of TV's "Seinfeld" fame directed. He achieved some tension with the simple plot of Borat coming to American and making a road trip across the land to California to meet and hopefully mate with Pamela Anderson. That was pretty funny. I understand that some of the scenes were staged and scripted, for example the book signing scene with Miss Anderson was at least partly staged. But other scenes were play-as-you-go with Cohen just making up stuff and saying provocative things to get reactions from the innocents. The scene in the bathroom with the woman from the Magnolia Fine Dining Society was pretty funny as she explains to Borat so seriously and so sincerely how to wipe himself.

Bottom line here is, should you bother to watch? My answer: maybe if you can stand the crudities, and maybe if you don't squirm at satire directed at Americans. On the other hand, this is not in my opinion in the same league as some other famous comedic movies. Certainly it is not nearly as good as *Blazing Saddles* (1974), which I was watching the other night. Finally, the techniques used by Cohen and Charles are interesting in their own right because of the reaction of people who were taken in, or somewhat taken in, and so that they ended up saying some outrageous and embarrassing things.

*You were right on...*_____
*You were totally unfair...*_____

Brazil (1985) 7

Mary Poppins did not influence this film

There's a lot to like and a lot not to like in this Monty Python cum Citizen Kane Orwellian Kafkaesque Luddite comedic satire of a Rube Goldberg bureaucracy in a retro-future. Throw in a little sword and sorcery, a remembrance of some bad video games from the eighties, a bit of Star Wars, perhaps the sci-fi novels *Level 7* and *We*, sprinkled with Hitlerian mustaches on underdeveloped characters and you get the picture.

What's good is a script full of witty one-liners finding the right target, the corporate and governmental bureaucracies, our preoccupation with petty power in the pecking order, and our fear of ageing (face lifts) or looking irregular (braces). What's bad is that Director Terry Gilliam never got it under control. I'm reminded of what Mark Twain said about his magnum opus, "Anyone attempting to find a plot here will be shot." The story is slight, lacking any tension and the sets are dark and cluttered to a point past annoyance. I would say the film needed editing for focus, but that would only have spotlighted the poverty of the plot.

Here's the problem in a nutshell: recall the line of billboards on both sides of the road mile after mile without a break. Now that's a nice satire of where we're headed as corporate interests increasingly dominate the environment; however like a Rube Goldberg contraption, they don't work since the billboards are too close for anybody to read them as the cars fly by! In a way the world depicted here is like a parallel universe in which everything is essentially the same but differs in a thousand details: the weird little cars, the ridiculous maze of ducts and cables for air conditioning, the oversized bills on the baseball caps, the single desk sliding between two cubicle rooms, etc.

We can see how Gilliam has grown as a film maker by comparing this to *12 Monkeys*, produced a decade later. In *12 Monkeys* there is not only an interesting story and a subplot, but the characters are developed into flesh and blood. What I think Gilliam has realized is that no director, regardless of how brilliant, can long survive without catering in some way to the mass audience. Although *Brazil* ranks in IMDb's top 250 that is only because movie enthusiasts naturally reward creativity. Poll the mass audience however and you'll find a significant percentage that couldn't even sit through this film. Notice too that while Gilliam wasted the talented Robert De Niro in *Brazil* he wised up and used star Bruce Willis to the maximum in *12 Monkeys*.

It will be interesting to see what Gilliam does next.

You were right on..._____
You were totally unfair..._____

Breakdown (1997) 6

Kurt Russell kicks redneck butt, etc.

What we have here is a breakdown in probability, which is an advance on the usual thriller development, which is a breakdown in logic (although there's enough of that too). We also have the most incredible heroics known to humankind performed by Kurt Russell in the rescue of his wife, such heroics as would make Superman turn kryptonite green with envy.

Psychologically this is another yuppie nightmare to engage the fancy betwixt the consommé and the brie. Upscale young couple from Massachusetts driving to California get targeted in the redneck desert by some degenerate locals. First their shiny new Jeep Cherokee just stops running out in the middle of nowhere. Then the wife (Kathleen Quinlan) disappears after accepting a ride from a trucker (J.T. Walsh) who then denies he ever saw her. It's hard for hubby Kurt Russell to understand what's going on. Did J.T. kill her? Was it a sex crime? Next Russell himself is waylaid. But fear not. Our hero, now properly worked up, escapes, and against all odds, and I mean all odds, fights his way into the chase. We soon see that these evil guys are evil to the very core of their being. At one point they put Quinlan in the freezer, after she's already had a bad day and night tied up with tape over her mouth in a mummy's shroud stuffed into a side storage compartment of a traveling truck. They shut the freezer, lock the storm shelter door, lock the barn door and go to breakfast where, with hardy appetites, they swap stories and make merry.

Remember the old cowboy bit where Roy Rogers or Tom Mix crawls under the stage coach as the horses are galloping under the whip of the driver, and manages to climb up the side of the coach as the dust flies to emerge at shotgun position to fight the villain holding the reigns? Well, we've got the same thing here, only Kurt Russell with arms of steel and strength to shame Mighty Mouse, climbs under the roaring truck doing seventy MPH over the asphalt and emerges behind the cab where he endures a twelve-hour drive to later position himself to fight the villains. The man's will and fortitude are the envy of the known universe. Actually I laughed out loud at the absurdity of the some of the heroics.

The crash scenes sparkle, but the pièce de résistance is the final scene with the sixteen wheeler hanging precariously off the bridge above a rocky canyon stream WAY BELOW with Russell and Walsh crawling over it like ants as they try to murder one another.

At points I was reminded of the seminal Spielberg TV flick, *Duel*, in the use of the menacing truck, while the isolated and inbred western locale trapping our couple recalled to mind Oliver Stone's *U Turn*.

Incidentally, the map shown beneath the opening credits is fake: there is no such configuration of roads and towns in the United States. Actual scenes were shot in Utah and California.

You were right on..._____
You were totally unfair..._____

Breaking and Entering (2006) 7

Intriguing story marred by some careless direction

Anthony Minghella, who won an Oscar for *The English Patient* (1996), wrote and directed this interesting film starring Jude Law as an architect who gets involved with a Bosnian ex-pat (Juliette Binoche) and her son. I found it mostly satisfying, but somehow unconvincing. The fact that Jude Law is a few years younger than either Robin Wright Penn, who played his wife Liv, or Binoche who played Amira was not the problem. What bothered me was the incompleteness of Will Francis's character. To make this work, Will had to be a philandering sort of guy who this time gets involved in something more than the usual sexcapade. We need to see Will fooling around before he gets involved with Amira, otherwise his insistence on quick sex with an exotic woman just doesn't make sense. Not only that but the lesson he presumably learns from the experience is not as compelling.

And as much as I admire Juliette Binoche I really thought her character could have been spiced up a bit. She needs to look more exotic and to have a kind of saucy streak above the strait-laced mother and seamstress role she is forced to play. We needed to see her as sexually frustrated, yes, but also as someone who is awakened by being made love to by Jude Law! For some reason Minghella underplayed this possibility. I think she should have just gone bananas over Will, and that would have created the kind of emotional conflict that allowed her to feel guilt about arranging to have the photos taken of her and Will in bed together. Although this was blackmail for her son, it was—or should have been—a betrayal of love. Instead of exuding such a goody-goody persona, Amira should have projected a more compromised person, someone who would cynically sleep with a guy and conspire to photograph him in a compromised position instead of first asking him if he would help her son.

There were some schlocky details that Minghella did not pay enough attention to that detract from the effectiveness of the film. First, it is not clear why Will should be able to sleep so soundly in the afternoon in adulterous bed of Amira's friend that her friend can enter and take a dozen or so shots of him with Amira moving around on the bed in different poses. I kept expecting to see something showing us he was drugged!

The fact that the police detective befriended the boy was okay. Cops sometimes do that sort of thing. They like to play big brother (in a positive way), but I could not believe that Will would refuse to help Amira's son when she is literally on her knees begging him. Minghella played it in this artificial way so as to set up the climactic scene when Will and Liv arrive together at the hearing. In real life Will could not say no when Amira is begging him because (1) he does want to help the boy, (2) she still has the power to embarrass Will and his wife even though she has given him the incriminating photo negatives, (3) it is totally out of character for him to suddenly care so much about the affair coming out, and (4) he immediately confesses it to his wife anyway.

In the scene when Will returns to his wife after the stakeout smelling of the prostitute's perfume, we have Liv smelling it, and then when he opts for a shower, she pulls him close for immediate sex. I think he should have explained it. After all, he was not involved with the prostitute. He rejected her and that would be believable. In fact in his place I couldn't resist talking about this strange prostitute (played very enticingly by Vera Farmiga in a bit part). It would be interesting. Apparently Minghella was making some point by having Liv want to have sex with him immediately; however that was never developed. We are left imagining that the perfume or the thought of her husband with a prostitute somehow aroused her, which seems unlikely, but if that was the case, it needed to be developed.

Why the robbers would come back to the scene of the crime a third time to commit yet the same crime in the same manner is beyond, I would think, the reach of most of the world's dumbest criminals, and these guys weren't that dumb.

And there were some dangling strings: why DID the prostitute steal his car and then return it? Why was the boy so lost and then suddenly so repentant and seemingly on the right track? This was underdeveloped.

The scene with the autistic daughter Bea at Will's workplace was played so heavy-handedly that we knew what was going to happen before it happened—and what was the point? By the way, her relationship with Will was also not fully developed. (Perhaps Minghella's script was too demanding for the director!)

I am sorry to be so critical but this could have been an outstanding movie, and I get irritated when directors go to print so quickly. Minghella is never going to be a great director until he takes a page from Stanley Kubrick's book and polishes every scene and irons out the wrin-

kles. As it is, *Breaking and Entering* is a pretty good film, and certainly no Jude Law fan should miss it.

You were right on..._____
You were totally unfair..._____

Breaking the Waves (1996) 6

Very difficult to watch

Emily Watson's performance is extraordinary, and Stellan Skargard is very good, but this is without a doubt the most degrading, depressing and tragic movie I have seen in a long, long time. I had to force myself to watch it, hoping that somehow something redeeming would transpire. Two and one half hours later I can say that it did not. I wish I could say that this was a great work of art, but it is not. It is a sad, very sad commentary on the madness of human beings, a twentieth century "tale told by an idiot, full of sound and fury signifying nothing." Particularly depressing were the church fathers in their beards and their stupidity. And be forewarned, the sexuality is degrading, and the very essence of human love is willfully and repeatedly perverted.

In making this movie, Director Lars von Trier no doubt sought a kinship with the tragedies of Shakespeare and the Greeks in which the fates destroy the protagonist because of a so-called "fatal flaw," a flaw the protagonist cannot help. Bess's fatal flaw was her childlike nature twisted by circumstance. In the great tragedies the essential purpose is to bring the audience, through its involvement and its identification with the protagonist, to a catharsis, a catharsis that cleanses the emotions and allows us to see the world as it really is, free of self-delusion. But Von Trier's bizarre and pathetic ending with those ridiculous bells in the sky was closer to bathos than anything else, and steered us not toward catharsis but into a kind of emotional limbo where not even emptiness is felt.

You were right on..._____
You were totally unfair..._____

Brokedown Palace (1998) 7

Don't let this happen to you

The story of friendship tested is interesting, the characters are engaging, the sets are beautiful, the acting is good to excellent, but somehow this tale of two American girls unjustly jailed for drug tracking in Thailand doesn't quite convince. It's hard to say just what director Jonathan Kaplan might have done differently to make this promising movie an outstanding movie. But maybe it has something to do with the wrong kind of detail, the accumulated effects thereof.

First we have the sight of the pretty American girls, just out of high school, Alice Marano (Claire Danes) and Darlene Davis (Kate Beckinsale) dressed in USA young miss outfits that show off their figures like models on a runway. You'd think they would dress down a little for the natives, remembering that when in Rome do as the Romans do. I've watched the Globe Trekker on PBS and the young women there never wear tight skirts and lipstick. The girls prance about the streets of Thailand on display as though looking for Mr. Right.

Well, of course this being the nineties and not the fifties, they instead find Mr. Wrong. He charms them and divides them by invoking jealousy, the one of the other. All of this makes for an interesting premise. And then we have a nice (if predictable) twist, and the girls end up in prison.

The prison sets are beautiful in a dark and somber way, full of open spaces and diffused colors, guards in pressed uniforms, the other prisoners mostly healthy—pretty even—in clean uniforms with neat tags like charms hanging from the necks. The fruits and vegetables stacked in the corner of the mess area that the girls are tricked into sampling are fresh and attractive. Strange. A palace as a prison.

Somehow—perhaps it was the beauty of the sets—I never really felt the kind of outrage and horror and near hopelessness that such a situation might evoke. It seemed clear that everything would work out, and the girls would go home soon, leaving the misadventure behind them.

That is not exactly what happens.

See this for Claire Danes who gives a fine performance and almost sells the not-entirely plausible ending.

You were right on..._____
You were totally unfair..._____

Dangerous Beauty (1998) 5

True love triumphs over the Inquisition

Yes, and Santa Claus is coming to town. And there is somewhere a woman true and fair.

Veronica Franco (Catherine McCormack), a woman with a venerable family name but no cash, learns the oldest profession from her mother after experiencing the considerable shock of seeing a young woman in the nunnery (her first choice since she can't marry the man she loves) getting her golden locks shorn. No danger of that for Veronica, whose mane flows free even when she might dress down a little to hide from the hoi polloi, who are blaming her sinful ways for the plague that visits 16th Century Venice.

Rufus Sewell plays nobleman Marco Venier who loves her but must marry someone else for the good of the family fortune. He plays the role like a caddy to McCormack,

which is the way men appear in romance novels. McCormack herself gives only a workman-like performance that cannot lift this historical romance above the usual paperback issue. (We really needed Kate Winslet, but perhaps she read the script.) The rather routine indictment of the Inquisition and soft revelations of the hypocrisy of the Venetian nobility can't disguise the fact that this is a women's fantasy-fulfillment indulgence all the way and nothing more. The movie is also politically correct in the tiresome manner of the 1990's, when women must be shown as triumphing over men through the sheer power of their cleverness and superior moxie, or, put another way, through having bigger balls.

Once again Hollywood celebrates the high class whore as being ahead of her time. We see her gain admiration and riches as she develops a worldly sophistication second perhaps only to that of the Pope. Yet there is some truth to this stale notion. To make it work though, we needed to see Veronica's seamy side, to experience the crudity of her lascivious and exploitive nature. Instead we have a fairy tale princess whore, Snow White turning tricks in gorgeous gowns sans syphilis, sans beatings, sans pimp.

Jacqueline Bisset is competent as the mother who teaches her daughter how to exploit men. As a pep talk she tells Veronica that courtesans are the best educated women, and you are following in the footsteps of Cleopatra. I think the historical fact (if fact it is) that the only women who were allowed to read in 16th century Venice were courtesans, confused the designers of this tale into thinking that courtesans were the superior ladies of Venetian society. They were the only women allowed in the library because they were considered already corrupted. The whole movie suffers from this sort of "gee whiz this is so eye-opening for our times" treatment. The climactic scene before the Inquisition in particular is embarrassing in the melodramatic naiveté of its phony development. Hollywood is again attempting to re-write history in light of the current PC agenda. Alas, wasn't it always thus?

You were right on..._____
You were totally unfair..._____

Dead Ringers (1988) 6

A bit of a sick film with a great performance by Jeremy Irons

Jeremy Irons has a penchant for playing bizarre sorts of men. He played Humbert Humbert in Adrian Lyne's *Lolita* (1997) and the creepy Dr. Claus Von Bulow in *Reversal of Fortune* (1990). Here he gets to play two creepy guys. One is named Beverly. Now I ask you, if you had twins boys and you named one of them Elliot and the other Beverly, what did you have in mind?

"Dead Ringer" is an old title. There are a number of movies by that name (IMDb.com lists four; this one of course is "Dead Ringers"), and clearly the titles suggest twins.

Genevieve Bujold plays Claire Niveau, a celebrated actress who has a fertility problem and a great desire to have children. Elly and Bev are gynecologists who work with barren women in more ways than one. She becomes Elliot's or Beverly's patient. She has an extraordinary uterus, which they explore—I know, I know, this is pretty funny in a sick sort of way. The movie in fact is sort of sick but not funny—at least not intentionally. But it is interesting—appalling but interesting.

Anyway, Claire has the obligatory affair with both of them without realizing that there are two of them. They do the doctor thing with kinky sex and pills. At one point she begins to get the idea that Dr. Mantle is a bit—she calls him schizophrenic, which is, of course, for all you shrinks out there, a bit of a misnomer for what she means. Yes, one is nice and one is not so nice, one is slick with women and the other isn't, one is commanding and the other isn't, and yes it gets more complex than that by quite a bit. They are like Siamese twins joined with a long umbilical cord.

The problem for our boys, who have played this game with women many times before, is that Bev, who is always taking (you know what kind of) "seconds" actually falls in love with Claire. And she with him. And she knows the difference, once she finds out that there are two of them. And she is not pleased.

I've already perhaps said too much, but this is the setup, and it is familiar. How it works out is really the key to this movie. Irons is very good and so is Bujold of course. Both are professional actors with a lot of experience. Claire is a feisty kind of character, primitive in some ways, but ultra-sophisticated in others. And very vulnerable, pathetically so it would seem. However, she is also strong. A nice contrast that gives Bujold ample range to show off her talent.

David Cronenberg, AKA "the King of Venereal Horror," directs. He has a history of serving up violence as a means of seducing the mass audience. Here he foreshadows something to come with something like forceps and other scary-looking steel instruments illustrated on the screen as the opening credits roll. Frankly I feel the pain and I don't have a uterus.

I was able to watch until Bev, now a pill-popping menace, about 95 minutes in, grabs the surgical steel instruments that he designed for use on a "mutant woman's body," jabs them into his coat and pants pockets on his way to a rendezvous with his beloved Claire, she of the triple uterus. That was enough. Knowing Cronenberg's love of blood-splattered violence, I ejected the DVD.

But you might, at your own risk, watch the ending. I've got a feeling that the title "Dead Ringers" involves a pun. You can send me a note telling me what happens. Or not. Preferably not.

Jeremy Irons gets to exceed the range of most actors even over their lifetime in this one film, and he does it very well. If you're a big Jeremy Irons fan, you wouldn't want to miss this. Otherwise, I suggest the Disney channel, quickly.

You were right on..._____
You were totally unfair..._____

Death and the Maiden (1994) 6

Intense, disturbing, depressing

I would not recommend this for most people. It is painful to watch and artificial, very stagy (not surprising since it was adapted from a stage play written by Ariel Dorfman), and ultimately not redemptive (as the video jacket claims), but perverse and depressing.

Sigourney Weaver gives a raw-edged performance almost entirely in one key. She plays a woman (Pauline Escobar) who was raped and tortured by a Nazi-like doctor named Roberto Miranda played by Ben Kingsley in some unidentified South American country. Since Dorfman is from Argentina, we'll assume it's Argentina. Certainly this sort of thing happened there during the time of the "Disappeared." The other member of the three-person cast is her husband (Gerardo Escobar) played by Stuart Wilson. Roman Polanski directed.

The title comes from Franz Schubert's string quartet of the same name which was played by the doctor as he tortured Pauline.

This is a polarizing film. Women who have ever suffered anything at the hands of men will identify with Weaver's character and may find the film brilliant. Most men will not even be able to watch it.

There is some ambiguity in the ending, as to whether Roberto really was guilty as charged. My opinion is that he was without doubt. The final scene (which I can't describe since it would give away too much) is really a statement about the nature of horror and how it can live on amidst the most familiar settings, a man patting his son on the head, some people attending a concert.

I thought Wilson gave the most balanced performance. He had the most difficult role since it required subtlety and that he walk a fine line between accepting something monstrous in his presence or disbelieving his wife. He also had to be a weak sister, as it were, to the dominating presence of Sigourney Weaver who played most of the film with a gun in her hand. Yet he had to provide the strength of character and to symbolize the sense of justice. Kingsley looked very much the part of a sneaky little sickie, and his usual caged intensity was much in evidence.

Bottom line: any film that exposes the atrocities committed by the right wing dictatorships that dominated South and Central American during the Cold War is on the side of the angels; however most viewers I think will find this too intense and disturbing. Beware of some crude sexuality.

You were right on..._____
You were totally unfair..._____

Dick Tracy (1990) 5

Yes, that's Dustin Hoffman mumbling in the corner

The story doesn't matter. The plot doesn't matter. How could we identify with these fake characters anyway? What matters here is fidelity to the comic strip and the interesting effects on our eyes as we see what a cartoon looks like come to life, so to speak. The shadow of Dick Tracy thrown large against the warehouse wall, the sharp brim of his hat, his square jaw, the drawn gun preceding him, as Chester Gould so often drew him—this is what counts. Combining cartoon drawings, such as city streets and building facades and billboards in the background, with flesh and blood characters in the foreground makes for an interesting montage. The little shack, made small by the night sky and the big city towers, as in a Taoist drawing, is also true to a Gould frame. The intense contrasting and clashing colors, especially Tracy's yellow top coat and yellow hat, and Tess Trueheart's red, red dress and red hair—all these intense reds and greens and blues treat our eyes to something different.

Problem is, who cares? Or "so what?" as Popeye used to say. Madonna does her one-millionth Marilyn Monroe imitation. It's okay, although I would prefer the real thing. Al Pacino, with the prodigious proboscis, aptly burlesques his character, but what's the point? Warren Beatty (did he reject a fake jaw to stay pretty?) works hard to be the square-jawed, taciturn Tracy, and that's a handicap because then there is nothing to do except swing fists and spray bullets. Glenne Headly, trying to project some heart felt emotion, comes off as terribly out of place, since how can you weep for the love of a cartoon?

The gutter snipe kid befriended by Tracy, played memorably by Charlie Korsmo ("Suck eggs, copper!"), stands out somehow as the only one who seems real; and maybe that's right because only a kid could find involvement in such a shallow, if decorous enterprise.

Sharp-eyed movie aficionados will have fun picking out the star-studded cast behind the cartoon faces.

You were right on..._____
You were totally unfair..._____

Don't Say a Word (2001) 5

Better yet—don't watch

I think the rule for a Michael Douglas film has to be if he plays a bad guy (as in, for example, *A Perfect Murder* 1998) or when the film's director has enough prestige to actually direct Douglas (e.g., *Traffic* 2000 directed by Steven Soderbergh) the movie might be worth watching, otherwise forget it. Here Douglas is Dr. Nathan Conrad, god's gift to psychiatry and the good life, with a beautiful wife, a darling eight-year-old daughter, an opulently-decorated apartment, and a thriving practice—so much so he does some "pro bono" shrinking. In short he is an all-around good guy, fabulously successful, admired by all.

Of course in a movie these fantasy-world advantages might be a little hard to overcome. Usually heroes like this are the sort of pabulum fed to artistically unsophisticated middle-aged execs so that they will have something to fall asleep to in front of their hotel room TV. I think this would have worked better if Douglas's character were a little compromised, maybe make him a womanizer or somebody who abuses his practice or at least cheats on his income taxes.

The subject of his pro bono work is the catatonic Elisabeth Burrows played fetchingly by Brittany Murphy. In addition to being catatonic she is also quick with the multiple personalities and can job the shrinks to distraction. Enter the complication: the girl holds some numbers in her head that some crooks want. They give Conrad until five p.m. to shrink it out of her or they will kill his daughter whom they have kidnaped. Right, this could happen. Meanwhile they have magically installed cameras in Conrad's apartment and at the asylum lock-up, god only knows how. Furthermore, Conrad's wife (Skye McCole Bartusiak) is temporarily bed-ridden because of a skiing accident. Every time either she or Conrad makes a move a phone rings and it is the bad guys (led by Sean Bean) on the other end saying Big Brother is watching and if you don't behave we will kill your daughter.

Aside from the absurdities of the premise, there is the direction by Gary Fleder to consider. He might have made a passable made-for-TV kind of production if he had just played it straight, but no, he wanted to be creative (like Christopher Nolan of *Memento* fame, perhaps) and so chopped up the time sequence. Perhaps this was an attempt to camouflage the fatuous plot. No doubt Fleder and the clueless producers liked this because it allowed them to begin the movie with an inane action/adventure scene including a fire-balled vehicle and some "authentic" football-betting talk. After about twenty minutes of "Huh?" action, Fleder then allows the players to talk the plot and we realize that there are two time lines ten years apart. No doubt he also reveals how Bartusiak broke her leg, but I didn't stick around for that.

Bottom line: there are at least a thousand movies better. Pick one.

*You were right on...*_____
*You were totally unfair...*_____

Eight and a Half Women (1999) 4

Bizarre sexual comedy

There's a kind of French farce/Marquis de Sade/Japanese porn feel to this self-indulgent romp from Brit auteur Peter Greenaway. It's kind of a "God, I'm bored and I've got so much money and what the heck let's turn the Geneva mansion into a bordello, a different woman in every room and Dad and I will have lots of fun and bond" thing. "I mean mom's gone now, Dad, and you never really got out and now it's time to live." So father and son go naked a lot with lots of babes who are also naked a lot.

Matthew Delamere (Storey) is the son and John Standing (Philip) is the father. It's a bit creepy seeing them sharing the same bed naked. In fact it's a bit creepy seeing John Standing naked, period. But that's part of the Greenaway intent. Let's shock the bourgeoisie. It's such fun to do stuff that will make them squirm.

They hissed at Cannes when this was shown (I understand; I wasn't there). It was first released in the Czech Republic, which says something, but I'm not sure what. It was banned in Malaysia—but that's pretty standard. The women are bizarre but, to be honest, intriguing. The story isn't much of a story. The rationale for suddenly taking on the life of the libertine is slight (Philip's wife dies) and a bit late in the coming. (And no pun intended.)

The story starts in Tokyo with Storey helping Simato, a pachinko addict played by Annie Shizuka Inoh, avoid financial trouble in exchange for sexual favors. But never mind. As I said, the story doesn't matter. What matters is the outrageousness of the events (mostly sexual) and the beautiful sets. That's it.

Most interesting thing in the film is Polly Walker who has both sex appeal and charisma. Most grotesque is that pig with its pinkish white skin so very human looking—and of course that was a sight joke and a comment upon humanity. But again, never mind.

By the way, the 8 1/2 in the title is because Fellini's famous film somehow inspired Storey and Philip toward their debauchery.

*You were right on...*_____
*You were totally unfair...*_____

Everyone Says I Love You (1996) 7

Diverting, fun, wonderfully shallow

Woody Allen courts Julia Roberts. (I wonder if Woody writes his own dialogue these days or just chalks it in and improvises. Maybe he gives a signal to the other actor(s) that it's their turn.) Yes, I am eating my heart out, but believe it or not–and I swear this is true and Julia Roberts herself will vouch for this–she was once courted by an orangutan. True story. You could look it up. It was a PBS special. I'm serious. You think I could make up something like this? She even held a baby orangutan in her arms and he went wee wee on her. I kid you not.

Anyway, this is a kind of satirical take off on Broadway musicals, but half on the square. It features a lot of show tunes and dance numbers, some beautifully choreographed. Goldie sings, Alan Alda sings, Julia sings and of course Woody sings. (Drew is dubbed, I understand). Ed Norton also sings, but the difference is, he's actually good. Goldie Hawn is the mom, Woody is her ex and Alan Alda is her current. They are all rich and privileged and spend their time in places like New York and Paris and Venice. Goldie is a flaming, bleeding heart liberal who thinks that prisons ought to have a cuisine at least, and Alda is an establishment lawyer and doctrinaire liberal. His son consequently devours the National Review and is a member of the National Rifle Association, and thinks that welfare mothers ought to get a job, etc. Woody Allen is Woody Allen of course. I haven't seen one of his films in decades, but watching him put the moves on Julia brings back memories. You almost believe it. In fact, you DO believe it. And lament.

Tim Roth plays an ex-con, just released from prison, invited to a family dinner by Goldie. (Extended family dinners involving kids and grandparents and eccentric relatives stirred by light-hearted family politics are a staple of the Woody Allen canon, as I recall.) Roth's "animal" magnetism and his "interesting" kiss entice Drew away from her intended (at least temporarily). The story is narrated by Woody and Goldie's daughter (Natalie Portman, I presume), who finds herself falling in and out of puppy love with the regularity of the rising sun. Everything is played as a light satire of the intended audience, a technique perfected by Oscar Wilde in his play, *The Importance of Being Earnest* over a century ago. In a sense Woody Allen's effort amounts to a gentle massage of psyche of the New York liberal establishment.

Some highlights: The Marx Brothers song and dance number done *en francaise* near the Seine in Paris allowing Woody to do a fine Groucho impersonation; Drew's peach satin dress; Julia jogging in Venice; the intensive care unit choreography; mannequins coming to life in song and dance.

All in all, there's some cute fun had with Broadway show traditions, people breaking into song at odd moments, mostly standards from the pre-rock and roll era, e.g., "My Baby Just Cares for Me," "Making Whoopie," (yes, that is where Whoopie Goldberg got her moniker), and the beautiful "I'm Through with Love," (sung not badly by Goldie Hawn), a few good gags, a cute cast—enough of interest to divert one after an afternoon of hard-core shopping at Neiman-Marcus and Sak's Fifth Avenue.

You were right on..._____
You were totally unfair..._____

Flatliners (1990) 6

Don't try this at home

The premise of this horror lite venture in movie making is that if one is dead for only a few minutes and then brought back to life before the brain damage sets in, one might very well experience what it's like being dead, and that experience might be glorious and one might learn something nobody else knows, or at least something to tell them about on Sixty Minutes. Anyway, this is what med student Nelson Wright, played with energy and intensity by Kiefer Sutherland, thinks. Somehow he convinces four other med students, Joe Hurley (William Baldwin), David Labraccio (Kevin Bacon), Rachel Mannus (Julia Roberts), and Randy Steckle (Oliver Platt) to help him out.

Problem number one is that I don't think director Joel Schumacher sold this shaky premise sufficiently. We really need to believe that this group of med students could be flaky enough to risk their careers and their lives for an iffy few minutes of a supposed after life experience. For me it just wasn't happening, and I think that is why this movie starts slow and remains relatively unfocused for the first twenty minutes or so.

Problem number two is the casting of Julia Roberts as Rachel Mannus. This was the same year she did *Pretty Woman* (1990) with Richard Gere and became a box office sensation. She looks gorgeous in the dark red and blue tinted lights, but it's not enough to put some specs on her and make us believe she's a daredevil premed student. And let me ask you this, mightn't all that serious hair get in the way when she slices into those cadavers? She is one of my favorites with that face like no other, but her work here was limited, inconsistent and a bit preoccupied. Still Julia is always worth watching.

Problem number three is the lighting. All that dim lighting just doesn't mesh well with med school chic. Med students like to see what they're doing when they're digging into all that viscera. And if your job is to bring a friend back from the dead, you want a clean, well-lighted room, please.

Okay, putting all that aside, and accepting the premise, just how bad was this movie? Well, not all that bad really. The cast does a good job, particularly Sutherland who was apparently psyched for the part, and Bacon. The idea that we are responsible for our actions and must pay the consequences for evils done to others is a compelling

notion well illustrated. I particularly liked the haunting of Joe Hurley by all the girls he hustled and told lies to and videotaped without their knowledge. Those babes are looking a little ugly now, dude. Call it karma. The little boy who stalks Nelson Wright is chilling and Rachel Mannus's depressing father is very sad. After a bit the movie even gets a little scary. But I had a thought en route: What if we substitute the post death experience of the participants in this little star chamber club with some bad acid trips? How much would their experiences differ, really?

Bottom line: I don't think TV's "Fear Factor" is going to be featuring this one anytime soon. But wouldn't they love to do it? Think of the ratings. Anyway, this is a mild diversion for a rainy afternoon, thanks mainly to a fine cast.

You were right on..._____
You were totally unfair..._____

French Kiss (1995) 7

Predictably adorable

In my never ending endeavor to evaluate all the adorable movie stars (I'm sorry, I can't help myself) I've seen yet another Meg Ryan movie and I must say I'm beginning to be smitten. She is just so darn cute. And ageless. And perky. And actually a wee bit sexy when she gets in the right mood. And anyway since the movie takes place mostly in France (the stomping ground of my partially misspent youth) the scenery is nostalgic, the title is cute, and believe me, the food is delicious.

But what carries this movie is a beguiling performance by Kevin Kline and his very oo, la, la French accent. I also liked the concierge who takes Meg's 100-Franc note (worth about twenty bucks) as his God-given concierge right with nothing more than a belated, *merci* you vile American *touriste*.

Okay, I have to confess. I have a love/hate relationship with Meg. I just want to take her home and tuck her into bed, but all she cares about is being cute on screen and teasing me.

Director Lawrence Kasdan (*Body Heat* 1981, Anne Tyler's *The Accidental Tourist* 1989, writing credits with George Lucas sagas, etc.) has a few jokes with the nearly all female theater audience and their drag-along beaux. (Actually this video is currently being viewed on the couch across the nation by Roseanne Barr and John Goodman look-alikes with Roseanne making sarcastic remarks about Meg's eye shadow and scrawny physique while Goodman chortles with squinty eyes as he anticipates the action to come *après le flick*.) I especially liked the vast vineyard (Meg is drooling) that Kevin DOES NOT HAVE due to his wild and crazy ways (he says, but shows it to her anyway). I mean, RESOURCES are what a real woman wants in a man, dodo brain. What are you doing, playing hard to get?

Anyway, as all romance movie fans know, boy meets girl (cute), boy and girl cannot get it on just yet for 1001 wacky reasons, and finally boy gets girl or actually girl gets boy, and boy turns out to be worth getting as he naturally comes up with *beaucoup des ressources* of a very special kind. Etc.

See this for Kevin Kline, an underrated actor who has a lot of fun behind the five o'clock shadows and the French pastry while proving he can Can Can with the best of them.

You were right on..._____
You were totally unfair..._____

Frequent Flyer (1996) 5

How to juggle three wives.

Nick Rawlings, airline pilot, played with a clean-shaven smile and mindless amorality by Jack Wagner, has his bigamous lifestyle crash just as he weds wife number three, the youngest and blondest of the trio (Nicole Eggert). Somehow he was able to fool wife number one (Shelly Hack) for sixteen years, and wife number two (Joan Severance) for three years before they got wise. Neither wife seemed quite that dumb, but this is Hollywood. In reality these women wanted to be fooled of course, or didn't give a damn; but it makes a diverting story this way with wife number one only catching on after she finds a receipt in the trunk of his car for a nine thousand dollar ring that he does *not* give to her for their anniversary. When she discovers that it's an engagement ring for someone else, she hires a PI, cancels all his credit cards, sells his car, etc.

It's kind of fun to watch it all play out even if the characters are pure surface. The real problem (aside from Jack Wagner who has all the charm of a snake; but perhaps that's intentional) is the ending. How to sew it up and make the audience feel they've experienced the travails of bigamy? Turns out that real engagement with the subject was not even considered. Perhaps to the credit of director Alan Metzger it can be said he didn't even try. How horrible it would have been had he manufactured some phony catharsis and half baked it with some sort of deep philosophy. Instead Metzger had the cast walk through the production like it was a high school play: say your lines, look pretty, wear your costume and take a bow. For the audience it was kind of like cotton candy when what you really want is a steak.

Still this movie did demonstrate beyond any shadow of a doubt that one man is not enough for three women. However, that's a "duh."

You were right on..._____
You were totally unfair..._____

Hubble: Fifteen Years of Discovery (2005) 6

Sadly this is mostly just a puff piece

I was more than a little disappointed with this considering the fact that the Hubble telescope is one of humankind's most spectacular technological and scientific achievements. Instead of giving the viewer specific detail about what Hubble has achieved we get instead a kind of generalized, gee whiz hype about what a wonderful instrument it is. More—much more—information about how it was built and how it works and what its features are and what it has discovered and taught us could have been including in the narrative.

In fact, the narrative is dumbed down to an annoying degree. For example we are told that Hubble has discovered the most distant object ever seen, but we are not told how distant that object is. It's as though the narrative were written for people who just want to trip out on the images without being burdened with any specific knowledge.

Also annoying is the way the magnificent photos of the heavens are just displayed on the screen usually too quickly for any real contemplation and without detailed information about what is being shown or why it was photographed in the first place. ESA and NASA should have hired somebody knowledgeable to write an image-coordinated script for this that would inform and really entertain, and they should also have hired a professional to read the script, somebody with more enthusiasm and skill than Bob Fosbury displays. The images need to be explained so that we can understand what we are seeing. The clouds and nebulae, the points of light, the halos and the shapes are not self-explanatory. And when the images have been augmented or enhanced in some way, that needs to be explained as well. Some side by side contrasts between what is seen in the visual spectrum and, say, the infrared would be nice. Distances should be revealed.

There are two discs, one a DVD video, and another a CD audio which plays the soundtrack. There is a booklet full of statements like, "The planets of our Solar System have captured the imagination and interest of scientists and thinkers from the earliest times." Or, "Stars are social objects. They like to hang out together in star clusters or as large islands of stars..." This sort of empty expression or anthropomorphic nonsense is typical of what is heard on the video. It's as though the entire production was aimed at children. Actually what I think happened is the production was designed by a committee of ESA and NASA political types who just wanted to massage the public and were afraid that too many facts and numbers and ideas would simply turn them off.

It pains me to have to say this, because I love astronomy and cosmology, but shame on you ESA and NASA!

*You were right on...*_____
*You were totally unfair...*_____

Irreconcilable Differences (1984) 6

One of those that could have been good

Ryan O'Neal plays a tweedy east coast grad student who finds success in Hollywood first as a film editor, then as a writer, and finally as a director in quick succession, thanks in large part to his talented wife (Shelley Long) who is the one who really knows how to write—which makes me wonder how much of this is autobiographical since the script was co-authored by the husband and wife writing team of Charles Shy and Nancy Meyers.

Success immediately goes to his head and O'Neal trades Long in for a younger model (Sharon Stone, in her debut, looking slightly Latino and very cheap, but already in possession of that unique Sharon Stone quality of the evil femme fatale). Long is devastated at being replaced and loses all her self-esteem and unravels. Without his wife, however, O'Neal's scripts are not so good; and of course Stone is only using him to further her own ambitions. His solo film flops and he goes broke, but Long bounces back and writes a revenge best seller.

Drew Barrymore plays the nine-year-old daughter who, finally disgusted with their vanities and being neglected, hires a lawyer and "divorces" her parents for her nanny (the "clever" premise of the film).

The script shows a lot of workmanship, and lectures Hollywood from the pulpit nicely, but starts too slow and is a little too predictable in places. The movie might have worked if somebody else had played the leads. If you can stand Shelley Long, and I've tried and I can't, you might like the movie. Not that Long is on vacation or isn't trying. She tries as hard as she can, and has moments, but any difference between her and the character she played on "Cheers" is not discernible. Well, I take that back. They never put Diane Chambers in a fat suit and had her stuffing herself with half gallons of supermarket ice cream. Ryan O'Neal manages to look a lot like Ron Howard here; perhaps Howard is his idea of a director. And Drew Barrymore, bless her heart, is too goody-goody to be real.

If they could have gotten, say, Meg Ryan and Tom Cruise to play the leads, they might have had a smash. As it is, it's a frustrating movie.

*You were right on...*_____
*You were totally unfair...*_____

Joe's Apartment (1996) 5

Don't eat the popcorn

This is really a cartoon. The characters are caricatures without any depth, and the story line is beyond silly. The roaches have most of the good lines, delivered staccato-fashion so that it's hard to pick them up, just the thing for repeat and cult viewers. Amid the Loony Toons slapstick there are some good sight gags and some diverting hijinks. Mercifully, the roaches are not quite as disgusting as possible.

Jerry O'Connell plays a Wayne's World kind of sweet guy who spends a lot of time on his back surrounded by the Lilliputian roaches who even tie him down. But he gets the girl, the very pretty Megan Ward, who has little to do other than mug, which she does very prettily.

Nonetheless there is a strange pull to this loser-ID flick: perhaps it is a metaphor for the world in which we live, surrounded by filth and the ever-present reminder that cockroaches will inherit the earth.

*You were right on...*_____
*You were totally unfair...*_____

Kiss or Kill (1997) 6

Natural Born Killers on a budget down under

The opening scene of this lovers on the lam, Aussie style, noir thriller is designed to arrest our attention. Mommie answers the door only to have gasoline tossed on her and lighted while her four-year-old daughter Nikki watches. This accounts for Nikki's life of crime and explains why one night she doses her lover boy with the same stuff. However she doesn't light him up; it's only an exciting little joke.

Anyway, our lovers, Nikki and Al, have a little scam. They target business men at their hotels, Nikki as bait, Al to finish them off. An overdose of the mickey kills one of their victims and the lovers hit the road, chased by the cops and by a rugby legend whose pedophile video starring himself they have accidentally acquired. He has to keep *that* secret. So we have a chase for most of the movie, a kind of imitation *Natural Born Killers* (1994) cum *Wild at Heart* (1990) with some original spin and some diverting down under culture clips including the cops using sunscreen to protect the tips of their ears from skin cancer while the hole in the ozone layer grows.

Francis O'Connor, who plays Nikki is a little on the ugly/sexy side, mostly ugly, but Matt Day, who plays Al, adores her as a little boy might adore his mother. His problem is a homicidal temper and a blatant disregard for human life, except his own and Nikki's. He kills whenever the opportunity presents itself, it seems. Her problem is she kinda likes killing these men. Neither one of these

Aussie trash types is overly bright, but then neither are the cops.

Bill Bennett's story is derivative and banal but there are some witty elements. The scene in which one of the cops pretends to be kosher is funny, and the couple living on a nuclear testing site is amusing. The leg of kangaroo and the way Nikki has to get out from under the mark's dead body are nice touches. Alas, we have the ending. Bennett had a little fun with it, but his spin comes off as stupid and in sharp contrast with what proceded it, which was mostly realistic.

Bothered by the jump-cuts? It's just a mannerism. Bennett will get over it.

*You were right on...*_____
*You were totally unfair...*_____

Legally Blonde (2001) 6

Pure schmaltz...

But I liked it—well, I liked Reese Witherspoon. This might be seen as a continuation of *Election* (1999) as a slightly dingier Reese Witherspoon graduates from "CULA" (sic) and goes on to Harvard Law School. There's a kind of irony here—the real Reese Witherspoon with her drive and intelligence could actually do it. Her character in the movie: I don't think so. In fact, just about everything in the movie requires the maximum use of the suspension of disbelief option on the part of the audience because virtually nothing in the movie is real.

Well, the dogs are real, but I think they were drugged, they seem so passive. Witherspoon, of course, is real, but her performance was a little weary in parts, as though she is tired of playing ditzy blonde airheads and would like something more serious. This script understandably was very difficult to turn down since it amounts to a vehicle for her, and her character triumphs over every obstacle and ends up with a choice of two attractive men and a fast track career.

Selma Blair, whom I recall from *Cruel Intentions* (1999), provides fine support as the other girl. Robert Luketic's direction while undistinguished is crisp and even witty at times and gets a lot out of a mediocre script. However those who enjoyed *Election* might find the pandering to a mass audience in this one annoying. Certainly there is no comparing the scripts. However there are some funny bits and if you're a little, shall we say, relaxed, this might wash over you like a pleasant massage.

By the way this is clearly superior to *Legally Blonde 2* (2003) which, from what little I could stand, seemed beyond stupid.

*You were right on...*_____
*You were totally unfair...*_____

Lost Highway (1997) 6

Lacks the originality and coherence of Blue Velvet

In *Lost Highway*, David Lynch returns to some of the things that worked so well for him in *Blue Velvet* in 1986. Unfortunately, he doesn't have a very good script here, and to make up for that he tries too hard to be mysterious and arty. The first part of the film plays like an experimental low budget amateur venture (although the acting is professional). The sets are too dark and the games with the lighting lead to nothing. The long takes on the faces of the actors add nothing, and the long time spent fading to black creates nothing more than a mood of impatience. The supernatural hooey is strictly grade "B." The barroom lighting in most of the interiors recalls the apartment in Blue Velvet, but the apartment in *Blue Velvet* worked well because of its lay out and how it was set up to work effectively in the plot of the movie. Here we just have a lot of barroom lighting with little purpose.

Robert Blake, with his white clown face makeup as the "mystery man," expands on the cameo character of Dean Stockwell in *Blue Velvet*, but he is not so interesting as we eventually see he is another tired personification of some kind of Lucifer. Patricia Arquette plays the female sex animal as Isabella Rossellini did in *Blue Velvet* and she is as sexy as sexy can be, but not as interesting as Rossellini because she is a little too perfect physically, and too psychologically familiar. Lynch's idea that women are evil temptresses leading men astray is worked on here, but yields nothing new.

Main problem besides the script is Lynch has no Dennis Hopper. And he has no contrast. Laura Dern in *Blue Velvet* was a perfect foil to Rossellini, really etching their contrasting characters for us, but against Arquette plays only a variation of herself. Bill Pullman is good in a grim, spiritless role. Balthazar Getty, with more to do, does it very well.

The movie is also very poorly edited. A lot of the first half hour could have been profitably tossed. The film only gets going after the prison scene. (The "road rage" scene in the Hollywood Hills was good.) The desert scene where Arquette seems to turn into Blake was a wonderful opportunity lost. Instead of sex by the headlights of the Mustang in front of a dreary wooden structure (I don't think the crew got farther than Victorville) how about sex among the cacti in the blazing sun in front of something adobe? And the Lost Highway Hotel? Gee, how did everybody end up there apropos nothing and without rhyme or reason? How convenient for the requisite gore to follow.

Lynch lost his way here as he self-indulged to overdose. It's a shame. He needs some new ideas.

*You were right on...*_____
*You were totally unfair...*_____

The Matrix (1999) 6

An action/adventure future?

What can I possibly say about this movie that hasn't already been said? There are over thirty-three hundred comments at IMDb and another three thousand plus at Amazon. There even seems to be some block "reviewing" from young Christian groups enthusiastically pointing out all the parallels to Christ's life: Neo, "The One," "Trinity," saving humankind, and being lifted up to heaven, etc. I would add that directors Andy and Larry Wachowski touched some other religious bases as well. Note that Gloria Foster is "Oracle" (Greek mythology), that Lawrence Fishburne is Morpheus (of the Underworld) and that Joe Pantoliano is "Mr. Reagan" (a little secular allusion here). The band of heroes are also referred to as "freedom fighters" to recall our ex-prez's words. (But never mind.)

The main thing to understand is that this is one very popular and very arresting movie, the sort of thing Hollywood producers love; in fact all of Hollywood loves *The Matrix* because it gave work to so many. Scrolling the credits takes longer than your mother's phone good-bye. *The Matrix* is an industry in itself, something like *Star Wars* and *Rambo*.

But is the movie any good?

Well, it's not much on video. The DVD is undoubtedly an improvement, and on the silver screen it might lean you back in your seat. The cinematography, sound and special effects are first rate.

But I mean philosophically speaking?

I think we can get a hint from a review that began (and I quote) "Why can't all movies be this good? –A 12-year-old viewer." Indeed, this is the question all those marketing minds in Hollywood are asking. The true blockbuster action/adventure/sci-fi movie aims at a male viewer of about 18. Ideally the range would include 12-year-olds to thirtysomethings. Any philosophy beyond that mental age is burdensome.

So you don't think it is a philosophically interesting movie?

Actually I do. I just don't think it's original. I mean Plato's cave allegory is over two thousand years old. And let's not forget *The Wizard of Oz* (1939) or even *The Truman Show* (1998). Any science fiction buff can point to half a dozen precursors.

Isn't that stretching it a bit?

Okay, how about this short story from half a century or so ago called something like "The Perm-Machine." Every-body in the future society is working their nine-to-five tails off for a TEMP—that is, for a few hours in the box hooked up to the feelie machine complete with 3D screen, surround sound and electrodes attached to your every neuron so that the complete, thrilling, all senses experience of the greatest adventures in life are theirs, including sex, drugs, heart-pounding action and other sensual pleasures. But what everybody really wanted was a PERM, which would place them in the box permanently hooked up to the electrodes and intravenous drips, etc. for the rest of their lives, a kind of virtual reality heaven on earth.

What about the acting?

Forget the acting. It was okay. Consider this instead: we are going to become software. There isn't going to be any "warfare" between man and machine with the human spirit triumphant. Instead, we are going to become more and more attached to our machines, our computers, our chips, until at some point (see Ray Kurzweil's *The Age of Spiritual Machines: When Computers Exceed Human Intelligence* or Pierre Baldi's *The Shattered Self: The End of Natural Evolution*) the line between us and machine will be completely blurred. And then, molecule by molecule, we will DISAPPEAR, and at no time will we even realize it happened!

The Matrix is a vision of the future, but it is a hopelessly anthropomorphic vision, a kind of action/adventure director's scan, extrapolated from the present. Where artificial intelligence, virtual reality and the prospect of quantum computers is taking us cannot be envisioned at all. Some people call this the "singularity" factor. The future (and by the way, most of the audience of *The Matrix* will live to see this) is like the horizon of a black hole that we accelerate toward, never able to see beyond that horizon until we are *in*.

You were right on..._____
You were totally unfair..._____

Natural Born Killers (1994) 7

Another romantic comedy for the grunge set

One night Oliver Stone was watching David Lynch's *Wild at Heart* (1990) and he thought, "I'll show that half talent how a romantic comedy for the nineties is REALLY done," and he made *Natural Born Killers*. It was a lot of fun. Well, actually he also watched *Kalifornia* (1993) and thought, "Juliette Lewis is kind of sexy and she has potential. She doesn't really need to be THAT dumb." And so he reprised her role from that film, and saw that it was good.

Juilette Lewis as Mallory is Laura Dern on speed, and Woody Harrison as Mickey is Nicolas Cage tweaked. This is one bad ass film. Ah, but there's a deeper layer. Oliver Stone has targets. Somebody has to be satirized or what's the point? Well, TV's Geraldo gets it with both barrels, that is obvious as Robert Downey Jr. plays Wayne Gale, a sort of Geraldo with a Brit accent. (It plays since the British invented sleaze journalism). But beating up on Geraldo is too easy. What is really being satirized in this film is the audience! Ah, yes, pick their pockets and laugh at them. As Red Cloud in the film says, we've—that is us, Mickey and Mallory in our dreams—we've been watching too much TV. Mickey replies (innocent of being the target) "It's kind of like the twilight zone." Yeah, that's TV, the twilight zone. Red Cloud further says we're (again we are M and M) "lost in a world of ghosts"—the ghosts of TV and the movies and the tabloids. Funny in support of this satire is the Japanese media girl who remarks as a commentary to the "Drug Zone" drug store capture of Mickey, "He has a rather large gun." And when Mickey has to surrender, she adds, "He's now rendered impotent."

In case we miss the attack on the media, we are surrounded in our motel room by images from the TV coming through the windows. (We are literally surrounded by this crap!) It should be pointed out that we get the media we deserve, just as we get the politicians we deserve. Somebody's buying those supermarket tabloids; somebody's watching Jerry Springer and the nightly news. As M and M get ready to do the mating dance, on the small TV plays animal shows with lions and beetles and such doing the wild thing. Attacking animal shows! Is nothing sacred? Of course not. Stone's main purpose is to satirize the American psyche and get paid for doing it. And he does. And it's fun.

There are so many nice touches: "Route 666"; Wayne Gale's vain use of a nose hair clipper; his calling M and M "the most charismatic serial killers ever"(!) for his TV show "American Maniacs," which is logo'ed like "American Gladiators"; the adoring crowds cheering our psychos on like the Beatles in their prime. But what I especially loved was the sit-com clips near the beginning with Rodney Dangerfield as a "Father Knows Best," "Married with Children," burlesque of a psycho dad.

But it's really sad how Oliver Stone loses his concentration toward the end of his movies. Here we have something close to a satirical masterpiece, but he just can't finish. The absurd near-finale as they break out of prison dodging bullets as in an old time Western just wasn't up to the quality of the rest of the film (although Tommy Lee Jones had fun as the warden). The tacked-on little sit-com ending with Mickey as something like Chevy Chase in a Land Cruiser with a pregnant Mallory as his wife in maternity garb (with a cute little boy and girl already in tow) was precious and should have been expanded to replace the silly shoot 'em up at the prison.

Philosophically speaking (and of course an Oliver Stone movie has a philosophic position, otherwise where's the pretension?) we really are just animals who kill anything that gets in our way, the rain forests, all those cows and chickens (burp!), any other species, each other—what the hey, death's not that big a deal. It happens to everybody.

The Leonard Cohen recording, "The Future" played into the trailing credits has just the right tone and feel for this cynical look at the American mass mind as we enter the third millennium of the current era. May God have mercy on our souls.

You were right on..._____
You were totally unfair..._____

Never Been Kissed (1999) 5

Sure. And neither have I.

The premise of this romantic comedy/teen escapist fare is, what would it be like to go back to high school a few years later? Would you with your worldly wisdom triumph over the brutal social structure that so onerously held you down, and would you join the socialites at the prom with the cutest guy? Daydream believers want to know.

First of all, we want to know how Drew Barrymore, the sweet, trashy siren of the first *Poison Ivy* (1992), and the way accomplished actress and sex symbol of sixty (count 'em) other flicks, could be cast as a "Josie Grossie" nerd of a clumsy, socially inept wallflower? Make-up, yes. Good editing of course. And some fine acting by Barrymore, an actor not afraid to look her worst, and indeed she does look her worst here. Alas. The clinging gowns, the ratty hair, the make-up emphasizing her worst features (a nose looking a little on the Miss Piggy side, shot from slightly below) and down-playing her best, her pretty eyes, her sensual mouth. Instead of looking pleasingly plump, Drew comes off as plainly fat. But this is all the better for the metamorphosis to come.

I didn't stick around for that, secure in the knowledge that it was inevitable (but you might want to see for yourself). Incidentally, Drew was the executive producer, which shows she has guts as well as some loose change for such ventures.

Second question: does Drew sell out her chess and math club friends to join the cheerleaders? And if so, how does Director Raja Gosnell pull that off without making the darling of *E.T.* (1982) look like a shallow social-climber?

I'm not sure that was pulled off as well as it might have been, again not sticking around for the finale, but you might want to check it out. Also worth checking out (if you're a girl) is Michael Vartan who does a fine job playing Drew's sympathetic teacher.

Bottom line: Connoisseurs of Drew will find much worthwhile here, as will 15-year-old home alones on a Saturday night plotting their eventual triumph; but experienced movie-goers will probably want to watch reruns of

"Seinfeld" or "Just Shoot Me." Or better yet, if you're looking for a girl-nerd flick that really is funny and painfully sad and true-to-life in a totally original way, I highly recommend *Welcome to the Dollhouse* (1995) which really is brilliant.

You were right on..._____
You were totally unfair..._____

Palmetto (1998) 7

A steamy tale of greed and murder

This is a male-ID flick (definitely NOT a "chick flick") with Woody Harrelson as a jaded small town Florida newspaper reporter just released from false imprisonment having his choice of three sexy babes and a fake kidnaping scheme. He tries all four with varying degrees of enthusiasm, but of course makes no real move on the underaged kidnapee, played very sexily by Chloe Sevigny, who calls his lack of initiative "a shame." This steamy tale of greed and murder overcomes an unlikely plot thanks to her, Woody, Gina Gershon and Elisabeth Shue who keep us interested.

Shue plays a psychopathically sensual murderess with a studied lack of consistency, as though discovering the interpretation *in medias res*. Her final scene coming down the staircase a la Norma Desmond in *Sunset Boulevard* (1950) seems more than a bit contrived, as is the tentative voice-over frame from Woody via Joe Gillis from the same classic movie. Still, Shue, as always, is better than a drunken sailor's dream.

You were right on..._____
You were totally unfair..._____

The Pelican Brief (1993) 7

Star-powered escapist fare

I have seen other movies made from John Grisham novels, *The Client* (1994) and *The Firm* (1993). I would say this is on a par with those movies, and is typical of the mass market "thriller" genre. For me it's like watching TV, or an airline movie: the treatment is predictable, the plot includes a lot of unlikely action morphed out by various CIA, FBI, and other serious types according to the general expectation of the audience on a simplistic level, with some creativity but certainly nothing original. This is a movie for a tired CEO to fall asleep to. Yet it stars Julia Roberts and Denzel Washington with an interesting cast that includes the very talented Sam Shepherd. Alan J. Pakula, who directed and penned the script from Grisham's novel, has a number of important movies to his directorial credit including *All the President's Men* (1976) and *Sophie's Choice* (1982), and some as a producer, most notably the celebrated *To Kill a Mockingbird* (1962). So what happened here?

Just the usual gravitation toward the mean. If you make a movie aimed at a mass audience, what's the point of doing anything they wouldn't appreciate anyway? Roberts and Washington are here for their star power, not because of their considerable acting talent. Yet, perhaps inspired by one another, they both give strong performances that carry the movie and make this definitely worth watching.

Julia Roberts plays a Tulane law student who gets an idea about who assassinated two Supreme Court justices and why, and she writes a brief about it, the "Pelican Brief." We see her deep in the stacks at the library doing research, sporting several hair-dos at a little table under various lighting changes, so that we know its daytime and then night, etc., a clear device about as original as the pages flying off a calender. Tulane law professor Thomas Callahan (Sam Shepherd) is her mentor and bed mate. She's twenty-four and he's about forty, but a girl can learn a lot from such a man and he's warm and loving. Nonetheless we are scratching our head about this match up, especially when he begins drinking heavily (one of the justices was his mentor), and we know now for sure he's not in love. Well, the guy that gets Julia Roberts sure as heck can't be wishy washy about his love for her, we know that.

We are also scratching our head because Denzel Washington, the ace of spades of leading men, an actor of power and accomplishment, is usually found in more serious venues, a guy who's played Steve Biko, apartheid victim and martyr in *Cry Freedom* (1987) and Malcolm X in *Malcolm X* (1992). So what's he doing in this mid-brow flick? He plays a beltway reporter, right out of the annals of the Bernstein and Woodward legend, but there is little real acting for him to do. So why is he here? It's to play opposite Julia Roberts of course!

So what we have here is a very expensive "entertainment" starring two real actors. (I wonder how much money it made considering what they had to pay Grisham, Roberts and Washington.) Surely the subplot has to be romantic. How IS Hollywood going to play the racially mixed duo? Inquiring minds want to know. (Hint: with great subtlety.)

Julia is running, since the bad guys are after her. Notice that the plot conveniently gets rid of the "too old for her" guy. Try not to notice the other contrivances, the mysterious guy in the background who appears at exactly the last moment, for example. Just as one of the bad guys is about to blow our Julia away, he somehow blows the hit man away—by the way, getting blood on our girl. (It's enough to mention one plot contrivance per review, unless it's unusually bad, but there are others.) Well, Julia's getting the picture and it's pretty scary. She's on the phone as she's running from hotel to hotel, spending cash instead of using traceable credit cards. She can't trust anybody. Even the president of the United States is suspect, played incidentally with a kind of glee by Robert Culp as though impersonating Ronnie Reagan halfway into his dementia. Strange thing, Julia actually thinks you are supposed to really ACT in a thriller! Denzel knows better, managing a kind of controlled emotion throughout, saying as little as possible, using his eyes and making a lot out of silence, which is something an accomplished actor does when the script doesn't give him sparkling lines. Julia really does look scared, her face rubbery with a mean crease down the middle of her forehead. Watching just her, one could mistake this for an artsy-smartsy "serious" flick. Not to worry. There are some nice explosions and plenty of chases and all sorts of shadowy red herrings lurking about.

Bottom line: If this is your genre, and you've just got to get away from that pile of papers you brought home to work on, go for it. This is standard issue escapist fare, true, but the stars really do shine.

You were right on..._____
You were totally unfair..._____

The Perfect Storm (2000) 6

Uneven, Hollywood-ized

This is not as bad as I feared. I would never have watched it except that it was mentioned twice in a noncommittal way in a book I had just finished reading, Stuart Pimm's *The World According to Pimm: A Scientist Audits the Earth* (2001). It starts out like something from any of half a dozen big project Hollywood directors, e.g., James Cameron (*Titanic*) or Lasse Hallstrom (*Chocolat*), with faux realism and intrusive atmospheric sights and sounds and bits of background sound-bite conversations played too loud. I'm already shifting in my seat when I realize that Wolfgang Petersen, who produced and directed *The Perfect Storm* is none other than the very same Wolfgang Petersen who produced and directed the internationally acclaimed German language classic, *Das Boot* (1981), one of the best war movies of all time. So now I'm thinking, how bad can this be?

Turns out that *The Perfect Storm* is one of those movies that can't decide whether it's a man's action flick or a woman's relationship saga. Petersen spends an inordinate amount of time giving each of his crew members some kind of relationship before sending them off into the mother of all storms, reminding me of movies where the guys go away to war and the women stay behind keeping the home fires burning. Enough time is spent in the bar to make me think we're watching "Cheers" or we're on shore leave before the final assault. Strange thing about this is that Petersen, in making *Das Boot,* didn't care in the slightest about establishing relationships or engaging the female audience. But times have changed. Today's Hollywood director knows that to get people into the theaters you've got to make sure that women's issues and interests are addressed.

"Not that there's anything wrong with that!" (A quote from Jerry Seinfeld in a different context, that you might recall.) But imagine how diluted and unfocused *Das Boot* would have been had Petersen spent half an hour delineating each of the crew's fraus and frauleins. However, some of the work was worth the effort. The relationship between Irene and Bugsy (Rusty Schwimmer and John Hawkes, both doing a good job) was different and compelling: "I wish it was night so I could say, Goodnight, Irene." He speaks true corn. "There'll be a time for that" she rejoins, to the point and suggestively. (I'm paraphrasing from memory.) But the relationship between male and female fishboat captains (George Clooney and Mary Elizabeth Mastrantonio) never got off the ground, and I yawned through the all too familiar quandary of young lovers, Mark Wahlberg and Diane Lane.

Anyway, at last we are out the harbor and onto the fishing grounds. I was hoping for some real authentic, little known color about long-line fishermen, and I got some: the storage cells where the fish are packed with ice, the lines going out baited, the shark on deck, still biting...but that was about it. I was also hoping for some fisherman point of view on the world-wide controversy about over fishing and the "Tragedy of the Commons," but all we get is that they're not making as much money as they would like, and the boat's owner gets more than seems fair.

Okay, so let's see the storm. And we do and it's a monster, with massive waves throwing people all over the place threatening to swallow up the little fishing boat. Best action shot: the wave blasting the cargo containers off the deck like toys (actually they *were* toys). But I kept thinking, who really knows what it was like on that boat in the middle of that storm? The boat flips over and flips upright and then flips again. Nobody knows who tried to get out and who didn't. And were the lights still on? I would think it would get pitch black at night under the water. What I'm saying is, the cheap cutouts used for some of the water scenes in *Das Boot* were more effective than the millions spent on special effects for *The Perfect Storm*. At least in the former we knew they were merely simulations. Here the attempt at realism underscores the fact that I'm watching a movie. Oh, and the musical score: not only intrusive, but unnecessarily directive in the sense that it's telling me how I should feel about what I'm watching.

Bottom line: This is just interesting enough to keep a drowsy couple awake on a Sunday night, but be forewarned. The kids will want to stay up and see the storm.

You were right on..._____
You were totally unfair..._____

Pleasantville (1998) 7

Becomes an unconscious parody of itself

The premise of *Pleasantville* seemed irresistible (another "sure fire" Hollywood idea), but the execution turned out to be not so easy. The problem is, it is very, very difficult to sustain a satire over an entire movie (although Kubrick did it in Dr. Strangelove); things can get especially confused if you try to make the satire into a morality tale with a "pleasant" ending, as Director Gary Ross does here. He knows that life is too complex for easy answers, and that seemed to be one of the things he was trying to say, e.g., monogamy is not necessarily superior to, or inferior to, adultery. Ditto for chastity and fornication. Rain for a change is nice.

But he got confused somewhere along the way and ended up with a smug, sappy movie with ideas as shallow and black and white as the 50s milieu he was trying to satirize. The "feel good" ending is beyond redemption, in its way even sappier than the mythical sit-com it tries to improve upon. Yes, it is kind of neat to see things turn from black and white to color accompanied by stirring orchestral strings, especially as a result of something—like socking a bad guy in the jaw—that pleases one's prejudices. But where are the shades of gray? Not all red is fire engine red nor all blue, baby blue.

Reese Witherspoon plays a skanky teen (Jennifer) who teaches (as Mary Sue) the Pleasantvillians to fornicate (and her TV mom to masturbate) while she learns that reading is worthwhile. Tobey Maguire plays her brother David/Bud who begins as a nerd, but ends up heroic, attractive to the opposite sex, and wise beyond his years. (Yes, and we live in the best of all possible worlds.) Strange how this movie manages to satirize itself.

Joan Allen is grim as the stay-at-home sit-com housewife, and William H. Macy is appropriately bland as her simpleminded husband. Jeff Daniels as the soda jerk/*artiste*—and her unlikely lover—is tolerable.

Meandering through the film is a kind of confused extract of the Biblical story of the Garden of Eden. In the Bible, eating the fruit from the tree of knowledge of good and evil forever removed humans from paradise. In Pleasantville, knowledge of anything outside of town or of anything unpleasant has the same effect, while bestowing wondrous color. We even have a very red apple presented to Bud by his TV girl friend Margaret (played with wholesome sexiness by pretty Marley Shelton).

What began to wear on me was the easy choice of target. Going after fifties-style prudery and conformity is like shooting fish in a barrel. I should add here that human desire is infinite: "too much is never enough." So perhaps it is better to start modestly with a soda at the soda fountain holding hands (the 50s style made fun of in the film) instead of immediately coupling below the dashboard with legs in the air (90s spin on same, lauded in the film).

Gary Ross, for your next flick, how about taking aim at today's violent, mercenary, duplicitous society? Bring a cannon.

*You were right on...*_____
*You were totally unfair...*_____

Prelude to a Kiss (1992) 6

Actually it's mostly the aftermath

I tried to watch this, I really did. I mean, Meg is adorable and Alec has nice hair on his chest. But I just couldn't get interested. I mean, Meg is cute and kinky (kinky in a nice way of course) and she sincerely worries about bringing children into this troubled world, and Alec's character has had a troubled youth. So their characters have depth, I'm sure. And he meets her parents and gets warm with her mom and watches dear old dad's embarrassing antics with his dog tattoos, and they drink beer out of the bottle and you know it's going to be true love and all that.

But somehow I didn't feel any chemistry between them. I mean how would Spencer Tracy and Katharine Hepburn play this? (*Would* they play it?) How about Tony Randall and Jack Klugman? What the hey, how about Abbott and Costello? And then I saw the old guy who was going to kiss her (I knew the premise) and I didn't want to see THAT. He (Sydney Walker) gets on a train at random and goes to a random destination and is fated to arrive at their wedding at exactly the right time, etc.

Anyway, after a while I figured it was probably just me. After all, this is Meg Ryan who is adorable and can still play ingénue types at forty-something (she was only 31 when this was released), not to mention that this is adapted from a hit Broadway show of the same name from playwright Craig Lucas. And I guess I should add that Kathy Bates, who is a fine, fine, underrated actress (how I loved her in the film version of Stephen King's *Misery* 1990; boy wasn't she a nasty), is going to have a part. (Turned out to be a small part.) But still, let's face it, I'm just not the right guy to fully appreciate such a film.

But then, recalling that I am an intrepid reviewer and realizing I have an obligation to my public who need to see cutesy movies trashed—that, and noticing that today's rerun of Seinfeld is one I've seen three times—I flicked the DVD back on and tried to watch with my eyes closed. That didn't work, so I tried it with the sound off. I thought it might be interesting to try and guess what they were doing by just watching. (You can observe a whole lot by just watching, I've been told. In fact, Yogi Berra told me that.) Then I decided I better turn the sound back on because I knew that this kiss by an old man is going to turn the bride into somebody with the mind of the old man or something like that, and I had better catch what's going on.

Okay I'm still hanging in there and this is actually getting good. No, I mean it. Meg is now an old man (in her soul) and they're in Jamaica and she's dressing old man weird and loving life and Alec is wondering what happened to the woman he married.

I won't say any more except that Meg handles her new persona rather well, and Alec is very professional. Still I have to warn you that it gets syrupy at the end and there's a deep layer of what it means to be in love with someone over and above their sexuality—and that's good. However what really bothered me about this movie was that Meg Ryan was too skinny. She needs to quit stressing and relax a little, have some chocolate mousse and realize it's okay to be thirty-something then and forty-something now.

You were right on..._____
You were totally unfair..._____

Ransom (1996) 6

Average

Mel Gibson could hardly resist doing this picture since it not only amounts to a vehicle for him, but is exactly the kind of slightly off-beat but heroic part that he likes (cf., *Conspiracy Theory* 1997). He does a good job although his tendency to overact is not under consistent directorial control. But Ron Howard directing Mel Gibson is a bit like Spike Lee directing Danny DeVito. (Huh?) Or how about Oprah Winfrey directing Whoopie Goldberg? Or, John Wayne directing Clint Eastwood?

Gary Sinise as Jimmy Shaker, a cop gone not just bad, but sleazy psycho bad, also does a good job although just why he is such a sickie and why nobody noticed before is not developed or even explained. Rene Russo does her best (alas) as the suffering wife and mother condemned to a dreary role of one dimension. I was thinking, how about some creative casting? Instead of Lili Taylor as the bad girl, how about having her play Gibson's trophy wife and make Russo the girl gone bad? Taylor is talented enough to pull it off with panache and Russo would be an arresting sight among the degenerates.

Ron Howard clearly worked hard to hi-tech the old ransom plot with cell phones and cell phone tracers, infrared goggles, voice-distorters, helicopters and electronic homing devices. He provides plenty of shoot 'em up and gives the tale a twist with Gibson challenging the kidnappers. He also affords us a lot of satisfying revenge stuff at the end.

I do have a couple of questions though. Was his portrait of the FBI inspired by the real life FBI's fine work at Ruby Ridge and Waco? I mean at no time in this movie did the FBI do anything positive. I'm not crazy about today's FBI any more than anyone else, but was this a fair and realistic take on how they might handle such a case? Also what was police detective Jimmy Shaker's motivation for the kidnapping in the first place? After x number of years on the force he suddenly gets a yen for a lot of money and balmy climes? Finally why doesn't he just take his cleverly and murderously earned reward a couple of days down the road instead of showing up prematurely at the Mullen place and giving himself away?

Bottom line: this picks up after a slow beginning, and there's some clever business along the way, but don't examine it too closely.

You were right on..._____
You were totally unfair..._____

Rushmore (1998) 8

Clever, original and droll, but why all the cigs?

Wes Anderson has a nice light touch in the comedy department. He also has a unique style. Whereas most prep school coming of age stories attempt a kind of been-there realism, what Anderson achieves here is something close to a kid's fantasy framed in realism.

Jason Schwartzman stars as 15-year-old Max Fischer whose claim to fame is flunking most of his classes at Rushmore prep while being a boy genius who leads a dozen extra curricular activities including writing and directing his own plays. He's a kind of dark browed Woody Allen in the making. Bill Murray, slightly subdued and under comedic control, gives support as Herman Blume the millionaire entrepreneur who is impressed with Fischer's accomplishments and style. Olivia Williams is the grade school teacher they both adore.

Well, if you are a slightly nerdish boy (or were one) this movie is going to just pop your tart. So wish-fulfilling is the story that at any moment I expected Max Fischer to hop into a phone booth and come out in leotards and cape. Even the plays Max writes embody a boy's dream of being a man: Serpico as played by teens, Platoon (or Apocalypse Now) in the high school gym. But I have to say anybody who watches this movie and doesn't feel a bit of nostalgia for childhood needs to have his bedpan changed.

Max is a slacker who doesn't slack. Max is to be preferred to Blume's own idiot kids. Max can lead the boys at public or private schools. It doesn't matter. Max can almost win the girl, even though she is a dozen or so years older and six inches taller. Max can take a punch. Max has inexhaustible energy. Max is a leader and liked and respected by all but the school bully (whom he wins over and puts to work). Max probably will get into his safety school, Harvard, by scoring a perfect 2400 on his SATs. Humm, maybe that's a good idea for a sequel—oh, too late for a sequel, and anyway *The Royal Tenenbaums* (2001) certainly is better than any sequel.

Well, how about Max grows up and becomes an astronaut, the first man on Mars? Or better yet, Max grows up and becomes—Wes Anderson!

I have one MAJOR problem with this movie. What is with all the cigarettes? Wes, did you get some backing from Phillip Morris? I am so tired of cigarettes in movies where they serve no plot or character purpose, where they are planted merely to entice young people into a lifetime of addiction. Wes Anderson, now that you have found some fame and fortune, please remember: smoking cigarettes causes cancer and taking money from cigarette companies is, at the very least, Bad Form.

You were right on..._____
You were totally unfair..._____

Scattered Dreams (1993) 6

Politically correct all the way.

This is what might be called a poor white trash nightmare, circa 1951. Illiterate Florida tenant farmers are thrown in jail for not paying a mostly bogus debt. Never mind that debtor's prison was one of the things this country did away with, and that poverty is no crime. This is based on a true story, which allows us to imagine how things REALLY were. The three youngest of the five Messenger children are made wards of the state. The Florida cops, prison guards and social welfare people are mostly stereotypical degenerate sadists usually found in black oppression films set in places like ante bellum Mississippi or mid-twentieth century South Africa. One of the points being made here is that prejudice in the south against poor whites was sometimes as bad as prejudice against blacks.

The thing wrong with this movie and so many like it is that the unrelenting oppression of the central characters by the state is predictable, and their struggle against that oppression is admirable and heroic. The truth is not so simple. To give director Neema Barnette credit we can see that Kathryn Messenger, played with palpable, almost painful veracity by the wide-eyed Tyne Daly, was clumsy and crude and did stupid things (like trying to bribe a welfare clerk). Her husband, sadly impersonated by Gerald McRaney, groveled a lot. There is not a hint of alcohol or drug abuse by the poor Messengers; their only faults appear to be ignorance and poverty. Perhaps it was so.

Alicia Silverstone has a minor part as the 15-year-old daughter in a paper thin house dress like a ripe tart from a Faulkner novel or a Tennessee Williams play, but manages to keep covered up. There's a hint of inbreeding with all that white flesh being flashed about, and the constant suggestion of impending rape and/or sexual abuse, but it's mostly a tease to keep the audience from falling asleep.

You were right on..._____

You were totally unfair..._____

Seven Years in Tibet (1997) 6

A little too long

For the audience, that is.

There's an attempt here to capture the symbolism of the child as the spiritual leader of humankind. After all, the child is older than the adult by a generation and therefore, evolutionarily speaking, the adult's elder.

The idea that a child might be wiser than the adult is plausible since the child is not yet corrupted by the prejudices and delusions of the current society, and may see things more clearly than we can. If I had made this film, I would have worked on those ideas. Still I doubt success since what is really necessary is an illumination of Tibetan Buddhism, which is beyond the reach of a general audience.

What Jean-Jacques Annaud does is keep the camera on his star, Brad Pitt, and hope Pitt's charisma will carry the film. It does not, although Pitt does a commendable job, his accent fading in and out notwithstanding. It's just that without any real tension in the story, the film is just a picturesque travelogue, and not a very good one at that. There is no attempt to come to grips with Tibetan society nor with the issues surrounding the Communist aggression. Annaud does work hard on the relationship between Harra and the Dalai Lama, achieving unfortunately a sort of Western mid-brow comprehension. I was going to say news magazine comprehension, but it doesn't even reach that. Harra shows the kid how to work gadgets and trades some superficial knowledge of the world while learning humility and social responsibility. The unavoidable irony that Harra plays the father to the Dalai Lama instead of to his own son was agreeable although acted out with entirely too much familiarity. Worse fault though is to just present the child as the Dalai Lama without attempting to show why a child is chosen in the first place. Just to illustrate how far from the reality of Tibetan Buddhism this film was, let me ask the question, why not a girl?

You were right on..._____
You were totally unfair..._____

Single White Female (1992) 6

Majorly slick and sick psychodrama

This horror thriller directed by Barbet Schroeder is fairly tightly wound with some interesting psychology around an apartment and a ménage à trois. Jennifer Jason Leigh is the mousy, dykey new roommate (and such a beauty she used to be! almost a clone of Elisabeth Shue) interested in Bridget Fonda and Steven Weber (Fonda's semi-cheating fiancé). What we have is women's sex/fear fantasy and titillation all the way with the obligatory "all men are dogs" theme thoroughly worked in. Leigh actually says "men are pigs," which amounts to the same thing, although I guess we could say women are pigs and men are dogs and call it even.

There's some male titillation as well, of course, but Schroeder is primarily interested in spilling blood and out-dyking the dykes. Fonda is kind of cute and sexy, which is why I was able to watch the whole thing. She is, by the way, another one of those children of a star, like Liza Minelli, who would never but never have made it except for the family's stardom, yet achieved a certain appeal: Bridget can be striking in a gutter animal kind of way. The young stuff of her heartbreak on finding that her fiancé slept with his ex bored me, and the sickie blood and slashing by Leigh and her psychotic mind was too familiar and predictable. There were some good touches though, e.g., when Fonda kisses her when she takes off Fonda's gag, knife at Fonda's throat.

The scene where Leigh gives Weber head was ridiculous, but amusing in a campy sort of way. Weber is sleeping in his apartment and Leigh sneaks in in the dead of night, takes off her trench coat to reveal her nakedness (we see her breasts a lot, but get only glimpses of Fonda's, a clue to who has the status: the actress who doesn't have to show her breasts has the status—or at least that used to be the case), climbs into bed with the still-sleeping and unaware Weber, her hair cut and dyed just like Fonda's. She hugs his back and he turns and all he can see is her bowed carrot-topped head. Just as he's about to climax he realizes that something's different and she looks up at him and says "No, it's me." He moans and she brings him off. The poor guy should have known he was dead right then and there, because a really heroic guy, worthy of the heroine, would have thrown her off and saved himself for the heroine. Alas all men are dogs, even the good ones, and a few moments later Leigh buries her stiletto heel in his eyeball.

There was some other corny stuff, like the knockdown, drag out, blood flying fight between Leigh and Fonda at the end, etc., that made this slick psychodrama majorly sick. Another annoyance was portraying Fonda as such a wonderful career girl, fighting the good fight in the world of sexist and harassing men: the woman as male Hollywood hero.

You were right on..._____
You were totally unfair..._____

Sliding Doors (1998) 6
Do you like your Paltrow with light hair or dark?

Two things are essential if you want to watch this movie. One, you have to like Gwyneth Paltrow, because you're going to see a lot of her; and two, it helps to be a girl. Since I only half qualify I am not the best audience for

this corny, but clever, three-quarters cute, romantic comedy. Most of it is standard faire: London girl Helen (Paltrow) has to choose between puppy-eyed loser Gerry (John Lynch) and Good Guy James (John Hannah). Circumstances make the Good Guy look bad while the puppy-eyed loser pouts real well and looks emotionally helpless, so it's tough on our good girl, who's kind of like a Brit Mary Tyler Moore for the nineties. But "she's gonna find true love." Count on it. It's just that we have to sit through an hour and a half of misdirection before she does.

Paltrow isn't able to display anything close to her full range here, even though the film amounts to a vehicle for her. The clever plot idea is to show her life under one set of circumstances (she misses the train and doesn't meet James) and "a road not taken" (she catches the train and does meet James) in alternating cuts. Surprisingly it works fairly well. To keep us from getting confused, her hair goes short and blonde in one set and long and dark in the other. I like her better with dark hair. She looks more glamorous. I was surprised to notice that back-to-back adoring reviews on Amazon were written by eleven and twelve-year-old girls. When I think about it, that's kind of nice, since this is a sweet movie and those tough little critics are an appropriate audience (along with me, I guess), and this is an advisory tale about the nature of men, illustrating that you have to be careful about who you choose when you're following your heart.

Most fun in the movie is the dirty deeds done by Lydia, (Jeanne Tripplehorn) Helen's rival for Gerry. To humiliate working girl Helen she has her deliver sandwiches and then claims she got food poisoning. To really trash her, Lydia sends her on a phony job interview at her apartment in time to catch her with weasel-willed Gerry while announcing that she's pregnant by same. Our girl's knees buckle, but she stands tall through all the heart-break.

You were right on..._____
You were totally unfair..._____

Sling Blade (1996) 5
Too much Billy Bob

Billy Bob Thornton plays Karl Childers, a mentally retarded man who, as a 14-year-old boy, murdered his mother's boyfriend (with a sling blade) because he mistook the man's having his way with her for a violent attack. When she apprized him of the facts, he killed her too.

Mmm hmm.

So Karl spends twenty-five years in the state mental institution and then they let him go. He has improved himself and learned to read. He's read the Bible and he reckons he understands it, mostly. He meets a boy and they become best buds showering one another and the audience with "idiot savant" and "precocious lad" bits of phony wisdom. Sometimes it gets so corny you just want to blush for the players. This is not to say that the script has no redeeming qualities. It does, especially the first, last and penultimate scenes—and there are some nice touches in between. But overall it's heavy-handed and insufferably preachy.

The main problem is Billy Bob himself, who also wrote the script and directed. If it can be said that the man who acts as his own lawyer has an idiot for a client, then perhaps it can be said that the star who directs himself has no guidance as an actor. Thornton's performance (upper lip buried in lower, dead pan voice, etc.) is more mannerism than substance. In the beginning he had the timing down very well when Karl was saying little, but later on when Karl started dispensing all that wisdom, he had to talk faster and it started to come out phony. There's a great temptation, when writing of the down-trodden to cover ourselves with them, like the flag, and unabashedly champion the underdogs of society without regard for reality. When that happens we have a political movie, an "I'm in favor of motherhood" editorial instead of a film. Thornton falls into this trap as he attempts to catapult the second class citizens of our society halfway to sainthood over the straw body of bigots and the usual small town mentality. Consequently, both Karl and the boy become far too wise, too sensitive, too loving and frankly, too saintly to be believed.

I'm not sure that anything could have allowed this movie to live up to the PC adoration given it, but Thornton might have helped his cause by cutting some of Karl's more goody-goody pronouncements, and by giving more time and scope to the other characters, especially the boy's mother (Natalie Canerday) who is too narrowly presented. He had a very fine cast: he should have used them more and himself less.

Dwight Yoakam was properly despicable as the insufferably self-centered, woman-battering, bigoted boyfriend of the boy's mother. John Ritter was close to brilliant as a small town, thirty-something gay. J.T. Walsh, as a psychopathic rapist/murderer, was sardonically humorous, and Robert Duvall's cameo as Karl's falling-down poor white trash father was good (as far as it went). Lucas Black, who played the boy was excellent. In short, the cast carried the film, and if Thornton had given them more depth and himself less he might have had a work of art.

You were right on..._____
You were totally unfair..._____

Sliver (1993) 6

Underdeveloped

Sexually inactive book editor Carly Norris (Sharon Stone) gets a new apartment in a Manhattan high rise before learning that the previous tenant went over the railing to her death. She does a little microfiche sleuthing and finds that other tenants have met untimely ends. Seems that evil is aloft. Meanwhile she meets two guys intent on releasing her from the sexual doldrums, one a bestselling macho writer (Tom Berenger), the other a pretty boy with charm (William Baldwin). Somebody mysteriously gives her a telescope so she can check the action through the windows of the high rises around town. Meanwhile we are flashed shots of the tenants as though on video tape. Stone opts for Baldwin who seduces her. This is interesting: Stone cries tears of joyful release as she climaxes. Afterward it is revealed that he owns the apartment and has set up surveillance cameras in the walls to spy on the inhabitants.

I forget what this is ripped off from—maybe *Crawlspace* (1986)—but believe it or not, there was a man in Alaska a few years back who actually did this sort of spying on a modest scale. He had a four-plex or the like with peep holes in the bathroom, etc. It was on the news. Here we have high tech spying from a war room with monitors along the wall and an easy chair. Charming boy truly likes to watch.

The main problem with this film is the source material. Ira Levin, who penned the novel, never presumed to literature while managing a very successful career shocking the book club set with such made-into-movie hits as *Rosemary's Baby* and *The Stepford Wives*. His first success, and perhaps the only genuine book he ever published, was *No Time for Sergeants* from the fifties. The other novels suffer from flashy fake premises that lead to psychological waters never fully navigated. In *Sliver* what is not engaged is the character of a man who would choose to spy on his neighbors as a way of life. It is like throwing him in a grab bag to make him into your standard issue psycho killer. As such he is left unexplored.

A secondary problem is Phillip Noyce's uninspired and underdeveloped direction. We can see, even without reading the novel, that heroine Carly Norris was a somewhat frumpy, sexually fallow woman headed straight for matronhood. If only they had the guts to play her full out like that. But Stone seemed ill at ease in such an unfamiliar role and Noyce couldn't be bothered with nuances.

A tertiary problem is the casting of Stone in the first place. It might be said that Miss Stone, with her on-screen rapacious sexual appetite and her success at any cost cinematic persona, is truly a woman for the 'nineties. (If so, it makes me long for the woman of the 'oughts.) At her best Stone is a professional without charm, but unless she is cast as a slutty, evil, predatory female, she just doesn't cut it at all. In the war room she reverts partially to her usual persona as she goes along with Baldwin's sick program, and she comes to life. Here we glimpse what might have been done with the premise: the surveillance cameras strip away all privacy and for a moment the man who welds them is exposed as a Nazi-like monster, while she is confronted with her own compromised nature.

A final problem is the ending. It's an inappropriate joke told by someone insensitive to any context. Yet I can see how Noyce thought it might work: Carly Norris not only looks like his mother, but now she punishes him as a mother would, by destroying his toys and telling him to grow up. She actually says, "Get a life." Maybe she should have given him a spanking as well.

You were right on..._____
You were totally unfair..._____

Smilla's Sense of Snow (1997) 5

Fade to white

The Inuit people of the north are said to have a myriad of ways to say snow. There is snow in the morning, snow in the evening, snow that has freshly fallen and snow on the ground for a week. Snow seen and snow felt. Snow that has turned to ice. Just as we have many ways to say money—moola, loot, cash, dinero, lucre, wampum, etc.— because it is so important to us, so it is with snow for people who live in it all year round. Thus we have the seminal idea for this flick: Snow-savvy Smilla (Julia Ormond) knows that the six-year-old boy she had befriended didn't just fall off of a roof to his death. She can tell that he was running from someone in fear of his life because of the appearance of his footprints in the snow on the roof. (If only the logic of the rest of the movie were as plausible.)

In some ways Julia Ormond as Smilla reminds me of the French *La Femme Nikita* (1990) starring Anne Parillaud. Smilla, who was born and raised in Greenland and therefore knows all about snow, affects a snappy anti-social stance, an abiding cynicism and a foul mouth while displaying the physical prowess of a lioness. She also has Nikita's abhorrence of being locked up. But I wouldn't want to make too much of the comparison since this movie, which begins sprightly enough, soon deteriorates into a murky, cliché-enriched, murder yarn that eventually morphs into a grade "B" science fiction thriller gone astray. The striking sense of originality (obviously the product of the popular novel by Peter Hoeg) gives way, under Bille August's direction, to a tiresome vapidity reminiscent of bad TV.

This is not to say that this movie doesn't have some redeeming qualities. Ormond does a creditable job although we can see from the shots of her running in the snow that she's not exactly a world class athlete and therefore not capable of some of the heroics of her character. She's nice to look at, though, and director Bille August keeps the camera on her interesting face as much as possible. The edgy, amusing and psychologically veracious relationship between her and her father's very young wife is one of the highlights of the movie and might have been

expanded. The snow is beautiful and affecting, and the work of some of the bit players is excellent. Vanessa Redgrave's cameo, however, seemed unconnected and extraneous.

Bottom line: let this fade to white before the final credits and catch up on your sleep.

You were right on..._____
You were totally unfair..._____

Speechless (1994) 5

Semi-cute

Also shallow and predictable—very predictable. This romantic comedy about speech writers in opposing political camps is fluff and cotton candy, kind of like something from Neil Simon without the bite and with only a quarter of the wit. The candidates and the issues are trivialized and made into clichés. (But that's good.) Must have been written by a speech writer! She's a liberal Democrat and he's an amoral Republican hired gun. It might have been more interesting if they had switched them around. It's all surface and sound bite mentality including the performances by the leads, Geena Davis and Michael Keaton, who together produce enough chemistry to rival cold dishwater. If you're really, really bored and it's a choice between, say, a rerun of "Suddenly Susan" and this, flip a coin. Or better yet, go scrub the kitchen floor. This is the sort of mush that will turn your brain to cottage cheese.

Some observations: Christopher Reeve is sadly miscast: he makes a very soft heavy. Geena can smile and smile and smile and occasionally frown. Big deal. Poor Bonnie Bedelia. They made her look so dowdy, so as not to upstage Davis. It must be frustrating to know that not only are you more talented than the star, you are even better looking; but for an actress in Hollywood, younger always wins out.

Uh...Michael Keaton, next time, so as not to look like the leading lady's younger brother, try elevator shoes.

You were right on..._____
You were totally unfair..._____

The Stepford Wives (2004) 5

PC sellout

The ending here is beyond redemption, but otherwise this remake of the 1975 film from the novel by Ira Levin is not (entirely) bad. It's a different sort of film than the original and probably would amuse (if not offend) Ira Levin if he were alive today. But to put it bluntly, the film is a sellout to politically correct mentalities and could quite easily be called "Revenge of the Stepford Wives." (Actually there was a TV movie from 1980 by that name that I haven't seen.)

The original Stepford Wives starred Katharine Ross and Paula Prentiss and was a dark science fiction satire with only a few chuckles and a decidedly dark ending. This film is played mostly for laughs and is full of all sorts of silly (shall I say stupid?) updates, like having a gay couple instead of a black couple and making the wives (prior to their coming to Stepford) very accomplished—CEOs, scientists, etc., while the husbands are Neanderthal nerds. Nicole Kidman's Joanna Eberhart was a top TV exec while her husband Walter Kresby (played sheepishly by Matthew Broderick—note that Joanna did not take his last name) is a kind of ordinary joe and caddy to his wife.

But what about the premise? Let's be honest guys. Wouldn't it be wonderful if our wives were totally devoted to our comfort and pleasure? If they obeyed us and always kept the house and themselves spotless and catered to our every whim? If they didn't get moody and were always rational, etc.? Isn't it the natural state of the human male to be king of his castle and to have dominion over all he surveys?

Well, at any rate here's my update on the Stepford Wives for the new millennium, an expansion of the concept, if you will. Every man has not only a totally devoted and loving wife, but a totally devoted and loving mistress (or two). They would be robots of course, manufactured as consumer goods by General Electric, Microsoft and Intel. But here is the zinger: every woman would have a slavishly devoted husband and secret lover, etc. And while we are at it, they would have loving, appreciative and accomplished robotic children. In other words, nobody would actually interact with other living, breathing human beings. Instead all humans would interact only with perfect robots perfectly designed to make their world a heaven on earth.

Or, more likely we would just be hooked up to an elaborate software program with an utterly convincing virtual reality in which we would have a loyal and loving spouse, two extracurricular lovers..., etc.

Fly in the ointment? I think it would be called extinction.

Bottom line on this film: a few laughs, a good cast wasted, but a nice documentation of film land executive stupidity.

You were right on..._____
You were totally unfair..._____

Suspect Zero (2004) 6

Just another serial killer movie...?

Another serial killer movie... I can't believe I watched the whole thing. Well, it stars Ben Kingsley, one of the outstanding actors of our time, and he does a good job; and Aaron Eckhart, one of the most underrated actors of our

time; and the intriguing Carrie-Anne Moss whom you may recall from The Matrix films.

The gimmick here is that the serial killer is obsessive-compulsive. Well, it seems that way. We are shown massive numbers of sick black and white line-drawings done presumably by the serial killer and massive amounts of numerals up and down the page, on drinking glasses, all over the map of the US, etc. I mean this dude is obsessed, and as FBI agent sent to the hinterlands, Thomas Mackelway (Eckhart) says, he is smarter than us. Love those genius serial killers.

But wait. Let's not jump to conclusions. Even though we see Kingsley from the very beginning seemingly doing some very bad deeds, maybe, just maybe, that isn't the whole story. And anyway Eckhart clearly is a bit of a loose cannon. He was suspended for six months. So let's just keep viewing and see what happens.

Okay, why am I bothering to write a review about an American obsession, about some Hollywood types trying to make a buck? Do I want to write yet another review on just how sick the audience is that craves this stuff? And after all I watched the whole thing, although I must say in my defense that (1) this is not as gruesome as some other serial killer movies (sorry); and (2) I mostly turned away when they showed the bodies; and (3) Eckhart, Kingsley and Moss are very good. Do I want to say yet again, how sick is it to exploit the human weakness for watching this stuff? I mean, humans understandably are fascinated with death in all its forms and rightly so since knowledge about how death can occur, especially violent death, might be valuable. Such knowledge probably was valuable in the prehistory when our emotions were formed.

Anyway, what I really want to say in this review is what a shame it is that Kingsley, Eckhart and Moss have to waste their talent on something like this just to make a living. But this is the sadness of movies. How few, how very few, are really works of art or at least attempts at being works of art. Instead we have entertainments, seductions of the audience, emotional manipulations and so on. Seeing the bigger picture we may come to the conclusion that a serial killer movie is no worse than teen angst BS, or black exploitation, or uplifting, feel-good alien cartoons, or revenge, "make my day" dramas, or chick flicks, or musicals or any of the one hundred and one standard Hollywood commercial ventures.

But I was thinking as I watched this: could this inspire young minds (or deranged older minds) to kill? How about some poor smuck who desperately longs to be Somebody? Might not this give him some sick inspiration?

It might, but I suspect if I interviewed director E. Elias Merhige and asked him that question he would say something like, "Whoa, dude. Did you not notice that the bad guys got their just deserts in the end? Does that always happen these days? I think not. So cut me some slack. And besides, where is it written that I have to make some kind of socially correct movie? As soon as I am told what themes I am allowed or not allowed to pursue it's the same as censorship. You may not think this is art, but I'll tell you this: telling us what kind of movies we can and cannot make will guarantee that it isn't art."

And so let me say, this isn't bad as serial killer movies go and in fact better than most.

You were right on..._____
You were totally unfair..._____

True Crime (1995) 6

Couch potato sexual fare for two

Alicia Silverstone, yes, she of the pouty, sensuous mouth and the soft chubby thighs, stars here as nerdy cum sexy Mary Giordano, a Catholic school girl, daughter of a cop killed in the line of duty. She's attired in a plaid-skirt uniform to tease us with those pretty thighs. She wears glasses and makes all sorts of unsex, nosex, "I'm a nerd girl" expressions with her pouty mouth—to no avail of course: I can't take my eyes off of her.

There's been a murder of a classmate. She's "investigating." The head cop, who has helped her with some class projects, is black and gruff (women's sexual fantasy number one—totally under-played of course). He's a father figure. She decides to "become" the dead girl and goes swimming as the dead girl did. Immediately Kevin Dillon appears sweet talking some 14-year-olds. He's all in black and looking menacingly sexy. The girls giggle. She follows him to his home, and from across the street in some bushes takes pictures of him as he poses behind a conveniently opened window. He even takes out a gun and looks sinister.

Okay, obviously we have woman's fantasy number two rolling. This of course is the one the audience wants up front. The black daddy number is strictly "no speakie." Dillon seems "questionable," heightening woman's fantasy number two, but actually kicking in The Fundamental Woman's Ambivalence Sexual Fantasy Question, namely, is the sexy guy a good guy or a bad guy? We get our first clue when they go into the convenience store to quiz the clerk. Dillon flashes his junior cop badge and demands answers. Alicia watches. The clerk says he's answered these questions before and turns up the volume on the acid rock, in reply to which, Dillon sweeps the radio onto the floor and cracks the guy across the face and pins his arm behind his back and applies a little pressure. Outside, Alicia says "I can't believe what you just did!"

Okay, now we've got the sexual tension full force. On the one hand we have the sexy dude/star: I mean, kiss her! is what the audience wants; but on the other hand, he looks like a cold-blooded, mass rapist/murderer, so maybe don't. It's the usual dilemma with men: the only interesting ones are the ones you can't be sure of.

They return to his pad and he's having a beer, want one? Okay, this is a good question, allowing Alicia to show how grown up she really is. She says yes and they sit on his bed and tip back their long-necked brewskis. Now the nerdy expressions are gone, and the Alicia of the Aerosmith video comes to life. She laments that she is not pretty (right! sure!). They go outside and he begins to kiss her in earnest. He presses her up against the car (and yes, he removes her glasses) and she presses back big time and he guides her into the car still kissing her and (although the camera stays above the neck) makes with some obvious groping. Oh boy, ...and Doris Day this is not! He's not only kissing her, but he's feeling her up, and now he has her in the back seat of the car, laid out, and she is just giving in to it, and...fade to black.

Well, it's ninety-nine percent clear that they did the wild thing, and just where does that leave us vis-a-vis his possible villainous nature? It used to be the rule in Hollywood that the girl may be tempted, and she may even kiss and like the kiss a little, but she would never, ever, ever, lie down with a mass murderer. I mean, that's how we know the guy is a mass murderer. But this is the nineties and all bets are off. You *can* get carried away, if the guy is persuasive enough, sexy enough and knows how to do the deed. It could happen to anybody, even Doris Day were she nineteen today! We have *reality* today.

Now they have a suspect, a carnival Ferris wheel man. Yes, my sweet lord, they actually do a carnival in this one, and drag out some carny types, including women's sexual fantasy number three, the carny guy himself, who has a deformed right hand and a thick mustache and a leer to match, but biceps and an animal nature with which he favors Alicia as he tucks her into the Ferris wheel car. Later Alicia and Dillon follow the carny to a recycling plant and watch through a curb-side window as the one-handed carny puts some serious sex moves on a frail blonde in a white slip, circling her neck with his good, but formed-into-a-claw, left hand.

Finally we have the finale at a recycling plant. The centerpiece is a vat of swirling broken glass being churned by a giant meat grinder! Of course they climb up, up, up until they are above the swirling churning grinder of glass and Dillon is moving in on her. Her face is a mass of scream/cry/wet with tears. But she hits him with a plank of wood, knocking him out over the grinder. He grabs hold of a gunny sack rope and swings above the broken glass in the grinder, holding on for dear life. Now we have the moment of moral truth. He has one toe on the platform. The gunny sack rips a little more. Can she give him the final shove? He certainly deserves it. But no, her heart is too big. She reaches out for him her slender hand. He says, "I was inside you..."

Oops. Yes, he did say *that*, and yes, that fact has been in the audience's mind for an hour, and yes, it was her virginity, and yes, the stupid bastard is stupidly rubbing it in, and so...

Well, I can't reveal the ending, alas.

*You were right on...*_____
*You were totally unfair...*_____

Wild at Heart (1990) 7

It's the brain damage, dude

A romantic comedy for people who would never admit they like romantic comedy: a romance for the grunge set replete with lots of flowing blood, guns going off, cigarettes a-puffing, and slimy bit characters met on the lam. David Lynch directs with snap and shock and a devious sense of humor, but I think he ought to have the courage to make a romantic comedy straight out. He splashes guts and rubs our face in vomit to disguise the simple love story so his leather and chains audience can imagine they're seeing life in the raw instead of being seduced as their parents so often were by yet another Hollywood romance.

Nicolas Cage plays Barry Gifford's Sailor like a dumbed-down Elvis Presley (and that was before he grabbed the microphone), and Laura Dern as Lula captures well the mentality of a sweet, shallow, but meat-eating little thing who just wants to have fun. When I first saw her in Smooth Talk (1985) (from a story by Joyce Carol Oates) I thought she was just flat out sexy, but here she seems a little dull even if she does have "breasts that stand up and say hello." Diane Ladd, as Lula's mother, employing some Phyllis Diller shtick, is funny as the wicked witch of the west on testosterone.

What saves this movie from the ridiculous is the fact that the poor saps, Sailor and Lula, really love each other. He makes her "hotter than Georgia asphalt," and he finds her "dangerously cute." They have a whole bunch of mindless love—but maybe that's the best kind.

*You were right on...:*_____
*You were totally unfair...*_____

Working Girl (1988) 6

Who's afraid of Sigourney Weaver?

Working girl Tess McGill (Melanie Griffith, sporting some serious hair) is continuously being mistaken for a "coffee, tea or me?" kind of person when in fact she works hard, reads widely and studies nights to get ahead in the business world. But the sexist, class-conscious business world just won't take her seriously. Finally she hooks up with Katherine Parker (Sigourney Weaver), a successful but vulturous deal-maker with an elevated opinion of herself who knows how to use people. They set up a mentor relationship with Tess getting the coffee and Katherine spouting the words of wisdom. When Tess comes up with a good business idea, Katherine steals it.

Enter soon after Jack Trainer (Harrison Ford) and we have our triangle. Katherine has broken her leg skiing and Tess has to fill in for her. When Tess discovers that Katherine has ripped off her idea, she decides to assume Katherine's accouterments, including her lavish apartment, her wardrobe, her hairstyle, and as it turns out, her boyfriend. Will she succeed, and will she find true love and happiness with the leading man? Inquiring minds want to know.

Director Mike Nichols, auteur of a number of film land successes of more than average sophistication, including *Postcards from the Edge* (1990), *The Graduate* (1967), *Who's Afraid of Virginia Woolf* (1966), etc. with help from screen writer Kevin Wade and Melanie herself, manages to create enough sympathy for Tess that we want her to win. Sigourney Weaver does such a fine job of being a kind of sociopathic villainess that we want her to lose. Guess what happens?

While this is not on the same level as the three Mike Nichols flicks mentioned above, either in terms of cinematic significance or craftsmanship, it is clever and witty at times, and the story is one that most American women will find easy to identify with. And of course the winner gets Harrison Ford, displaying his usual bodice-busting charm. Only problem (aside from some smarmy pandering to a chick flick audience) is that the chemistry between Melanie Griffith and Harrison Ford is lacking.

See this for Mike Nichols whose direction here can be described as just a working guy trying to make a buck and not doing a bad job of it.

*You were right on...*_____
*You were totally unfair...*_____

Young Doctors in Love (1982) 6

A movie as a sit-com as a parody of a soap opera

There are some yucks in this burlesque of TV's "General Hospital," but you've got to concentrate. What is interesting is the cast and what has become of them since, and what they were before, especially in TV land.

Michael McKean, who plays the lead, has had a fine career, but I remember him best as Lenny Kosnowski on TV's "Laverne and Shirley"; Michael Richards who plays a bumbling mafia hit man became Cosmo Kramer on "Seinfeld"; Patrick Macnee was John Steed of "The Avengers" from the sixties; and although I'm sure you recognized Dabney Coleman, do you remember him from "Mary Hartman, Mary Hartman"?

Director Garry Marshall directed both "Laverne and Shirley" and "Mork and Mindy," which explains why *Young Doctors in Love* plays a little like a scattered sit-com. Nostalgic in a cameo was Jacklyn Zeman, who, last I heard, is still "Bobby" on "General Hospital"; and eye-popping in another cameo was Demi Moore, looking, I swear, a little like Monica Lewinski with muscles. (Moore was at the time also a regular on "General Hospital.")

This was the year (1982) in which the beautiful Sean Young, who plays the female lead here, was also presented in the classic sci fi *Blade Runner*. Who can ever forget those close-ups as Harrison Ford examined her eyes to see if she was a replicant?

The prize for best acting, however, goes to little known Pamela Reed as frigid mousy Nurse Norine Sprockett, who is sexually awakened by being romanced for her key to the drug cabinet, a surprising bit of dramatic reality amid the general mayhem.

You were right on..._____
You were totally unfair..._____

You've Got Mail (1998) 6

You've got corn syrup

Director Nora Ephron is obviously the kind of woman who believes you can't be too cute. I mean this is one cute movie. To begin with, Meg Ryan practically defines cuteness. Even at thirty something she is cute enough to fawn over, bless her heart; and Jean Stapleton as her bookkeeper and her mother's bookkeeper—adorable. The clever old gal even bought Intel at six—just adorable! And can Tom Hanks ever handle this? Play a male lead with property and money and a bad dye job? Piece of cake. I

mean, just behave and you are plenty eligible and totally adorable yourself. Throw in a dog and some cute kids and a fairy tale New York, and what have you got? You've got corn syrup! That's what you've got. My lord, even Dabney Coleman is cute in this! (And don't you just love the way his bad dye job mustache matches Hanks' bad dye job hairdo?)

This is a diabolical, cynical seduction of sappy-hearted lovers everywhere. Indulge. This is femme porn. Bring a box of Kleenex (actually the Ephrons anticipated this and put a few on screen, bless their hearts) and some bonbons. Know that the female lead will find true love, money and life-long security simultaneously after going through some real fun misdirections en route. Muggers in New York? AIDS? Cockroaches? Crack cocaine? Summer swelters? Dirty snow? Garbage strikes? Smelly, polluted Hudson? Odoriferous poverty? I mean, get real! Even the two roommates that our lovers dump are going to live happily ever after. Do we experience heartaches? Does love bite? Diss off! This is the yellow brick road in Olde New York, and it feels just like nirvana.

Best line: As Hanks reveals himself to Meg he uses her email handle and says, "Don't cry, Shopgirl" while the sound track prompts our tears with "Somewhere over the Rainbow." I mean, this is a BIG HANKY kind of movie!

In summation, the "cute" speed limit was greatly exceeded in this Pollyannish feel-gooder, and I am imposing the following fine on Director Nora Ephron: 200 hours of community service in the ladies powder room of the Bronx welfare office, and a promise never to do anything like this again, no matter how great the temptation.

You were right on..._____
You were totally unfair..._____

Chapter Six:

Read the Book, See the Movie

or

See the Movie, Read the Book?

Here are 14 movie reviews along with reviews of the books from which the movie was adapted. The question arises, why is the book always better than the movie—except once in a while when it isn't? As in the chapter on movie remakes, just for fun, I'll keep score to see if the books in these cases really are better than the movies. You might want to contradict me.

Movie review first, then book review, alphabetically by movie title.

1

The Big Sleep (1946) 8

Classic private eye tale with Bogart and Bacall in fine form

This classic of American cinema, actually made during the war and released in 1946, got a whole nation of young men affecting Bogey mannerisms, raising their eyebrows or showing their teeth while grimacing, and especially pulling on their earlobes while deep in thought, a smoking cigarette dangling between their lips. It was the genius of Howard Hawks, who directed, to do everything possible to make Humphrey Bogart a matinee idol, including having Lauren Bacall slump down in the car seat so as not to tower over him. With this movie a new kind of cinematic hero was created, the existential PI, a seemingly ordinary looking guy gifted with street smarts and easy courage, admired by men, and adored by women.

Hawks fashioned this, part of the Bogart legend, with a noir script penned by William Faulkner, et al., adapted from Raymond Chandler's first novel, that sparkled with spiffy lines, intriguing characters, danger and a not entirely serious attention to plot detail. Hawks surrounded Bogie with admiring dames, beginning with the sexy Martha Vickers who tries to jump into his lap while he's still standing (as Marlowe tells General Sternwood), and ending with the incomparable Lauren Bacall, looking beguiling, beautiful and mysteriously seductive. In fact, every female in the cast wants to get her hands on Bogie, including a quick and easy Dorothy Malone, bored in her specs while clerking at a book store. Hawks also employed some very fine character actors, most notably Elisa Cook Jr., and Bob Steele, the former as always, the little guy crook, (Harry Jones), and the latter, as often seen in westerns, the mindless heavy with a gun (Cani-no). Charles Waldron played the world-weary general and Charles D. Brown was the butler.

I was reminded somehow of the old Charlie Chan movies with the dark, mysterious, ornately-decorated interiors heavily carpeted and studded with ethnic statuettes, especially the house on Laverne Terrace that Bogie keeps coming back to, and the glass-paned doors and glass-separated cubicals of his office and others. The atmospheric L.A. created here has been much admired and imitated, cf., *Chinatown* (1974) and *L.A. Confidential* (1997), two very superior movies that continued the tradition.

In comparing this to the book, I have to say it's a little on the white-washed side, and not as clearly drawn—"confused" some have said. Of course liberties were taken with Chandler's novel to make it romantic. Chandler's novel emphasizes cynicism, and romance takes a back seat to manliness and loyalty to the client. An especially striking difference is in the character of General Sternwood's younger daughter, Carmen. She is vividly drawn in the book as something of monster, a degenerate sex kitten who would try and do just about anything. She is twice encountered butt naked by Marlowe, once in his bed. Being the sterling guy he is, he turns her away. (Right. I could do that.) Another difference is in all the sleazy details about the low-life underworld of Los Angeles that are omitted or glossed over in the film, including Geiger's homosexuality and his gay house guest, Carol Lundgren. (Of course there was a code in those days.) Bacall's character in the movie is actually a fusion of Vivian and Mona Mars from the book, made nice for movie fans. In the book, Marlowe kisses Vivian, but turns down her invitation for more intimate contact. In the movie, of course, there is no way Bogart is going to say "no" to Bacall. In the book Marlowe seems to prefer whiskey to women.

Most of the sharp dialogue comes right from Chandler's novel, including Bogart's grinning line, "Such a lot of guns around town, and so few brains." Interesting is the little joke on Bogart in the opening scene. In the novel, Chandler's hero is greeted by the purring Carmen with the words, "Tall, aren't you?" Well, the one thing Bogie ain't is tall, and so in the movie Carmen says, "You're not very tall, are you?" Bogart comes back with, "I try to be." In the novel, Marlowe says, "I didn't mean to be."

By the way, the film features Bacall singing a forties tune and looking mighty good doing it.

Chandler, Raymond *The Big Sleep* (1939) 8
Pulp fiction at the apex

This was Chandler's first novel, written when he was 51-years-old, although he had published a number of hard-boiled pulp fiction stories in the six years previous. The title refers to his hero, Philip Marlowe's idea of death. Not very original, but apt enough.

I read this to compare it to the famous Humphrey Bogart, Lauren Bacall film directed by Howard Hawks released in 1946. The structure of the book and the movie are very similar, but there's a subtle difference in the characterizations that gives the movie and the novel an entirely different feel.

The movie is a romantic mystery with something like a happy ending. The novel is an existential slice of one man's life as a worldly wise straight-shooter in a corrupted world of thieves, murders, predatory females, and assorted grifters. In the movie the part of Vivian Regan, General Sternwood's older daughter, is prettied up and expanded for Lauren Bacall so that she and Bogey can work on the romantic chemistry. In the book romance takes a third tier seat to manliness, cynicism, and loyalty to the client. Indeed, Marlowe prefers Mona Mars, whom he calls "Silver-Wig," to Vivian. But what he prefers even more than any of the women who are constantly throwing themselves at him is hard liquor and nicotine. He drinks morning, noon and night, always hard stuff, whiskey, rye, brandy. He spends a lot of time lighting and smoking tobacco and describing others doing the same. He even smokes a pipe, as did Chandler himself. With prohibition just a bad memory, and lung cancer something ugly that happened to coal miners and old people, the mass American mind thought it sexy and oh so sophisticated to toss back a few and indulge in the ritual of the cigarette, a ritual for tough guys that included striking the stick match with a thumbnail, dangling the cigarette out of one side of the mouth while talking out of the other, or pausing to eye the babe before flipping open the Zippo. Such an innocent world it was then.

Chandler wrote the novel in a white heat from chapter one to #30 at the end of the text on the last page in about three months. He had intended to make a few bucks, this being just a longer short story, but a funny thing happened. His unconscious took over and Chandler ended up projecting not only a hauntingly atmospheric Los Angeles during the thirties and a reflection of the entire culture, but a nearly heroic notion about right and wrong personified in his alter ego, the shamus Philip Marlowe. Note above all that Marlowe is a highly moral person who doesn't take advantage of women, refuses money that doesn't belong to him, and is something close to fearless in the face of personal danger. In a short Introduction to the Modern Library Edition of this book, it is noted that when Chandler himself fell on hard times in 1912, he borrowed money from an uncle and made a badge of paying it back, "Every penny...with six percent interest." Chandler never imagined at the time that he was writing "literature." Indeed he would have scoffed at such a notion and pretended not to know what it is, just as Marlowe pretends not to have heard of Proust.

So perhaps the secret of Marlowe's appeal is that Marlowe is the man Chandler would be on his best days, an essentially honest man, a very worldly man, a courageous straight-shooter, loved by women and admired by men, a man who is true to himself and his code. The average reader and moviegoer could easily identify with such a man, and his character became a formula for success in the private eye genre for another four or five decades. One reviewer insightfully recalled the Harrison Ford character from *Blade Runner* (1982). I am thinking of James Garner's "Jim Rockford" in the long running—it's still running, actually, in between infomercials on channels with numbers in the fifties—"The Rockford Files," whose character bears more than a token resemblance to Chandler's creation.

Besides this creation of an existential hero, the other striking feature of Chandler's novel is the sharply observed first person narrative spun out by Marlowe, and his quick, hard-boiled wit. He was not only brave, but had an eagle's eye for detail and more street smarts than an alley cat, and a nasty habit of speaking his mind in a way that penetrated. He describes the characters with precision, right down to their tie pins, and the scenery with enough verisimilitude to spring it to life, and he cuts through the crap with the repartee of a swordsman. His running analysis of the motives of others and his observations about himself are immediate and to the point.

There are of course contrivances. Marlowe does indeed seem to observe more than his fair share of action, and he seems to be where he should be nearly all the time. The scene (not in the movie) at the oil sump with Carmen near the end could never have been anticipated, not even by Sherlock Holmes and Charlie Chan working in tandem, and yet Marlowe did anticipate it, and was able to recreate an unlikely sequence of events to unravel the last mystery.

The Big Sleep is pulp fiction at the apex, a novel squarely between a fancy Bel Air hotel and a skid row flophouse, eagerly read by the clientele of both establishments.

Hard to choose here. I gave both works eight stars.

Your scores: Movie_____ Book_____

2

The Conformist (1970) 10

Stunningly beautiful, sensual and complex

Marcello Clerici (Jean-Louis Trintignant) is a fascist when the fascists are in power but becomes an antifascist when the fascists lose power. Hence he is the conformist of the title of this extraordinary movie adapted by Italian film legend Bernardo Bertolucci from Alberto Moravia's novel. But more significant than his political conformity is his ability to bend his sexual nature to what is acceptable. The defining event of his childhood is his incomplete seduction by a gay chauffeur, whom he more or less accidentally kills. When conformity to the fascist rule in Italy under dictator Benito Mussolini becomes the norm, Marcello marries the ordinary (but very pretty) Giulia (Stefania Sandrelli) whom he describes as "all bed and kitchen." Marcello thereby sentences himself to a boring but secure petite bourgeois existence. He will simply suppress his "abnormal" instincts.

In a sense this is a character study using a familiar theme, that of sexual repression leading to repressive political expression, such as psychoanalytic theory assigned to the fascist mentality. But Marcello is less interested in sadistic expression as he is with as a secure existence. He is something of a shrewd coward, cold, calculating, and indifferent to the feelings of others. We see this strikingly in the scene in the woods when Anna Quadri (Dominique Sanda), who is being chased by fascist thugs, pounds desperately on his car window. But he is completely unmoved and just stares at her with consummate indifference.

But what really enhances this film, making it one of the best I've ever seen, is the beautiful cinematography by Vittorio Storaro and the extraordinarily designed sets and scenes envisioned by Bertolucci. I am reminded of Michelangelo Antonioni's gorgeous *Blow Up* (1966) and Swedish director Bo Widerberg's stunningly beautiful *Elvira Madigan* (1967) from the same era. I think Bertolucci wanted to make a film that was politically and psychologically significant but also one that was strikingly beautiful. He used not only sumptuous settings but hired two of the most beautiful actresses in Sanda and Sandrelli. And because this movie is about sex (as it almost certainly must be, having been adapted from a novel by Moravia who was a master at expressing human sexuality) Bertolucci made the movie sexy and sensual. Sanda, whom I previously saw in Vittoria De Sica's

The Garden of the Finzi-Continis which came out a year after El Comformista (1970) where she played the beautiful, enigmatic, but icy Micol Finzi-Contini, here plays Anna the bi-sexual wife of one of Marcello's college professors—the man whom Marcello has been instructed to help kill. Sanda is exquisitely sensual as she works to seduce Giulia while at the same time both teasing and rejecting Marcello's advances.

Sandrelli is not be outdone. She too is beautiful and sensual even if the character she plays is a bit ordinary otherwise. The scene on the train where she describes to Marcello how she was ravished as a teen by an older man (the family lawyer) is very moving sexually, and very revealing because Marcello takes her description as a guide in how to make love to his wife! We can see clearly that he needs some instruction since he apparently is not really moved by her beauty.

While the film itself stands alone as an artistic achievement, I want to compare it to the novel from which it was adapted. The main difference is that in the novel we learn so much more about the character of Marcello because of Alberto Moravia's use of an interior monologue throughout. Rather than merely a conformist, in the novel we see that Marcello's character is that of someone who seeks the trappings of conformity and normality because he rightly fears he is not the entirely normal person he would like to be. Ironically it is Giulia who nearly always conforms to what is considered normal behavior and who harbors uncritically the knee jerk beliefs and opinions that she has learned from church and state. Marcello is attracted to her not so much because she is pretty but because she is authentically ordinary and therefore by association he too is not abnormal. It is abnormality that Marcello fears.

The ending in the novel is also different than in the movie although the sense of who Marcello is does not change. In the novel Quadri is a hunchback and his wife is clearly a lesbian who has married him for convenience and security, whereas in this film she is bisexual and he is more like someone she might marry for love. Another difference is in how what happens to the Quadris and the extent to which Marcello is responsible. Bertolucci chose to have Marcello at the scene, whereas in the novel he has no direct experience of their fate. Of course the novel, which is over a hundred thousand words long, goes more deeply into the character of Marcello than is possible in a film. The true psychological complexity of his character comes through, especially his struggle with sexual ambiguity. We see more clearly why he embraced fascism.

But the film is true to the novel in most respects and certainly in the main sense that Moravia intended, that of showing how a particular type of fascist mentality arises and is maintained. But Marcello, although an authentic fascist is not necessary a typical one. The idea that fascists in general follow the herd and adopt a superficial and uncultured world view is no doubt largely correct, but the essence of fascism is the belief in authoritarian rule, the stratification of society, intolerance of diversity, and a willingness, even an eagerness to use force and violence to obtain such ends. The psychology underlying the portrait by Moravia and Bertolucci is the idea that Marcello sees in himself violent and selfish tendencies and so it is only natural that he should adopt a political philosophy that condones and acts out such tendencies.

Moravia, Alberto *The Conformist* (1952) 10
One of several brilliant novels by Moravia

The Conformist is a psychologically complex novelistic study of an Italian fascist, although not necessarily a typical fascist, done in an existential style with intense interior monologues and introspection by Alberto Moravia's protagonist, Marcello Clerici.

No doubt Moravia intended Marcello as the conformist, but ironically it is his wife Giulia who nearly always conforms to what is considered normal behavior and who harbors uncritically knee jerk beliefs and opinions formed by church and state. In fact, that is part of the reason he married her. In contrast, Marcello struggles mightily with what he considers his abnormal tendencies. As a child he killed lizards for sport as any boy might, but felt uneasy about the wanton slaughter, and so sought from a friend and his mother some indication that killing lizards was okay. Later he kills a cat, although this is mostly accidental, and as a young teenager shots a homosexual limo driver named Lino. He feels something akin to consternation for these actions, not guilt exactly, but an unease since doing such things is not what he thinks normal people do.

It is his need to be—or at least to appear—"normal" that drives Marcello to conform to society's mores and persuades him to embrace fascism. He only feels really at ease when he sees himself as part of the common herd, on the installment plan, buying ordinary furniture, living in an apartment like a thousand others, having a wife and children, reading the newspapers, going to work, etc. He is not a peasant of course, but an educated functionary in the Italian Secret Service, a man with impeccable manners who seldom says more than is absolutely necessary.

The idea that fascists in general follow the herd and adopt a superficial and uncultured world view is no doubt largely correct, but the essence of fascism is the belief in authoritarian rule, the stratification of society, intolerance of diversity, and a willingness, even an eagerness to use force and violence to obtain such ends. The psychology underlying Moravia's portrait is the idea that Marcello sees in himself the violent and selfish tendencies and so it is only natural that he should adopt a political philosophy that condones and acts out such tendencies.

Moravia treats fascism in the person of Marcello more kindly than I believe he imagined he would when he began the novel, given Moravia's hatred of the fascist movement that seduced much of Europe following the First World War. But this is the necessary consequence of being an objective novelist. In drawing a living, breathing portrait of Marcello, Moravia allows us to see him as a complex person with strengths and weaknesses who deals with the trials of life sometimes in a despicable way, and sometimes, indeed often, in a way that most of us would choose were we in his shoes. Therefore it is impossible not to identify with him to some degree. It is an artifact of Moravia's artistry that we do in fact in the end identify with Marcello and may even realize that in his situation, we too might have embraced fascism or at least tolerated it.

A secondary theme in the novel is that of unrequited love or of desire that is not returned. All of the main characters, Marcello, Lino, Giulia, Quadri and Lina love someone who does not return their love. Marcello briefly falls madly in love with Lina who is a lesbian who despises him. Lina in turn is desperately in love with Giulia who only has eyes for her husband, who does not really love her. The inability of the characters to love the one who loves them is played out partly through a disparity in personality and political belief, and partly through differing sexuality. Lino and his latter-day incarnation in an old British homosexual who drives around Paris picking up indigent young men seldom if ever find their love returned although they might temporarily quench their desire. No one in the novel experiences love both in the giving and the receiving.

Part of Marcello's unease with himself comes from his ambivalent sexuality. He cannot return the intense passion that Giulia feels for him although apparently he does manage to perform his husbandly duties adequately. Perhaps even more to the point, he seems to project a need for the "abnormal" experience. He is twice mistaken for a homosexual, and he falls in love with a homosexual of the opposite sex—thus the "Lino" and the "Lina" of his life. Marcello seems to have a blindness about invert sexuality just as he has a blindness about human morality. He is a man who does not what he thinks is right but what others think is right. He fears his natural impulses. Moravia illustrates this by occasionally having him nearly give into what he feels inside, as in the case of Lina, only to have him realize that to act from his heart is dangerous.

In the final analysis Marcello finds that "the normality that he had sought after with such tenacity for so many years...was now revealed as a purely external thing entirely made up of abnormalities" (quote from near the beginning of Chapter Nineteen).

Moravia (born Alberto Pincherle) is in my opinion one of the great novelists of the 20th century and *The Conformist* is representative of his best work.

Again I called it even, ten stars apiece.
Your scores: Movie_____ Book_____

Matches:

    Movies: 0   _____

    Books: 0 _____

    Ties: 2   _____

Stars:

    Movies: 18   _____

    Books: 18   _____

3

Copenhagen (2002) 10

Brilliant, moving, cathartic

Most viewers of this extraordinary play believe that it doesn't answer the question of why Werner Heisenberg came to Copenhagen in 1941 to visit his mentor Niels Bohr. And this is true: playwright Michael Frayn does not give a definitive answer to that intriguing question. But he does give an interpretation.

We must go to the "final draft" of their recapitulation of what happened—the "their" being the three of them, Heisenberg, Bohr and his wife Margrethe, who appear as ghosts of themselves in the now empty Bohr residence. In the climatic revisionist scene, instead of walking away from Heisenberg in the woods, Bohr contains his anger and confronts his one-time protégé. He tells Heisenberg to do the calculation to determine how much fissionable material (a "critical mass") would be necessary to sustain a chain reaction.

Heisenberg had believed without doing the calculation that the amount was somewhere in the range of a metric ton. As he does the calculation in his head he realizes that the amount would be much, much less, only 50 kilos. This changes everything because it made the bomb entirely possible. Frayn's point is that it is far better that Bohr did not tell Heisenberg to do the calculation because if he had, it is possible that Nazi Germany would have developed an atomic bomb under Heisenberg's direction.

But this does not answer the question of why Heisenberg came to Copenhagen. Margrethe has her own answer: he came to show himself off. The little man who is now the reigning theoretical physicist in Germany had come to stand tall and to let Bohr, who was half Jewish, know that he had the ability to save him from the Nazis.

This is the "psychological" answer and it plays very well. Heisenberg, like most Germans felt humiliated by the defeat in the Great War and had suffered severely in the economic deprivations that followed. And like most Germans Heisenberg, who was not a Nazi, compromised his principles by acquiescing in Nazi rule because he believed that it would return Germany to "its rightful place" as an economic and military leader in the world. He came to Copenhagen in 1941 in triumph. His triumph, understandably, was not well received.

The more blunt question of did Heisenberg expect to find out whether the Americans were making a bomb or to get Bohr to help with the German project is also answered in a psychological way. The answer is no, because he knew that Bohr would not help him even if he could. As it turns out at the time Bohr had no knowledge of what the Allies were doing. The other question, a question that would haunt Heisenberg for the rest of his life, was did he delay the German bomb project in order to prevent the Nazis from acquiring the bomb—as he claimed—or was the fact that they were not able to develop a bomb just a matter of not having the ability? To this question playwright Frayn's answer is that Heisenberg would have developed the bomb if he had been able. This answer is the generally accepted one based on the historical evidence, part of which comes from some careless words from Heisenberg himself that were recorded by British intelligence after Heisenberg was captured and sent to England. What Frayn does so very well in his brilliant play is show us that Heisenberg's need to succeed and his need to feel national pride would not allow him to behave otherwise.

The direction of this PBS production by Howard Davies relies heavily on an interesting device. Bohr's wife becomes an objectifying factor who is able to step back from the emotional situation and to see both men clearly and to guide the audience toward an understanding of their relationship. Over the years, she and Niels Bohr served as surrogate parents to Heisenberg. He was the little boy who came home to his parents in 1941 to say, Look at me. I am a great success. Only problem was his "success" could not be separated from the Nazi occupation of their country, and Heisenberg was too obtuse and insensitive to see that.

In truth, Heisenberg was not entirely aware of his own motivation. He did not know why he came to Copenhagen. Neither did Bohr. But Margrethe did. An accompanying point to this idea is the story of Bohr bluffing Heisenberg and others during a poker game some years before. It appeared from the fall of the cards that it was extremely unlikely that Bohr had made a straight that would win the pot, and yet he kept on betting until all the others threw in, and then when he showed his hand, he had no straight. He had fooled himself. Frayn's position is that in believing he had come to Copenhagen for innocent reasons, Heisenberg was unconsciously fooling himself. Furthermore the fact that he had not done the calculation was equivalent to Bohr's not looking back at his hole cards to see what he really had.

This is not an easy play. I have seen it twice and benefitted from the second viewing. It is not, however, a play only accessible to intellectuals. The ideas are presented in a clear manner so that any reasonably intelligent person can understand them. Frayn employs an elaborate metaphor involving Heisenberg's famous uncertainty principle to elucidate the relationship between Bohr and Heisenberg. They are particles that will collide: Heisenberg the elusive electron, neither here nor there, the very essence of uncertainty, Bohr the stolid neutron. Davies has the two circling and circling one another, even chasing one another, as in a dance while Margrathe watches.

I found the play brilliant, moving, and ultimately cathartic as all great plays should be. Davies' direction and the sense of time and place greatly facilitated my enjoyment. And the acting by the three players, Stephen Rea (Bohr), Daniel Craig, and in particular, Francesca Annis, was outstanding.

Frayn, Michael *Copenhagen* **(1998)** 10
The play and a fascinating postscript

This book contains the text of Michael Frayn's Tony Award-winning play (94 pages), a fascinating 38-page Postscript, and a two-page word sketch of the scientific and historical background to the play.

The play itself is and is the kind of play that can be fully appreciated simply by reading it. There are no stage directions, no mention of props or stage business. There is simply Frayn's extraordinary dialogue. A photo from the cover suggests how the play might be staged on a round table with the three characters, Danish physicist Niels Bohr, his wife Margrethe, and German physicist Werner Heisenberg, going slowly round and round as in an atom. This symbolism is intrinsic to the ideas of the play with Bohr seen as the stolid proton at the center and the younger Heisenberg the flighty electron that "circles." Margrethe who brings both common sense and objectivity to the interactions between the ever circling physicists, might be thought of as a neutron, or perhaps she is the photon that illuminates (and deflects ever so slightly) what it touches.

At the center of the play (and at the center of our understanding of the world through quantum mechanics) is a fundamental uncertainty. While Heisenberg and Bohr demonstrated to the world through the Copenhagen interpretation of quantum mechanics that there will always be something we cannot in principle know regardless of how fine our measurements, Frayn's play suggests that there will always be some uncertainty about what went on between the two great architects of QM during Heisenberg's celebrated and fateful visit to the Bohr household in occupied Denmark in 1941. There is uncertainty at the heart of not only our historical tools but at the very heart of human memory (as Frayn explains in the Postscript).

"The great challenge facing the storyteller and the historian alike is to get inside people's heads... Even when all the external evidence has been mastered, the only way

into the protagonists' heads is through the imagination. This indeed is the substance of the play." (p. 97)

The three characters appear as ghosts of their former selves, as it were, and begin immediately an attempt to unravel and understand what happened in 1941. The central question is Why did Heisenberg come to Copenhagen? Was it an attempt to enlist Bohr in a German atomic bomb project? Was it to get information from Bohr about an Allied project or to pick his brain for ideas on how to make fission work? Or was it, as Margrethe avers, to "show himself off"—the little boy grown up, the man who was once part of a defeated country, now triumphant?

The play leaves it for us to find an answer, because neither history nor the recorded words of the participants give us anything close to certainty. With the conflicting statements of the characters Frayn implies that the truth may be a matter of one's point of view, that is, it may be a question of relativity. Ultimately it may even be that Heisenberg himself did not know why he came to Copenhagen.

Also being asked by Frayn's play is a moral question. Is it right for scientists to build weapons of mass destruction to be used on civilian targets? Heisenberg contends that this is the question he wanted to ask of Bohr. It is ironic that although Heisenberg was condemned by physicists around the world for his (presumed) unsuccessful attempt to build a fission bomb for Hitler, his work killed no one, while the universally beloved and admired Bohr had a hand in the Manhattan project that resulted in the bombs that were dropped on the Japanese cities.

As the electron is seen and then not seen, its speed measured and then not measured, but never both at the same time, so it is with Heisenberg's character in life and in this play. We are never sure where he is. Is he working for the Nazis or is he only pretending to? Is he working on a reactor or is he working on a bomb? Did he delay the German project intentionally (as he claimed), or was the failure due to incompetence, or even—as Frayn suggests—to an unconscious quirk of Heisenberg's mind?

In the Postscript Frayn recalls the historical evidence he used in constructing the play and cites his sources and gives us insights into what Bohr and Heisenberg were like. He quotes Max Born, describing Heisenberg as having an "unbelievable quickness and precision of understanding," while "the most characteristic property" of Bohr, as described by George Gamow, "was the slowness of his thinking and comprehension." One can see where Frayn got his metaphor of the atom with its heavy nucleus and its speedy electron. But Bohr was also thoughtful and thorough while Heisenberg was "careless with numbers." And of course these are relative terms since both men were Nobel Prize-winning physicists, brilliant men who reached the very pinnacle of their profession.

Bottom line: one the great plays of our time on an epochal subject, fascinating and cathartic as all great plays should be.

Again I gave ten stars apiece.

Matches:
    Movies: 0   _____
    Books: 0 _____
    Ties: 3   _____

Stars:
    Movies: 28   _____
    Books: 28   _____

4
    This is an example of an increasing common phenomenon, a documentary made from a nonfiction book.

The Corporation (2004) 10

The corporation as psychopath

This extraordinary documentary is based on the book *The Corporation: The Pathological Pursuit of Profit and Power* (2004) by law professor Joel Bakan. His thesis is that the corporation is a psychopathic entity.

In his book he notes that the modern corporation is "singularly self-interested and unable to feel genuine concern for others in any context." (p. 56) He adds that the corporation's sole reason for being is to enhance the profits and power of the corporation. He shows by citing court cases that it is the duty of management to make money and that any compromise with that duty is dereliction of duty.

Directors Mark Achbar and Jennifer Abbott bring these points and a slew of others to cinematic life through interviews, archival footage, and a fine narrative written by Achbar and Harold Crooks. The interviews cover a wide spectrum of opinion, from Michael Moore and Norm Chomsky on the left, to Nobel Prize winning economist Milton Friedman on the right. Friedman is heard to agree with Bakan that the corporation's duty is to its stockholders and that anything that deviates from that duty is irresponsible.

What emerges is a view of the corporation as an entity working both for and against human welfare. Designed to turn labor and raw materials efficiently into goods and services and to thereby raise our standard of living, it has been a very effective tool for humans to use. On the other hand, because it is blind to anything but its own welfare, the corporation uses humans and the re-sources of the planet in ways that can be and often are detrimental to people and the environment. Corporations, to put it bluntly, foul the environment with their wastes and will not clean up unless forced to.

An interesting technique that Achbar and Abbott use is to go down the list of behaviors cited in the Diagnostic and Statistical Manual of Mental Disorders that identify the psychopathic personality and show how the corporation has all of those behaviors including a criminal disregard for the welfare and feelings of others and a complete absence of guilt. Indeed corporations feel no compunction when they break the law. Their only concern is whether breaking the law is cost-effective. The result is a nearly constant bending and breaking of the law. They pay the fine and then break the law again. The corporation, after all, has no conscience and feels no remorse.

Bakan notes that "corporations are designed to externalize their costs." The corporation is "deliberately programmed, indeed legally compelled, to externalize costs without regard for the harm it may cause to people, communities, and the natural environment. Every cost it can unload onto someone else is a benefit to itself, a direct route to profit." (pp. 72-73) We are shown how rivers are polluted, environments destroyed and people placed into something close to servitude by the corporation's insatiable lust to profit.

The answer to this, as presented in the film, is to make corporations pay for their pollution. What many people are proposing is the creation of bills or certificates that would allow the barer "the right to pollute." The cost of these bills would reflect the societal and environmental costs of the pollution. This sounds scary, but what it would do is make those who pollute pay for their pollution instead of having the costs be externalized as they are now. Consequently, to protect their bottom line, corporations would pollute less.

Another problem with the corporation as emphasized in the film is that the corporate structure is essentially despotic. It is not a democracy or anything close. The owners hire officers to exercise control over everyone who works for the corporation. This is in direct contrast to democratic governments whose officers are elected and who are subject to the checks and balances of a constitutional government with shared powers. It is true that if you are a shareholder of a corporation you may be able to indirectly vote for the CEO. However, such a "democracy" is a democracy of capital in which the electoral power is inequitably distributed. Some people have hundreds of millions of votes. How many does the average shareholder have?

Bakan, Achbar and Abbott play fair, and give both sides of the case—although that is not to say that the weight of evidence or sentiment is equally distributed. After all, who's in favor of pollution or the destruction of the environment? The pathological corporation doesn't care about such things, but its officers should. Some do, but feel constrained by their fiduciary duty to their stockholders. Consequently it is our responsibility as the electorate to get our government to make the corporation socially and morally responsible. The way to do that is make the fines for breaking the law large enough to change corporate behavior. Furthermore—and this is essential—make management responsible—criminally if necessary—for the actions of the corporation.

This is absolutely one of the most interesting, most compelling, and, yes, entertaining documentaries that I have ever seen. But beware of some graphic footage.

Bakan, Joel *The Corporation: The Pathological Pursuit of Profit and Power* (2004) 10
Striking thesis convincingly presented

The modern corporation, according to law professor Joel Bakan, is "singularly self-interested and unable to feel genuine concern for others in any context." (p. 56) From this Bakan concludes that the corporation is a "pathological" entity.

This is a striking conclusion. The so-called pathological personality in humans is well documented and includes serial killers and others who have no regard for the life and welfare of anyone but themselves. But is it really fair to label the corporation, managed and owned by normal caring and loving people, in this way?

Bakan thinks so. He begins with a little history showing how the corporation developed and how it came to occupy the dominate position that it enjoys today. He recalls a time before "limited liability" when shareholders were legally responsible for the actions of the corporation, a time when corporations could not own stock in other companies, a time when corporations could not acquire or merge with other corporations, a time when shareholders could more closely control corporate management.

Next he shows what corporations have become, and finally what can be done about it.

Bakan's argument includes the point that the corporation's sole reason for being is to enhance the profits and power of the corporation. He shows by citing court cases that it is the duty of management to make money and that any compromise with that duty is dereliction of duty.

Another point is that "corporations are designed to externalize their costs." The corporation is "deliberately programmed, indeed legally compelled, to externalize costs without regard for the harm it may cause to people, communities, and the natural environment. Every cost it can unload onto someone else is a benefit to itself, a direct route to profit." (pp. 72-73)

And herein lays the paradox of the corporation. Designed to turn labor and raw materials efficiently into goods and services and to thereby raise our standard of living, it has been a very effective tool for humans to use. On the other hand, because it is blind to anything but its own welfare, the corporation uses humans and the resources of the planet in ways that can be and often are detrimental to people and the environment. Corporations, to put it bluntly, foul the environment with their wastes and will not clean up unless forced to. (Fouling the environment and leaving the mess for somebody else to clean up is exactly what "externalizing costs" is all about.)

Furthermore, corporations are amoral toward the law. "Compliance...is a matter of costs and benefits," Bakan writes. (p. 79) He quotes businessman Robert Monks as saying, "...whether corporations obey the law or not is a matter of whether it's cost effective... If the chance of getting caught and the penalty are less than it costs to comply, our people think of it as being just a business decision." (p. 80)

The result is a nearly constant bending and breaking of the law. They pay the fine and then break the law again. The corporation, after all, has no conscience and feels no remorse. Bakan cites 42 "major legal breaches" by General Electric between 1990 and 2001 on pages 75-79 as an example. The fines for maleficence are usually so small relative to the gain that it's cost effective to break the law.

Bakan disagrees with the notion that corporations can be responsible citizens and that corporate managers can act in the public good. He believes that corporations can and sometimes do act in the public interest, but only when that coincides with their interests or because they feel the public relations value of acting in the public interest is greater than the cost of not doing so. He adds "business is all about taking advantage of circumstances. Corporate social responsibility is an oxymoron...as is the related notion that corporations can...be relied upon to promote the public interest." (p. 109)

As for corporations regulating themselves, Bakan writes, "No one would seriously suggest that individuals should regulate themselves, that laws against murder, assault, and theft are unnecessary because people are socially responsible. Yet oddly, we are asked to believe that corporate persons—institutional psychopaths who lack any sense of moral conviction and who have the power and motivation to cause harm and devastation in the world—should be left free to govern themselves." (p. 110)

Bakan even argues (and I think he is substantially right) that "Deregulation is really a form of dedemocratization" because it takes power away from a government, elected by the people, and gives it to corporations which are elected by nobody.

Some of the book is devoted to advertising by corporations, especially to children, and the effect of such advertising. Beyond advertising is pro-corporate and anti-government propaganda. Bakan quotes Noam Chomsky as saying, "One of the reasons why propaganda tries to get you to hate government is because it's the one existing institution in which people can participate to some extent and constrain tyrannical unaccountable power." (p. 152)

What to do? Well, for starters, make the fines large enough to change corporate behavior. Make management responsible—criminally if necessary—for the actions of the corporation. Bakan includes these among his remedies on pages 161-164. He also wants the charters of flagrant and persistent violators to be suspended. He writes that corporations are the creations of government and should be subject to governmental control and should NOT (as we often hear) be "partners" with government.

He would also like to see elections publically financed and an end to corporate political donations. Indeed if we could take the money out of elections, our representatives would not be beholden to the corporate structure and would act more consistently in the broader public interest. I think this is one of the most important challenges facing our country today, that of lessening the influence of money on the democratic process.

Bottom line: a seminal book about one of the most important issues facing us today.

Again ten stars each. Four straight ties.

Matches:
    Movies: 0   _____
    Books: 0 _____
    Ties: 4   _____
Stars:
    Movies: 38   _____
    Books: 38   _____

5

Double Indemnity (1944) 10

One of the very best film noir

This is a terrific movie, beautifully directed by Billy Wilder, one of his better films, and he made some very good ones. *Sunset Boulevard* (1950); *Stalag 17* (1953); *Some Like It Hot* (1959); *The Apartment* (1960) come to mind. Note the range: a psychological mystery, a prisoners of war movie, a comedy with song and dance, and a "sophisticated" comedy. He could make any kind of film. He had a knack for getting the best out of the players and he never forgot his audience.

Double Indemnity is no exception. Fred MacMurray stars as Walter Neff, a morally-compromised insurance salesman who just couldn't resist the opportunity to out-smart the insurance business, and he was never better. Most people remember him from more light-hearted fare, e.g., *The Shaggy Dog* (1959); *The Absent-Minded Professor* (1961); and perhaps especially *The Egg and I* (1947) with Claudette Colbert. Barbara Stanwyck, whose career spanned six decades, was also excellent as the sociopathic Phyllis Dietrickson. Edward G. Robinson, who practically defined the Hollywood gangster from the thirties and forties, switches type and does an outstanding job as Barton Keyes, a sleuthful insurance claims manager.

The script was adapted from James M. Cain's second novel, a follow-up to his enormously successful *The Postman Always Rings Twice* (1934). That too was made into a movie, in fact two movies, but neither one was anywhere near as good as this classic film noir. Wilder employs the convention of the voice-over (something he would use again very successfully in *Sunset Boulevard*) by having Walter Neff ("Walter Huff" in the novel) tell the story into a Dictaphone as a confessional memo addressed to his admired pal and mentor Keyes. He didn't get the girl and he didn't get the money, he says. Strange but we can see he didn't really want the girl or the money. What he wanted was the admiration of Keyes. At any rate that's the way Wilder played it, and it worked big time. If you read the book you'll discover that Wilder (along with Raymond Chandler, who co-wrote the script) changed a number of things from the way Cain had them, especially the ending—all to the better. In fact the movie is significantly better than the novel, which isn't usually the case.

One of the things I was thinking while watching this was that it was actually as "perfect" a murder scheme as you'll see on the silver screen, although everything had to go just right. There was only one flaw, as Wilder saw it. He has Edward G. Robinson express it something like this: When a man buys an accidental death insurance policy and then dies an accidental death a few short weeks later, it ain't no accident.

Don't miss this one, one of the all-time best film noir and a jewel in the crown of Billy Wilder, one of filmland's greatest directors. Would that we had another like him.

Cain, James M. *Double Indemnity* (1936) 6
Raw material for a film noir

This is another of those James M. Cain novels that you can read in an hour with one hand tied behind your back.

Let me try that again. This is another of those James M. Cain novels that you can read in an hour without breaking a sweat.

Okay, how's this? This is another of those James M. Cain novels that you can read in an hour even if you're the kind of person who moves your lips when you read.

This is not to imply that Cain is the kind of writer who mixes his metaphors or hasn't gotten beyond primer prose. I mean, Shakespeare mixed his metaphors. I guess what I'm trying to say is that if Cain wrote literature then it was by accident. Come to think of it, Shakespeare was only trying to turn a shilling, please a patron or give an actor some range. I guess real literature comes about when you're just trying to make ends meet and somehow you get inspired and don't even know it.

Cain didn't think much of this, calling it something like tripe and saying it would never be published as a book. He wrote it to appear as a serial in Redbook magazine, but Redbook rejected it so it appeared in *Liberty* magazine in 1935. It didn't make hardcover until the forties just before it was made into an excellent movie by Hollywood great Billy Wider starring Barbara Stanwyck, Fred MacMurray and Edward G. Robinson. In fact, to be honest, the movie is better than the book, which as everyone knows, is usually not the case.

He also wrote this to take advantage of the surprising success of his first novel, *The Postman Always Rings Twice* (1934), which Knopf published to critical acclaim on its way to bestsellerdom. Cain's stream-lined and hard-boiled faux Hemingway style charmed the critics and made the dime novel reader feel like he was reading Nathanael West or maybe F. Scott Fitzgerald. Re-reading Cain's first person narrative today is a lot like watching a movie from the forties, mainly because the movies so often imitated him with their film noir voice-overs and desperate crimes for love or money. Indeed a number of Cain's novels have been made into movies, *Double Indemnity*, *Postman*, and *Mildred Pierce*, the most memorable.

Here we have a painstakingly planned murder for the insurance money. It is so perfectly conceived that it would take a miracle for everything to fall into place. And yet it does, and yet something goes wrong. In the Wilder movie, insurance salesman Walter Neff (Walter Huff here) does it mostly out a irresistible desire to put something over on the insurance business he has worked at all his adult life, while in Cain's novel, Huff explains his motivation to Phyllis Nirdlinger, sociopathic wife of the intended: "Just pulling off some piker job, that don't interest me. But this, hitting it for the limit, that's what I go for. It's all I go for."

He means that the "accident" has to take place on a train so that they can collect a double indemnity from a standard clause in the policy. Today's amoralist might proclaim that he did it for the rush of doing something almost nobody ever got away with.

My problem with the novel is not the convenient way everything fell into place for the murder to work, or with how unlikely it was that Keyes figured it out so neatly, but with the stupid ending. You've got to read it to believe it, actually. Billy Wilder changed the ending in the movie to something more plausible. He, along with Raymond Chandler, who worked on the script with him, actually improved on the Cain novel in several places. As in *Postman*, Cain's antihero does his dirty work from the back of the car while the wife drives and the victim rides shotgun. Here he applies the kind of brute strength usually attributed to mobster heavies. (The contrivance needed to get him into the back seat strains credence but Wilder fixes that.) In truth, Cain was right: this novel needed a little work. He does NOT, however, repeat the sexual "celebration" beside the car after the murder in *Postman*, a scene that so shocked depression era readers. Indeed, here the two murderers are already beginning to sour on one another.

What Cain does so well is to probe into our dark psyches and to let loose the dogs of dirty deeds done dumb so that we might experience vicariously the hell they might lead to. Notable in the novel is the character of Phyllis, an ex-nurse with the psychopathic mind of a serial killer. (In fact, she IS a serial killer.) That part was played down in the movie. In the movie Cain's antihero is given human dimension through the mutual affection he has with Keyes. In the novel that affection is muted, but Cain humanizes him by showing the sincere, but apparently hands off, love he has for the dead man's 19-year-old daughter.

I don't exactly recommend that you read this, but it's worthwhile to compare it to the movie and to see how two great screenwriters (Wilder and Chandler) handle material from a novel. It is also worth reading for the snapshot of pre-World War II Los Angeles afforded. Of course any true film noir fan or student of American lit ought not to miss this. I suggest however that you write your own ending.

I liked the movie a lot better, 10-6.
Matches:

Movies: 1	___	
Books: 0	___	
Ties: 4	___	

Stars:

Movies: 48	___	
Books: 44	___	

6

The English Patient (1996) 9

[Review is on page 19.]

Ondaatje, Michael. *The English Patient* (1992) 8
Not the masterpiece I had hoped for, but good anyway

Poetic and engaging. I like the way he handles time, as though painting in layers, going back to a point and elaborating on it, coming back to a "present" and then going back again and again, and then finally moving forward to the end, although I don't think the last parts of the book live up to the promise at the beginning.

I have remarked elsewhere that the book disappoints with its phony PC notions about how Kip and some others might have reacted to the atomic bombing of the Japanese cities. I'll add here that I was more horrified by the booby trap bombs left behind by the Germans that Kip had to disarm because they were left especially to murder people whereas the atomic bombs had at least one clear and laudable purpose: to end the war and to end it as quickly as possible and with a minimum of lost life.

But that is not the novel's only conformance with the current politically correct climate. *The English Patient*, like the preponderance of contemporary novels focuses on a woman, in this case the nurse Hana, surrounded by various interesting men, mainly because that is what the market place requires. My point is that even the most skillful and accomplished artists, and Ondaatje is one of them, must conform to the dictates of their age in commercial terms or not be published at all.

I saw the movie first and then read the book, something I almost never do, and I was reminded of a remark by a student of mine who said that she preferred to read the book first because that way she drew in her mind her own picture of what the characters were like. I found myself greatly influenced by the actress who played Hana (Juliette Binoche), so much so that I did not form any independent conception of the way Hana appeared in the book. I think my student was right: form your own view and then compare it to Hollywood's and the actor's interpretation.

Good book, but not the masterpiece I had hoped for.

A close win for the movie, 9-8.

Matches:

Movies: 2		_____
Books: 0	_____	
Ties: 4		_____

Stars:

Movies: 57		_____
Books: 52		_____

7

Fatal Vision (1984) 8

Superior made-for-TV movie

Although director David Greene is known almost exclusively for his work in television, this movie is several notches above most TV fare. Running a full three hours and twenty minutes in two parts, *Fatal Vision* is just about as riveting as the book of the same name from which it was adapted. The screenplay by long time Hollywood pro John Gay amounts to an indictment of army

Captain Dr. Jeffrey MacDonald, but then again so did the book.

Gary Cole gives a convincing performance as the former Green Beret army officer who was accused, and then some nine years after the fact, convicted of the murder of his pregnant wife Collette and two young daughters. Karl Malden plays Freddy Kassab, Collette's father, with his usual skill, while Eva Marie Saint plays Kassab's wife.

Since it is still being debated to this day whether Jeffrey MacDonald really was guilty of this horrendous crime (as he continues to serve his prison sentence), perhaps we should appreciate this movie strictly as a study in sociopathology.

The story begins February 17, 1970 with MacDonald phoning the police to report that his wife and two daughters had been brutally murdered by a marauding gang of hippies who broke into his home shouting "Kill the pigs, acid is groovy." He claims he tried to fight them off and was injured and knocked unconscious.

In contrast, the story presented by the prosecution and detailed in McGinniss's book, portrays MacDonald as having, in a fit of temper injured or killed a member of his family, and then to cover up that crime killed all of them, and then fabricated a crime scene to support his story including the infliction of superficial wounds upon himself.

The question most people would like answered is WHY would a previously upstanding member of the community, a successful doctor as well as a decorated army Captain, go to such a horrendous extreme to cover up a crime no worse than manslaughter, if that?

The answer is in the character of Jeffrey MacDonald himself who is depicted as a psychopath possibly under the influence of amphetamines, a man so callous and unfeeling about the pain and suffering of anyone except himself, that he would murder his own family in an attempt to divert the blame from himself. This was the answer that McGinniss came up with after spending a lot of time with MacDonald and after initially believing him to be innocent. This is the answer that the jury believed, and this is the answer given in the character that Gary Cole so vividly portrays.

There are many kinds of truth—legal truth decided by a jury, scientific truth decided by experiment and confirmation, spiritual truth, etc. And there is cinematic artistic truth, decided by the viewer. I think the business-like direction from Greene and his adherence to McGinniss's "vision," along with the fine performance by Gary Cole make us aware of the reality that there are sociopaths among us who can charm and kill with equal ease.

Regardless of the true facts of the case (which we will never know for certain) it is this singular truth that makes this movie worth seeing.

McGinniss Joe *Fatal Vision* (1983) 10
One of the classics of the true crime genre

This is one of the most chilling of true crime tales, and one of the most intriguing. Former Green Beret officer Dr. Jeffrey MacDonald (still in prison last time I checked) called the police early one morning to report that his pregnant wife and two young daughters had been murdered by a marauding gang of hippies shouting "Kill the pigs, acid is groovy" while he received some superficial wounds trying to fight them off.

Joe McGinniss who at the time was best known for his Nixon campaign book (*The Selling of the President* 1968) jumped on the case and made arrangements with Mac-Donald to follow him around and interview him. McGinniss has said that initially he believed MacDonald was innocent, but as he grew to know MacDonald, and as he sifted through the evidence he began to change his mind until in the end he believed along with the prosecution and the jurors that MacDonald had murdered his family. McGinniss reports all this in such a compelling manner that the reader is lead step by step to the same horrific conclusion (or at least most readers are). Also changing their minds about MacDonald were the wife's parents who at first refused to believe that he could have done something like this. Yet in the end they too were convinced.

Not convinced however were MacDonald's many supports including as I recall members of the Long Beach, California police department, many of MacDonald's co-workers, and a number of women who found the doctor very attractive.

All of this is interesting but what I think most fascinated McGinniss and what most fascinates me is an answer to the questions of Why did he do it? and How could any human being do something like that?

The most plausible theory (this is basically McGinniss's theory as well) to explain why he did it goes something like this: In a rage (possibly induced in part by amphetamine use) MacDonald badly or fatally injured one of his family. Rather than own up to this and face the consequences he had the "fatal vision" (thought to have been conjured up in part from an *Esquire Magazine* article or in remembrance of the Mason family murders) of acid-crazed hippies breaking into his home and attacking his family with him in heroic defense. To make this work he would have to kill everybody except himself and construct a crime scene that would support his story. The prosecution and McGinniss careful show how MacDon-ald's crime scene construction failed. Readers interested in forensic science will find this aspect of the book absolutely fascinating, even if not entirely convincing.

But to convict a man of murdering his family based on circumstantial evidence especially when the motive is not another woman, or money, but is instead merely a desire to hide what at worse would be manslaughter, seems quite a stretch for any jury, or so MacDonald apparently figured. But what went wrong was not only the evidence, but his personality.

As McGinniss spent time with MacDonald he came to realize that Dr. Jeffrey MacDonald was not like other people. He was charming and very bright but there was a cold aspect to his personality, what in autism is called a "lack of affect." Obviously he was not autistic, or perhaps his is a form of autism. Anyway, according to the current psychiatric wisdom, such a person is called a psychopath or a sociopath. The words mean approximately the same thing, that is, a person who values only his or her own life and welfare, a person who has no real feelings of warmth for others, a person who has no compunction about taking the life of another if he or she can gain from it and get away with it.

The compelling psychological argument for me (and perhaps for the jury that convicted him) is that ONLY such a husband and father could have done that. The fact that he fit the psychopathic personality type was what led to his conviction as much as the forensic evidence. I should add that even though over the years there have been tips about, and bizarre manifestations of, possible hippy suspects, MacDonald has remained the only real suspect.

But did he do it? This book makes a powerful case that he did. Followers of sensational crimes such as the Jon Benet Ramsey case or the current case of Scott Peterson (reported as "laughing and joking" with his attorneys in court today as I write this) will see similarities here. In the Jon Benet case there is the sense of an attempt to cover up some violence inflicted on a member of the family because somebody (probably the mother) lost her temper, while in the Scott Peterson case there is the phenomenon of the sociopathic personality to explain an otherwise unthinkable crime.

I originally thought that MacDonald was guilty and I still do, but I admit there is some doubt. Whether that doubt is "reasonable" is for you to decide. The jury has already decided. Someday there may be another trial. If so, that jury will decide. You might also want to read the "answer" to this book, *Fatal Justice: Reinvestigating the MacDonald Murders* (1992) by Jerry Allen Potter. Or go to the various Websites. I think you'll discover, as I did, why we have trials by jury in which both sides present their arguments. Just hearing one side seems so convincing until you hear the other side.

Bottom line: one of the very best true crime reads, the book that made McGinniss's career and helped to end MacDonald's: one of the classics of the genre.

First win for the books, 8-10. Movies still in front.

Matches:
- Movies: 2 _____
- Books: 1 _____
- Ties: 4 _____

Stars:
- Movies: 65 _____
- Books: 62 _____

8

Girl with a Pearl Earring (2003) 9

Exquisitely beautiful adaptation of the novel

One of the things that Tracy Chevalier wanted to do in the novel was to make the relationship between Griet and Johannas Vermeer nonsexual. Olivia Hetreed's script and the direction by Peter Webber adhere to this ideal. In her imaginings of what the girl with the pearl earring was like and what her life was like, I believe Chevalier thought it would be romantic in an artistic sense to have Vermeer's interest in her be artistic and not carnal. It is obvious from the exquisite beauty of the painting (actual title: "Girl in a Turban") that he very much admired her. It is difficult for me to believe that in that admiration he did not also feel some desire for her.

Be that as it may—and I certainly respect Chevalier's interpretation and in fact think it makes for a more interesting story than if there had been some sexual involvement—Vermeer's wife, Catharina, sees in the painting beauty that she herself does not possess. She also cannot help but wonder just what it is that her husband and the pretty young girl do during all those hours upstairs. Yet, the emphasis is on Catharina's jealousy of Griet's beauty and not on any imagined infidelity. I think this is consistent with Chevalier's interpretation of what the relationship between the maid and the great artist might have been.

This movie surprised me in how beautiful it is and how carefully Peter Webber, whose previous credits are in television, reconstructed 17th century Delft, Holland. If you go to the IMDb you will see that there were some goofs and anachronisms, such as a person in the background in one scene riding a bicycle. However, the Holland of 340 years ago seemed authentic and graphically atmospheric, including all the chores Griet had to do and the errands she had to run—note her red and bruised hands. (They used lye in soap in those days.)

Still the open air market could have used a few more flies (ha!) and the butcher boy (Cillian Murphy) was entirely too pretty (ha!), but Vermeer's studio seemed magical and I love the mixing of the colors and the way the light came through the windows. There are at least three Vermeer paintings in which we see the same light from the same window: the title painting; the painting he was working on without the chair in the foreground that Griet removed called, "Young Woman with a Water Jug"; and "The Painter's Studio." If I made a list of the most beautiful films I have ever seen, *Girl with a Pearl Earring* would make the list, along with, e.g., Zhang Yimou's *Raise the Red Lantern* (1992) and Stanley Kubrick's *Barry Lyndon* (1975) and maybe a dozen more.

As for Scarlett Johansson who had the title role I must say she won me over. At first I thought she was a bit too voluptuous for the part. (It is interesting to compare the reconstruction of the painting with Johansson with the original shown at the end of the movie. The real girl was a bit more delicate and of course not as sensual as Johansson.) Johansson won me over because of the subtly of her interpretation and because of the hard work she obviously put into the part. She is an actress we will see a lot of in the future. If you want to see her in less severe garb, catch her in Sofia Coppola's *Lost in Translation* (2003) where her sensual beauty is more fully presented.

Colin Firth very much caught the intensity of the artist and seemed to do so almost without effort. His eyes beheld Griet and indeed all the world not in a carnal way, but in the penetrating way of the artist who wants to see the world as it really is, not as our needs demand. We see this in the scene in which he insists that Griet see the real colors in the clouds, not just the white that we think we see. Note too (continuing Chevalier's theme) that it would be inopportune, careless and threatening to his artistic career for Vermeer to have an affair with the maid since with his mother-in-law in the house (her house, her money), and his wife and some nosy, tattling children, he would have been caught. Vermeer only completed about 40 paintings in his lifetime. His wife (or most especially his mother-in-law) was indeed his most important "patron." An artist without a patron sleeps in the streets, especially in such a mercantile world as a small town in 17th century Holland.

Catharina Vermeer (Essie Davis in an underappreciated role) provided exactly the right counterpoint with her vile, snake-in-the-garden-of-artistic-eden presence and her purely burgher mentality and her oppressive jealousy and her high-handed treatment of her servants. Without Davis's excruciatingly vivid performance this movie would have flat and lack in tension.

As for the ending and for the inevitable comparison with the novel, let's say the ending here (and the question of Griet's future life with the "butcher boy") is more open to interpretation than in the book where more is explained. (See my review, or better yet read the novel.) The strength of the book is in how deeply we can go into the mind of Griet and into the artistic intimacy of her relationship with Vermeer, whereas in the movie we can more fully appreciate the atmosphere and the beauty of the artist's vision.

By the way, in the novel it is clear that Griet does indeed desire Vermeer but realizes that his station is too much above hers, and his circumstances with five children and a sixth on the way leave no room for her. Also clear in both mediums is the fact that Vermeer's exquisite portrait is, in effect, his way of making love to her.

Chevalier, Tracy *Girl with a Pearl Earring* (1999) 10
A romantic historical novel of grace and power

In this radiant novel we are introduced to the minutia of family life in 17th century Holland as seen through the eyes of the maid Griet, a sixteen-year-old girl who became the subject of a famous painting by Johannes Vermeer. This is in fact the story of how she became his subject. As such it is a fiction fused into history, an imagination of Vermeer and the life of one of his models. It is a tale that makes us see with alacrity the poverty of choices that a girl without means had in that world, a world caught between feudalism and the rise of the mercantile class. Indeed, Griet had only her cleverness to stay her as she maneuvered among the men and women of privilege who would control her life.

Novelist Tracy Chevalier has a gift for expression and a great talent for telling a tale and weaving into the fabric of her story the poignant details of everyday life. Somehow she makes those details and the acting out of the petty politics of domestic life utterly enthralling. Her first-person narrative of an illiterate girl charms and disquiets by turns. Although this may seem a far-fetched comparison, I was reminded of Mark Twain's Huck Finn, also illiterate, who nonetheless waxed poetic with not just a novelist's but a painter's eye for detail. The words they use are everyday words, but spun out so beautifully, so aptly that they become something close to poetry, all the while maintaining plausibility. In truth no maid nor elegant lady of learning could express herself so well as this girl, but that is the novelist's license, and Chevalier uses it well.

Griet has these choices: a butcher's son with blood under his fingernails; Vermeer, who has a wife and five children (and a sixth on the way); and van Ruijven, Vermeer's rich and lecherous patron, who also has a family. She cannot move to another city, although sometimes she vaguely expresses this childish dream. She, like the vast majority of humankind before the Industrial Revolution, was fated to live and die in the town of her birth. Her life was controlled by the choices she had in men; and what would become of her depended on how she handled those choices. She could not take a job and live alone. She could not abandon her poverty-stricken parents. She could only steer between the rocks and the shoreline, torn between her heart's desire and her good Dutch rationality. Thus, on one level, this is a disturbing tale of how people, especially women, were subject to the dictates of property and privilege, without real choice, working six days a week, from sunup to sundown, for subsistence wages in economic subservience to the privi-

leged few. On another level this a Horatio Alger story of how one might, through hard work, right morality, a bit of clever common sense and—in this case—a pretty face, rise above one's predicament in life. Or, perhaps how one might try. This is also a tale of how our emotions lead us to ends both desirous and disastrous. Griet loves her master, as all good maids should, almost inevitably. Hers is a restrained and protracted love, beyond her control, so that she is caught. In this sense Chevalier's book is a romantic novel, a woman's interest tale of how the heart's desire may or may not be fulfilled. The beloved is a station above Griet; he is an accomplished artist, and he is taken—consumed in a sense—with his work and his large family, and yet she, as her brother points out, "wants him."

One of the nice things about this book is the reproduction of the celebrated Vermeer painting, "Girl with a Pearl Earring" on the cover. As one reads, one can easily refer to the painting again and again; and this is valuable because part of Chevalier's story is an imagination of how the work was painted through an intense study of the painting itself. Those in the visual arts I imagine will find this part of the novel fascinating, and may speculate on how closely Chevalier came to a truth about the process of artistic creation. Chevalier's interpretation includes the idea that the painting was the artist's way of making love to the girl. There can be no doubt of that.

I wish I could write with such grace and with such a feel for the felicitous detail and the absolutely apt phrase that is the hallmark of Chevalier's prose. I also wish I had the cunning to construct a novel so carefully. I knew I was in the thrall of a master as early as page nine when Griet learns that she is to clean Vermeer's studio without disturbing anything so that every object is returned to exactly where it had been. Chevalier has Griet remark: "After my father's accident we had learned to place things where he always knew to find them. It was one thing to do this for a blind man, though. Quite another for a man with a painter's eyes." Or, on page 163, Griet is home visiting her mother, and a "neighbor, a bright-eyed old woman who loved market talk," was there amid the rumors that Griet would appear in a painting alongside the lecherous van Ruijven. Griet tells her mother, "my master is beginning the painting that you were asking about. Van Ruijven has come over...Everyone who is to be in the painting is there now." Griet then observes that the gossipy neighbor "gazed at me as if I had just set a roast capon in front of her." Griet adds, "That will take care of the rumors."

Such skilled and subtle writing moves the reader along with a sense of deep involvement, and opens wide the eyes of other writers, who might learn from the very accomplished and gifted Tracy Chevalier.

Very close but I gave the nod to the novel, 9-10.

Matches:
>> Movies: 2 _____
>> Books: 2 _____
>> Ties: 4 _____
> Stars:
>> Movies: 74 _____
>> Books: 72 _____

9

> *There are two movie versions of Vladimir Nabokov's famous novel. My movie reviews are in the Memorable Remakes chapter. Here I give the book review. I'll score the movie as an average of the two movies = 9.*

Lolita (1962) 10

[Review on page 51.]

Lolita (1997) 8

[Review on page 52.]

Nabokov, Vladimir *Lolita* (1955) 10
A masterpiece on several levels

Vladimir Nabokov's *Lolita* is one of those rare books that is both a commercial and an artistic masterpiece. Like Joyce's *Ulysses* it is a tour de force of language seldom encountered in English outside the works of Shakespeare. It is a carefully crafted novel rich in irony and atmosphere, a novel of great psychological insight and poignancy, a novel to rival the masters of the nineteenth century and those of the twenty-first. Some have called it "The Great American Novel," that mythical tome of authorial genius that everybody was trying to write after the second world war, and the best novel about America ever penned. Certainly *Lolita* can feel comfortable alongside *The Scarlet Letter*, *Huck Finn*, *Moby Dick* and a few others as a top drawer classic of American literature.

Of course what sets *Lolita* apart from other novels, at least at the time of its publication in the fifties, is its theme. A grown man making love to a pre-adolescent girl was quite a shock for a prudish America weaned on Ozzie and Harriet and Dwight Eisenhower. As such it was a courageous novel and a bit of a derring-do. It was the novel of a man ravenous for the fame and fortune he thought his talent so richly deserved, and so he took a chance.

Originally Nabokov had intended to withhold his name from the title page while dispersing throughout the narrative cryptic evidences of his presence, should he later want to claim authorship; but somehow, even before the novel's first publication in France, he was persuaded to admit paternity. Even so he remained uneasy about *Lolita* throughout most of his life, maintaining that other, less appreciated works of his were superior, especially *Ada* and *Pnin*, while insisting that Humbert Humbert, his nymphet-enchanted antihero, was no part of himself,

merely a puppet on the master's string. After the rush of fame had subsided and he was comfortably ensconced *en chateau* with his fortune, Nabokov even grew weary of the attention *Lolita* commanded from critics and public alike, attention he saw as detrimental to his scholarly work, his autobiography (the splendid *Speak, Memory*) and his other works of fiction. I wouldn't be at all surprised to learn that more than once he spoke aloud the ancient warning and lamentation: "Beware of what you wish for. You may get it."

Still, one can survive such annoyances, and nowhere in Nabokov's life was he seen as more than slightly troubled by the very real belief that such a penetrating revelation of character (Humbert's) could only be achieved by having part of that character as one's own. This he denied to his dying day—as well he might. The "biographical fallacy" has a place in literary criticism, perhaps, but not here. His denial, while politically correct, was unnecessary since girls are desirable, and one can feel that desire without being a lecher. What is needed is the understanding, as with avocados and the rising of the sun, that there is a time appropriate to every purpose.

While reading *Lolita* for the first time, as with any rich piece of literature, do yourself a favor and don't try to catch all the subtleties. Just read it through. Those familiar with Nabokov know full well that he plays games with the reader just as he does with his characters. He likes to show off, and besides few of us are as erudite as the very learned professor himself. You might want to take a note or two to record how you feel about Humbert and his little charge, and then compare those notes to how you feel after a second reading. Like others, I found myself moved from the amusement and tolerance of a first reading to a fully sober appreciation, after a second reading, of what a "brute" (Lo's fair description) Humbert Humbert really is. It is a curious coincidence perhaps, but this is exactly what happened with the cinematic interpretations of the novel. The first, by Kubrick from the sixties, is a brilliant comedy that has us identifying with the tragedy of Hum's obsession, while the second, Adrian Lyne's more graphic recent production, makes it clear how violated and used and ultimately destroyed Lolita really was.

If you're writing a paper, buy the annotated Lolita with notes by Alfred Appel Jr. Although the annotations add only a little to an enjoyment of the novel, and in some cases seem a bit of a pedantic stretch, they will satisfy a scholastic urge.

> *Movies 9, novel 10.*

> Matches:
>> Movies: 2 _____
>> Books: 3 _____
>> Ties: 4 _____
> Stars:
>> Movies: 83 _____

10

Memoirs of a Geisha (2005) 8

Beautiful but somehow incomplete

In Arthur Golden's beautiful novel from which this movie was adapted there is the sense that the geisha exists in a fairytale world removed from harsh reality. Even though the kimonos have their seamy side that is not for us to see. The fact that Chiyo was sold into slavery and then charged for room and board and for her education in the pleasing arts, is made clear to the audience, and yet the treatment of the story is very much that of a fairytale. Chiyo is a Cinderella kind of character, beautiful, graceful, tactful and intelligent, courageous, morally correct and even heroic.

This is a good thing and perhaps why the producers worked so hard to get a PG-13 rating. And maybe it is a good thing that such a movie may be seen by teenaged girls and can afterwards discuss the movie with their mothers. The geisha as a role model...

And then again perhaps I am too harsh. My problem is that what made the novel so interesting, so much a work of art beyond its commercial success was the fine line that Golden walked between the fairytale and the reality, between the preserving and the selling of Chiyo/Sayuri's virginity, between her rising above the life of a fishmonger's daughter and that of becoming someone who sells herself to the highest bidder. In the movie this play between the fantasy and the reality is not sufficiently realized. Certainly director Rob Marshall tried. But I think the movie falls short of its potential mainly because the contrast was not made sharp enough. Or perhaps I have become jaded and don't realize that the harsh realities only need to be alluded to.

At any rate, the geisha's story (told in the first person by the geisha as an older woman looking back—Shizuko Hoshi does the voice over) is a strange and touching story of love spanning decades and ending in happiness and fulfillment. But primarily it is a fairy tale, and like all fairy tales there is beneath the surface an underlying current of the dark nature of humanity that can only be glimpsed through the use of symbolism. Just as the wolf in grandmother's bed represents something more than a wolf, so it is with the men attended by the geisha. And so it is with her as well. She projects the image of fairytale beauty and an attentive loveliness, but is in fact a woman of business whose attentions are bought and sold, just as with any commodity. This is the illusion and the pretense, and the soft, embroidered veil between us and the truth that is paid for.

At one point in the film Mameha (Michelle Yeoh) who is mentoring Chiyo tells her that "we are geishas not courtesans. We sell our skills not our bodies." No doubt this is true to some very real extent. It is also true that courtesans sell more than their bodies and even common street walkers might be looked upon as workers in a sex industry or even as physical therapists.

When I wrote the review for the book some years ago I speculated that this might be made into a epic quality movie, and indeed it was rumored that Steven Spielberg was to direct. I even thought that in might be made into a Broadway musical or even an opera (and it still might). Such is the familiar yet universal appeal of the central psychology of the story, that of a young and beautiful, but ordinary girl being thrown into an alien culture, where she experiences abuse, jealousy and unrequited love, but manages to triumph over such antagonists.

The direction by Rob Marshall, who directed the award-winning musical Chicago (2002), is competent with a nice emphasis on grace and beauty, which is certainly appropriate. Especially excellent was the final scene. It is touching and Ziyi Zhang plays her part to perfection. However I didn't like the blue lenses that she had to wear (and I understand she didn't like them either!). I realize that her eyes were supposed to provoke a sense of a "water person," but I think that could have been achieved without the artificiality of the lenses. They were particularly grotesque in the final scene with its lengthy close up.

Li Gong (or Gong Li—this is the Chinese way in which the last name goes first, or so I am told) was outstanding as always as Hatsumomo, the mean geisha who is jealous of Chiyo; and Suzuka Ohgo who played Chiyo as a little girl was adorable and did an excellent job. Ken Watanabe as The Chairman captured the sense of a wise and compassionate statesman very well, and Koji Yakusho as Nobu was entirely believable as a man of strength and character.

In the final analysis I guess the reason I was not thrilled with the movie is that I thought there was something lost in the adaptation, a subtlety of artistic intent and purpose to show an entire life both before and after World War II, from the time of the Emperor through the hardships that everybody had to endure as the rising sun set. Perhaps this works better in a 400-page novel than in a 145-minute movie. On the other hand maybe it is just that I read the book first. Some people say it is better to read the book first because you are then able to form your own idea of what the characters look like. Others say it is better to see the movie first because when you read the book the greater depth that is usually there is better appreciated.

Anyway, this is an excellent movie although not the masterpiece it might have been.

Golden, Arthur *Memoirs of a Geisha* (1997) 10

The Great American Novel as a Japanese love story

This begins as Charles Dickens might have written it, had he such visions, continues as a fairy tale, and concludes as a strange and touching story of love spanning decades and ending in happiness and fulfillment. But primarily this is a fairy tale, and like all fairy tales there is beneath the surface an underlying current of the dark nature of humanity that can only be glimpsed through the use of symbolism. Just as the wolf in grandmother's bed represents something more than a wolf, so it is with the men attended by the geisha. And so it is with her as well. She projects the image of fairy tale beauty and an attentive loveliness, but is in fact a woman of business whose attentions are bought and sold, just as with any commodity. This is the illusion and the pretense, and the soft, embroidered veil between us and the truth that is paid for.

This is also a beautiful novel, charming and witty with just the barest touch of satire, an original work of a cunning genius, as readable as a best seller, as satisfying as a masterpiece. Although written as realistic fiction and presented as the memoirs of someone who really did exist, the story and especially the action are veiled reality. Notice that Sayuri is fifteen when she first learns of the significance of her virginity. Since her captors would have put a very high price on maintaining that virginity until they could sell it, they would have taken very careful measures to ensure that she could not lose it; consequently, being the clever girl that she was, Sayuri would have understood what that meant. And to suppose that she knew nothing of sexual intercourse until Mameha's story of the lonely eel and the cave... Well, this is part of the contrivance and illusion maintained by geisha and its tradition. But make no mistake, the girls know, but their knowledge must be expressed and understood euphemistically.

There are a number of other "contradictions" in the novel that are of no real import because the world of the geisha is the world of illusion and fairy tale. Although Chiyo never says so directly, she knew quite well what was being done to her sister in the house of ill-repute that she visited in the poor section of Kyoto. There is something wonderful and alluring about this duplicitous view of human sexuality found in all cultures. One of the wonderful things about Golden's novel is how he shows us its expression in the Japanese tradition. When Hatsumomo's vagina is forcibly investigated by Granny and Mother looking for evidence of semen (and Chiyo is about ten years old) she understands what was found because she had seen the man between Hatsumomo's legs in the dim light through the partially opened door. Adults find comfort in the illusion of a sexless childhood, comfort that can only be maintained through the artifice of self-deception. Please note that this is not a criticism of the novel; on the contrary. It is part of Golden's vision to realize that a fairy tale view of Chiyo's sexuality was necessary. Note also the scenes with Mr. Tanaka when she appears as a naked nine-year-old. Read carefully we can see that his sexual desire for her is apparent and is

symbolically acted out through the device of her sister with the Sugi boy and Mr. Tanaka's bare touch of her cheek. Incidentally Nitta Sayuri's narrative is coy by design, and it is this structure that allows Golden to so beautifully present this fairy tale world with its illusion of a foreign and bygone reality.

But the fairy tale ends three-quarters of the way through, and then begins a counter point as the war and the hardships are brought home to the Japanese people and to Sayuri personally. Now we have a tale stripped of illusion, devoid of symbolism, replete with the harsh reality of a civilian population with dwindling resources, impending loss, and the sound of bombers overhead...

This is the kind of commerically and artistically successful novel that makes other novelists despair of ever coming close. The exquisite style, the confident scholarship, the ample energy so gracefully expended, the unerring sense of what is appropriate, the generous and apt use of metaphor, the clever plotting, the rich detail, the sure commercial feel: a publisher's dream, an agent's adrenal rush! I expect a lavish movie production, an Andrew Lloyd Webber musical, and perhaps even the first important opera of the twenty-first century to follow.

Or maybe a Disney cartoon in the tradition of Snow White and Cinderella. On second thought, probably NOT.

I didn't think the beautiful movie lived up to beauty and depth of the book, 8-10.

Matches:
　　Movies: 2　　_____
　　Books: 4 _____
　　Ties: 4　　_____
Stars:
　　Movies: 91　_____
　　Books: 92　_____

11

No Country for Old Men (2007) 9
Lean, mean adaptation of the Cormac McCarthy novel

The way the last quarter of so of this movie was cut makes me wonder, who did the cutting and what was the rush? We see Llewelyn dead but we don't see him die. We can presume the money went to Mexican drug dealers but we don't see that happen. Or—because Chigurh gives the kid a hundred dollar bill for his shirt—maybe HE got the money. Whether Carla Jean (Kelly Macdonald) is still alive as Chigurh walks out the door is unclear—intentionally unclear since the psychopathic fatalist gave her a coin flip. However she wouldn't let Chigurh avoid responsibility for her death by calling the coin flip. What's a madman to do? We never find out. Or—since we see Chigurh checking the bottoms of his boots for something (blood?) as he leaves her place—maybe he did kill her.

I also wonder about keeping such a sickie alive as the closing credits run. I wasn't keeping count but Chigurh wantonly killed somewhere around a dozen people, mostly just because he could. I think this kind of character—a psychopath with a code (you harm, insult or even inconvenience me and you die)—plays well in this age of violence in which we live. He is something like shock and awe made flesh.

Don't misunderstand me. This is a riveting flick, as one would expect from Ethan Coen and Joel Coen. The acting, especially by Javier Bardem and Josh Brolin is superlative. Bardem, with the thick pageboy hairdo and the big malevolent eyes and the no nonsense conversational style, is particularly good. Brolin becomes the country and cocky Llewelyn Moss very well. He is much more likeable in the movie than in the book.

One thing that the movie cleared up for me was the business with the money in the air conditioning shaft at the motel. Llewelyn puts it there in the first place to hide it. When he comes back to the motel he sees that the drapes are a bit parted and he knows somebody's in there waiting for him. So he rents the room on the other side and manages to pull the suitcase out. The Mexicans who were waiting for him didn't have the tracking device (transponder) so they didn't know the money was nearby. Chigurh knows of course, but by the time he is through shooting the Mexicans, Llewelyn is gone.

A problem in the very beginning of the movie comes up when Llewelyn acknowledges that he is about to do something incredibly foolish. He goes back to the bloody scene in the scrub desert to bring the dying Mexican some water. The fact that he says it's foolish doesn't excuse it as a plot device. The guy was just about dead when Llewelyn left him many hours earlier. Coming back now with water isn't going to save him. Furthermore, Llewelyn was originally indifferent to his thirst. There must have been some water or something to drink somewhere in all the vehicles on the scene, but Llewelyn doesn't bother looking. It's curious that Llewelyn didn't realize that bringing the man who had been bleeding for many hours some water wasn't really going to help. If he wanted to help he could have dialed 911.

By the way, this device, which has the effect of giving Llewelyn a "fatal flaw" in the Greek dramatic sense, was also in Cormac McCarthy's novel. If Llewelyn doesn't return to the scene, the story would play out a bit differently, to say the least. Since Chigurh has the transponder he would locate the money and possibly take Llewelyn by surprise.

What are the chances that Carson Wells (Woody Harrison) is able to go to the exact spot where Llewelyn threw the money over the fence and into bushes? Close to zero,

I would say. I suspect that the Coens were going to do something with this unlikely plot event but as it turns out, they didn't. In fact, there is a lot they didn't do or show, so much so, I just think they got overwhelmed with all the footage they had and the time constraints and just sliced it up near the end.

Now, why this is called "No Country for Old Men"? Cormac McCarthy took his cue from the poem "Sailing to Byzantium" by William Butler Yeats. Here is the opening stanza.

That is no country for old men. The young
in one another's arms, birds in the trees
—Those dying generations—at their song,
The salmon-falls, the mackerel-crowded seas,
Fish, flesh, or fowl, commend all summer long
Whatever is begotten, born, and dies.
Caught in that sensual music all neglect
Monuments of unageing intellect.

The theme of Yeats' poem is the impermanence of this world, and so he set sail "To the holy city of Byzantium" where things are made of more permanent stuff such "as Grecian goldsmiths make" and where things are eternal like ideas.

One of McCarthy's points is that the bloody violence of the border towns of West Texas about which he writes resembles more "the mackerel-crowded seas" than the holy city of Byzantium, and the "sensual music" is the sound of bullet hitting bone from those dying generations at their song. Additionally, the old men in the story, Ed Tom Bell (played very effectively by Tommy Lee Jones), Roscoe Giddens (Rodger Boyce), and Ellis (Barry Corbin), feel estranged from the lust of the young after money and drugs.

The premise of the movie centers around a dope drop in the semi-desert gone bad that Llewelyn Moss stumbles onto some time after the shooting has stopped. Bodies everywhere. Bullet holes in vehicles, blood, etc. Moss is wondering, where's the money? He follows the bloody trail of someone carrying something heavy and finds him and it. It's a carrying case with $2-million in hundred dollar bills.

Needless to say that kind of cash attracts a lot of flies.

McCarthy, Cormac *No Country for Old Men* (2005) 9
An artistic and commercial triumph

McCarthy takes the name of his novel from the first line of William Butler Yeats' famous poem, "Sailing to Byzantium," the theme of which is the impermanence of this world. (For more, see the movie review above.)

But what has this to do with Cormac McCarthy's mesmerizing and seductive narrative?

Well, perhaps not as much as McCarthy thought when he came up with the title or when he began his tale. One thing is clear, the bloody violence of the border towns of West Texas about which he writes resemble more "the mackerel-crowded seas" than the holy city of Byzantium, and the "sensual music" is the sound of bullet hitting bone from those dying generations at their song.

The novel is a triumph, both artistically and commercially for the gifted Mr. McCarthy, one of many. What I think aspiring novelists can learn from this is that the power of voice, story and character easily triumphs over any kind of defect that might exist in technique or composition. McCarthy makes his own artistic rules as spins out his tales like shining dimes shimmering across a waxed counter—or dimes thrown in the air to land on heads or tails to decide if you live or die, which is what happens to a couple of the characters in this tale.

Anton Chigurh is the ironically triumphant character in the novel, with the passably human Llewelyn Moss his counterpoint and foil. Chigurh is a psychopath with a code: you harm, insult or even inconvenience me and you die. (Maybe sometimes just for sport I'll flip a coin and if you call it right I'll let you live.) Moss is a fated character who made one fatal error. He's tough and tenacious but a bit out of his league versus Chigurh who is something like the terminator made flesh. All behave like driven animals with the exception of Sheriff Bell who is reflective and philosophic. He is the old man who learns that this is no longer the country for him.

The plot centers around a dope drop in the semi-desert gone bad that Moss stumbles onto some time after the shooting has stopped. Bodies everywhere. Bullet holes in vehicles, blood, etc. And one guy still alive begging for agua. I aint got no water, Moss tells him. Shrewd and with an eye to gaining something big, he's thinking about other things, like where's the money? He follows the bloody trail of someone carrying something heavy and finds him and it. It's a carrying case full of used hundred dollar bills.

He takes the case and heads home to his wife, has a beer, etc. But in the middle of the night he returns to the scene, and it is here that McCarthy begins to allow the plot to get a little shabby and the logic to go south. Why does he return? He says, "Somethin I forgot to do." Apparently what he forgot to do is give the dying Mexican some water. Funny thing about that. It's 12 hours later at one o'clock in the morning when remembers this and its another hour and fifteen before he reaches the Mexican who is now freshly dead with what appears to be a brand new bullet hole in his forehead.

When reading this I thought Moss had returned possibly to get the heroin or maybe to shoot the Mexican who might be able to identify him. But no, Moss's fatal flaw is his kindness.

His kindness! I guess he didn't realize that bringing the man who had been bleeding for a day or two some water wasn't really going to help. If he wanted to help he could have dialed 911.

There are some other minor plot problems and loose ends, but they really don't matter. What matters is McCarthy's brilliant prose, the flawless dialogue, the masterful sketches of the land, and especially his lean narrative that makes the action and the characters vivid and indelible.

Although I have termed this an artistic and commercial triumph I would not call it an unqualified success. The loose ends, the mixed narratives in which Bell appears both in the first person and in the omniscient third, the slight development of most of the characters—although what is developed is very good—and the admixture of an existential ending with Bell's attempts to find a greater meaning are disconcerting. But I don't think McCarthy was much worried about any of this. His intense involvement with the struggles and experiences of his characters is what probably gave him the most artistic satisfaction. Straightening up the details would not be as important.

By the way, the Coen brothers of Fargo (1996) movie fame, violence meisters themselves, whose first film, Blood Simple (1984), was set in Texas, have made a film adapted from McCarthy's novel set for release August 7, 2007. It will star Josh Brolin as Moss, Woody Harrelson as Wells, Tommy Lee Jones as Bell, and Javier Bardem as Chigurh. It should be a doosie. The screenplay must have been easy to write since McCarthy's novel is so very visual and so full of clever stuff.

I have to say I don't like the fact that one of our most successful and brilliant novelists is a master of violence. Is it an accident that the public has rewarded him, or is it the case that he is a product of his times and rides the Zeitgeist? We are living in an age of escalating violence and perhaps that is reflected in our literature.

Both the movie and the book are superlative entertainments with some real depth flawed by a plot hole or two, 9-9.

Matches:

Movies: 2		_____
Books: 4	_____	
Ties: 5		_____

Stars:

Movies: 100	_____
Books: 101	_____

12

= 7.

Again I'll average the ratings of the two movies

The Postman Always Rings Twice (1946) 6

[Review on page 44.]

The Postman Always Rings Twice (1981) 8

[Review on page 45.]

Cain, James M. *The Postman Always Rings Twice*
(1934) 8
Hemingway accelerated

I spent some time trying to find out why this potboiler turned literature is called "The Postman Always Rings Twice" since at no place in the novel is a postman even mentioned. At first I thought it might be an echo of Eugene O'Neill's *The Iceman Cometh*, dreamt up by Knopf, Cain's publisher, to lend some literary pretension to a novel they weren't sure about; but that play wasn't written until some years after Postman was published in 1934. It was recently suggested to me (by Joseph Feinsinger, one of Amazon.com's best reviewers of literature) that it might be a rejoinder for the saying "opportunity knocks only once," which was the sort of pabulum given to out of work people during the depression. Cain's original title was "Bar-B-Que," which is entirely appropriate for a couple of reasons (the café, the burning car), but was perhaps a little too morbid for Knopf's sensibilities.

At any rate, the title finally chosen is somewhat magical as is the novel itself, the first of Cain's hard-boiled, loser tales that somehow caught the imagination and psyche of depression America. Re-reading the novel today one wonders why, but then again, I can see why.

First there's the raw sex with Frank forcing himself onto Cora, biting her lip, etc. and she loving it that was somewhat shocking for its time. Ditto for the spontaneous sex they have in the dirt outside the car after Frank has beamed Nick. Then there is the fascination we have with stupid people doing vile deeds rather clumsily (with whom we might identify). But more than anything else it's the style. Cain raised the dime novel to something amazing with his no nonsense, no time to chat, no description beyond the absolutely necessary—a pared-down to raw flesh and bones writing style that made even some of the icons of literature sit up and take notice. Edmund Wilson, long the dean of American literary critics, was intrigued by the novel, as was Franklin P Adams who called it "the most engrossing, unlaydownable book that I have any memory of." (Quoted from Paul Skenazy's critical work, *James M. Cain* (1989), pp. 20-21). And Albert Camus said that his internationally famous masterpiece *The Stranger* was based in part on Postman. The alternate English title, "The Outsider," perhaps reveals its debt to Cain more clearly. Today the sex seems rather tame and the terse style seems almost a burlesque, having been so often imitated. I personally think that Cain, who was a one-time editor of *The New Yorker* and a relatively sophisticated literary man, was actually taking Hemingway's primer-prose style to its logical conclusion by simply cutting out all of Hemingway's poetic repetitions and anything else that didn't move the plot.

Well, how well does this stand up after almost seventy years? It was made into two movies, a 1946 version starring John Garfield and Lana Turner and a 1981 version starring Jack Nicholson and Jessica Lange, which you might want to compare. You can read the novel faster than you can watch either movie. I read it in an hour and I'm no speed reader. There was also a play and, believe it or not, an opera. The atmosphere is suburban naturalistic, set in the environs of Glendale, California, just north of L.A. where there really are (or mostly were) oak trees. (The name of the café is the Twin Oaks.) The story is a little confused in parts, and a little unlikely elsewhere (Cora really would not be such an adept at gun toting, and the Frank would not be so quick to fall for the D.A.'s line of chatter, nor could Nick be quite so blind to the hanky-panky going on behind his back). But what Cain got so, so very right was the underlying psychology. This is a classic triangle, the old guy with the resources who can't cut the mustard anymore with a young wife who longs for love, a little excitement and to be rid of "that greasy Greek." Even deeper (and this is characteristic of Cain) is the suggestion that Nick encouraged Frank and kept him around, using his presence to spice up his own libido. Furthermore, Frank is a kind of depression-era anti-hero, who beat up on the hated railway dicks, the kind of guy who has become a film noir staple, a man who acts out his basic desires in an amoral, animalistic way. I see woman. I take woman. I eat when I'm hungry, drink when I'm dry, and sleep when I run out of gas, a kind of natural man on the run, the kind of guy we think we would like to be for a change (a brief change) in our daydreams around two p.m. on a blue Monday afternoon.

Cain followed this up with *Double Indemnity* (using some insurance fraud research he had left over). *Double Indemnity* appeared as a serial in Liberty magazine after being rejected by Redbook. It was also made into a classic Billy Wilder movie starring Barbara Stanwyck, Fred MacMurray and Edward G. Robinson in 1944 a year after it finally appeared in book form.

Cain, along with Raymond Chandler, Dashiell Hammett, Nathanael West and later Ross MacDonald created a kind of southern California milieu that Hollywood has mined again and again with such postmodern films as, e.g., *Chinatown* (1974) and *L.A. Confidential* (1997). Read this (during lunch) for its historical value as a precursor of film noir and the hard-boiled detective novel.

Another win for the book, 7-8. Books pulling away.

13

Siddhartha (1972) 7

Not bad, but fails to capture the resplendence of the novel

No movie that is even marginally true to the story that Nobel Prize-winning German author Hermann Hesse told in his novel *Siddhartha* (1951) is without merit; and this modest film is no exception. The problem is that while Conrad Brooks, who wrote, directed and produced the film, is true to the storyline of the novel and even in some respects true to the spirit of the novel, he fails to bring the power and the resplendence of Hesse's philosophic and spiritual masterpiece to the screen.

What made the novel one of the best ever written is the character of Siddhartha himself. Patterned after the Buddha both in temperament and in experience, Hesse's Siddhartha, "the Accomplished One," grew up amid extravagant wealth and privilege only to dump it all in an effort to find himself. Brooks fails almost immediately when he leaves out the scene from the book in which the young Siddhartha, not wanting to directly disobey his father (and to demonstrate his resolve) stands up all night waiting patiently for his father's permission to leave their splendid estates. This is one of the greatest "coming of age" scenes ever written and an early insight into Siddhartha's strength of character, but Brooks gives it barely a notice!

Also skirted over too quickly are Siddhartha's years with the samanas in the forest where he practiced meditation and austerities. This part of Siddhartha's life was essential in making him the man he was and in showing us his character. He spent six years with the shamans and gurus of the forest (along with his companion Govinda) and in the end learned everything they knew and more, and yet had not found the answer he sought. (This parallels the experience of the "emaciated" Buddha.)

Brooks does do the meeting with the Buddha well, having us hear his voice but not see him, and then follows that up with Siddhartha's reasons for not following the Buddha, even though he finds no fault with the Enlightened One's teachings. Note that without his actually meeting the Buddha, the life of Siddhartha (which is one of the traditional names of the Buddha) would so closely parallel that of the Buddha that some people might think that Hesse had written a profane life of the Buddha, which might not set well with some Buddhists!

Siddhartha's life with the courtesan Kamala and the merchant Kamaswami and his spiral into debauchery and sloth is well depicted, although again the ultimate disillusionment that Siddhartha experienced is not as well presented as in the novel. Which brings me to Shashi Kapoor who plays Siddhartha. Although he would go on to be the veteran of well over a hundred films, and although he is appropriately enough Indian as well as tall, dark and handsome and a good actor, he fails to evoke the passion that Siddhartha must have. Siddhartha felt everything in a profound manner, even boredom was profoundly experienced by the Brahmin's prodigal son. Kapoor, especially near the end of the film when he plays an old man, occasionally made me feel that he could be "the Accomplished One," but more often he made me feel that he was holding something back.

Finally, the poetic scene near the end of the novel when, after living with and being guided by Vasudeva, the ferryman, Siddhartha becomes one with the river and falls spiritually into its wisdom, is only a bland shadow of what appears in the novel!

Part of the reason for the failure probably has to do with a limited budget. The film is 83 minutes long, but could easily be twice that long. Part has to do with the selection of scenes and the emphasis on those scenes, and finally part of the reason has to do with the relative inexperience of Brooks who was only directing his second major film (and apparently his last). Certainly the on-location in India cinematography by Sven Nykvist who worked on so many films with Ingmar Berman is not to be faulted. Although not spectacular, Nykvist's camera conveys both the exotic beauty and the poverty of a landscape that could have been India 26 centuries ago.

Hesse, Herman *Siddhartha* (1951) 10
Beautiful, poignant, uplifting: a great novel

This beautiful and poetic novel about the life of the Buddha is not about the life of the Buddha, per se, or so Herman Hesse (it's a German name: the final "e" is pronounced like a soft English "a") would have us believe. "Siddhartha," meaning "the accomplished one" is one of the traditional names of the Buddha, but in this novel Siddhartha (from the Sanskrit so that the "h's" are silent) encounters the Buddha in his travels and gains by what he learns from the Enlightened One. Yet the life so wondrously depicted here is closely patterned after the traditional life of the Buddha, and where it is not, it is highly plausible. I think Hesse started out to write a life of the Buddha but at some point realized that his sometimes spiritual, sometimes profane depiction might offend some Buddhists, and so he had Gotama, the Perfect One himself, appear as a separate character while keeping the life and the traditional name for his hero.

At any rate, this is one of the great novels of the twentieth century, or any century for that matter. It begins with Siddhartha's royal birth in India in the Sixth Century BCE into a Brahmin's life of privilege and wealth, continues through Siddhartha's traditional discovery of poverty, death, disease and pain as he wanders outside the royal estates, and his consequent desire to conquer or somehow come to terms with what he sees, things he had been sheltered from since birth. Thus we have the fundamental tenant of Buddhism: Life is suffering. The scene where the young Siddhartha confronts his father and stands up all night to show his resolve is one of the greatest "coming of age" scenes ever written.

And that is what really makes this novel: the character of Siddhartha himself. Hesse has created a seeker who is a real life hero: kind, brave, strong of will and decisive, intelligent, modest, confident, honest, hardworking, un-prejudiced, self-questioning and sometimes self-doubting, somebody we can identify with and admire. He goes through the temptations and the travails of life, sometimes weakening and sometimes distracted, finally finding salvation only after he has tried not only asceticism, but indulgence, not just renunciation, but a Tantric-like embracing of all things social and profane. In a sense this is a generalized life of the true seeker after spiritual enlightenment, a life that pleases not just Buddhists, but Christians and Hindus and those from other faiths as well because it is a portrait of humanity at our finest and our truest, out of the entangled bank and toward the stars.

The deceptive simplicity of the story makes it accessible to readers of all ages and walks of life, and greatly rewards a second and a third reading. In the United States it is often part of a superior high school curriculum. It is inspirational not only for the spiritually inclined, but for young people of all ages, and in writing it, Hesse did a service for humanity greater than a thousand sermons.

I should add that the English translation of the German by Hilda Rosner is itself a work of art, graceful, balanced, every word so natural that one is unaware that the work was written in another language.

The story ends with Siddhartha finding the peace that passeth all understanding, learned from a simple ferry boatman as he listens to the timeless voice of the river as it flows, expressing all that is or has been or will be.

This novel is a treasure.

Big win for the books, 7-10.

Matches:

Movies: 2	____	
Books: 7	____	
Ties: 4	____	

Stars:

Movies: 114	____	
Books: 119	____	

14

The Talented Mr. Ripley (1999) 9
Excellent interpretation of the Highsmith mystery classic

It's interesting to compare director and screenwriter Anthony Minghella's interpretation with the source material, mystery writer Patricia Highsmith's 1955 novel of the same name. That novel was an intense but somewhat euphemistic psycho/sexual study of a sociopath of ambiguous sexuality done as a third-person narrative from a limited point of view (Ripley's). As such we were forced to identify with Highsmith's antihero, all the better to set us up for her ironic and daring "resolution." Minghella has changed the ending, but without changing its spirit. He has Ripley committing an additional murder while throwing in a character not in the novel, Cate Blanchett's Meredith Logue. Miss Logue serves two purposes, one, she helps unravel the plot and two, she helps to objectify Tom Ripley's ambivalent sexual nature.

The simplistic question, is Ripley gay? is not answered in the Highsmith novel. But Minghella, by adding the bathtub scene with Dickie and the scene aboard ship with the clearly gay Peter Smith-Kingsley, decides that Ripley is indeed gay. Nonetheless the psychological heart of the story, that of a man who loathes himself so much that he can only love himself by assuming the identity of another man whom he admires, is left intact. Minghella's script and direction remain true to the spirit and broad form of the novel, while improving on the dramatic quality of the story. (I don't think most movie audiences would have the patience for Highsmith's more leisurely exposition.)

Some other changes by Minghella include making Dickie's passion jazz music instead of painting, and emphasizing the rich boy/poor boy dichotomy (somewhat reminiscent of the chasm in *The Great Gatsby*) by making Dickie a Princeton grad and Tom a piano-playing kid who had a menial job at the university. In the book Dickie and Tom actually knew one another before Europe, while Minghella has Tom pretend that Dickie and he had previously met. Also in the book Marge Sherwood's character is almost stupid. In the movie she is intelligent and insightful. Dickie loves her and they are to be married. In the book she is just a girlfriend.

The success of this movie in large part is due to Minghella's ability to translate the novel to the screen, but also because of a very superior cast. Matt Damon as the murderous Mr. Ripley is creepy and vulnerable and entirely believable. Jude Law as the rich and spoiled, but likeable Dickie Greenleaf, is outstanding. He is an actor of charisma and subtlety. Gwyneth Paltrow does a good job in a somewhat limited role as Marge Sherwood. Cate Blanchett, whom you may recall from her outstanding work in *Elizabeth* (1998) is particularly good as the straight-laced and somewhat inhibited Meredith Logue who has designs on Tom Ripley's morally corrupted heart (although she thinks he's Dickie Greenleaf).

She, more than anyone conveys the look and feel of the fifties. And Phillip Seymour Hoffman, whom I recall from his small part as Lester Bangs, the cynical rock critic in *Almost Famous* (2000), is superb as Dickie's somewhat boorish friend, Freddie Miles.

In some ways this is better than the book. (And in some ways it isn't, of course.) Minghella, who brought Michael Ondaatje's difficult novel, *The English Patient,* to the screen, proves once again that he knows the difference between a novel and a screenplay and how to translate the one into the other without losing the essence of the original. Incidentally, the spiffy line spoken by James Rebhorn as Dickie's father, Herbert Greenleaf, "People say you can't choose your parents, but you know you can't choose your children either," is not in the book (nor in Bartlett's *Quotations*) and so I presume was penned by Minghella.

Another very good movie version of the Highsmith novel is the Hitchcock-like *Plein Soleil* ("Purple Noon") released in 1960 from French director Rene Clement.

Highsmith, Patricia. *The Talented Mr. Ripley* (1955) 9
Splendid psycho/sexual study of a sociopath

Patricia Highsmith, one of the *grande dames* of the mystery genre, as usual transcends that genre in this meticulously wrought study of a sociopath. The action is set in Europe in the fifties, mostly Italy, at a time when the Yankee dollar bought a whole lot of cappuccino, and an American accent still commanded some respect. In her intense exploration of the 25-year-old Tom Ripley, Highsmith implicitly asks the question: Is the difference between a sociopath and a "normal" person only a matter of degree, or is there a distinct difference between "us" and "them"?

First published in 1955, *The Talented Mr. Ripley* has since been made into a couple of excellent movies, the first a Hitchcockian venture by French director Rene Clement entitled *Plein Soleil* "Purple Moon" (1960) and recently the interpretation by Anthony Minghella using Highsmith's title. Neither picture was entirely faithful to Highsmith's novel, yet both caught the spirit of the sexually ambiguous Tom Ripley, who might more properly be called, "The Murderous Mr. Ripley."

In effect, Highsmith asks, is Ripley's love of self so complete and exclusive that it precludes any other love? Note that his love for the rich and spoiled Dickie Greenleaf takes form as a step by step assumption of Dickie's life and personality. It is only when he becomes Dickie that Ripley is able to love Dickie and thereby to love himself. In other words, to love himself Tom Ripley must destroy the self-loathing that he has always felt. He does this by becoming Dickie Greenleaf and assuming Dickie's witty, confident personality and all the accoutrements of wealth, leisure and status that Dickie enjoys. While we note Ripley's repulsive feelings toward Marge and a kind of identification and interest in gay men, an interest that Dickie finds disgusting—witness the scene on the beach with the men making human pyramids—our answer to the simplistic question, is Tom Ripley gay? is...not really, and anyway it doesn't matter. He is interested only in loving himself, and finding ways to do that.

There is a strong sense of the psychoanalytic approach in Highsmith's somewhat euphemistic study, which is not surprising considering that the 1950s were perhaps the heyday of Freudian analysis and suppositions, at least in the popular culture. The movie *Rebel Without a Cause* (1955) and Robert Lindner's popular, *The Fifty Minute Hour: A Collection of True Psychoanalytical Tales* (1954) come quickly to mind, and Hitchcock's Psycho (1960) was not far off. But Highsmith does not allow us to draw any set conclusions about her anti-hero.

The ending is disturbingly ironic and daring, surprising both us and the slippery Mr. Ripley.

Yet another win for the books, 8-10. As expected the books easily beat the movies.

Final score: Matches:
Movies: 2 _____
Books: 8 _____
Ties: 4 _____
    Stars:
Movies: 122 _____
Books: 129 _____

Chapter Seven:

Not for Women Only?

Obviously some movies might be of more interest to women than to men. Here's a chapter full of them in three parts. The question is, are they really for women only? Whether you are a man or a woman, after each review you can address that question by making some strategic check marks—or, if you really want to get involved, go to the Amazon.com or IMDb.com sites and express yourself. (Civilly, of course.)

I

Mother–Daughter Dynamics

or

If I Don't Get My Way, I Will Hate You until the End of Time

Anywhere But Here (1999) 10

Brilliant performances by Sarandon and Portman

The mother-daughter bond, especially with an only child, is one of the strongest human bonds there is. Some say it's stronger than husband and wife. It tends to be intense and it almost always develops into a situation where neither side has the clear upper hand because both are vulnerable.

And they fight. Tooth and nail. And they love each other intensely. For the mother it is scary because everything is in the daughter and for the daughter, especially when the mother is divorced or single, as is the case here. For the daughter it can be a nightmare because the mother is the adult and has the power and is a total embarrassment. This is especially true when the mother is delusional or dysfunctional as is Adele August (Susan Sarandon).

The story from Mona Simpson's novel is familiar in plot and theme although the details here are unique and especially well done. Adele's judgment is more than suspect and she's careless with other people's feelings, and she's shallow and dresses funny. And she isn't completely aware of, nor has she sufficient respect for the needs and wants of her daughter, Ann (Natalie Portman). She, the mother, wants to leave behind the small town, Midwestern existence and embrace Hollywood and all things glamorous. Ann would rather stay in Bay City, Wisconsin with her friends and family. Mom buys a Mercedes and forces Ann to go with her to make a new life in Beverly Hills.

I thought Wayne Wang's direction was excellent. He used visual clues to introduce the scenes: shots of a still apartment, shots of part of a person, shots of the beach or the highway, etc., and then a focus on—almost always—Sarandon or Portman. And then at some time, the camera backs away and we see the larger scene: the desert sand and scrub, the ocean and the sunrise, the other diners at the restaurant, the mourners at the funeral, the crossway over the freeway, and so on. The scene in which Adele is hiding under the covers from heartbreak, and Ann pulls them off, is shot from above because such an angle so beautifully reveals Adele's limbs pulled in close to her body as though in catatonia or in a return to the safety of the womb. Sometimes the sounds precede the shot as when Adele is in Bay City trying desperately to get in touch with the dentist in California who doesn't want her, and we hear her desperation before we see it in her face.

I also liked the way the film was cut. As soon as the point of the scene was made, we moved on to another scene, which is again introduced visually with just the right kind of lighting, giving us a moment or two to imagine what transpired in-between. However the real strength of the film is in the brilliant work by Sarandon and Portman.

Sarandon is deliberately annoying, flighty, self-delusive, and deeply vulnerable while Portman is powerful, sensitive, and one step ahead of us. Indeed Natalie Portman is one of the most gifted young talents in all of cinema.

She absolutely commands the camera, and, as it stays on her face, she reveals to us a full set of emotions and responses, layered like things very deep. If she wants to she can become one of the great stars of the screen. She has the talent. I understand however that she is pursuing a career as a doctor. Whatever she does, one has the sense that she will do it very well.

A couple of irreverent questions for director Wayne Wang:

How *did* Ann's audition go? Did her projection of her mother's personality win her the part?

And, what *is* it that the man does in bed only with a woman he feels special about? Inquiring minds want to know (rather than make stupid guesses).

Anywhere But Here can be compared with some other dysfunctional mom and wise-beyond-her-years daughter films, for example, *Mermaids* (1990) with Cher and Winona Ryder, *Postcards from the Edge* (1990) with Shirley MacLaine and Meryl Streep, *Mommie Dearest* (1981) with Fay Dunaway and Diana Scarwid, *Terms of Endearment* (1983) with Shirley MacLaine and Debra Winger, and some others I have forgotten.

For the record I would rate these in this order:

Terms of Endearment (1983)
Postcards from the Edge (1990)
Anywhere But Here (1999)
Mermaids (1990)
Mommie Dearest (1981)

At IMDb they are rated in the same order but with *Anywhere But Here* at the bottom. Too bad, but that allows me to say that this is very much an underrated film.

See it for both Susan Sarandon, who is as good or even better than she ever was—and that is very good indeed—and for Natalie Portman, who is very appealing, and as an actress, mature beyond her years.

I am a man and I admit to having seen this movie and I am the better for it___. Not!___.

It doesn't matter what my sexual orientation is. This is a movie definitely worth seeing___. Not!___.

Autumn Sonata (1978) 8

Bergman directs Bergman

Before she was an international star of incomparable charisma and beauty, and even before Ingmar Bergman became a legendary director of films bleak and intense, Ingrid Bergman played in the Swedish cinema. So it is entirely apropos that someday Bergman might direct Bergman.

Ingrid plays Charlotte, a concert pianist who has, upon the recent death of her longtime lover, Leonardo, returned to her native land to visit her daughter Eva (Liv Ullmann), whom she hasn't seen for seven years, and Eva's husband Viktor (Halvar Bjork), who is a minister. Ullmann is frumpish in specs with her hair up and her dress loose and ill-fitting. She is Ingrid's nerdish daughter who has been throughout her life entirely overshadowed by her glamorous mother. Eva has an unpleasant surprise for mom. Her other daughter, Helena (Lena Nyman), who suffers from a crippling disease, perhaps muscular dystrophy, is on hand. Eva didn't tell her mother that Helena was now living with them. She says she didn't tell her because she knew that, if she had, Charlotte would not have come. And so we can guess that there are issues that will come out, issues between mother and daughter that have been festering for decades.

I got goose bumps seeing Ingrid Bergman as an elderly woman, and seeing the smooth, graceful style again, the elegant presence, a hint of the old gestures, the sly glances, the tentative smiles... It was really wonderful and at the same time disconcerting to examine her face (Sven Nykvist's intense close ups expose every inch of skin) and sigh and remember and understand the effect of the passing years. Ingrid is elegant but she has been robbed of her beauty so now we are able to see her character; unfortunately Ingmar's script allows little of the real Ingrid Bergman to appear. Hers is not a pleasant part to play. She is an entirely selfish and self-centered woman who has put her career before her family, but is unaware of what she has done. Eva seizes this opportunity to punish her mother by dredging up the neglect of her childhood to throw it in her mother's face (which perhaps explains why Charlotte hasn't been home in seven years). The sheer cold hatred that Eva expresses is enough to make the devil himself cringe. After a bit one begins to feel sorry for Charlotte, despite her failures as a mother, to have a daughter so unforgiving and so hateful.

Liv Ullmann is rather startling in this portrayal, with her penetrating eyes, her hard, Neandethalish forehead, the severe specs, and the uncompromising tone of her voice. Charlotte is ashamed and begs for forgiveness and tries to defend herself, but it is no use. Eva is too strong for her. This is one of the more intense scenes in cinema, and one not easily watched. Meanwhile in the upstairs bedroom and then in the hallway and down the staircase, Helena has heard them arguing and is pulling her crippled body over the floor, desperately trying to reach them. She cries out, "Mama! Mama!" but is not heard.

Viewers might want to pick sides between mother and daughter to say who is more at fault. Indeed, it is hard to say who Bergman himself found more at fault. Perhaps there is no fault, only human weakness and stupidity. Such scenes are usually followed by a greater understanding, forgiveness and a willingness to start anew. However, although Charlotte wants that, it is not clear in Bergman's script that anything good will come of what has happened. Charlotte leaves, the minister returns to looking at his wife, (having overheard the argument, about which he has said nothing) and Eva writes a letter to her mother. It is not clear whether she wants to patch things up or to gain another opportunity to pick her mother to pieces. The viewer is left to decide.

Perhaps the best scene in the film is the one that follows dinner the night of Charlotte's arrival in which Eva plays the piano, a Chopin prelude. She has worked hard on it and hopes to please her mother. Alas, her play is not so good. After all, the mother is a genius, the daughter only the daughter of a genius. Charlotte sits down next to Eva and takes the keys to gently demonstrate how the piece should be played. We see and feel at once the inadequacy of the daughter in her mother's eyes. It is a great scene filmed with a tight focus on the faces of the two women. When Eva turns to stare at her mother, who is, of course, playing brilliantly with great finesse and touch, the expression on Eva's face, held for many long seconds, is unforgettable.

Not to second guess the master, but I would have liked to have seen the entire movie played in this, a more subtle key than that which followed. However when it comes to dysfunction and disease, Ingmar Bergman is unrestrained.

Ingrid Bergman was nominated for an academy award for best actress in this, her last feature film (she had already been diagnosed with cancer), but lost out to Jane Fonda in *Coming Home* (1978).

I am a man and I admit to having seen this movie and I am the better for it___. Not!___.

It doesn't matter what my sexual orientation is. This is a movie definitely worth seeing___. Not!___.

A Kidnapping in the Family (1996) 6

Tracy Gold gives a balanced and believable performance

This ABC "Original," "based on actual events," the kind behind the mail flyers showing the missing child "last seen with" and "age progression by...," might be subtitled, "Grunge Girl versus Batso Mom." When Grandmother Dede, sporting a sadistic smile, played with witch-like frigidity by Kate Jackson, can't have absolute control over her grandchild and slightly slutty daughter, Sarah, played by Tracy Gold, she drums up some satanic child abuse accusations against the leather-wearing, cigarette-smoking, bar-hopping ingrate. When that fails, Batso Mom escalates...

Subplot: Sarah meets handsome, long-haired hunk Jack at art class. This guy is so good he might be called "the

saint who loves you." But Sarah disses him a little, and when he proves to be a good puppy dog, she throws him a little sex, and in the morning taunts him with the marriage question. He surprises by saying he thinks that would be okay. She never pretends to love him, but after he works seventy hours a week and buys the big house and puts up with her insensitive behavior and gets her pregnant, she learns to love him. Not only that, but she loses the leather and no longer waves a cigarette around. For unexplained reasons, it is Grandma Dede who sucks on the weed in the final reel.

This is no work of art, but more important in a MOW than artistic integrity or even artistic cleverness is how the movie plays according to the current politically-correct wisdom. Since most child-nappings are known to be by family members, this fits; and since virtually all "satanic abuse" charges are patently false, they got that right too. What they didn't get right is the casting and the sets. Everybody is too pretty to be real, and Sarah's apartment and then her house are like middle American dream homes when in reality they should reflect her low-rent, high school dropout, no-housework-for-me persona.

I am a man and I admit to having seen this movie and I am the better for it___. Not!___.

It doesn't matter what my sexual orientation is. This is a movie definitely worth seeing___. Not!___.

Manny & Lo (1996) 7

No men allowed

This is the sweetest film. It's definitely a "chick thing" with Manny and Lo and Elaine bonding around an infant to be (Lo's). No men are allowed in this paradise. One appears and he gets bopped over the head, gagged and hog-tied. This is a femme-family made on the run. Lo (Aleska Palladino) in her high teens runs away from a foster home with her younger sister, Manny (Scarlett Johansson). It's a Thelma and Louise crime spree made as a movie for children. Well, not quite. Turns out Lo's pregnant. She has been hiding this from 11-year-old Manny, who has the eye of Sherlock Holmes and is the brains of this team. They find a rather nice, used only during the ski season, cabin in the woods and hole up to await the stork. They spot Elaine (Mary Kay Place), a lonely spinster working in a baby clothes shop and kidnap her to help deliver the baby. Everybody, despite gruff exteriors, has a heart of gold, and togetherness and loving concern prevail. And what's wrong with that?

Nothing really. But I was thinking: this is the obverse of male war movies where none or few women appear, men doing their manly thing killing one another, women irrelevant. I think that's the key word here for director Lisa Krueger: in the reproductive game that is war by other means, men are irrelevant. Or almost so. In war it doesn't matter how many men are killed. As long as there are some left the population will quickly spring back. Kill the women, though, and you have a serious population problem. Manny and Lo and Elaine prove that you really don't need the male: his sperm will do, and that way you don't have to put up with his loutish behavior.

I think I got this right. Anyway, it's a cute movie.

I am a man and I admit to having seen this movie and I am the better for it___. Not!___.

It doesn't matter what my sexual orientation is. This is a movie definitely worth seeing___. Not!___.

Mermaids (1990) 7

Cute and funny

Cher plays a free-spirited, uninhibited and saucy mother of two. Charlotte (Winona Ryder) and Kate (Christina Ricci), who are about 15- and 8-years old respectively, are her daughters. Cher's behavior and appearance is an embarrassment to Charlotte who is trying to think "pure thoughts" on her way to becoming a nun. Ironically (considering Ryder's recent troubles) the part she plays has no interest in new clothes and even refuses new shoes, content with her old square boots that look like they were made in the former Soviet Union during the reign of Stalin. This is a nice (but increasingly familiar) switch on the mother who is embarrassed by her daughter's precocious sexuality, and Cher and Ryder play their parts well.

The story, from a novel by Patty Dann, begins with the trio moving into yet another town, this time somewhere in New England. They are always on the run, so to speak, because Cher is afraid of commitment or of staying around long enough to lose her heart to some guy. Enter predictably a man (Bob Hoskins) with the right stuff to win her over and a cute guy (Michael Schoeffing) to rearrange Charlotte's priorities. Director Richard Benjamin plays it as a romantic comedy cum coming of ager with wit and charm. Ryder is adorably cute as a conservative Christian miss goody two shoes who is always lecturing mom while Cher is voluptuous as the kind of woman who says yes, early and often, but underneath it all has strength and a kind of intuitive wisdom about herself and the people around her. Little Ricci really is the mermaid since she likes to practice holding her breath under water.

Part of the strength of the film is in the dialogue and the sharp repartee between Ryder and Cher. My favorite line is from Charlotte who is always dialoging with God. After seeing Schoeffing, who drives the school bus, and realizing what she is feeling, prays "Oh please God, don't make me fall in love and want to do disgusting things!"

I am a man and I admit to having seen this movie and I am the better for it___. Not!___.

It doesn't matter what my sexual orientation is. This is a movie definitely worth seeing___. Not!___.

Postcards from the Edge (1990) 9

One of the best Hollywood "insider" movies

The insider here telling all is Carrie Fisher (of Princess Leia fame), daughter of crooner Eddie Fisher and songstress Debbie Reynolds. Carrie adapted the screenplay from her best-selling novel of the same name in which she tells us what it's like (through her protagonist Suzanne Vale) to drug rehab Hollywood style. As a writer she has a sharp eye for the hypocrisy of movie land culture, dysfunctional relationships, and a splendid gift for cutting one-liners. Her dialogue made the book, and is the heart and soul of the movie. Here are a few examples:

"Instant gratification takes too long." (A takeoff on, and a reinvention of, the doper's "Too much is never enough.")

"...Endolphin rush." (Annette Bening corrects with, "You mean enDORphin rush.")

"I am so glad that I got sober now so I can be hyperconscious for this series of humiliations." (Suzanne Vale on her life without the deadening effect of drugs.)

Playing Carrie Fisher's alter ego is Meryl Streep, one of the great actresses of our time, while Shirley MacLaine, another outstanding star, plays the mother.

Streep is nearly flawless as always. She just demands the camera, and she has extraordinary talent. In the finale she sings a country and western song (from Carly Simon, by the way) and she does a great job. But she seems almost absurd in the police uni (playing a part in a movie within a movie). She doesn't seem to be achieving a comedic effect and then she does, just this side of the ridiculous. But, as usual with Steep, when the camera gets on her face, we believe her.

Particularly telling was the opening scene, nicely directed by Mike Nichols. I could see the familiar Palos Verdes cliffs and the shots of the ocean below. As I waited for the SoCal scene to unfold (actually it was supposed to be Mexico) I thought, "Gee, this looks like a cheap MOW set," and I continued to be fooled as Streep is hauled from customs by the customs officer and slapped. It is only when they go to "cut!" and the movie within the movie is exposed that I realized why the set looked cheap. (Because it was supposed to!)

Streep sold the scene within the scene, and irony, she was supposed to be doing a terrible job because of her character's drug dependency.

Somehow a scene with Meryl Streep in it never drags. Maybe she guides the direction and the editing. Thinking back (this is the first movie of hers I've seen in years) to *Sophie's Choice*, for example—1982 best actress Oscar and other honors—she hasn't changed much except that she's a little more relaxed, and while her concentration is still total, there is a touch less urgency in her performance. I've heard people complain about her mannerisms, that head to the side so that the corner of the mouth goes up, a little defensive smile, and then the flash of eyes, comes to mind, and some others; but compared with say, Dustin Hoffman or (horrors) John Wayne, she's as pure as Olivier.

I liked her timing on the "..And you weren't wearing any underwear" line (talking about the embarrassment of her drunk mother showing her legs at a party in the past).

Shirley MacLaine is, if anything, even better here as—dare I say it?—"Debbie Reynolds," one part alcoholic, one part stage mom, and one part frustrated actress jealous of her daughter's youth and talent, all parts overbearing. I recall Shirley MacLaine as a young woman. I can see her in *Can-Can* (1960) showing off those gorgeous legs (she shows her legs here too, but I cringed along with her daughter). She was pretty, healthy and busting her bodice as a young actress, and I liked her, but she was never more than a popular actress. Then came, *Terms of Endearment* (1983).

Shirley MacLaine is the classic example of the actress who really learned how to act as she got older, not unlike Betty Davis, who also got better as she aged. Shirley MacLaine (Warren Beatty's sister, one recalls) did get an academy award nomination for *The Apartment* (1960) with Jack Lemmon, but did not win.

I liked the hospital scene here at the end, mother and daughter renewing their bonds, Shirley without her wig, and no make-up. You know you've got a serious actress when she will let herself look naturally terrible for the camera!

This is a true tinsel town original in which Hollywood self-analyzes in public, to be ranked in the vicinity of *Sunset Boulevard* (1950) and *The Player* (1992)—in different ways, of course—for giving us a glimpse of what it's really like to live the dream. (Or is it a nightmare?)

I am a man and I admit to having seen this movie and I am the better for it___. Not!___.

It doesn't matter what my sexual orientation is. This is a movie definitely worth seeing___. Not!___.

Ghost River (La Vie Promise) (2002) 8
The flow of the ghost river

The story here is a little bit specious and even cloying at times. Isabelle Huppert plays Sylvia, a druggie prostitute who seems to care only about her booze and pills. She plies her trade on the streets of Nice. Her 14-year-old daughter, Laurence (Maud Forget) appears out of nowhere, having run away from her foster home. Sylvia tells her to get lost. She doesn't, and in the next scene, trying to protect her mother from a couple of pimps who are starting to beat her up for some money, the 14-year-old somehow stabs one of them. The other runs out the door. The stabbed man is dead, and mother and daughter are on the run as in a Hollywood on the lam movie.

I don't think I need to tell the reader that mom is going to find the love she really feels for her daughter in addition to finding her own heart, and so I won't, because it isn't that simple. The story though is rather ordinary and predictable and is told with a number of loose ends just left lying about, not the least of which is the dead man.

No matter however because:

(1) Isabelle Huppert is brilliant and very convincing as a low-class, trashy kind of person who lies almost habitually, even when she doesn't need to, a person lacking social skills or really any kind of skill. Her hair is too too blonde and she dresses like a tramp.

But it is amazing how comfortable Huppert looks in the role. Again I am very much impressed with her ability. I wonder if there is a more talented actress working anywhere in the world today. She is almost obsessive in the way she becomes the characters she plays. I've seen her in half a dozen films and in everyone she was a distinctly different person.

(2) The movie is beautifully shot with arresting scenes of earth and sky, unlike anything one usually sees in a domestic French movie.

(3) The music, some of it American country and western, some of it classical, was wonderfully chosen and coordinated with the story of the film in a way that enhances our appreciation. That is what is usually attempted of course. The idea being that music should help to trigger our response; but often the attempt is only halfhearted or too obviously directive. Here the music helps to bring the film to life.

(4) The story is uplifting and redemptive.

One more thing: the title in English, The Promise Life, is not a good translation of what is intended by the French, *La Vie Promise*. Better would be "The Promised Life," although that would be inaccurate. Also unsatisfactory would be "The Life of Promise." What I like is the title sometimes given to the film, "Ghost River." There is a beautiful line in the film that refers to "The flow of the ghost river" that I think somehow illustrates the life Sylvia has lead.

By all means see this beautiful if somewhat sentimental film for Isabelle Huppert, one of the great stars of the modern cinema.

I am a man and I admit to having seen this movie and I am the better for it___. Not!___.

It doesn't matter what my sexual orientation is. This is a movie definitely worth seeing___. Not!___.

II

Testosterone-Free Zone

You know how there are movies, especially war movies, in which no women appear, as though the business at hand is too important to include any women? Well, here are a few movies almost completely without men, or if there are men, they are inconsequential.

8 Women (2002) 7

Farcical who done it with chanson

This farcical "who done it" is funny, absurd, campish, and silly all at the same time. Starring a kind of premiere selection of leading ladies of the French cinema, *8 femmes* reminds me of similar tongue-in-cheek "who done its" such as Agatha Christie's *Ten Little Indians* and especially Neil Simon's *Murder by Death*.

Adapted from the play by Robert Thomas, which accounts for the stage play feel to the production, this one begins—as a proper murder mystery might—with a murder in a well-appointed house out in the country. Somehow everyone is stranded there and of course under suspicion. While Neil Simon made fun of detectives in *Murder by Death*, and Agatha Christie made fun of murder, period, here the fun is on the players themselves. What follows, as all point fingers away from themselves, is a whole lot of dirty laundry and closet skeletons being tossed about.

The scandalous revelations, including interracial lesbianism, same- and heterosexual incest, etc., are particularly ironic since the film is set in the staid fifties. (Note Suzon's pink/orange pony skirt.) To quote a line from the film, "it's a sad family affair" played for laughs with a kind of absurdist delight. Yet, there is no nudity or anything resembling sexual titillation anywhere in the film. Strange.

In another sense this is a celebration of some of the French cinema's leading ladies who get to strut their stuff and play it for laughs.

Catherine Deneuve heads the cast as Gaby the wife of the murdered. She looks stately, beautiful and more than a bit spoiled. Danielle Darrieux at 85 steals a few scenes as the mother, Mamy. Isabelle Huppert makes herself into a neurotic, dotty old maid named Augustine while Emmanuelle Beart plays Louise, the sexy maid. Fanny Ardant is Pierrette, Gaby's scandalous sister-in-law. The cast takes turns doing lightweight song and dance numbers which tends to fluff out the production in a sweet fifties-ish way. In a kind of gender joke, no men appear in the movie, although we do see the back of Marcel (Gaby's husband) a couple of times.

You will not be able to guess who done it, but I will not tell you why.
See this for Danielle Darrieux, one the grande dames of the French cinema whose film credits go back to 1931—yes, 1931. She has a lot of fun in a juicy part.

I am a man and I admit to having seen this movie and I am the better for it___. Not!___.

It doesn't matter what my sexual orientation is. This is a movie definitely worth seeing___. Not!___.

Story of Women (Une affaire de femmes) (1988) 10

Abortion in Nazi-occupied France

Claude Chabrol's stark and unsentimental masterpiece about the last woman to be executed in France—she was guillotined for performing abortions in Nazi-occupied France during World War II—forces us to see a side of war not often depicted. What does a woman with two little children do when her country is occupied by the brute forces of the enemy? How is she to find enough to eat, to buy the increasingly scarce and costly necessities of life? How is she to find joy in life? Women often turn to prostitution during such times, but Maire Latour does not. Instead she aborts the foetuses of the prostitutes and of other women impregnated, often by the Nazis. In a sense this is her "resistence." However she prospers and takes up with a Nazi collaborator. In the process she reduces her husband to frustration and humiliation.

Isabelle Huppert as Marie Latour is mesmerizing in a role that allows her talent full latitude. She is clear-headed and sly as a business woman, warm and ordinary as a mother, cold and brutal as a wife, childish and careless as an adulteress, resourceful and fearless as an abortionist, and unrepentant as she awaits the executioner (foreshadowed, by the way, by her son, who wants to be an executioner when he grows up). Francois Cluzet plays her husband Paul, and he is also very good, especially at rousing our pity. Chabrol makes it clear that both Marie and Paul are victims, not only of war, but of their divergent natures. Paul wants the love of Marie, but she wants only a man that represents success and power, a man who is clean-shaven, not the menial worker that he is. Marie Trintignant is interesting and convincing as a prostitute who becomes Marie Latour's friend and business associate.

While abortion is indeed "Une affaire de femmes" this film is about much more than that. No doubt the title is there to emphasize Chabrol's point that men really do not (did not then, and do not now) really understand abortion and why it is sometimes a horrible and abject necessity. When Marie is taken to Paris for a show trial she exclaims to a woman in jail with her, referring to the court that will pass judgment on her, "It's all men...how could men understand?" We can see that men really can't, and that precisely is what this movie is all about: showing us just how horrible pregnancy can be under the circumstances of enemy occupation.

A secondary story here, not quite a subplot, is Paul's story. What does a man do when he and his children are dependent on a woman who doesn't love him, a woman who rejects him and even goes so far as to arrange for the cleaning woman to sleep with him? It is not only Marie who humiliates him, but it is the defeat of his country, the easy surrender to the Nazis that has so reduced him. This is made clear in a scene late in the film between two lawyers who voice their shame as Frenchmen in a time of defeat.

What Paul does is not pretty (and I won't reveal it here), but so great is the provocation that one understands his behavior and can forgive him.

I am a man and I admit to having seen this movie and I am the better for it___. Not!___.

It doesn't matter what my sexual orientation is. This is a movie definitely worth seeing___. Not!___.

The Business of Strangers (2001) 8

Edgy, daring, unconventional

Near the beginning of this imaginative film when Paula Murphy (20-year-old Julia Stiles) and Julie Styron (Stockard Channing) meet in earnest, Paula tells Julie

what she really does in life: "I'm a writer," she says. I write short stories about things that I experience. Non-fiction. "Fiction is too stupid, too neat. I like the sloppiness of real life." What we don't know at the time is that Paula is about to improvise just such a tale involving Julie, a tale that challenges the middle-aged executive's lifestyle and her assumptions about herself and inspires her to do things she wouldn't normally do.

This is the "business of strangers." And this is the story within the story. Paula is the diabolical kind of person who is dedicated to introducing people to themselves so that she can watch them twist, a privileged, under-achieving Ivy League girl with machinations. Julie is a community college workaholic who never had time for a family, or love, or self-discovery, a lonely woman whose life is a parade of sterile hotel rooms, anonymous strangers, alcohol and pills. Although the story drags in a little in spots, the overall effect is edgy and fascinating, and the contrast between the principals keeps us wondering who is going to come out on top.

The action really begins when Julie, in an expansive mood with some booze and her promotion to CEO, shows some interest in the girl she just fired for being late to a presentation. It's not clear what sort of interest that is. Julie responds as a spider coaxing a fly into the web, but it's not clear what she's up to. They go to the pool and play around, get on the treadmills at the gym and run. They go back to Julie's suite and drink some more.

At this point I'm afraid that the film will deteriorate into a politically correct cliché of some kind, or a lesbian wish-fulfillment debacle, without anything really happening. Enter (or actually re-enter) Nick Harris (Fred Weller) who, Paula has confided to Julie, raped her best friend when they were undergraduates in Boston. This excites Julie's loathing and so the two women play out an improvised and drunken revenge scenario that is a bit over the top, but psychologically correct.

After some intense emotional interaction, the film resolves surprisingly and rather neatly, allowing us to see that Paula has indeed spun out a tale whose moral might be, "watch out for young foxes." The final scene in the airport emphasizes this, with Julie and Nick sheepishly sorting out last night's bizarre debauchery while trying to maintain their dignity, with Paula poised brazenly in plain sight wearing earphones, a smug silhouette in the distance.

Patrick Stettner wrote the script, which, judging from the series of stationary settings and the limited cast, I suspect was originally a stage play. He also directed in a business-like manner, getting a saucy and smirk-laden performance from Stiles, whose originality and talent is obvious, and a steady and believable one from veteran Channing. Incidentally, Channing is a Harvard graduate who is perhaps best known for her performance as Betty Rizzo in *Grease* (1978) playing a teenager when she was

32-years-old! Here she braves some close camera work that starkly reveals the 57-year-old actress beneath the makeup. Yet, as always, Stockard Channing pleases us.

But see this for Julia Stiles, a thoroughly professional player, whose arrogant, sneering, and edgy style add spice to, and partially disguise, her youthful mastery of the fine art of acting.

I am a man and I admit to having seen this movie and I am the better for it___. Not!___.

It doesn't matter what my sexual orientation is. This is a movie definitely worth seeing___. Not!___.

A Judgment in Stone *(La Cérémonie)* (1995) 9

Stark, naturalistic shocker, brilliantly presented

In this character study of two hateful middle-aged women (not so middle-aged in the movie, however, as in the novel by Ruth Rendell) we are made to fathom the bad that may befall the good.

Claude Chabrol's direction is clean, crisp and uncluttered—which isn't always the case, witness his *Madame Bovary* (1991), which is a bit too leisurely and *L'Enfer* (1993) which muddles a whole lot. Maybe it's the editing. Anyway this is more like his quietly brilliant *Une affaire de femmes* (1988) with a fine script and striking performances by Sandrine Bonnaire and Isabelle Huppert, handsomely supported by Jacqueline Bisset, Jean Pierre Cassel and the very pretty Virginie Ledoyen.

Bonnaire plays Sophie, an intense taciturn woman harboring dark secrets, whom the Leliévres have hired to cook and keep house at their country home. Bisset is Catherine Leliévre and Cassel her husband. They exist in bourgeois heaven avec matrimonial bliss with two teenagers, a family so closely knit and so charmingly together that they watch a two-part production of Mozart's *Don Giovanni* on TV, just the four of them cosily on the couch.

Well, this sort of unobtainable happiness doesn't sit well with Jeanne (Huppert) who is a lowly postal clerk living alone whose past includes the (accidental?) killing of her four-year-old daughter. Jeanne takes a fancy to the Leliévre's strange new maid with the idea of showing her something besides work. They strike up a fateful friendship that we know is leading to something horrible.

Huppert is as good as I've seen her, which is very good indeed. She is particularly striking here in an uncharacteristic role as a spiteful, working class woman with a heart of vengeance against anybody better off than she is. There is just a touch of sly irony in her performance suggesting that she is having a particularly good time playing the nasty. Bonnaire's stark performance as the unbalanced and humorless, reclusive Sophie will remain

etched in your brain. Apart they are like inert, harmless chemicals. Together they catalyze one another and become brazen and explosive.

The story, filled with little foreshadowing of the tragedy to come, gilds the lily of our *tristesse* by making the Leliévres so very, very nice. We are reminded of the violent hatred by the proletariat toward the privileged classes, in this case acted out by two loonies against an innocent, but representative family, echoing not only the Russian Revolution but even more so the French Revolution, now two hundred years old.

What I am trying to figure out why this is called *La Cérémonie*. Maybe it is a ceremony of execution.

I am a man and I admit to having seen this movie and I am the better for it___. Not!___.

It doesn't matter what my sexual orientation is. This is a movie definitely worth seeing___. Not!___.

High Art (1998) 9

Lesbo druggies exposed!

Just kidding. Actually this is very good film whose only fault is a tendency to take itself a little too seriously at times.

Ally Sheedy plays Lucy, a lesbian photographer with a serious drug problem, but an even more serious inability to cope with the rapacious New York City commercial art scene. Lucy struts and poses her cocaine-trim limbs while her mind stoops to degeneracy. She is controlled by the deep-throated German has-been actress, Greta (Patricia Clarkson) her long-time lover, and by her own falling-down habits. The mercantile world is too much for her pure artist's nature, and so she forsakes it for the haze...

Radha Mitchell plays Syd, an assistant editor at *Frame*, a glitzy photo art mag, who is seduced by Lucy and by her own need to succeed. Gabriel Mann plays James, her boyfriend, who can see the handwriting on the wall, and splits.

Sheedy is outstanding and Mitchell is very good, but what makes this an intriguing and worth-while film is the uncompromising eye of Director Lisa Cholodenko, who depicts the sad, dreary NYC "high art" drug scene without a trace of sentimentality or any hidden sexist agenda. True, the women in the film are vastly more interesting than the men, who are merely passive appendages, of little notice. But that is because those in focus—Lucy, Syd and Greta—are strong people who shape their own lives, for better or for worse. Notice that the hangers-on, on the couch, male or female, are shallow and empty regardless of sex.

The lesbian sexuality displayed seemed authentic but somehow limited—although, how would I know? Maybe it's the code. The dependency passing for love between Lucy and Greta also struck me as real. Syd's loss of innocence was the main point, however, and it was not her sexual seduction that did it, but her discovery of her own very complex nature. The look on the face of the receptionist reading Dostoyevski after Syd appeared on the cover of the magazine, her hungry interest and then Syd's realization of being looked at in a different way, was just a marvelous piece of cinema incisively rendered.

I am a man and I admit to having seen this movie and I am the better for it___. Not!___.

It doesn't matter what my sexual orientation is. This is a movie definitely worth seeing___. Not!___.

Persona (1966) 10

Beyond Interpretation

Someone who has read a biography of Ingmar Bergman would probably be able to offer an intelligent interpretation of this very personal film by the great Swedish director. Since it stars his two most famous protégés, Bibi Andersson and Liv Ullmann, and is an intense focus on their faces as though to look into their souls, and further since during the film their personas merge as one—given all this, perhaps it could be speculated that Bergman is suggesting that his perfect love would be a composite of the two. Certainly part of the erotic power of this stunningly filmed masterwork (black and white cinematography by the gifted Sven Nykvist) is the evocative display of the two Swedish actresses, who were respectively, 30- and 26-years-old, when the film was made. It is curious however that Bergman is very deliberate in downplaying their sexuality. They are never coquettish, nor openly sexual. Very little skin is exposed and that only incidentally. It is their differing power as actresses that is explored with some, no doubt, deliberate and unavoidable revelation of their real life personalities.

I was particularly impressed with Bibi Andersson's performance. She plays, Alma, a young and naive nurse who is called upon to help rehabilitate Liv Ullmann's Elisabeth Vogler, an actress who suddenly stopped talking. Andersson has a beautiful and expressive voice that should be heard, so avoid a dubbed version (if it exists). It is true that the subtitles are occasionally ungrammatical and full of typos (and at one point a misleading term is used to avoid a gross sexual expression), but it doesn't matter because everything is very clear; indeed one could view this without the subtitles and without knowing Swedish and still get a fair idea of what is going on. Liv Ullmann is also brilliant in a part that has her on camera for most of the film but without a single speaking line! Nurse Alma does all the talking and something curious happens. She becomes the "patient," spilling out

the intimate details of her life while Elisabeth becomes in a sense the (superior) shrink, and a "transference" takes place. This is no doubt a Bergman joke (he was no fan of psychotherapy), but it is also a statement about the power of silence. Elisabeth stopped speaking during a performance of the Greek tragedy Electra, and of course we have all heard of the Electra Complex, the female equivalent of the Oedipus Complex so beloved of psychoanalytic theory. However what Bergman's point here is, I have no idea. I do know that in the last two Bergman films I have viewed, this and *Autumn Sonata* (1978) with Ingrid Bergman as a concert pianist, the star is a selfish woman who does not love her children. Here, we have Alma tearing into Elisabeth with the accusation that she hates her son and wishes he was dead. Since Ingmar Bergman both wrote and directed this film, one might reasonably ask what this has to do with the psyche of the master. The fact that an older man makes love to both women is also grist for the mill of an autobiographical interpretation.

However, I am Against Interpretation in this case (although clearly a film like this cries out for it) and more in favor of experience. A work of art can always be interpreted and sometimes should, but always it is essential to first experience the work. If I ever see this film again, and after reading up on the life and loves Ingmar Bergman, perhaps I will look for what *Persona* says about him. Meanwhile, I am content to observe that this is an original work of art, and as always with Bergman, an emotionally draining experience.

I am a man and I admit to having seen this movie and I am the better for it___. Not!___.

It doesn't matter what my sexual orientation is. This is a movie definitely worth seeing___. Not!___.

Raise the Red Lantern (1991) 10

Brutal politics in a marriage of concubines

Raise the Red Lantern is one of the most extraordinarily beautiful movies I have ever seen. The sets are exquisite tableaux carefully arranged, decorated and framed, and then shot from an attractive angle. The scene as they drag the third mistress, kicking and screaming to the tower of death, with the snow falling so peacefully onto the rooftops, was chilling in its effect. The startling blaze of color, light and detail within the houses set against the drab simplicity of the courtyards, continually provided a contrast between life within the protection and at the favor of the master, and life without. This dichotomy is symbolized in the vibrant red lamps and the somber blue hue of the lamps when they are covered. In this manner, the mistresses are controlled. I was also struck by the sonorous beauty of the accompanying Chinese music.

But more compelling than the beauty of the film is the story Director Zhang Yimou tells, a tale of paternity and imperious privilege set in early twentieth century China. He begins with the newly arrived fourth mistress, 19-year-old Songlian, a university student who, because of the death of her father, is forced to quit school. She chooses to marry a man of wealth. She is warned by her stepmother that she will be a concubine. She replies, isn't that our fate? Her cynicism and then her robust energy in seeking her ascendancy over the other sisters engages us and we identify with her struggle.

What is extraordinary about Zhang's direction is how easily and naturally the personalities of the characters are revealed. The first mistress ("big sister") is too old to be of any sexual interest to the master, yet she is the mother of the eldest son. The second mistress, who has given the master only a daughter, still dreams of having a son. Her devious schemes and plots are hidden by smiles and fake good will toward her sisters. The third mistress, an opera singer still vibrant and beautiful (in a fascinating performance by the intriguing Caifei He), uses her allure in vying for the master's attention. Songlian, in spite of herself, finds herself caught up in the competition with the others.

Gong Li, who plays Songlian, is very beautiful with a strength of character that one quite naturally admires. She has the gift, as does, for example, Julia Roberts, of being able to express a wide range of emotion with just a glance of her very expressive face.

Serving as a foil to the mistresses, and perhaps as the most poignant victim of the concubine system, is the servant girl Yan'er, played with a compelling veracity by Kong Lin. She is occasionally (how shall I say this for Amazon?) "touched," to use Songlian's term, by the master, and so she dreamed of being the fourth mistress. But when the fourth mistress arrives, her dreams are shattered, and in her jealousy she hates Songlian and plots against her. One of the most memorable scenes in the movie is when Songlian, thinking Yan'er has stolen her flute, forces open the servant girl's room and finds it flooded with.... Well, you should see.

Note well that the master is only hazily observed. He is a personage, a man of wealth. That is enough to know about him. He is as interchangeable as the harem masters on a beach of elephant seals. But because he has wealth, he can engage concubines who must compete with one another through him to find their station in life. One gets a sense of what it might be like in the harem system practiced by gorillas and the sheiks and warlords of old. One pleases the master not because one loves the master (although one does of course because humans tend to love their masters) but because in pleasing the master one rises above the others. Thus the triumphant call, "Light the lanterns in the third house!"

Most people no doubt lament the life of the mistresses. Yet women in poor places may wish such a life upon themselves. But concubines are just prostitutes, really, one might say, trapped by a system of male privilege. But I would remind those who see only that, that for every wife the "master" has, that is one wife another man will not have. The system does NOT favor males. It favors wealth and privilege. In such a system there are many men without wives, fomenting unrest, which is why modern states forbid polygamy. What does a man do with the capital he accumulates or inherits? If the system allows, he spends it on women and the assurance of his paternity. And why is that possible? Because many women—Songlian is our example—would rather be the fourth wife of a rich man than the first and only wife of a poor man. Many women would rather be used by a man of wealth than rule the household of a nerd. This is the way humans are, and any sexist interpretation of this movie misses this truth.

The real horror depicted here, though, is in the brutality used to maintain the system, not in the polygamy itself. The women who follow the rules and beget the master's children, especially if they are sons, enjoy a pampered and secure existence Those who do not are dealt with severely, branded as mad, or even murdered. Note the similar experience of the wives of Henry VIII, for example, within the English system of serial monogamy.

This is a great movie, like a timeless novel fully realized, directed by a visual genius, from a script of great psychological power. Don't miss this one. It's one of the best ever made.

I am a man and I admit to having seen this movie and I am the better for it___. Not!___.

It doesn't matter what my sexual orientation is. This is a movie definitely worth seeing___. Not!___.

III

Movies to Watch While He's Out Playing Poker

or

Yes, this IS a chick flick, and yes, I'm eating chocolate chip cookie dough ice cream, and would you please shut up so I can watch this.

Or while he's watching football in the other room, or baseball or basketball or wrestling. (Yes, you know he actually watches wrestling when you're not around.) Or maybe he's on a weekend fishing trip. If so here are some he'll never want to watch with you. Indulge, some of these are actually pretty good.

A Lot Like Love (2005) 6

Cute and semi-smart

The time-honored Hollywood formula for romantic comedies gets a nice work out here. First you have to have "Boy meets girl, cute." Well, it's hard to get cuter than the guy starts to walk out of the bathroom at thirty-seven thousand feet and gets shoved right back in by the girl who locks the door behind her and initiates him into the mile-high club. (Considering that it was Amanda Peet doing the shoving, how lucky can a guy get?)

Next you've got to have kinky and cute—either the guy or the girl. Amanda Peet as Emily is clearly cute and (ahem, kinky), while Ashton Kutcher, the ditzy but adorable heartthrob of TV's "That Seventies Show," plays it mostly straight as still-living-at-home Oliver Martin. It seems that she was just on the rebound as she rushed him into the mile-high club, so it didn't mean a thing. She was just proving to herself that she is still attractive. And so, dude, good-bye.

Yes, you've got to have complications, lots of them, to keep the lovers apart until the final reel. Shakespeare had 'em. Katharine Hepburn and Spencer Tracy had 'em, Audrey Hepburn had 'em, and God knows Meg Ryan and various beaux had 'em galore. Here Emily really doesn't see Oliver as quite the alpha male she had in mind, but three years later when she finds herself dumped and without a date for New Year's Eve she comes across his phone number (he wanted her to call him in six years to find out that he was a great success with a beautiful wife, etc., and no longer living at home). So she calls and asks him out.

Well, enough about the specifics of the plot. It doesn't matter. The plot is just a way to throw them together so that they find out after many mishaps, heartbreaks, misadventures and just plain old-fashioned boy and girl fun that they are truly in love. After all wasn't it the Bard who said that "The course of true love never did run smooth"? (from A Midsummer-Night's Dream)

Although I am a little (just a little) too old for this movie, I did find it enjoyable. Peet is as pretty as pretty has any right to be, and tall, handsome Kutcher has an infectious, likable quality about him, so even though the movie was not as clever or as smart as some romantic comedies, it was nonetheless a step above eye candy, and a nice diversion for a dateless Saturday night—or actually, I think it would work even better as a first-date kind of movie or even a been-married-for-five-years movie for the both of you. But beware guys, this IS a chick flick.

I am a man and I admit to having seen this movie and I am the better for it___. Not!___.
It doesn't matter what my sexual orientation is. This is a movie definitely worth seeing___. Not!___.

Antonia's Line (1995) 8

Bring a couple of hankies

This is an incredibly seductive movie with a strong sense of the spirit of Demeter and Dionysus throughout. There's no Hollywood glamour here. Instead we have an unabashed celebration of life ("This is the only dance we dance") in which love, community and simple hard work prevail. The simple are seen as the equal of the gifted, and everybody (except for rapists and hypocrites) are appreciated for their strengths and forgiven their faults. Intellectualism is seen as quaint and unsocial (as in the person of Crooked Finger) possibly leading to a morbid cynicism. And brain power (as in the person of the prodigy Therese) is just another talent, like being able to laugh or to bale hay or to have lots of children.

This is the Dionysian view of life that doesn't allow for Apollo, and there's a lot to be said for it. But I couldn't help but reflect that during the time span depicted in this movie—five generations in Holland during the twentieth century—Europe experienced some of the most horrific events known to humankind, two world wars, genocide, concentration camps, poison gas, fire bombings, political repression, and the death of millions of people. But perhaps that is director Marleen Gorris's point, to see life at its most elemental, locally and without the horror of war and the delusions of generals and politicians.

What's not to like about that? Well, not to rain on anyone's love-fest, but we have vigilante justice here and a murder, seemingly justified and certainly agreeable to the audience since the victim was a brutal rapist. Men are not exactly banished, but they are put in their place, serving or (literally) servicing women. What is banished is orthodox religiosity in the form of a hypocritical cleric who (with his disciples, we are told) goes to town and becomes a social worker (!).

This is also an ode to feminism and a deliberate tearjerker that manipulates the emotions of the audience. Yet, somehow Gorris, who also wrote the script, manages not to offend my sensitivities. I think it is because the movie amounts to a very effective sermon against prejudice of any kind, and because of the gentle humanity of her tale.

You'll forgive me, however, if I say that my favorite part was the handstand! It was just perfect.

I am a man and I admit to having seen this movie and I am the better for it___. Not!___.

It doesn't matter what my sexual orientation is. This is a movie definitely worth seeing___. Not!___.

Bridget Jones's Diary (2001) 8

Corny but cute

What really makes this movie stand out from a long list of other working girl fantasies is the familiar but one-of-a-kind personality of the irrepressible Bridget Jones. Created by novelist Helen Fielding, who also wrote the script, and brought to life by the talented and zany Renée Zellweger, Bridget Jones is a 32-year-old pleasingly plump London working girl, a "...verbally incontinent spinster who...dresses like her mother" (to quote Colin Firth's character, Mark Darcy). She is also clumsy, the kind of girl who might spill sauce on her blouse, a little overweight, smokes, drinks too much and sometimes says what she thinks without consulting her brain. She is also very good at improvising on the spot, a talent that charms not only the two leading men, Hugh Grant and Colin Firth, who vie for her affection, but also the five o'clock news audience who like her bum and knickers just fine.

Director Sharon Maguire, in her first outing, combines Brit witticisms, slapstick pratfalls, raunchy, sharp and realistic dialogue, and a blatant but inoffensive senti-mentality into a romantic comedy that surely has Nora Ephron and Julia Roberts paying close attention. She keeps us guessing about who will get the girl (and who really *deserves* the girl) with the usual misdirections and misunderstandings characteristic of the genre. There's a little dead time about half way in, and the uncertainty about whether Bridget wants Hugh Grant or Colin Firth is milked a bit overmuch, otherwise this is nicely paced entertainment sure to chase away a blue afternoon.

Hugh Grant and Colin Firth are both very good, and Gemma Jones as Bridget's mother is a charming, dotty sight to see. Bridget's friends are funny as a kind of foil to the tired glamor of Yank TV's "Friends." And there's a darling "home movie" sequence during the closing credits purporting to recall Bridget at four and Mark Darcy at eight, that retrospectively and adorably frames the movie.

Should a "CHICK FLICK ALERT" be declared here? No doubt, but thanks to a warm, bubbly, funny and decidedly unprudish and unaffected (and I must say, somewhat daring) performance by Zellweger, we'll ignore it because we "like her just the way she is."

I am a man and I admit to having seen this movie and I am the better for it___. Not!___.

It doesn't matter what my sexual orientation is. This is a movie definitely worth seeing___. Not!___.

Como Agua Para Chocolate (1992) 6

Do not watch this on an empty stomach

This is a Mexican romance novel set in the early part of this century masquerading as a naturalistic melodrama with supernatural overtones, penned by director Alfonso Arau's wife, Laura Esquivel. We can see from the frequent narrative voice overs that her novel was beautifully, if idiotically, written. Although "Chocolate" strains credulity at times and offends my sensibilities, it provides moments of pleasant diversion. I am reminded of Dickens, somehow. I think it is because the mother is so bad, and so many years pass before she gets her comeuppance, which is the way Dickens used to do it. She is truly a mommy from hell. She even comes back to haunt her poor last-born daughter.

Tita, the youngest daughter, played sympathetically by Lumi Cavazos, is a sort of Cinderella to her two older sisters and her evil mother. She has to work in the kitchen and is constantly abused by her mother while forbidden to marry since it is a family tradition that she must take care of her mother in her old age. Consequently, her true love, Pedro, a wooden pretty boy, is given to her sister instead of her. He goes along with this since it allows him to be close to Tita. One gets the sense that Pedro figures he's getting two for the price of one, although initially he acts out a celibate role, the better to whet the appetite, I suppose.

The scene where the oldest daughter is carried off by a swashbuckling rebel, butt naked on his horse, reveals the romance novel heart of the movie. Further swells the fancy of the feminine heart when she returns years later as a revolutionary general (!) in tweed jacket wearing bandoliers of bullets, still beloved by her handsome abductor.

As is the rule in women's POV fairy tales, the men in this movie are without personality: they just fill the roles as heroes, lovers and villains. What counts is the interaction between the women and the fulfillment of romantic notions. Nonetheless, there are a number of nice touches, especially the sumptuous feasts including such delectables as baked quail with rose petal sauce, chillis with walnuts, and corn fritters with syrup.

I am a man and I admit to having seen this movie and I am the better for it____. Not!____.

It doesn't matter what my sexual orientation is. This is a movie definitely worth seeing____. Not!____.

Hanging Up (2000) 8

Meg is adorable

Of course. But she is particularly adorable here mainly because she is so sweet to her poor old dad (Walter Matthau) and is so good and long-suffering compared to her sisters Diane Keaton (self-obsessed tycoon, Georgia) and Lisa Kudrow (irresponsible soap actress, Maddy).

Yes, this is a Nora Ephron chick flick, and yes it takes dead aim at a female audience and hits the bull's-eye; however the combination of realistic family dynamics and the all too true characterizations lift this above—quite a bit above—the usual exploitation fare. Personally I think this is superior to the Ephron/Meg Ryan/Tom Hanks hits, *You've Got Mail* (1998) and *Sleepless in Seattle* (1993). There is, as part of the plot, this curious thing that Ephron has with communications media. In *You've Got Mail* (a remake, by the way, of *Shop Around the Corner* (1940) starring James Stewart and Margaret Sullivan) it was the Internet that figured in. In *Sleepless in Seattle*, it was the radio. Here it's the telephone. Hence the title, "Hanging Up."

[Imagined dialogue from real life:
Delia Ephron: (Staring incredulously at her cell phone in hand): Geez, everybody's always hanging up on me!

Cut to:

Nora Ephron (hanging up the phone; speaking aloud to herself): You know, that would make a great premise for a movie: Plucky, earnest younger sister always getting hung up on! Ha! (Grabs personal organizer.) Make a note...]

Matthau as the senile old rake of a dad behaving badly is funny and lovably pathetic; Kudrow is annoying as usual (= "good casting"), and Keaton is adequate as the "thinks only of herself and her career" magazine publisher. (The name of her new fashion 'zine is "Georgia." Enough said.) But the star here is Meg Ryan, make no mistake about that. Director Diane Keaton dresses her oh so cute and has her do gumby kind of stuff and be vulnerable and caring and keeps the camera on that pixie face as much as possible. (There are a couple of shots of her in an agreeably tight white tank-top style blouse. But never mind.) As the sweet, earnest, slightly ditzy Eve, Meg Ryan, looking younger than springtime (although she was 38—it's amazing how she looks younger at 38 than she did at say, 32, when she made *Sleepless*), will steal your heart. If you like her you will love this cute movie about the trials and tribulations of some of America's well-to-do ladies even if you're a 18-year-old male stoner with rings through your nose.

Yes Diane Keaton directed this, not Nora Ephron, who produced and co-wrote the script with her sister Delia Ephron, and I have to say Keaton did an excellent job and ought to take a spin as a director more often. Of course the movie is distinctly an Ephron affair. Nora's influence is obvious, and it is no coincidence that Henry Ephron had, like King Lear, three daughters who undoubtedly loved him well but with less than equal fervor. (The third Ephron sister is Amy.) So the family dynamics and dysfunctions are to some extent fictionalized bits from the life of the Ephron clan. I wonder which sister is Meg? Clearly Georgia is Nora.

But enough of the "biographical fallacy." It doesn't matter one whit about where the material came from. The fact remains this is a highly entertaining movie. Besides, believe it or believe it not, for those who want to know more, there is a TV documentary entitled *The Making of "Hanging Up"* (2000) in which Ryan, Keaton and Kudrow appear. Two of the three Ephron sisters also get acting credits. (I wonder what the story is with Amy? Hmm... I guess Maddy is Amy.)

But see this for Meg Ryan (anagram of her screen name: "Germany"), one of the top stars of our time and always a delight to watch. And did you know that there's a PBS-style documentary of her riding elephants in southeast Asia? Yes, and having fun doing it. Julia Roberts, take that.

I am a man and I admit to having seen this movie and I am the better for it____. Not!____.

It doesn't matter what my sexual orientation is. This is a movie definitely worth seeing____. Not!____.

How to Make an American Quilt (1995) 7

Women as Darwinian animals?

This is a syrupy orgy of social and sexual need with a strong message and some redeeming artistic value, beautifully photographed. It's sad to see Jean Simmons, who was once a fine actress as well as an intriguing, voluptuous beauty, reduced to this. Ditto for the other Grand Dames here who fret about and wallow in their past loves while spying lustily on the loves of others.

I saw this to study Winona Ryder's face. She plays Finn Dodd, a Berkeley grad student writing her thesis on the lives of the quilt makers while debating a marriage proposal. Sometimes she seems to be posing, and at other times I find her as subtle and as natural as a great actress. As beautiful as she is, I found myself wondering if her interpretation of a selfish and duplicitous young woman was more a projection of her own true heart than a demonstration of any acting skill. She certainly doesn't give the slightest hint that she cares about the loves and heartaches of the quilt makers: she seems totally absorbed in present titillations and in the working out of the pre-matrimonial angst. But it may be that *that* is the reality of who her character is, and if so Ryder plays her to a perfect fit.

Totally captivating is the scene in the orange grove where the 26-year-old Finn gets laid by mesomorphic Leon who provokes her to a swooning imitation of a Victorian maiden being touched for the first time. (Winona's face is VERY sexy.)

In a sense the Darwinian nature of the human animals depicted here is correct, and on that level director Jocelyn Moorehouse is having a good laugh on all of us. Her assertion is that what humans really practice is "serial monogamy," an insight from evolutionary psychology increasingly accepted these days. Her answer to the vexing question, "Can men and women be friends?" is clearly no. From a woman's point of view—and this film is clearly from a woman's POV—I suspect she is correct.

The quilt symbolizes the human institutions and the social and political bonding that enable women to collar their animal nature and live in harmony with others.

Memorable are the oaks and the orange groves and the rolling hills of the California countryside; a black crow that hops; a wind devil that tumbles a white plastic chair and blows the pages of Finn's thesis out the door; and an old Ann Bancroft stoned on marijuana and cognac.

I am a man and I admit to having seen this movie and I am the better for it___. Not!___.

It doesn't matter what my sexual orientation is. This is a movie definitely worth seeing___. Not!___.

Moscow Does Not Believe in Tears (1979) 10

What a great movie!

This is one of the most captivating love stories I've ever seen on film. It starts with a young woman (Katya, played by Vera Alentova) reporting to her Worker's Dormitory friends that she has flunked by two points the exam to get into university. It ends with the most incredible sweetness of life.

It is like a French film done by a Russian company (which is what it is). The Moscow we see that does not believe in tears does believe in love, and it is not a Moscow of politics, although some people do call one another "comrade." This is a woman's point of view film that transcends any genre cage. It begins slowly, almost painfully dull in a way that will remind the viewer of all the cliches about Russia, the unstylish dress, the worker's paradise that isn't, the sharp contrast between Moscow and the peasants who live outside the city. Katya works in a factory. She works at a drill press. She is obviously underemployed. Lyudmila (Irina Muravyova) works in a bakery. She is probably gainfully employed for the time and place. They are friends, twentysomethings who are on the make for a man, but not a man from the sticks. They pretend to be university post docs or something close to that and they impress some people as they house-sit a beautiful Moscow apartment.

This is how their adult life begins in a sense. Lyudmila falls in love with an athlete; Katya becomes infatuated with a television cameraman. One thing leads to another and before we know it they are forty. Neither relationship worked out. The athlete becomes an alcoholic, the cameraman, in the sway of his mother, believes that Katya is beneath him (once he finds out that she works in a factory). How wrong he is, of course.

But no more of the plot. I won't spoil it. The plot is important. The characterizations are important. The story is like a Russian novel in that it spans lots of time, but once you are engaged you will find that the two and a half hours fly by and you will, perhaps like me, say at the end "What a great movie!"

My hat is off to director Vladimir Menshov and to Valentin Chernykh who wrote the script and to the cast. I've mentioned Vera Alentova and Irina Muravyova, but Aleksey Batlov who played Gosha was also excellent. I don't want to say anymore. Just watch the film. It is one of the best I've ever seen.

I am a man and I admit to having seen this movie and I am the better for it___. Not!___.

It doesn't matter what my sexual orientation is. This is a movie definitely worth seeing___. Not!___.

Nathalie (2003) 8

French style chick flick with some depth and surprises

Fanny Ardant plays Catherine, a gynecologist of a certain age, who discovers that her husband Benard (Gerard Depardieu) is cheating on her. She wonders if this is a onetime thing or something he does regularly. So she hires a prostitute (Emmanuelle Beart as Marlene/Nathalie) to test him. When the test turns up positive, Catherine wants to hear the intimate details which Marlene agreeably supplies.

The details of exactly what they do would seem a bit hard to take for the spouse who is being cheated on, and Catherine does find some of the descriptions unsavory. However she insists on hearing them. The viewer begins to wonder if Catherine is not being sexually aroused by these details (which is what Marlene thinks) or is of a masochistic frame of mind.

As Catherine and Marlene draw closer together the viewer now begins to wonder if Catherine herself would like to have a sexual relationship with Marlene. Since a lot of the tension in the movie relies on just what it is that Catherine wants, I won't reveal the answer. She claims to love her husband but as the details get seamier and seamier she decides she no longer knows whether she loves him or not.

How this will resolve itself is what kept me watching. The ending is a bit of a surprise. See if you can guess it.

Ardant is excellent, although her long suffering face may become a bit tedious for some. Beart is very good as a skillful and opportunistic prostitute, almost too good perhaps because I found her a bit creepy. She was 40-years-old when this was released and there is nary a line on her face. Ardant's look was natural and, for me anyway, more agreeable. Both women are of course two of the most celebrated stars of the French cinema as is Depardieu, whose part is rather modest. Anne Fontaine's direction is clear and focused.

While not your typical "chick flick"—certainly it is not like American chick flick faire—this is nonetheless very much a woman's point of view movie with the kind of agreeable ending that will please most viewers regardless of sex.

Best line and typical of the kind of psychology presented is this from Catherine as she is talking to Marlene: "Jealousy. For men it's a reflex."

See this for Fanny Ardant who has that Catherine Deneuve quality of growing more beautiful as she gets older, a very talented actress who always carries herself well.

I am a man and I admit to having seen this movie and I am the better for it___. Not!___.

It doesn't matter what my sexual orientation is. This is a movie definitely worth seeing___. Not!___.

Something to Talk About (1995) 6

Familiar but pleasing nonetheless

Director Lasse Hallstrom attempts to combine two venerable Hollywood genres and several subplots in this nonetheless agreeable morality tale about the bad effect adultery can have on your marriage. Part women's POV romantic comedy and part Dixie family dynamics saga, this is a generational story about what it takes to make a marriage work. It's a little scattered and loose fitting and underdeveloped in parts, but there's enough warmth and bright comedy to make up for the defects, and the cast is fun to watch.

The script by Callie Khouri is familiar but clever with some good human observations and some nice twists. I notice that Khouri also wrote Thelma and Louise (1991), which may explain why, in this flick, it is the men who learn (and need) most of the hard lessons. Robert Duvall plays the still feisty patriarch, Wyly King, who really needs to learn to loosen the reigns a little, while Dennis Quaid, who plays Grace's adulterous husband, needs to appreciate what he's got and to stop catting around. Kyra Sedgwick as Grace's sister helps him by kneeing him right where it hurts the most, and Grace, accidentally on purpose, nearly poisons him. (All part of his well-deserved and to be continued penance.) Sedgwick sparkles while being careful not to upstage "America's Darling" too often while Gena Rowlands as the mother is steady and sure.

Julia Roberts has become a great star and a great actress, and she is one of my favorites, but there is no question that she felt not entirely comfortable in this part. From the details of the script you can see that she is supposed to be a somewhat ditzy and naively outspoken woman, a southern belle with spunk, a mind of her own, and a desire to be something more than her father's daughter or her husband's wife. Julia got most of it right except for the ditzy part. She either wouldn't bend (maybe her agency advised against looking too weird) or Hallstrom didn't insist because Julia played this like Bogart always played Bogart, just like herself. You can see that the character of Grace Bichon is a bit out in left field because she leaves her daughter places or forgets to take her as she drives off in the morning. And then there was that outrageous confrontation at the woman's club where she stands up and demands to know how many other women have been sleeping with her husband. Something to talk about indeed!

But Julia stays Julia, and so the character is never developed as written. Nonetheless Julia Roberts is always wonderful, and although there is not here the effortless and nearly flawless style she was then developing, a style that culminated in her Oscar winning performance in *Erin Brockovich*, there is the undeniable down to earth charm and warmth that has made her so beloved by audiences that she can command something like twenty million dollars per.

Robert Duvall obviously had a lot of fun with his part, but I wonder if he realizes how much he looks like a bantam rooster in those riding tights!

I am a man and I admit to having seen this movie and I am the better for it___. Not!___.

It doesn't matter what my sexual orientation is. This is a movie definitely worth seeing___. Not!___.

Thelma and Louise (1991) 8

More than an exercise in male-bashing

This is an important commercial film aimed at blue collar women who feel victimized by both society and the men in their lives. Directed by Ridley Scott, who directed the science fiction classics, *Alien* (1979) and *Blade Runner* (1982), *Thelma and Louise* is an on-the-lam chick flick (with chase scenes), a kind of femme *Butch Cassidy and the Sundance Kid* (1969), somewhat akin to *Wild at Heart* (1990) and *Natural Born Killers* (1994) but without the gratuitous violence of those films. Ridley Scott walks the razor edge between femme-exploitation and serious social commentary. Incidentally, the script is by Callie Khouri who wrote *Something to Talk About* (1995) and *Divine Secrets of the Ya-Ya Sisterhood* (2002) which should give you an idea of how men are depicted here.

Susan Sarandon is Louise, a thirty-something Arkansas waitress with an attitude and some emotional baggage, and Geena Davis is Thelma, a cloistered ingénue house-wife with a yearning to breathe free. Both do an outstanding job and carry the film from beginning to end. The characters they play are well-rounded and fully developed and sympathetic, in contrast to the men in the film who are for the most part merely clichés, or in the case of Darryl (Christopher McDonald), Thelma's boorish husband, or the troll-like truck driver, burlesques.

I have never seen Geena Davis better. Her unique style is melded very well into a naive woman who never had a chance to express herself, but goes hog wild and seems a natural at it when the time comes. Sarandon is also at the top of her game and plays the crusty, worldly wise, vulnerable Louise with tenderness and understanding. Note, by the way, her pinned up in back hair-style, directly lifted from TV's Polly Holliday ("Kiss my grits!") who appeared as a waitress in the seventies sitcoms "Alice" and "Flo."

Harvey Keitel plays the almost sympathetic cop, Hal Slocumb, and Brad Pitt appears as J. D., a sweet-talking twenty-something who gives Thelma the script for robbing 7-11s as he steals more than her libido.

This movie works because it is funny and sad by turns and expresses the yearning we all have to be free of the restraints of society and its institutions (symbolized in the wide-open spaces of the American Southwest) while representing the on again, off again incompatibility of the male and female heart. The male-bashing is done with a touch of humor and the targets are richly deserving of what they get. The ending is perhaps too theatrical and frankly unrealistic, but opinions may differ.

Best and most telling quick scene is when Thelma phones Darryl to see if he has found out about their escapades. Weasel-like, he is trying to help the cops locate them, but he is so transparent to her that all she has to do is hear his voice. "He knows," she says to Louise and hangs up.

Best visual is when the black police helicopter appears suddenly, menacingly like a giant fly beneath the horizon of the Grand Canyon. Also excellent were the all those squad cars lined up like armored battalions aimed at the girls on the run.

I also liked the scenes at the motel with J.D. and Louise's boyfriend. They were beautifully directed and cut, and very well conveyed by Sarandon and Davis, depicting two contrasting stages in male-female relationships.

I am a man and I admit to having seen this movie and I am the better for it___. Not!___.

It doesn't matter what my sexual orientation is. This is a movie definitely worth seeing___. Not!___.

Venus Beauty Institute (*Vénus beauté (institut)* (1999) 9
Very pink

This stars Nathalie Baye, not Audrey Tautou, of *Amélie* (2001) fame. (She has a supporting role.) Baye is Angèle, a 40-year-old Parisian beautician who has loved and lost a few too many times. Indeed, as the film opens we (and Samuel Le Bihan as Antoine) watch and hear her being dumped once again. Well, she *is* careless with men. She is perhaps too "easy." She picks up men, the wrong ones. She is aggressive in her desire. And now she has become cynical. All she wants now are one-nights stands, no more love, no more unbreak my heart. Love is too painful.

So when Antoine falls in love with her at something like first sight (I do have a weakness for love at first sight: it is so, so daring, and so, shall we say, unpredictable) she rejects him out of hand even though he is a vital and handsome artist, confident and winning. What IS her problem? But he pursues her even though he is engaged to another (Hélène Fillières). And when she gets drunk and wants some casual sex with him, he says no. He wants her fully in control of her faculties.

So this is a romantic comedy of sorts centered around a beauty parlor. However any resemblance to Hollywood movies in the same genre (*Shampoo* (1975) and *Hairspray* (1988) come to mind) is purely coincidental. Here the salon is brightly and colorfully lit with a tinker bell as the door opens, and the clientele are eclectic to say the least: an exhibitionist who arrives in a raincoat and nothing else; a rich old man lusting after Tautou; a woman with oozing pimples on her...(never mind)...etc.

What makes this work so well is a completely winning performance by Baye, sharp direction by Toni Marshall, and a kind of quirky and blunt realism that eschews all cliché. Tautou fans will be disappointed in her modest part, but she is just adorable in that role. The voyeur scene in which she is willingly seduced by the rich old guy may raise your libido or your envy depending on where you're coming from. Ha!

See this for Nathalie Baye who gives the performance of a lifetime, simultaneously subtle and strong, vulnerable and willful. She makes us identify with her character and she makes us wish her love.

I am a man and I admit to having seen this movie and I am the better for it___. Not!___.

It doesn't matter what my sexual orientation is. This is a movie definitely worth seeing___. Not!___.

Chapter Eight:

Sex, Sex Kittens,

Pretty Babies, Budding Starlets,

and Femme Fatales

The films reviewed here represent more or less a totally male chauvinistic pig mentality with the emphasis almost exclusively on young, delectable members of the fair sex.

Beginning here a space is provided after each review so that you can give your own evaluation of the film, if you've seen it, or indicate whether you want to see it. You can also rate my review as worth reading (or not).

I

Sex without Love

Claire Dolan (1998) 8

Sex without love or tenderness

For those of you who have seen this and are looking for a message, I can say that the brutal facts of life, that is to say, an animal existence, will out. Whether we are talking about sexual desire and sexual release, or about reproduction—especially that—it is the fundamental animal drives that control our lives and dictate our actions.

This movie offers nothing beyond that, and it shouldn't. It is perfect as it is. There is no phony sentimentality to entice us to delusion, or any sort of Hollywood ending. There is no redemption here. There is no spirituality. There is only desire and fulfillment; desire and frustration; desire and the end of desire which comes with... The movie doesn't say.

I don't know if this makes my top ten of the nineties—I have seen a lot of movies—but it makes my most memorable. I will not forget this stark performance by Katrin Cartlidge, who plays Claire Dolan. She does not have the charisma of a great actress, and the range of what is required here is limited, but within that range she is stunning. A good part of the credit surely goes to director Lodge Kerrigan, who emphasizes the tight, washed out lines of desperation on her face, along with her intense sexual desire and the stark, rapacious environment of the urban jungle in which she plies her trade. This is a movie that might well be viewed following Pretty Woman (1990). I wonder how many people who allowed themselves to identify with Julia Roberts as a whore,

would like to identify with the high class prostitute of this film. Could they even watch it?

I was mesmerized by the sharp cuts and the film verité editing, the effective use of line and shadow, sound and silence, the clean, focused camera work. Our modern cities in all their indifference—the hard concrete and steel, the harsh lighting and intrusive sounds—are captured brilliantly. The script, cut lean and without comment, surprises us by turns, and keeps us on the edge of our seat throughout. The sex scenes are raw, intense and numerous. This is not a film for the kiddies. And that is an understatement.

Vincent D'Onofrio, who is an actor of suburb balance, plays the cabby who loves women, especially perhaps those in great need of his love, and he plays his part with subtlety and control. Colm Meaney plays the psychopathic pimp, a brutal man without conscience who uses force when necessary and a kind of cheap charm when it isn't. He has the type of the animal trainer, who plies the whip and the carrot, which he uses on women. Note well how Kerrigan has ironically emphasized this despicable man's ability to reproduce himself, making him the father of four children.

If I could sum up the life that Claire Dolan leads, I would say she lives among the wolves with a burden...her sexuality. She has a flat affect, strangely bereft of normal human expression. She is a kind of woman seldom seen on the silver scene, presented without an ounce of sentimentality. She feels life most strongly through sexuality, and only smiles at the result of sexual behavior, children. There is something profound in the realization that she is only really freed from her almost maniacal desire when she is with child. Meaney's character says he has known her since she was twelve and she has always been and always will be a whore. She will die a whore, he says. If true—and again, the movie lets us decide for ourselves—the question is, how did she become that way? The implication is that she was led or forced into prostitution at twelve. That is why she cannot feel about sex the way others feel, and that is why she finds it so difficult to feel affection for others. Hers has been an animal existence. She is always on her guard, and she shies away from a world that seems always about to hurt her brutally.

I've seen this and I give it____stars.
I want to see it___. I'll pass___.
The review was worth reading___. Not___.

Diabolique (1996) 7

Feeding the male libido

This is a sexploitation thriller but not all that bad, mainly because it is played somewhat tongue-in-cheek so that the plot absurdities might be overlooked in the interest of high camp, or at least in the interest of a mild diversion, and also because the women are diabolically diverting each in her own way.

Especially effective in a satirical performance is Sharon Stone as Nicole Horner, a duplicitous siren teaching math at a boy's boarding school. (Just the thought conjures up visions of a vampish Mary Kay Letoureau, although director Jeremiah Chechik studiously avoids *that* angle.) Her partner in crime is French actress Isabelle Adjani who plays Mia Baran, an ex-nun who is the owner of the school unhappily married to (after being seduced by, it appears) the school's sadistic task master Guy Baran played with a steady macho malevolence by Chazz Palminteri. Adjani, whom I recall (vividly) from Truffaut's *L'Histoire d'Adele H.* (1975) in which she played Victor Hugo's daughter Adele who was obsessively in love with an English army lieutenant who didn't want her. The masochistic persona employed there is revisited here as Mia is used by both her husband and Nicole Horner, who is also Guy's mistress.

Coming lately onto the scene is Kathy Bates as a man-despising, middle-aged, slightly butch Nancy Drew who doesn't let a partial mastectomy slow her down as she sleuths about looking for clues. She has some fine one-liners, but perhaps the best in the film comes from Sharon Stone. Two of the school's middle-aged bores have just come upon Stone and Adjani in the courtyard. Stone's ever-present cigarette inspires this from one of the men: "Don't you know that second-hand smoke kills?" Sharon Stone maneuvers past him, blows smoke in his face, and replies, "Not reliably."

This is a remake of *Les Diaboliques* (1955) starring Simone Signoret which I have not seen. My guess is that the French version played it straight and made the ending at least plausible. Here we have not only a ridiculous ending but a plot in dire need of a plot doctor. I have also not seen the TV version, *Reflections of Murder*, starring that quintessential sex-kitten (and personal favorite) Tuesday Weld. Anybody got a copy?

Bottom line: see this for Isabelle Adjani, whose over the top performance is garnished with an au naturale glimpse, and for Sharon Stone who is at her diabolical best. Be aware however that if sexual exploitation of the male libido is not your cup of tea, you will not like this movie, and even if it is, you may find the story more than a bit silly.

I've seen this and I give it____stars.
I want to see it___. I'll pass___.
The review was worth reading___. Not___.

Hard Candy (2005) 7

Totally sick, but compelling

This is a taunt drama of the man bites dog sort in which a precocious 14-year-old girl Hayley (Ellen Page, who was so delightful in Juno (2007)) has her way with photographer Jeff Kohlver (Patrick Wilson) a 32-year-old sickie who specializes in under aged girls. And her way is...well, way extreme. But apparently she has cause.

The vibrant tension that glues us to our seats can only be resolved by finding out if she is right in her accusations or if he is an innocent victim. She is certain. But director David Slade (using a diabolical script from Brian Nelson) keeps us guessing. Hayley seems not merely precocious intellectually, but emotionally more like a grown woman than a 14-year-old. Jeff appears to be a sweet, clever guy any girl would love to love. But she has anything but love in mind. Her scheme of vengeance is well thought out and very well executed. Everything is a twist on the Internet chat room stalker scenario. Instead of the older dude seducing, drugging and taking advantage of the young girl, the young girl turns the tables on him in a horrifying way. What is it that should happen to guys who take advantage of under-aged girls? They should have their balls cut off. That is exactly what Hayley has in mind.

Or so it seems. Actually, although she says at one point that death is too good for him, she finally settles on getting him to commit suicide. But will he?

I was hoping that Nelson and Slade would have the nerve to really turn the tables and make Hayley the villain and Jeff the innocent victim, and it seems for perhaps three-quarters of the film that this is still possible. We learn that he does have a thing for under aged girls and that is not good, but is that enough to justify what he is going through and will go through? And Hayley seems to be some kind of monster with a sick desire of her own. But this all washes out when we discover that no he didn't actually kill the girl. No, he only—as he confesses—FILMED the killing. (Nice diabolical touch, that.) And no Hayley does not go through with her Third Reich surgery (although she has brought along a blue surgeon's gown for the operation and has donned it). That would make her just too, too unsavory. Instead she uses her wiles and her physical and psychological control to get him to jump off a roof with a rope around his neck. (Yes, I warned you about spoilers.)

I mention all these essential details because I want to make a point. This is a seduction of the audience film and a kind of black comedy that isn't funny until perhaps you see it for the second or third time—which I am not planning to do. It is absurd in the slasher/horror film manner in which gross human behavior is depicted for the titillation of the audience while maintaining a politically correct stance. A politically incorrect stance would have been to end the film with Jeff innocent and Hayley the sickie. I suspect this film would have met with boycotts from women's groups had Slade done that.

Still the violence is mostly imagined or alluded to. Slade eschews any blood splattering or outright torture. The balls in the garbage disposal are, after all, only in our imagination. And Jeff really does deserve his fate. However there is no getting around the fact that Hayley is not your everyday 14-year-old. I don't think any future suitor would feel comfortable with her knowing what she did to Jeff, evil as he is. In other words, her brand of vigilante justice could only come from somebody who was a bit sick herself.

I think what mesmerized me most about this exercise in fantasy revenge wish fulfillment was the performance of Ellen Page. I thought she was a bit creepy but very effective. She actually could have passed for a 14-year-old (she was 18 when the film was released) yet the words put in her mouth and the actions she performed were well beyond the reach of the vast majority of fourteen year olds. The intense close ups of her face and that of her co-star Patrick Wilson helped to make the characters larger than life, which is one of the things that film can do so very well.

I've seen this and I give it____stars.
I want to see it___. I'll pass___.
The review was worth reading___. Not___.

Holy Smoke (1999) 8

Can Kate deprogram the deprogrammer?

Kate Winslet plays Ruth Barron, a young Australian woman who goes to India and becomes smitten with the touch of a charismatic guru, so much so that she changes her name and forsakes her family to stay in India and attend to and worship the guru. Her parents become alarmed. Her mother goes to India to trick her into coming back to Australia so that she can be deprogrammed by a professional from the United States that they have hired (P.J. Waters as played by Harvey Keitel).

What director Jane Campion does with this once familiar theme is most interesting. She puts the deprogrammer to the test, so to speak, and initiates a struggle of will between the deprogrammer and his young charge. The key scene arrives as Ruth comes naked into P.J.'s arms in order to test his professionalism (and her sexual power). I don't know about you but I think a naked and passionate Kate Winslet would test any man's motivation and make him think twice about what he really wants to do.

The psychological idea behind the story is this question, What is the nature of the guru's hold on his flock? Is it spiritual or is it profane? Do the young women who follow him desire him as an alpha male or is it spiritual deliverance they seek? Naturally Ruth believes the latter and the deprogrammer the former. But what is the deprogammer's motivation? Is this just a job for him or does he feel he is helping to free his clients from some kind of mental slavery? Or is he just another sort of phony guru himself?

Keitel in black hair and black moustache and devil's mini goatee dressed in black with a menacing look and a lot of physical energy (despite being 60-years-old when this film was released) contrasts sharply with Winslet's youthful beauty and beguiling voluptuousness. Strength of character is something Kate Winslet brings to any role, even including her outstanding performance as Ophelia in Kenneth Branagh's *Hamlet* (1996), a role that is usually played wiltingly. Here one senses that her strong will and determination are going to be quite a match for the deprogrammer who gives himself three days alone with her to break her attachment to the guru.

Two questions: One, if he is successful, will that just mean that she has transferred her allegiance from the Indian guru to him? Will it mean that his psychological strength is greater than that of the guru in far-off India? Two, in what respect is such a forced confinement with someone who is in physical control going to lead to a variant of the "Stockholm syndrome" experienced by some women held hostage, e.g., flight attendants on hijacked planes, and the famous case of Patty Hearst? Will the captive become enamored of her captor?

Campion handles this most interesting theme by focusing on the sexual and carnal nature of the relationships. The test of will between P.J. and Ruth becomes a question of Can she seduce him and thereby strip him of his professionalism? The movie is candid about sex and sexuality in a way that emphasizes the power dynamics of sexual relationships. There is some full frontal nudity and the sex scenes are steamy beyond what one usually sees in an R-rated film. (If seeing Kate Winslet naked might offend you, I recommend you close your eyes.)

Harvey Keitel did an outstanding job in a very demanding role and was entirely convincing (despite being a little too old for the part); but as usual Kate Winslet completely took over the film with her commanding countenance, her superior acting skills, her great concentration and her mesmerizing charisma. If there is a better, more captivating actress working today, I don't know who she is.

Her role here might be compared with her performance in Hideous Kinky (1998) in which she goes to Morocco to find enlightenment among the Sufis. That is a more charming film, and she is outstanding, but this one gives greater range to her skills.

Notable (and watchable!) as a counterpoint to Winslet's Ruth is sexy and sleazy Sophie Lee as Yvonne who is so taken with P.J. that she fairly begs him to make love to her. Also impressive is Julie Hamilton as the woebegone and stumbling mother.

Of course I would say see this for Kate Winslet, and if you are a fan, you sure don't want to miss *Holy Smoke* since it includes one of her best performances; however, what really impressed me is the original and daring conception and direction by Jane Campion who is best known for *The Piano* (1993), a film that received an Oscar nomination for the best direction and starred Holly Hunter, Harvey Keitel and Sam Neill.

So see this for Jane Campion who is not afraid to show human nature in the raw.

I've seen this and I give it____stars.
I want to see it___. I'll pass___.
The review was worth reading___. Not___.

Last Tango in Paris (1972) 10

Stunning performance by Brando

On the cover of the paperback edition of my novel *A Perfectly Natural Act* there is the blurb: "As compelling as Last Tango in Paris!" (This is not a shameless plug since my novel is long out of print.) When your work is touted as being "like" some earlier, successful work, you can be sure what is really being said is your work is not all that good and needs some hype to move it off the shelves.

So it took me 33 years to finally get around to watching "Last Tango..." and that is all to the good because if I had watched it when I was young, the barbarous sexuality would have sorely distracted me. Well, Maria Schneider (Jeanne) would have. She is very sexy and is shown complete ("she comes complete"!) in a number of scenes.

Her acting ability has been challenged by some, but I thought she did a nice job in a difficult role.

Problem was she was paired opposite Marlon Brando (Paul) who was busy giving one of his greatest performances. Brando said some time afterwards that he never wanted to do anything like this again. Presumably he was referring to the depressing nature of human sexuality portrayed in the film. This is ironic since most of the really raunchy and degrading lines are spoken by Brando who improvised them himself! He later commented that some of the lines written by director Bernado Bertolucci were not to his liking. What I think happened is Bertolucci wanted to live out as a director one of his youthful fantasies (raw, anonymous sex with a young beauty) and Brando, with his ultra-sophistication about such matters, played his part with a brutal satirical edge, perhaps making fun of Bertolucci's fantasy, turning it into an unpleasant, hard reality.

But the "reality" was a bit over the top for everybody. The infamous "Get the butter" scene, which was improvised by Brando and Bertolucci (to Schneider's dismay), made it clear that Paul considered Jeanne an animal that you used and nothing more. The dead rat scene and all the pig talk, ditto. Brando was also projecting his own feelings. He was 48-years-old when the film was released and was getting a paunch and losing his muscle tone. All the sex scenes but one are filmed with Brando clothed so as not to make the decline of his physical prowess obvious. He projected his own feelings about the decline of his body by referring derisively to his hemorrhoids, his prostate, and his paunch. When Jeanne wanted to get back at him she called him fat.

What Brando does so very well here is become that animalistic, but thinking brute who has his way with women because they cannot resist his alpha male prowess regardless of the gray in his hair. The early scene in the apartment when the nameless Brando just takes the nameless Schneider without so much as a spoken word or a caress might make women say "if only more men could be so commanding," and men say "I wish I had that kind of confidence." I am reminded Brando's Stanley Kowalski in *A Streetcar Named Desire* (1951) except that here little is left to the imagination. The Brando that was Kowalski at twenty-seven (with an I.Q. upgrade) could easily be the Brando that was Paul at forty-eight.

Almost all the discussion about this movie is about Brando, and that is certainly understandable since, despite all the ugliness of the film, it featured one of Brando's greatest performances. However, the movie was and is Bertolucci's. He wrote it and directed it. His original cut runs something like four hours. The version here rated NC-17 runs 136 minutes. The problem is that just about everything in the movie that does not included Brando is a bit of an anticlimax or an irrelevancy. Jean-Pierre Leaud (Tom) of Truffaut's *The 400 Blows* (1959) fame plays a film maker and Jeanne's intended. He was possibly chosen for the film because his boyish style and demeanor would contrast so sharply with Brando's commanding style. Two lovers had Jeanne: one was easy and boring, the other was scary and exciting. But I think Bertolucci was also having some fun with the French cinema and especially with Francois Truffaut. Perhaps it is only a coincidence that a year later Truffaut would release *Day for Night* (1973) (*La Nuit americaine*) in which Truffaut plays a director directing Leaud in a kind of pleasing but lightweight film contrasting sharply with the dark psychosis of Last Tango.

I don't think I could sit through the four hour version but it might be a good learning experience for young film makers. At any rate, perhaps some of the seeming illogic of the film might become reasonable, including the all too easy and not entirely explicable ending. I rate this film very highly because it was innovative (rather shocking for its time), with a fine jazz score, but mostly because of Brando's stellar performance and the sensual beauty of a 20-year-old Maria Schneider. By the way, the film is in French and English with subtitles. Brando's French is amusing, and whoever dubbed Schneider's English has a cute and witty voice.

Another excellent (and very beautiful) film by Bertolucci is *The Conformist* (1970) starring Jean-Louis Trintignant, Stefania Sandrelli, and Dominque Sanda. Interestingly enough Sanda was originally picked for Last Tango, as was Trintignant, and she would have given some needed depth to Jeanne's character, but she declined I guess because of all the nudity. Ironically a few years later Schneider was tabbed to play the lead in Luis Brunuel's *That Obscure Object of Desire* (1977) but dropped out during the filming reportedly because of a nude scene! Maybe she was afraid of becoming typecast.

I guess the bottom line on Last Tango is that it is an uncomfortable film illuminated by a veracious Parisian feel and a truly stunning performance by one of the greatest actors to ever grace the silver screen.

I've seen this and I give it____stars.
I want to see it___. I'll pass___.
The review was worth reading___. Not___.

Romance (1999) 8

Who's perverted?

Is Marie (Caroline Ducey) perverted because she wants to be used and abused, or is it her boyfriend Paul (Sagamore Stévenin) who is perverted because he denies her the love she craves because of his need to control? Or is it Robert (François Berléand) who has spent a lifetime chasing and seducing women? Or is it director Catherine Breillat herself who in France is sometimes known as a "*porno auteuriste*"?

Or, better yet, is it the debased mind of the censor, the prude and the hypocrite who would deny the range of human sexuality?

From Breillat's point of view, it is the censors who create the concept of obscenity.

I have to say however that some movies are so graphically sexual that it is difficult to watch them without being aroused, and this is such a movie, the most pornographic movie that I have ever seen that was not pornography per se.

Candor about sexuality is not what most people want. Even rarer is it for a woman to be candid about her sexuality in a forum that might include men. The fact that Catherine Breillat directed this film does not mean in any way that the sexuality of the central character is Breillat's sexuality, but it does mean she understands that sexuality; and since it is presented in a sympathetic manner, it means that she believes it is true at least for some women, at least some of the time.

In effect the movie asks the politically incorrect question, do women want to be used and abused? Breillat's cinematic answer is a bit of equivocation. I think what she is saying is, it depends. For even asking such questions Breillat has experienced hatred and been denied funding. But she says "All true artists are hated. Only conformists are ever adored."

Marie's boyfriend, who is pretty and very attractive to most women, will not have sex with her. Not completely. He frustrates her for no apparent reason. He seems almost pathological in his disinterest in her. She feels not just rejected but inadequate and of course frustrated. She is crazy about him and does everything she can to interest him, but to no avail. A game begins: but we see only her side of the game. His side is hardly present, but there is this blond-haired male friend that he likes to hang out with. Perhaps Paul is gay and doesn't know it or doesn't want to admit it.

Marie first tries a guy in a bar. It doesn't work out because there is no feeling on her part aside from...aside from what? From a desire to hurt Paul? To prove to herself that she is attractive? Then there is Robert the older man who claims to have had sex with 10,000 women although he is anything but handsome. This reminds me of the French novelist Georges Simenon who made the same claim in much the same way. Incidentally 10,000 women is approximately one a day for thirty years, which (pre Viagra) is sometimes thought of as the length of a man's sexually active life. Some readers may recall these lines from the poem "Go and Catch a Falling Star" by John Donne:

Ride ten thousand days and nights,
Till age snow white hairs on thee,
Thou, when thou return'st, wilt tell me,

All strange wonders that befell thee,
 And swear,
 No where
Lives a woman true, and fair.

Or the reader may be reminded of the "ten thousand things" from the East. In other words, ten thousand is a number that means "many," but many in a very human way.

At any rate, this man Robert is past the time in his life when he can, shall we say, perform. But he knows women and he discerns Marie's desires which are to be taken completely. He ties her up and she finds that she likes it, etc.

Well, what's the resolution? How should this end? Should Paul wake up and really love her? Or will she finally get completely disgusted with him and leave? Or will he wake up and then be found boring. Is that what he is afraid of?

The way Breillat chooses to end the film is both a bit too easy and yet seems apt. Notice that the title "Romance" is a kind of sardonic take on the "pornography" of romance novels. Romance novels fulfill the wishes of the feminine reader but in a euphemistic and unspecific way. The "hard" sex that Breillat presents (in a mostly soft way) in this film is only hinted at in romance novels.

On the other hand, clearly in keeping with a good ending from a woman's point of view (in so far as a "good" ending is possible in this film) is the fact that Marie ends up with what in evolutionary psychology is called having her cake and eating it too. She receives superior genes (or at least very attractive genes) for reproduction while winning the support of the man who will take care of her and her child. In this case these are two different men. Guess which one is which.

Be forewarned that this is a MOST explicit film sexually speaking and will offend many viewers.

One final question: did she have to kill the cat?

I've seen this and I give it____stars.

I want to see it___. I'll pass___.
The review was worth reading___. Not___.

To Die For (1995) 9
This one will stay with you a little bit

This is a clever story with more depth that appears at first blush, directed with irony and a sardonic sense of humor by Gus Van Sant. Nicole Kidman plays an especially shallow TV weather person who gets some grunge kids to kill her husband for her. Her motive is, as Illeana Douglas, who plays the sister-in-law, says, "He got in her way." This is a nice study of narcissism metastasized into psychopathology. Kidman's character is headstrong, motivated and rather stupid. She thinks only of herself and would do anything for herself and would do anything to anybody who got in her way. And amazingly, she does.

Matt Dillon is wasted as the husband (in more ways than one). I'm surprised he agreed to do the part. Kidman is mesmerizing and makes us believe in a slightly unbelievable character. We've all known narcissistic little darlings who would kill you for the right shade of eye shadow, but to see it acted out so coldly and with such appalling stupidity, yet with a psychology so bizarre that it has to be real, fairly takes your breath away. It was especially apt that she had him killed so that her pointless little docu-drama "Teens Speak Out" could become newsworthy enough for national exposure. Consciously she doesn't realize this: she has no introspection; she just acts.

Also cute is the way the picture is framed: a pseudo-documentary within a pseudo-documentary. Everything is so well orchestrated that when Kidman's character gets her surprising, but entirely appropriate comeuppance at the end, we are quite pleased.

I've seen this and I give it____stars.
I want to see it___. I'll pass___.
The review was worth reading___. Not___.

II

Starlet Debuts

or

Yes, You Can Star in This Movie

But No You Can't Watch It

Because You're Too Young!

It is a curious fact that in some of the movies reviewed in this section the leading "lady" was so young that she wouldn't be allowed into the theater (at least in the United States) to view her own movie!

36 Fillette (1988) 8

Transcends the American brat style

This is a love story off the beaten track clearly in the tradition of Louis Malle and Francois Truffaut, told without prudishness or gratuitous violence.

The title refers to a children's dress size that the 14-year-old central character, Lili, played with snap by Delphine Zentout, is bursting out of. Billed as a "French Lolita," Zentout is not all that fetching at first glance. She's a chubbette with light skin and thick black hair and not exactly pretty. But she has intriguing eyes and a saucy way about her.

Lili is "discovering" her sexuality, but won't let herself be impregnated. The playboy, played with grace and economy by Etienne Chicot, falls in love with her in spite of himself and "tolerates" her reluctance while being partially satisfied in other ways, one of which we used to call a "cold f..." They are a believable match because sexually they are equal: she precocious, he experienced.

Catherine Beillet directs without sentimentality while guiding Zentout to an interpretation that transcends the American brat style and leads us to a thoughtful view of feminine sexuality.

I've seen this and I give it____stars.
I want to see it___. I'll pass___.
The review was worth reading___. Not___.

Pretty Baby (1978) 10

Only Louis Malle could have made this film

Brooke Shields is as gorgeous as a little girl can be. Her beauty really rivets you to the screen. Louis Malle keeps the camera on her as often and for as long as possible, reminding me that some years ago Brooke Shields was the most photographed model in the world. Susan Sarandon gets considerably upstaged. However as far as acting goes, Brooke ranged from amateurish to competent to flashes of delight. She was good, so good I would say in comparing her to later roles that she has regressed. But perhaps it was Louis Malle's direction that made her seem so natural.

Sarandon was flawless and seamless as usual (and never looked better). The long takes on the faces of the characters was noticeable but short of annoying. The sets were almost magical. They seemed so natural without all the usual, "Look folks, this is 1917!" kind of feeling you usually get with period piece photography. The milieu of the whore house in New Orleans in which little Violet wanders about in every room and every nook and at any time, day or night, seems natural and unforced. It's a huge child's playground in effect for the twelve-year-old who yearns to out-do mommie in being desirable to the johns.

The story line is strangely reserved. You keep expecting some real horror to explode in your face, and then you expect a heart sickening tragedy, Violet to be mutilated by one of her johns or perhaps exploited by some sick man, but the worst she gets is deflowered and slapped. The madame of the house (played brilliantly by an actress whose name I don't know) has her whipped for something, but she skips away from that saying it didn't hurt and runs off to the photographer she likes, played perhaps too Victorianly by Keith Carradine. I got the feeling he couldn't make up his mind whether he was Toulouse Lautrec, Vincent Van Gogh or Professor Henry Higgins and decided to go with all three. I expected to see him grovel a little for Brooke, or debase himself à la Philip in *Of Human Bondage*, but Malle spares us that.

The defining sequence in the movie, and the part that reveals the real tragedy of the little girl is when she goes to the photographer's house and they begin living together and he leaves her a note that she can't read (because she is illiterate) and we see her standing behind his iron fence watching the sailors walk by (perhaps the sailors are in her future). When he comes home and we see that her child's view of the world is so different than his, we know their relationship is doomed. But we also know that she has lost her childhood and will never have a normal adolescence. That is her tragedy.

The cinematography is beautiful without calling undue attention to itself. The whore house seems real enough as a sort of French salon cum New Orleans brothel, cum Dodge City saloon. We see Brooke as close to naked as perhaps we would want. The point of the photography is to show her physical beauty, but in a naturalistic, almost nonsexual way, to show the awkwardness of the child who is about to become a woman. She never looks worse than when she's painted up and thick with lipstick. We get the point. In the scene where she is deflowered we are "threatened" with horror (she screams, the john sneaks out and they discover her motionless on the bed). But she's only joking and they all get choked up at this "rite of passage." Malle makes it like a first kiss, which for her (his point) it is.

He gets to tell it like it is sometimes with young girls and men but spares us a lot of the shock by making it clear that Brooke Shields as Violet the 12-year-old prostitute is an exception to the general rule. Yet nothing is hid from us. The slavery of the prostitute's life and bondage to her trade is made clear. The tragedy of growing up in a whore house is not glossed over; it's just that the tragedy is sugar coated like our memories of childhood, and indeed the little girl has a lot of fun in the old whore house and we know that some of her memories will be fond ones.

Finally, Violet's mother comes back for her. She has made a successful marriage with her rich respectable husband. Violet goes to her and although her photographer husband objects, he knows it's inevitable: he must lose her. She asks "Can't you come too?" We, along with Keith Carradine, get to fathom that for a long moment or two before he lets her go. The great thing about this scene is that the arrival of the mother and her rich husband just destroys their "marriage." Kaboom. We immediately see that the child's higher loyalty and greater love is to and for the mother and not her husband and her marriage, a relationship she does not understand.

It's a strange tale, bravely told with a touch of gentle genius. I'm glad I didn't have to see all the warts, but I know they were there behind the gloss and Malle left them out on purpose: and the nearly idyllic world of the child prostitute is nothing like his fairy tale, but I thank him for it anyway; after all, these things have to be told in the form of fairy tales or myths otherwise we can't accept them.

I've seen this and I give it____stars.
I want to see it___. I'll pass___.
The review was worth reading___. Not___.

The Professional (1994) 7

A different kind of "Lolita"?

Take away the elaborately staged shoot 'em ups and the spilled blood and the rest of the mayhem, and what we have here is a love story, of sorts.

Jean Reno stars as Leon, a cold-blooded professional hit man sans people skills who doesn't know how to read. He plays a kind of reluctant Humbert Humbert to 12-year-old Mathilda (Natalie Portman in her screen debut), a kind of Lolita for the mean streets. Owing a little to Jodie Foster's portrayal of a street urchin/nymphet in *Taxi Driver* (1976) and not much to the teenaged stars of the two movie Lolitas (Sue Lyon and Dominique Swain) who were really too old to be genuine nymphets, Natalie Portman yearns to become a "cleaner" so that she can get revenge on Stansfield, a psycho drug enforcement agent who killed her little brother. Played with psychotic zest by Gary Oldman, Stansfield is the kind of guy who pops pills and delights in a Beethoven overture while he tortures his various victims.

Okay, it is not surprising that this is more or less a French film done American style. After all the underlying story did not and will not ever play in the Heartland of America like a Chevy commercial. (It needed to be disguised as an action thriller.) After all Portman really *is* 12-years-old (as Nabokov's Lolita was in the book) and she and Leon really do live together and declare their love for one another, although there is no sexual hanky-panky between hit man and pre-adolescent, and nary a kiss on the lips.

What French director Luc Besson (best known in the States for his very interesting and original *La Femme Nikita* 1990) has accomplished here is a kind of elaborate joke on the movie establishment. He has made a cold-blooded killer into a sympathetic character and has played peek-a-boo with the censorship system with some "cute" shots of his very pretty little star. One wants to ask, "What's a nice Jewish girl [Portman was born in Israel] like you doing in a movie like this?"

What makes this movie work (if you can stomach the premise and the mayhem) is the fine acting by Reno, Portman and Oldman with support from Danny Aiello, and some really outrageous shtick infusing a quirky plot. Some highlights:

The scene in which Mathilda goes to the concierge and declares proudly of Leon, "He's not my father. He's my lover." (And their subsequent hasty departure from the concierge's establishment.)

Reno's obsession with milk drinking and with cleaning his plant (his only friend).

Stansfield's predilection for touching his victims almost lovingly (like a carnivore) before or after he kills them and his bizarre body-shudder as he pops his pills. In the funniest and most crowd-pleasing scene in the movie, he lingers a little too long over the body of his last bloody victim, long enough to hear the fatal words, "This is from Mathilda" as he looks down to find a strange piece of metal in his hand... (Yes, this is really vague, but you have to see the scene to appreciate it, and anyway, I can't give it away in a review! Those who have seen the movie know what I mean.)

One last word: this is another of those ironic R-rated films in which one of its stars (Natalie Portman) would not be allowed into the movie theater to see her own film!

Okay, one more last word: if you want to see how Natalie Portman has developed as an actress, in addition to her work in *Star Wars* and in *Cold Mountain*, see her in *Anywhere But Here* (1999) an entirely different sort of film in which she co-stars with Susan Sarandon.

I've seen this and I give it____stars.
I want to see it___. I'll pass___.
The review was worth reading___. Not___.

Xiu Xiu, The Sent-Down Girl *(Tian yu)* (1998) 9

A beautiful and brutal film

Joan Chen, who has had a modest career as an actress in American films and TV, makes her directorial debut here in this brutal, poignant and beautiful Mandarin language film. Starring Lu Lu as Xiu Xiu, a teenaged girl from the city sent to the country during Mao's cultural revolution, and Lopsang as Lao Jin, a castrated Tibetan nomad who is to teach her horse husbandry, *Tian yu* is not so much an indictment of communist China as it is an indictment of human nature. Xiu Xiu is brutalized by small-minded bureaucratic males as has happened throughout human history, be they communist or feudal, her innocence and youth traded for an apple, her buoyant hope for life dashed by blind political and economic forces, and her self-respect stolen from her by the twisted logic of rape and lust.

What elevates this story above what we have seen many times before is the striking beauty of the Tibetan countryside and the fine characterizations of both Xiu Xiu and Lao Jin. Lao Jin is a "gelding," made fun of by others, a man of quiet disposition who falls in love with his beautiful young charge, but stands aside because of his impotence. Xiu Xiu has an imperial nature natural to favored girls everywhere, be they Japanese "princesses" or American "valley girls," a nature very well depicted by the script and very well acted out by Lu Lu, whose delicate beauty and spicy temperament clash well with Lao Jin's Taoist stoicism. At one point he remarks wisely that "every place is the same," meaning of course that it is what we bring to the place that really matters. But his wisdom is completely lost on the teenaged girl who wants and needs society and all that it has to offer. And so, the underlying "love affair" between the two can never be...except...as it is in the end.

Lopsang's performance is entirely convincing and Lu Lu is fascinating to watch. Joan Chen did a fine job with both of them while managing to keep politics and political agendas in the background. She concentrated on the human tragedy and made it universal. Both of her central characters had flaws that in some way led to the great sadness that they experienced, and yet they were not to blame. In this naturalistic expression we are reminded of the tragedies of novelists Thomas Hardy and Theodore Dreiser; and of course Chen was influenced by the work of Chinese director Zhang Yimou, in particular his sad, but captivating *Raise the Red Lantern* (1991) in which a beautiful girl is consumed and brutalized by societal forces of a different nature.

This film misses being a masterpiece because of a hurried resolution leading to an ending that needed a bit more shaping. Nonetheless this is an arresting and compelling drama, beautifully filmed and sensitively directed. But be forewarned. "Celestial Bath" is a disturbing film not easily shaken from the mind.

I've seen this and I give it____stars.
I want to see it___. I'll pass___.
The review was worth reading___. Not___.

Welcome to the Dollhouse (1995) 10

I even liked the song

This is a very funny comedy about the indomitable spirit of an 11-year-old junior high school girl, Dawn Wiener, played with geekish verve by Heather Matarazzo, who overcomes real life horrors the likes of which would make war heroes shutter. How would you like to be courted by a guy whose pick up line is "I'm going to rape you at three o'clock. Be there."? Or have a mother who splits your chocolate cake in front of your watering eyes into two pieces and adds them to the plates of your brother and sister? Or have your dream lover tell you he can't be a member of your Special People Club because it's "a club for retards"?

It gets worse. You're taunted daily by choruses of "Wiener Dog!" and "Lesbo freak!" and bullied at school by everybody including some teachers and the principal. And at home, your siblings tear down your club house. And when you're missing from home for a day and phone home, you're told to call back later, mom and your spoiled little sister are mugging for the TV cameras.

Ah, but Dawn can overcome the night. She turns the would-be rapist into a macho-posturing little boy who really only wants to be affectionate ("I make the first move!" he boasts) and demonstrates that no matter how hard they hit her, she'll be back tomorrow, undaunted. Matarazzo does a great job, but she isn't alone. Brenden Sexton stands out as the posturing macho boy who loves her but can't admit it, as does Eric Mabius playing Steve Rogers, the self-absorbed high schooler/rock star wanna be (and Dawn's first love). The rest of the cast is also good, especially Victoria Davis in a bit part as the foul-mouthed, sexually ambiguous 12-year-old Lolita who corners Dawn in the bathroom. Incidentally that scene in which Lolita slyly tells Dawn "You didn't come in here to wash your hands," and insists that she do what she intended to do is just a great piece of preadolescent camp. Another fine (and subtle) scene is when Dawn in her bedroom hears Steve Rogers sing for the first time (in the garage with her brother's "band"). The expression on her face, as she rises up enthralled and follows the sound, suggests someone in the throes of a first awakening. And I loved the bit where Dawn, after being told by one of Steve Rogers's ex-girlfriends that they "finger-...(you-know-what)" one night and that was all, is inspired to demonstrate her finger work on the piano to Steve and then to show him her hands, fingers spread so he can see them. Of course he hasn't a clue to what she's thinking—and we're not too sure either!

Now some people may think there is some exaggeration here, and they're right. I mean, nobody wears a pirate's black eye patch after getting hit in the eye with a spit ball! And teachers, even bad ones, know better than to deliberately humiliate their students (although some do it unconsciously). Nonetheless, while the action may not be entirely realistic at times, its spirit is totally true. Just ask anybody who remembers junior high school. Which brings me to the question: how did director and script writer, Todd Solondz, get it so right? Did he take notes when he was still in junior high to use when he grew up? Did he steal his daughter's diary? Clearly *somebody* lived this script. I'm guessing that "Dawn" is "Todd" at least in spirit, and the striking capture of the psychology of the world of being twelve-years-old is due to his having been there and done that, "big time," as is written on Dawn's locker.

Whatever, this full color world of the middle child is an adorable, witty, psychologically honest, beautifully directed and edited, masterfully conceived entertainment, winner of the Grand Jury Prize at Sundance, 1996, and sure to steal your heart.

Final irony: this is a movie for and about 12-year-olds (it would appear) yet it is rated "R" and so, in effect, junior high school life is not only "not suitable" for those under thirteen, they can't even view it!

I've seen this and I give it____stars.
I want to see it___. I'll pass___.
The review was worth reading___. Not___.

III

Pure Titillation

or

Yes, I <u>Do</u> Know Why

I Watched the Whole Thing

What we have here for the most part is a director in adoration of his beautiful young star (often also his girlfriend or wife) so that the film amounts to showing her off to the world. Directors can do that and the young stars find such exposure very agreeable and career-enhancing—usually.

Barbarella (1968) 5

Roger Vadim does Jane

For decades I had been meaning to watch this to see if Jane Fonda was as gorgeously displayed by Roger Vadim as advertised (and as reported by my horny friends). Well, yes. But the rest of the movie—high camp? Interesting sci-fi spoof? Satire on the genre? Well, no, but there are some eyebrow-raising and rather bizarre flights of fancy by Vadim including some creepy children in an icy landscape who bean Fonda with a rock, knock her out and tie her up. They have little dolls with piranha teeth that they sic on her luscious tied-up bod, drawing some very red blood to contrast with her white skin. You get the picture.

Another interesting idea is that of the labyrinth containing the "good" people outside the city of all sins. Vadim reverses Dante's Inferno and puts the angels and other people in hell while the evil doers live in their decadence in the not so fair city. Fonda rides on the back of an angel with wings (John Phillip Law) while shooting down the "leather" storm troopers from the city in their flying machines. Ka-boom! Jane doesn't miss but of course she does get captured and...well, scantily clad Jane in chains or rather ropes in the city of evil. You get the picture.

Roger Vadim gained international fame as the director of "Et Dieu... créa la femme" (1956) starring the amazingly beautiful Bridget Bardot. He seemed to have a way with actresses, especially young, beautiful and aspiring ones. It was quite a coup to somehow capture the heart or perhaps it was the ambition of the young and beautiful Jane Fonda. One can see that part of his technique was to really put the lady on display. Here in Barbarella, Fonda more or less undresses for the camera as the opening credits roll. It's a kind of "you gotta have a gimmick" strip tease as she is turned upside down and sideways by the seemingly lack of gravity in her spaceship as she dodges behind the text of the opening credits. This peek-a-boo would be quite titillating were I still 19 years old (or what the heck, 50). Regardless the point is the full (as much as possible) display of Fonda who does indeed look gorgeous. But that would not be enough, not nearly enough for the actress that Jane would become. She exclusively holds the camera for much of the first part of the movie in her space ship as she re-robes, talks with the President of Earth, and moves about and begins her space faring mission looking for "Duran Duran" (yes, they got their name from this flick). Her skin is flawless, her limbs elegant, her eyes beautifully made up in the dark sixties style. The camera loves her, Vadim loves her, the audience loves her, Jane loves her.

To be candid I did not watch the entire movie. But that is more a problem of age (mine) than it is of the movie which was at least as good as most sci-fi spoofs and a bit more creative. However if you don't find Jane Fonda attractive, you won't even be able to watch as much as I did.

I've seen this and I give it___stars.
I want to see it___. I'll pass___.
The review was worth reading___. Not___.

Devil in the Flesh (Il diavolo in corpo) (1987) 6

See it alone and bring a towel

I watched "the original X-rated theatrical version" (gee, lucky me) and I can tell you Maruschka Detmers has headlights that point very sharply in the direction they want to go. She is also very pretty, although I'm not sure she is prettier than her co-star, Federico Pitzalis. Clearly, she is taller. Yes, this is a very sexy movie, which some might say is its *raison d'etre*, but that's really beside the point. What matters here is school-boy wish fulfillment, a little self-indulgence by Director Marco Bellocchio.

Well, why not? It isn't often that the boy gets the beautiful woman, especially when in competition with his suave father, a handsome and distinguished psychiatrist, and her fiancé, a well-heeled and attractive terrorist. I mean, this could happen, couldn't it?

I didn't see the original French version of 1946, in which the terrorist was a soldier in World War I. I understand it was better. I'm willing to bet that Bellocchio saw it and had the sort of relationship with it that a later generation had with Star Wars, e.g., and just had to relive the fantasy.

Nonetheless, and having said all that, this is not a bad movie. I'm not sure who is supposed to be the "devil in the flesh," but Maruschka is worth the price of the ticket and then some.

I've seen this and I give it___stars.
I want to see it___. I'll pass___.
The review was worth reading___. Not___.

The Disenchanted (1990) 8

Parisian girl leaves adolescence behind

This is a charming little film made in the agreeable French tradition of Vadim, Techine, Kieslowski, et al, in which the film itself reflects the director's adoration for its pretty young star. In this case we have Director Benoît Jacquot adoring Judith Godrèche, who plays a poor but principled 17-year-old Parisian girl disenchanted with her life, in particular with the choices she has in males. Her boyfriend tells her she should sleep with somebody ugly. Just why isn't clear. He is referred to as "whatshisname." She meets an interesting man, Alphonse, played by Marchel Bozonnet, but he is too old for her and, at any rate, still enamored of another. And certainly she doesn't want her mother's lover, referred to as "Sugardad," who is in his sixties.

Godrèche herself is as natural and unself-conscious as a child. Dressed mostly in thin house dresses that cling lightly to her body, she displays the clear eyes, the clean jaw line and sculptured arms of youthful innocence. The camera adores her face and stays with her throughout. Clearly she is good and good to look at, but I would not say she is as enchanting as Krzysztof Kieslowski's Irène Jacob (*La Double vie de Véronique* (1991); *Trois Couleurs: Rouge* (1994)) nor as talented as Juliette Binoche in Andre Techine's *Rendez-Vous* (1985). And of course not nearly as sexy as Brigitte Bardot in Roger Vadim's *And God Created Woman* (1957).

But comparisons are said to be odious. This is a good film in its own right. The treatment suggests a short story from a literary journal, original, with quiet, unexpected tableaux of daily life leaving one to ponder. The climax appears without one's knowing it until the film begins the closing credits and then one understands what happened. There is a dark symbolic element throughout suggesting the bondage to the material world that comes when a girl is no longer a child.

Vietnamese-French actor Hai Truhong Tu is excellent in a small part as Godrèche's Chinese friend.

I've seen this and I give it____stars.
I want to see it___. I'll pass___.
The review was worth reading___. Not___.

The Double Life of Veronique (La Double Vie de Véronique) (1991) 8
Beautiful, but somewhat unaffecting

Much of this is an adoration of French actress Irène Jacob by Director Krzysztof Kieslowski; in a sense it is a homage to her, one of the most beautiful actresses of our time and one of the most talented. If you've never seen her, this is an excellent place to begin. She has an earnest, open quality about her that is innocent and sophisticated at the same time so that everything a man might want in a young woman is realized in her. Part of her power comes from Kieslowski himself who has taught her how she should act to captivate. He has made her like a little girl fully grown, yet uncorrupted, natural, generous, kind, without pretension, unaffected. She is a dream, and she plays the dream so well.

The movie itself is very pretty, but somewhat unaffecting with only the slightest touch of blue (when the puppeteer appears by the curtain, the curtain is blue, and we know he is the one, since she is always red). The music by Zbignew Preisner is beautiful and lifts our spirits, highlighted by the soprano voice of Elzbieta Towarnicka. But the main point is Irène Jacob, whom the camera seldom leaves. We see her from every angle, in various stages of dress and undress, and she is beautiful from head to toe. And we see her as she is filled with the joy of herself and her talent, with the wonder of discovery and the wonder of life, with desire, and with love.

Obviously this is not a movie for the action/adventure crowd. Everything is subtle and refined with only a gross touch or two (and no gore, thank you) to remind us of the world out there. Véronique accepts the little crudities of life with a generous spirit, the flasher, the two a.m. call, her prospective lover blowing his nose in front of her. She loves her father and old people. She is a teacher of children. She climaxes easily and fully. To some no doubt she is a little too good to be true. And she is, and that is Kieslowski's point: she is a dream. And such a beautiful dream.

An actress playing the character twice in a slightly different way has occurred in at least two other films in the nineties: there was Patricia Arquette in David Lynch's *Lost Highway* (1997) and Gwyneth Paltrow in *Sliding Doors* (1998). It's an appealing venture for an actress of course and when the actress is as talented as these three are, for the audience as well.

Note that as Weronika/Véronique is in two worlds, Poland and France, so too has always been Kieslowski himself in his real life. It is interesting how he fuses himself with his star. This film is his way of making love to her.

Kieslowski died in 1996 not long after finishing his celebrated trilogy, *Trois Couleurs: Bleu* (1993); *Rouge* (1994) and *Bialy* (White) (1994). We could use another like him.

I've seen this and I give it____stars.
I want to see it___. I'll pass___.
The review was worth reading___. Not___.

Poison Ivy (1992) 7
Is Drew worth an ocean of calamine lotion?

This is primarily a vehicle to exploit the generalized sensuality of Miss Drew Barrymore, an excellent actress and heir of a great acting family. Drew, who was so cuddily in E.T. when she was six years old or so, is now oh so cuddily and then some to a more varied audience. Here, as a scheming little poor girl, she seduces dad, mom and daughter (in psychologically different ways) before slipping into murder. She is sexy, trashy and very pretty.

Sara Gilbert (from TV's "Rosanne") plays the dweeby poor little rich girl daughter with veracity and some wit. Tom Skerrit is the father without a clue; and Cheryl Ladd, looking rather fetching despite the role, is the dreary mother. Yes, old TV stars can find work! Best scene is when Sara and Drew go to the tattoo parlor. Drew makes a few ugly remarks causing Sara to get up to leave, but Drew draws her back tenderly (to pay the tab), pulls her close, and kisses her. When the beer-bellied tattoo guy tries to join in, the girls give him an "ugh!" and split.

The slow-motion seduction of Skerrit seems a little drawn out. Even after Drew kisses and licks his cut hand, Skerrit just looks off into space in befuddlement. Later things heat up though, and then take a kinky turn when Mom, through a drug and alcohol haze, dimly notices Drew wearing her sexy dress and doing some love numbers on her husband.

Second best scene is after the funeral with Drew sleeping in Cheryl Ladd's bed where she is discovered by Sara. Drew urges her friend, the distraught daughter, to join her. "Pretend I'm your mother," Drew says. As they lie in bed, Sara confides to Drew that what she couldn't say to her mother was "I love you." Drew kisses her head and holds her close.

What was intended here was a psychological study of a teenaged girl without much of a home or much of a family who is drawn to adopt her own family among those of her friends, and in doing so assumes the role of the mother in toto. What we get is a semi-pornographic focus on a very sexy screen darling, a ridiculous murder, and an even more ridiculous finale, the details of which you might want to see for yourself.

I've seen this and I give it____stars.
I want to see it___. I'll pass___.
The review was worth reading___. Not___.

Rendez-Vous (1985) 7

A very young and vital Juliette Binoche carries this

Notice how the jackets of just about every video, especially the French ones, SHOUT how SEXY the movie is. In Krzysztof Kieslowski's "Blue," *par example*, Juliette Binoche and the film are touted as being so, so sexy. But it wasn't, and neither was she. However in "Rendez-Vous" you will see a Juliette Binoche with enough sexual power to awaken a dead man—not to say that this movie is as good as Kieslowski's "Blue." It isn't, but it's not bad.

Binoche is full of energy as a provincial French girl with a flair for the stage new to the lights of gay Paree. She plays fast and loose (and natural) with the men she meets, and dodges some serious trouble before working it out with the man she really wants. Characteristically, Director André Téchiné leads us close to the dark side of sex without really offending our sensibilities.

Jean-Louis Trintignant appears in a small role that anticipates his triumphant creation as the admiring older man in Kieslowski's "Trois Couleurs: Rouge" nine years later.

I've seen this and I give it____stars.
I want to see it___. I'll pass___.
The review was worth reading___. Not___.

Three Colors: Red (Trois Couleurs: Rouge) (1994) 9

Red is the color of love

This is a sometimes clever, sometimes corny, but always beautiful story of predestined love.

Jean-Louis Trintignant plays a retired judge, corrupted by an all-consuming cynicism, who meets a beautiful girl, but doesn't fall in love with her. Instead, his reincarnation does, and he mystically orchestrates their predestined meeting. The girl is played by Irène Jacob, who is earnest, warm, uncorrupted and beautiful. She's a French model unloved by her boyfriend (fool that he is) with a demeanor proud, but not vain, vulnerable, but not weak.

The judge is so pathetic that he spies on his neighbors' phone conversations to spice up his lonely and pitiful existence. Their love affairs, their spats, their crimes are piped into him as he sits alone in his house. But she has the genius to appreciate him and to understand him, and so frees him from his bitterness.

We see in this, the final third of director Krzysztof Kieslowski's trilogy, something reminiscent of his countryman, Roman Polanski, in his passion for young actresses and his ability to bring out the best in them. We see further in the character of the retired judge a projection of ideas about how an old man, past any pretense, might love a young woman: wisely, delicately, from a slight distance, without a hint of lechery.

Irène Jacob makes us believe that innocence and instinctive goodness are wondrous qualities, regrettably not much touted these days. More often depicted are women who would rather sing proudly of being bitches while acting out violent, two-fisted, emulations of a bogus masculinity, e.g., see "Single White Female," etc.

Red is for her lips, for the color of curtains and theater seats, for the color of her true love's utility vehicle (often in her sight, but not yet recognized), for doors and panels and for the warm beat of her heart. Her name is Valentine. She is the dream of the worldly man who has known many women, whose head is not easily turned. And red is for the ringing of the phone, heard in its urgency as red.

I liked this better than Blue or White, both of which were very good; but the clash of innocence and cynicism here, with youth and age so aptly contrasted, along with a clever plot (Kieslowski loves to surprise us), highlighted by captivating performances from the leads, make this the best of the three.

I've seen this and I give it____stars.
I want to see it___. I'll pass___.
The review was worth reading___. Not___.

Chapter Nine:

Film Noir:

Is that a Gun in Your Pocket?

or

Did I Miss Some of the Plot?

I take a rather broad view of film noir here. My notion of the genre emphasizes the existential man in a brutal world. This man is urban and realistic. He's a bit compromised. He is tough and he is essentially alone. He isn't necessarily a private eye or a cop, and the film did not have to be made in America in the '40s or '50s. Dark brooding and the lack of a happy ending are important elements. Note that the first film reviewed here could also be called a fantasy or a sci fi. For me the fact that its protagonist, Chow Mo Wan (Tony Leung), gets by on his own devices amid a mostly indifferent world is the key.

Note that some other films noir appear elsewhere in this book, e.g., The Big Sleep *(1946) and* Double Indemnity *(1944) appear in the chapter "Read the Book, See the Movie...."*

2046 (2004) 9

What is real and what is make believe?

Chinese film maker Wong Kar Wai weaves a stylish web of romance and fantasy in this somewhat disjointed story about a writer whose fiction begins where his life leaves off—or vice versa. Starring Tony Leung, who played Broken Sword in Yimou Zhang's *Hero* (2002), as Chow Mo Wan, the writer, and Ziyi Zhang as Bai Ling, the vulnerable and gorgeous prostitute, "Two Oh Four Six" mystifies as it beguiles. Worth watching just as eye candy and to hear the music in the background, 2046 appropriately enough moves between Hong Kong and Singapore, two great Asian economic tigers, and then into the future which will be (let's face it folks) Chinese, very Chinese.

This is the first of Wong Kar Wai's films that I have seen. He reminds me a little of Zhang Yimou in that he strives for beauty in his production, in the sets, the scenes and the costumes. His interiors are darker than Zhang's and his scenes are more cosmopolitan, and unlike Zhang he does not aim to make any kind of social statement. There's more than a touch of American film noir in his story that focuses on Chow, the existential man who makes his living by writing newspaper articles and mass market fiction while meeting and pleasing the ladies, especially the ladies of the evening. Tony Leung's easy charm and confident manner make him a natural for the part, a deeply introspective man who likes the night life. I thought it was interesting—and maybe this is just

me—that he looked a bit like Clark Gable with that thin moustache and surefooted way with women.

Ziyi Zhang is fascinating to watch, but so are the other actresses, including Li Gong who has a modest part as Su Li Zhen, prostitute turned professional gambler, and Jie Dong and Faye Wong who play different aspects of Wang Jie Wen. The sense I get from Chow's point of view is a succession of beautiful women moving before his eyes and in his memory, women he had loved but somehow never possessed. As he says, "Love is all a matter of timing. It's no good meeting the right person too late or too soon."

One of the ideas touched upon here is that of the android lover. I have little doubt that once humans are able to create life-like androids or robots, one of the first enterprises will be to make them experts at pleasing people sexually. Another idea is that of impermanence, of time as our master, of time as fickle and malevolent with change as our enemy. Everybody wants to go to 2046 and never return because nothing ever changes in 2046. Or so it is said because nobody really knows since nobody ever returned from 2046—except Chow. We can guess he returned to find somebody in the past, to recapture something he missed.

In this way, Wong Kar Wai plays with time and human emotions. The result is a gorgeous movie that transcends cultures and leaves the viewer wondering what is real and what is make believe. Here's a question, where is that country from which no one returns? Is such a place a metaphor? And for what? Here it is from Shakespeare's Hamlet: "The undiscover'd country from whose bourn/No traveler returns..." This is from the "To be or not to be" speech, and that country is death.

I've seen this and I give it____stars.
I want to see it___. I'll pass___.
The review was worth reading___. Not___.

Behind Locked Doors (1948) 6

Interesting grade B thriller

It seems like everything done in black and white in the forties, unless there was some singing and dancing in it, is now a film noir. (Well, excluding Olivier's 1949 *Hamlet*, I suppose.) When this "Poverty Row" production came out in 1948 I'm sure it was billed as a mystery/suspense tale, but never mind. "Film noir" is now a growth industry.

There's a gumshoe, Ross Stewart played by Richard Carlson, whom I recall most indelibly as Herbert A. Philbrick of TV's cold war espionage series "I Led Three Lives" from the fifties when HUAC had us all looking under our beds for commies. Lucille Bremer, near the end (which was also near the beginning) of a very modest filmland career, co-stars as Kathy Lawrence, a newspaper woman with a story idea. She needs a private eye to do the investigative dirty work.

Ross Stewart has just hung out his gumshoe shingle and had the frosted glass door of his office lettered and is paying the painter when Kathy Lawrence shows up. (I love all the private eye movies which begin with the dame showing up at the PI's office needing help. So logical, so correct; so like a noir "Once upon a time.") She wants him to pretend to be insane so that she can get him committed to a private sanitarium where she believes a corrupted judge is hiding, thus the locked doors in the title.

What I liked about this is the way the low-budget production meshed with the gloomy and aptly named "La Siesta Sanitarium," the scenes shot in rather dim light giving everything a kind of shady appearance. The story itself and the direction by Oscar "Budd" Boetticher defines "pedestrian," but there is a curious and authentic period piece feel to the movie that can't be faked. Postmodern directors wanting to capture late-forties, early fifties L.A. atmosphere would do well to take a look at this tidy 62-minute production.

Tor Johnson, the original "hulk" (perhaps) plays a dim-witted but violent punch drunk ex-fighter who is locked in a padded cell. He comes to life when the fire extinguisher outside his door is sadistically "rung" by one of the attendants with his keys, thereby springing the hulk

into shadow boxing imaginary opponents. Could it be that he will get a live one later on...?

See this for Richard Carlson who made a fine living half a century ago playing the lead or supporting roles in a slew of low budget mystery, horror and sci fi pictures, most notably perhaps *The Creature from the Black Lagoon* (1954).

I've seen this and I give it____stars.
I want to see it___. I'll pass___.
The review was worth reading___. Not___.

Blood Simple (1984) 7

Diverting and original, but a little too slick

Joel and Ethan Coen made their cinematic debut in this well-plotted, diabolical thriller about a Texas saloon owner (Marty, played by Dan Hedaya) who hires a morally deranged private eye (M. Emmet Walsh) to murder both his two-timing wife (Abby, played by Joel Coen's significant other, Frances McDormand) and her lover (Ray, played by John Getz).

This is one of those movies that looks good as you're watching it; it's even amazing how it all fits together; but later you look back and see how contrived it was. Everything is set up a little too well, with the viewer aware of so many things the characters are not, for example where the Zippo lighter is and how many bullets are left in the revolver and how the gun got to be where it is. That's the sort of thing good writers are supposed to do: start, or at least place themselves, at the end and then work backward. Problem is, you can get too cute, and that's what happens to Coen and Coen here. If everything is too pat and works too well, the viewer is left with an empty feeling of having been hustled by contrivance.

McDormand, seen later as the homespun pregnant police chief in *Fargo* (1996) also directed by Coen, does a good job here of looking like a cheap and easy woman with strong survival instincts. Getz seems just about as stupid as his character needs to be. (His attempted cover-up of the murder was worthy of an appearance on "America's Dumbest Criminals.") Hedaya as the sleazy saloon keep is particularly slimy, and M. Emmet Walsh in his VW beetle with the doll with lighted boobs hanging from the rear view mirror is fully degenerate in that good old Southern style.

Some annoyances: Why do Abby and Ray sleep and mate with the blinds up so the P.I. can conveniently photograph them? (Who does THAT?) Did I lose track of the number of bullets left in the revolver or was there a gap in their placement, and even if there really was one left at the end why doesn't Abby wait until she can see him to shoot, and how come she doesn't check to see if the gun is loaded? And how come the window is about four inches open, instead of closed or open more, after Abby climbs out the bathroom window into it; and how come Walsh is feeling around in the window? Is he using his hand as bait?

Coen and Coen admitted in an article in the *New Yorker* that this was not their best work, and had they been more experienced, they would have done it differently. Of course. But there is an undercurrent of black humor and irony and a whole slew of original touches (the car and the car's tracks in the farmer's field at break of day, the quiet rural Texas roads at night, the dead fish on the desk, etc.) that suggest a rare cinematic talent in the making. *Fargo* (1996) was a mature expression of that talent. It will be interesting to see what they do next. Regardless, this is already a cult classic and the kind of movie that aficionados understandably like to own. If you're a film noir fan, you should definitely see this, despite its acknowledged shortcomings.

I've seen this and I give it____stars.
I want to see it___. I'll pass___.
The review was worth reading___. Not___.

Body Heat (1981) 8

I'm sweating

This is a very cleverly contrived sexploitation thriller/film noir, penned and directed by the talented Lawrence Kasdan. It stars Academy-Award winner (*Kiss of the Spider Woman* (1985)) William Hurt with a mustache and a dangling cigarette as Ned Racine, a not overly bright Florida lawyer smitten by Matty Walker (Kathleen Turner in her steamy film debut) a rich housewife with a husband she hates, and a yearning to breathe free. Shades of James M. Cain's *The Postman Always Rings Twice* and *Double Indemnity*, both triangle murder tales made into film noirs.

Kasdan is cribbing, but I forgive him since in some ways his film is an improvement on both the novels and the films they inspired, plus his is a kind of satire on those films with numerous witticisms. I especially liked it when Matty describes her husband, Edmund, a hard-nosed and successful financier played repulsively by Richard Crenna: "I can't stand the thought of him. He's small and mean and weak." Ned gives this some serious thought and then kisses her on the head like she's a good little girl.

Not too much later, after the first mention of the murder, immediately in the very next scene, Kasdan does a little foreshadowing with lawyer Ned visiting the jail. The steel door clangs shut behind him, startling him and causing him to jump in fright. I also liked the fog on the night of the murder, and I especially liked it when Ned, after putting the body in the trunk, closes the lid to reveal Matty standing there directly in our line of sight, a kind of visual witticism. I also liked the scene in which the lawyers are sitting around the varnished wood with

Matty and the woman she has shrewdly cheated, and the lead lawyer asks if anyone would like to smoke. Everybody (except Ted Danson) eagerly and immediately lights up. Ted says he'll just breathe the air. This is a little in-joke satire by Kasdan on the fact that Hollywood movies of the day were financially encouraged by the tobacco companies to show the players happily puffing away as often as possible.

William Hurt really is excellent, almost as good as he was in *Kiss of the Spider Woman*, and that was very good indeed. Turner is completely believable as a voracious and greedy femme fatale with a wondrous criminal mind. The dialogue is sharp and clever throughout; especially interesting are the dueling "pick-up" rejoinders by Ned and Matty when they first meet. Noteworthy is the performance of Ted Danson of TV's "Cheers" fame as a prosecutor in black-rimmed specs. He has some spiffy lines of his own and he does a great job, as does Mickey Rourke as Teddy Lewis, Ned's fire-bombing buddy.

The plot twists are in some sense anticipated, but the exact nature of their unfolding is fascinating to watch. Indeed, Kasdan's snappy direction of his diabolically wicked tale is practically seamless. This is not to say that it was perfect. I have to point out that the scene in which Matty is in the tub with Ned and he dumps more ice cubes in to cool her off is a little on the contrived side since they surely had air conditioning. She claims to a natural body temperature of 100, reminding me of the classic rock lyric, "I'm hot-blooded, check it and see/I've got a temperature of a hundred and three." Also Matty's seduction of Ned was a little too fortuitous. I don't think she would have left so much to chance. But I liked the beginning anyway because it led us to believe that this would be a tale of sexual obsession (which in part it is) and not just an adulterous murder thriller.

Be advised that the sex is indeed steamy. If explicit sex offends you, you will be offended. Of course I was not. Indeed I found it somewhat refreshing to see a movie in which there is only sexual appetite without any pretense of love or redemption, just lust and its accompanying disillusionment.

This is film noir for 1981 just before the rise of AIDS and the sexual self-censorship that Hollywood embraced (as it switched to more explicit violence). See it with your mistress.

I've seen this and I give it____stars.
I want to see it___. I'll pass___.
The review was worth reading___. Not___.

Dark Passage (1947) 7

Agreeable, but not Bogey and Bacall's best

This is the one in which Humphrey Bogart is not seen on camera until the movie is about a third over. (He's an escaped con who is going to have plastic surgery.) We see his "old" face in a newspaper photo, and then we see Bogart in bandages, reminding me a little of Claude Rains in the original *The Invisible Man* (1933), and finally we Bogey's face when Lauren Bacall removes the bandages.

Although *Dark Passage* is representative of one of my favorite eras in film, namely the late forties/early fifties, on display here is not the best work of either of the principles. Two better films starring Bacall and Bogart are the Howard Hawks production of the Raymond Chandler novel, *The Big Sleep* (1946), and John Huston's *Key Largo* (1948), both classics. Delmer Daves, who went on to direct a number of mid-brow indulgences that achieved some box office success, including *Broken Arrow* (1950), *Kings Go Forth* (1958), and *A Summer Place* (1959), is here the victim of a mediocre script and his own tendency to disregard plausibility and plot logic in favor of moving on to the next scene. On the plus side, Dark Passage is free of the heavy-handed schmaltz and imbedded social messages that sometimes marred Daves' later films—that is, until the bus station scene, when, for a brief moment, I guess he couldn't control himself.

Lauren Bacall is shown to advantage, and when she gets misted up, she is indeed beautiful. But there is little challenge in the part she plays. Bogart is his usual self of course, and manages, once he gets the bandages off, to continue that very fine portrayal. However, the chemistry between Bogart and Bacall doesn't amount to much (although Bacall certainly is trying) until the phone call from the bus station.

What Daves does manage well is the atmospheric feel of mid-century San Francisco. (I wonder if Florshiem Shoes and The Owl Drug Store paid for the shots that lingered on their lighted marquees...) Bacall's apartment with the winding staircase and the hi fi record player console, and the suits and hats of the men, and Bacall's languid, sleek dresses with the boxed shoulders, the cigarette cases and the pre rock and roll pop tunes on the radio (especially Mercer and Whiting's, "Too Marvelous for Words," sung by Jo Stafford) offer a nostalgic sense of time and place. Also good is the work of some of the supporting characters including Tom D'Andrea as the cabby and Houseley Stevenson as the plastic surgeon. Agnes Moorehead is memorable as Bogey's villainous ex. Perhaps the highlight of the film is the corny, but entirely agreeable, finale at the Peruvian cantina.

I've seen this and I give it____stars.
I want to see it___. I'll pass___.
The review was worth reading___. Not___.

Detour (1945) 6
Grade B, but one of the most memorable of film noirs

"What kind of dames thumb rides? Sunday school teachers?"

I guess this would be the most appropriate tagline for this black and white grade B noir from 1945. Al Roberts (Tom Neal) is the one asking the rhetorical question, although it could have been Charles Haskell Jr. (Edmund MacDonald) who has some nasty scratches on his hand to prove he can speak from experience. The lady in question is Vera (Ann Savage) who can turn on you like a cornered rat and strike at you like a rattlesnake, which is what she does to Roberts after he's picked her up hitchhiking. In a scene as startling as any I've seen in quite a while, Vera wakes from a nap and suddenly, without warning, but in retrospect with plenty of foreshadowing, viciously tears into Roberts who finds himself caught in a deadly vice of his own making.

Roberts plays it passively, a born loser who knows he's losing again. A pianist who once dreamed of Carnegie Hall, he just knuckles under to Vera who comes off as a domimatrix. But Roberts can't get a yen for her since he's still in love with his sweetheart, a night club singer named Sue Harvey (Claudia Drake). Too bad, if he had, he might have gotten the upper hand in his relationship with Vera because she certainly wants him. Hell hath no fury like a woman scorned, it is said, and 'tis true, I can tell you, but Vera had the fury from first glance.

Some of the dialogue is pretty lame, dime novel realistic you might say, the kind of talk that is written on the fly without imagination. E.g., "As I drove off, it was still raining and the drops streaked down the windshield like tears," which might not have been half bad except that the windshield wipers were flapping and there were no tracks of anybody's tears... Or, how about this: "Life's like a ball game. You gotta take a swing at whatever comes along before you find it's the ninth inning."

Strange to say though, sprinkled among the prosaic and the banal are such gems as the one at the top of this review and this: "So when this drunk handed me a ten spot after a request, I couldn't get very excited. What was it I asked myself? A piece of paper crawling with germs. Couldn't buy anything I wanted."

Sociologically speaking, this is a bit of a retrofit from the Depression era which featured gritty tales about guys down on their luck hitchhiking and looking for that one big shot at something, anything, love, money, half a break. And Roberts, even though a pianist of some talent, is like a James M. Cain protagonist, an ordinary Joe who gets involved with a dame (or two) and somehow makes the wrong moves and ends up in the deepest of deep quagmires. And like many another antihero, we can sympathize with him although we know and can see it's mostly his own damn fault. Fate has dealt him a bad hand that he should have tossed in, but he plays it out with the kind of fatalism that would befit a minor Greek tragedy.

I've seen this and I give it___stars.
I want to see it___. I'll pass___.
The review was worth reading___. Not___.

Elevator to the Gallows| (*Ascenseur pour l'é-*

chafaud) (1957) 10
Top floor film noir from one of the greats

This was Louis Malle's first full-length feature. Previously he had worked with Jacques Cousteau on "The Silent World" (interestingly enough) and now tried his hand at film noir. Several things fell into place to make this debut a memorable one.

First, he was able to get Jeanne Moreau to play Florence Carala. She had previously been mostly a stage and B-movie player who was obviously very talented, but as Malle put it, not considered really photogenic. What she becomes after her performance here is a premier star of the French cinema partially because of the way she is photographed, and partly because she was so perfectly suited to the character, which I suspect she helped to create. She does a lot silently or with just a few words in the scenes where she walks the streets of Paris, frantic because her lover and fellow murder conspirator, Julien Tavernier (Maurice Ronet) has stood her up and she cannot understand what has happened.

Second, Malle's collaboration with screenwriter and novelist Roger Nimier adapting a *roman* thriller by Noel Calef to the screen turned out to be exactly right for the material, especially because they used mostly just the plot of the novel and expanded Moreau's role.

The third factor was the fortuitous jazz score by Miles Davis. Davis happened to be in Paris as the movie was being edited and Malle was able to talk him into doing a trumpet-centered original score, said to have been composed on the fly late one night and early the next morning as Moreau drank champagne and listened.

"Ascenseur pour l'echafaud," like so many American film noirs that it frankly resembles, is a murder done for love and money gone wrong. It is both a mistake by the murderer and fate itself that traps Julien Tavernier. But there is an intriguing complication in the person of young Louis (Georges Poujouly) who steals Julien's car and takes the flower girl (who admired the dashing Tavernier from afar) on an ill-fated joy ride. Unlike most of Malle's work to come, this is clearly a plot-driven, commercial flick (but oh, so exquisitely done!) without a hint of the usual autobiographical elements for which Malle is so well-known.

The Criterion Collection two disc set features interviews with Moreau, Malle and others, and includes Malle's student film, "Crazeologie," (after a Charlie Parker tune) a "theater of the absurd" little ditty about which I can only say I would never have guessed that Louis Malle was the *auteur*. "Elevator to the Gallows" itself is a beautifully restored high-definition black and white transfer with new and excellent subtitles. There is a booklet with an insightful review by Terrence Rafferty and part of a very interesting interview with Malle conducted by Philip French.

By the way, Malle was 24-years-old when he made this film and commented that he was very worried about his ability to work with actors since he had "spent four years" previously "filming fish"! (quoting from the Philip French interview). He gives Jeanne Moreau credit for being "incredibly helpful" until he lost his fear of actors.

So, see this for Jeanne Moreau, one of the legends of the French cinema, who displays here a kind of magnetic sexuality that had me thoroughly intrigued.

I've seen this and I give it___stars.
I want to see it___. I'll pass___.
The review was worth reading___. Not___.

The Grifters (1990) 7

Great cast amid some plot contrivances

What Lilly Dillon (Anjelica Huston in a long tight dress) is doing in this movie is laying off a bookie's bets. But, like a lot else in this plot-challenged movie, it's not really realistic. The way it's supposed to work is this: the bookie takes in some big time money on a long shot. This understandably scares the bookie since the fix may be on (or the nag might win legitimately) and if so, he's out a whole lot of money. So to protect himself, HE bets on the nag (using a confederate at the track).

This is called hedging. Hedging, whether in sports betting or in the stock or commodities markets works like an insurance policy. But it comes at a price. Take a simpler case. The Yankees are entertaining the Dodgers at Yankee Stadium. The line on the game is Yankees -200, that is, the Yankees are about a two to one favorite. If you want to bet on the Yankees you've got to put up $200 to win $100. If you bet on the Dodgers you put up $100 to win $200. (Actually, the "spread" or "vig" reduces that to $180.) Now suppose the bookie gets a couple of $10,000 bets on the Dodgers. Since his daily handle is usually about half that, he begins to sweat. Sure, he'll have a $20,000-day if the Yankees win, but what if the Dodgers win? Then he's out $36,000 dollars and maybe out of business. So what does he do? He hedges; that is he goes to a bigger bookie or to his Lilly in Las Vegas and lays off the action with a $20,000 bet on the Dodgers. Now if the Dodgers win he breaks even and lives to book another day. If the Yankees win, he still breaks even (instead of winning $20,000). But that's the price he pays for laying off, for hedging. Call it insurance.

Now the problem with all this in the movie is that Lilly cannot be at every race track in the country. So for Director Stephen Frears to make the action plausible he needs to show that Lilly's regular job is to hang out in California (by the phone!) to cover the West Coast tracks in case a lot of strange money comes in that the bookie needs to lay off. Presumably this is what Lilly is doing in the movie. For more realism, Frears could have shown Lilly hanging by the phone, working for several bookies.

Frears has a great cast and they do a fine job. But the plot contrivances keep this from being a really top notch noir flick. Worse stupidity is the scene in which Myra (Annette Bening) finds a motel key on her 100-plus key ring to open Lilly's motel door. Even though Lilly is on the run, apparently she doesn't bother with a second lock, or the chain lock. (Sure.) Second worse stupidity is Lilly sitting in the track's parking lot in full view of the grandstand overhead (although admittedly many feet away) with the trunk of her car open and a drawer full of money exposed for all the world to see. She doesn't have to play with her money in the parking lot. She can wait until she gets to her motel. But this contrivance allows Myra to see the money with binoculars. And as for Roy Dillon (John Cusack) hiding his money inside some strangely thick clown paintings in his living room...I don't think so. And Dillon finding one die on the floor of the dining room car of the train doesn't work either because later he has to "find" the other one (an action we don't see) so he can fleece the sailors with his loaded dice.

Not all the action is unrealistic however. Roy Dillon's little hustle with the flashing of the twenty and the switch to the ten is an actual con done innumerable times; and the reaction of bar keep who catches Dillon in the act is perfect, illustrating how people who work at cash registers feel about people who work little cons on them. And the business beginning when Lilly doesn't lay off the money on "Troubadour," and hears the very sad news on the radio that the horse actually wins the race, and then gets punished by her boss, is realistic because he is out some serious money. By the way, a person in Lilly's position, in effect becomes a bookie herself, if she wants to. She can bet a little less on the nag and pocket the change when the nag loses, as the nag usually will. Of course if she bets nothing, the tote board odds don't go down and so the bookie will know. Worse is when she doesn't bet and the nag comes in. Now she has to pay the bookie out of her own money. In the case of Troubadour, a 70 to one shot, obviously she couldn't afford to pay off and so had to take a beating, literary. The dialogue between her and Bobo (Pat Hingle) is perfect if you understand that he knows that she steals a little, here and there.

Be forewarned that the subplot is Oedipal and spicily played in parts. I'm sure Huston and Cusack had a few laughs off camera, but we are left not really knowing whether Lilly really is his mother or not. (Perhaps that's a good thing.)

All in all there's some nice grifter atmosphere in the movie and Cusack is interesting as a baby-faced little hustler, and Bening is sleazy, sexy and desperate, while Huston is both fawning and cowardly, and sneaky strong. In short, the cast is interesting and they do a great job. See this for Anjelica Huston who makes a complex character real.

I've seen this and I give it___stars.
I want to see it___. I'll pass___.
The review was worth reading___. Not___.

The Hot Spot (1990) 8
Steamy film noir

The hot shot (not to be confused with the hot spot of the title, which is located...well, on the person of Dolly Harshaw, as you'll see) is Harry Madox (Don Johnson) who has just arrived in Podunk, Texas. What he's hot about is selling used cars and bedding floosies. He scans the small town scene to see what's available. He's a hunk with a gift of the macho and an ability to move clunkers off the lot. What he finds is the used car lot of George Harshaw (Jerry Hardin) in need of a salesman. George has a bad heart and a young and sexy wife, the aforementioned Dolly Harshaw (Virginia Madsen, who once played in a movie called "Zombie High" or "The High School that Ate My Brain"). She's a woman who always gets what she wants, and once she sets her rapacious eyes on Harry, Harry is what she wants.

Harry has other plans however. There's this bank in town that he just happens into as there's a fire going down the street. The bank is wide open and there's nobody there but this blind old black guy and the bank manager. Seems that the surveillance system isn't working and what's more all the tellers are off fighting the fire because they all belong to the volunteer fire department. This gives Harry ideas.

One more complication. Doing the books for George is Gloria Harper (Jennifer Connelly at 19) looking about as tasty as pie a la mode and as ripe as a peach about to fall off the tree. Harry soon discovers that she's as sweet as Tupelo honey and nearly as innocent as a small town girl can be with one strange problem. It seems that a country degenerate named Frank Sutton (William Sadler) has got some kind of hold on her.

So what we have here is a setting for film noir circa 1990 done up in color with a lot of upper body and tail end nudity and plenty of steamy sex. Will Harry pull off the bank job and retire to the Caribbean? Or will he put on George's shoes and service the very serviceable Mrs. H? Or will he succumb to the charms of Gloria? Or will he end up afoul of the local law or meet foul play at the hands of Frank Sutton? Stay tuned. I know I did even though this is not exactly a masterpiece.

Top three reasons to see this diversion are:

(1) Virginia Madsen, who is as hot as the barrel of an AK-47 as it unloads, with a mind devious enough to delight the devil himself.

(2) Jennifer Connelly, who is pretty enough to awaken the libido of the dead.

(3) The nice twist at the end in which we learn that life has a certain perverse logic to it, proving that the hero may not get what he wants, but hey, things could be worse.

I guess I should also mention the direction of Dennis Hopper who has garnered over 200 film credits in a career going back to the fifties. Can you believe he played in the classic teen angst film *Rebel Without a Cause* from 1955? Here he just panders shamelessly to the prurient interest of the audience while moving the action along at a spritely pace.

One problem for today's sophisticated viewer: beware of being overcome with a constant stream of cigarette smoke. I mean, did the tobacco industry front the cash for this?

I've seen this and I give it____stars.
I want to see it___. I'll pass___.
The review was worth reading___. Not___.

Key Largo (1948) 8
Edward G. Robinson at his best

Key Largo is just one of John Huston's many memorable films that somehow always seem to transcend the intention—the Hollywood intention being to make a few bucks—and to this day still plays very well and indeed appears as something close to a work of art. It features what I think is one of Edward G. Robinson's finest performances as Johnny Rocco, a sociopathic gangster holding the off-season personnel of a seaside hotel hostage as he concludes a counterfeit money deal.

The story begins as Major Frank McCloud (Humphrey Bogart) pays a visit to the family of one of his G.I. buddies who was killed in Italy during WWII. He finds the welcome from the hotel's only "guests" chilly except for Gaye Dawn (a funny and perhaps prescient Hollywood stage name) played by Claire Trevor who is drunk and befriends him. After a bit McCloud discovers that the hotel's owner Nora Temple (Lauren Bacall) and her invalid father-in-law James Temple (Lionel Barrymore) have been tricked into allowing Rocco's gang to stay and now, as a tropical storm begins to blow, are being held at gunpoint. McCloud's delicate task is to keep the mega-lomaniac and murderous personality of Rocco under some control so that he doesn't murder everyone.

Note that this is a splendid cast, and they all do a good job. Note too that Huston adapted this from a play by the versatile American playwright Maxwell Anderson. So the ingredients for a good film are clearly in place; and aside from some self-conscious mishmash with the Seminoles of Florida, this is a success. Anderson's desire to explore the psychopathic personality (some years later he adapted William March's novel *The Bad Seed* into a stage play) finds realization in Huston's direction and especially in Robinson's indelible performance. The utter disregard for the lives of others and the obsessive love of self that characterize the sociopath reek from the snares and callous laughter of the very sick Johnny Rocco. I especially liked the crazed and thrilled grin on his face when he emerges from the hold of the boat in the climactic scene, gun in hand, imagining that he has once again fooled his adversaries and is about to delightfully shoot Humphrey Bogart to death. What I loved about this scene was that Huston did not think it necessary to contrive a fight in which the good guy (Bogart) beats the bad guy by fighting fair. What happens is exactly what should happen, and without regard for the fine points of Marquis of Queensberry-type rules. Also good is Rocco beginning to sweat in fear of his life as the storm moves in while Bogey gives us his famous laugh and grin as he assesses the essential cowardice of the petty gangster.

Lauren Bacall, in one of her more modest roles, does a lot without saying much, and Lionel Barrymore is very good as the cantankerous old guy in a wheelchair. Claire Trevor actually won an Academy Award as Best Supporting Actress for her work, and she was good as the alcoholic moll with a heart of gold. Robinson won nothing, but he really dominated the picture and demonstrated why he was one of Hollywood's greatest stars.

Bottom line: watch this to see the gangster yarn meld into film noir with overtones of the psychoanalytical drama that characterized many of the black and white Hollywood films of the forties and early fifties.

I've seen this and I give it____stars.
I want to see it___. I'll pass___.
The review was worth reading___. Not___.

The Killing (1956) 8
Script Writing 101 by Kubrick

The "killing" in the title refers to "making a killing," which is what ex-con Johnny Clay (Sterling Hayden) wants to do as a kind of last heist before running off to matrimonial bliss with his girlfriend Fay (Coleen Gray). This early work by Stanley Kubrick qualifies as a film noir, I suppose, since we are compelled to identify with the bad guys, especially with Clay who is a regular kind of joe who just happens to be a stick up artist. The Hollywood "code" that demanded that all bad guys get their just desserts before "The End" (yes, they still ran "The End" in 1956) was apparently still in effect, so I'm not so sure. I recall that Hitchcock in his television series used to make fun of the code by sometimes ending his weekly episode with the bad guy getting away clean, only to appear himself after the commercial and tell the audience that the bad guy was, alas, run over by a truck after helping an old lady cross the street, or something like that.

The Killing, aka, "Clean Break" from the novel by Lionel White, is a tightly plotted thriller, scripted and directed by Kubrick in a very instructive style. By that I mean Kubrick demonstrates just how tension can be created and maintained by aiming all the action and characterizations toward a single event, in this case the seventh race at (either Hollywood Park or Santa Anita, I couldn't figure out which). This "spokes all pointing toward the hub of the wheel structure" (if I may call it that) has been much admired and imitated. I am thinking in particular of Quentin Tarantino's *Reservoir Dogs* (1992). It looks easy to do and it plays so well, but if we don't care about or identify with the characters, it won't work. Kubrick makes us identify with his second-rate hoods by giving them dimension and motivation. Elisha Cook Jr., in perhaps his greatest role, plays the little guy loser to perfection. I say "perhaps" because I have only seen about a dozen of the over one hundred films in which this great character actor has appeared. His desperate face with the wide, round eyes (as he's about to be hit or blasted away) is not to be forgotten. Marie Windsor plays his two-timing, money-hungry wife, the dame that gums up the works.

This is a superior venture not only because of the tight plotting but because of the vivid atmosphere created and because of some memorable scenes and some clever "movie business" attached to the scenes. I am thinking of the black parking lot attendant who thinks he is being befriended (or perhaps more) by one of the hoods, and the middle aged woman carrying on the conversation with her dog at the airport (a kind of Hitchcockian aside, actually). I was amused by the appearance of a chess and checker parlor ("15 cents an hour") because Kubrick was an avid chess player, although he wasn't very good. It's too bad he never made a film with Humphrey Bogart who loved to play chess on the set between scenes.

Most modern thrillers have several plot red herrings not only to keep us guessing but to divert our attention away from the loose ends they never manage to clean up. Kubrick's rather brutal method of tying up all the loose ends lacked subtlety, but at least he cleaned them up. And there were only a couple of red herrings. One was having the money man show up at the track drunk so we'd think maybe he was going to somehow screw things up, and the other was when Marie Windsor's character intimates to her jealous husband that Clay had his way with her, which makes us expect that Cook will gum up the works in a fit of jealousy.

The final sequence at the airport and what happens to the contents of the suitcase is not to be missed, after which Clay's final words of profound exasperation are just perfect.

I've seen this and I give it____stars.
I want to see it___. I'll pass___.
The review was worth reading___. Not___.

Killer's Kiss (1955) 8

Early Kubrick, definitely worth seeing

This is a tidy little opus that Kubrick wrote, directed and filmed himself on a $40,000 borrowed budget. It comes a year before *The Killing* (1956), a more substantial film noir that marked Kubrick as a film maker for whom you might want to front some real money.

Killer's Kiss runs sixty-seven mostly taunt minutes in New York City gritty black and white, featuring some stylistic variations on some standard Hollywood noir elements: the fight game, bare-knuckle toughs, a chase scene, a good guy/bad guy fight (the bad guy, Vincent Rapolla played by Frank Silvera, swinging a fireman's axe, the good guy, Davey Gordon—Jamie Smith—coming up with what looks like a pointed flag pole), a blond beauty to be fought over, Gloria Price (Irene Kane AKA Chris Chase), and a very satisfying ending.

The film is framed as a first person flashback from Davey Gordon as he waits for a train to Seattle. He's a prize fighter with eighty-plus fights under his belt, but a guy with a weak chin near the end of a mediocre career who serves as a tune-up for contenders. Gloria Price is a dancehall girl controlled by the dancehall manager, the bad guy, Vincent Rapolla, a kind of swarthy masher. All the action takes place in a two to three day period following Davey Gordon's last fight. The last scene neatly takes place at the train station.

Kubrick doesn't dwell on the fight game much. We see the gym where the fighters are working out and Gordon's last fight against "Kid Rodriguez" which is over quickly (although three minutes in the ring is an eternity for the fighters). Andy Warhol would have loved the later fight scene which takes place in a storeroom full of hundreds of white, naked manikins that the combatants toss at each other to ward off axe and pointed flag pole. Hitchcock (and others, by the way) would have smiled at the scenes in which Gordon and Gloria can see the action in the other's apartment through conveniently opened apartment windows. (But this was before most people had air conditioning.)

Irene Kane reminded me a bit of Grace Kelly, not quite as tall or as graceful, but a bit more sensuous with similar features.

I was struck by Kubrick's clear, tight direction and by his use of the camera to highlight the mundane but very telling artifacts that surrounded the lives of the characters: the cheap, tiny apartments, the hard indifferent streets of the city, Gloria's old doll, the glitter of the marquees ("The Queen of Sheba" was playing at one theatre), the window shade that flies back up, the not really pretty dancehall girls, and the repeated focus on important elements, like the axe and guns. I was amused to think that even the very young Kubrick exhausted the actors, especially in the fight scenes.

This is a film by a young man who impresses with his knowledge of the psychology of film noir while displaying his artistic talent. I predict a great career.

I've seen this and I give it___stars.
I want to see it___. I'll pass___.
The review was worth reading___. Not___.

L.A. Confidential (1997) 8

Classy film noir thriller with atmosphere

"L.A. Confidential" is a "guy thing," a well-directed, fast-paced thriller with an atmospheric feel comparable to say "Chinatown" and "Sunset Boulevard." Director Curtis Hanson brings the fifties L.A. milieu to life with music, authentic appearing sets and a story that focuses on crime and corruption, false glamour and moral disillusionment as only the City of Angels could play it. Things get a little bit comic book toward the end, but the characters and story and the rapid-fire one-liners will keep you glued to the screen. There's a lot of Raymond Chandler's L.A. here.

"Confidential" was the name of an "exposé" magazine published in the fifties in the L.A. area. I recall seeing it as a kid in liquor stores at some distance from the comic books. It used green lettering on its first page (the only page I ever saw), and amazing as it may be, I recall a headline once seen: "Youth Attacks/Rapes Own Mother." In this film the magazine is called "Hush-Hush," and Danny DeVito is appropriately cast as its sleazy editor and publisher.

Kim Basinger appears as a Veronica Lake look-a-like prostitute and plays it like Lauren Becall from a Bogey film, but without any wit or grace. James Cromwell is the personification of evil as the morally sick Capt Dudley Smith. Russell Crowe as Bud White, the justice-dispensing cop with a brutal temper and a soft heart for battered dames, gives an excellent performance. Guy Pearce as Ed Exley, the cop with glasses who doesn't care what the other cops think is also very good. Kevin Spacey as Jack Vincennes, the cop whose thrill is to be

part of the TV production "Badge of Honor" (that's the old "Dragnet" series with Jack Webb from the fifties) is also good.

In short, the cast is excellent and is probably the main reason this classy "shoot 'em up" is so over-rated. It was number 27 on IMDb's top 250 last time I looked. Recent movies and especially male-ID films tend to be overrated on this site. As the Internet and IMDb acquire a greater feminine voice, the ratings of thriller/action/adventure flicks will tumble.

A question to ask while watching this is, was the LAPD really this corrupt? Quick answer: yes. Next question, why? Answer, because all police departments, like all governments eventually become infested with corruption and must to cleaned out or overthrown. Why? Quick, but non-illuminating answer: human nature. Even you and I, if we had to deal with criminals on the one hand and the bureaucracy of the justice system on the other, day after frustrating and cynical day, might very well take on the values and persona of our surroundings.

Some authentic period piece phrases heard in the movie: "Just the facts, Jack"; "taco bender"; "just another Hollywood homocide"; "maybe that's why he's under a house in Elysian Park and don't smell too good" and of course the sleazy tabloid tag: "off the record, on the QT and very hush-hush."

One last thought for Director Hanson: Here's a lyric from a fifties tune that should have made the sound track: "Confidential as a church at twilight/Secret and moving as a lover's prayer/My love for you will always be/Confidential to me." They used to moon over that one in the barrios, circa 1955.

I've seen this and I give it___stars.
I want to see it___. I'll pass___.
The review was worth reading___. Not___.

Laura (1944) 9

One of Otto Preminger's best

This is film noir played in part as a comedy of manners. (Incidentally, a comedy of manners gets its name from the satirical possibilities in the differing class views on proper behavior—manners—exploited by playwrights to the delight of an audience placed in a superior position, they think, of social discernment. Here we can see the differentials, but they are not played for comedic effect.)

Gene Tierney (at twenty-four) stars as Laura Hunt, a beautiful career girl who, as the picture opens, has been murdered. (Shot in face with a double barreled shotgun, a point of information not dwelled on by director Otto Preminger. Today's directors, of course, would have begun with a full facial shot of the corpse.) Dana Andrews is the leading man, playing Mark McPherson, a hard-boiled police detective with a soft heart. Vincent Price, who before he became a maven of horror, was actually a soft-spoken, hunkish lady's man, plays Shelby Carpenter, who could afford to have his reputation blemished, but not his clothes. He is a man about town who would fit nicely into a British comedy of manners at the turn of the nineteenth century.

But the surprising star is Clifton Webb who plays Waldo Lydecker, venomous columnist and radio personality, who against his first impressions, falls madly (and of course hopelessly) in love with Laura and becomes her mentor. This was before the genteel and very precise veteran of the musical stage was Mr. Belvedere, and before his triumph in *Cheaper by the Dozen* (1950), that is to say, before he was typecast as an irascible but lovable middle aged man—but not before his fiftieth birthday; strange how the fortunes of actors may go. By the way, George Sanders's Oscar-winning performance as the cynical critic in *All About Eve* (1950), owes something to Webb's work here.

The strength of the movie is in the intriguing storyline featuring surprising but agreeable plot twists, and especially in the fine acting by Webb, Andrews, Tierney and Price. Webb in particular is brilliant. I think this is another example of Otto Preminger getting a lot more out of his actors than he is usually given credit for. See *Anatomy of a Murder* 1959, starring James Stewart and Lee Remick, for another example. Known for turning commercial novels into commercial movies (e.g., *The Man with the Golden Arm* (1955); *Exodus* (1960); *Advise and Consent* (1962)) Preminger is at his best when he lets the material have its way. I call that the invisible style of directing and he follows it here. Add the beautiful score by David Raksin and this movie is a special treat.

As a mystery however it is a little predictable. We know from the beginning not only who will get the girl, but with a very high probability who pulled the trigger. What we don't know in the first case is how, since she is presumably dead, and in the second case, why. The lack of motive hides the killer's identity from us. But rest assured, all is unraveled in the final reel.

See this for Clifton Webb whose improbable Hollywood success, beginning with this movie, started when he was in his fifties and ended when he was in his sixties. If I were a thirty-year-old actor running to auditions, I would call that inspiration.

I've seen this and I give it____stars.
I want to see it___. I'll pass___.
The review was worth reading___. Not___.

The Maltese Falcon (1941) 10

Classic gumshoe tale with a great cast

This was John Huston's first film and some say his best. It features a most interesting cast led by Humphrey Bogart who, one can see, had a great time playing the devil-may-care and cynical private eye, Sam Spade, a creation of mystery novelist Dashiell Hammett, who also created another cinematic favorite, *The Thin Man* (1934) (and sequels) starring William Powell and Myrna Loy. Playing opposite Bogey as the tearful and treacherous Brigid O'Shaughnessy is Mary Astor, at the time in her mid-thirties and a veteran of many films going back to the silent era. Interestingly enough one of the films was *The Runaway Bride* (1930). In Hollywood the films never change, they just get make-overs.

Peter Lorre plays the perfumed and villainous Joel Cairo in a style both humorous and sinister. His distinctive high pitched voice has become a staple of cartoon villains. Sidney Greenstreet, the rotund one, who catches up on his reading while they await the delivery of the falcon, plays Kasper Gutman, art connoisseur and sly crook. Elisha Cook Jr., the eternal little man with a gun, whose face seldom changes expression from that of hurtful vengeance, plays Wilmer Cook, Gutman's bodyguard.

What makes this film the favorite of so many is the supremely confident manner in which Sam Spade deals with not only the motley assortment of crooks and con artists, but with the police, tearful women and the district attorney. He's a man's man whose rationality and good old fashioned common sense allow him to spot deception in the twinkling of an eye and give him the power to turn his back on love if there are strings attached. The cosmopolitan air and the sophisticated script allow the players full scope and they are fascinating to watch. Astor's fake tears and feigned innocence cause both Bogey and the audience to grin broadly. And the tête-a-têtes among all the characters, but especially between Greenstreet and Bogart and Lorre and Bogart—the big eyes, the greedy grabbing of guns—are the kind of scenes you can watch again and again with pleasure.

Some see greed as the theme of this film, and indeed John Huston is very good at delineating the psychology of greed—witness also his *The Treasure of the Sierra Madre* (1948)—but in the existential character of Sam Spade we see an American legend come to life. He is the thinking man of action living life by his wits and an independent code, the kind of man who takes life as it comes but without ever losing his sense of humor, the kind of guy we'd all like to be.

There are a couple of earlier version of this film, *The Maltese Falcon* (1931) with Bebe Daniels and Ricado Cortez, and one starring Bette Davis and Warren William called *Satan Met a Lady* (1936), neither of which I've seen, but I understand that the 1931 version is very good. With help from a script by Truman Capote, Huston made a kind of a spoof in *Beat the Devil* (1954).

Incidentally, in this and in *The Big Sleep* (1946), Bogart never really plays the gumshoe with the kind of hard-nosed disregard for conventional morality as envisioned in the novels, but is politically-corrected for the mass movie audience. Note here however that the first thing Sam Spade does when he gets the guys unconscious is to go through their wallets.

Bottom line: a classic and a treat. Don't miss it.

I've seen this and I give it____stars.
I want to see it___. I'll pass___.
The review was worth reading___. Not___.

Mississippi Mermaid (1969) 8

A *thriller noire* from Truffaut

Although *Mississippi Mermaid* was considered one of Truffaut's losers, it has charm, and the personalities of the characters will stay with you. It's clearly better than its reputation. Said to be influenced by Hitchcock and then rendered in the Truffautian style, it is a little off the beaten track, and the coincidences are a little ridiculous. Nonetheless Catherine Deneuve is outstanding and strangely at home in a role considered by many to be out of character for her, as though Grace Kelly might play Bonnie in "Bonnie and Clyde."

This comes five years after Deneuve charmed audiences in *The Umbrellas of Cherbourg* (1964), and two years after her success in *Belle de Jour* (1967). She stars here as a skanky ex-home girl with a murderous heart. (Truffaut gives us a flashback to the dorm where they slept with the lights on and had masturbating contests.) For all her elegant beauty Deneuve does manage to look cheap and almost sleazy. In some ways she comes to life in this role more than in any other I've seen. Certainly I've never seen her sexier.

Co-star Jean-Paul Belmondo is engaging as a slightly sweet and naive tobacco farmer from Reunion Island (near Madagascar) who gets Deneuve as a mail order bride, she and her bad boyfriend having first dumped the real mail order bride overboard en route. If you've never seen Belmondo you should since he was a sensation in his prime, something like a French Marlon Brando.

I've seen this and I give it____stars.
I want to see it___. I'll pass___.
The review was worth reading___. Not___.

Rififi (1954) 9

Film noir meets New Wave

Or vice-versa.

This is a French film noir directed by an American film maker (Jules Dassin) who had to leave the country because of being blacklisted by Hollywood thanks to HUAC. The premise of the story is rather familiar—one last jewel heist for Tony le Stephanois and his buds—and so is the ending with everybody getting... Well, no spoilers here, for sure, since this is the sort of film in which tension toward the ending is important.

Dassin filmed in realistic lighting in black and white on the streets of Paris using actors and actresses who are not glamourous. The engaging—sometimes intruding—score by Georges Auric nicely enhances the movie and will remind viewers of many a similar score from American film noirs from the forties and early fifties. Jean Servais plays the hardcore, consumptive lead in a fedora much as Humphrey Bogart might have played him. Tony's recently out of prison, past his prime, but still tough and decisive when he has to be, his mind still sharp when focused, the kind of anti-hero whose eyes water even though the tears will never fall.

Dassin plays the Italian safecracker and would-be lady's man who knows the rules but gets careless.

In film noir we are forced by the logic and focus of the film to identify with the bad guys. Often there are levels of bad guys, the "good" bad guys we are identifying with and the "bad" bad guys who are out to do in our good bad guys, and then maybe there's a really bad, bad bad guy or two. (Here we have Remi Grutter, played by Robert Hossein, a slightly sadistic druggie.) Then there are the cops who are irrelevant or nearly so. In more modern film noir the bad guys are not even "good" bad guys, and they get away with it or something close to that. In the old film noir, which evolved from the gangster films of the thirties, the usual motto, following the old Hollywood "code," was "Crime Doesn't Pay," with every criminal having to pay for his or her crime before the end of the movie.

Probably the most impressive feature of Rififi is how nicely the film moves along. The plot unfolds quickly and seamlessly much the way the great film directors always did it, directors like Stanley Kubrick, Louis Malle, and the best of Hitchcock. Some have actually compared this to Kubrick's The Killing (1956) and suggest that Kubrick stole a little. Well, directors always steal if need be, and there are some perhaps telling similarities, such as it being "one last heist" for the protagonist, and having the girl gum up the works. The similarities may go deeper because as this film was nearing its end I suddenly thought, oh, no! the suitcase in the back seat is going to fly out of the convertible, hit the ground, burst open, and all the money is going to fly into the air! Those of you who have seen The Killing may recall what happened to the money near the end of the film! Which reminds me of another film with something bad happening to the money: Oliver Stone's *U Turn* (1997) starring Sean

Penn. There the money in his backpack gets blown to smithereens by a shotgun blast. Ha, ha, ha!

Getting the dubbed version of this film would be an act of sacrilege since the dialogue (when there is some: the heist itself is done entirely without dialogue, about 30 minutes worth) is terse and easy to follow requiring only an occasional glance at the subtitles, which, by the way, are quite utilitarian and guiding as opposed to having every word spelled out.

One other thing: all the brutality is done as sex used to be done in film, that is off camera. A guy gets his throat slit. We don't see it. I kind of like this approach. We don't have to see the gore. You could almost let your kids see Rififi—almost.

Catch this one now and be on the lookout for a Hollywood reprise starring Al Pacino and directed by Harold Becker coming out next year in which you can be sure that the violent scenes will be played out in full.

I've seen this and I give it____stars.
I want to see it___. I'll pass___.
The review was worth reading___. Not___.

Sorry, Wrong Number (1948) 8

Classic film noir, slightly diluted

The title is dialogue spoken at the diabolical finish to this classic and famous film noir based on the radio play of the same name. It stars Barbara Stanwyck as Leona Stevenson, a rich invalid who overhears a telephone conversation between two men who are plotting the murder of an unidentified woman. Alone, from her sickbed she desperately tries to find somebody who will listen to her story and stop the murder from happening. Burt Lancaster co-stars as Henry Stevenson, Leona's handsome husband from the wrong side of the tracks.

Stanwyck's performance is excellent, although according to what I understand (not having heard the radio play), she is not as good as Agnes Moorehead was in the original. Be that as it may, Stanwyck grows in the part until as the story ends she is totally authentic and believable.

Lancaster too does a good job in one of his earlier roles. He went on to star in scores of important films, perhaps most notably in From Here to Eternity (1953) and Elmer

Gantry (1960). Here he is a bit tentative, his enormous screen charisma held in check playing a compromised character.

The screenplay by Lucile Fletcher, based on her radio play, was expanded for the silver screen and consequently the story loses a bit dramatically as the tension is diffused as the end is delayed. Fletcher uses flashbacks to fill us in on the story of how Henry and Leona met and how the murder plot developed and why.

I thought director Anatole Litvak did a good job with the flashbacks, but frankly their artificiality was noticeable. I would have preferred starting the story at the beginning when Leona and Henry first meet and then telling it chronologically without flashback. But that would have been a great departure from the structure of the very successful radio play.

Because of the added material, the movie becomes something more than the original intention. Indeed the theme is expanded, that of the possible consequences of marrying for money, and the consequences—from Leona's point of view—of marrying someone who may or may not love you. I thought this was well done. It is especially interesting to see how trapped Henry feels working for his father-in-law and even living in his father-in-law's house. Also interesting is how Leona's insecurities regarding Henry's love are manifested in psychosomatic symptoms.

When Hollywood once again reprises this (and you can be sure they will, but perhaps they will use email and not the telephone) I suggest that they concentrate on both the dramatic and psychological aspects of the story and tell it straight.

Bottom line: Despite some awkwardness and dissipation of tension, this is one of the best film noirs from that classic era of the genre, the late forties and early fifties. See this for Barbara Stanwyck, one of Hollywood's celebrated stars whose career spanned half a century beginning in the silent film era.

I've seen this and I give it____stars.
I want to see it___. I'll pass___.
The review was worth reading___. Not___.

Chapter Ten:

Some Documentaries Worth Seeing

Not included here are the many nature documentaries available in DVD and on television. I have not included them because I haven't reviewed them even though I've watched just about every major nature documentary made during the last dozen years or so and many before that. I didn't review any of them except for The March of the Penguins *(2005) (the review is in part III of this chapter) mainly because I didn't feel competent to say anything worthwhile except "Wonderful!" (and most really are wonderful); but also because it is good to watch something some of the time without having to take notes or think about what to write.*

Nonetheless I have included in a later chapter from memory a list of the best nature documentaries that I have ever seen.

I

Artists

Andy Goldsworthy: Rivers and Tides:

Working with Time (2003) 10

The timeless and the ephemeral

As the jacket proclaims, this film is "Gorgeously shot and masterfully edited," and, yes, it is mesmerizingly beautiful. The timelessness that we perceive in stoic rock and in the unceasing ebb and flow of water frames the ephemeral works from Goldsworthy's hands so that in their very transitoriness they point to eternity.

And so the beauty of his compositions haunt us with just a touch of melancholy woven in—or in the words of Matthew Arnold from his poem "Dover Beach":

Listen! you hear the grating roar
Of pebbles which the waves draw back, and fling,
At their return, up the high strand,
Begin, and cease, and then again begin,
With tremulous cadence slow, and bring
The eternal note of sadness in.

At one point near the end of the film Goldsworthy says that "Words do their job, but what I'm doing here says a lot more." As a wordsmith myself I take no offense and not for a moment do I think him immodest because the combination of form and time and change and texture and color and composition that Goldsworthy painstakingly and intuitively creates, is indeed something more than mere words can say.

At another point he remarks on "What is here to stay...and what isn't." That is his theme.

I think that artists sometime in the twentieth century became acutely aware of how ephemeral even the greatest works of art are compared to the vast expanse of cosmic time; and so they began to reflect this understanding by composing works that were deliberately ephemeral. The idea was, that by emphasizing how short-lived are even the mightiest works of humans, a sense of the timelessness of art would be expressed.

Perhaps part of the effectiveness of Goldsworthy's work is in this sort of expression. He painstakingly composes some form of straw or leaves where the tide will reach it, or places it in the river where it will be swept away; and in this process is merged both the composition and its ephemerality.

Both the transitory and the timeless are necessary for us to understand our world and our place within it. And it is important that these works be done within the context of nature so that what is composed is set within what is natural. Thus the walls of stone and the eggs of stone that Goldsworthy constructs are silent and solid; yet we know that they are not monuments to eternity, but instead will stay for some undefined length of time and then dissipate and return to a state much like that which existed before we came along.

This is art as art should be, akin to the spiritual.

In a sense Goldsworthy's work is an unarticulated understanding. It is an experience purely of time and form. In a sense his work "answers" Shelley's famous poem "Ozymandias" by saying, even as the tide washes the work away, and even as the river dissipates the expression, even so the art lives on because of our experience of it. Similarly one thinks of Tibetan sand paintings so carefully composed and measured out, and then just as they are so beautifully and preciously finished, they are given to the wind, so that we might know that all is flux.

Yet, in the modern world these works of art endure in photos and videos. Goldsworthy is an accomplished photographer (of necessity I would say) and all his works, even the unsuccessful ones, he tells us, are photographed so that he can look back at them in a more reflective mood and see what he has accomplished and what he has not.

This cinematic production directed by Thomas Riedelsheimer with the beautiful and appropriately haunting music by Fred Frith is not to be missed. It is one of the most beautiful documentaries that I have ever seen and one of the most spiritual.

I've seen this and I give it____stars.
I want to see it___. I'll pass___.
The review was worth reading___. Not___.

Crumb (1994) 10

A degenerate genius?

Will comic book artist Robert Crumb—best known as "R.Crumb" of "Keep on trucking" fame—someday be recognized as a great American artist of the 20th century? Will future generations speak of him in the same breath as Picasso and Michelangelo? Is he really *that* good? Is the comic book a legitimate art form? Or is he just an ephemeral phenomenon of the American popular culture, to be placed somewhere among Andy Warhol, Tiny Tim, Thomas Kinkade, and Paris Hilton?

Director Terry Zwigoff in this documentary about Crumb's life and work makes a strong affirmative case. He works hard at showing us an iconoclastic genius who, because of his own demons, was able to expose our own. And if genius is, as somebody once said, an infinite capacity for taking pains, then R.Crumb clearly is a candidate. Zwigoff reveals him as a man who draws and observes with an incredibly practiced (left) hand and a most penetrating eye. His big-bottomed women with their legs of knotted muscle that so obsessed him, his black-faced jungle bunnies, like something out of a degenerate southern racist's mind, his demented tales of childish lust for sex and blood—the entire oeuvre of his work seems to cry out to us: *Save me. I am sick. Stop me before I draw again.*

I am reminded in a sense of the bitter work of George Grosz who so effectively depicted the sleazy, gluttonous degeneration of the German middle class between the world wars. There is the same almost juvenile need to shock and smear the bourgeoisie, to rub our faces in our animal nature, and to test the limits of what the burgh-

ers will tolerate. Grosz wisely fled Nazi Germany and Robert Crumb has fled the United States.

I wonder, could it be for similar reasons? There is a point in Zwigoff's film where he shows us a particular comic book created by Crumb in which the story is of pornographic incest involving children. If such a comic book were published today it would be seized by the FBI, and the artist and publishers thrown in jail. Could it be that Crumb was ADVISED to leave the US? I also wonder if Zwigoff is in any danger himself, having produced this documentary which shows part of the verboten action. Will the morality police go after the film maker? What is the statute of limitations on child pornography?

On the other hand, would they dare? The Supreme Court has defined actionable expression as being utterly without redeeming social value. There can be little doubt that the work of Crumb and Zwigoff is of estimable value to us as a society in that it puts a mirror up to our faces so that we can see our darker, seamier side, an animalistic side that we hide with our clothes and our vehicles or sheltered behind our Venetian blinds and closed doors. A function of the artist is to tell us what nobody else in the society will tell us. Art is not propaganda extolling the virtues of the state or a medium to foster social cohesion or to make us feel good about ourselves. On the contrary, art must penetrate the facade of respectability and reveal us as we really are, perversions and all.

Crumb does this. He is compelled to do this. He takes the infinite pains to exaggerate what we look like so that we can see what we really are. Of course society as seen through the lens of the artist is always to some extent a distortion filtered through the psyche of the artist. In Crumb's case we can see, thanks to Zwigoff's fine work, that a dysfunctional family life, combined with a difficult experience as a child and teen, sowed the bitter seeds that would spring up in the sunshine of his accomplished adulthood. This is why Zwigoff needed to set up his camera in the Crumb household, to show us Max in his messiness at home still living with his mother, taking his meds and staying indoors with his rotting teeth. And that is why we needed to see his talented brother Charles, pathetically upon his bed of nails prior to his suicide. And that is also why Robert Crumb's sisters declined to participate in the filming. They knew what it would reveal. And that is also why R.Crumb himself is reported to have hated this documentary and why he had to be dragged along to get it finished. He was torn. The artist in his soul wanted to see the truth of his life expressed. The everyday Robert Crumb knew that he would regret the exposure.

One thing though that I think has to be a positive for Crumb is that the film makes it clear that he is anything but a sick soul, that he is not only a wizard with his pen, but he is nobody's fool. He comes across as geeky but intelligent and worldly wise with an ability to laugh good-naturedly at humanity's foibles.

Nonetheless we hear Crumb claim that he never loved anybody—lusted after some babes, his two wives, some girlfriends, but he never loved them—until, that is, he fell in love with his daughter. But Zwigoff gives us a hint of what that relationship is like when his camera catches Crumb bestowing a kiss upon his daughter's cheek, a kiss that she immediately wipes off as something annoying. I think that this scene, perhaps more than any, is what R.Crumb regrets about this all too-telling documentary.

My opinion: R.Crumb will indeed be recognized by future generations as a great artist. They will look back at our times and remark how accurately Crumb captured our hypocrisy, and how he was able to project the crimes and misdemeanors of our hidden hearts onto the comic book page with a skill and originality and a brutal honesty only possible from the mind of an artist.

I've seen this and I give it___stars.
I want to see it___. I'll pass___.
The review was worth reading___. Not___.

The Gleaners and I (2000) 9

Artistically done

At one point in this unusual and very interesting documentary by French New Wave director Agnes Varda (born, 1928!) she ties it together by showing art made from "gleaned" articles—that is, trash thrown away and made into objects of art by artists.

Of course it is trite to recall that "one man's trash is another man's treasure," but it is so. How dearly archeologists love ancient midden sites, and how much we can learn about the ancients from their trash. But Varda is here to show us that we can also learn a lot about modern people from what they throw away, and from what is gleaned, and from the gleaners themselves. I thought the guy who ate (grazed almost) as he went through the market place after closing was interesting. Clearly going through the trash is something instinctive with humans: no doubt it comes from our prehistoric past when we were hunters and gatherers.

The main focus here is on gleaning fruits and vegetables left behind by mechanized pickers. It is interesting to note that there are laws going back hundreds of years that regulate gleaners. (Varda puts a French lawyer on camera to quote some relevant law.) I was fascinated to see that there are dumpster divers in France. In America dumpster diving has been a big deal since at least the sixties. Today there are Web sites devoted to dumpster diving, and I personally know some people who dumpster dive for fun and profit. It was also interesting to see just which fruits and vegetables are gleaned from the ground and from the trees and vines and plants left after the harvest, and to hear from the people who do the gleaning. Varda shows mounds of potatoes left behind, and we learn that both potatoes too small and potatoes too big are discarded by the producers. (In America, large potatoes are not only not discarded, they bring a higher price.) Interesting too were her interviews with French gypsies and others who derive a good part of their subsistence from gleaning.

I enjoyed seeing parts of France not normally seen on the screen or by tourists. In fact in some ways this documentary could serve as a kind of travelogue so widely does Varda and her camera travel about the French countryside and cities.

See this for the Grande Dame of French cinema, Agnes Varda, *auteur* of the innovative documentary *Cléo from 5 to 7* (1961) and other films who is now 77 years old and still going strong.

I've seen this and I give it___stars.
I want to see it___. I'll pass___.
The review was worth reading___. Not___.

My Kid Could Paint That (2007) 10

A matter of interpretation

This documentary ends with the credits rolling down the screen and Bob Dylan singing "Everything's gonna be different when I paint my masterpiece." The sense of yearning and a kind of dissatisfaction with what you know that life is going to bring that Dylan expresses in his song is the way so many parents feel about their children. They want everything for them. They want to give them advantages they never had. They see in their children the good genetic parts of themselves and their spouses (and in-laws!) and yet sometimes they want to yell at themselves: Stop that! Let the child be. Let the child be a child.

This is the way Laura Olmstead no doubt felt about her daughter Marla. Four-year-old Marla loved to paint and seemed to have some kind of unusual facility for color and expression. Her paintings came out like little works of art, and then bigger works of art, and then suddenly they were selling for tens of thousands of dollars and little Marla was having art shows in New York City.

Abstract impressionism is considered by some to express the inner workings of our consciousness, to describe in form and color a deep artistic and human truth. To others it is a scam. Mark Olmstead, Marla's father—not exactly an ingénue when it comes to art—encouraged his daughter in her work. He bought paints and took the time to be with her while she was painting. At some point he began to put the canvas on the floor. Occasionally he allows (late in the documentary) that he taught her to PULL the brush, not push it. But he swears he never finished or touched up her work.

Marla became famous and the family garnered some $300,000 from her paintings, with millions more offered if and when she would paint some more. Laura had misgivings, was uneasy, but she wasn't sure why. Mark saw no downside. Little red dots appeared beside her paints at show, indicating that the paintings had been sold. Indeed all her paintings had sold. Curiously a friend named Anthony Brunelli, ironically himself a painter working in photo realism, which I suppose is as far as you can get from the abstract, served as a sometime broker and dealer. It was as though the artist, four-year-old Marla had indeed painted her masterpiece and was living the life of a princess in a fairytale.

And then came a "Sixty Minutes" piece on Marla the prodigy showing her at work. But somehow something wasn't quite right. A child psychologist was interviewed who had looked at the video and said that it didn't look like this child was doing anything that a normal child of her age wouldn't do, and intimated further that you could clearly see the father's guiding hand. The implication was that Mark had "finished" the paintings or had authored them himself!

Marla is a pretty and vivacious little girl. Her mother seems the very embodiment of common sense. Mark seems like a loving and nurturing father. But they become targets of hate mail. Amazing. A segment of the public believes that the parents are scam artists and have bilked a gullible public.

Enter documentary film maker Amir Bar-Ley. He convinces the Olmsteads to allow him into their home with the idea that while making his documentary he will film an entire sequence with Marla at work on one of her masterpieces from start to finish with no help from Dad or anybody else to prove that she is genuine. What we see at times is a reluctant Marla who wants her dad to draw a face or to suggest something.

Mark is caught, not in a lie, but in the logic of his situation. Yes, he had to have "helped" her and there is no doubt (at least to this observer) that in some of the works he guided her choice of colors and painting instruments, which would only be natural. But in the esoteric world of art collecting, if that is admitted, the value of her paintings would plummet. Not only that, but Marla's integrity as a prodigy and his reputation as someone presenting her art, would be compromised as well. So he is caught. And so also is Laura, who wants to tell us that she would love to take a lie-detector test to prove that she in no way misrepresented her daughter's work or her involvement in it.

Whether Mark went further than guiding her is a question that the documentary leaves open to interpretation. The one work shown as completely Marla's (as evidenced by its composition being recorded on film) called "Ocean" may be seen as not on the same level of achievement as her other works. Again this is a matter of interpretation.

In a sense this is also a story about people who buy abstract art for high prices. It is about the vanity of collectors.

How does it end? See for yourself, but of course it may not end until Marla is old and her parents are gone, and even then, what really happened, and what it really means will continue to be—as is always the case with art—a matter of interpretation.

(For what it's worth, I have little doubt that Marla was "marketed" especially by her father and Anthony. Just ask yourself, who chose the names for the paintings, "Ode to Pollock," Asian Sunrise," etc.? Not Marla, that is for sure. And when Marla says, I'm done. It's your turn, Dad, I think we get the picture. But I would tar with the brush of "human, all too human" only Mark, Tony and the art collectors, not Laura who knew they would be compromised in some way, and of course not little Marla who was as pure as gold throughout.)

I've seen this and I give it____stars.
I want to see it___. I'll pass___.
The review was worth reading___. Not___.

II

War and other Unpleasantries

I barely touch the surface of what is available in war documentaries. The documentaries in this section addressing war deal with it primarily from a political standpoint. The great documentaries that focus on strategy, weapons and archival footage are clearly beyond my sphere of competence to review. (I know, I know: that never stopped me before.)

Radio Bikini (1987) 7

From the dawn of the nuclear age

What I found interesting about this documentary is the glimpse it gives us of the state of mind of the United States just after World War II, now sixty years past. We see in the newsreel and other film footage the style and substance of America in the afterglow of our greatest victory. But mostly we see ordinary soldiers and sailors who were stationed on or near the Bikini Atoll in the Marshalls in the South Pacific. We also see some of the islanders whom the United States military displaced so that the capabilities of the atom bomb could be explored.

An old uneducated Bikini islander recalls how his people were told that in the interest of "science" (but actually in the interest of weapons development) they would have to leave their home island and be relocated. Then at some point they were told that they would not be able to return to their island since it was "poisoned."

Director Robert Stone shows us the big media build up orchestrated by the US to justify dropping the bomb on Bikini. (Actually one bomb was dropped. Another was exploded under water in the Bikini lagoon.) Dignitaries and scientists from all over the world were invited to watch. Stone shows them arriving and being greeted by the officer in charge as a voice-over gives their names, country of origin and their titles. I found that interesting. Two from India, a couple from the USSR, some Asians, etc. Ah, yes, the US was going to make the world safe from nuclear power by experimenting with nuclear power.

Or some such argument. I thought the dignitaries were positively drooling. Not drooling were the goats and sheep (sheared so that the scientists could see the effects of the radiation on their bare skin) who were trapped in little stalls aboard strategically placed ships near the island. Also not drooling, but having a good time were the sailors who with dark glasses viewed the blast from some safe distance on their ships. They were happy because it looked like an easy duty, and were told that there was no danger. Radiation was never mentioned, and in those days, the dangers of radiation were only just becoming public knowledge. Stone has footage of an interview with one of the sailors years later, only his head and shoulders shown for most of the documentary until near the end when the camera retreats a little and we can see what grotesque things the radiation poisoning did to him. It's pretty shocking footage, and you won't forget it.

We see the blasts and the mushroom clouds and the magnificent glory of the power of the bomb. Unfortunately some observers were down wind and radioactive dust fell upon them. Unfortunately some observers boarded the ships that suffered damage from the blasts (but were far enough away so as not to be destroyed) and got radi-oactive dust on their clothes and skin. Stone shows the sailors exploring the damage while being scanned by Geiger counters going crazy monitoring the radiation. One is struck by the innocence and playfulness of the sailors as the radiation begins its work on their bodies.

In other words this is a snapshot from the dawn of the nuclear age, strangely innocent and diabolical at the same time. I don't think this is a great documentary, but I will say it is effective. For the complete story of what happened at the Bikini Atoll and especially what happened to the islanders who lost their homes and to those exposed to the radiation, the viewer will have to look elsewhere. This is merely an introduction.

I've seen this and I give it___stars.
I want to see it___. I'll pass___.
The review was worth reading___. Not___.

Control Room (2005) 6

The spin war within the war

While this is not by any means a prize-winning documentary it is still worth seeing because of the perspective gained. To see the war through Arab/Muslim eyes is what is gained. It is a bit chilling. Most of us watched the war through the eyes of CNN or Fox or PBS or one or more of the networks, and we saw a biased view. The real carnage was withheld from us because it was believed that to show the bleeding and mangled bodies was to (1) inflame opinion (2) give assistance to the enemy.

It was almost impossible for an American news source to present the war as it really was. No American network executive could do that. But for Al Jazeera, no such reluctance existed. And that is the value of this documentary: it allows us to see what our own news media dared not show, although that too was only part of the story.

Filmmaker Jehane Noujaim uses interviews and footage from inside Al Jazeera's "control room" and footage from the communications center of the coalition forces to show how the reporters worked. Reports from the US authorities, Rumsfeld and the generals, the media officers in the field and at the communications center, are contrasted with actual footage and reports from Iraq. It is clear that the news was managed by both Western services and by Al Jazeera to conform to the expectations and interests of their differing audiences.

Frankly I was surprised that the bias wasn't greater (on both sides). I came away feeling that, given that modern wars are won or lost to some extent by how well the combatants manage the news, this war within a war was a toss-up. And indeed despite Bush's declaration of victory aboard the aircraft carrier, the war on the ground as it exists today is still very much a toss-up. Coalition forces roared into Iraq and found very little resistance. And then began the insurgency. What does it mean to win? How does one side lose? As in Vietnam, victory or defeat is to some extent in the eyes of those watching. In the field there was and is no victory. There is only carnage. And so the combatants try to spin the war to their advantage, because it is in the spin that one may find victory regardless of what happens in the field of battle. In this case, Saddam Hussein and the insurgents had no media. But the Muslim/Arab world needed such a media, and thereby arose Al Jazeera to spin the other side. This documentary affords us a quick look at that network.

However I don't think this documentary was very effective. It lacked focus and continuity. It seemed hastily thrown together. We are shone some interviews, some on-camera reportorial and editorial activities, some footage from the field, from Baghdad, from Mosul. An Al Jazeera reporter is killed by an American missile. The people at Al Jazeera are deeply saddened and outraged. They think it was on purpose, to "punish" them for reporting what Rumsfeld doesn't want reported, and they may be right; but somehow the loss seems almost trivial compared to the rest of it: the tens of thousands of people dead, the uncounted maimed and wounded, the hundreds of billions of dollars spent like buckets of water poured upon a vast and seething desert. Somehow the "news" of the news reporters themselves seems somewhat irrelevant, almost, I thought, a vanity show. We have the power to report what happens, they are telling us. Therefore we have the power to create what happens.

As was famously said, "In war, the first casualty is truth." One thing this documentary does do well is demonstrate the truth of that adage.

I've seen this and I give it____stars.
I want to see it___. I'll pass___.
The review was worth reading___. Not___.

The Fog of War (2002) 10

The life and times of Robert McNamara

Back in the late sixties and early seventies Robert McNamara was a much hated man since it was widely believed that he was the architect of the buildup in Vietnam and therefore personally responsible for one of our country's most disastrous military engagements. After all, he was Secretary of Defense under both Kennedy and Johnson.

But there's a limit to what one man can do no matter how high his office, and that is especially true in a democracy with governmental checks and balances. Moreover, according to the spin of this brilliant documentary by Errol Morris (director of the almost equally brilliant *The Thin Blue Line* 1988), it was really President Lyndon Baines Johnson who insisted on the buildup and slowly, like somebody inching his way blindly into a quagmire,

get stuck in a trap of his own making. Still McNamara, Boy Wonder, now a man in his prime, originally chosen by the ill-fated JFK to be Secretary of Defense, has some serious culpability, even though he is on record as telling President Kennedy in 1963 that we ought to get out. By the way, being offered the job by JFK was an offer he couldn't refuse, even though he protested that he wasn't qualified. JFK knew better. Errol Morris shows this point cleverly by having McNamara say he hadn't yet agreed to take the job as he stood by JFK even as the President publically announced that McNamara was the new Secretary of Defense.

Here then is Morris's technique: Robert McNamara, who at the time this film was made was 85-years-old, long in tooth and watery eyed, yet full of an acute sense of history and of his place in it, was put on camera as he was being interviewed. Again and again the camera holds tight and close on his face and we can see that face asking for understanding, as an overwhelmed parent might ask of his children. Meanwhile, juxtaposed between shots of the man were scenes from his past, B-29s taking off and dropping bombs on Japanese cities, and then jets from the Vietnam era firing rockets and tracers at targets on the ground, bombs falling, falling, falling, and bursting and bodies lying in the rubble.

McNamara would explain. He would justify himself. Or he would offer no excuses. There is the fog of war, he said, and Vietnam was enormously complex not just from a military point of view, but from a political and global perspective. And there was always Lyndon Johnson who could never be persuaded to get out of the bog even as the slime rose to his waist and then to his neck. Incidentally, as far as I can tell the phrase, "the fog of war" is a paraphrase of something Karl von Clausewitz wrote in his famous treatise *On War* (1833).

Included in the voice-overs are recordings made in the Oval Office that were not available to reporters until recent years. Listening to them, I was stuck again and again at the Machiavellian personality of President Johnson as revealed in the verbatim tapes, and at the Iago-like influence of Robert McNamara at his side—Iago in the sense that he whispered in the President's ear, and in the fact that they shared confidences they did not share with others. But Johnson was no easily-led Othello. Instead, Johnson was his own man, a stubborn man, and while he listened eagerly to McNamara, in the final analysis he went his own way down, down into the quagmire.

This is also in a sense a biography of the public Robert McNamara. He talks about his childhood and his days as an undergraduate at Berkeley. There is a shot of him as a young man at the stove of an apartment with his young wife. There is his experience in World War II analyzing bombing effectiveness under General Curtis E. LeMay (who doesn't look good here), and then his phenomenal run at Ford Motor Company where he turned a floundering auto maker into a leader of the industry. There is also his remembrance of the Cuban missile crisis in which he makes it clear that we were—holding his finger and thumb less than an inch apart—"this close" to nuclear war.

McNamara comes off as enormously hard-working, brilliant yes, but with the modesty that comes from hard experience. He seems confident that he did the best he could in a job that required everything he had. He allows that he made mistakes and he reminds us that people in high places who make mistakes make mistakes that can have horrific consequences. He now assures us that he knows war is the wrong way if it can be avoided since in the fog of war we all lose our way. I would add that the logic of war always takes over and has its way with us, regardless of intention. Once the dogs of war are let loose, they run and run and run until they are exhausted. And only then do they come home.

In addition to being an extremely informative and revealing portrait of one of our most controversial secretaries of defense, this is also a marvelous artistic achievement, a film carefully collaged, and sharply edited employing all sorts of archived media with a haunting score by Philip Glass. Of course it doesn't tell us the whole story or anything close to the whole story, and certainly were Lyndon Johnson and Curtis LeMay alive today, they might very well tell it differently.

What I liked most about McNamara here is his willingness to be mostly candid and not only admit errors, but to reveal some of the very human processes by which monumental decisions of state are made. We can thank him for appearing in front of the camera and exposing himself so boldly for all the world to see.

The Fog of War won the Academy Award for Best Documentary Feature in 2003.

I've seen this and I give it___stars.
I want to see it___. I'll pass___.
The review was worth reading___. Not___.

Iraq for Sale: The War Profiteers (2006) 10

Actually it's America for sale and it's a no-bid contract

The war dribbles on, hundreds of billions of dollars dumped into the Iraqi sand, over a hundred thousand people dead, millions made homeless, Halliburton stock triples, Bush has his hair styled, Cheney shoots caged birds thrown from the bed of a pickup truck, heroically I guess or ain't it fun to watch the bird bodies splatter? Meanwhile, somebody somewhere has that "Mission Accomplished" banner. It should go for some serious bucks on Ebay someday. Karl Rove is writing his memoirs: "There's a new reality, the reality of power. Power makes its own reality. (And I—I!—was at the pinnacle: indeed I was the Power and the Glory. Myself. Me.)"

Rumsfeld ditto. But Rummy writes of "shock and awe" and how the generals in the field bungled his best laid plans. And soon George W. himself will be writing his memoirs. The advance will be several million. The lies will probably not exceed that number.

Of course there is no way that I at my computer can find the words to really make clear the stupefying waste and the horrific immorality of what the Bush administration has done in the name that was once America. Robert Greenwald's documentary does it better, much better by focusing on the profiteering by KBR, Halliburton, Blackwater et al. He uses the camera to show the images of human carnage, of the weighty mass of trucks and equipment, of Bush administration officials lying through their teeth on TV, of Bush himself strutting, waving, smiling. There are graphs of profits going up, up, up, street level shots of the stately office buildings of the profiteering companies, silver and glass, sunlight on well-tended lawns. Condi and Rummy, and Dick and Bush lying, lying, and lying some more. And for what? Cheney will be dead soon himself. Bush will be bored (perhaps to drink), their ill-gotten millions of no value to their dying souls.

I liked the way Greenwald predicted the Blackwater scandal, more or less with his focus. (You should check it out.) All those macho guys with their military pensions in their back pockets finding Soldier of Fortune jobs at Blackwater, toting their guns, shooting the enemy in self-defense, making an additional six figures a year. Pallets of hundred dollar bills forklifted off of military transport planes...

Well, Greenwald didn't get THAT shot (too bad), but he did show EMPTY trucks, a convoy, on an Iraqi highway (paid for as LOADED according to the contract). The contract of America with Halliburton. Halliburton with America. What's good for Halliburton is good for America. He shows the hundred dollar a meal meals contracted for those inside the Green Zone. It's surreal and then some. We airlift the PX, the movie theaters, the gym equipment, the computers, the TVs, the Pepsi Cola—well, actually Halliburton was able to substitute some local Iraqi cola at a fraction of the cost. We create a virtual reality army base inside Bagdad where our forces can hang out in safety. Who gains? Those doing the transporting.

More than any war in history, this documentary shows the influence of privatization. With no-bid contracts, of course. Bush hates big government. The way to reduce government is to make it go broke. How do you do that? You create a useless war and sell the contracts to your buds at inflated prices. It's amazing but this is what has happened. And Greenwald documents it.

Problem is, this fine documentary will be lost in the vast sea of information that we ourselves are lost in. Hide in plain sight is what the profiteers have been able to do.

Your stock triples, it's reported on the five o'clock news and in the pages of the New York Times ("our paper, man") but who can see it amid the myriad details of other stock prices or of the endless parade of other numbers, and words, words, words. A billion dollars lost here and there. Pentagon accountants clueless. Just another story on CNN, spun out of sight by Fox News.

You can watch this without the sound. The images tell the story.

This is another fine piece of work by Greenwald. He also directed *Uncovered: The Whole Truth about the Iraq War* (2003) and *Outfoxed: Rupert Murdoch's War on Journalism* (2004). He does a great job with the visuals, the interviews, and the narrative.

I have one tiny criticism. No captions. No English subtitles. Every film and documentary on DVD should have subtitles. That way we can be sure of the exact phrasing of the lies.

I've seen this and I give it____stars.
I want to see it___. I'll pass___.
The review was worth reading___. Not___.

Relentless:

The Struggle for Peace in Israel (2003) 9

Eye-opening

For those who might be sitting on the fence as regards the Israeli-Palestinian conflict this documentary is an eye-opener. I've always found the Palestinian position untenable because of their use of terror. There is no excuse for using your children to kill other people's children regardless of the grievance. It is particularly horrific to use such tactics when peaceful ones—such as those championed by Gandhi and Martin Luther King, Jr.—could be employed with great effect, and indeed might win over much of the world to the Palestinian cause.

After viewing this documentary I am even more disgusted, appalled, sickened and horrified by Palestinian leadership, especially that of the Palestinian Authority under Yasser Arafat. His two-faced, lying persona in which he pretends to be for peace when in fact his actions actually escalated terror are well known from the historical record. However what this documentary shows is that the increase in terror is only one way in which the Palestinian leadership has made it clear that they do not recognize the right of the Jewish people to exist. They still want to drive all the Jews from the lands in the Middle East, even if that means killing them.

"Relentless" begins by outlining the conflict from the establishment of the Jewish state by the Allied powers following WWII. There was one very large problem with

that creation: many Palestinians were displaced. Like so much that is wrong in the Middle East and elsewhere in the world, the fault began with miscalculated actions by the colonial powers. Having acknowledged that fact—and this documentary, to the credit of its authors, does indeed do that—one must, some sixty years later ask, what is to be done now?

One answer was the Oslo accords to which both the Palestinians and the Israelis agreed. However, as this film makes clear it was only the Israelis who lived up to the agreement. The Palestinians did not. Not only was the terror escalated (perhaps the Palestinian leadership thought that the accords were a "reward" for their use of terror), but there was an escalation in the indoctrination of the Palestinian children so that even the youngest children might hate Jews and want to kill them. This film shows Palestinian children reciting words of hatred and singing songs of hatred and violence toward Jews and asserting that what they want to do with their lives is kill Jews. One little girl of about six says that the highest calling of all for her is to become a martyr who kills Jews and dies doing it.

Personally, I think the Israelis were foolish to believe anything Arafat said or to enter into any sort of agreement with him. Of course that is hindsight, but could have been easily discerned by just looking at his record. Now the question is what about the current Palestinian leadership? Has anything really changed? There seems little hope for peace because the vast majority of the people of Palestine have been totally indoctrinated with hatred of the Jewish people, so much so that the majority of them actually believe things that have no basis in reality. For example, a majority of the Palestinian people believe that Jews were the ones who flew the planes into the World Trade Center buildings. They are taught by their religious leaders that Allah wants them to kill Jews. This is insanity on a grand scale. While this mind set prevails I am afraid there will be no peace in the Holy Land.

Well, what about the faults of the Israelis? What about the wall and the settlements and the inescapable fact that Jews have displaced Palestinians, many of whom now live in camps or in Jordan or elsewhere and are subject to checkpoints that restrict their movements?

I would note that the Sunnis displaced Kurds in Iraq, that Europeans displaced Natives in the Americas, that Europeans displaced Aborigines in Australia, and if we go far enough back we can note that Cro-Magnons displaced Neanderthals. None of this is good, but we cannot turn back the clock. We cannot send the Europeans or others back to their homelands. The vast majority of people alive today in Israeli had nothing to do with the establishment of the Jewish state, no more than I had anything to do with slavery in the US. What is necessary is a compromise between what is best for the displaced and those who have displaced them. That is what the two-state solution attempts. But when one party to the prospective agreement teaches its children genocide, then what agreement is possible?

One last point from the film: If the Palestinians laid down their arms their prospects for an improvement in their lives would probably actually increase. If the Israelis laid down their arms, they would be slaughtered.

I've seen this and I give it____stars.
I want to see it___. I'll pass___.
The review was worth reading___. Not___.

Six Days in June: The War that Redefined the Middle East (2007) 10

Clear, very watchable account

This DVD is taken from the WGBM production directed by Ilan Ziv. It is admirably objective considering that Ziv was born in Israel and fought in the Yom Kippur War of 1973. He came to the US and graduated from New York University's film school soon afterwards.

The film consists of interviews with soldiers and politicians from both the Arab and Israeli side along with footage shot during the war. I say the film is "admirably objective" but of course there is no such thing as absolute objectivity in such matters, and I am sure that Arab viewers will find the production disagreeable. This disagreement may stem largely from the fact that the Six Day War in June, 1967 was an unmitigated disaster for Syria, Egypt, Lebanon, and especially for Palestine.

However, Israel's swift and decisive victory brought with it no lasting peace. It did however humiliate the Arabs who imagined that they should be able to defeat such a tiny nation as Israel with Allah on their side and great leadership from Egypt's charismatic President Gamal Adbel Nassar and Jordan's King Hussein. To save face Arab leaders have done two things. One, they have inculcated the faithful with the notion that Israel won only because the US and other allies helped them; and Two, they have refused to acknowledge defeat holding onto the notion that the war is not over and that the Arab nations will yet achieve victory.

Ziv's film emphasizes the political nature of the conflict, revealing the thinking of leaders on both sides, showing how Moshe Dayan assumed a position of power and influence just prior to the war and how Nassar deluded himself (or was deluded by his military people) into thinking the combined forces of Egypt, Syria and Jordan could defeat the Israelis. In the United States President Lyndon Johnson was advised by his military people that if the Israelis struck first they would win in a week or so, if second, it would take them perhaps two weeks. Johnson remarked (at the time mired in Vietnam) that his generals did a great job of analyzing prospective wars in

which they would not be involved, or words to that effect.

Ziv reminds the viewer that the war could have escalated into a much wider conflict, possibly bringing in the Soviet Union on the side of the Arabs and the US on the side of Israel. Some teletype messages between Soviet Premier Aleksei Kosygin and Johnson are recalled.

Some facts gleaned from the film:

Israel struck first with well-timed, precision bombing of Arab airfields so that the Arab states were left with no air power. The war was, effectively speaking, over then within hours of its start. However, when the report of the air disaster reached Nassar, instead of seeking peace as fast as possible, he ordered propaganda broadcasts repeat with fictitious "victories." Black and white film clips show the Arabs in jubilant celebration. How cruel it was when the truth came a few days later.

Israeli's preemptive first strike was prompted by the military buildup by Egypt and Nassar's closing of the Strait of Hormuz, which most authorities consider an act of war. The film strongly suggests that if Israel had not acted first it would have suffered many more casualties, especially from Arab air power.

And then there is the famous phone call from the Arab states that never came. The Israelis were willing to trade land for peace, but the Arabs decided to pretend that the war would continue and so they did not negotiate a peace treaty. The reason the actual fighting ended is because the super powers and the United Nations demanded that Israel halt its advances.

There is some almost nostalgic footage of Moshe Dayan, Israeli's heroic Defense Minister who led the armed forces to victory, and some of indecisive Prime Minister Levi Eshkol. Ziv recreates the story of their difference of opinion on what Israel should do and how Dayan's position prevailed.

The real losers in the war have turned out to be the Palestinian people who have been under occupation since the war ended. The Arab states that were instrumental in bringing about this human tragedy seem content to blame Israel while doing nothing substantive to help the Palestinians. Indeed a significant portion of the terrorism directed at Israel and the West is motivated by spiteful spasms of revenge by Arabs who are desperate to somehow erase what they see as a humiliating defeat. How much wiser it would be to realize that what happened in 1967 reflects not at all on the manhood of anyone living today, or even then for that matter. Israel won because it could not lose. "Manhood" and heroic acts of valor or lack thereof have nothing to do with it.

Sadly, as many others have noted, Israel may win all the battles and all the wars and yet never achieve peace.

Theirs is an unenviable position. As long as they exist in the midst of Arab nations who hate them and teach their children to hate, they will always be on a military footing. Only when the old hatreds die, some many years from now, will there be lasting peace in the Holy Lands.

I've seen this and I give it____stars.
I want to see it___. I'll pass___.
The review was worth reading___. Not___.

Uncovered: The Whole Truth about the Iraq

War (2003) 10

Blistering

Watching the talking heads in archival news clips from TV in this documentary one is just amazed at how obvious it is that the Bush administration lied about its reasons for invading Iraq. Of course we have the benefit of hindsight and know for a fact that the weapons of mass destruction were not there. But the really striking thing is that all these so-called leaders of our country—Bush, Cheney, Rumsfeld, Rice, and yes, Colin Powell—KNEW they were lying.

As Al Franken so succinctly said, "It's one thing for a President to lie about his sex life. It's another to lie about why we are sending our young men and women into battle."

What this documentary does through interviews with leading experts in government, the military, and the intelligence communities, juxtaposed before, between and following the many dire pronouncements from the administration, is demonstrate beyond a shadow of a doubt that what they said was propaganda, disinformation—the Big Lie—dished out to the Congress, the Press and the American people.

The real question is why? What were the real reasons for Bush's invasion of Iraq?

Before I attempt to answer that question, two things, One, this documentary is utterly convincing in its indictment of the Bush administration and will be almost impossible to watch by those who supported the war and continue to support the war. The evidence for the massive mendacity is so vividly expressed by knowledgeable and experienced people within and without the government—people like former Ambassador Joe Wilson, former Director of the CIA Stansfield Turner, anti-terrorism expert Rand Beers, former Assistant Secretary of Defense Philip Coyle, retired Col Patrick Lang, and at least a dozen more—that only the most hardened neocons and faith-based True Believers could doubt the subterfuge. Incidentally, it was Wilson's wife, an undercover agent for the CIA, who was deliberately exposed by leaks from the Bush administration in order to punish Wilson for his expression of the truth about WMD.

Two, the real blame beyond the Bush administration lies with the Press and with the Congress. If medals were given for cowardice, members of the Press and the Congress would have chests ablaze with bronze, silver and gold. The Press simply abdicated its Fourth Estate responsibility through fear of reprisals from the Bush administration, while the Congress dared not go against the Bush propaganda machine for fear that it would be labeled anti-American. In fact their cowardly and irresponsible behavior was deeply anti-American while it was solidly pro-Bush. They both kept the American people in ignorance about the real reasons for the war.

Okay what were those reasons?

Oil? Of course this was a factor. Notice that other horrendous dictators elsewhere in the world are not removed from power by an American invading force.

To right the wrong that the first president Bush did when he kept Saddam Hussein in power after the Gulf War? Yes, but here is the beginning of the stupidity. The senior Bush pulled up short of deposing Saddam Hussein because keeping him in power was considered in the best interests of the United States. We had good control over him and he served as buffer to Iranian theocratic ambitions.

To demonstrate to the world the awesome might of the US military (the "shock and awe" that had Rumsfeld practically drooling) and show our willingness to use force if necessary? Yes. This is probably the most important psychological and geopolitical reason for invading Iraq. That it was immoral and likely to further alienate our allies and turn the vast majority of Muslims throughout the world into enemies didn't seem to occur to Bush and the neocons. Notice that another effect has been to convince Iran that it needs to acquire nuclear weapons, since it is obvious that the Bush administration isn't about to invade a country that has them (e.g., North Korea, Pakistan).

To mollify the American people, so many of whom naturally felt a great need after 9/11 to see some kind of action taken, any action to Show Strength, like a bull whirling around, swinging its horns at anything near.

To smoke-screen our failure to get Osama bin Laden and the general failure in Afghanistan? Absolutely. Blowing up great mounds of dirt in Afghanistan was NOT satisfactory, and going into nuked-up Pakistan to get bin Laden was not palatable.

To provide business for Halliburton and other corporations close to Bush and members of his administration? Well, that was one of the effects of the war.

To subconsciously get into the minds of soccer moms and make them feel safer by making US soldiers (who get paid for this sort of thing) the target for terrorists in Iraq instead of civilians at home? Possibly. Again, that was part of the effect of the war.

To help Bush win in 2004? Without doubt. Being a "war time" president would give Bush a big advantage over any Democrat. A quick "victory" over Iraq (celebrated aboard an aircraft carrier with Bush in pilot's gear strutting around with a helmet tucked under his arm shaking hands) would allow him to go one up on his father who abdicated such a possible advantage and lost the next election. By the way, film of the Bush strut is shown in the documentary more fully and more embarrassingly than the nightly news dared show it at the time. You have to see it to believe it.

I think this last reason is the most compelling reason that Bush went to war, whether he realizes it or not: he desperately wanted to win, not so much the war on terror, but the next election.

I've seen this and I give it____stars.
I want to see it___. I'll pass___.
The review was worth reading___. Not___.

Weapons of Mass Deception (2004) 9

How the American media failed

This is an excellent documentary showing how the Bush administration cowed, seduced and used the media to sell the Iraqi war to the American public. It is also an indictment of the media for its failure to accurately report the news during the build up to the war and during the war itself. The media, from the lofty New York *Times* to the unfair and unbalanced Fox News, bought hook, line and sinker the administration's tale of weapons of mass destruction in Iraq and helped Bush and the neocons prepare the American public for the invasion. A nice piece of war-prep irony revealed in the DVD was the administration's disinclination to call the plan "Operation Iraqi Liberation" since that would have led to the unfortunate (and perhaps telling) anagram "OIL."

The media turned the war into a "militainment." Bottom line, the news networks stood to make mass bucks by covering the war, by playing it up in red, white and blue sets, and playing on the public's need to escape from the usual TV fare. Exciting graphics were designed by people who worked in the computer game industry. Curiously the rule, "if it bleeds, it leads" was suspended because there was way, way too much gore to show the public, especially while they were eating dinner; and anyway it would not serve the purposes of the administration to show all those dead and dying Iraqis (especially the children) smeared with blood and gaping wounds, nor ironically would it serve to show the maimed American troops. In fact, it would be considered down right unpatriotic to do so. (You'll recall the flap over photos of flag-covered coffins of dead American soldiers.) The war had

to be sanitized and made palpable. Consequently what prevailed was "best bomb" footage showing really awesome explosions—buildings blown to bits, cars flying into the air as Rumsfeld enthused over "shock and awe." The fact that the shock and awe resulted in human casualties was very much beside the point. As has been said, "In war the first casualty is truth."

The tactic of "embedding" reporters with the military was a stroke of genius by the Bush administration because it ensured one-sided and biased reporting on the war. Being embedded (not precisely to say "in bed with") the young, idealistic American soldiers for weeks at time, being supported and protected by those soldiers and sharing their experiences forced the reporters to identify with the soldiers and to assume a similar point of view. As the documentary points out there was also some "Stockholm syndrome" psychology at work.

Sadly, the media swallowed the administration's disinformation about the never-found weapons of mass destruction without noticing that the primary justification for the war was a sham. There was also no link between Al Qaeda and the Saddam Hussein. Osama bin Laden hated the B'athist regime of Saddam Hussein almost as much as he hates Israel and the United States since Saddam Hussein is about as Islamic as say Rupert Murdoch. And of course Saddam Hussein had no use for bin Laden since he would be uncontrollable and dangerous to his regime. So that rationale was also a sham. The idea that we would be doing the people of Iraq a favor by getting rid of Saddam Hussein was also a sham because (1) any invasion would bring more misery to the people than the continued presence of Hussein; and (2) the Iraqis would rather be ruled by a dictator than be occupied by a foreign power (which is the case for practically any country in the world, including our own).

And finally the idea that by invading Iraq we would be fighting the war on terrorism (which became the administration's johnny come lately justification for the war) is not only a sham and a lie, but is actually counterproductive. The invasion of Iraq has been a setback in the war on terrorism, and actually a diversion from it. It could be argued that Bush invaded Iraq because after the invasion of Afghanistan he had no plan to go after Al Qaeda and so created a diversion—a very costly and stupid diversion.

The mainstream media failed not only as news sources, but editorially, and as news analysts. Like Bush and the neocons in the White House, the news media failed to look beyond "best bombs" and "shock and awe" and "mission accomplished" to the aftermath. The media also failed to educate the public on just how absurd the idea is that you can force democracy onto a mostly Islamic country, especially a country artificially formed from such diverse elements as the Shi'a, the Sunni and the Kurds. Furthermore, because the Shi'a are in the majority, even if a democracy is formed, it may be voted out with an Iranian style theocracy the likely result—not exactly what the White House had in mind. Another likely result is another dictatorship following a bloody civil war.

Director Danny Schechter also points to how the press was controlled and manipulated during White House press conferences. Any reporter who asked a tough question of the press secretary or the president would not be called upon again. In order words, the press conferences were (and largely still are) propaganda opportunities for the Bush administration.

It should never be forgotten that however mainstream or "liberal" or enlightened the individual reporter may or may not be, it doesn't matter because the media is controlled by conglomerate interests (think Rupert Murdoch) that own the stations, magazines and newspapers, and those guys are conservative and want support for their man in the White House, and they will not long tolerate anything else.

Question: with the consolidation of media into fewer and fewer hands, are we witnessing the beginning of the death of a free press in the United States?

I've seen this and I give it____stars.
I want to see it___. I'll pass___.
The review was worth reading___. Not___.

Why We Fight (2005) 10

Much better than Michael Moore's 9/11

There's a sense of dreadful irony suffusing this documentary about Bush's war in Iraq. There's the case of the guy (Wilton Sekzer) whose son was killed in the 9/11 attacks. Fired with a desire for revenge, he writes the Pentagon to get his son's name put on a bomb that he hopes is dropped on those who killed his son. He's a retired cop and a Vietnam vet. He gets to see a photo of the bomb with his son's name on it. The terrible irony is the bomb is not dropped on somebody who might have killed his son. Instead it likely falls on civilians in Iraq.

This up close and personal irony mirrors the larger one: Bush had little interest in getting bin Laden and those responsible for the 9/11 murders. Instead he used those attacks as a rationale to pursue a personal agenda of shock and awe so that he might be in a position to avoid the fate of his father, who was a one-term president.

An even greater irony is in the title. "Why We Fight" is the name of a series of World War II films made by Frank Capra aimed at American soldiers going overseas to fight the Nazis or the Japanese imperialists. The irony is that in WWII it was clear why we had to fight. In

Bush's war there was and is no clear necessity, moral or strategic, no sense of doing the right thing, of going against an enemy that would conquer us. Instead, there is just the terrible sense of waste, waste of over one hundred thousand human lives (and counting), waste of hundreds of billions of American dollars (that could have been put to better use at home)—all seemingly for the aggrandizement of one man and the twisted dreams of a handful of neocon chicken hawks drunk with power.

Another irony is that of the intelligence/information officer, Air Force Lt. Col. (ret.) Karen Kwiatkowski, who learned that much of the information that she was required to disseminate and swallow was misinformation and outright lies. And then there is the irony of the young pilots who were interviewed, who dropped the bombs. One is lead to say what an honor it was to drop one of the first bombs in Operation Iraqi Freedom, an operation he saw as liberating a people, an operation that had previously been called (with telling dramatic irony) Operation Iraqi Liberation (OIL).

As the documentary reminds us, World War II was fought for oil as well, but it was the Japanese who started it to secure the oil fields in the South Pacific so that they could fuel further expansion in Asia, and by the Nazis who also had little to no domestic crude to fuel their maniac dreams of world domination.

What sets this documentary apart from some others (especially the somewhat shallow exercise by Michael Moore) is how the war is put in historical perspective. Director Eugene Jarecki shows how the illogic of the present meshes with that of the past as we see Rumsfeld making nice with Saddam Hussein in the days when we supported him as our dictator in the Middle East. And further removed we see the grainy ghosts of Vietnam past: John F. Kennedy, LBJ, Nixon... And then there are the many mendacious statements of Bush, Cheney, Rumsfeld, Richard Perle, Paul Wolfowitz, et al., juxtaposed against the damning analysis of military and political experts.

In the final analysis Jarecki makes it clear that we fight to feed the vast military-industrial complex that Eisenhower warned us about. As someone (Chalmers Johnson, I believe) remarks, with so much profit to be made in war, you can be sure that war will follow. How else to use up the munitions so that others might be manufactured and sold?

I've seen this and I give it____stars.
I want to see it___. I'll pass___.
The review was worth reading___. Not___.

III

Miscellaneous

Bowling for Columbine (2002) 7

Can a man be a man in America without a gun?

Did Charlton Heston get blind-sided by Michael Moore? Yes, but he's definitely old enough and savvy enough to know better. Did Moore gain entry to the Heston Hollywood mansion using false pretenses? No, he told the one-time celluloid god of the waters that he was a lifetime, paid-up member of the National Rifle Association, and once inside even showed his membership card. And, although the average guy in the street might be disarmed by Moore's folksy style and declasse dress code, Heston knew that Moore was a big time media guy (previous film: *Roger and Me*; book: *Stupid White Men*).

But Heston never misses a chance to spread the Second Amendment gospel. He just thought he could handle the situation. There's no fool like an old fool, they say. To his credit, when he realized that he had fallen into a trap, he moseyed off, putting one gimpy leg carefully in front of the other as he carried a bent back and a 79-year-old frame off camera.

Well, was this fair? Indeed, was the entire film fair? No, of course not. This is Michael Moore simultaneously making a buck, building a rep, and working a cause. The cause is something like 11,000 dead-by-gunshot Americans every year (a pretty good cause), and the target is indeed Charlton Heston, long-time spokesman not only for God, but more significantly, the NRA, and of course gun and ammo manufacturers and sellers. So at least we can say that Michael Moore was after big game.

He mostly bagged them too (and made Dick Clark look heartless), but somehow I didn't gain much satisfaction. I don't care much for Charlton Heston, either as an actor or a proselytizer, but I am finding, after watching this and *Fahrenheit 9/11*, that I don't care much for Michael Moore either. I think all good, right-thinking liberals should continue to play fair even though the opposition might not. This film preached to the choir and a good time was had by all who agree with Moore's point of view. The cover on this DVD even quotes Time Magazine as saying the film is "hilarious."

Somehow though I don't think those on the right thought it was all that funny. And I wonder if those in the middle were swayed one way or the other. It is indeed heartbreaking that kids in this country pick up guns and shoot each other, and the fact that they do it much more often per capita than any other country in the First World does indeed call for an explanation. Ironically, I think Heston actually had the answer. This is a violent country with a violent history relative to other industrial nations. Moore and Heston agreed that our history isn't more violent than, say, Germany's, but they got their ideas confused. In Germany the violence was by the state and its armies and its police. We have plenty of that as well of course, but in the US we also have a tradition of the handy six-shooter in the holster for a quick draw and a further tradition of celebrating the rugged individual who stands up against the state and anyone wanting to take his arms away.

Personally I think there's a lot to be said and not said for both sides in this all too American debate. The Freudian implication that would-be macho guys need guns symbolically to feel like men is very real. It was no accident that Heston let slip the "multi-ethnic" rationale for explaining all those dead by firearms in the USA, a rationale that is usually interpreted to mean fear of a big black dude breaking into one's home. Or actually that is often a sort of "make my day" fantasy indulged in by some randy militia types as they sip a little Jack Daniels on the front porch swing as they fondle their weapon.

Well, what's the answer? There is no answer. It is a gradual process from the jungle to civilization, and the US, in this gun-toting regard, is just a little behind the rest of the West. If Michael Moore wants to focus on some people who really adore their weapons, he should take a trip to Iraq or Afghanistan, or just watch the nightly news.

Still this is worth seeing as a kind of Americana snapshot portfolio. Marilyn Manson proves a fine foil for Charlton Heston, and the Afro-American elementary school principal can be balanced against the poor little black kid who shot the little white girl, who can be contrasted with the members of the NRA who think the black kid should be tried as an adult, who can be contrasted with the kids at Columbine who were just there when it happened. And the mentality of Moore and his crew in imagining that they won a "victory" against K-Mart when it agreed to take the ammo off it shelves can be contrasted with the young dude who was disappointed that he wasn't named a number one collaborating suspect. (Actually the ammo sales are small potatoes to K-Mart which has big management and bottom-line problems.)

But see this to study the techniques used by Moore. Oh, where, oh, where has the concept of objective journalism gone—or did it ever exist in the first place?

I've seen this and I give it____stars.
I want to see it___. I'll pass___.

The review was worth reading___. Not___.

Enron: The Smartest Guys in the Room

(2005) 10
Actually the most morally deranged guys in the room

Bethany McLean, who along with Peter Elkind, wrote the book from which this documentary was adapted, is clearly satisfied with herself as she sits on a couch relating what she knows about the fall of Enron. And she should be. She was the one who first really pursued the question, "How does Enron make money?" What she didn't know when she first asked the question is that they make money the old-fashioned way, they steal it.

What I was most forcibly struck with while watching this fascinating story is how much all the posturing and lying and misrepresenting of the talking heads, Jeff Skilling, Kenneth Lay, et al., reminded me of George W. Bush, Dick Cheney, et al., in the White House. The key similarity is the use of their power over the media and in front of a podium to mislead the minions and the public to their advantage. Without the ability to lie to large numbers of people at the same time, and to stifle and belittle contrary voices, they would not have succeeded.

But also there is the complacency and the complicity of not just the greedy stockholders and the adoring employees, but the greater public who failed to ask not "why?" but "how?" In the case of Enron, how can a company exceed not only all expectations, but something like the law of financial gravity? If it looks too good to be true and nobody can give you a clear answer to how it's done—guess what? It is too good to be true. It may seem a stretch, but the same kind of mentality continues to persuade Nigerian scammers and "Congratulations: You've Won!!!" emailers that there are still fat bank accounts in America just waiting to be emptied. Nobody wanted to look too closely because nobody wanted to prick a bubble. Instead everybody wanted to believe that things that go up never have to come down (at least not now), and that the smartest guys in the room really were, and thanks to them we are all going to get rich, or at least we can applaud and admire from the sidelines.

Another failure is that of not looking critically at the cultural climate and the mentality of the traders and their bosses, whose morality (in the form of emails and public pronouncements) was that of people who would cheat their best friend, who would steal from widows and orphans (no exaggeration: they did) and laugh about it.

And the bankers and the brokerage firms, the federal watch dogs and the Congress—where were they? Lapping it up like lap dogs, getting paid off or having their campaigns funded by the robber barons at Enron. Greed is good! It's the American way! Deregulate everything! The police force, the army; and free enterprise and the magical, invisible hand of the marketplace will bring us unprecedented and unparalleled riches. Burp!

No, the honchos at Enron were not the smartest guys in the room. They were the sickest. Smart guys would have made a good living, maybe even enough to buy that house on the hill, a vacation home in some warm clime, while having banked and invested enough to send the kids and grandkids to good schools, and been satisfied. They might even have taken some pride in the work they were doing. But how can you take pride in your work when you are essentially stealing from others, especially when you are stealing from the very people who work for you and trust you? The smartest guys in the room would not have thrown so much time and energy into ripping people off, into gratifying a warped desire to financially lord it over others. They would not be those who cared more about ratcheting up their millions than they did about anything else in life. People who care about winning so massively and so cruelly are not smart. They aren't even well. They are morally deranged.

Alex Gibney (who also wrote and produced the excellent *The Trials of Henry Kissinger* 2002) is to be commended for making the kind of documentary that informs, enlightens and appalls. The footage from corporate meetings, press conferences, company skits (oh, what fun they had!) and interviews with the principals and those they ruined make for a most engaging moral lesson. The story unfolds like some kind of pathological tragedy from inside a fascist state or like the neoconned White House where public pronouncements are made with only one goal in mind: deception. What fools these morals be. And the biggest fools are the greediest whose lives are lived in empty pursuit of nothing more than naked power with which they can buy nothing of value that they didn't already have.

I've seen this and I give it___stars.
I want to see it___. I'll pass___.
The review was worth reading___. Not___.

The Farmer's Wife (1996) 10

One of the best social documentaries ever made

Although six and a half hours long, *The Farmer's Wife* never drags. It is amazing that independent film maker David Sutherland could choose as his subject a young Nebraskan farm family, Juanita and Darrel Buschkoetter and their three daughters, and out of their lives create such a masterpiece of documentary. How he got them to be so natural and so open and so sharing of the intimate details of their lives; how he got such stark, clear, and engaging footage of their lives, and how he was able to edit it so that it plays like a movie is something to behold, literally.

Somehow Juanita and Darrel became themselves in front of the cameras, somehow they were able to open their hearts and minds to us, and to show us what it is like to be family farmers in America's Midwest in the 1990's. We watch them raise their family while they struggle to make ends meet despite a capricious marketplace that cares for them not at all, and all the while, almost naked to the world, they are able to maintain their human dignity, indeed to set an example of strength and courage for all of us. To see Juanita slop the hogs with one arm while cradling her two-year-old in the other, and to do so with grace and skill and a kind of old fashioned dignity will set your heart and mind to spinning. This is as real as it gets.

Sutherland shows the Buschkoetters, warts and all, but at no time does he demean them or make them look less than heroic. Yes, heroic in the sense that theirs is a life lived fully in a way that humans have lived for thousands of years, a way of life too hard and too demanding for most of us to bear, certainly too much for me. It is a poignant story, the stuff of country ballads and short stories from literary magazines, done with the skill and vision of a great film maker. If this doesn't touch your heart, you, like the tin man, need to see the Wizard of Oz.

I've seen this and I give it____stars.
I want to see it___. I'll pass___.
The review was worth reading___. Not___.

Jesus Camp (2006) 8

Indoctrinating the kids

As the closing credits roll we hear Norman Greenbaum's "Spirit in the Sky." The lyric goes something like, "I got a friend in Jesus...He's going to set me up with the spirit in the sky...when I die...I'm going to go to the place that's the best."

A similar point-blank irony suffuses this engaging documentary by Heidi Ewing and Rachel Grady. Norman Greenbaum had his tongue firmly in cheek, of course, but Becky Fischer and her fellow molders of children are serious. She believes in indoctrinating the children and she says so. She points out that in Muslim lands the children are similarly indoctrinated, and even more so. It is a war. The word "war" is used repeatedly at Jesus Camp which was located (ironically, I guess) in Devil's Lake, North Dakota. It's a war that must be won, and implicitly the war is against liberals and mainstream American culture, but explicitly against science, especially biological evolution, and against other faiths. Becky pretends to apologize before telling us that Christianity has The Truth and therefore should triumph over other religions, creeds and cultures. She believes that. There can be no question about the sincerity of her beliefs.

What struck me most powerfully is what was REALLY being taught at Jesus Camp. That is, methods of indoc-trination. Behind all the rhetoric about Jesus and being saved was the political agenda for the fundamentalist movement. Part Nazi rally, part revival meeting, part Brainwashing 101, what really came across were all the persuasive techniques that Becky Fischer, Ted Haggard and the others had perfected. Suffer the little children indeed. Get 'em while they're young, Becky tells us. The impressions made and beliefs instilled in children before the age of, say eight, will last a lifetime, she tells us.

She says she loves America. We see out of a car window the endless sameness of asphalt roads, telephone poles and electric wires, KFC restaurants and car dealerships that form the main streets of most any American town. I doubt that she loves the America of the Museum of Modern Art or the America of Benjamin Franklin or Thomas Jefferson or the redwoods or the Grand Canyon. Becky says that she loves America, and then she says she prays to get away from this awful world—or words to that effect.

I find it tough to find credence in people who devote their lives to manipulating the emotions of children in an effort to create a new generation of opportunists (or zombies) to mindlessly champion the slogans of their political and social agenda. How sad it was to see young Levi O'Brien—bright, talented and impressionable beyond his years—being molded into a future TV evangelist. He will learn the clever deceit practiced not by people like Becky Fischer, who as I said, is a true believer, but more like Ted Haggard himself or any number of moneyed evangelical personalities who preach one thing in public and in their private lives do something else. He will learn the same techniques that Becky and Ted have learned, techniques of rhetoric and persuasion, of indoctrination and the manipulation of emotions. He will learn what leads to success in evangelical land, that truth comes from religious authority and political and economic power, and that anyone who thinks differently is an enemy.

Becky Fischer thinks liberal America will be worried after seeing this documentary. Her ability to mold children into her brand of Christianity should scare us, she thinks. But revivalist America comes and goes with the passing of time. We've seen it all before. What is different today is that evangelicals were able to elect somebody like George W. Bush and to control the Congress and cow the media. I think America has seen where that leads, to the weakening and embarrassment of America; and I am betting that America has learned its lesson and that the politicians who would do the work of the faith-based, ignorance-based, head-in-the-sand, evangelical movement will lose out to more enlightened leadership. After all, unlike Becky, most of us and our children must live in this world without the fantasy of imminent rapture, and therefore must work toward making the world a better place for all of us.

I've seen this and I give it____stars.

I want to see it___. I'll pass___.
The review was worth reading___. Not___.

The March of the Penguins (2005) 10

Emotionally compelling, gorgeous and epic

The penguins are exquisite. They almost look unreal they are so precisely sculptured and painted, their graceful bills sliced from the rim of the moon, their red and black lines like something from a designer of fine tuxedos, their round, dough-boy bodies with their flippers like little wings, their stoic non-expressiveness otherworldly and heroic.

The desolate and forbidding Antarctic landscape with its immovable walls of blue-white ice and its black, rocky outcrops and the great blue and black sky above is awesome and awe-inspiring, beautiful and frightening, clearly another world as distant from our experience as another planet.

And the story of the seventy-mile trek away from the ocean in which the penguins are so wondrously at home, where they fly through the water like something propelled, quicker than cats in their pudgy streamlined costumes, where they are expert and gluttonous fishers of fish, is nothing short of epic. At first they march together (and glide when they can over the ice like snowmen on their bellies), male and female to the place of their birth seventy miles inland, taking tiny child-like steps. And then they pair off and mate (the graceful courtship shown, the actual mating tastefully framed so that what we see is no more graphic than shared hugs), and then, as they stand huddled in a great mass against the wind and cold, the fertilized egg develops within the female and at length the egg is laid.

And here the story becomes especially instructive for modern human parents. The egg is carefully, oh, so carefully and with some haste transferred from the feather-covered warmth of the mother's pouch to that of the father's. The transfer must not be careless or too slow because the fierce Antarctic cold will freeze the egg and the chick within in seconds. Then the mother leaves her mate and her egg behind and begins the trek back to the ocean so that she can eat once again, and can return with rich, oily, protein-packed food from her belly to regurgitate to the chick that will be born in her absence.

Meanwhile the fathers stand together in their living mass against the cold and wind and snow, rotating in some semi-automatic manner so that each penguin spends some time on the periphery of the mass and sometime in the warm interior. And they do not eat. Months go by, and they do not eat. Finally the eggs begin to hatch and the chicks are born.

And now the time for the mothers to return is nigh. And the chicks peer out of their downy pouches as though looking for their mothers, and they chirp. The fathers grow worried (I imagine) as they wait for the mothers to return and feed the hungry chicks. Each father has exactly one egg. Those who lost their eggs or never had an egg have left to return to the sea and to fish. When things get very desperate, the fathers exude from their mouths a little bit of mysterious white nourishment, enough to last the chick for a day or two, a crucial day or two.

And then at long last the mothers return, one at a time in a line from over the horizon they come. And how welcome we can imagine they are!

So this is a very human story, a story of monogamous parents who give everything they have to their progeny, whose struggles against the elements (and quick and hungry leopard seals in the sea) remind us of our own, except that ours seem relatively tame and not nearly as onerous.

It is a gorgeous movie, best seen on a big screen of course with a beautiful score, a film that might be a little too emotionally demanding for small children, but one that will surely captivate older children and their parents. Highly recommended.

I've seen this and I give it___stars.
I want to see it___. I'll pass___.
The review was worth reading___. Not___.

Outfoxed: Rupert Murdoch's War on Journalism (2004) 10

On the growing threat from managed "news"

Robert Greenwald, who directed the scathing documentary *Uncovered: The Whole Truth about the Iraq War* (2003) in which he demonstrated beyond any shadow of a doubt that the Bush administration repeatedly lied to the American people as it manipulated the Press and the Congress to get them to support its invasion of Iraq, now takes dead aim at one of Bush's most staunch supporters, media mogul Rupert Murdoch.

Using the same technique that worked so well in "Uncovered," Greenwald plays clips from Murdoch's Fox News to show that Fox News is anything but "fair and balanced." From the clips of Bill O'Reilly verbally abusing his "guests" and telling them to "shut up" to Brit Hume mouthing the Republican Party line in the guise of objective journalism to slanted stories directed from above (that would be from Mr. Murdoch himself in some cases, like some worshipful filler about Ronald Reagan or some non-news from Bush's standard stump speech) to the daily email directives telling the staff at Fox News how to slant today's selected stories—from the glitz and the directive music and the flags in the background to the character assassinations of Republican opponents, to the "feel good" misinformation about the war in Iraq and Afghanistan, Greenwald shows that Fox News stands for propaganda, spoon fed to the American masses.

Interspersed with the clips are sound bites from ex-Fox employees (some of them with their voices and faces disguised or hidden for fear of reprisals from Fox) and media experts and even some progressive politicians. From the employees we get a glimpse of the stifling Fox News "culture" that subtly but unmistakably requires everyone on staff to slant the news as directed or find work some place else. What emerges is a portrait of a media empire that is dead set on destroying journalism as we know it. And that's the way Murdoch wants it. He wants to control events through the power of the media, to stifle contrary opinion and to keep the masses in couch potato ignorance.

Thus there is a specter haunting the American democracy, and that specter is media control by anti-democratic corporations. It is not just arch-conservative Rupert Murdoch and his vast media empire, it is CBS, NBC, ABC, CNN, etc. that are becoming more and directed from above, and more and more divorced from actual reportage in favor of the kind of spin and slant that pleases the corporate heads. Even National Public Radio is coming under greater and greater corporate influence and control.

What's to be done?

We must elect public officials that will prevent the consolidation of media. If we don't, those who own the media will soon own the government. The airwaves belong to everyone. No one should have a monopoly on their use. Traditionally the media has served as "the Fourth Estate," a watchdog on government. More and more it has abdicated that responsibility because its purse strings are controlled by its corporate sponsors. In the case of Murdoch, more and more media is falling under the control of a single ideology. Can a fascist state be far behind?

I am not panicking yet. The Democrats saw what can happen when the other side controls most of the media (almost all of it, actually), and fiscal conservatives are learning that social conservatives may not be their best allies, especially faith-based evangelicals whose first order of business is a return to ignorance and superstition on the way to establishing a theocracy in the United States like something out of Margaret Atwood's "The Handmaid's Tale." As the mass mind becomes more and more dumbed down and indoctrinated into mindless consumerism while being massaged by a dictatorial media, greater and greater grows the threat to democracy.

The real test will come after Bush is out of office. The next administration must take steps to break up ClearChannel, etc., and prevent the further consolidation of Murdoch's empire. The airwaves must be a public utility because to control media in the modern society is ultimately to control elections.

This documentary is a clarion call to wake up and smell the newsprint because if Murdoch has his way there will only be the comic page and Murdoch-slanted news stories, editorials and canned opinion.

I've seen this and I give it____stars.
I want to see it___. I'll pass___.
The review was worth reading___. Not___.

Regret to Inform (1998) 8

Looking back with tears in our eyes

Some have called this documentary "propaganda," and I can understand that point of view since there is no mention of Viet Cong atrocities here; but since this was made some thirty years after the war was over, it can hardly be propaganda. It does present a limited point of view, that of the women who suffered because of the war, but that was film maker Barbara Sonneborn's intention. She wanted to show how she personally suffered because she lost her husband in the war and how she has come to grips with that loss, but more than that she wanted to show how other women also suffered and what the war meant to them, including, and perhaps especially, the Vietnamese women. After all, it was their homes that were bombed, not ours.

Imbedded within and at the heart of Sonneborn's reflections is the story of Xuan Ngoc Nguyen, the Vietnamese-American woman who served as her translator. Nguyen tells her personal story beginning with the sight of the bombs falling on her village and that of her five-year-old cousin being shot by an America soldier (who became horrified at what he had done). She tells of her stint as a prostitute for G.I.'s, her marriage to an American soldier and her coming to America, the end of her marriage, and the implications of her life afterwards, raising her son and becoming Americanized, and finally her return with Sonneborn to the country of her birth. She is the heroine of this film, a woman who faced the horrors of war, did what she felt she had to do, somehow survived in one piece, and now looks back with tears in her eyes.

Sonneborn's documentary owes part of its effectiveness to the contrast between the black and white and fading colored film shot during the war and the brilliant rush of greenery so beautifully photographed today. The effect of seeing the verdant fields of today's Vietnam contrasted with a land torn apart by bombs and sickened with Agent Orange is to show that despite all the damage and death of the war, the fields and those who tend the fields, recover. In this sense—and John Hersey used the same idea in his book, *Hiroshima* (1946), when he described how the grass grew back after the atom bomb—the futility of war is demonstrated. We kill one another with a ferocious abandonment; nonetheless, the greenery returns, even if, as Carl Sandburg implies in his poem, "Grass," it is fertilized by our blood.

Consequently this film cannot but play as an indictment of the war in Vietnam, and for some, as an indictment of all wars. I will not argue with that. As anyone who has really thought long and hard about war knows, from Sun Tzu to General Powell, it is always best to avoid the war if that is possible, but there comes a time and a circumstance in which one has no choice. The jury has long since rendered its verdict on the war in Vietnam. We are reminded of that every time we hear a commentator say, "We don't want another Vietnam." But there is an enormous difference between the horrendous stupidity of our involvement in Vietnam and the absolute necessity of defending ourselves against the aggression of the fascists and imperialists during World War II. And the war being fought today against terrorism is also one that cannot be avoided.

I see Sonneborn's film as a reminder not only of the horror of war, but of our responsibility to be sure that our cause, as Bush has it, "is just" and our methods restricted to the task at hand, and that the suffering of those involved be ended as soon as humanly possible.

I've seen this and I give it____stars.
I want to see it___. I'll pass___.
The review was worth reading___. Not___.

Spellbound (2002) 9

Spellbinding

Hitchcock did not direct this and it does not star Ingrid Bergman and Gregory Peck. *Spellbound* (1945) and *Spellbound* (2002) have in common the fact that they both won Academy Awards and both are spellbinding.

Director Jeffrey Blitz's approach to making this most interesting documentary is straight-forward: pick eight contestants. Produce a mini-documentary on each one of them with scenes from family life, school. Interview their teachers, their parents, and some of their friends so that we get to know the contestants. Show the town they live in and the land they grew up on. Cut each mini-documentary to a few minutes and run them one after the other before taking us to the National Spelling Bee in Washington, D.C.

Film the spelling bee and show the eight in action along with some of the other 242 or so who made it to the Capitol. Start with round one. Show the officials, the people who read the words to the contestants and answer questions about the words, such as word origin, definition, pronunciation, and root. Show the eager parents. Show the kids on stage with wrinkled brow and sweaty hands—well, you can't show the sweaty hands, although one mother reported that her hands got all wet when her daughter's turn came and then got all dry afterwards. Get some shots of the kids talking. Show the faces with the thrill of victory and the agony of defeat

And guess what? The film plays itself. It's a natural. We identify with the contestants, perhaps have our favorite. The tension builds. The hour and a half flies by. The spelling bee is a great spectator sport!

Another thing I liked about this was the fact that although the eager parents would put your usual stage moms or little league dads to shame in the way they pushed their kids, when it was over, it was over. A couple of the kids said they were disappointed not to have won, but what a relief it was not to have to study the dictionary anymore! Of course there is always next year, but unlike baseball and the Broadway stage, you can grow too old to compete in the spelling bee—although now that I think about it, I wouldn't be surprised to find that they have adult spelling bees, maybe even spelling bees for senior citizens.

Another nice thing is the view Blitz gives us of the Heartland. The film amounts to a glimpse of America the melting pot near the beginning of the 21st Century (the contest is from 1999).

Also educational were insights into the way the kids learned to be excellent spellers. They memorized, yes, but they also learned which letters were likely to be correct for certain sounds based on the language of origin of the word. Greek words—there a lot of scientific Greek words in the dictionary—almost always have every letter pronounced (although watch out for those silent leading "m's"!). French words are just the opposite. I used to teach honors English and I can tell you that half the kids could out-spell me. The best kid I had just seemed to do it naturally. I realized however after talking to him that his approach was phonetic to start. That was the default. Every word that could be spelled correctly phonetically he noted and put aside in his mind. (His habit was to notice the spelling of every new word he encountered.) If the word was not spelled phonetically, it was an exception and he noted why it was an exception and dreamed up some mnemonic—silent leading m!—device to remember the exception. I could never spell a word like "lieutenant" (French) until I also developed a mnemonic device. In this case I made a sentence out of the word: "Lie-u-tenant" or I found the little words within: "lie," ... "ten," "ant."

Spellbound won the Oscar for Best Documentary in 2002, and it's that good. People and especially young people can identify (or not!) with kids their own age, and they can choose their favorites to root for.

I've seen this and I give it____stars.

174

I want to see it___. I'll pass___.
The review was worth reading___. Not___.

Super Size Me (2004) 8

Please don't

This documentary film by Morgan Spurlock asks the intriguing and topical question: What would happen to a normal 33-year-old man in perfect health who stands six feet two and weighs 185 pounds if he ate nothing but McDonald's fast food for thirty days?

Well, it is not recorded that he shrunk. In fact, Spurlock, forsaking his vegan girlfriend's healthy cuisine, gained about 25 pounds and saw his cholesterol level shoot up to dangerous levels as he huffed and puffed his way three times a day through myriad Big Macs and fillet o' fish sandwiches, milk shakes, sodas, fries and other not-so-delicate items from the menu of the world's largest purveyor of fast food. He had hired three doctors and a registered dietician to check his vital signs and give him a thorough physical exam prior to this experiment in not-so-fine dining. Before the gorging was done all three doctors and the dietician advised him in the most uncertain terms for the sake of his health to stop eating the sugar-laden, fat-smeared, nearly fiber-free "diet." But Spurlock, trooper that he is, amid the McTingles and the McPukes, hung in there until the very end.

I can report that he survived the experience. Whether the viewer will is another matter. If you yourself (God help you) are seriously overweight you might want to pass on this excruciatingly detailed misadventure under the Golden Arches. All that fat slapping against those waddling thighs (Spurlock mercifully fuzzed out the faces of his subjects, allowing us only body shots), all that jiggling flesh under those XXXL garments might be too uncomfortably close to home for some sensitive viewers.

But was this a fair test of the harmful consequences of eating Happy Meals and being super sized? After all, Spurlock eschewed exercise during the experiment, and of course nobody actually eats every meal at McDonald's as Spurlock did. Furthermore he actually doubled his normal caloric intake from about 2500 calories a day to about 5000. Regardless I think we can say that his experience was indicative.

The real question to be asked here (and Spurlock asks it) is whether McDonald's (or as some have dubbed thee) whether McDeath's can be or should be held responsible for the epidemic of obesity that is sweeping the country. Spurlock implies that McDonald's should be held responsible at least for its advertising aimed at children. I agree with this. But I also think that adults ought to know what they are doing. If they choose to chow down at a place that loves to super size and under nourish them, perhaps they themselves should be held responsible for the consequences. However, some people feel that the advertising has been so insidious for so long and the food so addictive to susceptible individuals that McDonald's ought to be taken to court just as the tobacco companies have been.

For more information on the epidemic, its consequences, and what can be done about it, I refer the interested reader to The Hungry Gene: The Science of Fat and the Future of Thin by Ellen Ruppel Shell; Fat Land: How Americans Became the Fastest People in the World by Eric Critser; and Fast Food Nation: The Dark Side of the All-American Meal by Eric Schlosser. Schlosser appears in one of the bonus features being interviewed by Spurlock. This interview is one of the highlights of the DVD. Schlosser is articulate, candid, and very well-informed.

Spurlock of course is a performer as well as a film maker. His directorial style owes something to that of Michael Moore, and his playful on-camera muggings remind me of Ian Wright of PBS's Globe Trekker series.

See this as an introduction to this most serious threat to the nation's health, especially as it affects children. Morgan Spurlock is to be commended for bringing the reality of the epidemic to the attention of the general public.

By the way, "McTingles" are those highflying, scary feelings you get after rapidly injecting massive amounts of pure sugar and caffeine into your system, usually by gulping your way through a 64-ounce McCola—and to think when I was a kid, Coca-Cola came in six-ounce bottles. However did we survive? "McPukes" are self-explanatory.

I've seen this and I give it___stars.
I want to see it___. I'll pass___.
The review was worth reading___. Not___.

The Thin Blue Line (1988) 9

Stunning depiction of a gross miscarriage of justice

This is an extraordinary documentary in which film maker Errol Morris shows how an innocent man was convicted of murdering a policeman while the real murderer was let off scot free by the incompetent criminal justice system of Dallas, Texas. The amazing thing is that Morris demonstrates this gross miscarriage of justice in an utterly convincing manner simply by interviewing the participants. True, he reenacts the crime scene and flashes headlines from the newspaper stories to guide us, but it is simply the spoken words of the real murderer, especially in the cold-blooded, explosive audio tape that ends the film, that demonstrate not only his guilt but his psychopathic personality. And it is the spoken words of the defense attorneys, the rather substantial Edith James and the withdrawing Dennis White, and the wrongfully convicted Randall Adams that demonstrate the corrupt and incompetent methods used by the Dallas Country justice system to bring about this false conviction. Particularly chilling were the words of Judge Don Metcalfe, waxing teary-eyed, as he recalls listening to the prosecutor's summation about how society is made safe by that "thin blue line" of cops who give their lives to protect us from criminals. The chilling part is that while he is indulging his emotions he is allowing the cop killer to go free and helping to convict an innocent man. Almost as chilling in its revelation of just how perverted and corrupt the system has become, was the report of how a paid psychologist, as a means of justifying the death penalty, "interviewed" innocent Randall Adams for fifteen minutes and found him to be a danger to society, a blood-thirsty killer who would kill again.

This film will get your dander up. How the cops were so blind as to not see that 16-year-old David Harris was a dangerous, remorseless psychopath from the very beginning is beyond belief. He even took a delight in bragging about his crime. As Morris suggests, it was their desire to revenge the cop killing with the death penalty that blinded them to the obvious. They would rather fry an innocent man than convict the real murderer, who because of his age was not subject to the death penalty under Texas law. When an innocent man is wrongly convicted of a murder three things happen that are disastrous: One, an innocent man is in jail or even executed. Two, the real guilty party is free to kill again. And, three, the justice system is perverted. This last consequence is perhaps the worst. When people see their police, their courts, their judges condemning the innocent and letting the guilty walk free, they lose faith in the system and they begin to identify with those outside the system. They no longer trust the cops or the courts. The people become estranged from the system and the system becomes estranged from the people. This is the beginning of the breakdown of society. The Dallas cops and prosecutors and the stupid judge (David Metcalfe), who should have seen through the travesty, are to be blamed for the fact that David Harris, after he testified for the prosecution and was set free, did indeed kill again, as well as commit a number of other crimes of violence.

The beautiful thing about this film is, over and above the brilliance of its artistic construction, is that its message was so clear and so powerful that it led to the freeing of the innocent Randall Adams. Although the psychopathic David Harris, to my knowledge, was never tried for the crime he committed, he is in prison for other crimes and, it is hoped, will be there for the rest of his life. Errol Morris and the other people who made this fine film can pride in these facts and in knowing that they did a job that the Dallas criminal justice system was unable to do.

I've seen this and I give it____stars.
I want to see it___. I'll pass___.
The review was worth reading___. Not___.

The Trials of Henry Kissinger (2002) 7

The ironies abound

This is an indictment. You'll have to read Kissinger's memoirs for the defense. I'm not planning on doing that myself, time constraints and other things to do being what they are.

In this 80-minute documentary, director Eugene Jarecki follows the intent of the book by Christopher Hitchens, which was to put Kissinger on trial before a world court with himself as prosecutor. By the way, note the slight, but perhaps significant difference in the title: the book is *The Trial* [singular] *of Henry Kissinger*. In a strange way the plural title of this documentary almost suggests The *Struggles* of Henry Kissinger, which would be irony number one.

I also thought it strange that Jarecki doesn't include Hitchens in the credits. I would say, one wonders why, but I really don't care.

What I care about here is:

First, the incredible irony of Kissinger being a winner of the Nobel Peace Prize. But then one recalls that Yasser Arafat also won one of those. Maybe I should win the literary prize for writing this review.

Second, the bizarre irony of Kissinger being a German Jew with relatives who died in the concentration camps becoming a man who ends up regarding his fellow human beings with the same sort of cattle to the slaughter mentality that characterized the Nazis. I think Henry called it "realpolitik."

Third, the slippery irony of Kissinger working for Democrat Lyndon Johnson, liberal Republican Nelson Rockefeller, and conservative Republican Richard Nixon, while having loyalty only to his own lust to power and his delight in exercising it.

Fourth, the comedic irony that now in the 21st century, decades after the fact, with Kissinger in his eighties, we get a call for a war crimes trial. Is this some kind of joke?

Fifth, the theoretical irony of realizing that it is Kissinger himself who believed that heads of state (and their top lieutenants) operate according to laws different than those imposed on private citizens because people in such elevated positions are often faced with only "a choice of evils," and so inevitably end up doing evil themselves.

Sixth, the media circus irony of Henry Kissinger being thought of as sexy and a Playgirl kind of centerfold because "power is the ultimate aphrodisiac," an image that delighted Kissinger who was quoted in the New York *Times* (Jan 19, 1971) as saying "Power is the great aphrodisiac."

Seventh, the judicial irony of Kissinger being put on trial for war crimes when it was his boss, the President of the United States, Richard Nixon, who had the ultimate responsibility for what happened in, for example, Cambodia.

Finally, it may be a kind of historical irony that it is George W. Bush who is most adamant that the US not give authority to a World Court that might try American government officials.

This is an easy documentary to view, done according to the "Sixty Minutes" formula. We are shown official documents with blacked out lines, archival footage, and interviews with some of the people who are still alive. There's Nixon's one time Chief of Staff Alexander Haig who sticks up for Kissinger (his old boss), but there is also the son of Chilean General Schneider who was assassinated in order to bring the horrific Pinochet to power and to protect American interests. And of course, the documentary reports that the principal indictee himself, Henry Kissinger, refused to be interviewed.

However I think the emphasis in any documentary that covers the material that this one covered should have been on our Cold War foreign policy itself (hardly original or unique to Kissinger), a policy that led the United States to commit and support the most amazing atrocities in the name of anti-communism, atrocities for which we are still paying the cost in world opinion, especially in the Middle East.

I should note that there's something wrong with the DVD in that it gives great close ups of the talking heads, but truncates their names and titles.

I also didn't care much about that.

I've seen this and I give it____stars.
I want to see it___. I'll pass___.
The review was worth reading___. Not___.

Who Killed the Electric Car? (2006) 9

Let's suck some serious amps

Probably the most alarming thing about this story of how the electric car was literally destroyed is what it reveals about the power of corporations to control our lives. Film maker Chris Paine, himself an EV1 owner, makes it clear that it was big corporations, especially big oil, and most especially General Motors itself, that woke up one day and asked themselves the multi-billion dollar question: Is an economical and efficient electric vehicle really good for business? In the case of the oil companies, obviously not since such a vehicle would not be burning any gas or needing any motor oil. In the case of the car manufacturers themselves, especially GM, which actually spent some very serious bucks on developing the EV1, the answer came as a bit of a surprise. First of

all, they asked themselves, in the long run are you going to make more money building small efficient vehicles or behemoths like the Hummer? It didn't take long for them to figure out that the profit margins would be higher with the bigger vehicles. And then they realized that with the EV1 they wouldn't be able to sell many of their combustion-engine parts like oil filters and such. Furthermore, the EV1 was built to comply with California law. Doing some more thinking, GM realized that it would never do to allow some state government to tell them what to manufacture. If things worked out in California, before you know it, the whole nation might very well go plug-in.

So, as shown so vividly in this documentary, the car manufactures and the oil companies bought up or scared enough politicians so that the law requiring zero emissions in California went the way of the dodo. Meanwhile GM, which had been leasing the EV1, recalled them all and literally destroyed them. Paine has some nice footage showing the brand new and near brand new cars being crushed while EV1 lovers protested in vain. Nationally of course we know about the bills congress passed allowing truck-sized vehicles to continue to guzzle gas (mostly SUVs) and how 6,000-pound vehicles were given massive tax breaks for small business owners (mostly anybody but a wage earner).

There is of course plenty of controversy about whether the story presented by Paine (narration by Martin Sheen, by the way) is fair and accurate. I did a little research—there is a ton of information on the Web—and what became obvious after not too long was that the electric car not only is a viable alternative to the combustion engine car but really is the wave of the future whether General Motors and the other car manufacturers know it or not. For now, however, they are not about to change their ways. They have too much of a vested interest in business as it is.

The hydrogen fuel cell red herring is addressed, and, with help from Joseph J. Romm, who wrote *The Hype about Hydrogen: Fact and Fiction in the Race to Save the Climate* (2004), which I highly recommend, got fed to the dogs. Naturally there is a clip of George W. Bush pretending to support the hydrogen fuel cell car, even though I am sure he knows that economically it's not even close to a match for the electric car. Getting the Great Prevaricator to advance the propaganda put out by the oil and vehicle companies surely is something close to proof positive that it's BS.

Especially watchable is the clip from Huell Howser's PBS show in which we get to see the EV1s not only being crushed but pulverized into little bits for recycling.

So, what's it all about, Alfie? It's just as Eisenhower warned: beware not just of the industrial-military complex taking over our lives, but beware of corporations in general buying up all the politicians and writing all the laws. In fact, with the way the mass electorate is influenced by advertising, only politicians pre-approved through campaign donations from big corporations have a chance of even getting the nomination of either of the two main political parties. And without that nomination, effectively speaking, they can't win.

Regardless of all the machinations by GM, et al., I think our grandchildren will be driving mostly electric vehicles with nary a gas station in sight. And they will be inundated with "green" ads in the media with lots of flowers and little girls paid for by General Motors and Toyota, telling us how they are responsible for the shiny, new clean world.

I've seen this and I give it____stars.
I want to see it___. I'll pass___.
The review was worth reading___. Not___.

With God on Our Side (2004) 8

Scary

The real danger is that someday the evangelicals will gain so much power that they will turn this country into a theocracy. You can believe that the likes of Jerry Falwell, Pat Robertson, James Robison and others, if given the choice of a country under their power or a country under the power of the people, would not hesitate to install themselves or someone who would do their bidding.

Well, would this be a bad thing for America? The astonishing thing is that many people would say "No, it wouldn't be a bad thing for America." The more amazing thing is, it could happen.

Democracy and the rule of law, the idea of equal rights for all citizens and a government of checks and balances is actually something new in the world if one takes a long view. Throughout most of human history most rulers were tyrannical and told the people that they derived their power and authority from God. Whether they were European kings, Japanese emperors, Islamic ayatollahs or Easter Island chieftains, they all spoke for and were to spoken to in a privileged way by God. It is only in the last two centuries or so that democratic leaders have risen to rule their countries without the claim that they rule by the authority of God. Thanks to the Enlightenment and the rise of education for the masses it has become increasing difficult to persuade the majority of people that any individual should rule because that individual (and his supporters) say he is God's choice. After all, who decides who is God's choice, and how can we know? Who speaks for God?

That is the real question. In Iran the ayatollahs speak for God. In America it is often the TV evangelist. But they speak in different tongues and they say diametrically opposed things. Both have the Truth and the Light. Both have God on their side.

Today's evangelical Christians claim that it is they who speak for God and it is they who know God's will. Ah, to know God's will. Such arrogance. And in their arrogance they would turn this country into a theocracy in which their will would be done in the name of God.

The problem with having God on your side is that you can't be wrong. Not only that but with God on your side it is easy to persuade yourself that the ends you believe in justify the means you will use to achieve them. If someone is against you, it is easy to see that they are against God. Since you can't be wrong, why should there be any discussion? Why should anyone be allowed to stand in your way?

This is why it is dangerous for the rest of us to allow the evangelicals to take over the Republican Party on their way to taking over the country. You can be sure, given the power, they will usher in an Age of Ignorance and Superstition to rival that of the Middle Ages and (by the way) initiate an apocalyptic war with Islam and any other religion or creed that tries to oppose their Truth. After all, to them this life on earth is only a brief period of time before the Judgment. And those who do not follow their beliefs will be in eternal damnation anyway. So what does it matter what we do today or tomorrow or the next when the Rapture is coming and Christ again and the Day of Judgment?

Question: By what authority does Pat Robertson speak for God?

Answer: By the same authority that Osama bin Laden speaks for God.

This documentary—like no other documentary that I have ever viewed—will appeal simultaneously to both the evangelicals and those who oppose them. Both sides will see in this documentary evidence that supports their point of view. The evangelicals will see their glorious and upstanding heroes triumphant, and others will be disgusted at the very sight on screen of the carefully coiffured liars and hypocrites and those who lust for power. It will also explain why George W. Bush became the President of the United States, and send a warning. What sort of person might the evangelicals elect next?

I've seen this and I give it____stars.
I want to see it___. I'll pass___.
The review was worth reading___. Not___.

Chapter Eleven:

Foreign Language Films

One advantage of watching films in languages you don't understand is that you don't have to have the sound on loud, you can crunch corn chips, the air conditioning can be going full blast, etc., and you can follow the film with your hearing aid off.

A disadvantage is that in following the subtitles you miss some of the nuances, especially those conveyed in facial expressions. It takes some experience to learn to give the subtitles exactly the attention they deserve and no more. Many foreign language films are sparse on dialogue so as to better travel internationally.

I

Jewels of the French Cinema

My favorite foreign films are French, perhaps because I lived in France in the Sixties and have some experience with the language and culture; but also because I love the way the French cinema focuses on relationships and in the relatively honest, non-violent way most French directors deal with human sexuality.

The reviews are in alphabetical order by English title. I've included the French title as well as my rating from one to ten stars. Again you can do your own ratings in the space provided after each review.

Alias Betty (*Betty Fisher et autres histoires*) (2001) 9
Engaging, character-driven thriller

I am somehow reminded in the storyline of this film of the work of mystery novelist Patricia Highsmith (*The Talented Mr. Ripley*; *A Game for the Living*, etc.) There is the same slightly genteel sense of mystery, realism and a women's point of view that characterizes Highsmith's work. In this case we have a young woman who loses her four-year-old son and then unexpectedly gains another. This intensely personal experience is set in the strata of contemporary French society. There are people in the projects, there is the underworld of petty criminals and prostitutes, and in contrast there are those who live in country homes beyond the suburbs. It is there that Betty, who is a novelist who has just published a best seller, lives.

What director Claude Miller has done with this material is to make it dramatic and to tell the story through the medium of film. That may seem obvious, but how many film makers fail to understand the differences in media and end up with too much talk and too little use of the camera to good effect? Miller shows us commonplace scenes of the projects and contrasts them with the fine homes of the well-to-do. He shows us the long limbs and slightly gawky beauty of his star, Sandrine Kiberlain, who plays Betty, and he contrasts her to the fleshy woman of the streets and bars, Carole Novacki (Mathide Seigner) who is the mother of the boy that Betty gains. He also compares and contrasts the craziness of Betty's mother Margot (played with a fine fidelity by Nicole Garcia) with similar, more muted manifestations in Betty herself. There are interiors of luxury and grace, and those of people living temporary lives in high rise block apartments. One gets a sense of France in the twenty-first century adding texture and place to a woman's story that could happen in almost any city in the world.

The opening scene shows Betty as a little girl on a train with her mother. We are told that her mother is suffering from some compulsive mental illness. We see her stab her daughter in the hand. And then we are fast-forwarded to the present and Betty is with her son Joseph, a scar on her hand, without a husband, going to her house in the countryside. Mother re-enters and we see that she is indeed a mental case, absurdly self-consumed and insensitive. When the boy falls out of a window and dies from the brain damage, Betty is in something close to catatonic shock, but her mother thinks only of her own welfare and seems indifferent to anything else.

And then comes the twist.

I won't describe what Margo does now because it is so interesting to see it unfold. At any rate, Betty is forced to come out of her depression and embrace new love and new responsibilities and to indeed commit a most criminal act, that of running away with another's child. And yet somehow we are made to feel—indeed the events of the plot compels us to feel—that she does the right thing in spite of her initial feelings and in spite of what would normally be right. Later on in the film there is another nice twist when the father of the dead boy returns and wants his share of Betty's success and fortune.

What I think many viewers will appreciate here is that the players look and act like real people, not like people from central casting. Alex Chatrian plays the second little boy and he is a charmer, and beautifully directed by Miller. Kiberlain's laconic and wistful portrayal of a woman with so many choices won her Best Actress awards at the Montreal and Chicago film festivals. She has the kind of beauty that grows on you, yet is not glamorous or glittery, but when she smiles, as she so seldom does in this movie, she lights up the whole screen. And Seigner looks like a common woman, not like a Hollywood star dressed up like a prostitute.

The men are also interesting and also very real. Luck Mervil, who plays Carole's boyfriend, is restrained like a volcano that one knows will eventually go off; and Stephane Freiss, who plays the father of the dead boy, and Edouard Baer who plays a scheming lower-class gigolo, are two very real varieties of men who prey on women.

The ending is witty and satisfying, and I can tell that Claude Miller has seen Stanley Kubrick's *The Killing* (1956) starring Sterling Hayden since part of this scene recalls the finale in that American film noir with the money flying out of a suitcase during a chase scene at an airport. Or perhaps that bit is from Rendell's novel (which I haven't read) and it is she who recalls Kubrick's film.

This is a thriller that manages to also be an engaging chick flick, if you will, a commingling of character and story that is in the best tradition of film making.

I've seen this and I give it____stars.
I want to see it___. I'll pass___.
The review was worth reading___. Not___.

Amélie (*Le fabuleux destin d'Amélie Poulain*) (2001) 9

Very funny, heart-warming and strikingly original

This is a delightful romantic fantasy of love and comedy, of vivid color and some preposterous antics of love and friendship that will send mawkish tears down your cheeks while making you laugh out loud. If not, turn in your headset for a heart.

Audrey Tautou is Amélie, a fashion-sharp Parisian wait-ress with an impish heart of gold and a shyness born of a bizarrely restricted childhood. She is cute and inno-cent, but not too innocent.

Her father, who was a physician, thought she had a defective heart because every time he put the stetho-scope to her little chest it was beating wildly. A voice-over explains that this was caused by the excitement that Amélie felt because her frigid father, whom she wanted so much to hold her, although he never did, was actually touching her. Because of an imagined heart condition she is kept out of school and tutored at home.

After her mother dies from being hit by a falling body (an actual human body on its way to the pavement from a tall building) we are flash-forwarded to the present where we find little Amélie all grown up. She still has no love in her life. But one day while listening to a news report of the death of Princess Di she drops something on the floor of her apartment. It rolls against a tile in the bathroom, dislodging the tile. Amélie pulls down the tile and finds in a hole in the wall a little tin box full of a boy's childhood mementoes from many years ago. In a characteristic bit of inspiration she decides to find that little boy, now grown into middle age, and give him the box. But she is shy and so must invent a stratagem. She arranges to call him when he is near a public phone booth in which she has placed the box. So delighted with the joy she has given him, Amélie sets off on a series of inventive and pixie-like intrusions into the lives of others in order to bring them happiness and even love.

While this R-rated fantasy would delight children there is too much actual sex in it for most American moms to tolerate for their little ones. In fact in the French style sex is made innocent, and of course that will not set well with those of a prudish nature.

Favorite corny pun: "Even artichokes have hearts." Fa-vorite elaborate joke: sending her father's garden gnome on the world tour that he won't take himself, and having the gnome photographed at tourist sites and the photos sent airmail to a very perplexed dad. Favorite joke: the beggar refusing a handout saying he takes Sundays off. Favorite scheme: reconstructing through cut and paste and photocopy the words of the landlady's beloved, and then fashioning a last love letter to her from him that was lost in the mail for forty years.

The two disc set includes a wealth of information to delight afficionados. There's an interview with director Jean-Pierre Jeunet, some footage on how *Amélie* was made, filmographies of cast and crew, audition footage, etc., etc.

Bottom line: very funny, heart-warming and strikingly original.

I've seen this and I give it____stars.
I want to see it___. I'll pass___.
The review was worth reading___. Not___.

Autumn Tale (*Conte d'automne*) (1998) 9

Rohmer knows relationships

And he knows how to write dialogue that is revealing, engaging and realistic, no small feat; and it is perhaps this talent more than anything else that has made Eric Rohmer the great director that he is. Here uses France's Cotes du Rhone wine country as a backdrop and symbol to help him explore not only autumn love, but the enduring friendship of two very different women. Isabelle (Maire Revière) is an elegant, tall, fair haired, blue-eyed haute bourgeoisie and her friend Magali (Beatrice Romand) is a short, earthy, dark-haired petite winemaker originally from Tunisia. Isabelle is happily married; Magali is divorced. They are both forty-something.

Isabelle's daughter is to be married. But the focus of the film is not on the bride and groom, but on the older generation, on Isabelle and Magali. In this way Rohmer combines the warmth and enchantment of the celebration of autumn life, when the grapes are ripe for harvest, when love has its last chance, when Dionysus has his festival, when the heat of summer is over and we are ready to reflect and realize what is really important before it's too late.

Isabelle feels this strongly and wants her friend to find happiness before another winter comes. But Magali, because of the vineyard, doesn't have much of an opportunity to meet men, although she allows that she would like to. She is at that delicate age when one can try again or shrug it off. Isabelle intervenes by going to a dating service and placing an ad. She meets Gerald (Alain Libolt) and they have lunch (she insists on lunch) two or three times and she evaluates him. He is modest, somewhat suave and amazingly diplomatic. They share a certain attraction.

Meanwhile, Rosine (Alexia Portal) who is dating Magali's son and who is very close to Magali, perhaps more so that she is to her son, also wants to find a mate for Magali. She proposes her philosophy professor, Etienne (Didier Sandre), who is in fact sweet on her. He is the kind of man who, as Magali observes, likes them younger as he grows older. But maybe she will be the excep-

tion. Maybe he will finally grow up. Both arrange for their choices to meet Magali at the wedding.

As usual Rohmer explores humanity and how we relate to one another, and finds both love and a kind of sweetness that is liable to bring us to tears. The resolution of the film is followed by a most endearing anticlimax in which there is a dance of joy.

I've seen this and I give it____stars.
I want to see it___. I'll pass___.
The review was worth reading___. Not___.

The Aviator's Wife (*La femme de l'aviateur*) (1981) 9

Rohmer really does know relationships

In this bittersweet tale of disconnections and possibilities perhaps we have the essence of the art of Eric Rohmer. If you have only one Rohmer film to see, perhaps you ought to make it this one because it is so very, very French, so interestingly talkative (one of Rohmer's trademarks) and so very, very Rohmer.

The aviator's wife, incidentally does not appear except in a photograph, but that is all to the point. Everything is a bit off stage in this intriguing drama: love especially is a bit off stage. And yet how all the participants yearn.

Marie Riviere stars as Anne who is in love with the aviator. We catch her just as she learns that he no longer wants her. He tells her that his wife is pregnant and so he must return to her. Meanwhile, she is being pestered by Francois (Philippe Marlaud) who is in love with her. However he is a little too young and "clinging." Truly she is not interested. It is a disconnection as far as she is concerned.

The heart of the film occurs when Francois is following the aviator and the blond woman. Francois is obsessive and jealous. He follows because...it isn't clear and he really doesn't know why except that this is the man that Anne loves. As it happens while he is following them he runs into a pretty fifteen-year-old Lucie (played fetchingly by Anne-Laure Meury) who imagines that he is following *her*. She turns it into a game, and again we have a disconnection. She is fun and cute and full of life, but he cannot really see her because he pines for Anne. Meanwhile Anne of course is pining for the aviator.

Rohmer's intriguing little joke is about the aviator's wife. Who is she and what is she like? We can only imagine. And this is right. The woman imagines what the other woman is like, but never really knows unless she meets her.

Maire Riviere is only passably pretty, but she has gorgeous limbs and beautiful skin and a hypnotic way about her which Rohmer accentuates in the next to the last scene in her apartment with Francois. We follow the talk between the two, of disconnection and off-center possibilities, of friends and lovers with whom things are tantalizingly not exactly right and yet not tragically wrong. As we follow this talk we see that Anne's heart is breaking or has broken—and all the while we see her skin as Francois does. She wants to be touched, but not by him. And then she allows him to touch her, but only in comforting gestures, redirecting his hands away from amorous intent. And then she goes out with a man in whom she really has no interest.

Such is life, one might say. Rohmer certainly thinks so.

One thing I love about Rohmer's films is that you cannot predict where they will go. Another thing is his incredible attention to authentic detail about how people talk and how they feel without cliché and without any compromise with reality—Rohmer's reality of course, which I find is very much like the reality that I have experienced.

See this for Eric Rohmer whose entre into the world of cinema is substantial, original, and wonderfully evocative of what it is like to live in the modern world with an emphasis on personal relationships and love.

I've seen this and I give it____stars.
I want to see it___. I'll pass___.
The review was worth reading___. Not___.

Band of Outsiders (Bande à part) (1964) 9

Light, playful with a gray undertone

Even though I haven't gotten around to finish watching Jean-Luc Godard's celebrated *Breathless* (1960) despite trying a couple of times, I'm pretty sure I like *Band of Outsiders* better. Main reason: Anna Karina. I have little doubt that most women would prefer *Breathless* since it stars Jean-Paul Belmondo who, as cinematic history has it, anticipated Richard Gere's performance in Truffaut's American *Breathless* (1983).

What I love about Karina's Odile is her incredible naiveté. Although 20-years-old playing perhaps an 18-year-old, Karina, then Godard's wife, manages the complete and total personality of someone say 12-years-old. It is her naiveté that makes the film work as two petty, would-be criminals, Arthur (Claude Brasseur) and Franz (Sami Frey), seduce her into helping them rob a surprisingly large number of francs from her Aunt's house. At least they think they're going to score. We'll see how the fates feel about that.

They meet in a beginning English language class. Obviously it is not just Godard who admires American culture; our three beginners in life do as well. Appropriately enough the film is adapted from *Fools' Gold*, an American novel by Dolores Hitchins. In a sense this is a French film imitating not an American film but an American attitude toward life, a free and easy world in which riches are liable to just fall into your lap, where it's chic to be young and run with the wind and drive your convertible onto the sidewalk when you feel like it and in crazy circles for no reason at all, and it is especially fun to jump into the vehicle without opening the doors while it is moving. It is an existence in which you feel spontaneous and uninhibited and can dance the Madison without looking at your feet.

Well, Odile and Franz can. Arthur watches his continuously. And this tells us something about Arthur, who is a bit mean and a bit shallow, but intent on getting his and getting it right. It is he with whom Odile falls into puppy love. She is attracted to his confidence and his crude masculinity, and his interest in her, nothing more. She is further seduced by the joy of finding friends and something exciting to do. She hasn't a clue about who they are or who she is, and that in part is the charm of the film.

She has lovely limbs that we do not see. She runs gracefully, stretching her legs out like a colt. She delights in sitting in the front seat of the Simca, the men on either side of her. Steal the money she has spotted in her uncle's closet, money that she herself would never think of stealing? Okay. And then we go to England or better yet, South America like Butch Cassidy and the Sundance Kid.

Childish, very childish and charming because Odile is so pretty, just that, pretty as every young girl should be. But surely something tragic is going to happen. Surely this is a cautionary tale about how innocence is lost.

There are gray day shots of Paris and the suburbs now covered with concrete and asphalt. There's a nine-minute run through the Louvre, young people just having fun; and then the denouement and tragedy. Of some sort. And then the fantasy life returns as the film ends.

Godard's story, his plot, isn't to be taken seriously, but his characters are. Arthur is the bad guy, the primitive, just an animal acting out his animal life. But Franz is sly, reflective, reads books, is well-mannered, and is finding himself. Odile is a child who will be a woman soon.

The Criterion Collection DVD is nicely presented with some of the usual extras, including excerpts from interviews with Godard and Anna Karina. The subtitles are excellent. There's a booklet with a review by Joshua Clover and part of an interview by Jean Collet from 1964 entitled, "No Questions Asked: Conversations with Jean-Luc Godard."

I've seen this and I give it____stars.
I want to see it___. I'll pass___.
The review was worth reading___. Not___.

The Beat that My Heart Skipped (De battre

mon coeur s'est arête) (2005) 9
Fast, tense with outstanding acting and a clever story-line

Jacques Audiard, who previously gave us the very interesting *Read My Lips* (2001) and the cute and clever *Venus Beauty Institute* (1999), manages to create here a story about a character who is both a petty gangster and a pianist. Not exactly your usual combination of talents. Romain Duris plays Thomas Seyr who is that character. Duris brings an animal sensuality and an artist's sensitivity to the part. He is an actor of unusual skills and vitality. Audiard gets the most out of him.

In the beginning Tom Seyr is in apprenticeship to take over his father's way of life in a French version of the protection racket. Their particular hustle involves getting properties condemned by trashing them or infecting them with rats or some other vermin, forcibly throwing out squatters or tenants, then buying the property on the cheap, and then finally selling it at a nice profit. In the end...well, I can't give you the ending, but I can say that it is entirely agreeable and surprising with just a little twist on what we might expect.

Neils Arestrup plays the father. There are some other interesting characters and a lot of macho action, a bit of blood here and there, some quick and easy sex. And then there is an old piano teacher that Tom happens to run into one day who invites him to an audition. Tom has not played the piano seriously for years, but just seeing his old teacher brings back the thrill and the deep intimacy he once had with music, and recalls to him the career of his deceased mother, who was once a concert pianist who had hoped that her son would be too. He had the talent.

But of course playing the piano at that level is not something you can take up, let go, and then go back to. But Tom thinks maybe he can do it with a little practice. But he needs a teacher to prepare for the audition. When he tries to get one he is effectively laughed at since he is 28-years-old and is very much out of practice and indeed never really practiced that much. But by chance (there are a number of plot furtherances in this film that come about by chance—but that is not a problem because the chance meetings seem natural and are events that would probably happen eventually)—and so by chance he is hooked up with a young woman fresh from China who speaks no French, but is an expert pianist who needs a little money. She agrees to help him. Her name is Miao Lin. She is played brilliantly with subtlety and finesse by French-Vietnamese actress Linh Dan Pham, whom I previously saw in *Indochine* (1992) playing the adopted child of Catherine Deneuve's character.

The acting ability of Romain Duris and Linh Dan Pham are what carry this film. Audiard's direction is a bit scattered at times and especially in the beginning lacks focus, but a clever storyline and his ability to get great performances from the players overcome these faults.

See this for Romain Duris who gives a virtuoso performance and for Linh Dan Pham who captivates with restrained intensity.

I've seen this and I give it___stars.
I want to see it___. I'll pass___.
The review was worth reading___. Not___.

Blame It on Fidel (La faute a Fidel) (2006) 9
Cute and vital growing up story from a little girl's POV

This debut film by Julie Gavras, daughter of famed Greek-born director Costa-Gavras (e.g., *Z*, 1969), was nominated for the Grand Jury Award at the Sundance Film Festival in 2007. In addition to directing, Julie Gavras also collaborated with Arnaud Cathrine on the script which they adapted from a novel by Italian novelist Domitilla Calamai. What is striking about the story is the way it reconstructs how girls become social, how they learn about their world, how they question it, and how they reconcile the contradictions, and how they grow up.

Doing the growing up is nine-year-old Anna de la Mesa, played with fidelity, wit, and skill beyond her years by Nina Kervel-Bey. She is bourgeois to the core, following the lead of her maternal grandparents, who own a vineyard in Bordeaux, and her favorite nanny and housekeeper who lost everything to the Communists when Fidel Castro came to power in Cuba. Her parents, however, are infatuated with the Left, especially with the rise of Allende to power in Chile. The year is 1970-71.

Anna loves their house and garden and going to Catholic school. She is proper and sensible. When they lose their house, and have to let the nanny go, and end up renting an apartment in Paris, Anna is upset and demands to know why things have changed. When it appears that they don't have as much money, Anna begins turning off the lights and turning down the heat to save money. When they want her to transfer to the public school, she demurs and a compromise is made: she can continue to go to Catholic school but she is not allowed to take Bible studies. So when that time of the day comes, she has to stand up and go outside the classroom door and wait.

But Anna is strong emotionally and intellectually. She questions everything and is not self-conscious about being singled out. The other girls may laugh, but when she gets into a fight with one of them, she manages to win her over afterwards so that they are friends, even though their parents are not.

There is in the background the political disputes between the Right and the Left, between parents who change the subject when the question how babies are made is brought up, and those who tell the truth, in short between the bourgeois and the bohemian. One gets the sense that Gavras and Anna are wiser than the disputants, and that there is something to appreciate in both ways of life.

It is impossible not to identify with little Anna, partially because she herself is so fair, and partially because it is such a thrill to see the psychology of the socialization process displayed so well and true in a movie, but also because Nina Kervel-Bey is such a powerful little actress who was so wondrously directed by Julie Gavras. This is one of the best performances by a preteen actor that I have ever seen. Kervel-Bey simply dominates the film and commands the screen.

Will Anna shed her petite bourgeois ways and embrace the politics of her parents? I highly recommend that you see this film and find out.

I've seen this and I give it____stars.
I want to see it___. I'll pass___.
The review was worth reading___. Not___.

Claire's Knee (Le genou de Claire) (1970) 10

Warm, sensual and beautifully presented

The title of this charming film by Eric Rohmer is perhaps too provocative. It really gives the wrong impression, yet Claire's knee is exactly the central point of the film, although in a way that will surprise you.

This is the story about a thirty-something year old diplomat, Jerome Montcharvin, who encounters two pretty girls, sixteen and eighteen years old, while on vacation at Lake Annecy in France (near Lake Geneva, Switzerland) a month before his wedding and finds that they affect him more strongly than he might have expected. It is especially Claire who brings out a side of his personality that is seldom exposed, much to the merry interest of his friend, Aurora, a writer, who has guided his interest in the girls, ostensibly as material for a story she is writing. The film, it need be said immediately, has not so much to do with the pretty girl's knee as it has to do with the protagonist's self-perception.

Jean-Claude Brialy, who plays Jerome Montcharvin, brings a veracious mix of smug confidence and little guy vulnerability to the part spiked with a clear case of self-delusion that illuminates his character very well. And the girls are indeed very pretty, with Laura, played with coquettish innocence by Béatrice Romand, also being clever and slyly sophisticated, vulnerable and honest. In contrast Claire, played by Laurence de Monaghan, whose fawn-like beauty is perfect for the part, seems superficial and ordinary and a bit distant. I found myself more attracted to Aurora, played with a gentle and understated irony by Aurora Cornu. She provides the ob-

jectifying point of view for us to realize that while Jerome imagines he is a man in touch with his feelings and has an objective understanding of himself, he is really a man who fools himself about his motivation, a man who can be ugly when frustrated, as he is by Claire's lack of interest in him.

The dialogue, written by director Eric Rohmer, which some have found excessive is anything but. It is instead clever and witty and at times profound as Rohmer relentlessly explores the nature of love, sex, sensuality and self-delusion. The cinematography of the lake and the French alps in the summer time is luscious, and the privileged, softly indulgent life style of the characters living around the lake provoked a twinge of jealousy in my soul. This is a beautiful film, worldly wise, warm, sensual and subtle as a dinner by candlelight.

I've seen this and I give it____stars.
I want to see it___. I'll pass___.
The review was worth reading___. Not___.

Day for Night (La nuit américaine) (1973) 9

Delicate but penetrating

La Nuit Américaine is an interesting movie with celebrated French director Francois Truffaut playing a director making a movie. He proves to be a modest and convincing actor himself while patiently weaving a tale about how movies are made and how intense the emotional interactions among those making the movie can be.

Don't give up on this one too soon. It starts slow and seems almost amateurish because of the relatively low-tech way the film within the film is being shot. Truffaut gives us a glimpse of how the production crew works together (and sometimes at odds) while showing us some of the things that can go wrong while making a movie. He begins with the technical details of the production but before long begins to concentrate on the personalities of the movie-makers and their individual stories. Each story is carefully crafted in a somewhat leisurely way almost like the characterizations in a soap opera (without of course the phony drama and mass market sentimentality seen on TV). Truffaut's fine sense of emotional conflict and how conflict might be resolved makes the various stories touching without being maudlin.

Jacqueline Bisset who stars as English actress Julia Baker who plays the title role in the film within the film (*May I Introduce Pamela?*) doesn't make her appearance until about a fourth of the way in. She is a delight as an actress with a heart of gold recovering from a nervous breakdown married to an older man whom she does indeed love. Jean-Pierre Leaud, whom most viewers will recall as the running boy in Truffaut's *The 400 Blows*, plays a young and not entirely confident actor who gets jilted by the script girl who runs off with the stunt man during production. Bisset's warm and sisterly befriending of Leaud is, shall we say, entirely French (which gets her into trouble with her husband). This really is a skillful showcasing of Bisset since she gets to play something like an ingénue with her husband and the older woman with Leaud. Be careful you might fall in love with her.

Valentina Cortese in a fine supporting role does a most convincing job of playing the temperamental Italian actress just past her prime who quaffs champagne while working, who forgets her lines and can't find the right door, but when properly indulged gives a great performance.

My problem with this movie is I saw the dubbed version and of course that is disconcerting because one is constantly trying to reconcile the visualized actor with the dubbed one. To see Jacqueline Bisset who is beautifully fluent in both English and French speaking French while at the same time hearing someone else speaking English for her is just a bit too much to take.

Truffaut is the kind of director who allows the audience to penetrate not only his characters to see what makes them tick, but also the stars who play those characters. He does a particularly beautiful job with Bisset who is warm and wise and something close to heroic, and with Leaud whose childishness seems natural and whose pettiness forgivable. Don't believe those reviewers who think this is a slight film. It is carefully crafted and very well thought out and is a fine example of the work of the one of the great directors of the French cinema. See it for Truffaut whose delicate genius is evident throughout.

I've seen this and I give it____stars.
I want to see it___. I'll pass___.
The review was worth reading___. Not___.

Diary of a Chambermaid *(Le journal d'une femme*

de chamber) (1964) 10
A dark comedy of brilliance

This is my favorite Buñuel film. The story is stunningly presented, an absolute work of art, unbelievably subtle but always concrete. It is like a great symphony: every note is perfect.

Surprisingly (considering the title) *Le journal d'une femme de chambre* is not about sex, nor is it a journal for that matter. It is about politics, sexual politics of course, but also domestic politics, manor politics, and nation-state politics. The time is the thirties as fascism moves toward its mesmerizing stranglehold on a decadent Europe. The place is France (Normandy, I imagine) where the republicans hold power. In the streets are those who would be brown suits and among them is Joseph (Georges Geret), groundskeeper for a petite bourgeois family of degenerate eccentrics. He is an incipient Nazi, a xenophobic anti-Semitic man who worships

brute force, an ignorant man that every French moviegoer knows will be a Nazi-collaborator once France is under the occupation.

The story is seen from the point of view of Celestine, a chambermaid of some sophistication (and an abiding, but understandable duplicity), a Parisian who has come to work for the family in the country. She is played by the incomparable Jeanne Moreau of the plastic face, a woman of many guises, many moods and an ability to depict with a glance any emotion. She is a great star of the French stage and screen who plays the part effortlessly, with finesse and a fine subtlety. The screenplay by Buñel and the brilliant Jean-Claude Carriere (who penned so many outstanding films, *Belle de Jour* (1967), *The Discreet Charm of the Bourgeoisie* (1972), *Valmont* (1989), *The Ogre* (1996), etc.) is an adaptation of the novel by Octave Mirbeau. There is a Hollywood film of the same name starring Paulette Goddard, Burgess Meredith and Judith Anderson, directed by Jean Renoir that I haven't seen, released in 1946. I understand the treatment was more comedic and conventional.

Surrealist Luis Buñuel's film is perhaps best described as a *comédie noire*, a genre antecedent to the familiar (and somewhat similar) film noir. In the latter the comedy is usually incidental and there is no attempt at any great philosophic or symbolic significance. Here Buñel not only makes a statement about the nature of the relationship between bourgeois Europe in the thirties and fascism, but even delves into the primeval nature of women and gives us a sharp look at a woman's place in bourgeois society. Celestine is duplicitous because she has to be to survive. She uses men the way the society uses her.

Be sure and pay close attention to the final scene inside and outside the café and consider the implications of what is being shown. What is being suggested? Will Joseph finally get the punishment he so richly deserves? Or did Celestine make the choice she made out of fear? Is the union between Joseph and Celestine symbolic of that between the fascists and Europe?

For those interested in this last theme I highly recommend Vittoria De Sica's brilliant *The Garden of the Finzi-Continis* (1971).

I've seen this and I give it____stars.
I want to see it___. I'll pass___.
The review was worth reading___. Not___.

The Discreet Charm of the Bourgeoisie *(Le*

charme discret de la bourgeoisie) (1972) 9
Surreal dreams running into an absurd reality

The title is certainly intriguing, suggesting something ultra sophisticated, and we can guess that "discreet" will be exposed as "hypocritical," and the charm will be superficial. In this we are not disappointed. I should also say this reminds me of the theater of the absurd that had its heyday in the postwar period in Europe and the US with *Rhinoceros, Six Characters in Search of an Author, Waiting For Godot, The Birthday Party,* etc., and then more or less disappeared, Roberto Benigni's more recent cinematic venture, *La Vita e Bella* (1997) notwithstanding. Most critics however would refer to *Le charme discret de la bourgeoisie* as an example of surrealism, an aesthetic movement in art, theater, cinema, etc. that grew out of Dadaism in the twenties. But the theater of the absurd is later, taking its rationale from the existential work of Camus—see especially his collection of essays, *The Myth of Sisyphus* (1942)—and Sartre, while getting its name from a book entitled, *The Theatre of the Absurd* (1960) by Martin Esslin. Regardless of how we tag this, Spanish/French director Luis Buñuel's treatment is indeed charming and funny.

Fernando Rey stars as a diplomat from the country of "Miranda" who, along with his five constant friends, cannot seem to ever finish a meal. They are the bourgeoisie who are discreet in their sexual activities and their illegalities (Rey's character apparently smuggles cocaine) while maintaining a sort of absurd decorum in which good manners are paramount. A café runs out of tea, well, they will content themselves with coffee. No coffee, well, water will be fine. Guests arrive a day ahead of time, well, we'll go out instead, won't you join us. When a company of soldiers on maneuvers shows up at the house just as they are sitting down to dinner, they are invited to join them, and when the police come to arrest Rey, they all politely intercede only to follow him to jail. When the one finds that his wife is in his friend's bedroom, he is too polite to object.

Buñuel's technique runs realistic scenes into dream sequences without warning. When a soldier sits down to tea to tell his story of horror, all listen politely. When, for the umpteenth time they *are à la table,* a curtain parts and they find themselves on stage in front of an audience, they discreetly excuse themselves, saying they have forgotten their lines.

Of course Buñuel must have his little satire of the church, and here he uses a *monseigneur* who becomes a gardener who hears a last rites confession that reveals that the confessor murdered his, the *monseigneur's,* parents many years ago. The *monseigneur* politely and without being ruffled, allows that Jesus forgives him and leaves him in a state of grace, which soothes his conscience as he then picks up a shotgun....

So seamlessly does Buñuel weave his tapestry that it's sometimes hard to tell when reality ends and the dreams begin, but that is perhaps the point. Our dreams are absurd of course, but then again so is our reality.

I've seen this and I give it____stars.
I want to see it___. I'll pass___.

The review was worth reading___. Not___.

The Dream Life of Angels (*La vie rêvée des anges*)

(1998) 10
A sad and beautiful movie

Two French girls who are "not the chosen ones" (to recall a Cyndi Laper lyric) befriend one another after meeting at a sweat shop where they operate sewing machines. One of them, Marie (Natacha Régnier) is apartment-sitting for a mother and her daughter who are in the hospital, victims of an accident. The other, Isabelle (Élodie Bouchez) has been living day to day with her backpack on her back, sometimes selling handmade cards on street corners. Almost immediately there is an affinity, and they find joy and adventure in one another's company.

Part of the power of Erick Zonca's forceful and precise direction is to make us not only identify with his two heroines, but to force us see the world from their point of view. They are tossed about by strong emotions, powerfully projected by both actresses. Their lives and happiness are at the whim of forces beyond their control, the most powerful of which are their own feelings.

When I was a little boy and went to the movies I would see three films, bang, bang, bang, one after the other, and when I came out, five or six hours later, I was transformed. I had grown, and I could see the world in a different way. Of course I was a little boy and every little bit of experience was amazing and added to my knowledge of the world. Now, such transformations, like moments of Zen enlightenment, are rare and precious. *The Dream Life of Angels* is one of those rare and precious films that has the kind of power to make us see the world afresh as though for the very first time.

Bouchez and Régnier shared the Best Actress award at the 1998 Cannes Film Festival for their work in this movie. Indeed it is hard to choose between them. Both are wonderful. Bouchez's character, Isabelle, has a gentle, fun-loving, child-like nature, tomboyish and sentimental. Marie is cynical, uptight and wired. Her emotions swing wildly from deep pessimism to a tenuous hope for something better in this life. When she is seduced, rather forcefully, by the arrogant and predatory Chris (Grégoire Colin) who owns nightclubs and is accustomed to having his way with women, she is stunned to find that she wants him, needs him, loves him. But she knows (and is warned by Isabelle) that he is just using her and will dump her. She hates herself for loving him and therefore lashes out at Isabelle who is a witness to her humiliation.

As a counterpoint to the raw animal love that Marie finds in Chris, there is the tender, dreamlike love that Isabelle finds for the daughter of the woman who owns the apartment. The mother dies from her injuries, but the daughter, Sandrine, lives on in a coma. Isabelle finds Sandrine's diary and reads it, and is touched by the sentiments expressed by the girl, and falls in love with her. A nurse tells Isabelle: "You can talk to her. She's sleeping, but she can hear you." Whether she can or not, we don't know, but to show her love Isabelle visits the comatose girl in the hospital and reads from her diary to her.

In a sense we feel that the dream life of angels is the dream of Sandrine, who is dreaming the life of the young women who are living in her apartment. She is an angel and they are her dream, a troubled dream of raw emotion contrasted with her state of quiet somnolence.

The Dream Life of Angels is beautifully shot in tableaux of pastel interiors in which the characters are sometimes seen at offset as in portraits. In one scene we see one of the girls in the apartment while in the right upper corner is a window through which we see in clear focus a car pass in front of a picturesque building, so that the scene is seen in layers, so that we experience the inner life and the outside world at once. In another scene, Isabelle is reading Sandrine's diary, which we see over her shoulder. Just as she reads the words that excite her passion for the girl, there is just the slightest quickening of tempo as Isabelle flips the page to see what Sandrine writes next, and in that small gesture, we feel the emotions of the girls, the one who wrote the words and the one who reads them.

As a foil to the smooth, but bestial Chris, we are given Charlie (Patrick Mercado), fat motorcycle dude who is gentle and wise. This enlightened juxtaposition of character is part of director Erick Zonca's technique. We see it also in the contrasting characters of Marie and Isabelle.

Obviously this is a work of art, but it is also a triumph of film making in a directorial sense. Zonca's careful attention to detail and his total concentration throughout turn something that might have been merely original into a masterful work of art.

I've seen this and I give it____stars.
I want to see it___. I'll pass___.
The review was worth reading___. Not___.

Entre Nous (1983) 9

Honest, sad, beautiful and very touching

Michel (Guy Marchand) falls in love with Jewish refuge Lena (Isabelle Huppert) at first sight and offers marriage as a way she can avoid being sent to a German concentration camp. She accepts, and although she doesn't love him, they have two children and are still married when we pick up the action again in Lyons in 1952 when Lena is 29-years-old. There she meets the sophisticated and well-to-do artist Madeleine (Miou-Miou) who

awakens her to the drabness of her existence as a housewife with a loutish husband who now runs a gas station. The attraction between Lena and Madeleine is very strong, and very threatening to the men, especially to Michel.

Huppert's poignant and bittersweet portrayal reminds me of her delicate work in *Madame Bovary* (1991). There is the same listlessness expressed along with a vague desire for something better out of life, and the anticipation of the sadness that we know will come of such desire. Miou-Miou is sharp and cynical with perhaps a streak of the manic-depressive about her. The love they spontaneously feel for one another is real and beautiful and makes us want it to be fulfilled. But Lena holds herself back because of her family, and then it is the men and propriety that get in the way.

Of course this is very French and Lena and Madeleine hold hands and comfort one another while telling each other their innermost secrets including the infidelities of their spouses, etc. (The men have no such communication.) Director Diane Kurys exercises more restraint in showing the physical nature of their mutual attraction than would be displayed today. Lena says to Madeleine at one point, "I want to kiss you," but we do not see them kissing. The most explicit scene sexually is the startling, but delicately expressed, meeting with the soldiers on the train where we discover the full extent of Lena's frustration.

This is not quite a great movie. The pace is a little slow in spots and sometimes the focus is not as sharp as it could be. But it is an extraordinarily honest movie, and I'll take that over sharp technique any day. Huppert is not only at her best here, but her exquisite and subtle beauty is shown to great advantage. Miou-Miou is also very pretty of course—this is the first time I've seen her—but I would say her strength of character is perhaps her strongest suit. This is a human tragedy on a small, intimate scale, one that we can't help but feel could have been averted had those involved understood one another better, had they been a little wiser. We've all been there before and so we can share the sadness and the sense of loss.

I've seen this and I give it____stars.
I want to see it___. I'll pass___.
The review was worth reading___. Not___.

Forbidden Games (*Jeux interdits*) (1952) 10

A masterpiece with a somewhat misleading title

In French the title of this movie is perhaps appropriate, but in English it is misleading. What is "forbidden" about the games that the children play has nothing to do with sex (the usual designation of "forbidden" in English). Instead what 11-year-old Michel Dolle (Georges Poujouly) and 5-year-old Paulette (Brigitte Fossey) do that is forbidden is they steal crosses: from the cemetery, from the top of a horse-drawn hearse—Michel even attempts to steal the rector's crucifix. They do this as a way of coping with death. The crosses are for dead animals, her dog, some chicks, a worm, etc. that they have buried in a little plot under the mill near a stream.

But this is not a horror show or anything like it. Instead, René Clément's celebrated tale of childhood love is actually a strongly religious anti-war movie of incredible delicacy, laced with humor and poignancy.

It begins with an air attack on a stream of people (presumably Parisians running from Paris) along a country road trying to escape the encroachment of the Nazi army. Little Paulette is in a car with her parents and her little dog, Jock. They are gunned down by a German fighter plane. Paulette's parents and the dog are killed. Paulette is left alone carrying the dead dog in her arms. Eventually she wanders onto a farm where she is met by Michel who takes an instant liking to her and becomes her protector and her friend. His is a peasant family of farmers who really don't need another mouth to feed, but they take her in. She is so clean, they exclaim and she smells so good. She is from Paris. She has just undergone the most horrible terror, the death of her parents and her dog, and now she must somehow come to grips with that loss. What transpires is a child's interpretation of the healing power of religious ritual and symbol.

Clément uses the world of the children as a counterpoint to the war in the background and as a gentle satire on the church. The children make a game of religion and in doing so demonstrate the healing power of ritual and sacrament.

What makes this totally original and deeply symbolic film work is the uncluttered and naturalistic vision of Clément and his wonderful direction of his two little stars. Fossey in particular is amazing. She is completely unaffected and natural, an adorable little girl suddenly alone in the world who must make a new world for herself against great odds. Her sense of personal integrity and her strong will makes us believe that somehow she will succeed. Incidentally, Fossey's performance here in conveying the creative world of the child should be compared with 4-year-old Victoire Thivisol's performance in Jacques Doillon's *Ponette* (1996), as should the skill and vision of the directors. Both are deeply religious films that rely on the pre-socialized world of the child to show us our own spirituality.

Also very good is Poujouly as the farm boy who loves little Paulette and shows that love by assuming the psychological and spiritual responsibility for helping her to overcome the tragedy of being so brutally orphaned. He is himself experiencing a pre-adolescent coming of age, a transition exemplified by rebellion and a growing independence of mind and spirit. Poujouly is intense and

fully engaged, so much so that in one scene we can see him mouth in unison Paulette's lines in preparation for his time to speak. Clément left this in perhaps because he knew it would further characterize Michel's intensity.

This film won the Grand Prize at the Venice Film Festival in 1952 and an Academy Award the same year as best foreign film. It is one of the wonders of the French cinema, a masterpiece of the human spirit not to be missed. See it for the children, whose strength of character can inspire us all.

I've seen this and I give it____stars.
I want to see it___. I'll pass___.
The review was worth reading___. Not___.

The 400 Blows (Les *Quatre cents coup*) (1959) 9
Sympathetic and engaging

An idiomatic translation of the French title of this movie, *Les quatre cents coup*, would be something like "Raising Hell," understood ironically. Twelve-year-old Antoine Doinel, played very winningly by Jean-Pierre Leaud, doesn't suffer "400 blows," although he does get mistreated quite a bit, and he doesn't mean to raise hell or to be a problem to his parents or society. He's just a boy being a boy. Unfortunately his mother (Claire Mauier), who is more like a wicked step-mother than the boy's biological mother (although she is that) would like to be rid of him so that she can spend more time pursuing her hobby, which is adultery. His cuckolded step-father (Albert Remy) is no help, although he seems to care more for the boy than his mother. And the institutions of society, as represented by his school, the Parisian police, and the social services people, seem intent on turning poor Antoine into a criminal. Truffaut ends the movie at a spot where it is still far from clear where Antoine is really headed, but we can guess that his spirit will be undaunted.

Some have called this, Francois Truffaut's first feature, realism, but if it's realism, so is Charles Dickens. This is an extended slice of life, a coming-of-ager stopped before the boy does become of age, and in this sense original. Truffaut paints everybody but the boy and his best friend in such a negative hue that we cannot help but identify with Antoine. This is not realism, but it doesn't matter because this is a splendid film, perhaps not as great as some have claimed, but very much worth watching because of Leaud's fine performance and Truffaut's original and charming presentation of Paris in the 1950s. In one sense Truffaut makes the City of Light a child's playground, and in another, it is a repressive, indifferent monolith. Antoine's transgressions—ditching school, telling lies, stealing from his grandmother—are trivial. But Truffaut wants to make sure we don't misunderstand so he has the boy get into trouble for (1) having a magazine passed to him in class, (2) unconsciously memorizing Balzac (he is accused of plagiarism by his fascist teacher) (3) returning a typewriter, which admittedly he had lifted, and (4) lighting a candle in honor of Balzac (which starts a fire).

My favorite scene is the one with the psychiatrist in which we hear her questions, but the camera stays on Antoine. His candid, eminently reasonable and entirely sane answers to her questions demonstrate that he is a completely normal, even admirable boy, and that it is society and its stupid adults that are off the mark.

The faces of the children at the Punch and Judy show are wonderful and the sequence of Antoine running and running so gracefully and seemingly with little effort symbolizes the longing that all children have to be free.

While I think this famous movie is perhaps a little over-rated, I can tell you that if you haven't seen it you are in danger of being labeled a cinematic illiterate.

I've seen this and I give it____stars.
I want to see it___. I'll pass___.
The review was worth reading___. Not___.

Girl on the Bridge (*Fille sur la pont, La*) (1999) 9

An erotic, funny and original romantic comedy

The old Hollywood formula, Boy Meets Girl, Cute, is given a nice French twist is this very funny and intriguing romantic comedy starring Daniel Auteuil and Vanessa Paradis. Paradis is Adele, a twenty-something waif who looks like a Parisian model except for the charming and disarming gap between her two front teeth. She's *sur la pont* and looking to jump off into the Seine. Auteuil appears as Gabor, a forty-something carnival knife thrower, looking for a new and more exciting target. He taunts her a little, shames her a bit. She gets insulted and jumps. He jumps in right after her.

Well, I have it on good report that Nora Ephron is jealous as hell. I mean wouldn't, say, Meg Ryan and Mel Gibson just be adorable meeting like this?

I...don't...think...so. For one thing, this would never work in the American cinema since one of the essentials is that the "boy" be twenty years older than the "girl" so that his patience with her frequent liaisons is plausible, and that's too great an age difference for standard Hollywood faire. Hollywood would have to find another slant on their relationship (something banal no doubt) and alter the ending to make it more romantic. But Hollywood can do that! Watch for the remake—a Nancy Meyers film, directed by Ephron—in theaters everywhere, circa 2015.

Since the script, containing some very witty dialogue by Serge Frydman, and the fine acting by Auteuil and Paradis, carry the show, Director Patrice Leconte was able to film this on the cheap in glorious black and white, which

doesn't detract from the film at all. I didn't really notice there was no color until about twenty minutes in because I was so taken with, first, Paradis as the girl who could never say no, and then Auteuil who is funny, commanding, and obviously having a great time. By the way, the device of her being interviewed to open the film makes us think for a moment that we are being shown a video recording of that interview. Following a well-established cinematic convention of rendering video recordings in black and white, this makes our minds accept the black and white cinematography without question.

Paradis is child-like and sexy by turns. The scene after the train passes and she says to Gabor something like, "You KNOW what I want to do, and I want to do it NOW," leads to a rather strange, but clearly erotic, symbolic sexual experience. Paradis plays her part very well.

The theme is the mystery of capricious luck, believed in passionately by those who feel they have none, which is how Adele and Gabor feel before they meet each other. Together, however, they can call the number at roulette, win at the lottery, and find gold on the ground!

The enigmatic and rather predictable ending warrants some pondering. Are they going to live happily ever after as man and wife, lovers, or as a kind of father/daughter team? It's not clear, and that's deliberate. Draw your own conclusions, but don't miss this one. It's definitely worth seeing.

I've seen this and I give it____stars.
I want to see it___. I'll pass___.
The review was worth reading___. Not___.

Goodbye Children (*Au revoir les enfants*) (1987) 10

A work of genius

This is a masterpiece of cinema, a work of genius by one of the greatest directors, Louis Malle. He does everything with the barest touch, just the slightest emphasis, without rancor or any loading of the deck. He understates and plays fair always. He has complete control of his story and of the audience. He knows what they believe and what they expect. He respects that, but he doesn't cater, and he is very gentle about leading us to the conclusion. He makes it beautiful although it is horrible.

Gaspard Manesse as Julien and Raphael Fejto as Jean are unforgettable and a reminder that in film it's important to have a good cast. Yet, I suspect Malle could have made geniuses of any number of talented young boys in their parts. This is your Catholic boys school coming of age film without lecherous priests or the brutality of children; that is, no more than is necessary, just what is real and seen in perspective, the context being the Nazi occupation of France in 1944. It is amazing how Malle manages to show the bestiality and brain dead stupidity of the Nazis by presenting them at their most gentle. If one can damn by faint praise, one can destroy by contrast. Compared to what is human and natural we see the Nazis, as their pretentious Reich is falling apart, chasing after children, obsessed with psychotic racist delusions. Through the objective eyes of the children we see the evil. Malle need only let the facts speak for themselves.

I think artists working in any medium would benefit from studying this film. What it says to us is be honest, be fair, keep it simple, but not too simple. Use not a brush stroke more than necessary, and pay attention to every detail, especially the small ones. But while we can learn from and appreciate, it takes genius to pull it off. It can't be done by connecting the dots.

I am struck by a little irony on the jacket of the video. It has an early Siskel and Ebert quote: "One of the year's best films." That's a little embarrassing unless the year is a hundred years long.

Incidentally, the sublime, beautiful and very talented Irène Jacob made her debut here in a small part as a piano teacher.

I've seen this and I give it____stars.
I want to see it___. I'll pass___.
The review was worth reading___. Not___.

A Heart in Winter *(Un Coeur en Hiver)* (1992) 10

A little masterpiece

Un Coeur en Hiver is primarily a work of art and not a commercial film. Only a genius could have written the subtle and very affecting script. In this case there were two geniuses: Jacques Fieschi and Claude Sautet, who also directed. There are no PC gods being cow-towed to here, and no pandering to the mass-mind of the audience. No tantalizing or graphic sex scenes. In fact the lovers, she, a young, gifted violinist played by the beautiful Emmanuelle Béart, and he, a cynical genius of violin repair (!) played by the enigmatic Daniel Auteuil (whose heart is in winter) never even kiss! Yet the powerful emotion felt by both is manifest.

The story line is original and rather striking. Strong performances by the leads and seamless, invisible direction make this a ten-star film and a modern classic.

I Loved You So Long *(Il y a longtemps que je t'aime)* (2008) 10

Beautiful and touching story about the love between sisters

I need to watch a movie like this once in a while. Otherwise I might never cry. And crying is cathartic.

French cinema is about relationships. I wonder how it became so intensely about relationships in a way that no other national cinema is about relationships. I don't know. This one is the about the relationship between sisters done in a way that I have never seen before. And that I like. I am so bored with reprises and remakes of themes, as good as they sometimes are. This is not about sisterhood politically. And thank you for that. It is about real sisterhood under confusing and difficult circumstances, when there is estrangement for very good reasons, yet there is love to overcome whatever it is that causes the distance.

In this case Juliette (Kristin Scott Thomas) has been released after 15 years in prison. Her younger sister Lea (Elsa Zylberstein) who always adored her and looked up to her takes her in. She has her own family, two adopted Vietnamese girls, a husband and a father who is old and can no longer speak. Naturally bringing Juliette into their household is risky. What has Juliette done and why? It is really unspeakable and yet Lea believes like all "bleeding hearts" that her sister is essentially good and whatever happened happened for a reason, and so do we in the audience. Kristin Scott Thomas plays this part of the film with a long, suffering face and the sort of resignation that comes with complete defeat. So we know. Whatever happened to her, whatever she did was forced upon her by the fates. What we don't know is exactly what that was.

I cannot say enough about the exquisite performances by both Kristin Scott Thomas and Elsa Zylberstein. The direction by Philippe Claudel was, in the French manner, focused on people and who they are, done unobtrusively in the best invisible style in which the story and the characters are what we see without directorial distraction. We are lost in the story and the existential conflict between what we are and what is thought of us by others. We are caught between the appearance of life and the reality.

I've seen this and I give it____stars.
I want to see it___. I'll pass___.
The review was worth reading___. Not___.

Indochine (1992) 9

Foreshadows the American failure in Vietnam

There is some difference of opinion about whether this is a good film or not. Some have called it a "soap opera" beautifully filmed. (Both Leonard Maltin in his *Movie and Video Guide* and the good people at Video Hound used that designation.) But I don't think that is correct at all. Beautifully filmed yes, stunning at times like something from David Lean; and in fact this film has more in common with the Hollywood panoramic epic than it does with the tradition of the French cinema. But it is certainly not a soap opera. In a soap opera the important element is a narrow focus on things material, social, and sexual played out in a banal, cliché-ridden and bourgeois manner. In *Indochine* the focus is on political change and why it came about.

The story begins in Vietnam in 1930 and concludes on the eve of the communist revolution in 1954—presaging the tragic American involvement a decade later. Catherine Deneuve plays Eliane Devries, the strong-willed owner of a rubber plantation in Vietnam, then part of the French colonial empire. Having no children of her own (or a husband) she raises the Vietnamese girl Camille (Linh Dan Pham) as her own. She conducts secret affairs and even visits opium dens while maintaining the appearance of respectability. We are shown the decadence of the French living in Vietnam and the exploitive evils of colonialism, hardy the stuff of soap opera. We are made aware of the social unrest stirring amongst the population and even shown what amounts to a slave auction conducted by the colonial powers with the aid of the French military, in particular, the French navy.

Enter Jean-Baptiste (Vincent Perez), a handsome French naval officer who, despite the difference in their ages, initiates an affair with Eliane. She is at first put off, then reluctant, and then madly in love. Perhaps this familiar progression is what some think of as soap opera material; and perhaps it is, although their affair is only a small part of the film, and at any rate, such behavior is entirely consistent with Eliane's character and that of Jean-Baptiste, and is necessary for the plot developments to come.

Deneuve was nominated for Best Actress by the Academy but didn't win (Emma Thompson won for *Howard's End*), but the film itself won as Best Foreign Film. In truth Deneuve's performance is a little uneven. Regardless, this is one of the most important roles in the career of an actress who was as beautiful in 1991 when this film was made as she had been in *The Umbrellas of Cherbourg* (1964) at the beginning of her career. Indeed, I would say even more beautiful. My favorite Deneuve film, by the way, is *Mississippi Mermaid* (1969) with Jean-Paul Belmondo directed by Francois Truffaut.

Also uneven is the direction by Regis Wargnier. The scenes set in Saigon involving the French and the Mandarins at their pleasures amid their wealth as they maintain their privilege are done with strikingly beautiful interiors splashed with the kind of color seen in, for example, the films of Chinese director Zhang Yimou. The scenes amount to indictments of the French and demonstrate why the communists eventually came to power. Note that the privileged are always decked out in the most amazing displays of color while the workers and the peasants are brown and dirty.

The panoramic cinematography of the Vietnamese country is also strikingly beautiful. We are shown the sheer cliffs falling into tranquil waters dotted with junks, the rock outcrops nestled in verdant growth, the angry skies, and the deluge of the monsoon. But the trek of Camille across the land to find her beloved is not realistically done. Her quick incorporation in a peasant family is also not convincing. And the following scene in which she and Jean-Baptiste escape from the slave market defies probability. However what becomes of her and him is brutally realistic and consistent with what we know about those times, although I would like to have seen them being fed when they are rescued and some indication of how they spent their time in that Shangri-la-like hidden valley.

Despite the flaws and inconsistencies, this is a fine cinematic experience, enthralling, disturbing and visually beautiful. See this as a prelude to all other films about Vietnam and the Vietnam War. What will become clear is how foolish was our involvement and how doomed to failure it had to be.

I've seen this and I give it___stars.
I want to see it___. I'll pass___.
The review was worth reading___. Not___.

Intimate Strangers (*Confidences trop intimes*)

(2004) 9
An unusual love story, nicely realized

This is the most nuanced of Patrice Leconte's films that I have seen. Everything is carefully constructed at a measured pace with just enough revelation as we go along, but no more, so that we can follow the plot's development easily. The film is cut as close as a barber's shave and is as neat as a pin.

Anna (Sandrine Bonnaire), who is a bit of a tease, finds herself in what she thinks is a shrink's office. (There's a magazine on the desk whose title is partially obscured so that only the word "analyst" appears to her eyes, thereby confirming her expectations.) Behind the desk however is William Faber (Fabrice Luchini) who is a tax accountant and perhaps the last man in the building who could conceivably help Anna with her marital problem. He is after all something of recluse. He doesn't drive. He usually eats alone in his apartment, which apparently is the same place as his office, watching TV (in one scene it's Humphrey Bogart as Phillip Marlowe with French subtitles). He is only marginally experienced in the ways of human relationships and knows little about psychoanalysis. (The "analyst" magazine on his desk was on economic analysis.)

She flips a zippo cigarette lighter, lights a cigarette like someone new to smoking, and begins to tell a somewhat astonished Faber about the intimate details of her married life, mainly that her husband won't touch her anymore.

I previously saw Bonnaire in *La Cérémonie* (1995), directed by Claude Chabrol, in which she played a mean, hateful housemaid, and she was very good there. Here she is playful, almost childish at times, as she reveals her life to this stranger.

This is the first time I have seen Luchini who is very properly Parisian in his carefully knotted tie (worn even while preparing his solitary meal). His acting style is markedly laid back. He carries an almost continual look of surprise on his face—astonishment almost—with his eyes made big and round and his demeanor controlled and taciturn.

Because Anna is so direct and begins talking about herself almost immediately and because Faber is a most polite man who will not interrupt her, it is several minutes before he has the opportunity to advise her that she really wants the office down the hall where the psychoanalyst Dr. Monnier holds forth. By then he is intrigued with her and smitten, and is slow, very slow, to advise her of her error.

Also because Anna likes to talk about herself like a teenager and because William Faber is a practiced listener, there is a certain simpatico that automatically develops.

One can see where this is heading. She talks, he listens. She performs, so to speak; he appreciates. Faber is the kind of man, as his "ex" points out, who never makes the first move. This is good for Anna because it allows her to become comfortable with him before she has to respond.

The complications begin with the appearance of Anna's husband who first makes an unusual sexual demand of the very proper tax accountant, and then when that is refused, treats Faber to a most upsetting motel scene through a window across the way. Yes, it's a little contrived (as is the movie's premise). But I like the way Leconte didn't let us see the scene and only revealed later what Faber had seen.

Near the end of the film we see Faber for the first time sans necktie, which we can guess signals a change in the man. The film ends in a most artistic way with a shot from above as Anna lies stretched out on a classic analyst's couch in a cute frock with her ankles crossed and Faber... Well, we see the credits roll down the screen and we can imagine what will eventually happen.

My favorite Leconte film is *Ridicule* (1996). I also liked his *La Fille sur la pont* (1999). If you haven't seen his work you are in for a treat. He is witty in a sly way (especially here in *Confidence trop intimes*) and can be strikingly original. Like all good directors, he never loses track of the audience and the needs of the audience. His films are carefully cut so that we always know what is going on, but without any heavy-handedness.

See this for Patrice Leconte, one of France's most talented film makers.

I've seen this and I give it____stars.
I want to see it___. I'll pass___.
The review was worth reading___. Not___.

Jean de Florette (1986) 9

Guy de Maupassant would have loved this

The acting—pick any of the three stars, Yves Montand, Gerard Depardieu, Daniel Auteuil—is superb, and the supporting cast excellent. But what makes this and its sequel, Manon des Sources (1986), jewels of the French cinema is the story and the characterizations, which go hand in hand. There is genius in how naturally and almost inevitably the story unfolds. Although I haven't read the novel by Marcel Pagnol, I'm sure he's the genius. And this is not to slight Claude Berri's direction which is invisible and at the same time in total control, so that the film is simply a work of art.

The characters are true to themselves, and what they do seems natural because of who they are. Jean Florette (Depardieu) fails because he puts too much faith in science, knowledge and the good will and fairness of his fellow man. (He should have listened to his suspicious wife!) Ugolin (Auteuil), whose selfishness and little guy envy lead him to do the harm that he does, is not a despicable character. We do not hate him the way Manon understandably does. He is a man of weakness who gave into greed. Papet (Montand), believes in the lineage of man, in property, money—all the standard burgher values. He is led to do his dirty deeds because of who he is.

What is so, so superior in "Florette" compared to most movies is the lack of propaganda, the lack of adherence to some political or philosophic preconception. What shines forth is people living their lives and falling into some very human traps. I am reminded of Balzac and Guy De Maupassant in the depiction of the petit bourgeois life of the French peasantry and attendant psychology.

I've seen this and I give it____stars.
I want to see it___. I'll pass___.
The review was worth reading___. Not___.

The Lacemaker (La Dentellière) (1977) 9

Huppert is brilliant in this very sad love story

I understand that this is the film that brought Isabelle Huppert, already the accomplished veteran of over 20 films and yet just 22-years-old, to the forefront of the French cinema. It is not hard to see why. She is apple sweet in her red hair and freckles and her pretty face and her cute little figure playing Pomme, a Parisian apprentice hairdresser. She is shy about sex and modest—just an ordinary French girl who hopes one day to be a beautician. Along comes François (Yves Beneyton) a tall, handsome, young intellectual from a petite bourgeois family who sweeps her off her feet.

They set up housekeeping and eventually he gets around to introducing her to his family. Alas, Mom finds the girl "decent," and ...well, it's rather predictable. You should watch. I've seen the story a number of times, and I find it rather painful, especially because in this case Huppert is so incredibly sweet and adorable. It is a naturalistic love story, like something from a nineteenth century novel, sad, compelling, bittersweet and ultimately tragic in an all too familiar way.

Claude Goretta's direction is lean and finely cut, and he does a great job with Huppert. There are moments of pure genius, especially the stunning final shot in which Pomme suddenly turns to the camera, on her face a vaguely hopeful, enigmatic expression. It lingers just long enough so that we realize this really is the end, and the lights are about to come up. The shot is especially effective because we can see the posters from Greece on the walls that reveal that what she just told François was a kind of proud make-believe story. Also very well done without undue emphasis is the scene where Pomme goes to him at the window in their apartment, presenting herself to him, so to speak, her naked little self so vulnerable, and he is not interested. Nothing more need to be said. It is like the turn in a sonnet: everything changes.

Without the beguiling child-like, but deeply experienced and finely expressed performance by Mademoiselle Huppert, this film would still be good, but nothing special. She carries the film: her timing, her intense concentration, her sense of who she is and how she feels at every moment is just perfect. She is exquisite.

For those of you familiar with the work of Isabelle Huppert, this is a film not to be missed.

I've seen this and I give it___stars.
I want to see it___. I'll pass___.
The review was worth reading___. Not___.

Manon of the Spring (*Manon des sources*) (1986)

10
A great film

This is just as good or even better that it predecessor, *Jean de Florette* (1986). It is amazing how well thought out the story is. Like a classic tragedy, everything falls into place, everything is accounted for as fate conspires with character to bring about retribution for those who did wrong. We feel sad and sorry for Papet and Ugolin, whose weaknesses and "crimes" are so like our own.

Daniel Auteuil, who plays Ugolin, is an actor with great range and sensitivity. He is unforgettable here as a not-too-bright peasant who suffers an excruciating and hopeless case of unrequited love. And Yves Montand, who plays his uncle is flawless, like an Olivier, as he experiences a very cruel turn of fate. Emmanuelle Béart, who plays Manon, is very beautiful, but she is also strange enough to be believable in an unlikely role as a solitary shepherdess of the hills of Provence.

Claude Berri's direction is so perfectly paced, so full of attention to detail and so unobtrusive and natural that the film just seems to happen without effort. Nothing fancy, just show what needs to be seen, no more. Use no more words than necessary, but all that are necessary. It's almost like magic, how easy it looks. The scene near the end when the blind woman reveals the cruel turn of fate to Papet is exquisite in its simplicity and its effectiveness.

In a sense this movie is a throwback to an earlier era in cinema when careful attention to the construction of a character-driven story was the essence of the art.

I've seen this and I give it___stars.
I want to see it___. I'll pass___.
The review was worth reading___. Not___.

Murmur of the Heart (*Le Souffle au Coeur*) (1971)

9
One of Louis Malle's best

Unbridled youth is very powerful in this somewhat tongue-in-cheek coming of age romp from the French master. The boys are your Menendez brothers *en petit*. They are arrogant, mean to the servants, sell the family jewels, paintings and carpets, drink to excess, attend whore houses with their stolen money and put up with lecherous priests in the day time. Mom has a lover and is bored with Dad, but she loves her little boy, 14-year-old Laurent, played with a "youth will be served" confidence by Benoit Ferreux, whose coming of age is perhaps a Louis Malle fantasy from his own youth.

There is the usual deft and warm Malle touch as he explores some verboten sexual ground and manages to have it all come out as charmingly sweet as a French musical farce. En route he parodies the post-war decadence of the French during the fifties as he satirizes Albert Camus, the war in Vietnam (pre-US involvement) and the Catholic church. One scene moves to another as though there was a fire to get to. Malle gives us what is necessary and runs into the next scene relying heavily on the camera to carry the story with minimal dialogue.

This film should be seen and contrasted with Malle's homage to a pre-adolescent Brooke Shields in his American film, *Pretty Baby* (1978) where the camera tends to linger. Here he celebrates the randy adolescent charm of Ferreux perhaps to excess. But I'm sure to some, 12-year-old Brooke Shields must have been a yawn.

I've seen this and I give it____stars.
I want to see it___. I'll pass___.
The review was worth reading___. Not___.

The Piano Teacher (*La pianist*) (2001) 10

Featuring a stunning performance by Isabelle Huppert

If it is true that sadomasochism is a two-sided coin which contains the whole in the diverse expression of its opposites, then the cinematic portrait of Erika Kohut has its reality. Professor Kohut treats her piano students with a kind of fascist sadism while longing for the same for herself. Her outward expression projects her desire. That is why she can hurt without guilt or remorse.

Along comes talented, charming, handsome young Walter Klemmer (Benoit Magimel) who is attracted to her because of her passion and her intensity. He wants to become her student so as to be close to her. She rejects him out of hand, but because of his talent the Vienna conservatory votes him in. He falls in love with her. Again she pushes him away, but he will not take no for an answer, and thereby begins his own descent into depravity and loss of self-respect.

The question the viewer might ask at this point is, who is in control? The sadist or the masochist? Indeed who is the sadist and who the masochist? It is hard to tell. Is it the person who has just been greatly abused both psychologically and physically, who is actually lying wounded on the floor in grotesque triumphant and fulfillment, or is it the person who is rushing out the door, sated, giving the order that no one is to know what happened.

But Erika is not just a sadomasochistic freak. She is a sex extreme freak. She wants to experience the extremes of human sexuality while maintaining the facade of respectability. Actually that isn't even true. She says she doesn't care what others think. She doesn't care if they walk in and find her bleeding on the floor because she is in love. Love, she calls it. For her sex and love are one and the same.

At one point Walter tells her that love isn't everything. How ironic such a superfluity is to her. How gratuitous the comment.

The movie is beautifully cut and masterfully directed by Michael Haneke who spins the tale with expert camera work and carefully constructed sets in which the essence of the action is not just clear but exemplified (as in the bathroom when Walter propels himself high above the top of the stall to find Erika within). He also employs a fine positioning of the players so that they are always where they should be with well-timed cuts from one angle to another. This is particularly important in the scene in which Erika, like a blood-drained corpse caught in stark white and black light, lies under her lover, rigid as stone. Here for the most part we only see her face and the stark outline of her neck with its pulsating artery. We don't need to see any more.

The part of Erika Kohut is perfect for Isabelle Huppert who is not afraid of extremes; indeed she excels in them. I have seen her in a number of movies and what she does better than almost anyone is become the character body and soul. Like the woman she plays in this movie she is unafraid of what others may think and cares little about her appearance in a decorative sense. What matters to her is the performance and the challenge. No part is too demanding. No character too depraved. It's as if Huppert wants to experience all of humanity, and wants us to watch her as she does. She is always fascinating and nearly flawless. She is not merely a leading light of the French cinema; she is one of the great actresses of our time who has put together an amazingly diverse body of work.

I think it is highly instructive and affords us a wonderful and striking contrast to compare her performance here with her performance in *The Lacemaker* (*La Dentellière*) from 1977 when she was 22 years old. There she was apple sweet in her red hair and freckles and her pretty face and her cute little figure playing Pomme, a Parisian apprentice hairdresser. Her character was shy about sex and modest—just an ordinary French girl who hoped one day to be a beautician. Here she is a self-destructive witch, bitter with hateful knowledge of herself, shameless and entirely depraved.

Huppert is fortunate in being an actress in France where there are parts like this for women past the age of starlets. In the American cinema, only a handful of the very best and hardest working actresses can hope to have a career after the age of about thirty. Huppert greatly increases her exposure because of her ability and range, but also because she is willing to play unsympathetic roles, here and also in *La Cérémonie* (1995) in which she plays a vile, spiteful murderess.

Do see this for Isabelle Huppert. You won't forget her or the character she brings to life.

I've seen this and I give it____stars.
I want to see it___. I'll pass___.
The review was worth reading___. Not___.

A Prophet (*Un prophète*) (2009) 10

Very superior "French mafia" type film

First the ending: the three cars. From what I understand the three cars represent the three drug gangs that Malik has united: the Arabs, the Egyptians and the Corsicans. Their ominous presence also suggests that Malik will live the life of a drug lord and die the life of a drug lord, which of course is his fate and what he deserves. There is also the echo from Francis Ford Coppola's *The Godfather* (1972) with Michael at the end.

Now to the idea that Malik is "a prophet." I can only guess that he is a prophet in the world of drug lords. There is the possibility that director Jacques Audiard, who has written twenty-some films and directed half a dozen including two very good ones that I've seen, *Read My Lips* (2001) and *The Beat that My Heart Skipped* (2005), meant to disparage (celebrate?) The Prophet by comparing his illiterate and up-by-his bootstraps hero Malik to Allah's Messenger—but I'll pass on that.

The real philosophic question to be answered in this most arresting film is does Malik represent what we might call "Existential Man" in his struggle to prevail in life after being dumped on this planet and told to sink or swim? Certainly to the drug gangs he is heroically triumphant, and to most of the audience as well. Malik represents a new kind of hero, a naturalistic creation who doesn't make judgments about what is good or bad, or question the way the world is run (or the way the prison is run), but makes the best of what life has thrown at him and learns not to be squeamish about what he has to do to prevail. French existential novelist Albert Camus famously said that the only important philosophic question is that of suicide. Malik chooses murder over suicide, but we cannot help but identify with him since his choices were indeed just those.

Malik's character combines underprivileged raw youth with something beyond street smarts with the kind of courage war heroes can only envy. That is how he wows his home boys and others. This is what they respect. But, looking around at all the dead bodies, and especially at Cesar Luciani (Niels Arestrup) the once powerful war lord who bows out of the movie a beaten old man, one can see that Malik will die by today's equivalent of the sword as did the ancients who lived the life of the war lord. Tahar Rahim, who plays Malik, would seem to have a great future as a film star. He does an outstanding job here in a very demanding role.

What I found most arresting about this film is the way the French prison system is depicted. Apparently corruption is rampant with the inmates in significant control of the guards and prison officials. Luciani runs his drug empire from within the prison. Prisoners favored by the drug lord powers that be get special privileges and are allowed to control the other prisoners. I understand that Audiard studied the French prison system before making this film. The film is an indictment of that system, which makes me wonder how they feel about this sensation film in France.

Also interesting is how the various ethnic gangs in French prisons relate to one another. Luciani's Corsicans were mostly in charge as the film begins with Malik just a low-level forced funky. By the end of the film the Muslim gang is mostly in charge it appears. I wonder if this reflects the reality in French prisons.

Finally, this is a brutally realistic film in which humans are seen primarily as animals. Even Malik's love for his teacher's child can be seen as unconsciously acting out a communal role that will result in his having many reproductive tries—indeed how sweet is the mother already on him as they walk together to the bus stop and presumably to her bed. The only law that seems to exist is that of the jungle, that of the stronger, with the laws of the state as kind of fact of nature that must be overcome or subverted, never respected. And the values of the larger society are irrelevant, immaterial, nonexistent and mute. This is a naturalistic film for the twenty-first century.

I've seen this and I give it____stars.
I want to see it___. I'll pass___.
The review was worth reading___. Not___.

Read My Lips *(Sur mes lèvres)* (2001) 9

Smell my shirt

For those of you who have seen this rather extraordinary romantic thriller noir, my review title is self-explanatory: this is *cinema verité* for the 21st century. For those of you who haven't, let me note that this begins slowly, so stay with it. You won't regret it.

What French director Jacques Audiard has done is create a taut noir thriller with a romantic subplot intricately woven into the fabric of the main plot, told in the realistic and non-glamorous manner usually seen in films that win international awards. In fact, *Sur mes lèvre* did indeed win a Cesar (for Emmanuelle Devos) and some other awards. For Audiard character development and delineation are more important than action, yet the action is extremely tense. The romance is of the counter-cultural sort seen in films like, say, *Kalifornia* (1993) or *Natural Born Killer* (1994) or the Aussie *Kiss or Kill* (1997), a genre I call "grunge love on the lam" except that the principles here are not on the road (yet) and still have most of their moral compasses intact.

Vincent Cessel and Emmanuelle Devos play the non-glamorous leads, Paul and Carla. Carla is a mousy corporate secretary—actually she's supposed to be mousy, but in fact is intriguing and charismatic and more than a wee bit sexy. But she is inexperienced with men, doesn't dance, is something of a workaholic who lives out a fantasy life home alone with herself. She is partially deaf and adept at reading lips, a talent that figures prominently in the story. She is a little put on by the world and likes to remove her hearing aid or turn it off. When she collapses from overwork her boss suggests she hire an assistant. She hires Paul, who is just out of prison, even though he has no clerical experience. He is filled with the sort of bad boy sex appeal that may recall Jean-Paul Belmondo in Godard's *Breathless* (1959) or even Richard Gere in the American remake from 1983. We get the sense that Carla doesn't realize that she hired him because she found him attractive. When Carla gets squeezed out of credit for a company deal, she gets Paul to help her turn the tables. From there it is but a step to a larger crime. Note that Carla is unconsciously getting Paul to "prove" his love for her (and his virility) by doing what she wants, working for her, appearing in front of her girlfriends as her beau, etc.

The camera work features tense, off-center close-ups so that we see a lot of the action not in the center of our field of vision but to the periphery as in things partially hidden or overheard or seen out of the corner of our eyes. Audiard wants to avoid any sense of a set or a stage. The camera is not at the center of the action, but is a spy that catches just enough of what is going on for us to follow. Additionally, the film is sharply cut so that many scenes are truncated or even omitted and it is left for us to surmise what has happened. This has the effect of heightening the viewer's involvement, although one has to pay attention. Enhancing the staccato frenzy is a sparse use of dialogue. This works especially well for those who do not speak French since the distraction of having to follow the subtitles is kept to a minimum.

Powering the film is a script that reveals and explores the unconscious psychological mechanisms of the main characters while dramatizing both their growing attraction to each other and their shared criminal enterprise. But more than that is the on-screen chemistry starkly and subtly developed by both Devos and Cessel. It is pleasing to note that the usual thriller plot contrivances are kept to a minimum here, and the surprises really are surprises.

See this for Emmanuelle Devos whose skill and offbeat charisma more than make up for a lack of glamor, and for Vincent Cessel for a testosterone-filled performance so intense one can almost smell the leather jacket.

I've seen this and I give it____stars.
I want to see it___. I'll pass___.
The review was worth reading___. Not___.

Ridicule (1996) 9

At the court of Louis XVI before the guillotine fell

This reminds me a lot of *Dangerous Liaisons* (1988) and *Valmont* (1989) in its cynicism and sharp wit. Set in France during the same time period (the eve of the French Revolution), *Ridicule* concentrates not so much on sexual intrigues (although there is plenty of that) but on cynical wit as though in homage to Voltaire, France's master of satire whose spirit is suffused throughout.

First a warning. Don't let the rather gross crudity of the opening scene mislead you. It is meant merely as satire, not as a presaging of further crudities to come. It is also meant as a kind of cinematic joke since there is no comparable female nudity in the entire film. Indeed, there is

no comparable, shall we say "expression," anywhere in legitimate filmdom that I am aware of. So let it pass or close your eyes.

Charles Berling stars as Gregoire Ponceludon de Malavoy, a country engineer who comes to Versailles to get financial backing to drain a swamp to save the peasants who are dying of mosquito-borne disease. ("Peasants feed aristocrats as well as mosquitos.") He discovers very quickly that a way to an audience with Louis XVI is through gaining a reputation as a clever courtier. Guided by M. Bellegarde (Jean Rochefort), a retired courtier himself, Ponceludon quickly picks up the games of wit and ridicule that reign at court. His quick and clever mind and youthful good looks gain the attention of the king's mistress, Madame de Blayac (Fanny Ardant) who demonstrates how access to the king can come through her bedroom. Ponceludon is sincere only in his desire to drain the swamp and so readily allows himself to become another of Blayac's lovers in exchange for a chance to present his program to Louis XVI.

At the same time he meets Bellegarde's daughter Mathide (Judith Godrèche), an idealistic beauty with a scientific bent, who is betrothed to a dying old man of wealth and position. They fall in love, but their differing agendas keep them apart.

What makes this film such a delight is the delicious way it satirizes the decadent court of Louis XVI. The dramatic irony is superb and absolute in the sense that at no time does director Patrice Leconte give even the slightest hint that any of the byzantine sycophants at court are aware that Danton and the Terror await them. Throw in the impending Industrial (and scientific) Revolution symbolized in the form of Ponceludon and Mathide, and the *ancien régime* with its antiquated feudal titles and corrupt privilege is seen for what it was, a parasitic anachronism, ripe to rot for destruction.

The sets, the direction and especially the acting are excellent. Veteran Rochefort is particularly good in a part that depends on a directive and expressive face amid the whispers at court. Berling is smooth and believable as a man with a noble mission, adroit at repartee, love and dueling, a modest and earnest hero.

Godrèche is good, but seems a little restrained here. She is an impossibly healthy, handsome beauty no man could resist. I first saw her as a 17-year-old in *The Disenchanted* (1990) where her adolescent charm was carefully and craftily displayed by director Benoît Jacquot. Here Leconte concentrates on her strength of character.

Fanny Ardant's Madame de Blayac is a Machiavellian mistress of love's duplicity, very much like the Marquise de Merteuil from *Dangerous Liaisons* and *Valmont*. Her performance compares favorably with that of Glenn Close and Annette Bening, respectively, although there is an earthy quality to Ardant that seems most realistic. Her character is also more vulnerable.

The sets are sumptuous without being artificially showy. The gray, high-topped wigs and the beaked-nosed masks at ball, along with the gilded attire, the caked makeup, etc., somehow suggest the true state of costume and personal hygiene circa 1784, reminding me that in those days people did not generally wear underpants or take showers.

Some bon mots:

"The soul of wit is to know one's place."

When asked by the king to say something witty about the king himself, Ponceludon returns: "The king is not a subject." The king asks if this is not a (lowly) pun, but is assured that it is a "play on words."

When Blayac discerns that Ponceludon is not entirely smitten with her, she responds, "Learn to hide your insincerity so that I may yield without dishonor."

The film closes with a scene in England on a cliff overlooking the English channel. Bellegarde and another reflect on the changes after the revolution: "Wit was the very air we breathed." "Now the bloated rhetoric of Danton rules in place of wit." Bellegarde's hat is blown off by the wind. His companion remarks: "Better your hat than your head."

By the way, the subtitles (and this is usually not the case) are excellent, inventive and faithful enough, while comfortably brief, to have been done by a professional translator instead of by someone handy who is passably bilingual.

I've seen this and I give it____stars.
I want to see it___. I'll pass___.
The review was worth reading___. Not___.

Stolen Kisses (*Baisers volés*) (1968) 9

Charming romantic comedy that really is funny

This is a delightful Truffaut movie starring Jean-Pierre Leaud who played Antoine Doinel, the running boy in Truffaut's famous *Les Quatre cents coup* (1959). He's a young man now just discharged from the army bouncing from one temporary job to another, from being a night watchman to being a TV repairman. He gets into scrapes and gets fired, but presses on (in-between impulsive liaisons with ladies of the evening).

He gets his big chance when he lucks into a job with a private detective agency. After some mishaps he is called upon to take a job (within a job, as it were) at a shoe store to find out why the owner is not liked. There he meets the owner's wife, Fabienne Tabard, played by Del-

phine Seyrig (*Last Year at Marienbad* 1961; *The Discreet Charm of the Bourgeoisie* 1972, etc.). He is immediately smitten by her. In typical French cinematic fashion it is not clear whether she is a goddess or a maternal figure for the thoroughly bewitched Antoine.

Meanwhile there is Christine Darbon (Claude Jade) who plays Antoine's real love interest. What makes this film so thoroughly agreeable is Truffaut's light-hearted wit and his studious avoidance of cliché in a genre (the romantic comedy) in which clichés abound. The humor is often tongue-in-cheek, and as subtle as a diplomat's compliment. Leaud's charm and his oh so earnest style make him the perfect foil for life's little jokes. Along the way detective agencies are satirized as are its clientele, including a guy who wants his magician boyfriend tailed only to find that he is (horrors!) married, or the aforementioned shoe haberdasher who hires a private eye (not a shrink!) to find out why he is not beloved.

Bottom line: see this for Francois Truffaut, whose keen sense of humanity's foibles and unique style, sometimes playful and sometimes penetrating, have made him one of cinema's greatest directors.

I've seen this and I give it___stars.
I want to see it___. I'll pass___.
The review was worth reading___. Not___.

That Obscure Object of Desire (*Cet obscur objet du désir*) (1977) 9

No fool like an old fool

Carole Bouquet is the thinner Conchita who is somewhat severe. Angela Molina is the one who dances and seems more natural.

Jean-Claude Carriere wrote the script. He may be the greatest screenwriter of all time. He has over a hundred credits and some of them are among the best movies ever made. Here's a brief list from those that I have seen: *The Ogre* (1996), *Valmont* (1989), *The Unbearable Lightness of Being* (1988), *The Discreet Charm of the Bourgeoisie* (1972), *Diary of a Chambermaid* (1964).

There's some symbolism in *Cet obscur objet du desir*. Sometimes Mathieu (Fernando Rey) carries around an old gunny sack. We find out what's in it in the final scene. It represents Conchita's virginity. The terrorists in the background seem rather contemporary although this movie is from 1977. Mathieu is rich and therefore represents the established European society. Conchita and her friends represent the underclass. Both Mathieu and Conchita are really character types. He is the masher, the rake who is always working on a new conquest, although he is somewhat naive. She is the tease who uses her wiles to get what she can from him. Buñuel plays this ancient theme as a burlesque, exaggerating her coyness and his foolishness. The ending may suggest that in some way he has won, or more likely that they are still at a standoff, even while the terrorists escalate the bombings.

The question of why there are two actresses playing Conchita has more to do with Maria Schneider, who originally was cast in the role, but left because of the nudity or because Conchita's character was too contrary, than it has to do with any plot or symbolic necessity. On the other hand, since she is that "obscure object of desire" (which really should be that "unobtainable object of desire"), and because Buñuel wanted to emphasize that Mathieu's desire for her had nothing to do with her personally, he used two actresses and made it clear that Mathieu didn't notice the difference! A bit of absurdity here, but Buñuel is comfortable with absurdity.

All in all this is an interesting treatment of an ancient theme, but not one of Buñuel's best, even though it was his last at age 77.

I've seen this and I give it____stars.
I want to see it___. I'll pass___.
The review was worth reading___. Not___.

Toto the Hero (*Toto le héros*) (1991) 9

A kind of naturalistic delight.

Thomas is a bitter old man who feels he has been cheated out of the life that was rightly his because he and another boy were switched at birth during a fire at the hospital. Alfred, the other boy, lives a life of privilege and becomes rich. Thomas is jealous. But in another sense Thomas needs to believe that he was switched because he falls in love with his sister Alice. If he really was switched, they are not related.

This is just one of the ironic witticisms spun out by Jaco van Dormael, who wrote and directed this striking and totally original bit of life triumphant. Veteran French actor Michel Bouquet plays Thomas as an old man, sneaking cigarettes in the old folks home, reliving his memories, plotting his revenge. Jo De Backer plays Thomas as a slightly nerdish young man, consumed by the loss of his beloved sister in a fire when she was about eleven or twelve. One day by accident he spots a woman who reminds him of his sister. He follows her, they fall in love, and it turns out she is married to Alfred! Thomas Godet plays the little boy Thomas with charm and a touching vulnerability. He is picked on and bullied by Alfred and his friends who taunt him with, "van Chickensoup!" (I wonder if the French Academie approves of this vulgar Anglais.) Sandrine Blancke plays Thomas's cute and impish older sister. Mireille Perrier plays Evelyne, who is the woman who reminds Thomas of his sister.

In a sense this is a romantic comedy, but be warned that in the French cinema a hint of incest is seldom looked on as shocking, rather as something almost akin to nostalgia. And certainly every woman should have a lover and every man a mistress. In another sense this is an art film that plays with time, using both flashbacks and flash forwards to present a story filled with spooky coincidences, punctuated with fantasy and a kind of naturalistic glorification of life epitomized in the catchy tune, "Boom!" that weaves its way in and out of the story, a tune you might have trouble getting out of your head, so be forewarned. ("Boom! When your heart goes boom! It's love, love, love!" written and performed by Charles Trenet.) There is also as aspect of sentimentality, especially in the resolution, that provides a sweet contrast with the naturalistic pathos. When the words that Alice spoke as a child are reprised by Evelyne (although she could not have known what Alice had said) we are delighted, and Thomas is a little rattled. ("Do you like my hands?" she asks, holding them up. "Which hand do you prefer?")

The bitter old man learns that he really had the better of it all along (and so he does somewhat the opposite of what he had intended) and indeed we in the audience realize that how we might feel about life, looking back on it, might really just depend on how we choose to feel about it. Dormael's message seems to be that love makes life worth living. We are left with the sense that there is a time for love, and that time passes, and we have to accept that and celebrate the memory.

Best scene: Ten-year-old Thomas sees his perhaps 11-year-old sister rising out of the bath tub. (We see only his widening eyes; this is a discreet movie.) He says, "I...didn't know you had breasts." She replies (deadpanning the pride of a pre-adolescence girl), "I thought you'd read about them in the newspapers."

I've seen this and I give it____stars.
I want to see it___. I'll pass___.
The review was worth reading___. Not___.

The Umbrellas of Cherbourg (*Les parapluies de Cherbourg*) (1963) 10

"I will wait for you."

Maybe not.

Les Parapluies de Cherbourg is one of the most beautiful movies ever made with an enchanting and haunting score by Michel Le Grande, and totally focused, sharp and creative direction by Jacques Demy. Catherine Deneuve gives a fine performance in pinkish white makeup with her blonde hair pulled away from her famous face, at twenty playing a seventeen-year-old shopkeeper's daughter who falls in love with a garage mechanic. He is called away to the war in Algeria after making her pregnant. Will she wait for him as the award-winning song proclaims? Will their love endure the long separation?

All the dialogue is sung. The script is terse with nothing extraneous to the bittersweet story. Because the dialogue is stripped to the barest essentials, the singing seems natural and enhances the dream-like quality established early with the rain falling on the umbrellas and the cobblestone streets of the seacoast town. The sets are splashed in vivid color. Everything is superficially romantic, but the events are the starkest realism.

When a young girl is forced to choose between love and security, which does she choose? It depends on the circumstances, and sometimes circumstances and the passage of time can change her heart.

I was a teenager in France when this was made in the sixties. The backdrops of the white Esso gas station, the red and yellow passenger train cars, the bouffant hair styles on the girls, their eyes heavily made up with mascara and black eyeliner, the ubiquitous bicycles and the little French "cigarette roller" cars all brought back vivid memories of youth as did the musical score.

A question: what ever happened to the "other" girl, Ellen Farner who played Madeleine? To be honest I found her more attractive than Deneuve who of course went on to become a great star and an acclaimed international beauty.

Some scenes made more effective by their simplicity: When Geneviève (Deneuve) returns home after a late evening with Guy, her mother (Anne Vernon) surveys her daughter and exclaims, "What have you done?" Geneviève retorts sharply, "Mama!" and it is clear what she has done. Also, as Guy is going off to the army Madeleine arrives upon the scene as he is saying good-bye to his stepmother who is ill. They exchange glances that reveal Madeleine's love for him. And then she sings out softly in the heartfelt regret of parting, "Adieu, Guy." We know these are not the last words that will pass between them. Additionally, the brief, beautifully structured, final scene at the shiny new Esso gas station is not to be forgotten.

The scenes with Roland Cassard (Marc Michel), the suave, traveling man of means who sells Madame Emery's jewelry so she can pay the taxes on her umbrella shop, are nicely staged so that we can see at a glance that he is enormously taken with Geneviève and that the mother will do everything possible to further his case. It is agreeable for those identifying with Geneviève that Roland is not only well off financially, but is as handsome as the garage mechanic. But will he still want her when he learns that she is pregnant with another man's child?

Jacques Demy who also wrote the script is to be commended for the effortless pace and tight focus of this romantic tale of star crossed lovers. I wish every director had such an ability to cut the extraneous and concentrate on the essentials without intrusion. The tale is an atmospheric tour de force of love lost and gained, of bourgeois values triumphant.

This might be a bit precious for some, but upon seeing this for the third time, I can tell you I was enchanted anew.

I've seen this and I give it____stars.
I want to see it___. I'll pass___.
The review was worth reading___. Not___.

The Wages of Fear (La Salaire de la peur) (1953) 10
Macho naturalism extraordinaire

This is an extraordinary movie. From the opening scene showing the squalor of a Latin American town with filth and vultures in the street and naked children begging for food amid the oppressive, fly-stirred heat, to the finale on a winding mountain road, it is just plain fascinating. True, some of the action does not bear close scrutiny. One does not siphon nitroclycerine nor does one avoid potholes or bumps in the road by driving at forty miles per hour. No matter. Let's allow a little license. And the title doesn't entirely make sense because the wages of sin are death, but the wages of those who followed their fear and did not seek to drive a nitroclycerine truck over 300 miles of bad road are life. Again, no matter. This is such an original movie, every scene like little or nothing you've ever seen before (and for sure will never see again), that the little inconsistencies and some stretching of what is possible are not important. This is man against nature, man against himself reduced to a simple task. It is life in the raw. One mistake and you are dead.

Yves Montand has the lead as Mario, a Frenchman stranded in this god-forsaken town with only one way out: get enough money to pay for airfare. Charles Vanel is the older, tin-horn dandy who ends up with a case of the shakes. Peter Van Eyck is the man with the nerves of steel who finds this little adventure a piece of cake after forced labor in the salt mines for the Nazis. And Folco Lulli is Luigi, the happy, singing baker who hopes to return to Italy with the two thousand dollars they are paying him to drive the nitro-loaded truck.

This is a film depicting the primitive nature of a macho mentality. There's a lot of posturing. Every event is a potential test of manhood. Status and privilege are flouted. The weak and the poor do not inherit the earth.

Henri-Georges Clouzot directs and somehow manages to come up with a work of genius. One wonders how. The story, on the face of it, would seem to belong in the slush pile of a ten-cent pulp fiction mag from the 1930's. The acting is good, very good in places, but not great. The cinematography is straightforward, but nonetheless very effective. It is lean and focused always, showing us what needs to be seen without drawing attention to itself: the invisible style, which is the best. Clouzot's direction is characterized by a vivid depiction of things that we can feel: the mud and filth in the streets, the desperation and the boredom, the cruelty and meanness of men, the oil on their bodies, the singular fact of a ton of nitro in the back seat so that every move is a neuron-exposing adventure. I think that the visceral experience from beginning to end and the fine pacing are the essence of what makes this a great film.

Clouzot's wife, Vera Clouzot, plays Linda who first appears scrubbing the floor in an open-air bistro. She is rather extraordinary herself, finely made up and creamy white like a star of the silent film era. She grovels a lot, especially for Mario. She provides the counter-point, the contrast for the testosterone action of the movie.

No student of film should miss this. It would be like missing *Citizen Kane* or *Dr. Strangelove* or especially *The Treasure of the Sierra Madre*, which it vaguely and strangely resembles. *La salaire de la peur* is, regardless of its flaws, one of the best ever made.

I've seen this and I give it____stars.
I want to see it___. I'll pass___.
The review was worth reading___. Not___.

The Widow of Saint-Pierre (*La veuve de Saint-Pierre*) (2000) 10
A moral tale

In this French language film (with English subtitles), Juliette Binoche plays what some today might call a "bleeding heart liberal," maybe even a head-strong bleeding heart liberal. Her name is Pauline and her husband Jean (Daniel Auteuil) is the Captain of a troop of soldiers on the island of St. Pierre off the coast of Newfoundland. The year is 1849.

One night two of the local peasants get drunk and have an argument about whether a certain man of the island is fat or just big. As a joke they go to his cottage and rouse him from his dinner table with calls of "fat!" and "big" until comes out to investigate with a knife in his hands for protection. In the ensuing confrontation one of the men holds the big guy from behind while the other (Ariel Neel Auguste, played by Emir Kusturica) knocks the knife from his hand, picks it up, and in a kind of madness cuts the man open to see—as they later testify at the trial—whether he is really fat or just big.

As it happens, Neel is condemned to death, but can't be executed because the law requires that he be beheaded and there is no guillotine on the island, nor is there an executioner. Since he can hardly run away from this snowy island, Pauline wants him out of his cell and at work helping her around the house, maybe as a gardener. Jean, who loves Pauline extravagantly, agrees and Neel becomes Pauline's protégé. She wants to reform

him and teach him to read, etc. The tension in the film builds as her good intensions run afoul of the island's governing authorities. Through it all Jean stands steadfast by his wife in a most heroic way.

I won't say any more about the plot. What interests me more is the motivation of Pauline in helping Neel. Is she motivated by generosity of heart or by her desire to be a person doing good? This is an ancient question. Do we do good because that is our nature or because we are fulfilling a desire to be good? Furthermore, is Pauline's heart filled with human love for Neel or does she in fact have a yen for him?

Director Patrice Leconte gives us plenty of reason to be skeptical. When Pauline is sitting practically on Neel's lap while teaching him to read, the camera closes in on their fingers as they trace the lines in the text. The fingers get closer and closer together until they touch and even mingle a bit.

Cut immediately to a scene through a bedroom door: two naked figures in vigorous sexual union. At first we can't see who they are, and it is hard not to imagine that it is Pauline and Neel in adulterous embrace. However, it is Pauline and her husband, Jean.

In another scene the bored women of the island are seen talking about how close Pauline and Neel have gotten and how this must inspire Jean to be a better lover; but in fact we can see that what the presence of Neel is doing is lighting a fire under Pauline.

Captain Jean is an entirely admirable character who loves his wife. Neel is also admirable in that he loves Pauline but doesn't make any moves on her. He becomes something of a hero when he saves the building of a café on wheels being moved from crashing. She is of course the most talked-about person on the island, the source of most of the gossip. As we watch the film unfold there is a sense of doom coming. We know something terrible is going to happen; we just don't know what or to whom.

In the final analysis I guess we can say that Pauline—who, in the framing device, narrates the events from memory—got not what she deserved—for no one deserves what happened to her; nor can we attribute what happens to some kind of fatalism. Instead the tragedy can be seen as the direct result of her compromised behavior. Or perhaps we can make a more generous interpretation and say that no good deed ever goes unpunished.

This film can also be seen as a tract against capital punishment since Neel is basically a good man who made a bad mistake. He is clearly a worthwhile member of the community. He is also repentant even to the point of believing that he must pay for his sin in accordance with the law.

See this for director Patrice Laconte who has a nice touch with historical period pieces and directs with the kind of attention to detail and story that rank him among the very best auteurs of the French cinema. I also highly recommend his *Ridicule* (1996) and *La fille sur la pont* (1999).

I've seen this and I give it____stars.
I want to see it___. I'll pass___.
The review was worth reading___. Not___.

II

Slightly Tarnished Jewels of the French Cinema

It may be nothing more than a matter of opinion separating the following French language films from the jewels in the first section of this chapter, but I think overall they're not quite as good. You might want to disagree in the space provided after each review.

Bad Girls (*Les Biches*) (1968) 7

Beautiful period piece

Les Biches is from the early middle period of Claude Chabrol's long career in film making. It is interesting but somewhat inexplicable. It features longtime French leading man Jean-Louis Trintignant as Paul Thomas, an architect who comes between wealthy playgirl Frederique (Stephane Audran) and her latest plaything, street artist "Why" (Jacqueline Sassard) with disastrous consequences.

Audran, who was Chabrol's wife at the time, sports spit curls down the side of her ears like sideburns which is apropos since her character is bisexual. She is a woman with a steely imperial manner who enjoys conquests above all. First she picks up Why, beds her, and then when Paul arrives on the scene showing an interest in Why, she seduces Paul and dumps Why.

The question is why? In the central scene (as far as the plot goes) the three get drunk with seemingly obvious intent only to have Frederique nix the *menage a trois* and shut the bedroom door on Why. Why, who has been desperately trying to look like Frederique, sits outside the bedroom door and listens to the drunken lovers inside and sucks on her fingers.

Obviously Paul would have gone along with this juicy arrangement, and certainly Why wanted it desperately. But Frederique is malicious and all conquering. Paul, who is anything but a heroic character does not insist on Why's joining them in bed not because he is madly, exclusively in love with Frederique but more likely because Frederique is the better catch because of her wealth. He is a cautious, opportunistic man.

The dialogue is sharp and witty but reserved and terse. One striking feature is the way the eyes of the women are so heavily made up. Clearly this signals a film made in the sixties. The scene in which Frederique hosts a poker game certainly anticipated the popularity of the game today. Interesting are the sycophantic gay guys that Frederique keeps around her chateau in St. Tropez for amusement.

The finish of the film is a bit of a surprise and really not that well foreshadowed. Also the title, Les Biches (translated as "Bad Girls" in English) is a bit of mystery. More appropriate might be "L'imperatrice petite" with the focus where it should be on the character of Frederique.

I've seen this and I give it____stars.
I want to see it___. I'll pass___.
The review was worth reading___. Not___.

Belle de Jour (1967) 7

See it with Gloria Steinem

This psychodrama seems a little dated viewed today, and would be an ordinary film except for the fact that it stars the legendary French beauty Catherine Deneuve and is directed by the incomparable Spaniard Luis Buñuel, although this is not his best work. The quasi-Freudian exploration of the character of a woman who can only be sexually aroused and satisfied by being treated as trash doesn't exactly play in today's world, nor would it appear on Ms. Magazine's most admired list.

Deneuve demands the screen and is fascinating to watch, and Buñuel's direction, while not flashy or completely intelligible, is intriguing and focused. Buñuel has done some great work including two I recall, *The Discreet Charm of the Bourgeoisie* (1972) and *That Obscure Object of Desire* (1977). His early work goes back to the silent film era. My favorite Deneuve film is *Mississippi Mermaid* (1969) followed closely by *The Umbrellas of Cherbourg* (1964).

Deneuve is your high class, slightly cool beauty, somewhat in the manner of Grace Kelly. She looks like butter wouldn't melt in her mouth and so directors have always tried to sully her up. Buñuel smears her both literally and figuratively here as a day-tripping prostitute addicted to debasement. I don't buy the psychology, but this sort of thing used to play well. I recall an Italian movie from the same period in which the hero couldn't perform with his sweet and beautiful wife, but had to go slumming to get it on. I think it was called "Bell Antonio" or something like that.

I've seen this and I give it____stars.
I want to see it___. I'll pass___.
The review was worth reading___. Not___.

Caché (Hidden) (2005) 8

A kind of mystery thriller artfully shot

To what extent are you responsible for something you did when you were six years old?

This is the central question of this strange thriller from French shock meister Michael Haneke. Another question is, How crazy do you have to be to seek revenge for something done to you by a child when you were a child?

Haneke, like the playwrights of an earlier generation, begins the movie by boring his captive audience (although with DVDs we aren't so captive) so as to make the excitement to come seem by contrast even more exciting. Hunger is the best cook, one might say. He even goes so far as to show us the back of Juliette Binoche's head for a few minutes before we see her face. I'm not enamored of such "techniques," but what I really don't like about Haneke is the excessive blood-spilling he is so fond of. Here he is actually (for him) in remarkable control.

This movie is about guilt, the guilt the privileged feel toward those who haven't had the same opportunities and the same advantages that they have had. It is about the French national guilt over the Algerian war that still lingers and is being rehashed because of recent events. Daniel Auteuil, he of the kind face and most noticeable proboscis, plays with his usual skill Georges Laurent, an intellectual who hosts a book-chat show on TV. Binoche is his wife, Anne. They begin to get videos, long boring shots of their residence, wrapped in child-like drawings in charcoal and red. Eventually in one of the videos Georges's childhood home is pictured leading him to believe he has figured out who is watching them threateningly and why. But he won't tell Anne because he says he isn't sure. There is a nice scene in which she demonstrates that not being sure is not a good enough reason since this is happening to her too! But the real reason he

will not tell her his suspicions is because he doesn't want to reveal something bad that he had done as a child.

Another nice scene is when he visits his mother, played with great subtlety by Annie Girardot, who reads him like a book and only frowns when she sees that he is lying to her.

Most of the movie is characterized by excellent work by the actors and realistic dialogue in a contemporary French milieu, emphasizing the contrast between today's French haves and have nots, between the elegant suburban home of the Laurent's and the simple apartment of the Algerian Majid (Maurice Benichou) from Georges's youth.

The movie begins very slowly, but stay with it. Once it gets rolling it is very good. One other thing: the question about their very pretty 12-year-old son Pierrot Laurent (Lester Makedonsky) and his seeming disdain for his parents will not make sense until the final framing scene in which we watch the credits roll down the screen in front of a set shot of Pierrot's school letting out. Watch that scene carefully and you will find the answer to who made the videotapes and how.

I've seen this and I give it____stars.
I want to see it___. I'll pass___.
The review was worth reading___. Not___.

Chloe in the Afternoon (*L'amour l'apres-midi*)

(1972) 8
Intriguing story about love and monogamy

Veteran French actor Bernard Verley stars as Frederic who is the kind of man who loves women with a great passion, but finds that he can direct all that love physically into one woman. Chloe is a woman, cynical about men, confident of her power of seduction, a woman who never wants to marry. They were friends and now they meet again. He is married, a successful businessman. She is single, living from day to day. What will happen? Will she entice him away from his wife? Will he find the French happiness with a wife and a mistress?

The title, while good, is misleading, as is the sexy cover on this video. (The French title, *L'amour l'apres-midi*, is better; but that title in English was taken by *Love in the Afternoon* (1957) starring Gary Cooper and Audrey Hepburn.) This is about as sexy as a Disney movie (although there is some backside nudity), yet it is an intriguing story about love, human sexuality and the question of monogamy. I can already see some of the other reviews: "Too talky." "Endless talk and no action." Ah, but they are wrong. This is a fascinating film in which the action is subtle and true and very interesting.

Francoise Verley plays Frederic's wife. She is not nearly as pretty as he thinks she is. Nor is she as removed from his life away from her as he naively believes. Eric Rohmer's subtle direction makes it clear that she knows more than she will ever tell him, that she loves him and perhaps prays that he still loves her. But she is above saying a single word. One gets the sense that she knows he is a man so attractive to other women that it is inevitable that he will stray. But does he? The final scene in which we know why she is crying—although ironically, he does not—is just beautifully done and ends the movie at exactly the right moment.

Zouzou plays Chloe who is Parisian, bohemian and quietly desperate. As usual with Rohmer there is a kind of realism in the movie that defies description. The people and the scenes and the events are real; there is no straining for effect, and everything is understated with a characteristic Rohmerian message about human nature.

This starts slow and never really speeds up, but do yourself a favor and stay with it. The denouement is beautifully turned and the revelation of the three principal characters is as clear and clean and agreeable as Chloe after her shower.

I've seen this and I give it____stars.
I want to see it___. I'll pass___.
The review was worth reading___. Not___.

La Femme Nikita (1990) 8

Accept no substitutes

This, the French *La Femme Nikita*, directed by Luc Besson, is one of the strangest, most bizarre, yet psychologically truest movies ever made. The story on the surface is absurd and something you'd expect from a grade "B" international intrigue thriller. Anne Parillaud plays Nikita, a bitter, drug-dependent, unsocialized child of the streets who is faster than a kung fu fighter and packs more punch than a Mike Tyson bite. She's killed some people and is given a choice between death and becoming an assassin for the French government.

This premise should lead to the usual action/adventure yarn, with lots of fists flying, guns going off, people jumping off of buildings, roaring through the streets in souped up vehicles, spraying bullets, etc., as blood flows and bones shatter. And something like that does happen. However there is a second level in which Nitika becomes the embodiment of something beyond an action adventure heroine. She is coerced and managed by society. Her individuality is beaten out of her so that she can be molded into what the society demands. She comes out of her "training" with her individuality compromised, her free and natural spirit cowed, but undefeated and alive, and she sets out to do what she has been taught to do. And then she falls in love. And she notices, somewhere along the way, amid the murder and the mayhem,

that there is something better than and more important than, and closer to her soul in this world than killing and being killed. She finds that she prefers love to hate, tenderness to brutality. She sees herself and who she is for the first time, but it is too late. She cannot escape. Or can she?

Parillaud brings a wild animal persona tinged with beauty and unself-conscious grace to the role of Nikita. Marc Duret plays Rico, the tender man she loves, and Tchéky Karyo is her mentor, Bob, whom she also loves. Jeanne Moreau, the legend, has a small part as Amande, who teaches Nikita lipstick application and how to be attractive.

Now compare this to the US remake called *Point of No Return* (1993), starring Bridget Fonda. (Please, do not even consider the vapid TV Nikita.) What's the difference? Well, Fonda's flashier, I suppose, but nowhere is there anything like the psychological depth and raw animal magnetism found in the original. The Fonda vehicle is simply a one-dimensional action flick stylishly done in a predictable manner. Besson's Nikita is a work of art that explores the human predicament and even suggests something close to salvation.

As always with a French film, get the subtitled version. The dubbing is always atrocious, and anyway there's really not that much dialogue.

I've seen this and I give it____stars.
I want to see it___. I'll pass___.
The review was worth reading___. Not___.

The Flower of Evil (La Fleur du mal) (2003) 8

Actually the flower is not so evil

This is a pleasant film by Claude Chabrol, nothing like the forbidding title "La Fleur du Mal" would suggest. I say pleasant in that there is nothing gross or ugly about it or really shocking, and it ends in a way that most viewers would find agreeable. There is some dark suggestion of family evil and a kind of playful non-incest and some skeletons in the closet from the Nazi occupation and one dead man at the end, but otherwise this is almost a comedy.

It is not, however, in my opinion his best work, but is very representative. My favorite Chabrol film is *Une affaire de femmes* (1988) starring Isabelle Huppert and Francois Cluzet. I also liked *La Cérémonie* (1995) featuring Sandrine Bonnaire, Isabelle Huppert and Jacqueline Bisset. Both of these are much darker works than *The Flower of Evil*.

As in many Chabrol films this starts slowly but manages to be interesting thanks to some veracious color and characterization blended with a hint of the tension to come. And then, also characteristic of Chabrol, there is an interesting finish.

Nathalie Baye plays Anne Charpin-Vasseur, who in her fifties decides to run for mayor. Her philandering husband Gérard (Bernard Le Coq) is not pleased. Benoit Magimel plays the prodigal son Francois Vasseur, just home after four years in the US, while Melanie Doutey plays his non-biological sister Michele. Francois apparently ran away to the States to cool his growing attraction to Michele (to her disappointment). Now on his return their love blooms.

This is very much approved of by Aunt Line (played wonderfully well with spry energy by Suzanne Flon who was 85 years old when the film was made). Their affair reminds her of her youth, a mixed blessing since she lived through some horrors.

The main plot concerns the opposition that Anne is getting as she runs for mayor. A leaflet accusing the family of collaboration with the Nazis during WWII is distributed that threatens to derail her campaign.

See this for one of France's great ladies of both film and the theater, Suzanne Flon, who died last year after a career that spanned five decades.

I've seen this and I give it___stars.
I want to see it___. I'll pass___.
The review was worth reading___. Not___.

Hell (*L'Enfer*) (1994) 6

Obsessive jealousy

Although Emmanuelle Béart (*Manon des sources* (1986), *Un coeur en hiver* (1992) etc.) is particularly beautiful in this Claude Chabrol film and entirely compelling in the role of a free-spirited wife suspected of adultery, and even though her co-star Francois Cluzet (*Une affaire de femmes* (1988)) does a fine job as a man obsessed with jealousy, this turns out to be an almost boring movie.

I think the problem is in the ambiguity about Nelly's infidelity that director and scriptwriter Chabrol relied on. Ambiguity by itself does not create tension. Artistic tension comes from an interplay within the mind of the viewer between an anticipated or expected result and its actual delineation. Thus in comedy we know that they will live happily ever after, and in tragedy, the fatal flaw will lead to something horrible. We can even know the end of the story, as in Shakespeare's *Romeo and Juliet* or in the Swedish film, *Elvira Madigan* (1967), or indeed in any number of war films, and still eagerly anticipate how it happens. In fact, I think it is always the case that we anticipate the end of a story at least in a general way: good will triumph over evil, the evil person will get his or her comeuppance, the British army will win the war, etc. In modern cinema this may not seem always true since

the bad guys sometimes triumph, as in *noire* movies. Nonetheless I think the ending of such movies is really what we expect, the revelation of the essential unfairness of the world. It becomes then only a question of just how this unfairness manifests itself. As in classic drama, the modern *comédie noire* may be seen as a tragedy, with society or the meek or the slow or the trusting being devoured by the wild animals of the city.

Regardless, here I think it might have been better to clearly reveal Nelly's infidelity or lack of it, early on, and then focus on its discovery or the revelation of a delusion. Obsessive jealousy is a theme that should work, but may be harder to put on film than Chabrol realized. I think too that the character of the irrationally jealous man be made manifest in some collateral way; perhaps we should see his insecurity beforehand somehow; perhaps he should have some obvious shortcoming of appearance or character or there should be something from his past that leads him to irrational jealousy. Clearly an older man with a young and beautiful wife may be jealous in anticipation of the inevitable; or any man with a flirtatious wife. This is not necessarily irrational.

Béart's Nelly reminds me of Brigitte Bardot from the days of her youth as in *And God Created Woman* (1957), a naturally warm and sensuous being, full of affection for others, very beautiful and impossibly sexy. The way Nelly walks and swings herself owes something to Bardot. The psychology of the Roger Vadim film from the fifties advanced the controversial argument that a woman like that needs a firm hand. Here the suggestion is that the husband's jealousy can only lead to pain and disaster, and that the only hope is complete trust.

What I am trying to say is that the psychology, like the tension of the film, seemed at loose ends. It is clear before we are halfway through that Nelly really loves her husband, the real question being, is he enough for her? I also think that Nelly's character should have included something negative in it (she seems a little too good to be true), something the viewer could relate to, perhaps a past infidelity or betrayal.

Charbol is a better director than this film might indicate. See the aforementioned *Une affaire de femmes* (1988) starring Isabelle Huppert as an example of what he can do.

I've seen this and I give it___stars.
I want to see it___. I'll pass___.
The review was worth reading___. Not___.

The Housekeeper (*Une femme de ménage*) (2002) 8

Only the French can make movies like this

I almost gave up on this one forty minutes in. Don't *you* do that. The ending is superb.

Premise: working class girl gets dumped by her boyfriend and seeks work by housekeeping.

Well, that can lead to something better if you keep house for the right person.

Jacques (Jean-Pierre Bacri) who recently got walked out on by his wife, and who, not so incidentally looks sixty—well, fifty-five—(actually he was barely fifty when this was made, but you get the point) gets his ad for a housekeeper answered by Laura (Emilie Dequenne) who is twentysomething—a young twentysomething.

I guess there is not much else to say, and to be honest I decided I would force myself to watch the inevitable. But the director is Claude Berri who directed two of the best movies I ever saw: *Manon of the Spring* (1986) and *Jean De Florette* (1986).

And so I stayed with it. At about the fifty minute mark the movie started to get interesting. I could feel that old guy/young girl love affair was going to take an unexpected fork in the road. (As Yogi said, if you come to a fork in the road, take it. The players have no choice.) Obviously, old guy/young girl can end only one way: young girl leaves old guy for young guy. This is biology. It will be painful.

Claude Berri knows all this, and probably a lot better than I do. And so guess what?

Well, I won't tell. But you will find that the last thirty-some minutes of this sexy romantic comedy delightful, and especially the very, very clever and most satisfying ending.

Just prior to that Laura asks Jacques for his blessing. He won't give it, but she is right: he should. And then when we get the final "life is so...lifelike" grimace on Jacques's face, we can only smile.

Emilie Dequenne is delightful as the strangely wise and very natural Laura, and Jean-Pierre Bacri is winning as the old guy who knows better, but on reflection should thank his lucky stars.

I've seen this and I give it____stars.
I want to see it___. I'll pass___.
The review was worth reading___. Not___.

Human Resources (*Ressources humaines*) (1999) 6

Management vs. Labor

I thought this was played in a rather too pedestrian manner until near the end when the unspoken conflict between the father and the son exploded. In a sense this is a story more or less a century behind its time. We have the factory and the bosses, and we have the workers whose labor is exploited by those who own and control the capital. We have the union organizers who are little different from those who long ago sought a worker's paradise while employing communistic tactics.

But where this is different is that it depicts the conflict in a contemporary setting with the institution of the 35-hour week as the bone of contention. Jalil Lespert plays Franck, the son who is home for the summer from college in Paris to serve as a management trainee at the factory where his father (Jean-Claude Vallod) is employed. The father is a throwback to the loyal worker of the 19th century who was wedded to the machine, who adored the machine, someone who has completely accepted his status as worker/cog in the greater machine that is the factory. Even in his off hours he works cutting wood using a large buzz saw in his garage. But he wants something better for his son.

The son is personable and talented. He puts together a questionnaire that allows management to see how its employees feel about the 35-hour week in order to better manipulate them. By accident he discovers that management is going to fire 12 workers, most of whom have spent their entire lives working for the company. This is the crisis point for the son.

Without going into plot details, what we discover at the end is that the father despises himself because he is nothing more than a man who feeds a machine while the son reveals that he at some level hates his father because he is a factory worker, a man who had neither the ability nor the gumption to raise about his station in life and a man who is afraid to question management.

Bottom line: slow and realist to the point of being mundane with professional, but uninspired direction by Laurent Cantet.

I've seen this and I give it____stars.
I want to see it___. I'll pass___.
The review was worth reading___. Not___.

Love on a Pillow (*Le Repos du guerrier*) (1962) 7

One of Bardot's best

A young woman named Genevieve Le Theil (Brigitte Bardot) while on a trip to Dijon to claim an inheritance accidently opens the wrong hotel door and finds a man named Renaud Sarti (Robert Hossein) lying unconscious on a bed. He has attempted suicide by taking an overdose of sleeping pills. Her intervention saves his life.

One would think he would be grateful and perhaps fall in love with his beautiful benefactress. What happens is just the opposite. She falls into a kind of obsessive, almost masochistic, love with him, but all he feels for her is indifference. He spends her money, drinks to excess, abuses her verbally and emotionally. But she can't let him go regardless of what he does. Yes, this is a familiar premise, and frankly I would not have stuck around long enough to see how it plays out except for Brigitte Bardot.

If you haven't seen her, you might want to watch this just to take a look at her. She is strikingly beautiful and amazingly sexy. She has pretty, almost perfect features and a soft and sweet way about her; but perhaps the most arresting thing about her is her figure. It is absolutely exquisite. She was a sensation in the fifties not only in France but in the US as the quintessence of the "sex kitten," in some ways even more so than, say, Marilyn Monroe or Tuesday Weld.

Roger Vadim, who would later direct Jane Fonda in *Barbarella* (1968) was married to Bardot at the time this movie was made. (He would later marry Jane Fonda.) Like some other French directors, Vadim liked to make movies which amounted to adorations of the beautiful young star. See Roman Polanski with, e.g., Nastassja Kinski in *Tess* (1979); Krzysztof Kieslowski with Irene Jacob in *La Double vie de Véronique* (1991) and *Trois couleurs: Rouge* (1994); and Andre Techine, with Juliette Binoche in *Rendez-vous* (1985) for some comparisons. Naturally if you make movies in which the camera adores the young actress and shows her in her best light, you are going to attract young actresses! Here Vadim directs in a studied manner designed to not only show off Bardot's exquisite beauty but to highlight her ability as an actress. Although not among the first rank as actresses go, Bardot performs well here. Perhaps this is her best film. She is elegantly dressed and coiffured, and Vadim treats us to many close ups of her lovely face. (If there is a more beautiful woman in filmdom, I haven't seen her.) But don't expect to see much of her equally lovely body or any kinky sex. This film could easily pass for PG-13.

Vadim creates an early sixties French atmosphere as he recalls the jazz/beat scene from that era, but he does so in a superficial, almost euphemistic way. In the elaborate scenes at Katov's apartment and then at his estate, we are given a hint of the decadent indulgence of a certain class of French society in which privilege, jazz, heroin, pot and easy sex are the rule, but Vadim keeps it all off camera except for one scene in which a joint is passed around.

Vadim's most famous film starring Brigitte Bardot is Et Dieu... créa la femme (And God Created Woman) (1956). This is not to be confused with Vadim's American version of the film from 1988 starring Rebecca De Mornay, which was not very good.

Bardot retired fairly young and devoted her life to helping animals.

I've seen this and I give it____stars.
I want to see it___. I'll pass___.
The review was worth reading___. Not___.

My Favorite Season (*Ma Saison Préférée)* (1993) 7
Good as far as it goes

This is an interesting but somewhat cryptic family-dynamics saga presented with characteristic French warmth and some charm. Daniel Auteuil plays a brain surgeon in love with his big sister (Catherine Deneuve). Apparently he has been pining away for her for decades since they are now middle-aged. She's no longer interested in sex, and he apparently never was, since he never married and lived alone. Meanwhile mom, who loved him best, can't live alone anymore because of fainting spells, and so goes to live with Deneuve and her family. But that doesn't work out and Auteuil won't or can't take her in, and so they send her to a nursing home, which she hates. All this occasions brother and sister to spend some time together. They recall with fondness their childhood; and when she breaks up with her husband, little brother rents a nice apartment for himself and her, all the better to live happily ever after.

Well, what a tease. That really doesn't happen. After a bit Deneuve gets seduced by a very aggressive and anonymous intern which reawakens her sexuality and makes her realize she can't live with her brother. And so she leaves him. He breaks into her house in an attempt to get her back....

I think Director André Téchiné did a good job with what he attempted, but could have attempted more. The cast is good, especially Marthe Villalonga as the mother and Deneuve, who has aged well. It's amusing to see that the cool and stately actress is still being sexually abused by the French directors for the audience. I wonder what they would have done if, instead of Hitchcock, et. al., THEY could have gotten their hands on Deneuve's cinematic American soul sister, Grace Kelly. It would have been interesting to see Grace Kelly in, say, Truffaut's Mississippi Mermaid (1969) with Jean-Paul Belmondo instead of Deneuve. Or, how about Grace Kelly as "Belle de Jour"?

But I digress.

I've seen this and I give it____stars.
I want to see it___. I'll pass___.
The review was worth reading___. Not___.

My Night at Maud's (*Ma nuit chez Maud)* (1969) 8
Rohmer at his most conversational

"The heart has it reasons which reason knows nothing of." —Blaise Pascal (1623-1662)

This is the Eric Rohmer film they warned you about. There is a lot of talk, talk, and more talk. But the talk is very interesting. One of the main topics of discussion is

Pascal's famous wager. Pascal believed that if there is even the slightest chance of the Christian heaven being true, then as a matter of probability, one ought to be a believer. Even a minuscule chance of everlasting paradise is worth the bet because infinity (eternity) times even a very small number is infinity. And, of course, if not believing puts one in however small the danger of eternal damnation, then again one should be a believer. But, as Vidal (Antoine Vitez) sagely remarks in the movie, infinity times zero is still zero.

Jean-Louis Trintignant stars as a 34-year-old Catholic mathematician who has a way with women. He runs into his old school chum, Vidal, who introduces him to Maud (Francoise Fabian), who has a way with men. Funny but they don't quite hit it off even though she manipulates him into spending the night with her. Their conversation is witty, subliminal and revealing. Maud believes in the supremacy of love, Jean-Louis in being morally flexible. Although a believing and practicing Catholic, he tells Maud that one is not going against God's will by chasing girls any more than one is going against God's will by doing mathematics.

The girl that Jean-Louis is currently chasing is 22-year-old Francoise (Maire-Christine Barrault) a blonde, Catholic girl that he has spied at church. At first it seems that although he is certain that she is perfect for him, she is reluctant. They too fence with words as they try to mislead and reveal at the same time, and the audience is intrigued, so much so that at times you might forget you are watching a movie. In this sense a Rohmer film is like a stage play. Whereas contemporary directors try to get by with as little dialogue as possible, to let the action itself reveal character, Rohmer is not shy about using dialogue to reveal character, plot, theme—the whole works.

The film begins with a long close shot of Francoise's profile as she listens in church, turning twice briefly to face the camera. She is pretty and intriguing. Although we won't realize it until the movie is mostly over, she is the focal point of the balance between the world views of Jean-Louis and Maud. After the night at Maud's during which Maud uses her intuition and sly intelligence to figure out Jean-Louis's character, he spends the night with Francoise. She uses her instincts to figure out not his character so much as his aptness for her. And then it is revealed how Francoise figures twice in the life of Maud. I won't anticipate the revelation, but be sure and watch for it. Suffice it to say that there are two reasons that Francoise is far from Maud's favorite person! The film ends, as French films often do, with the ironic affirmation of bourgeois values.

For today's DVD hound this movie will play slowly or not at all. The use of dialogue as something over and above the plot and action of the film will seem demanding and perhaps old fashioned. The deliberately drawn out scenes at church may cause you to yawn. But I recommend you stay with it. The movie has a quality that lingers long after the action is gone. The underlying philosophy about the nature of human love and how it conflicts or is compatible with reason and/or religion really does reflect to some extent the quotation above from Pascal, whose spirit is akin, although he denies it, to that of Jean-Louis, the careful protagonist of this very interesting film.

I've seen this and I give it____stars.
I want to see it___. I'll pass___.
The review was worth reading___. Not___.

Nelly & Monsieur Arnaud (1995) 7

The eyes of Emmanuelle Beart...

...are featured rather prominently in this ultra-sophisticated film by Claude Sautet, perhaps to the point of annoyance for some. Mlle. Beart, whom I first saw in Claude Berri's *Manon of the Spring* (1986), has the largest, most beautiful eyes one would ever want to see, and she is a fine actress with a smooth and subtle style. However I think that Sautet worked too exclusively with glances of nuance, raised and lowered lids, eyes widened and narrowed and such and such to further the story and to create character when he might have added a line of dialogue here and there.

Yet I liked this and certainly prefer such a style to the loud gestures and over the top hysterics that some directors might have employed. Nelly and Monsieur Arnaud (Beart and Michel Serrault) do raise their voices once—a lover's spat one might say, he to perhaps show he is still alive, she to show that she cares enough to get angry with him and has an independent spirit.

This then is a love story, super fine like gossamer and civilized to the point of something close to a burlesque of being civilized, and yet, and yet, because he is well past the age of retirement and she a vibrant young woman in her prime, the story must be presented in symbol and gesture: the back rub, the Platonic staying overnight, the little spat mentioned above, the muted jealousies, the stealthy triumph of the returning wife—in short it has everything a love affair might have, the bittersweet (their parting) and the bitter (a night with another, younger man) and the very sweet (the Sauternes, Chateau d'Yquem, no less, older than the woman herself, *apres diner*).

What Sautet does so well and so completely here is show how such a bloodless affair can touch the heart of both the old guy who knows that he can never express himself sexually and the young woman who knows that as well, how their love is emotional and deeply felt but like those two ships passing in the night, ephemeral and at some unavoidable distance. One could say—and I think we'll all felt this—that the two are soul mates separated by an implacable difference in age who by chance experience an intimation of their love together, and then it is gone.

I also liked the behavior in which Nelly says she has done something and then, only after she has said she has done it, does she do it! At first she rejects Arnaud's financial help. Then she tells her husband that she has gotten this money from an older man, gratis, and only then does she accept the money. Later in the film she tells Arnaud that she spent the night with the editor when she has not, and then afterwards, she does spend the night with him. Interesting psychology. I have actually known someone who would do that. It is like trying out an action to see how it is received before doing it!

See this for Michel Serrault, whose credits in 12-point type are longer than my arm (IMDb lists 155 as an actor) and for Emmanuelle Beart whose unique beauty is unforgettable.

I've seen this and I give it____stars.
I want to see it___. I'll pass___.
The review was worth reading___. Not___.

Nightcap *(Merci pour le chocolat)* (2000) 8

A short analysis of the film

Be forewarned that this review is in part an analysis of the movie *Merci pour le chocolat* and therefore contains several spoilers. So if you haven't seen the film and don't want to know anything about the plot development, please don't read this review.

Part of the problem with this very interesting movie is carelessness or deliberate ambiguity on the part of director Claude Chabrol. The celebrated French master of cinema really is a bit like Alfred Hitchcock in the way he put this film together. He doesn't care so much about the consistency of detail or logic, instead what he strives for, as did Hitchcock, is effect. Begin with a tantalizing premise, build tension, and then come up with a striking ending.

The premise, that of a psychologically disturbed woman of high social and economic status (Mika Muller, played with her usual haunting skill by Isabelle Huppert), whose bizarre nature forces her to poison those around her, satisfies the formula nicely. The tension is maintained by our need to find out exactly what she is doing and why and how it will affect the husband André (Jacques Dutronc), the son Guillaume (Rodolphe Pauly), and the young pianist, Jeanne Pollet (Anna Mouglalis). The ending which is heavily symbolic and deeply psychological however may disappoint some viewers. Note that as the closing credits run down the screen, Mika cries and then curls up catatonically on the couch next to a black Afghan in the shape of a spider web. She is the spider at the side of the web waiting for something to fall into it. She can't help herself. That is her nature.

And that is why she cries for herself. And notice that her husband does not hate her or rage against her. Instead he seems to have pity upon her as he plays a funereal piece on the piano.

Personally what disappointed me—although I still think this is an excellent film—is the way the ambiguity about Jeanne's paternity is handled. Obviously we can tell by the photos on the wall of the tragically deceased Lisbeth that Jeanne is indeed her daughter since she looks exactly like her. In fact in the next scene Jeanne unconsciously apes the pose in the photo by putting the palms of her hands to either side of her face as André watches. Another problem with the film is that nobody except the audience seems struck by the exact similarity.

Additionally, the truth of her paternity is obscured by Jeanne's mother saying that the mix-up at the maternity ward was straightened out to everyone's satisfaction, and besides (almost as an afterthought) she reveals that her husband was not the father, that instead she was inseminated by an unknown donor. This silliness could easily be resolved by DNA testing since the movie, which was released in 2000, is set in contemporary France. Chabrol uses a lab to establish what drug Mika is putting in the chocolate. Why not use a lab to establish paternity? Part of the reason may simply be that the novel upon which the movie is based *The Chocolate Cobweb* was written by the American mystery writer Charlotte Armstrong in the 1950's, before the age of DNA testing.

The real answer however is that Chabrol didn't bother, just as he didn't bother cleaning up some other ambiguities, like why the son does not confront Mika after he is told by Jeanne that Mika is drugging him. Or why Mika deliberately spills the drugged chocolate intended for Guillaume onto the floor, allowing her to be surreptitiously observed by Jeanne through a reflection in the glass of one of the photos. The spilling seems purely a plot device to allow Jeanne a reason to get the chocolate analyzed. Furthermore, we presume that Mika, who is very rich, remarries André because she loves him or admires him or wants to be with him. And it can be seen that he would want to remarry her because of her wealth, her beauty, her elegance, etc. However, it is revealed near the end of the film that he had all along suspected her of causing Lisbeth's death since he says something like "You also washed the glasses the night Lisbeth died." He knew.

One can even go to the extent of analyzing this by saying that Mika is the black widow and André finds her irresistible. Note the scene in which he suggests they make love to have a daughter and she puts him off by saying that he would be ineffective since he has already taken his Rohypnol. She says, next time before he takes his sleep potion they will do it. Furthermore notice that EVERY night he falls into a drugged sleep since he is addicted to Rohypnol. Perhaps this nightly occurrence is pleasant to Mika, in a sense an acting out of the black widow's mating ritual again and again.

Nonetheless, this idea of a woman helpless against her own nature seems a bit unsatisfying. We want something more. And what she does to satisfy her urges leaves us a bit mystified. It seems hardly enough. She drugs the chocolate that she lovingly makes for Guillaume and Jeanne. Why only this? Why this at all? The logic is that she needs to excrete her poison, like a spider. The very act of doing it is what satisfies her need. The fact that somebody could take the drug and then fall asleep at the wheel of a car really is beside the point.

This tale of the dark psychology within the human soul is the sort of thing that attracts Isabelle Huppert as an actress. She has played in her distinguished career a number of roles that require evil in the human soul. This is one of the more subtle ones. For one of the more striking, see her in *The Piano Teacher* (2001).

I've seen this and I give it____stars.
I want to see it___. I'll pass___.
The review was worth reading___. Not___.

Scene of the Crime (*Le Lieu du crime*) (1986) 7

Lacks focus, but interesting

The title is a bit misleading since *Le lieu du crime* is not a noir thriller or a mystery. It is a relationships movie with psychological undertones. Director André Téchiné is especially drawn to the exploration of family affairs featuring naturalistic depictions of human sexuality. For example see *Ma Saison Préférée* (1993), also starring Catherine Deneuve, in which the central tension, maintained for decades, is that of a brother's unrequited desire for his older sister. Téchiné is very good at exploring taboo situations without leaving us with a sense of the perverse, and he is able to hint at a deeper, non-expressed sexuality behind ordinary life.

Here Catherine Deneuve stars as Lili Ravenel, who has a 13-year-old son, Thomas (Nicolas Giraudi), who is not doing well at school, a father who no longer cares about people at all, including members of his own family, and a mother who is emotionally close and distant by turns. Lili is estranged from her husband, a man she no longer loves, if ever she did. She is a woman of a certain age who finds diversion in managing a night club. Thus we have the familiar psychology of the bored middle class woman who, we know, will be drawn irresistibly to the excitement of an outsider. Directors who find themselves in the enviable position of directing the beautiful, cool and stately Deneuve seem themselves irresistibly drawn to showing her in compromised situations. I'm thinking of *Belle de Jour* (1967) and *Mississippi Mermaid* (1969), directed respectively by Luis Buñuel and Francois Truffaut. In the former Deneuve is a day-tripping prostitute and in the latter she is a criminal on the run. For some

odd reason there is something deeply moving about seeing Deneuve give into her baser nature. (I think.)

Anyway, here she does indeed give herself to the rough young man who has killed his companion, and she does so without a hint of regret or lingering doubt. Incidentally in Téchiné's *Ma Saison Préférée*, mentioned above, there is a scene in which a young intern has his way with Deneuve using much the same approach that Wadeck Stanczack, who plays Martin, an escaped con, employs here. That Lili's sexuality is aroused by his crude demand is the psychology that Téchiné wants to concentrate on; but because one of the weaknesses of his movie is a lack of focus, the impact of her desire is not as strongly felt as it might be. For a most striking and stunning exploration of this theme see Vittoria De Sica's unforgettable *The Garden of the Finzi-Continis* (1971).

Another weakness of this movie is some unconvincing action and dialogue in places. The opening scene in which Thomas is threatened by Martin who demands money to help him escape is a case in point. Martin's threats seem mild and ineffective. One wonders why Thomas is compelled to return. I also wonder about the boy's response to seeing his mother in bed with Martin. His first reaction is to say, "He will kill you!" and then later he asks his father, "Is that love?" which doesn't seem like something a 13-year-old would say. A six-year-old, maybe. Also a puzzle is why Claire Nebout, who is interesting as Alice, the girl involved with the two escapees, stops her car in the rain to pick up Thomas only to throw him out a few minutes later. Why did she stop at all? As the scene was shot he seemed to be in the middle of the road, so she couldn't avoid him, but considering that it was dark and it was raining, I don't think that would happen. At any rate, the purpose of the scene is to show that Thomas, like his mother, is starved for excitement, begging Alice to take him with her.

My favorite Téchiné movie is *Rendez-Vous* (1985) starring a very young and vital Juilette Binoche, who is clearly adored by the director. It is, like this movie, uneven in places, but Binoche is incredibly sexy and captivating. If you are a Binoche fan, see it. You will experience a side of her not shown in her American movies.

By the way, when this was filmed Deneuve was about 43-years-old and had already appeared in at least 67 films. She is the kind of woman who grows more beautiful as she grows older. I found her much more attractive here than when I first saw her in the celebrated *The Umbrellas of Cherbourg* (1964), released when she was 21.

I've seen this and I give it____stars.
I want to see it___. I'll pass___.
The review was worth reading___. Not___.

The Story of Adele H. (*L'histoire d'Adèle H.*) (1975)

8

A story of obsessive love

Isabelle Adjani plays the title role, that of Adele Hugo, daughter of the great French writer, a woman obsessively in love with an English army lieutenant who doesn't want her. The scene is Halifax, Nova Scotia, during the time of the American Civil War. She has followed Lt. Pinson (Bruce Robinson) from her home in exile on the island of Guernsey to be with him even though he has rejected her. Adjani's sensual beauty and her intense and passionate nature command the screen and we are drawn to identify with her as she spirals toward madness as her abject pleas of love are unrequited. We watch as she debases herself in every way possible in a desperate attempt to gain Pinson's love, even to the point of giving him to other women. She is psychologically pleased with this because she thinks it shows that her love for him transcends sexuality. Of course the nature of obsessive love is always entirely selfish. If you really love someone who doesn't want you, you have to let them go. But of course she cannot.

Francois Truffaut directed and did a fine job of getting the most out of his young star. The maddening nature of obsession is well depicted and the story is focused and unfolds at a deliberate pace. Noteworthy is the setting itself, a cold and remote clime so that Adele is in isolation from her home, family and friends with little to do or think about every day except her obsession. It is easy to see how something like this can lead to complete madness.

Memorable is a little story within the larger tale, that of the fraudulent hypnotist whom Adele thinks might be able to turn Pinson's indifference into love.

I've seen this and I give it____stars.
I want to see it___. I'll pass___.
The review was worth reading___. Not___.

The Swindle (*Rien ne va plus*) (1997) 8

An interesting and restrained thriller

Although Betty (Isabelle Huppert, who was 43-years-old when the film was released) calls Victor (Michel Serrault, who was 69) "Papa" on occasion in this smooth and restrained thriller from Claude Chabrol, he is not her father by any means. The term is merely one of ironic affection. What they are are modern "gypsies" living on the fringes of society plying their ancient trade. Perhaps they were lovers in the past. Clearly they are a team, dependent upon one another. In particular what these small time con artists do is go to conventions, medical, dental, farm equipment salesman conventions, find a target and con the poor dupe out of some of his money.

Some. The film begins at a roulette table on the French Riviera with Betty stringing along a not entirely bright lawnmower salesman whom she invites for a drink. She slips some knockout drops into his drink and quickly invites him up to his room where, after he is out cold, Victor follows. They take some of his money. Victor insists on always playing it safe and using a rather strange but plausible psychology (which will figure later in the movie) of making the man think that perhaps he wasn't robbed, since if she had intended to rob him, would she have only taken part of the money out of his wallet? They do forge his signature on a check, but he will only find out about that later, and indeed might not be sure about how that happened.

So this is a small time con. Trouble begins for our vagabond thieves when Betty meets the CFO of a big corporation who is transferring five million Swiss francs in cash out of the country. She senses the chance for a big score, and after the mark falls in love with her (she thinks) she brings Victor into the scheme. With some tricky exchanges of the metal suitcase containing the money Betty and Victor end up over their heads in some very hot water.

The plot is a little on the unlikely side, as thriller plots tend to be, but the thing to keep in mind is the idea of taking only PART of the money. This is what fools the bad bad guys (as opposed to the good bad guys who are our vagabond duo, Betty and Victor).

Any movie starring the incomparable Isabelle Huppert (*La Pianiste* 2001; *Merci pour le chocolat* 2000; *La dentelliere* 1977, and many more) is worth seeing and any movie directed by Claude Chabrol (*Une affair de femmes* 1988; *Betty* 1992; *La ceremonie* 1995, etc.) will have something of interest in it. Add a fine performance by Serrault, one of the great veterans of the French cinema, and *Rien ne va plus* is definitely worth seeing. However the role played by Huppert does not challenge her and Chabrol's more famous films (some of them also starring Huppert) are decidedly more interesting.

But see this for the lighthearted chemistry between Huppert who is sublimely fetching and Serrault who is clearly past the age of any pretension. Such a quasi-Platonic union based on the love that still warms the embers in a dying fire has become almost a staple of directors past their prime. See Claude Sautet's *Nelly and Monsieur Arnaud* (1995) which also featured Serrault for another example.

I've seen this and I give it____stars.
I want to see it___. I'll pass___.
The review was worth reading___. Not___.

Three Colors: Blue (*Trois Couleurs: Bleu*) (1993) 8

See it with a fine arts major

She is the wife of a great composer, and the music plays in her head, because she is really the composer herself. After her husband and daughter are killed in a traffic accident, she tries to kill herself because the music is too beautiful and the memory of it too painful, but she can't swallow the pills. Then she tries to renounce the world but finds that she still cares. She is still of flesh. She says she wants no belongings and no memories, "No friends, no love. Those are all traps."

This is a beautiful film, perhaps too precious for some, understated and overdone by turns with artsy shots on common objects and blurred views filtered through liquid colors, especially of course the color blue. Sometimes the movie was so quiet for so long I became aware of the faint whine of the refrigerator.

Juliette Binoche, lately seen as the nurse in *The English Patient*, dominates the screen with her affecting countenance. The camera continually explores and re-explores her face—an interesting, almost androgynous face, kind and gentle, unassuming with a sweet undercurrent of power.

I liked this better than the overly clever "White" that followed, also directed by the talented Krzysztof Kieslowski. "Red" starring the incomparable Irène Jacob and featuring long-time French film favorite, Jean-Louis Trintignant, is the Kieslowski film I like best.

I've seen this and I give it___stars.
I want to see it___. I'll pass___.
The review was worth reading___. Not___.

Three Colors: White (*Trois couleurs: Blanc*) (1994) 8

Clever

Some of this is not done in a very convincing manner, and there's enough hokum to please a sit-com producer, but in the area of tricky plot twists and original story ideas this gets an A+.

Premise: Little Polish guy living in Paris, an adorable and prize-winning hair dresser, is divorced by his beautiful French wife, whom he loves passionately, because he can't...perform, or at least can't perform long enough. She is unhappy with him, VERY unhappy. She takes everything from him but a trunk and even calls the gendarmes and pretends he is burning down what is now her salon after he fails her one last time. I guess this is the ultimate fury from a woman scorned, although he sure wishes he wasn't scorning her.

He ends up on his knees in the Metro playing his comb for francs to get enough to eat. Then he arranges to get sent back to Poland in the trunk. After some mishaps he makes his fortune. It would be unfair to reveal any more of the plot since it is so, so clever... But the "white" of the title is for a Polish dinner roll and the snow of Po-

land and for sheets of legal paper and for the white walls of new enterprises and especially for the white light of her orgasm.

Julie Delpy, who plays the very frustrated wife, is pretty enough to go to extremes for, and Zbigniew Zamachowski who plays the lead, is convincing in a role that borders on the silly. Memorable for his sly portrayal of a bored with life, bridge-playing professional is Janusz Gajos.

This is the second in the "Trois Couleurs" trilogy by Polish cum French director Krzysztof Kieslowski. I have seen both "Red" and "Blue," and I would rate this one a little behind those two very excellent films.

I've seen this and I give it___stars.
I want to see it___. I'll pass___.
The review was worth reading___. Not___.

Time Out (*L'emploi du temps*) (2001) 8

Long, slow, and yet compelling

When I scanned the blurb on the cover of this DVD I thought that this film was a dramatization of the story of Frenchman Jean-Claude Romand from the book *The Adversary: A True Story of Monstrous Deception* (2000) written by novelist and screen writer Emmanuel Carrère. However, Carrère did not write the screen play for *L'Emploi du temps*, nor is the story in the film the same or even close to "A True Story of Monstrous Deception."

True, Vincent, the central character, does practice a deception, but it is hardly monstrous. In fact it is so ordinary and banal that many viewers may find it boring.

The film opens with a man pretending to be working while in fact he is just driving around in his car, talking on his cellphone and telling his wife lies about where he is and what he is doing.

What is going on?

I won't say anymore because part of the effectiveness of this very subtle film stems from not knowing why Vincent is driving around pretending to be working. If you haven't seen the film I recommend that you not read any reviews on it until you have, because it is difficult to write a review of this film without revealing something that will spoil it for the viewer. If I had known what Vincent's predicament was prior to viewing, I don't think the film would have held my interest as well as it did.

So let me compliment the director, Laurent Cantet, on his fine direction, make note of the interesting and professional camera work, and the fine acting by Aurélien Recoing who plays the lead with excellent support from Karin Viard as his wife, Muriel, and Serge Livrozet who plays a mysterious petty criminal. And let me add that the theme of the film involves the fear of failure and the dehumanization of life within the modern corporate structure, and that it is replete with the sort of vacuous dialogue heard in corporate biz-speak in which vague but seemingly impressive generalities are bandied about in lieu of saying anything specific for fear of giving away too much information.

In a sense this is a dismaying satire of the business world, to be compared (distantly) to such films as *In the Company of Men* (1997)—a sociopathic study within the corporate structure—and David Mamet's striking *Glengarry Glen Ross* (1992).

I had mixed feelings about the resolution of the film (which of course I will keep vague). It seemed that the movie could have ended the scene before the haunting scene in which we hear the voice of Vincent's wife on the cellphone telling him she loves him while we see him walking away from the headlights of his Renault van over the snow toward the blackness of the night. If the film had ended with that scene how different would our experience have been! I wonder if originally that was indeed the ending, with the other ending an afterthought. How different our understanding of Vincent the man would be depending on which ending we experience.

Of course if you haven't seen the film, this is way too vague, but I mention the endings because when you do watch the film you might think about how the ending affects the story and our understanding of the film. Most of the time for me the ending doesn't matter that much. It's the treatment and the development of the story and the theme, the artistry of the players and the camera work and the direction that count. Endings sometimes are even arbitrary. In this film however the ending is important.
See this for Aurélien Recoing who elicits our empathy over the course of a long and demanding role.

I've seen this and I give it____stars.
I want to see it___. I'll pass___.
The review was worth reading___. Not___.

Wild Reeds (*Les Roseaux sauvages*) (1994) 8

Sexual coming of ager

The slightly loose and episodic feel of this charming coming-of-ager doesn't matter because the characters and the conflicts are so well presented that we are enthralled throughout.

Three boys on the verge of manhood (with the French-Algerian conflict smoldering in the background) are in residence at a boarding school in the south of France in 1962. One is gay, the second is bi-sexual and the third is straight. Through their interactions we (and they) discover their sexuality.

Francois Forestier, played attractively by Gael Morel, is gay as he discovers one night when Serge Bartolo (Stephane Rideau), an athletic schoolmate with a natural style, awakens his sexuality by seducing him. For Serge it is just a school age sexual adventure; for Francois it is love so intense he is transformed. The third boy, Henri Mariana, who is from Algeria, is a little older and a little more cynical. He finds heterosexual love with his enemy, Maité Alverez, who is a hated communist. Elodie Bouchez, whom I recall from *The Dream Life of Angels* (1998) for which she shared a Cannes Best Actress award, plays Maité whose style is earnest, witty and brave.

As it happens I was in France during the period of this film, and a teenager as well. The Algerian conflict haunted the young men because as soon as they were of age they could be sent away to fight. Also the Communist Party was strong in France and an attraction to some who opposed what they saw as French colonialism in Algeria and Vietnam. Director André Téchiné who characteristically explores human sexuality in his films (e.g., *Rendez-Vous* (1985) with a young and vital Juliette Binoche; *Le lieu du crime* (1986) with Catherine Deneuve; and *Ma Saison Préférée* (1993) also starring Catherine Deneuve) attempts to integrate these larger issues into his film but I don't think is entirely successful. Serge's older brother is killed in Algeria and his teacher blames herself for not helping him to escape his military service and suffers a nervous breakdown. However this story is not well-connected with the rest of the film. Also more could have been done with the divergent views of Maité and Henri. What I loved was the club scene where suddenly the French girls are twisting to Chubby Checker's "Let's Twist Again" which propelled me back to 1962 when indeed the Twist was all the rage in France.

What makes this film superior is the warm and truthful way in which the sexual awakenings are realized. The kids seem absolutely real and the dialogue is sharp and authentic. Morel is very winning. I especially liked the earnest way he confronts and then accepts his sexuality. Interesting was the scene in which he seeks out the shoe salesman whom he knows is gay for his advice on how he should cope with unrequited homosexual love.
This is a film about young people for open-minded adults attractively done. For many it will strike a strong cord of recognition.

I've seen this and I give it____stars.
I want to see it___. I'll pass___.
The review was worth reading___. Not___.

III
Chinese Language Films

This modest section is dominated by the beautiful and affecting films of that great cinematic artist, Zhang Yimou.

Blind Shaft (*Mang jing*) (2003) 8

Evokes a stark picture of modern China

What happened at the start of this movie down in the mine shaft confused me so much I had to go back to the scene and view it again. That really didn't help because it seemed that three men—one very young; another older, perhaps in his early thirties; and the third perhaps in his forties—go down into the coal mine and after working for a while take a break in the semidarkness. And then after some talk the two older men bludgeon the youngest to death.

That in fact is what happened. Turns out that drifting miners Tang, the older, and Song have dreamed up a murderous scheme in which they recruit young men to go with them to work in the mines. They make the young man pretend that he is related to them. Then they kill him, fake a cave-in and demand hush money from the boss of the mine. We see this work one time, and then the two men are off to the town to spend their ill-gotten lucre. And then it's back to recruitment and a new mine.

Part of the logic of this premise is the fear of the mine operators that if there is an accident, there will be an investigation and the mine will be closed down. So they pay hush money to the families of those killed to keep the authorities away. How realistic this is I have no idea. The scam certainly is a brutal, bestial way to make a living that cannot go on for long.

In the next part of the movie Tang and Song find a poor 16-year-old country boy in the city who is looking for work. Director Li Yang carefully shows us a lot of interaction among the three as the next setup develops at a new coal mine. What makes all this so interesting are the glimpses we get of life in modern China, the wretched, dangerous coal mines, the cities teeming with all their poverty and industry, their hustles and indifference. The landscapes are not lush with greenery; instead it is cold and bleak and the ground is mostly barren. This is not a travel log for tourists, nor is this an ode to the communist state. What we see is a rural and agrarian society perverted by a forced industrialization.

We see the housing for the miners. We see them at meal times and at play. We see what they eat and drink, how they amuse themselves. We see the great dependence that China has on coal. There is a lot of coal in China and it is used for heating and cooking and for firing kilns and crematoriums. It runs the industrial state. Coal burns dirty and pollutes. Although Li Yang does not dwell on it or show us the poisonous clouds that hang over many Chinese cities, we nonetheless get the picture.

Perhaps the most evocative shot of all is the last one. A body with a blanket over it is shoved into the crematorium oven. The door is slammed shut; the fires incinerate. The camera pans up, up to the top of the smokestack and we see puffy tendrils of smoke emitting. That's it. Run the credits.

The simplicity of the story starkly told and the low-budget realism of the cinematography lend to this film a sense of truth and immediacy not found in more carefully contrived productions.

I've seen this and I give it____stars.
I want to see it___. I'll pass___.
The review was worth reading___. Not___.

Farewell, My Concubine (*Ba wang bie ji*) (1993) 8

A lavish, opulent, and intense film; bring your lunch

As far as story and content goes this owes more than a little to *The Last Emperor* (1987), which is not surprising since Director Chen Kaige was a member of the cast of that film and no doubt was influenced by its success. But stylistically, and especially as the film was directed and cut, *Farewell, My Concubine* is original and stands alone. If *The Last Emperor* was a Western movie about the Chinese political experience in the Twentieth Century, then *Farewell, My Concubine* is a Chinese movie influenced by the West about that same experience. While the former focused on the emperor and those around him, *Farewell My Concubine* focuses on two actors of the Beijing opera.

Admittedly, the film is long (I saw the 157-minute version) and sometimes strays from it intent, but gains and maintains power and keeps our interest mainly because everything is presented in a starkly-lit, intensely focused manner. The epic-like story itself is good if a little pedestrian at times. The lavish and stunning sets in opulent color and design are just fascinating to view. Everything from the extras in the crowds to the porcelain for tea is carefully chosen and presented. Particularly striking are the traditional costumes and makeup, shown to advantage through the fine camera work. But what makes the film is the glimpse we get of the world of the Beijing opera and its traditions. From the Dickensian boy's school for the actors to the intrigues with patrons and the political powers that be, there's the sense of a world beyond our experience.

The acting is also excellent. The beautiful Gong Li, who played Duan's wife, was captivating as she displayed a wide range of emotion. Leslie Cheung as Dieyi, "the concubine," and Fengyi Zhang as Duan, "the king," were also excellent. The boys who played the actors as children, especially the actor who played Douzi, were first rate.

I've seen this and I give it____stars.
I want to see it___. I'll pass___.
The review was worth reading___. Not___.

Goodbye Dragon Inn (*Bu san*) (2003) 7

An anti-film

This is the kind of film you see at an art film festival at some inopportune time after you've already watched twenty films. You start watching it and it seems so boring that you know it can't be THAT boring. You're missing something. You sit up and you concentrate. Nothing happens. There is this woman with a club foot. She sways and totters up and down like a boat caught in waves as she drags her foot down a sparsely-lit corridor. The camera is at one end of the corridor and it records her progress. Then after she is gone, the camera holds on the empty corridor for some long seconds, make that literally minutes, and then cuts to another scene.

This time the camera is looking out into a darkened movie theater. There are only a couple of people seated in the red seats. Finally some dialogue. It's from the movie being shown, a kind of sword and warlord melodrama set in the Ming Dynasty. (Actually it's King Hu's *Dragon Inn* (1967), a martial arts epic—hence the name of this movie). The camera watches the face of one particular viewer. He is just sitting there watching the movie. The camera watches him watching the movie. It watches him watching the movie for a long time.
At some later point the guy goes to the bathroom. He's actually a Japanese tourist. He stands next to some other guy at a urinal. Another guy comes in and stands at a third urinal. One guy smokes a cigarette. Some time passes. Then there is another scene. The woman with the club foot is in the bathroom. She opens one stall and flushes the toilet. She opens another stall and flushes the toilet. The camera stays on the scene until she has

flushed the last toilet, and then holds on the empty bathroom...

At this point you figure out what is going on. This is an anti-film. Everything is backwards. The film maker (Tsai Ming-Liang) is not trying to entertain you, to impress you, or to excite you, or rally you to some cause, dazzle you, invoke your tears, uplift you, scare you, redeem you—no, the film maker is doing exactly the opposite of what film normally tries to do.
And then there's another scene, as if to confirm your interpretation. The one guy and another stand in the corridor smoking cigarettes. There is after a bit some words from the second man. He says this theater is haunted. There is no response. He says "Ghosts." No response. The camera now gets a little closer so that you see the men from perhaps a few feet away. Their heads are turned away from the camera so that only the back of their heads and a little bit of the sides of their faces can be seen. The camera holds. No one says anything.

And finally near the end of the film after the theater has been closed for the night (actually forever, as this is about the death of the movie house), one guy puts his palm on a fortune telling machine. The machine says, "Enter your question." He punches a button. After a bit, the machine says, "Please take your fortune." A pause, and then the machine kicks out the fortune on a strip of paper. The guy takes it and reads it. And then he leaves. The camera does NOT show his fortune.

The part you like best comes at the end as a woman sings a Chinese song about "Half was bitter; half was sweet." Her voice is gorgeous and the melody is engaging. And then the title characters run down the screen.
Okay, this film really IS boring unless you are a true student of film, and then you can see that this anti-film about people watching a film is a statement about the film-maker's art. As you leave the theater, now having seen twenty-one films, you declare that this was very interesting, and you know you are going to vote this one higher than some of the others because it so deliberately bored you that you were not really bored at all, compared to some other films that took themselves too seriously and really did bore you. "Interesting," you say to your companion. "Really makes a statement," he says. "Beautiful in a way," you say. "Yes," he says.

Suddenly you have an angle on the film. You're thinking, *Goodbye, Dragon Inn* somehow reminds you of the lyric from the Elton John song about Marilyn Monroe. The lyric is, "Goodbye Yellow Brick Road." Same thing, you think—or at least the same melancholy idea.

I've seen this and I give it____stars.
I want to see it___. I'll pass___.
The review was worth reading___. Not___.

Hero (*Ying xiong*) (2002) 8

Merely beautiful?

"Hero" is a beautiful movie, as all Zhang Yimou movies are. There are spectacular outdoor, epic-like scenes, and wondrously colorful costumes and fabrics (and swords!) in addition to the choreographed sword play. I would also note that this movie was his most successful American box office flick—and therein lies a problem.

Zhang Yimou is a great artist. He uses the silver screen the way a Michelangelo or Rembrandt used a canvas. His sense of color and line and composition would cause Da Vinci or Picasso or any of the great Renaissance masters to sit up and take notice were they around today. His films are universally admired not only for their visual artistry but—and this is where I take exception to the direction in which that this film suggests that Zhang Yimou is going—their story-telling ability and their unusual sensitivity to the human condition. Here we have a fantasy of Chinese history brought to life. We have supernatural swordplay—beautifully, hauntingly done, to be sure: sword play as ballet—but what we don't have is a real human story.

This is more like a legend. The great King of Qin, threatened by three great warriors—Sky, Broken Sword, and Flying Snow—is now threatened by a third, the Nameless one (like somebody out of a Clint Eastwood movie), who has pretended to vanquish the other three as a means to get within ten paces of the hated King in order to slay him. This is history as seen from the point of view of Great Men, not history as the force of events and conditions greater than any single person. This is also history as myth. It is nationalistic: the great Chinese king unites "our land" in a great historical event in which the Chinese people can take pride.

It also glorifies war. The great gray mass of soldiers in the service of the king (Zhang Yimou actually used something like 18,000 soldiers from the Revolutionary Army of the People's Republic of China in the production) represents a force that will go on to triumph over lesser forces. The King of Qin can be seen as the ultimate warlord, the warlord with the largest army and therefore the one who will win.

Yet, there is a sense in which this does not sit well with Zhang Yimou. He likes the individual heroes, and indeed would have Nameless achieve his personal victory except that Nameless sees in the end that killing the king would not be a victory at all. Furthermore, Zhang Yimou celebrates in the choreographed sword dances of his heroes the indomitable human spirit that will in the long run, triumph over the forces of sheer might. We can see this in not only the beauty of the dances, but in the association of calligraphy—that uniquely human art form—with the play of the sword. He who practices calligraphy with his heart and soul also learns the secrets of the sword.

My problem with all this is that just prior to seeing this film I viewed *Hotel Rwanda* (2004) in which ironically the horrendous human slaughter in Rwanda was achieved in large part through the use of machetes made in China. Can we celebrate the sword about which it is said: if you live by the sword you will die by the sword? These are words that have only a tiny impact on us compared to what they meant to the people of 2,000 years ago who actually knew what it meant to die by the sword. Or should we more correctly celebrate the word, not the sword? For it is also said that the word is mightier than the sword.

I think Zhang Yimou knows this, and I suspect part of what he wanted to convey in this film is that sort of message. However, I think his love of beauty and his sense of what works cinematically overcame what he might have intended, and instead of a great film we have one that is merely beautiful.

But by all means see this. See this for his artistry of course. See this to compare it to the legendary kung fu movies. See this for Jet Li who plays Nameless and is a great favorite of the Chinese cinema, and for Daoming Chen who plays the king. And see this for the beautiful actresses Maggie Cheung, who plays Flying Snow, and Ziyi Zhang, who plays Moon. And last but not least, see this for Tony Leung Chiu Wai who plays the enigmatic Broken Sword.

I've seen this and I give it____stars.
I want to see it___. I'll pass___.
The review was worth reading___. Not___.

Ju Dou (1990) 10

Visually stunning, psychologically brutal

The title character, a peasant sold as a concubine to a cruel old man, is played by the beautiful Gong Li, one of the great actresses of our time who followed this brilliant work with spectacular performances in *The Story of Qiu Ju* (1991), *Raise the Red Lantern* (1992), and *Farewell, My Concubine* (1993). Li Wei plays her master, Yang Jin-shan, the childless owner of a dye mill in the agrarian China of the 1920s. Li Wei's fine performance combines craftiness with iniquity reminding me a little of the late great John Huston with scruffy beard. The third character in the tragic triangle is Jin-shan's nephew, Yang Tianqing, a modest man who does most of the work in the dye mill. The pent-up intensity of Li Baotian, who plays Tianqing, recalled to me at times the work of Ben Kingsley. Ju Dou falls in love with Tianqing almost by default, and it is their ill-fated love that leads to tragedy.

In some ways this visually stunning, psychologically brutal film about paternity and the old social order of

China was Director Zhang Yimou's "practice" for the making two years later of his masterpiece, the afore mentioned, *Raise the Red Lantern*, one the greatest films ever made. The theme of patriarchal privilege is similar, and in both films Gong Li portrays a young concubine required to bear a son and heir to a cruel and ageing man of means. Even though the setting in both films is China in the twenties before the rise of Communism, both films very much annoyed the ageing leadership of Communist China and were censured (*Ju Dou* was actually banned), ostensibly for moral reasons, but more obviously because of the way they depicted elderly men in positions of power.

Ju Dou is the lesser film only in the sense that Sirius might outshine the sun were the two stars placed side by side. Both films are masterpieces, but for me *Ju Dou* was difficult to watch because of the overt cruelty of the master, whereas in *Raise the Red Lantern*, Zhang Yimou chose to keep the more brutal aspects of the story off camera. In a sense, then, *Raise the Red Lantern* is the more subtle film. It is also a film of greater scope involving more characters, infused with an underlining sense of something close to black humor. (The very lighting of the lanterns was slyly amusing as it ironically pointed to the subjugation.)

In *Ju Dou* there is virtually no humor and the emphasis is on the physical brutality of life under the patriarchal social order. Ju Dou is beaten and tortured while we learn that Jin-shan tortured his previous wives to death because of their failure to bear him an heir. The terrible irony is that it is Jin-shan who is sterile. He feels shamed in the eyes of his ancestors because the Wang line will die out with him. But a child is finally born through Ju Dou's illicit affair with Tianqing. (Note that this conjoining in effect saves Ju Dou's life.) Jin-shan thinks the infant is his son and briefly all is serenity. However, while two may live happily ever after, three will not. Notice too that now that Jin-shan has an heir, nephew Tianqing will inherit nothing.

Will they kill Jin-shan? Will fortuitous events put him out of the picture? Will they find happiness? Will the boy learn the truth about his paternity? Zhang Yimou's artistry does not allow superficial resolution, you can be sure.

Note the two significant turns the film takes early on. One comes after Ju Dou discovers that Tianqing has been spying on her through a peep hole as she goes about her bath. At first she is mortified, and then sees this as a chance to show him the scars from the torture she endures daily, and then she shows him her body to allure him. The other turn comes as the child pronounces his first words by calling the old man "Daddy." Instantly Jin-shan, now confined to a wooden bucket that serves as a wheelchair, divines a deep psychological plan to realize his revenge. He embraces the child as his own, hoping to turn the boy against the illicit couple.

The strength of the film is in the fine acting, the beautiful sets, the gorgeous camera work, and in the unsentimental story that does not compromise or cater to saccharin or simplistic expectations. Zhang Yimou is a visual master who turns the wood gear- and donkey-driven dye mill of the 1920s into a tapestry of brilliant color and texture. Notable is the fine work that he does with the two boys who play the son at different ages. He has them remain virtually mute throughout and almost autistically cold. Indeed part of the power of this film comes from the depiction of the character of the son who grows up to hate who he is and acts out his hatred in murderous violence toward those around him.

Zhang Yimou is one of the few directors who can bring simultaneously to the silver screen the power of an epic and the subtlety of a character study. His films are more beautiful than the most lavish Hollywood productions and as artistically satisfying as the best in world cinema. The only weakness in the film is perhaps the ending which is played like a Greek tragedy for cathartic effect. One senses that Zhang Yimou and co-director Yang Fengliang in choosing the terminus were not entirely sure how this tale should end and took what might be seen as an easy way out.

I've seen this and I give it____stars.
I want to see it___. I'll pass___.
The review was worth reading___. Not___.

Not One Less (*Yi ge dou bu neng shao*) (1999) 9

A quasi-realistic fairy tale of modern China

Wei Minzhi (played by Wei Minzhi, essentially playing herself) is a 13-year-old peasant girl pressed into being "Teacher Wei" at a small rural elementary school when the regular teacher must take a month off. She knows one song (a Maoist propaganda song) and that not very well. She hasn't a clue about how to manage a classroom. Her arithmetic is suspect and her people skills are those of a self-centered beginner. It's not even clear that she wants to do the job. In fact she seems more concerned about the 50 yuan she's supposed to get than anything else.

Thus acclaimed Chinese film maker Zhang Yimou sets the stage for a most compelling fairy tale which illustrates how the determined spirit of a little girl might triumph over poverty, ignorance, and the hard-headed reality of the post-Maoist bureaucratic society.

And is she determined! She is given 30 pieces of chalk and warned not to waste any of it. The lesson plans are to copy some lessons on the chalkboard and to get the students to copy the copy. That's it! Both the regular teacher and the town's mayor point to the other as the one who will pay her. When the regular teacher starts to leave without paying her, she chases after him. She is told she will get paid when he returns, and if all the students are still enrolled, she will get a ten-yuan bonus.

Thus we have the movie's title and the source of "Teacher Wei's" determination. When one little girl is picked to go to a sports camp because she can run, Wei hides her from the authorities. When Zhang Huike, the class trouble-maker (played by Zhang Huike), quits school and heads for the city to find work, Wei schemes ways to get him and bring him back.

At this point the magic begins. With this common goal both teacher and the kids figure out ways to raise money to send Wei by bus to the city and back. They figure the cost for Wei's round trip and for Zhang Huike's one-way trip back, with the kids themselves taking the initiative at the chalkboard with the math. Wei makes them empty their pocketbooks, and when there is not enough she takes them on a field trip to a brick-making factory and together they move bricks to raise the cash. Again they calculate how many bricks they must move at so many "cents" per brick.

I mention all this because what is demonstrated, by the by, is some real teaching and learning taking place. In fact the mayor comes by and peeks into the classroom and is delighted to see that the substitute teacher knows how to teach math!

This sequence of events is very moving and is at the heart of the film. Any teacher anywhere in the world will recognize how brilliantly this is done. The kids become so eager to learn that they learn effortlessly, which is the way it is supposed to be. Furthermore, one of the phenomena of the profession is exemplified: that of the real teacher learning more (partly because she is older) than the students from the lessons they encounter.

Now, it is true that director Zhang Yimou does not show us the real poverty that exists in China nor does he point to the horrid dangers encountered by children who go to the city to work. Neither the little boy nor Teacher Wei is preyed upon in the manner we might fear. Recapitulations of the baser instincts of human beings are not part of Zhang Yimou's purpose here. This is in fact a movie that can be viewed by children, who will, I suspect, identify very strongly with the story. Zhang Yimou is talking to the child in all of us and he does it without preaching or through any didactic manipulation of adult verses child values. It is true he does manipulate our hearts to some degree, but with all the ugliness that one sees in the world today, perhaps he can be allowed this indulgence.

Although I would not say that this film is as good as Zhang Yimou's internationally celebrated films such as *Red Sorghum* (1987) (his first film) or *Raise the Red Lantern* (1991) (which I think is his best film) or *The Story of Qiu Ju* (1991) (which this film resembles to some extent), it is nonetheless a fine work of art exemplifying Zhang

Yimou's beautiful and graceful style and his deep love for his characters and their struggles. And as always his work rises above and exists in a place outside of political propaganda as does the work of all great artists.

Perhaps more than anything else, however, one should see this movie to delight in the unselfconscious, natural, and utterly convincing "amateur" performance by Wei Minzhi as a most determined and brave little girl. She will win your heart.

I've seen this and I give it____stars.
I want to see it___. I'll pass___.
The review was worth reading___. Not___.

Red Sorghum *(Hong gao liang)* (1987) 8

Barbaric and beautiful

Although I don't think this is quite as good as some of the other films that master Chinese film maker Zhang Yimou has made—e.g., *Raise the Red Lantern* (1991); *The Story of Qiu Ju* (1991); *Ju Duo* (1990)—*Red Sorghum* is nonetheless an outstanding film strikingly presented visually and thematically.

Gong Li stars as the betrothed of an old leprous wine maker. The film opens with her being carried in a covered sedan chair to the consummation of her wedding by a rowdy crew from the sorghum winery. It is the 1930s or a little before. They joust her about according to tradition and sing a most scary song about how horrible her life is going to be married to the leprous old man. Through a break in the sedan's enclosure as she sits alone in fear and dread she catches sight of Jiang Wen, a burly, naturalistic man with a piercing countenance. A little later after a bit of unsuccessful highway robbery during which she is released from her confinement, they exchange meaningful glances. The young man doing the voice-over identifies them as his Grandmother and Grandfather. (Obviously the leprous old man is going to miss out!)

Zhang Yimou's technique here, as in all of his films that I have seen, is to tell a story as simply as possible from a strong moral viewpoint with as little dialogue as possible and to rely on sumptuous sets, intense, highly focused camera work, veracious acting by a carefully directed cast, and of course to feature the great beauty of his star, the incomparable and mesmerizing Gong Li. If you haven't seen her, *Red Sorghum* is a good place to start. Jiang Wen is also very good and brings both a comedic quality to the screen as well as an invigorating vitality. His courageous and sometimes boorish behavior seems exactly right.

I should warn the viewer that this film contains striking violence and would be rated R in the United States for that and for showing a little boy always naked and for the "watering" of the wine by Jiang Wen and the boy.

Indeed the film is a little crude at times and represents a view of pre-communist China and its culture that the present rulers find agreeable. The depiction of the barbarity and cruelty of the Japanese soldiers is accurate from what I know, but I must say that this film would never have seen the light of day had communist soldiers been depicted in such a manner.

Nonetheless the treatment is appropriate since *Red Sorghum* is a masculine, lusty film suggesting the influence of Akira Kurosawa with perhaps a bit of Clint Eastwood blended in. There are bandits and tests of manhood. The men get drunk and behave badly. Masculine sexual energy is glorified, especially in the scene where Jiang Wen carries Gong Li off to bed, holding her like a barrel under his arm, feet forward, after having "watered" her wine as though to mark his territory. The camera trailing them shows her reach up and put her arms around his neck and shoulder as much in sexual embrace as in balance.

Obviously this is Zhang Yimou before he became completely enamored of the feminist viewpoint; yet somehow, although Gong Li is allowed to fall in love with her rapist (something not possible in contemporary American cinema), Zhang Yimou manages to depict her in a light that celebrates her strength as a woman. One can see here the germination of the full blown feminism that Zhang Yimou would later develop in the aforementioned *Raise the Red Lantern*, *Ju Dou* and *Qiu Ju*.

As usual in Zhang Yimou's films not only are the sets gorgeous but the accompanying accouterments—the pottery, the costumes, the lush verdure of the sorghum fields, even the walls and interiors of the meat house restaurant/bar and Gong Li's bedroom—are feasts for the eyes, somehow looming before cinematographer Gu Changwei's camera more vividly than reality.

There are some indications here however that Zhang Yimou had not yet completely mastered his art, and indeed was working under the constraint of a limited budget. For example there was no opening in the sedan through which Gong Li could see Jiang Wen, and there shouldn't have been one (a peephole maybe). The pouring of the wine (into presumably empty bowls that obviously already contained wine) by Jiang Wen needed more practice. In his later films Zhang Yimou would reshoot such scenes to make them consistent with the audience's perception. Additionally, Gong Li's character was not sufficiently developed early on for us to appreciate her confident governance of the winery she had inherited. "Uncle" Luohan's apparently jealous departure from the winery and his implied relationship with and loyalty to Gong Li were also underdeveloped.

However these are minor points: in what really matters in film making—telling a story and engaging the audience in the significance and the experience of the tale—in these things Zhang Yimou not only excelled, but gave

promise of his extraordinary talent that would be realized in the films to come. See this by all means, but don't miss his *Raise the Red Lantern*, in my opinion one of the greatest films ever made.

I've seen this and I give it___stars.
I want to see it___. I'll pass___.
The review was worth reading___. Not___.

The Road Home (*Wo de fu qin mu qin*) (1999) 9

A touching and compelling love story

This is not as opulently beautiful as some of Zhang Yimou's films but the story is compelling and wonderfully told with deep affection for the characters. It's a love story beginning in the present with the death of a beloved village school teacher whose widow demands that he be honored by having his body carried—not driven—from where he died to his home in the small mountain village where he taught for over 40 years. The expense seems extravagant and where will the pallbearers come from? Most of the young people have left the village for the cities.

Returning for the funeral is the dead teacher's son. He realizes how important this ancient tradition of actually, physically carrying the body home, and so he goes about making that happen for his illiterate mother who is now all alone.

The real focus of the movie however is the extraordinarily beautiful face of the then 19-year-old Ziyi Zhang (*Crouching Tiger, Hidden Dragon* 2000; *Memoirs of a Geisha* 2005) who plays Zhao Di, the mother as a young woman. We are flashed back to the teacher's arrival in the village and to the young Zhao Di doing everything in the exuberant way of first love that she can to catch his eye. Again and again Zhang has his camera focused tightly on Ziyi Zhang's face as she experiences love at virtual first sight and goes through all the emotions of love's labors. Pointedly Zhang Yimou shows only her face. Her body is covered in the padded winter clothes of the Chinese north.

In this focus on the skill, charisma and beauty of Ziyi Zhang one sees perhaps the influence of some Western directors like Ingmar Bergman, Krzysztof Kieslowski and Roget Vidam who made movies in homage to the beauty of their young stars, Bergman with Bibi Andersson and Liv Ullmann, Kieslowski with Juliette Binoche and Irene Jacob, and Vadim with Bridget Bardot and Jane Fonda.

As always in the films of Zhang Yimou one sees in the background or off to a side a gentle but penetrating subtext on the effect that communism has had on Chinese society. Here he gives not criticism but guidance as he carefully insists that the traditional ways have value and should not be completely shoved aside.

I've seen this and I give it____stars.
I want to see it___. I'll pass___.
The review was worth reading___. Not___.

Shanghai Triad (*Yao a yao yao dao waipo qiao*)

(1995) 10
Gangster politics in gorgeous color

This could be an American gangster movie except that it is so beautiful. Well, that and the fact that it takes place in Shanghai in the 1930s. Gong Li plays Xiao Jingbao ("Bijou") the moll, a self-centered, vain, mean, slutty songstress kept by the "Boss" (Baotian Li) of Shanghai's underworld. As usual with director Zhang Yimou every set is gorgeous and artfully planned, the story compelling, and the human psychology veracious.

We see the events through the eyes of Shuisheng (Wang Xiaoxiao) a 14-year-old boy from the country who, because he is a member of the trusted Tang family, is brought to the city to be a servant to Bijou. She treats him and everybody else like dirt while she plays the Boss for a fool. We can guess that her comeuppance will be severe. Oh, but HOW severe? In this Zhang Yimou goes beyond what one has seen in American gangster movies and gives us something from Machiavelli and Genghis Kahn.

The film is a little slow in parts and Gong Li plays her role so well that she is most disagreeable—that is, until what I might call the "turn." This occurs when she is forced to go with the Boss to the country after a rival has attempted to kill him. Bijou is bored. There is nothing for her to do so she goes to the house of a country widow named Cuihua (Baoying Jiang) with a nine-year-old daughter Ah Jiao (Yang Qianquan) to lord it over her and to amuse herself with these country bumpkins. But the surprise is that in the process she is returned to her childhood when she herself was a country bumpkin. Zhang Yimou plays this part of the film masterfully as we slowly realize that Bijou is jealous of Cuihua and her poor but idyllic life. But that is something she can never admit to herself as she spies on Cuihua with her lover. One almost gets the sense that Bijou would like to be in Cuihua's place with that crude country lover.

At one point Bijou makes Cuihua loan her some of her peasant clothes and then takes delight in wearing them. We can see that Bijou is in denial about how much of a slave to the master she really is and how unsatisfying is the life of a kept woman regardless of how well kept. She realizes that her life is empty. And now we see a certain generosity of spirit: she gives the boy some silver coins; she tells the boss to spare the woman, but it is too late. Because you talked to her she knows too much, he says. He adds, you see, it is your fault again.

This film sits well with the current communist government of China despite or perhaps partly because the Boss with his small round eyeglasses looks a little like a Chinese Trotsky. But more importantly Zhang Yimou's depiction of the criminal decadence of China in the 30s before the rise of communism is exactly what Maoists like to see. Communism freed the Chinese from all that is perhaps the idea.

This is not the only film of Zhang Yimou's to play to communist sensibilities. His *Raise the Red Lantern* (1991) also shows in a different way the moral corruption of what might be called the ancient regime. But Zhang Yimou can be forgiven for playing to the powers that be because he does it with subtle irony and for a purpose, the purpose being to give himself the celebrity and an international reputation so that he is able to make films that might in some way criticize the communist state while he maintains a position of loyalty to that state. Working from within, it might be said. We see this in his *To Live* (*Huozhe*) from 1994 in which the hardships under communism are not euphemized. To be more exact it might be said that Zhang Yimou sees the excesses of Mao's regime but realizes that Mao was a stage through which China had to pass; and at any rate, who would want to go back to the time of the capitalist gangsters?

The airy, white tops of the reeds wave in the breeze. The colors are straw and the cottage on the island is neat and holds out against the rain. Inside Cuihua cooks and weaves a basket. She is content. Bijou, in her red dress and her red lips, wearing her jewelry and her superior manner, is not. She recalls the mulberry trees of her childhood and how she would climb the trees and eat the tree-ripened fruit. All the riches in the world cannot bring back those days, nor can she return to them.

She would like to take nine-year-old Ah Jiao with her back to Shanghai. Ironically Ah Jiao in her innocence wants to be like "Miss," which is Bijou's "title." Ironically, however, it is the Boss who takes the little girl back so that she can grow into the next Bijou.

The ending of the film is as brutal as anything you might expect to see, and yet there is a kind of poetic justice in what happens. In part. Zhang Yimou is always about politics, even though the politics are sometimes "just" domestic politics, as in *Raise the Red Lantern*. But he does the politics in a way that leaves no doubt: justice or what comes to pass is shaped by those who hold the power, whether it is the power of the state, or the power of the gangster boss, or the power of the master of the house, not by those who do not hold power. And that is the trenchant reality behind the great beauty of any Zhang Yimou film.

I've seen this and I give it____stars.
I want to see it___. I'll pass___.
The review was worth reading___. Not___.

Shower (*Xizao*) (1999) 9

A little corny but wonderful all the same

This delighted audiences at a number of film festivals, and it is not hard to see why. Director Yang Zhang, with the help of some very nice work by the three principle actors, Xu Zhu as the father, Master Liu; Quanxin Pu as the elder son, Da Ming; and especially Wu Jiang as the irrepressible and lovable younger son, Er Ming, spins a tale that will warm the coldest heart.

The film starts with a man taking a shower in an automated booth in the middle of Beijing. He puts some money in a slot, opens the door, takes off his clothes and puts some of them on a conveyer belt to be cleaned, steps into the shower and gets cleaned with brushes and squirts of water and soap as though he's a car at the car wash. This is the future symbolically speaking, and the old bathhouse we will see in the next scene is the past. Agrarian China is giving way to industrial China.

Pollution? Cultural Revolution hang-over? Industrialization blues? No way. What we have here is a celebration of people and their kindness and love for one another, a celebration of goodness in the hearts of men. Yet I wonder how the Chinese government views this film. On the one hand, it clearly presents a pleasant view of China and its people. It is stringently nonpolitical without criticism of the present regime expressed or implied. Yet there is the slightest sense that the good old ways are going to be replaced by something that may not be as good. I think Yang Zhang had the wisdom to just let that be as it may. Tell a story about old men at the bathhouse where they get back rubs and massages, where they tell tall tales and reminisce about the good old days, where they can relax and play Chinese chess and stage cricket fights, where the Master is a spry and wise old guy and his assistant is his son, who may be retarded or autistic, but who does his job with glee and an infectious spirit of fun and good will.

Enter back on the scene the older son, Da Ming, who is polished, well groomed and taciturn. He is uncomfortable with what he sees as the unsophisticated behavior of his father and brother. He represents modern China with his tie and his briefcase, his cell phone and his education. He has only returned because he thought his father was dying. When he sees that this is not true, he packs his bags and is set to return to his wife and his career. But then a crisis ensues and it is during this crisis that Da Ming sees the value of the natural, people-centered life that his father and his brother have been living.

And so Yang Zhang reconciles the old and the new, and does so in such a charming manner that I will not object, especially since his style is so neat and so carefully expressed. One of the nice things he does that I miss in most movies is the way he dovetails the subplots within the larger story so that they are resolved before the picture ends. The bathhouse regular who sings "O sole mio" in the bathhouse as the water showers down upon him, much to the delight of Er Ming, finds that he can't sing in public because of stage fright. Near the end of the film he loses his stage fright and sings thanks to some inspired help from Er Ming. And the bathhouse regular who is losing his wife because...well, he tells a tale to Master Liu before he confesses the real reason. But Liu understands and again before the movie is over, husband and wife are reconciled.

This kind of "happy ending" movie-making is unusual in today artistic and international films, or in almost any film directed at adults. Some happy endings are so contrived as to embarrass not only their contrivers but their audiences. And some are so blatantly condescending that the audience is offended. Here however the audience is delighted.

See this especially for the comedic performance by Wu Jiang whose warm effervescence overcomes any handicap his character may have.

I've seen this and I give it____stars.
I want to see it___. I'll pass___.
The review was worth reading___. Not___.

The Story of Qiu Ju (*Qiu Ju da guan si*) (1991) 9

A parable of modern China

This is a story about saving face and winning face, and what can happen if you carry things too far. Gong Li stars as Qiu Ju, a peasant woman with child whose husband is kicked in the groin by the local chief. She wants an apology. The chief of course will not apologize since he would then lose face. Both are stubborn and obstinate. Proud and determined, Qiu Ju steers her way through the bureaucracy from the village to the district to the city; but the thing she desires, an apology from the chief, eludes her. He cannot apologize because he has only sired daughters. He has license (he believes in his heart) because he was insulted by her husband who said he raised "only hens."

The Chinese locales, from village roads to big city avenues are presented with stunning clarity so that the color and the sense of life is vivid and compelling. Director Zhang Yimou forces us to see. From the opening shot of the mass of people in the city walking toward us (out of which emerges Qiu Ju) to the feast celebrating the child's first month of life near the end, we feel the humanity of the great mass of the Chinese people.

In a sense this is a gentle satire of the bureaucratic state that modern China has become. But Zhang Yimou emphasizes the bounty of China and not its poverty. There is a sense of abundance with the corn drying in the eaves, the sheets of dough being cut into noodles, the fat cows on the roads and the bright red chili drying in the sun. There is snow on the ground and the roads are unpaved, but there is an idyllic feeling of warmth emanating from the people. One gets the idea that fairness and tolerance will prevail.

In another sense, this is a parable about the price of things and how that differs from what is really of value. So often is price mentioned in the movie that I can tell you that a yuan at the time of the movie was worth about a dollar in its buying power. (Four and a half yuan for a "pound" of chili; five yuan as a fair price for a short cab ride; twenty yuan for a legal letter.) Getting justice in the strict sense is what Qiu Ju demands. Her affable husband would settle for a lot less. He is the wiser of the two. Notice how Qiu Ju is acutely sensitive to price. She bargains well and avoids most of the rip offs of the big city. But what is the value of being a member of the community? This is a lesson she needs to learn, and, as the movie ends, she does.

I've seen this and I give it____stars.
I want to see it___. I'll pass___.
The review was worth reading___. Not___.

To Live (*Huozhe*) (1994) 9

Glory to the revolution...

Not.

What I think Zhang Yimou's message here is that the will of the people "to live," as in the title, to survive and overcome obstacles is what defines the Chinese people. They ride the ox of communism as a boat rides a wave. They adapt.

Consider that tall and thin Fugui (played with consummate skill by You Ge) says that a chick will become a chicken when it grows up, and then a sheep and then an ox and then the Communist Party. But as the film ends he tells his grandson only that the chick will become a chicken and then a sheep and then an ox. He doesn't mention communism. In this way we know that the people have tamed the ox.

Zhang Yimou's film is an epic parable of life in China in the 20th century. It opens before the communist revolution with protagonist Fugui as a wayward son who is gambling the family fortune away. His wife, Jiazhen (Gong Li) pleads with him to stop, but he cannot. He is addicted to vice. Symbolically he represents the old regime. He loses everything, wife included and goes to live in the streets. After some time the revolutionary war begins and he and his friends find it convenient to switch sides and join the revolutionary army—he as an entertainer for the troops, a puppeteer. He and wife reunite and become loyal and even enthusiastic communists. He is lucky to have lost his fortune for now he is recognized as a hero of the revolution, while the man who won his family's house at dice is declared a counter-revolutionary and meets a bad end.

As in every Zhang Yimou film I have seen, everything is beautifully and exquisitely done. His work is characterized by an artist's sense of color and form, by an engaging simplicity in the telling, and by a subtle sense of what is going on politically, and especially by a deep and abiding sense of humanity. Here the transformation of Chinese society from feudalism to communism to the capitalist/communism hybrid that exists today is shown through the eyes and experiences of the people; and what is emphasized is the endurance and the will of the people to survive, adapt and finally to flourish regardless of who might be in power.

I would compare Zhang Yimou to the very greatest directors, say, to Stanley Kubrick, to Francis Ford Coppola, to Louis Malle, to Krzysztof Kieslowski in sheer artistic talent. Like Malle he is warm and honest about human beings and what they do without being maudlin or sentimental. Like Coppola he has an epic-maker's vision, and like the Coppola of the Godfather films, a strong sense of family. Like Kubrick he is creative and always aware of the needs of the audience, and like Kieslowski he is clever.

This is in some respects Zhang Yimou's finest achievement because of the way he tells the story of communism in China. I am reminded of the way Louis Malle tells the truth about human sexuality without inciting the censors. Here Zhang Yimou tells the truth about the communist experience in China, subtly demonstrating its cruelties and stupidities without, amazing enough, incurring the wrath of the authorities. (Some of his films have been banned in China, but I understand they are readily available nonetheless.) Here the kids are smiling and happy as they work in the steel mill. The accident that kills Fugui's son is seen as just that, an accident and not the fault of the "Great Leap Forward." The members of the educated class, who are ridiculed, beaten and banished (and worse) during the Cultural Revolution, accept their fate as their just deserts—the doctor who insists that it is better to wear the placard shaming him that is hung from around his neck than it is to take it off. The local official who has preached and practiced the communist line faithfully, who finds himself being labeled a capitalist, also accepts his fate as though in doing so he is furthering a cause larger than himself.

In a way Zhang Yimou's international celebrity and reputation as one of the world's greatest film makers protects him. In another sense his depictions of the sins and excesses of the old regime before communism are so well done and appreciated by all, that such an expression also protects him.

Nonetheless, I do not personally consider this Zhang Yimou's best film. I prefer the startling beauty of *Raise the Red Lantern* (1991) and *Red Sorghum* (1987) as well as the charming *Not One Less* (1999) or the simple but powerful, *The Story of Qiu Ju*. However, this is an outstanding film.

Notable in a supporting role is Wu Jiang as Wan Erxi the strong young man with the limp who marries the mute daughter. I have seen him in *Shower* (1999) in which his personal charisma and strength of character are shown more fully. He is the younger brother of Wan Jiang who starred in Zhang Yimou's first film, *Red Sor-* *ghum.* Of course Gong Li, one of the finest actresses of our time, who is often featured in Zhang Yimou's films, is outstanding as always.

I've seen this and I give it____stars.
I want to see it___. I'll pass___.
The review was worth reading___. Not___.

Italian Language Films

Big Deal on Madonna Street (1959) 9

Madcap petty criminal hijinks in postwar Italy

Tall, handsome Vittorio Gassman stars as Peppe, the womanizing glass-jawed palooka who, along with several keystone criminals, stumblebum their way to...not much. Also featured in this comedy by Italian film legend Mario Monicelli are Marcello Mastroianni and Claudia Cardinale, who would go on to fame and fortune, but here have only modest parts. Mastroianni, who would later star in *La Dolce Vita* (1960), *Il Bell'Antonio* (1960), *Divorzio all'italiana* (1961) and many others, plays Tiberio a photographer without a camera, whose wife is in jail, who has a constantly crying baby to take care of with one of his arms up in a sling with a board under it. Cardinale, who would go on to become one of Italy's most famous beauty bombshells, plays Carmelina, a young woman locked up by her brother in order to protect her honor until she marries.

Also featured are Carla Gravina (Nicoletta), a very pretty 17-year-old who went on to only a modest career, and the veteran Toto who plays the incompetent safecracker, Dante Cruciani. Notable is Renato Salvatori as Mario who wins Carmelina's heart, Memmo Carotenuto as Cosimo who fails at purse-snatching, and Carlo Pisacane as Capannelle who looks like an aged member of the Bowery Boys.

The story begins when Cosimo is caught trying to steal a car. In prison he learns of a nice sting that he can pull off if only he can get out of jail. So he tries to hire a scapegoat to confess to the crime so he can be freed. Finally Peppe, after getting knocked out in the first round of a prize fight, decides he needs the money. However when he goes to confess, the police see through the ruse and throw him in jail without releasing Cosimo. But Peppe does get out, and he and the motley assortment of would-be jewel thieves plot their crime amid hilarious missteps, pratfalls and mass confusion as they break into an apartment that they have the keys for to knock down a wall (which wall?) to gain access to a safe they probably can't crack. Will they succeed despite all the mishaps?

There is a sense of both recovery and poverty in post-World War II Italy in the backdrops and the asides and the circumstances of the characters that lend to this comedy a realistic edge. We see the petty thievery as an understandable and almost acceptable way of life, at least for the time being. Mario always buys or steals three identical things for his "mother" who turns out to be three women who raised him at the orphanage. Tiberio has to sell his camera and then steal one. Skinny Capannelle is always eating. And in the jail several men share one cigarette while they blow the smoke into a bottle to capture it so that others might get a little nicotine as well! (Sure, and I have some gum I can recycle.)

The Criterion Collection DVD that I viewed has excellent yellow subtitles, but some of the lines come so fast and with such comedic as well as denotative intent that it is easy to miss something. Knowing Italian would help!

See this for all the "bumbling criminal" movies that it both imitated and inspired, and for the fine work by the talented cast.

I've seen this and I give it____stars.
I want to see it___. I'll pass___.
The review was worth reading___. Not___.

Divorce Italian Style (1961) 10

Actually Sicilian style

Divorzio all'italiana is a richly textured satire of Sicilian macho Catholic life styles starring one of Italy's greatest actors, Marcello Mastroianni. He is a bit Chaplinesque in this tongue in cheek exploration of how to dump your wife and marry your 16-year-old cousin. His wide-eyed, dead pan expressions combined with vulnerability and suave, leading-man good looks made him the heartthrob of women for decades. He plays a bored baron stuck with a baroness (played fatuously by Daniela Rocca) that he cannot abide. It should be noted that today it IS possible to get a divorce in Italy, but at the time it was very difficult, perhaps easier to get an annulment, and so we have the premise of the plot.

Stefania Sandrelli, who became one of the great ladies of the Italian cinema, plays the cousin. She was only 15 when the film was shot but could easily pass for, say, 18. She is sensual, sweet and a bit naughty. In the final scene, famous for its fitting irony, the last thing we see are her feet. I won't tell you more, but the movie is almost worth seeing just for that final scene.

Rocca's Rosalia on the other hand is more syrupy than sweet and would qualify as clinging. She could smother a lumberjack, and although it is not polite to comment unfavorably on a lady's looks, I must note that she seemed to be having a bad facial hair day, everyday. Her impersonation of a country baroness nonetheless was unforgettable. I also liked 16-year-old Margherita Girelli as Sisini, the maid. Her coquettish ways helped to lend a French bedroom farce flavor to the film.

But what really makes this one of the great monuments of the Italian cinema is the witty and delightful script by Ennio De Concini (it won an Academy Award in 1962) and the detailed, textured direction by Pietro Germi. The picture that Germi paints of life in a small Sicilian (or southern Italian, for that matter) village is picturesque, much imitated, and indelible. The crowded ornate clutter of the old estate, the sun-drenched streets and the monolithic stone and mason churches haunt our memory. True, the film starts a bit slowly and drags (at least for modern audiences) a bit at times, but don't make the mistake of giving up on this. The latter half of the film is wonderful. And remember, if you had to go to film school, Divorce Italian Style would be on the syllabus.

So see this for Mastroianni of course but also because no film education would be complete without having seen Divorzio all'italiana.

The Criterion Collection DVD includes a second disc with a documentary on Germi's career, an interview with Ennio De Concini, and screen-test footage of Stefania Sandrelli and Daniela Rocca that I just had to see. There is also a booklet with reviews of the film from Stuart Klawans, Andrew Sarris, and Martin Scorsese. Scorsese's review is adoring and nostalgic since he is from Sicily and since the film had made such a lasting impression on him as a 19-year-old. For him the film was not so much a comedy as a true reflection of a life he and his family had known. He writes, "Every detail in *Divorce Italian Style* is so truthful and right that all Germi had to do was heighten everything a bit to make it funny."

I've seen this and I give it____stars.
I want to see it___. I'll pass___.
The review was worth reading___. Not___.

Don't Move (*Non ti muovere*) (2004) 9

Brilliant and haunting performance by Penélope Cruz

Timoteo (Sergio Castellitto, who also directed) plays a surgeon whose car breaks down in a working class neighborhood of a great Italian city. Italia (Penélope Cruz) is a denizen of this part of town who lets Timoteo use her phone. She works as a cleaner of hotel rooms. She is crude, a little desperate, uneducated and so passive that she more or less allows Timoteo to rape her, a rape that she experiences without emotion, as something that society perhaps has taught her to accept as her due. Timoteo comes back a day or two later to apologize. He says he was drunk. He had drunk two vials of cold vodka while waiting for a mechanic to fix his car.

Italia sniffs at this privileged man who took advantage of her. There is nothing she can do. Her word against his. Just move on and forget it. But part of her is wondering if there is more to his interest than the quick gratification of lust.

He takes her again, this time though, it is clear that his passion is especially for her. It is something about her that turns him into a sexual beast, and not just the fact that she is a woman who cannot complain. It is interesting to note that when he returns and catches her carrying groceries home, she looks at him with some inquiry on her face, nothing more, no anger, no recriminations, no judgments. When he apologizes and says he was drunk, she swiftly picks up her groceries and turns away. She was looking for something deeper from him. She wants the reason that he raped her to be NOT that he was drunk but that he was so drawn to her that he couldn't help himself.

It is during the third scene a few days later that she accepts his passion for her and finds some of her own. And it is after this third scene as she serves him spaghetti that he realizes that he loves her. The moment comes when he reaches for the bottle of beer on the table at the same time she reaches to pour it for him. They accidentally tip the bottle over, spilling the beer onto the table and floor, and their hands meet. He holds her index finger in his hand for a moment, and it is at that moment that he knows he loves her. And she sees it in his eyes.

All of this is shown in flashback as Timoteo awaits the fate of his daughter who has suffered a massive head injury from a motorcycle accident and lies in a coma in his hospital. His meeting with Italia took place some fifteen years previously, or I should say it was a relatively brief but ultra passionate love affair that ended fifteen years in the past at the time his daughter, from the womb of his wife, Elsa (Claudia Gerini), was born. It was his passion for Italia that spilled over into Elsa that brought about the conception. Ironically—and this is part of the terrible tragedy of this story—Italia too becomes pregnant at nearly the same time. What Timoteo does not realize until it is too late is the depth of feeling that Italia comes to have for him. This is a love affair that, to quote the words of LA *Times* film critic Kevin Thomas, "makes most of today's screen romances seem undernourished by comparison."

Penélope Cruz's performance is nothing short of spectacular. I invite the reader to view the special feature on the DVD in which she discusses her character with Castellitto. Here we can see the incredible passion and attention to detail that Cruz brings to her performance, and also that of Castellitto, who is outstanding both as an actor and a director. Cruz, whose first language is

Spanish, must become this noble wretch of desperate woman who must speak Italian with a street accent and behave in way that belies her great beauty and the fine finish of her own character. It is a shame that most Americans only know Cruz from some television commercials and being Tom Cruise's ex. Penélope Cruz is without question—and she proves it in this deeply moving performance—to be one of the finest actresses working today.

A couple of other points. Elsa knows of course that her husband had fallen in love with someone else. She can sense it in the new passion he brings to making love to her. She can deduce it in his absences from her and from the change in his manner. But she never says a word. That is interesting. Perhaps she knows it will pass. And it does, but not before Timoteo performs a "marriage ceremony" at a hotel restaurant near the place of Italia's birth with Italia, and with the "reheated soup" and the wine and cheese as witnesses, and not before he fantasizes aloud with her of leaving his wife and newborn child and going to some far off place with her alone. Only tragedy, it would appear, prevents his leaving Elsa for the love of his life.

But time does heal this wound to their marriage, as Timoteo prays that time will heal his daughter. And the passion of yesteryear perhaps is the more glorious because, like a portrait, it does not age. And perhaps there is some solace in knowing that the love that one finds in a wife and a life's companion is different than that found in a fiery mania of long ago, but taken in total, no less deeply felt.

I've seen this and I give it____stars.
I want to see it___. I'll pass___.
The review was worth reading___. Not___.

Facing Windows (2003) 10

A bittersweet love affair in modern Italy

This is the best film I've seen in perhaps six months or more. The direction by Turkish/Italian director Ferzen Ozpetek is consistently interesting, intriguing, beguiling and ultimately satisfying both emotionally and intellectually. The film is beautifully cut, and the acting, particularly by the fascinating Giovanna Mezzogiorno who plays the young mother of two whose name is also Giovanna, is first rate.

The story begins in a bakery during World War II when Davide Veroli (Massimo Girotti) is a baker's apprentice. We see him among the great earthen ovens and the warm loaves as he makes what appears to be a sprint out of the cave-like establishment. But he is pounced upon by the baker. They wrestle, a knife is grabbed and apparently the baker falls and there is blood on Davide's hands as he runs out into the streets.

Cut to modern times as Giovanna and her working-class husband, Filippo (Filippo Nigro) are crossing a bridge in the city. They meet an old man who seems lost and disoriented. He can't remember his name and he has no identification. Filippo takes pity on him and against his wife's wishes takes him home with them to their apartment. We know because of the man's age that the mystery of who he is has something to do with the men in the bakery scene from World War II.

But his story is only tangential to the central story of the film which is about Giovanna's brief affair with the man next door, Lorenzo (Raoul Bova), whose apartment window faces hers. This is a love story, a bitter-sweet one—which all great love stories should be in some sense, since life itself is bittersweet. It is framed by, and contrasted with, another love story, that involving the older man from many years ago.

The tension in the film revolves around the resolution of the affair between the married Giovanna and the handsome man who will soon be leaving the city. Will she abandon her marriage and her family for the excitement of a new man? Because the police can find out nothing about the old man, and because Giovanna's heart softens toward him, and because he is an elegant man of refinement, especially in the pastry arts—Giovanna's dream is to be a pastry chef—the man is allowed to stay for a while and the two are drawn together into friendship, the old man and the young woman.

That's enough of the plot—the development, the denouement, and the resolution of which are beautifully realized in both an artistic and an emotional sense. Instead let me say that the feel of modern Italy with its racial tensions and its old world versus new world differences are nicely expressed as the past makes itself felt on the present. The dialogue is wonderfully expressive and gives us the sense of authenticity and the kind of realistic effect seen only in the very best films. This is the first film directed by Ozpetek that I have seen, but it won't be the last.

But see this for Giovanna Mezzogiorno whose beautiful and expressive eyes and natural demeanor will hold you to the screen.

I've seen this and I give it____stars.
I want to see it___. I'll pass___.
The review was worth reading___. Not___.

The Garden of the Finzi-Continis (1971) 9

Imperfect, but unforgettable

In this haunting work by Vittoria De Sica an aristocratic Italian-Jewish family, the Finzi-Continis, serve as a symbol of European civilization in the hands of the brown shirts on the eve of World War II. Seeing it again after thirty years I find myself saddened almost as much by the story of a stillborn, unrequited love as I am by the horror of the cattle cars to come.

Dominique Sanda with her large, soft eyes is mesmerizing as the beautiful, enigmatic, but icy Micol Finzi-Contini. Giorgio (Lino Capolicchio) is her childhood friend, a boy from a middle-class Jewish family, now grown up. He's in love with her, but her feelings for him are that of a sister. He is confused by her warmth, and then as he tries to get close, her cool rejection.

It has often been expressed metaphorically that Europe in the thirties was raped by fascism. However in this extremely disturbing film, De Sica is saying that it wasn't a rape, that the aristocracy of Europe (here represented by the Finzi-Continis of Ferrara, and in particular by the young and beautiful Micol) was a willing, even an eager, participant in the bestial conjoining.

The Garden of the Finzi-Continis is far from perfect; some would say it is also far from De Sica's best work. Certainly it comes after his prime. The editing is a little too severe in places, while some of the scenes are too loosely focused. Nonetheless this is an enormously powerful film that finds its climax in one of the most disturbing scenes in all of cinema. There is little point in discussing this film without looking at this scene. Consequently, for those of you who have not seen the film and do not want to risk having it spoiled for you, you should stop reading now and come back afterwards.

Everything in the movie works toward setting up the cabana scene. We see the dog several times, hinting at a crude, animalistic side to Micol. And there is the wall that separates the Finzi-Contini's garden of civilization from the brown shirts in the streets, a wall that also separates the rich from other people, particularly from the middle class who support the fascists (as we are told in the opening scene). We see Micol leading Giorgio by the hand about the estate, but always when he tries to caress her, she pulls away. Finally she explains to him why she doesn't love him. She says, "lovers want to overwhelm each other...[but]...we are as alike as two drops of water...how could we overwhelm and want to tear each other...it would be like making love with a brother..." But hearing these words is not enough. Giorgio goes to the wall one last time, sees a red bicycle there (red and black were the colors of the Nazi party) and knows that Micol is with someone else. He climbs the wall and finds the dog outside the cabana so that he knows she is within. In the opening scene she referred to the cabana with the German "Hütte," adding that now "we'll all have to learn German." What he sees when he looks through the window fills him with a kind of stupefying horror, as it does us. Not a word is spoken. He sees her, he sees who she is with and what the circumstances are. She sees him, turns on the light so that there can be no mistake and they stare wordlessly at one another. She projects not shame, but a sense of "This is who I

am. I would say I'm sorry, but it wouldn't change anything. This is what I'm drawn to."

What is expressed in this essentially symbolic scene, acted out in sexual terms, is what happened to Europe. Micol is at once the love he wanted so much, deflowered by an anonymous, but clearly fascist man, and she is also the aristocracy of Europe, polluted by fascism.

I wonder if it is just a coincidence that the famous poem by Robert Browning, "My Last Duchess," is also set in Ferrara. In that poem the narrator reveals himself through the unfeeling brutality of his speech and actions to be, although an aristocrat, an incipient fascist. I also wonder if De Sica is saying that the Jews in some sense contributed to the horror that befell them, and by extension, all of humanity. We see this expressed in the person of Giorgio's father who continually insists that it's not that bad yet, as step by step they lose their status as citizens, a prelude to the dehumanization that is the precursor of genocide. Certainly the closing scenes in which the Jews of Italy are seen to be compliant as they are led to the slaughter suggests as much. I know that the central feeling expressed by Jews after the war and especially in Israel was simply, never again. Nevertheless, there is a certain sense of the inevitable about this film that I find particularly disturbing. Passivity in sexual terms, a "giving in" to one's nature is one thing. A passivity in political terms is quite another, and yet it is part of the power of this film to show us how they are related in our psyches.

I've seen this___ and I give it___stars.
I want to see it___. I'll pass___.
The review was worth reading___. Not___.

Umberto D. (1952) 10

A masterpiece of neorealism

Having seen the film I read a bit about it. The Criterion Collection provides a booklet with an excellent review by Stuart Klawans and a bit of an interview with director Vittorio De Sica. What I learned was the Umberto D. was a big flop at the box office in Italy primarily because the Italian government didn't like the film because they thought it was insulting since it made Italy seem so unfeeling, poverty-stricken, and mercantile. I was struck by this because, yes, poor Umberto and his dog are pretty much set out to pasture without so much as some grass and a bone. But to say that such a film reflects upon an entire people is perhaps to protest too much.

Italy was devastated by the failure of fascism and was just beginning to recover from the war when this film was made, and nobody wanted any downers. Vittorio De Sica's film is perhaps not so much of a downer as the early critics thought. The ending is ambiguous and while not hopeful for Umberto is somewhat inspiring in the youthfulness of his dog and in the sweet humanity of the maid Maria who shoulders her situation with alacrity while showing affection and kindness toward a bitter old man.

I was not moved to tears as some have been in watching this. Umberto's troubles seem to me (from my privileged vantage point in time and place) somewhat of his own doing. I imagined that he supported the fascists, and I saw his poverty in his old age as a direct result of that support. Barring that, I imagined that he had planned poorly for his old age, and at any rate his values, represented by his always wearing a suit and tie and hat and his inability to beg or to take some kind of job, disqualified him for tears. Of course I was unfair.

Even so my sympathy was with him, and I respected the decision he finally makes—although whether he will be able to carry it out is unclear. I respect his dignity, and identify with him in his struggle with the Teutonic and utterly bourgeois landlord who holds sway over him, played with a deliberately heavy presence by Lina Gennari, whom De Sica photographs up close and low to her large body to emphasize her strength and to make it clear to us that Umberto has no chance in his struggle with her.

Both Carlo Battisti who played Umberto and Maria Pia Casilio who played Maria, were considered amateur actors, very much in keeping with the neorealistic school of film; yet for me they were both excellent and natural, whereas Gennari, who was a professional, seemed artificial. But that impression is an artifact of the neorealist school (which they say died with this film). The very fact of no flourishes and no modeling and certainly no flights of creativity by the actors, it was believed, helped to make the film realistic, about real people in real situations.

Today of course this is a celebrated film, considered one of De Sica's best. He himself believed from the very beginning that it was one of his best even though he knew it would be hard-pressed to make any money for its producers.

A word about the dog (the other professional actor in the film). Flike is extraordinarily well-trained, so much so he becomes part of the psychology of the film and is at the very heart of the denouement. The scene near the end where Umberto dips under the rail guard as the train approaches, Flike held close to his chest—and the scene after—is of one of the great sequences in cinema, and, ironically, as in a commercial film, stars a dog! Umberto D. is in fact one of the greatest dog films ever made. All dog lovers will appreciate the love that Umberto feels for his dog and the love that is returned AND the gutty realism that the dog displays.

The DVD includes a documentary about De Sica that I didn't have a chance to view, excellent subtitles, and a video interview with Maria Pia Casilio.

I would almost say, see this for the dog, but do see this for Vittorio De Sica, one of cinema's greats, here at his best, and for Cesare Zavattini who wrote the compelling script.

I've seen this and I give it____stars.
I want to see it___. I'll pass___.
The review was worth reading___. Not___.

The Icicle Thief (1989) 7

Original and misinterpreted

This offbeat Italian comedy uses the familiar black and white/color dichotomy to indicate different worlds, a technique always in danger of being overdone. Last time I saw it was in *Pleasantville* (1998) where it was so cloying it annoyed; the first time magically in *The Wizard of Oz* (1939). It was even done (to good effect) in Spielberg's *Schindler's List* (1993). Here the "film" is in black and white (as it's being shown on TV) and the commercials are in color. The characters bizarrely go from one "world" to the other while somewhere in between is the "real" world of TV viewers. Because the world of TV commercials is the more fantastic, I think the technique works well here.

Maurizio Nichetti, who might (and might not) remind you of Roberto Benigni, stars as Anotonio Piermattei, the icicle thief, the protagonist of the movie within a movie, which is a Bicycle Thief-like tragic film that the TV people manage to mangle into a TV-like romantic comedy. (If you're wondering how one can be an icicle thief, keep wondering. I'll never tell.) Nichetti also plays the auteur of the film being shown on TV who is invited to be interviewed but never gets to speak partly because the film critic who is to do the interview thinks they are viewing a different film.

The title notwithstanding, this is not a satire or a "spoof" of Vittorio De Sica's internationally acclaimed *The Bicycle Thief* (1948), although De Sica himself might be seen as being lightly satirized. Nichetti's *The Icicle Thief* is more like an identification as it attempts to stand with the art film solidly against commercialism. However any similarity between the film within a film here and De Sica's masterpiece is sycophantic. This is not to say that *The Icicle Thief* does not have its moments and its charm. It does.

Caterina Sylos Labini who plays Maria, Antonio Piermattei's singing wife, is charming as the archetypical Italian femme fatale, a dark, lusty, earthy woman who can cry and laugh at the drop of a hat. She is contrasted with Heidi Komarck, a colorized blonde model in a butch haircut who does TV commercials. Komarck looks like a member of the Swedish ski team draped in a lingerie outfit that leaves little to the imagination while speaking only American English. My favorite part of the film was the cute shtick with Maria's happy one-year-old daughter who crawls continually into mischief (grabbing a knife by the blade, putting an electric wire in her mouth, etc.) but somehow never has to shed a tear.

That this is a satire and spoof of TV (and not De Sica's *Bicycle Thief* or old-time neo-realism itself) is immediately apparent when the TV film critic has to ask the name of the film he is critiquing. On TV the only things that really matter are the commercials. So, to the extent that a "Big Big" candy bar jingle and a laundry detergent superhero triumph over a black and white neo-realistic film, we can see that triumph as a satire of television and its middle-brow audience.

I've seen this and I give it____stars.
I want to see it___. I'll pass___.
The review was worth reading___. Not___.

Life Is Beautiful *(La Vita e Bella)* (1997) 9

Remember the Theater of the Absurd?

Roberto Benigni's celebrated affirmation of the human spirit owes a little to "Rhinoceros," Ionesco's absurdist play from the Sixties. There's the same attempt to reduce the worse horror in human history to the absurd. Perhaps this is a way of comprehending something monstrous beyond comprehension. Benigni was criticized in some circles for trivializing the Holocaust, but that is not what he did. He sought to rise above it. I don't know whether he or Ionesco were really successful. On the other hand has anybody—any religion, philosophy or great artist—ever solved the problem of evil in this world?

There's something of Charlie Chaplin in Benigni's irrepressible hero, and in the camera work look for the influence of Orson Wells in light and shadow. The strange splashes of color on such places as the concentration camps walls reminded me curiously of Jacque Demy's *Umbrellas of Cherbourg* (1963), a wondrous French operetta from the Sixties (starring Catherine Deneuve, music by Michel Legrand).

La Vita e Bella drags a little at times and we miss a lot of Benigni's mugging as our eyes chase after the subtitles, but the central idea, that with our attitudes we create the world, and that life can be beautiful even in the midst of tragedy, is uplifting, if hard to believe.

I've seen this and I give it____stars.
I want to see it___. I'll pass___.
The review was worth reading___. Not___.

The Star Maker *(L'uomo delle stelle)* (1995) 9

Beautiful, original—an engaging work of art

Joe Morelli (Sergio Castellitto) is a flimflam man who is driving around the rural villages of Sicily shortly after World War II selling potential stardom for fifteen hundred lira. He has a motion picture camera and loudspeaker on his truck. As he drives through the villages he broadcasts to the people that he is from the film industry of Roma and he is giving screen tests in order to discover natural talent.

He sets up his truck and tent typically in the town square. His technique is to tell everyone that they have a wonderful face, hidden talent, that they are naturals and diamonds in the rough. He hands out fliers with some dialogue from *Gone with the Wind* on them that they should practice reading before appearing before his camera. He has discovered that people will fall for his flattery and pay him for the fake screen tests.

As we watch the film we discover that people will put their hearts and souls into the experience of appearing before his camera. They don't just read the lines from *Gone with the Wind*. They tell their life stories in miniature. They bare their hearts and souls to the flimflam man in the hope that someone will hear and see their anguish, their pain, their experience. To Morelli, who has been to Hollywood and failed, this is just a way to make a lira. He has a gift for the hustle and is blind to the real emotion that he evokes.

A woman believes her teenaged daughter has the talent to make it in the movies. She begs Morelli to take her to Roma. She even has sex with him and promises to allow him to be her daughter's first lover. But Morelli moves on to the next town. He is stopped by the local police chief, but Morelli manages to flatter him into appearing before his camera and then applauds the chief's performance. Three highwaymen stop to rob Morelli. He is able to convince them that Roma longs for their raw talent. And so on, as he travels over the cobblestones and over the winding roads.

Finally he meets beautiful Beata (Tiziana Lodato) who is 15 or 18. She isn't sure. She works in the convent, bathing the sick and scrubbing the floors. She exposes herself to the local tax man to raise the 1500 lira needed for Morelli's screen test. She is strikingly beautiful from head to toe, and the tax man exclaims, "You are a statue!" when he sees her body. Morelli is reluctant to get involved with someone so young even though she throws herself at him.

What happens after this I will not say since it would spoil the film for those who have not seen it. But watch for the con man to get conned, among other things. Despite his villainy, there is a sense that Morelli is a man that we can identify with and understand. I think it is this quality that director Giuseppe Tornatore has developed in his character that carries the film, and Sergio Castellitto whom I saw recently in *Non ti muovere* (Don't Move) (2004) really becomes the part.

Tornatore, who made a splash with the critically acclaimed *Cinema Paradiso* (1988) wrote the original material here and worked on the script in addition to directing. While I thought *Cinema Paradiso* was an excellent film, I liked this one even more. Both are original works of art, but I found *L'uomo delle stelle* more engaging.

Particularly striking are the beautiful village scenes, the faces of the people, and the photography of the Sicilian countryside and ruins.

I've seen this and I give it____stars.
I want to see it___. I'll pass___.
The review was worth reading___. Not___.

V

German Language Films

As Far as My Feet Will Carry Me (*So weit die Füße tragen*) (2001) 10
Compelling adventure drama

This is a German language film based on the novel by the same name which was based on a true story about a German POW in the aftermath of WWII who escaped a Siberia work camp and made an amazing 8,000-mile trek home to Munich to be reunited with his family.

I haven't read the novel, but of course it was a novel and so much of it was made up. It doesn't matter however, since what counts in a movie is simply the movie itself. I am always a little put off when the blurbs for a film scream out: "Based on a true story!" So what? Sometimes that's significant and sometimes it isn't. In this case the fact that there actually existed a German POW who managed such an amazing escape is important. The exact details of what happened to him would be wonderful to have. But in lieu of that, we do have this wonderful movie.

Bernhard Bettermann stars as Clemens Forell, and he is perfect for the part. To survive such an epic adventure the person has to be strong of body and strong of will. Bettermann looks as though he could actually do something like this, except for the fact that he is so tall and pale I suspect he would stand out and be easily identified as a foreigner in those strange lands through which he trekked. Also a bit not so realistic is the Soviet camp commander who personally chases Forell all the way to the Iranian border (although that resulted in a nice ironic scene on the bridge at the border between Iran and what—I think—is Turkmenistan). In reality there were probably several Soviet officers who played that part. And I would also liked to have seen a little more about how he found enough to eat. And finally it is clear that the last parts of his journey were sped up a bit as though the filmmakers were in a hurry. But these are small quibbles.

I don't know if this "coloration" (as I will call it) was in the book, but what director Harvey Martins does is make the tall and "Aryan" Forell experience some of the same horrors that the Jews experienced. In the beginning he is in a cattle car and nearly starved to death as he is taken to the Siberian lead mines. He is in rags and nearly frozen and gets kicked around by sadistic soldiers. If you saw just this part of the movie you would swear it was about the Jews being sent to a concentration camp. In the camp after Forell is caught in an early escape attempt he is shown being beaten by his fellow soldiers, who of course, were punished because he tried to escape. This was exactly the sort of thing the Nazis did in the occupied countries during WWII—if a single German was killed, that killing would be revenged many times over. Later, one of the people who helped Forell is a Jew who lost relatives to the Nazis. Nonetheless he helps Forell, and in doing so demonstrates not only a superior morality, but the kind of courage that is rare. And why did he do it? Because that is the kind of person he is, and that is the kind of persons we all should be.

While Forell is a positive, even a heroic figure, and a nice change for Germans who have to endlessly read about and see Germans portrayed in a most negative way throughout their whole lives, the movie itself tends to be neutral politically.

The scenes of the snow and the forests and the various places that Forell travels through are nicely done. The ending is exquisite and brought me to tears.

I've seen this and I give it____stars.
I want to see it___. I'll pass___.
The review was worth reading___. Not___.

Das Boot (1981) 10

A strong candidate for the best war movie ever

Das Boot is a taut, realistic drama, exemplified by a careful plot that maintains and releases tension incrementally so that we are riveted to the screen, and the two and a half hours the film runs seems like half an hour. Director Wolfgang Petersen (lately the director of *The Perfect Storm* (2000)) persuades us to identify with the German sailors crammed into their *Unterseeboot* as the depth charges blast all around them. Strange, take away the spoken German and this could be an American submarine dodging those depth charges. In fact there is no German insignia on the U-boat, and you have to look hard to find a swastika anywhere in the movie. Clearly Petersen wanted to disassociate himself and his movie from the Nazis, who had ruined his Germany, and seek a more universal identification for his crew. The somewhat eerie effect on the American viewer is not only to make us see the human waste of war, but to lead us to realize that yes, it was horrible for the Germans.

Great movies surprise you. Something creative happens and your eyes widen and your attention is arrested. For me it begins here when the U-boat's captain, played with superb subtlety and characteristic charm by Jürgen Prochnow, talks against "our masters in Berlin" as his men steal nervous glances at one another. You know they're thinking, "The captain is talking *treason*." But suddenly we, the audience, realize that he knows he's going to die (*probably* going to die, I should say, since we are told in a blurb following the opening credits that of 40,000 Germans sailors sent out in U-boats, 30,000 did not return); and so he feels free to speak his mind. And then to put an exclamation point on it, he tells the young journalist on board to write it up for the propaganda minister and then, as an ironic stab at the "Hitler Youth" officer, he orders "It's a long way to Tipperary" to be played on the Victrola, while they all sing along in glorious English!

One of the amazing things about this movie is how the U-boat and the destroyers seem to take on emotionally-charged characteristics. When the destroyer appears in the periscope out of the fog and the spray, it seem like a monster about to descend. And the way the depth charges are flung at the U-boat made me feel how much the Allies hated them and wanted to destroy them like vermin. I felt sorry for the German sailors cowering in their little boat, being hated so much, because Petersen made us see that those men were no different than you and I.

This is not only one of the greatest war movies ever made, it compares favorably with the classic anti-war drama (also seen from a German POV), Erich Maria Remarque's *All Quiet on the Western Front* (1930) directed by Lewis Milestone. I suspect that Petersen was influenced by that movie and by some American films about World War II, in particular *Run Silent, Run Deep* (1958), Robert Wise's excellent submarine drama set in the Pacific starring Clark Gable and Burt Lancaster.

I've seen this and I give it____stars.
I want to see it___. I'll pass___.

The review was worth reading___. Not___.

Downfall (*Der Untergang*) (2004) 9

Fascinating and uncompromising look at the final days

It was agreeable to see Hitler reduced to a bent, defeated, raving madman, and there is no question that Bruno Ganz looked the part. The endearments he gave to the children and to his bunker mates contrasted horrifically with his plan for them and his "love" for the German people. In a sense the way the final days are presented in this film reminded me of what the victims of the Nazis suffered, and that was also apropos and agreeable. Still most people do not like to see human suffering even to those who may, by all that is right, have it coming; and so it was essentially a depressing experience to watch this film.

Alexandra Maria Lara, who played Hitler's last personal secretary, Traudl Junge, provided the only bright spot in this necessarily grim picture. She is a fine actress, but somehow she seemed too normal, too smart actually to be the sort of worshipful underling that she must have been. Incidentally, it is from the book by the real Traudl Junge, *Biz sur letzten Stunde*, and from Joachim Fest's *Der Untergang* that this movie was adapted. The fine screenplay was written by Bernd Eichinger. Junge appears at the beginning of the film from an interview in 2001, a year before her death, to say a few words and at the end where she explains that she is essentially not that naive young person she once was who should have looked further than the fuhrer's face to see what was really going on. But she was with Hitler for three years and knew his philosophy well. Truth is she was so pleased to be his secretary that she turned a deaf ear to the truth that was in front of her.

Of course she was hardly the only one. An entire nation was seduced and led down the path to genocide, humiliation, starvation and near-starvation, and ignominious defeat. One thing the film does to help us understand how this could have happened is to show the blind loyalty that even some of the highest ranking officers felt toward Hitler regardless of his bumbling, his stupidity and his blatant disregard for the feelings and lives of anyone who got in his way—his essential immorality. Some say there was something in the German character that accounts for this blind obedience to authority regardless of how corrupted and evil that authority might be. Maybe in a more pluralistic and multicultural society something like this could not happen. There might be something to that, but I doubt it. Too many monsters have grown in too many different soils and in so many different cultures, I am persuaded it could happen anywhere, but perhaps not as easily and as completely as it happened in Germany.

It is interesting that Oliver Hirshbiegel, who directed, did not show the Red Army atrocities as they stormed into

Berlin. I don't think he wanted to dilute the sense of the moral culpability of the German people.

I was also struck by Hitler's obsession with loyalty. This is how all dictators, warlords and, unfortunately, some respected heads of state operate: they demand unquestioned loyalty, and they ruthlessly eliminate anyone they suspect of anything but that unquestioned loyalty while rewarding the loyal. And so in such governments the head of state becomes surrounded by sycophants and toadies who tell him what he wants to hear and who live in fear of their own lives should they somehow be seen as disloyal. Indeed they sneak around trying to undermine others in other to protect themselves. They live in secrecy amid lies, intrigue and murder.

The film is long, 155 minutes, the bunker is dreary and most of the characters are sickies of the worse sort. We as an audience are reduced to those who see inside a cave, the floor covered with bat guano crawling with despicable creatures who feed off of one another. The stench is overwhelming. We watch transfixed for a while at the ugly, unsavory spectacle and then we turn away.

Can it happen again? Can it happen here? Let's hope not, but that freedom that the right assures us is not free requires more than loyalty. It requires vigilance and a willingness to speak out, the kind of vigilance that can see the danger when the government begins to deal almost exclusively in lies and misinformation, that invades other countries for dubious gain, deals in propaganda and points fingers at perceived enemies and promotes only those loyal to the leader instead of those most qualified.

(I said I would write this review without mentioning a certain personage, and I did, but the allusions are probably more than obvious.)

See this for veteran Swiss-German actor Bruno Ganz who gave a fine performance as Hitler. By theway there are some take off on his almost wildly spirited performance to be found on UTube with funny English "translations" of the German.

I've seen this and I give it____stars.
I want to see it___. I'll pass___.
The review was worth reading___. Not___.

Revanche (2008) 10

"What could go wrong?"

This is a carefully orchestrated German language film set in and around contemporary Vienna. It is about how the desires and needs of men and women differ at the most fundamental level. The action concerns what can go wrong when you try to rob a bank, even when you use an unloaded gun.

There is an old saying in the theater that if you show a gun in the first act, it had better go off in the third act. Here director Gotz Spielmann plays a variant on that old stage business. We see something splash into a pond as the opening credits roll. It is not clear what it is. The camera lingers as the concentric ripples spread out and then are done. Later on in the film we see the same scene from the point of view of the person who threw the object into the water. It is near the end of the film, in what in the theater would be the third act.

"Revanche" in German means "revenge." We all know how hard it is to forsake revenge when we have been hurt. We want to strike out at some target. But what do we do when we have no target or when the target is innocent? And to what extent is the desire for revenge a way of absolving ourselves from what has happened? Revenge is a standard, even hackneyed, movie theme. Action movies and thrillers often employ the psychology of revenge as both theme and plot device, as a way of keeping the audience emotionally involved. Here revenge is used in a different and ultimately redemptive way.

Early in the film the camera lingers on a street scene. We see a narrow alleyway like an urban street tunnel. The camera holds that shot so that we expect to see someone or something emerging from that alleyway. But it is only later that the scene is revisited, and much like the pond scene mentioned above we see the scene from the opposite angle, and what transpires contains the central event of the movie. This sense of seeing scenes from different angles—opposite angles actually—is echoed in the opposing perspectives of the two women and the two men.

There is, for example, the symmetry of how the two men work off the psychological tension that they feel. Robert (Andreas Lust), who is a cop who has accidentally shot and killed a young woman involved in a robbery, jogs. Alex (Johannes Krisch), who is the boyfriend of the dead woman, a woman he loves very much, puts his physical energy into chopping wood—viciously. For one it is the cardio and the legs; for the other it is the upper body.

And then there are the two women: Tamara (Irina Potapenko) who is the young woman now dead, who was a prostitute, and Susanne (Ursula Strauss) who is the cop's wife. Both are very physical as women, both aware of the power of their bodies, but more significantly both are aware of their primeval need to understand men, and their ability to do just that.

Susanne, who is thoroughly bourgeois, does something that is condemned by society in the same way that prostitution is condemned. Yet she acts out of clear intent without a hint of shame or the sense that she is doing something essentially wrong. The prostitute acts out her societal role with a shrug of her shoulders as to society's hypocritical morality. Thus both women are morally and humanly the same.

This is Spielmann's point, not to make moral judgments about the worth of either man or either woman. The prostitute is the moral equal of the cop's wife, and cop's wife is the equal of the prostitute who sells her body. And the man who kills because his aim is bad is the same as the man who caused the death because of his criminal act and his carelessness.

And in a deeper, extended sense, the old man (Alex's grandfather) grows old and will die soon, but another life is stirring, and will be born to take its place in this world. And so it goes. It is not for us to pass judgment on the rightness or wrongness of any of this, except to say that revenge, as Susanne expresses it, is a "sin" whether you are a "believer" or not.

At any rate, this is a finely wrought and beautifully realized film by a gifted cinematic artist who explores the human condition with sensitivity and candor while eschewing clichés and easy answers. I hope to see more of his work in the years to come.

I've seen this and I give it____stars.
I want to see it___. I'll pass___.
The review was worth reading___. Not___.

Run, Lola, Run *(Lola rennt)* (1998) 8

She can scream too...

Loud enough to shatter glass.

There are three keys to the success of this remarkable German language film (with English subtitles): originality of conception, crisp direction and editing, and two attractive stars to play the leads.

The stars are Franka Potente, who plays ruby red-haired Lola, daughter of a banker. She is smitten with Manni, handsome young man played by Moritz Bleibtreu, who forgot to keep his grip on a bag containing 100,000 Deutsche marks belonging to his mobster boss. He is to hand over the money in twenty minutes, but he lost it on the train. (It was picked up by a homeless man.) Manni calls Franka and tells her the desperate straits he is in. He says his only out is to rob a store. She says no wait, she can come up with something. What that something is is dear old dad. She looks at the clock. It's twenty minutes until twelve. So Lola starts running to get to the bank and then to Manni before the stroke of noon.

If you've seen Truffaut's *Les Quatre cents coup* (1959) then you know where director Tom Tykwer may have gotten the idea of showing us a Lola who runs like the wind. Truffaut used a sustained shot of his young hero running to convey an uplifting sense of freedom amid action. It worked for Truffaut and it works for Tykwer. Franka, running in nicely fitted pants and tank top (with her white lace bra strap discretely showing) really is a delight to watch. And like Truffaut, Tykwer does not let us see the runner sweat. There is a kind of effortless release, without any straining of our lungs. It is like running in our dreams.

What Tykwer does with time is even more interesting. He has Lola run from her home to the bank to Manni three times, each time with a slight difference in the early events, leading to differences in the events to come. In the British movie *Sliding Doors* (1998) starring Gwyneth Paltrow, something of the same sort was tried with Gwyneth playing out two different permutations of her life based on decisions leading to differing scenarios. I'm also reminded of the brilliant American film, *Memento* (2000) directed by Christopher Nolan in the way some of the events are played over again. Here the scene as Lola runs by her mother on the telephone is the same three times, but then the differences begin. It might also be said that this movie is the "many worlds" interpretation of quantum mechanics brought to cinema. Or perhaps Tykwer was influenced by complexity theory in which a slight change in initial conditions can lead to large changes later on.

The story (or rather stories: there are three of them) strain credulity at times. The awful things her "father" says to her in the first accounting seems too harsh and stupid to be real. The co-incidence of Manni's spotting the bum on the bicycle in the third tale seems a bit too lucky to be believed. And the allotment of twenty minutes of time in the three sequences was a bit off. However some of the other events seemed to me to be plausible or at least very clever and therefore allowable in an artistic sense. That the man in the ambulance regains a steady heart beat because she holds his hand is something this old guy can believe. And the cops mistaking her for a bystander in the bank robbery seems like credible cop behavior to me. And for those who think that the casino event was too much to believe, consider this: Assuming that the roulette wheels in Germany have both a zero and a double zero, the odds against betting on the number twenty and hitting it on consecutive spins of the wheel are $1/36$ times $1/36$ which equals about $77/100,000$ or about 1300 to 1. It's a long shot, but nothing like winning the lottery. Incidentally she had in the bag 115,600 Deutsche marks (her initial 100 marks x 34 x 34).

For those of you who haven't seen this remarkable film, consider this: it lasts 80 minutes, but it will seem like fifteen. The "throbbing techno score" is haunting and there are some nice action sequences. This is the kind of (R-rated, however) movie you can see with your teenaged son, although he would probably prefer to see it with his buds.

I've seen this and I give it____stars.
I want to see it___. I'll pass___.
The review was worth reading___. Not___.

The Wannsee Conference (1984) 10

"Women and children are Jews too."

The Wannsee Conference is a German language film with white English subtitles. Sometimes the subtitles are superimposed over a white background and the words disappear. That is why state of the art subtitles are yellow so that they don't get lost in the background. Otherwise the subtitles are very good, translating what needs to be translated and ignoring the extraneous.

I also want to note that the somewhat miraculous script by Paul Mommertz is very much like a stage play with most of the action essentially confined to one set with the various players delivering their lines as the camera focuses on them, much as a spotlight might. I say "miraculous" because Mommertz forged his screenplay from the banal, bureaucratic and often euphemistic language used by the historical Nazis as they formulated the so-called "Final Solution." How to make such material dramatic was the problem Mommertz and Director Heinz Schirk faced. They achieved the nearly impossible through the subtle use of what I might call everyday "reality intrusions": the dog barking, the vainglorious Reinhard Heydrich tripping over a briefcase as he is posturing as the grand architect and fuhrer of the Holocaust, the stenographer flirting (and Heydrich's calculated, chilling affirmative response), the greedy drinking, the "Nazi rally" thumping of the table, the turf wars, the boorish jokes, etc. These served to highlight by contrast the horror that these men were so bureaucratically entertaining. Note too that when the stenographer asks if a verbatim report is desired, she is told that a detailed report will suffice. Thus the dumb brute reality could be edited later in a George Orwellian manner to further bureaucratize and euphemize what they were doing.

What a truly verbatim report might have revealed is the point of this film.

This is a work of art, and I want to say that real art, to the extent that it is didactic, fails. If the artist tries to teach a lesson or show us the way and the light through a human story, to that extent he or she loses control and becomes an advertiser, a propagandist, a preacher. We as audience or readers become not participants anymore but objects. A work of art is always a two-way street of participation between the artist and those viewing the art. We might agree with the message or we might not, but we are no longer equal participants in the experience.

Yet what a work of art does is demonstrate a human truth through form. It is almost always an emotional truth. The Greeks emphasized tragedy because they understood the cathartic emotional experience that tragedy brings. What Mommertz and Schirk have done is present the truth as best they could discover it, and then they ran the closing credits. What we as audience experience depends on how well we participated, and what we brought as human beings to the experience. How well we concentrate, how aware we are of what is going on, how alert—these too are important. *The Swannsee Conference* is a demanding film, but it is surprising how quickly it moves, how engaged we become. The tension is not in what will happen at the end, of course. Instead the tension is in how it happens. We are held in thrall of discovering the essential nature of this most horrific and incredible evil done by the Nazis. And what we find out is that it was above all else banal and bureaucratic.

This is its essence: the dehumanization of the objects upon which the evil is worked. It can be done no other way. It has been said that for good men to do evil it takes religious commitment. For ordinary men it is necessary to dehumanize. When Stuckart complains that women and children are being killed, he is told, "Women and children are Jews too."

I've seen this and I give it___stars.
I want to see it___. I'll pass___.
The review was worth reading___. Not___.

VI

Spanish Language Films

The Age of Beauty (Belle Époque) (1992) 8

Sweet country coupling

Although this is a Spanish production set during the Spanish Civil War in the thirties, it is a French bedroom farce all the way, and a delightful romp to be sure.

Warm and rustic with a light satirical air, "Belle Époque" plays like something from Molière with a touch of Cervantes and a dollop of Shakespeare folded in. Four young women, daughters of Manolo, an ageing Republican artist, played with warmth and a becoming rakishness by Fernando Fernán Gómez, converge one at a time on our very lucky hero (Jorge Sanz) so as to better help him decide which one he really loves. Director Fernando Trueba lets him try all four before a decision is reached. The sex scenes couldn't get by the Vatican, but are so charmingly done that we are delighted. None of your sick, violent Anglo matings here. No rapes, no drugs, no booze, just sweet country coupling all around.

The target of the satire is mostly the Catholic church and the Fascists, but the Republicans take some hits as well. The war is entirely in the background except for a little *comédie noire* scene at the outset where two stupido Fascists soldiers do themselves in. Our hero's foil is a Jerry Lewis sort of mamma's boy romancing one of the daughters with his inheritance and his mother. He flip-flops between the church and the Republicans trying to please mamma and Clara, his enchantress, second daughter of Manolo. Manolo's foil is the parish priest, a hypocritical libertine, who commits most of the deadly sins before expiring by his own hand when the Republicans win (temporarily) the war.

The title (in English, "The Age of Beauty") is ironic because of the war, but literal as it refers to the time of our youth. Is it not uplifting to recall our loves instead of our wars, to turn our political and religious hatreds into benign satirical jokes, and to see the beauty of our nature and not our bestiality?

The traditional comedy of course ends in marriage, but to whom? I'm betting on the beautiful Penélope Cruz, who was just eighteen when this film was released.

I've seen this and I give it____stars.
I want to see it___. I'll pass___.
The review was worth reading___. Not___.

All About My Mother (1999) 9

Unsettling and brilliant

This is my first experience with a film directed by the acclaimed Spanish film maker, Pedro Almodóvar. It is very complex on both a technical and emotional level.

It is first and foremost a kind of absurdist parody of contemporary life with Almodóvar simultaneously questioning bourgeois values and celebrating the community of those with alternative life styles. He makes the burghers in the audience feel uneasy in their assumptions, especially about questions of gender and about the lifestyle of cross-dressers and gender-unspecific/variable people, who, he wants us to know, live and breath and love and hate just like anybody else.

Cecile Roth stars as Manuela, who is a nurse at a hospital in Madrid where she helps to coordinate the organ donor programs. She is also an amateur actress who plays in the simulations that the hospital makes to educate staff and patients. Her 17-year-old son with whom she is very close tells her she is a great actress, but Manuela is modest. She is also secretive about his father's identity. After seeing a production of Tennessee Williams's *A Streetcar Named Desire*, the son and the mother await outside the stage door so that he can get an autograph from the actress who plays Blanche Dubois, Marisa Paredes, who is named Huma Rojo in the film. Tragedy ensues as the son is hit and fatally injured. In just one of a number of plot mixings that emphasize the sometimes tragic and often ironic nature of the human experience, the son becomes an organ donor before he dies, and Manuela, who had previously arranged for organ donations, now has to sign the papers to donate the organs of her beloved son.

Now she goes to Barcelona to look up the father, who had once played the crude and boorish Stanley Kowalski to her Stella, again from *A Streetcar Named Desire*. In Barcelona Manuela again sees the play, but this time meets the star, Huma, who is a grande old dame of the Spanish theater, a Lesbian genius who has taken her theatrical cue in life from Bette Davis (and her smoking habits as well). In a salute to Davis and a remembrance of one of her greatest roles, we see posters of Bette Davis from the classic Hollywood film, *All About Eve* (1950), and then a kind of take off on the action as Manuela becomes in a sense Eve Harrington as she befriends Huma and begins working for her. (Waiting outside the stage door for a autograph is also a scene from *All About Eve*.) Nina (Candela Peña) Huma's heroin-addicted lover becomes jealous and accuses Manuela of seeking Huma's friendship just so she can become a star herself, a la Eve Harrington. To top it off Manuela is called upon to play Stella when Nina cannot because of an overdose, and miraculously she relives her role from twenty years before, and does a great job, because she is, as her son knew, a gifted actress.

Okay, we can see the complexities. I have merely given the premise of the film. Enter now Antonia San Juan as Agrado, an old friend of Manuela's who is a professional transvestite. (San Juan is brilliant in the part as a woman playing a man playing a woman.) Enter also Penélope Cruz as a pregnant nun with AIDs. What evolves is a kind of sisterhood among variously gendered females. There is also a sense of a middle class, soap opera-ish even, action and resolution, but with Almodóvar's tongue firmly in cheek.

Men, however, do not come off very well in this film. The grandfather-to-be apparently has Alzheimer's and does not even recognize his daughter. Manuela's son is dead. A theater male is depicted as a kind of stagehand Stanley Kowalski, boorishly insensitive, seeking only his own pleasure; indeed Tennessee Williams's crude, animalistic Kowalski appears as a metaphor for men in this film. Manuela is his long-suffering Stella, and Huma has always, as she actually says, depended on the kindness of strangers. Finally, there is "Lola" a tall, handsome, gender-modified Kowalski, played inadequately by Toni

Cantó, in what may be a bit of purposely bad casting for effect by Almodóvar—or perhaps I should say, played shallowly and unconvincingly on purpose by Toni Cantó. It's hard to tell. Indeed part of Almodóvar's technique is a blurring of distinctions with ironic parallels, showing how some things are the same, but different depending on your point of view, the organ donors, Lola's father-hood, Manuela as Stella and/or Eve, etc.

Bottom line this is an unsettling film, brilliantly acted by Paredes, Roth and San Juan, and cleverly directed in a most original style by Almodóvar. It will not play well with Disney aficionados or with devotees of action cinema—and put the kiddies to bed, please.

I've seen this and I give it____stars.
I want to see it___. I'll pass___.
The review was worth reading___. Not___.

Amores perros (2000) 8

Stark depiction of modern Mexican society

There are a lot of dogs in this movie. And there are some dog-fighting scenes that dog lovers may not want to see. Be forewared, a lot of dog blood is spilled.

And why? Does director Alejandro Gonzalez Inarritu has some kind of obsession with dogs? I don't know but according to something I read at IMDb there's a blurb at the beginning of the film stating that no animals were harmed in making the film. I played the DVD back, but I couldn't find the statement. I wonder. They sure looked harmed, and at any rate must have been sedated for some of the scenes. There is a short documentary called *Los perros de'Amores perros* (2000) that explains it all for those who are worrying about the dogs. Personally I'm not too worried because I very much doubt that Inarritu would make a film involving so many dogs and allow them to be hurt.

Anyway, this is a violent movie with a lot of the violence happening to the dogs. It was Inarritu's first film, or at least his first big film. He has since made, most notably, *21 Grams* (2003). As in *21 Grams*, there are three stories here, connected only by chance and the dogs. The opening scene is a car chase in which, we later learn, the three stories collide. There was also an accident in *21 Grams* that help to hold the stories together.

Here we have (1) the story of Octavio (Gael Garcia Bernal) who is in love with his older brother's wife, Susana (Vanessa Bache); (2) the story of El Chivo (Emilio Chevarria), one-time guerilla fighter, now a hit man who dresses and behaves like a homeless person; and (3) the story of Daniel (Alvaro Guerrero) who leaves his wife and children for a lanky runway model, Valeria (Goya Toledo). All three stories include dogs. Octavio's dog Cofi becomes a big winner at the dog fights and makes money for Octavio which he gives to Susana to save so that

they can run away together. El Chivo lives with four dogs, and Valeria has a little dog Richie that somehow (I can't figure out how) gets stuck under the floor and put upon by rats after it chases a ball through a hole in the floor.

Presumably this film shows us the violence that is endemic in Mexican society, perhaps inherited from the Aztecs and the Conquistadors, who were pretty bloody in their time. Or perhaps Inarritu knows that violence plays with the young American audiences that go to the theaters, and what he has is a nice commingling of purpose. One thing for sure, Inarritu knows how to make a film that engages the audience with not just violence but the clash of character and aspiration. A lot of the credit for the success of this film must go to the outstanding cast, in particular Emilio Chevarria and Gael Garcia Bernal.

Best, most original scene: when El Chivo leaves the two men tied up with the gun equal distance between them, just out of reach.

Bottom line: not for the squeamish.

I've seen this and I give it____stars.
I want to see it___. I'll pass___.
The review was worth reading___. Not___.

Maria Full of Grace (Maria llenas eres de gracia) (2004) 10

Outstanding portrait of a young woman

"Maria llenas eres de gracia," is one of the outstanding films of the new century, and one of the best I've seen in months. Joshua Marston, who wrote the script and directed, took a commercial idea—that of telling a story about the "mulas" who smuggle drugs into the US by swallowing pellets of cocaine or (in this case) heroin wrapped in latex which they later excrete. Should one of them burst before it is passed out of the body, it is likely the mule will die. It's a risky business in more ways than one, and only somebody desperate or foolish would do it.

So the first thing that Marston must do is establish Maria's character in such a way that we can believe she would do something like this. She is, on the one hand, an ordinary 17-year-old Columbian girl who works stripping the thorns from the stems of roses in a factory. She lives at home with her mother, sister and her sister's baby. She has a boyfriend. She has to work to help support the family. On the other hand she is a head-strong person, a pretty girl with a head on her shoulders.

But Maria is not exactly desperate. She is a bit of a gambler, somewhat foolish, no doubt, but she is also a strong person with great personal integrity. Marston allows us to see in the beginning of the film that she will take chances that others won't. She climbs up onto the roof of a building, a climb her boyfriend is afraid to make. We see her tell her boss (more or less) to take this job and shove it when he won't let her go to the bathroom. And we realize shortly thereafter why she needs to go to the bathroom more often than usual. We watch her tell her boyfriend about her predicament, and she does it in such a way that we can tell that she is searching for how he really feels. And when she finds out he doesn't really love her, at least doesn't love her the way she wants to be loved, she leaves him.

But now she is in a fix. Her job helped pay for the family's bills. Now the situation is set. Her character is set. The premise of the film can unwind: and so she meets a young man on a motorcycle who tells her how she can make some serious money smuggling drugs into the US.

Imagine how the average Hollywood director would fashion a movie from such premise. There would be brutality, gun fights, car chases. Cardboard villains would exploit Maria and others like her. There would be some heroics and perhaps a knight in shining armor would save Maria.

But that is not how Marston plays it. He opts for realism and he doesn't wallow in the violence or the exploitation. He keeps the focus on Maria and her personal struggle to find herself and to deal with the circumstances she has gotten into. The characters are real, the situations are authentic, and the details are closely observed and realistic. We see Maria practice swallowing large globe grapes. We see the people in the drug-smuggling business and some of the other mules. We see the security people at the airport and the young men who watch the girls until the pellets are passed. There is no glamor among these characters. It is clear they are patterned after real people who could actually be in this ugly business. And in the end we see the triumph of Maria's character.

What makes this such an outstanding movie is not only the careful, clear and veracious way that Marston tells the story, but the compelling performance by Catalina Sandino Moreno who plays Maria. She is a very talented young actress who has the kind of beauty that suggests something close to nobility of character, if I may use such an old-fashioned phrase. It is this quality of hers that Marston captures and emphasizes. The result is one of the most arresting performances I've seen in quite a while. Moreno appears entirely real, completely divorced from any phony celluloid heroine. She became to me—and this is what all great actors can do—someone I know, someone I care about, and I was filled with emotion as the movie ended.

"This is a movie about a girl becoming a woman," is the way Moreno expressed it. Marston puts it this way, "I realized...I was making a film about a girl who was doing something universal in trying to figure out the meaning of her life." This is really what the story is about: becoming a woman in this world of risks and trade-offs, of dangers and obligations.

A movie that is a work of art and worthy of something more than the diversion of an evening should affect the viewer emotionally, intellectually and artistically. Maria Full of Grace is such a movie, a movie that comes along perhaps once a year, or perhaps only once in several years. It's that good.

By all means see this for Catalina Sandino Moreno who was nominated for Best Actress by the Academy in 2005 but lost out to Hilary Swank for her performance in *Million Dollar Baby* (2004). And see it for Joshua Marston who made it real.

I've seen this___ and I give it___stars.
I want to see it___. I'll pass___.
The review was worth reading___. Not___.

The Spirit of the Beehive (*El espíritu de la colmena*) (1973) 10
Through Ana's eyes: a masterpiece of childhood

Every once in a while I stumble upon a masterpiece. This is a masterpiece of childhood set in Franco's Spain in 1940. There are political allusions and asides that somehow escaped Franco's censors, or maybe they were indulged. It matters not because the bleak landscape surrounding the house with its honeycombed windows and its honey colored light says more than words could.

I would compare this favorably with two other masterpieces of childhood, the French films, *Jeux interdits* (*Forbidden Games*) (1952), and *Ponette* (1996) What is explored in all three of these films is the reality of childhood that we have forgotten, the intensity of first knowledge, of things experienced for the first time, the wonder and the horror that such experiences may contain. But more than that there is the unconditioned sense of life that the child experiences. When Ana sees the fugitive (from Franco, one imagines) who has injured his leg jumping off the train, she immediately knows what is essential in this situation. The man is hurt. He is hungry. He needs help. She gives him an apple from her lunch pail, which he eagerly devours. Although she has been scared by a Frankenstein movie and her sister's pretence of death and gloved hands around her face, she is not afraid.

This is the most laconic of films. Almost everything is done with the camera and the events. The children laugh and play and watch the world with wonder. They say a few words, direct and to the point. Six year old Ana (Ana Torrent) has dark eyes as big as saucers which she trains on the world as if to bore into the very nature of existence. Her older sister Isabel's eyes sometimes form slits of mischief or delight as she tests reality or teases her sister.

The pace of the film is deliberately slow. The essay by famed Spanish film expert Paul Julian Smith contained in the booklet accompanying the Criterion Collection two-disc set includes Smith's remark that when the film was first shown in San Sebastian in 1973 where it won the main prize, "Some of the audience, restless at the film's slow pace, even booed."

There is a technique in the theater, not so much observed today, that also works well in movies. Slow it down, begin with everyday, mundane events, and play them long like honey slowly oozing, so much the better to contrast with the events to come, and give those events the contrast they deserve as they have in real life. Director Victor Erice does this to fine effect. How drawn out seem the lessons at school, and how tedious. But such is the life of a child when every day is a little eternity, where so much happens that when the lights go out, the child falls into a deep, dreamless sleep for many hours at a stretch. We have forgotten this world of the child, but Erice reminds us.

I was not restless because, although the pace is indeed slow, the cinematography by Luis Cuadrado and the terse silent events of innocence set against the background of the late Spanish Civil War portended events to come. Just what those events might be it was impossible to guess; however it was clear there would be no compromise with audience expectations or any catering to any sort of correctness, political or otherwise. And this is part of what makes a great film.

Character, story, suspense, an important theme, beautiful visuals, truth—artistic truth of course, psychological human truth—and attention to detail: these are also what make a great film. And they are all here in *El espíritu de la colmena*.

Erice plays with our emotions of course. We are nearly terrified that something is going to happen to these beautiful little girls, and indeed once or twice it appears that our worst fears are realized. Are they or are they not?

It is said that Ana was traumatized by viewing the Frankenstein movie and by her sister's horrid joke, and then by the blood she sees in the old building by the well where the fugitive had rested. But I think it would be better to say that Ana was challenged by new-found knowledge of the ever close proximity of death, and in reaction she ran away into her own world to find an answer. Notice how the scene from James Wales' Frankenstein in which the monster kneels beside the water with the little girl is repeated in Ana's fantasy, and how she looks at the monster with big, wide-open, questioning, waiting eyes. What is life, and what is death? And, know this: I will always live in fear and dread if I do not know what they are and if cannot face them.

When she encounters the Frankenstein monster at the water's edge she has only her beauty to protect her. But that beauty resides in our head—in Frankenstein's head—and so she is safe. This is part of the deep psychology of the film, wondrously achieved, perhaps part by art and part by happenstance.

I believe that is what Ana experienced in her mind. But we do not know. We do not know the mind of the child. And we have forgotten what it is to be a child. Erice's masterpiece helps us to remember.

There is a documentary about the film on the second disc with interviews with Erice and with Angel Fernandez Santos who worked with Erice on the script, and others. We see Ana Torrent all grown up, which is what I most wanted to see. And we learn how the film was made. A masterpiece, it is my belief, whether it is in cinema or literature, in chess or music, or in some other art form always brings together unconscious elements that fuse with conscious intent. It is only later that we recognize what happened.

I've seen this and I give it___stars.
I want to see it___. I'll pass___.
The review was worth reading___. Not___.

Y Tu Mama Tambien (2001) 9

Oh, those randy Mexicans!

A translation of the title of this movie into English would yield something like "And Your Mother Too," which would echo a phrase often used in so-called "mother talk" or "wolfing." (If you're gonna wolf, you better wolf fast/ 'cause your old lady's got a face like a bulldog's Ask me no questions and I'll tell you no lies...)

Having been brought up in the United States and having attended the public schools I am no stranger to the phenomenon of teenaged boys being teenaged boys, having been there and done that myself, including the hazy, sunny obligatory motor trip to Tijuana and other points south. But what struck me while watching this fascinating film was how very like the guys I went to school with are Tenoch and Julio. In fact I was a little reminded of the song "Me and Julio Down by the Schoolyard" by Paul Simon. Not much would have to be changed to see this as an American movie about young people in America near the end of the 20th century.

But this is about Mexico and it takes place in Mexico and even though Julio and Tenoch rag on "Team America" there is no doubt that their lives and the styles they copy and take as their own are enormously influenced by American culture, for better or for worse.

Gael Garcia Bernal who previously starred in Alejandro Gonzalez Inarritu's *Amores perros* (2000) plays Julio, who is from a middle class family. Diego Luna plays his friend Tenoch (named after Tenochtitlan, Aztec founder of Mexico City) who is the son of a prominent Mexican politician. Both boys live the kind of lives of plenty and privilege that the average Mexican can only dream about. And so there is a certain decadent and hedonistic quality to the way they embrace life. But what director Alfonso Cuaron captures with these boys and their adventure to an imaginary beach with an older woman is the zest of youth that throws itself wildly and madly into sex, drugs and the search for experience and the fulfillment of youthful urges. What they learn from Luisa (Maribel Verdu) is something most young men really lust after, that is, how to please a woman sexually—well, at least they experience a first course.

Cuaron shows us teenaged boys as teenaged boys are: raunchy, randy, irreverent, and as an old army sergeant used to say, "young and dumb and full of come." Well, not dumb. Both boys are sharp and quick to learn about life, and as the movie ends and they go their separate ways, we know that both will go on to college and make a good life for themselves. In this sense this is a coming of age movie with Lusia as mentor to the boys.

Looking at the movie a little more deeply we have to ask, why does Lusia go on the trip with Tenoch and Julio, and why does she let herself go, so to speak? We learn that her husband has cheated on her (again, by the way) and had the temerity to call her up immediately after the fact and confess. Later we learn that she has an even more compelling reason to indulge herself in a youthful fling. (But of course you should see the movie to find out what that is.)

The sense of freedom and naturalness that Cuaron captures, not only in the area of human sexuality, but in the spirit of a vast country moving from a largely agrarian society to an industrial one, and the bewilderment that such rapid change makes people feel, is made especially vivid by the focus on the young, since they are the ones moving the fastest. (Of course this focus doesn't hurt at the box office, since young people make up the bulk of viewers, in Mexico as elsewhere.) However, despite what some reviewers have suggested, this movie addresses Mexican poverty in only a token way. This is a movie about privileged Mexicans who could, as I intimated above, pass for Americans or Europeans with only a minor cultural shift.

Be forewarned that the sexuality shown here is about as graphic as any you'll see this side of an X rating, which is okay with me. Certainly it is better than the usual violence that Hollywood serves up. In fact I hope this movie triggers a change in the movie industry away from the belief that you have to titillate the mass audience with violence in order to be successful. Sex will do just fine.

Bottom line: a vital, vivid romp that will delight especially the young. Clearly this is not a movie for prudes or social conservatives—and that's an understatement!

I've seen this and I give it____stars.
I want to see it___. I'll pass___.
The review was worth reading___. Not___.

VII

Swedish Language Films

Here the films of the great, incomparable Ingmar Bergman dominate.

Babette's Feast (*Babettes gæstebud*) (1987) 10
A bittersweet, redemptive northern masterpiece

Take the style of Ingmar Bergman, stir in some Lutheranism, add a dash of Guy De Maupassant, a pinch of Chekov (such a severe and forbidding brew!). Mix well with the grand cuisine of nineteenth century France and what do you have? Babette's Feast!

Our story (from an Isak Dinesen short story) is of two lovely maiden sisters from Jutland, the pious daughters of a stern and dictatorial minister, who spurn their

chance for love to remained devoted to their austere Protestant creed and to their puritanical and selfish father. We are subjected to the bleak, harsh winters, to the endless hours of knitting, to the long silences and the sighs upon sighs... Ah, the Danes, the Norwegians, the Swedes, how beautifully they brood! We see the barren beauty of Martina, who so enchanted the young cavalryman that when he could not melt her cold, cold heart, he instead vowed to be a success, and succeeded! And then there came the baritone from the Paris opera who heard her sister Phillipa's soprano voice at choir and fell immediately and hopeless in love with her, and sought to train her voice and carry her away. But no, he too could not melt the snows of her near Arctic heart, and so returned to Paris where he played out his (now) empty career.

Flash forward to the entrance of Babette, whom the opera singer sends many years later to the sisters to hide from the strife in France. She will be an angel of gastronomy, household management and common sense who will mend their souls and fill them with joy.

This is a tale of unrequited love, of love that festers and longs and does not die. How I adore the love stories where the love is never consummated! I love the years of yearning, the melancholy realization that it could never work, and yet, and yet... And then when they are old and past any pretense, how wonderful it is to know that the anticipation, the savoring, the longing, the utter lack of finality, how wonderful THAT was, and how superior to a banal consummation!

But then, such is not the usual taste. Speaking of tastes, this is not a movie to see on an empty stomach. The climatic feast of turtle soup, quail in pastry, rich sauces, dessert, fromage, fruit, etc., washed down with amontillado, champagne, etc. will wet your appetite. A little stunning for this modest epicure was the Clos de Vougeot, 1845 that the general so admired. Can you imagine how beautiful that wine was, and what it would fetch today!

This is also a tale of Christian piety, and a joining of the Protestant and the Catholic, of how a Lutheran might learn from a Papist, of how the temperate zone might warm the north. How food really is a sacrament.

Anyway, we know from the moment Babette comes to the austere, but grand old pious ladies to cook for them that she is something special. When the ladies show her how to precisely prepare the mundane Danish meals of bread soup and soaked, smoked flounder, we know immediately that she is a great cook; after all she is Parisian, and an opera star has signified her as such. But she modestly says not a word and learns the Danish names and follows faithfully the Danish recipes, as though she were an ingenue. She works for nothing, having lost her family to the bloodshed in France, and what has she to live for but to do what she has to do and do it right. And does she ever!

Babette's Feast is as heart-warming as a Disney tale would love to be. It is as uplifting as a stirring Sousa march, and as satisfying as a seven-course meal at the Grand Hotel in Paris. It starts like a novel from the nineteenth century, slow and studied, and before you know it, has captured your fancy. Director Gabriel Axel unfolds the story with precision and a careful attention to detail, but ultimately with an invisible simplicity and economy. What he is saying in the end, is what he has the general pronounce after the sensuous meal (which is quite a moral extravagance, perhaps even a sinfulness

for the pious flock): "Righteousness and bliss shall kiss one another."

Someday, one hopes in this world, they shall.

I've seen this and I give it____stars.
I want to see it___. I'll pass___.
The review was worth reading___. Not___.

Cries and Whispers (*Viskningar och rop*) (1972) 9

Sad, cold, cynical, but brilliant

To see Liv Ullmann, whose nature is so warm and natural, play a role in which her warmth is superficial and fraudulent, is a little offsetting; yet, great actress that she is, she pulls it off, so that if I had never seen her before, I would believe she was that way.

Cries and Whispers, much ballyhooed, I recall, when it appeared, seems too psychoanalytically cryptic today; dark and mysterious, beautifully filmed in an intense red—yes, very striking against the northern cold, but somehow not entirely convincing. The people are cynically presented as tortured animals caring only for themselves, without a scrap of genuine feeling for others. Anna, the maid, is the exception, so that she may serve as a foil for the rest of them.

Harriet Andersson gives a striking performance as Agnes who is dying of cancer. I have seen what she portrays, and can tell you she expressed it in all its horror and hopelessness. Ullmann plays Maria, one of her sisters who touches others easily, but without real feeling, so that the touches mean nothing. For those who grew up cinematically during the seventies, she was a great, expressive, sensual, flawless star of the screen, one of Ingmar Bergman's jewels. Bergman himself of course was already a legend by the time this film was made, a great master who did what he wanted and what he felt, yet never lost sight of the audience. What he seems to be saying here is we are desperate creatures living a cold and ultimately empty existence. The ending clip seems an afterthought that seeks our redemption, but it arrives too little too late. We are lost.

I've seen this and I give it____stars.
I want to see it___. I'll pass___.
The review was worth reading___. Not___.

Scenes from a Marriage (Scener ur ett äktenskap) (1973) 10

Compelling drama with a brilliant performance by Liv Ullmann

One of Director Ingmar Bergman's great talents was his deep understanding of women and his love for them. In Liv Ullmann he found a woman who could express that passion so that it could be felt by others. In the cinema that I most admire there is a collaboration of love and adoration between the director and the star that is expressed in the performance. We see this in the work of Krzysztof Kieslowski and to a lesser extent in the work of Roman Polanski and Roger Vadim. And I guess I might mention Benoît Jacquot and Andre Techine who first directed, respectively, Judith Godrèche and Juliette Binoche. But with Bergman there is a wider expression of this love and admiration to include the experience of pathos and tragedy. To understand what a woman is in the fullest extent of her being is what Bergman strives for, not just the revelation of a pretty girl. In Bergman we find the kind of all encompassing psychology characteristic of Shakespeare or Ibsen, in which the characters are fully fleshed and expressive of a wide range of human experience.

This begins slowly as a stage play and continues as something seen on television and then suddenly springs like a trap and we are immersed in a compelling drama about people who are interesting and alive, people like ourselves who have the longings and the frustrations that we live but seldom express. As Marianne and Johan watch their friends expose the sordid details of their failed marriage, they are understanding and quietly smug that they are different, especially it is Marianne who is proper and conventional, always alert to the necessities of propriety, who feels this way, and is so happy that their marriage, while not perfect, will last. And so it appears.

And then we have the scene in which Johan tells her that he is in love with a younger woman. It is nothing short of magnificent, one of the most memorable in all of cinema, and done with such subtly and power, infused with a deep underpinning of a wild and desperate, yet cunning expression of love from Liv Ullmann that would win over the devil himself. This is a woman at thirty-five, when everything that means anything to her is suddenly threatened, and this is how she responds, with genius.

Or, some might say, with madness. Johan's dull indifference is absurdist, and Marianne's incredible tolerance and "understanding" of his behavior is stunning. Yet when it happens to us, sometimes we are just a bit ahead of ourselves and we realize what has really happened, and like Marianne we are generous and sad instead of insanely jealous. And Johan's insufferable arrogance and "worldly" understanding of *himself* makes us want to scream. And then it turns and he says, "I'm beaten," and there is just a trace of a triumphant smile on her face. At forty-five, he is a beaten man. "You win," is what he is saying. And now he becomes a bit pathetic. His behavior, when it is she who has the upper hand, is crude and ugly. Of course hers was cunning and desperate when he had the upper hand. And then it turns again and then again, and we have twenty years of a marriage.

One thing I must say, this is a little too intense for TV! (The entire production, six hours worth, was originally made for Swedish TV.)

I was pleased to see the photos of Liv Ullmann as a child and then as a little girl and then as a teen and then as a young woman worked into the script. She is so beautiful and wholesome in a distinct way, like no other actress, and yet I knew her in the ninth grade in the person of a girl with the same red hair and the same white, reddish, freckled skin. The range that Liv Ullmann displays in this film is remarkable, but she is not alone. Co-star Erland Josephson is also outstanding. And they had better be since they command the screen for most of the 170 minutes this version runs. What Bergman does that keeps us glued to the tube is he tells the truth. It's a Bergman truth, but it is a truth so beyond the contrivances and superficialities of most movies that we are fascinated.

I've seen this and I give it____stars.
I want to see it___. I'll pass___.
The review was worth reading___. Not___.

Smiles of a Summer Night (Sommarnattens

leende) (1955) 10
My favorite Bergman film

Fredrick Egerman (Gunnar Bjornstrand) is a forty-something lawyer of precise calculation, a bit of a dandy among the mercantile. He has a young wife Anne (the very pretty Ulla Jacobsson) whom he married when she was sixteen, but somehow never got around to unintacting her virgo. He has a sometime mistress Desirée Armfeldt (the voluptuous Eva Dahlbeck) from whom he has recently been estranged. He has a son Henrik (Bjorn Bjelvenstam) full of angst and love's confusion who lusts after the saucy maid Petra (a blonde Harriet Andersson) while he studies theology and his father's wife.

The night for Fredrick and Anne (after a Platonic nap during which Fredrick inadvertently pronounces Desirée's name) begins with the theater; and who should be starring in the production but Desirée. Anne suddenly takes ill and they rush home. Fredrick now steals away to see Desirée. After a pratfall in some water he ends up in some night clothes that belong to Desirée's current lover, the militaristic Count Malcolm (Jarl Kulle as a sprung-steel bantam) who, as it happens, arrives upon the scene much to the merriment of Desirée and to the embarrassment of Fredrick.

The culmination of love's labors and intrigues takes place at the chateau of Desirée's mother, Mrs. Armfeldt (Naima Wifstrand). The action includes a most amusing duel, some hanky-panky atop a haystack, musical beds, an attempted suicide, some Chateau Mouton-Rothschild (if I caught the label right), the amorous kiss of young lovers, the triumph of the fairer sex, and the very proper lawyer's final humiliation.

If you haven't seen *Smiles of a Summer Night* you are in for a rare treat: a comedy by Ingmar Bergman. And it is no ordinary comedy. Shakespearean and Oscar Wilde-like in its sharp, satirical (and oh so worldly wise) dialogue, this playful romp with the Swedish landed gentry and servants of a hundred years ago is a delight that will satisfy the most sophisticated viewer as well as the most middlebrow.

Owing something to the French farcical tradition (in particular Molière), to light opera (maybe Mozart), and even the Greek theater, Bergman's romantic comedy sparkles with love's intrigues and pratfalls. According to Pauline Kael, whose review is part of a 24-page booklet that comes with the Criterion Collection DVD, Bergman had just finished directing a stage production of *The Merry Widow* which accounts in part for the fin-de-siècle setting and the genteel treatment that he finally settled upon for his comedy of manners. Also I think this examination and satire of the class structure with hilarious asides on the foibles of human nature owes something to Oscar Wilde's *The Importance of Being Ernest* which was set in approximately the same time period and had a similar cast of characters including a Grand Dame, an ingenue, some rustics, a clergyman, but most directly in the fact that both Wilde and Bergman aim their sardonic wit directly at the burghers and the bourgeois. Bohemians need not apply. Indeed the closest thing to a Bohemian in the play is the actress Desirée who is the very calculating and dominate personage of the film.

By the way, Bergman's future protege, Bibi Andersson, does appear in this movie, but only for a moment as an actress on stage at the theater.

The final, cynical bemusement comes as one reconsiders who ends up with whom. Not to spoil the plot, but notice that in every case there is something less than perfect in each romantic partnership, something slightly amiss that may cause problems down the road, something unsettled that suggests that nothing has really changed. As the French say, the more things change, the more they remain the same. It is this ironic underpinning to this delightful comedy that lends to it something of the timeless. Bergman is good at that.

I've seen this and I give it____stars.
I want to see it___. I'll pass___.
The review was worth reading___. Not___.

Wild Strawberries (*Smultronstället*) (1957) 10

When film was an art form

In this symbolic tale of an old man's journey from emotional isolation to a kind of personal renaissance, Ingmar Bergman explores in part his own past, and in

doing so rewards us all with a tale of redemption and love.

Victor Sjostrom, then 80 years old, stars as Professor Isak Borg whose self-indulgent cynicism has left him isolated from others. Sjostrom, whose work goes back to the very beginning of the Swedish cinema in the silent film era, both as an actor and as a director, gives a brilliant and compelling performance. All the action of the film takes place in a single day with flashbacks and dream sequences to Borg's past as Borg wakes and goes on a journey to receive a "Jubilee Doctor" degree from the University of Lund. Bergman wrote that the idea for the film came upon him when he asked the question, "What if I could suddenly walk into my childhood?" He then imagined a film "about suddenly opening a door, emerging in reality, then turning a corner and entering another period of one's existence, and all the time the past is going on, alive."

Bibi Andersson plays both the Sara from Borg's childhood, the cousin he was to marry, and the hitchhiker Sara who with her two companions befriends him with warmth and affection. The key scene is when the ancient Borg in dreamscape comes upon the Sara of his childhood out gathering wild strawberries. Borg looks on (unnoticed of course) as his brother, the young Sigfrid, ravishes her with a kiss which she returns passionately; and, as the wild strawberries fall from her bowl onto her apron, staining it red, Borg experiences the pain of infidelity and heartbreak once again. Note that in English we speak of losing one's "cherry"; here the strawberries symbolize emotionally much the same thing for Sara. Later on in the film as the redemption comes, the present day Sara calls out to Borg that it is he that she really loves, always and forever. Borg waves her away from the balcony, yet we are greatly moved by her love, and we know how touched he is.

The two young men accompanying Sara can be seen as reincarnations of the serious and careful Isak Borg and the more carefree and daring Sigfrid. It is as though his life has returned to him as a theater in which the characters resemble those of his past; yet we are not clear in realizing whether the resemblance properly belongs in the old man's mind or is a synchronicity of time returned.

Memorable is Ingrid Thulin who plays Mariana, the wife of Borg's son who accompanies him on the auto trip to Lund. She begins with frank bitterness toward the old man but ends with love for him; and again we are emotionally moved at the transformation. What Bergman does so very well in this film is to make us experience forgiveness and the transformation of the human spirit from the negative emotions of jealousy and a cold indifference that is close to hate, to the redemption that comes with love and a renewal of the human spirit. In quiet agreement with this, but with the edge of realism fully intact, is the scene near the end when Borg asks his long time housekeeper and cook if they might not call one another by their first names. She responses that even at her age, a woman has her reputation to consider. Such a gentle comeuppance meshes well with, and serves as a foil for, all that has gone on before on this magical day in an old man's life.

See this for Bergman who was just then realizing his genius (*The Seventh Seal* was produced immediately before this film) and for Sjostrom who had the rare opportunity to return to film as an actor in a leading role many decades past him prime, and made the most of it with a flawless performance, his last major performance as he was to die three years later.

I've seen this and I give it____stars.
I want to see it___. I'll pass___.
The review was worth reading___. Not___.

Elvira Madigan (1967) 9

As beautiful as advertised

This really is a beautiful movie, exquisite in detail, gorgeously filmed, directed with great subtlety and intensely focused. Nothing wasted or thrown away here. Everything counts. We feel the forebodings of tragedy first in the straight razor in Sixten's hand as he caresses the back of Elvira's head, and then again there is the knife on their picnics, stark, solid, sharp steel in the paradise of their love. Note too the shots on her belly. The child touches her stomach. She vomits from eating flowers...

To really appreciate this movie it should be understood that it was filmed in the sixties and it represented to that audience something precious and true. Note the anti-war sentiment seemingly tangential to the story of the film, but nonetheless running as a deep current underneath. He was an army deserter, like those in the sixties who fled to Canada to avoid the draft and the body bags in Vietnam. Note his confrontation with his friend from the regiment, a scene that many in the sixties lived themselves. He gave up everything for love, but it really is her story, her choice. She chose a man with a wife and two children, a soldier. She had many other choices, as the friend reminded her, but for her he was the "last one." What they did was wrong, but it was indeed a summer of love, the cold northern winter in the distance, ripe red raspberries and mushrooms to eat and greenery everywhere and the sun brilliant and warm; and then in the next to the last scene with the children when she faints as the child pulls off the blindfold of the game and is surprised to face Elvira's belly, there is just a little snow on the ground, perhaps it is from the last winter, not completely melted.

If you can watch this without a tear in your eye and a melancholy feeling about the nature of human love, you have grown too old. Theirs was a forbidden love, like that of Romeo and Juliet, a tragic love, doomed from the start, which is why the ending of the movie is revealed in the opening credits. Those who think a story is spoiled by knowing the ending, know not the subtle ways of story, of great tales that are told again and again. Knowing the ending only sharpens the senses and heightens the appreciation.

Pia Degermark who plays Elvira, who is a tightrope walker, a girl of gypsies, has beautiful calves (which is all we see of her body), a graceful style and gorgeous eyes, made up in the unmistakable style of the sixties, very dark with long heavily mascara'ed eyelashes. And she is a flower child, a fairy child of the forest, drawn to things earthy and mysterious, to a strong young man and a fortune teller who finds for her only small black spades in her future. In life we chase after butterflies. Sometimes we catch one.

I've seen this and I give it____stars.
I want to see it___. I'll pass___.
The review was worth reading___. Not___.

The Seventh Seal (*Det sjunde inseglet*) (1957) 10

Bleak, dark but with a ray of hope

BEWARE SPOILERS.

It really is impossible to consider an Ingmar Bergman movie without immediately running to an interpretation. At least for me that is the case. In particular *The Seventh Seal* seems to demand that we ask what was Bergman's intention. Was it to show that Christianity and superstition are brothers in arms? Was it to suggest a kind of fatalism that allows some to live and others to die without rhyme or reason?

The story, set in the 14th century during the time of plague, concerns a knight, Antonius Block (Max von Sydow) and his squire Jons (Gunnar Bjornstrand) lately returned to Sweden from the Crusades. Bergman combines realism with supernatural elements, such as the appearance of Death (Bengt Ekerot) with whom Antonius Block plays a game of chess, and the visions that the traveling troubadour, Jof (Nils Poppe) sees that nobody else can see including his wife Mia (Bibi Andersson). Block is haunted by death and has been assured that death is imminent, but hopes to put it off by beating Death at chess.

Meanwhile the inhabitants are also in fear of death and seek to blame someone. They seize a young girl (Maud Hansson) and brand her a witch for consorting with the Evil One. They hold her in a pillory prior to burning her at the stake. Notice that instead of denying that she has been with the devil, she tells us that she reaches out and touches him everywhere. The only bright spot in the movie is the family of Jof, Mia and their infant son.

Antonius Block goes to confession only to discover that the priest behind the window is none other than his adversary Death, to whom he inadvertently reveals his strategy in their game of chess. Block is searching for the meaning of life. He is trying to find God, whom he complains is always hiding. Instead he finds Death. Can they be one and the same? Jons is able and cynical and sees through humanity's many delusions. Jof plays at life and sings. Mia is filled with love for life. Guess who lives and who dies.

But of course the plague was the great leveler. Persons of stations high and low were brought within its compass, but Bergman gets to pick and choose who shall live and who shall die.

As usual with Bergman we have the most incredible study of human faces. I particularly liked the close ups of the women. The face of Gunnel Lindblom, who plays the young woman ("Girl" in the credits) that Jons saves from being raped, is particularly striking and intense. I recall her from *The Virgin Spring* (1960) in which she played Ingeri, the Odin-worshipping servant. The face of Bibi Andersson is a delight with her quick, pretty eyes and her engaging smile.

But Bergman also concentrates on the faces of the bit players, in the mead hall and at the burning and as they watch the traveling players at their song and dance. With Bergman people are intensely real, up close and always personal. And he knows what they think and how they act. He shows us here, as he does in all his films, human hypocrisy and stupidity, human love and frailty. The landscape is bleak, the shadows are dark and life is harsh. Humans take their quick pleasures and then they die. That is the message I think that Bergman is sending to us.

No student of film should miss this, one of the most talked about films ever made, and perhaps Bergman's first great work of art. He died only recently in 2007, not long after being voted (In Time Magazine, I think) as the greatest living director.

I've seen this and I give it____stars.
I want to see it___. I'll pass___.
The review was worth reading___. Not___.

Virgin Spring (*Jungfrukallen*) (1960) 10

A dark parable of sin and vengeance

A virgin spring would be an early spring when the days break bright and clear but the nights are still forbiddingly cold. As one of the characters says, The day began with such promise only to end tragically—or words to that effect. A virgin spring is also that time in a young maiden's life when she is still innocent and has no sense of the hardships to come or the beasts that dwell in the deep dark woods. And a virgin spring may be a miracu-

lous sign from God of clear spring water flowing spontaneously from an hitherto unknown fountain, a place on which to build a church to honor the God that one has offended.

All of these springs are in this riveting masterwork by one of cinema's greatest directors, the incomparable Ingmar Bergman. Light and darkness suffuse the 14th century landscape of a Sweden only partially given over to Christianity. Odin still rules the forests and the glades, the mountain tops and the cold, deep rivers. He is the god of darkness in this film, almost something akin to the devil, worshiped by the bridge keeper shaman with his herbs and by the dark-haired, dark-eyed young servant Ingeri (played with something close to demonic vivaciousness by Gunnel Lindblom). Lightness comes in the form of her privileged stepsister, Karin (Birgitta Pettersson) who is blonde and gets to wear fine clothes and is much loved by her father, Tore (Max von Sydow), and her doting mother, Mareta (Birgitta Valberg).

And so one bright spring day the two young women ride off to town, Karin in her finery carrying candles for the church, Ingeri in her rags many months pregnant with the child of someone who had forced himself upon her, her heart full of jealousy and hate. She has prayed to Odin for harm to come to Karin, for Karin to be taken against her will as she was, for Karin to suffer the humiliation and the pain that she suffered. In fact she has worked a little black magic with a toad in the bread that Karin takes with her.

She says to Karin, it could happen to you if a man puts his hands on your neck and around your waist. But Karin says no she would rebuff such a man, and when *she* is with child she will be happily married to a man of substance and privilege. But the man is stronger and will take you behind a bush and you won't be able to fight him off, Ingeri insists. Karin slaps her for such insolence.

This is a foreshadowing of events to come. But first they come upon a bridge keeper, an old shamanistic man living alone, a man who collects medicinal herbs and feeds the ravens. He represents the old Norse gods. While they are there Ingeri decides she can't go on. Karin leaves and the bridge keeper presses close to Ingeri to enthrall her with the black magic of the old gods. But she becomes frightened and runs away.

The thing that stays with me the most is the pure animal brutality of the two herders. They had only a sense of greed and ignorance about them. They raped and murdered and stole, and then stupidly sealed their own fate. They seemed almost subhuman.

Von Sydow's Tore is almost like a Norse God. And when he confronted God with "You saw this!" he spoke for everyone who has ever suffered a grievous harm and has wondered why God let it happen. Of course he represents along with his wife, Christianity.

The other thing that stays with me is the harsh life that these Swedes from the 14th century had to live. One imagines how short the spring and how long the winter. And one understands Karin's desire to have fun after being cooped up all winter. The terrible irony that is at the heart of the human condition is this hope of spring which everyone feels so powerfully; and then to have this senseless tragedy ensue defies explanation.

But an explanation is attempted. Bergman points to the girl's vanity and her naivety, to the mother's jealousy of the father who is more loved by Karin, to the way they look down on Ingeri and treat her like a serf who has sinned. Or even to the palpable presence of evil in the world. But the real explanation belongs to something naturalistic, primeval, something dark and cold and bestial in the Swedish woods, something before civilization and before the rule of law.

Indelible is Gunnel Lindblom's Ingeri, a woman-child of the devil almost (Odin would be like the devil to these medieval Christians), embittered and full of hate, but with such an animal presence. The carefully plotted story that allows her to watch her desire for revenge come to life in front of her eyes and then to have her cry out later in guilt and blame herself for what she had done heightens our involvement and deepens the complex tragedy.

Bottom line: one of Bergman's best and that is very good indeed.

I've seen this and I give it____stars.
I want to see it___. I'll pass___.
The review was worth reading___. Not___.

VIII

Other Foreign Language Films

Bad Guy (*Nabbeun namja*) (2001) 8

Disturbing and then some

This Korean film is what might be called postmodern naturalism. Director Ki-duk Kim tells a brutal story without comment and without mercy. He reminds us of some human truths that will make some viewers uncomfortable, and he invites controversy.

First, two things: Spoilers to come, so if you haven't seen this movie you might want to stop reading now.

Second, if you've seen the movie only once and are scratching your head, you're not alone.

Here's what happens: Han-ki (Jae-hyeon Jo), a street tough pimp walking along in a South Korean city spies this very pretty and privileged college girl, Sun-hwa (Won Seo), sitting on a bench waiting for her boyfriend. The girl is everything Han-ki desires. He sits down next to her. She pretends not to notice him while she talks on her cell phone to her boyfriend. When she does deign to notice him (and his desire for her) she shirks back in horror at his dirty, lower-class presumption and gets up. Her boyfriend arrives while she throws ugly glances at Han-ki. Han-ki can't take it anymore and grabs her and forcefully kisses her as the boyfriend ineffectually beats him about the head. Some soldiers arrive on the scene and beat the tar out of Han-ki. As a parting gesture, pretty girl spits on Han-ki as he is held by the soldiers.

That's "the setup." It's the kind of setup that cries out for revenge or at least a comeuppance, which is what I expected. Or perhaps pretty college girl and the bad guy will find true love and overcome their social differences. What actually happens is beyond expectation in a way that is likely to stun and totally engage the viewer.

Pretty girl is at a book store. She compromises herself (in the viewer's eyes) by tearing a page out of an art book and putting it in her purse. This can be seen as the fatal moral flaw that leads to her degeneration. Han-ki sees this. (He has been following her.) He is playing out a trap. Near her on the book display is a fat wallet. Pretty college girl grabs it, looks both ways, and puts it in her purse. This is the fatal moral flaw leading to entrapment and a descent into hell. She hurries to the bathroom and in the stall opens the wallet and takes out the money. Meanwhile the guy who lost the wallet is told (presumably by the bad guy) that she has the wallet and is in the bathroom. By the time he gets there she is gone. He chases after her and finally catches her. He roughs her up, calls her a pickpocket, and then forces her to go to a loan shark and sign an agreement (with her body as collateral) for money that he says was in the wallet.

This might be called "the turn" as the setup takes on a startling twist.

Next Sun-hwa is forced into prostitution by Han-ki She makes some feeble attempts to get away, but mysteriously has nowhere to go it seems, and anyway is too afraid to run. She realizes that she is going to lose her

21-year-old virginity so she begs her captors to let her lose it to her boyfriend. Han-ki and his fellow thugs mysteriously oblige. However, the boyfriend is confused and doesn't get the job done. They pull him out of the car, slap him around, dump him, and Sun-hwa is back at the showcase on the street. Through a two-way mirror Han-ki watches her lose her virginity to a forceful client.

Question number one: why doesn't Han-ki ever speak? Question number two: why does he watch her behind the two-way mirror instead of taking her himself?

The answer comes later in the film when we do hear him speak for the first time. His voice is a high shriek. Guess what his unique problem is.

And then comes the resolution. Yes, this is a love story of sorts and yes they do fall in love in a way that is debased and seemingly fated. He's a pimp and she's now a prostitute. This works out since he is able to vicariously experience her sexually and she is able to thereby serve the man she loves. And together they can make a living.

There is also a supernatural element in the film that suggests that the story is part wish-fulfillment fantasy by Han-ki. His ability to beat up the other guys and survive knife wounds fairly begs credulity. During the course of the film he loses enough blood to supply a small hospital. And the scene where both he and Sun-hwa appear together on the beach as if by magic is more mystical than realistic.

This is a haunting film done without any looking back or any compromise with the sensibilities of viewers. Director Ki-duk Kim's message seems to be that animal passion will win out in the end, and that humans are, despite the facades they put on, just animals doing animal-like things in the human jungle, and deliverance comes only when one realizes his or her nature and gives into it. Ki-duk Kim makes us identify with the bad guy and feel that he and pretty girl are no worse or no better than anyone else.

In short I found this movie disturbing like something from, say, novelist Cormac McCarthy. I am thinking especially of his novel, *Child of God*. That title is ironic in the sense that his anti-heroic protagonist really is, whatever we may say or think, or however bestial his behavior, a child of God, while Ki-duk Kim's title "Bad Guy" ("Nabbeun namja") is also ironic in the sense that Han-ki is by societal standards certainly a bad guy, but by naturalistic (or cosmic) standards no better or worse than the pretty college girl.

Bottom line: see this excellent and deeply troubling film at your own risk.

I've seen this and I give it____stars.
I want to see it___. I'll pass___.
The review was worth reading___. Not___.

Black Orpheus (*Orfeu Negro*) (1958) 10

A strange and beautiful film

Do they clean the streets in Rio de Janeiro? Well, of course they do. When this carnival is over.

And if you watch this movie you will see that they do it very near the end of the last reel, as in the morning when the truck comes round spraying water, just one of a thousand little details that director Marcel Camus got right, and one of the most insignificant. But it is from a multiplicity of detail that an edifice of cinematic genius is constructed.

The true brilliance of Black Orpheus lies in the people who live on the side of the cliffs overlooking the harbor at Rio. It is their energy that prevails. Then there is the color, the costumes, the pounding rhythms, the spectacular vitality of life that is depicted as a carnival of dance and song in which we are driven along as on a wave. And yet there is the constant reality of death. And it strikes in ways we cannot comprehend, fatalistically, and we are helpless to do anything about it. And then Orpheus sings, a new Orpheus perhaps, and the sun rises again, and a little girl in white, looking like Eurydice in miniature, begins to dance as the little boy Orpheus plays his guitar, telling us that time has come round again.

Well, that's the plot of this Portuguese language film as adapted by screen writer Jacques Voit from the play by Vinicius d Moraes as divined from the Greek mythology. Supporting this arresting conception is the music by Antonio Carlos Jobim and Luis Bonfa. I recall the former as the composer of bossanova who gave us "The Girl from Ipanema" and made the samba international. Starring in the title role as the streetcar conductor who is loved by all is Beno Melo, who might be seen as the natural man and native of paradise. The very pretty Marpessa Dawn plays Eurydice, an innocent from the country who falls in love with Orpheus and his song. Lourdes de Oliveira plays his intended, Mira who is hot blooded, vital and beautifully ordinary. But the actress I recall most vividly from the time I first saw this in the sixties was Léa Garcia who played Serafina. Her exuberance and comedic flair struck me as something completely different from anybody I had ever seen before. And then there are the boys who follow Orpheus around and emulate his every move. With their torn shirts and unflagging optimism, they represent the new day that will dawn.

If you haven't seen this strange and beautiful film, you are in for a singular experience. There is nothing else like it that I know of. And it is as fresh today as when it was made almost half a century ago.

I've seen this and I give it____stars.
I want to see it___. I'll pass___.
The review was worth reading___. Not___.

Paradise Now (2005) 10

Very much worth seeing regardless of your POV

For those viewers who are wondering whether this is a pro suicide bomber movie or not, I can say that it may depend upon who's doing the viewing. Director Hany Abu-Assad, who is a Muslim was born in Nazareth, which is a largely Christian city in Palestine. He moved to the Netherlands when he was a young man and currently lives in Los Angeles. He believes the film presents "an artistic point of view of...[a] political issue."

I tend to agree. The proof perhaps is in the fact that some Palestinians feel the film wasn't fair to their situation while some Israelis feel that the film glorified suicide bombers. Both sides can find evidence in the film to support their point of view, and the arguments can become heated.

Personally I find suicide bombings abhorrent and counterproductive. My belief has long been that the Palestinians would further their cause through a non-violent approach similar to methods used by Gandhi and Martin Luther King Jr. Using your children to kill other people's children while committing suicide is not only morally wrong, but not likely to win the hearts and minds of people who can help you. Furthermore the idea (expressed in the film by the suicide bombers and those who exploit them) that some people are superior because they are not afraid to die demonstrates a limited understanding of human nature and ignores history. The Japanese used suicide bombers in World War II for example to no good effect. And those men were not the "humiliated" and "oppressed" uneducated youths typical of suicide bombers in the Middle East. Instead some of them were the cream of the young manhood of a growing nation. Understand also that if the United States had the need it would have no trouble persuading countless Americans to commit suicide for God and country. Some of the combat missions in the Pacific Theater amounted to something close to suicide. No single people have a monopoly on tribalism.

What Hany Abu-Assad shows in this Arabic language film is that the justification for suicide bombing is at best suspect and at worse without any merit at all. "What happens afterward?" one of the bombers asks, and is told, "Two angels come and pick you up." This is not merely satire, it is a burlesque of the "Paradise Now" reasoning. Indeed the title of the film is itself satirical and ironic. Young men seeing this film will notice that it is THEY who are being used as suicide bombers, not the political leaders and the imams. Also the scene in which the suicide bombers make the obligatory video saying goodbye to family and friends and "I did it for God" with automatic rifle held on high, was played as farce, revealing the empty promise behind being used.

The fact that most of the anti-suicide rhetoric in the film comes from Suha (Lubna Azabal) who is the daughter of a privileged Arab and onetime opposition hero is seen as significant by some because in Arab/Muslim countries the political opinion of women is of scant value, and therefore Suha is seen as expressing a minority or discredited opinion. However, since her expression is so very well articulated and persuasive, it can be seen from the opposite point of view, as expressing reason and moral truth.

Hany Abu-Assad of course had more than an artistic intent in making this film. Clearly he wanted to put the tragedy of the Palestinians upon the silver screen (and DVD) for all the world to see. To be effective he realized that he could not poison the waters of his expression with subjectivity and one-sidedness. He had to work hard to be as objective as possible and to present both sides of the argument. That way his film would be viewed and discussed, and some sympathy and understanding might develop. He had to show suicide bombers as living, breathing human beings. Notice that the two depicted are relatively intelligent young men, not mindless robots.

I share with Abu-Assad the belief that if all the facts about what is happening in the Middle East become widely known and understood (in so far as it is possible to understand the lives of people living in different cultures thousands of miles away) this knowledge and understanding would help to bring about positive change. Ignorance is our only real enemy.

In short, Paradise Now is a work of art and an excellent film that clearly deserved its Golden Globe Award as the Best Foreign Film and its nomination for an Oscar as Best Foreign Film. Kais Nashif who plays Said, one of the bombers, and Ali Suliman, who plays the other, both do an outstanding job, particularly Nashif who manages to combine the look and feel of a disadvantaged youth with the strength of character of a young man who is determined to follow what he ultimately determines is his fate. His motivation goes beyond the ignorant and indoctrinated suicide bomber who is hoping to be rewarded with virgins in heaven. He has personal reasons for becoming a suicide bomber. He is the son of a man who collaborated with the Israelis, and consequently he feels that his fate is to compensate for what his father did.

The film was shot in Nablus and Nazareth and captures some of the atmosphere. The editing is crisp and the story unfolds clearly with a nice tension. The sense that the bomb around the bomber's waist could go off at any moment is one of the devices in the film that maintains that tension in a unique way.

All in all this a film very much worth seeing regardless of how you feel about the Israeli/Palestinian conflict.

Rashomon (1950) 10

Required viewing at most film schools

In the Bible, Pilate asks, "What is truth?" and, as Roger Bacon puts it, "would not stay for an answer."

I felt a bit the same way after seeing this remarkable film by Japan's celebrated film maker, Akira Kurosawa. It is set in 12th century Japan, and while most viewers would say it examines the nature of truth and finds it slippery, I think it more properly examines the nature of the feudal Japanese society.

We have as representatives of that society, a priest (Minuru Chiaki) and a woodcutter (Takashi Shimura) sitting out a rain storm in a place called Rashomon. It might pass for a ruined Greek temple except that its pillars and roof are made of wood. The priest and the woodcutter declare that they just can't understand it. They shake their heads and stare at the ground. Along comes a commoner (Kichijiro Uedo), a cynical man who asks what it is that they cannot understand.

They have witnessed an investigation into the death of a samurai, Takehiro (Masayuki Mori). He is in some ways the equivalent of a medieval knight. He has a horse and lady, Masako (Machiko Kyo). The accused is an infamous outlaw named Tajomaru (played brilliantly by Toshiro Mifune, who obviously had a lot of fun with the part). He tells his story. He admits to having his way with the lady, but lets the court know that she liked it so much that she began to embrace him while her husband was tied up watching. Afterwards he says that she insisted that they fight over her. Tajomaru obliges. He cuts the rope holding Takehiro and they sword fight. Tajomaru wins.

Next the wife tells her story. It is different of course. This causes the court to get a medium (Fumiko Honma) to tell the story from the point of view of the dead Takehiro. His story is different yet again. Finally the woodcutter reveals to the priest and the commoner that he saw the whole thing, and he then gives his version, again different of course.

The commoner has some terrifically cynical lines. Here are three:

"It's human to lie. Most of the time we can't even be honest with ourselves."

(To the priest:) "Not another sermon! I don't mind a lie if it's interesting."

"Man just wants to forget the bad stuff, and believe in the made-up good stuff. It's easier that way."

He speaks for the natural or animalistic man.

His counterpoint, the priest, opines, "If men don't trust each other, this earth might as well be hell."

He speaks for moral man.

Near the end of the film a baby is discovered crying. The woodcutter, who has five or six children of his own, takes the baby home.

He represents civilized man.

Masako represents the samurai's view of the nature of women when she is heard to say, "A man has to make a woman his by his sword."

What impressed me most about this film is the way Kurosawa was able to create an emotional atmosphere in each of the sittings. "In the Grove" we feel the trees and the light that sparkles through the leaves, and the disturbed serenity. At Rashomon in the rain we feel the men isolated and waiting, and in the sterile court scene we feel the severity of the tragedy.

Tampopo (1985) 9

The Wild Bunch at the noodle shop. Slurp!

There are any number of very funny scenes in this lightly plotted and highly episodic romantic comedy from acclaimed Japanese director Juzo Itami. You may recall him as the guy who got in trouble with the Yakuza, the Japanese "mafia," because they didn't like the way he made fun of them in Minbo no onna (1992). You may also know that he committed suicide at the age of 64 in 1997 after being accused of adultery. He is the son of samurai film maker Mansaku Itami. I mention this since one of the things satirized here are samurai films.

But—and perhaps this is the secret of Itami's success both in Japan and elsewhere—the satire is done with a light, almost loving touch. Even though he also takes dead aim at spaghetti westerns and the Japanese love affair with food, especially their predilection for fast food noodle soup, at no time is there any rancor or ugliness in his treatment.

If you've seen any Itami film you will be familiar with his star, his widow, Nobuko Miyamoto, she of the very expressive face, who is perhaps best known for her role as the spirited tax collector in Itami's The Taxing Woman (1987) and The Taxing Woman Returns (1988). She has appeared in all of his films. Here she is Tampopo ("Dandelion"), a not entirely successful proprietor of a noodle restaurant. Along comes not Jones but Tsutmu Yamazaki as Goro, a kind of true grit, but big-hearted Japanese urban cowboy. He ambles up to the noodle bar and before long establishes himself as a kind of John Wayne hero intent on teaching Tampopo how the good stuff is made. Along the way Itami makes fun of stuffy bureaucrats, macho Japanese males, heroic death scenes, Japanese princesses attempting to acquire a European eating style, movie fight scenes, and God knows what else.

The comedy is bizarre at times. The sexual exchange of an egg yoke between the man in the white suit (Koji Yakusho) and his mistress (Fukumi Kuroda) might make you laugh or it might just gross you out. The enthusiastic description of the "yam sausages" from inside a wild boar is strange. Surely one is not salivating at such an entre, but one can imagine that such a "delicacy" might surely exist and have its devotees.

Indeed an Itami film has a kind of logic all its own. An exemplary scene is that of the stressed and dying mother of two young children, who is ordered by her husband to "Get up and cook!" This (reasonably relevant) scene is juxtaposed with the one with the college professor which is about being and getting ripped off—which seems to have little to do with the rest of the movie, yet somehow seems appropriate, perhaps only because they are at a restaurant. Another typical Itami scene is the businessmen at supper. They hem and haw until their chief orders and then they all pretend to debate and consider, and then order exactly the same thing except for one brash young guy who dazzles (and embarrasses) the old sycophantic guys by order a massive meal in French with all the trimmings.

The climax of the film comes with plenty of musical fanfare. As Goro and others sit down at the counter, they are served Tampopo's final culinary creation, the noodle soup now hopefully honed to perfection. As the tension mounts, a musical accompaniment, reminiscent of something like the clock ticking in High Noon (1952), rises to a crescendo. All the while Tampopo sweats and frets and prays that she will triumph, which will be in evidence if, and only if, they drain their soup bowls! (Do they?)

The final credits roll (after some further misdirections and some further burlesque) over a most endearing and ultimately touching shot of a young mother with a beautiful and contented infant feeding at her breast.

Perhaps this is Itami's best film.

I've seen this and I give it____stars.
I want to see it___. I'll pass___.
The review was worth reading___. Not___.

City of God (*Cidade de Deus*) (2002) 9
Authentic and indelible

This Brazilian Portuguese language film set in the slums of Rio de Janeiro, the so-called "City of God," is a mesmerizing coming of age gangsta drama second to none you'll ever see. At the same time it is a tale of redemption and the triumph of relative good over relative evil.

Representing evil is the psychopathic L'il Dice/L'il Zé (Douglas Silva/Leandro Firmino da Hora), who kills people just for the joy it gives him. Representing the good is the story's narrator, Rocket (Alexandre Rodrigues), who will grow out of the slum to become a newspaper photographer. And representing something in between is the charismatic Benny (Phellipe Haagensen). The acting is excellent, including that by the "runts," actual kids from the City of God; but what carries the film is sharp direction by Fernando Meirelles from an outstanding script by Braulio Mantovani from a novel by Paulos Lins.

I think Hollywood directors ought to note well that it is the authentic realism of the film as seen from within the City of God by one of its own that makes this such a compelling experience for the audience. None of this can be faked. True, the story is a bit romanticized as a (very talented) kid might tell it to his friends, but that is all the better because the world view of those kids is part of what makes this film so effective. Additionally, all the little side stories: the woman at the newspaper who takes Rocket home with her for, shall we say, personal reasons; the story of the girl Rocket loves; the desire of the "runts' to be men, etc., add layers of genuineness that also can not be faked or dreamed up by any filmland script writer. These things have to be lived.

Last time I looked Cidade de Deus was rated #17 at IMDb, ahead of hundreds of great films. There's not much I can add to that. Is the film over-rated? I think so, and I think it will fall in the standings as time goes by. Good recent films tend to get a lot of attention, and then reach their level after some years have passed and they can be evaluated more objectively. Regardless, this is a watermark film for the Brazilian cinema and especially for director Fernando Meirelles who because of it rocketed from obscurity to world-wide fame almost overnight.

I've seen this and I give it____stars.
I want to see it___. I'll pass___.
The review was worth reading___. Not___.

The Eel (*Unagi*) (1997) 8
Flawed, but haunting

This is a film about human sexuality. It is not pleasant. Takuro Yamashita, played very effectively by Koji Yakusho, gets an anonymous letter telling him that his young, pretty wife is entertaining another man while he is out fishing at night, this after she lovingly prepares and packs his supper. He goes fishing but returns home early in time to catch them in medias res. In a cold rage he knifes his wife to death. He bicycles to the police station and turns himself in. Eight years later he gets out of prison. This is where our story begins.

Yamashita, now embittered toward others, and especially women, is on parole. He sets up a barber shop in a small town. He keeps a pet eel because he feels that the eel "listens" to him when he talks. One day he discovers a woman (Keiko Hattari, played by the beautiful Misa Shimizu) in some nearby bushes who has taken an overdose in a suicide attempt. He brings help and she is saved. She then enters his life as his assistant. Her presence challenges the emotional isolation he is seeking and forces him to face not only his future but his past.

The eel itself (a wet "snake") symbolizes sexuality. When this sexuality is confined it is under control. When it is let loose it is dark and deep and mysterious. Director Shohei Imamura's technique is plodding at times, and striking at others. His women are aggressive sexually even though, in the Japanese "princess" style, they may look younger than spring time. His men can be brutal. Their emotions, confined by society as the eel is confined by its tank, sometimes burst out violently.

For many viewers the pace of this film will be too slow, and for others the sexuality depicted will offend. For myself and others who are accustomed to seeing the faces of the players in long close ups on TV and in Western movies, Imamura's medium shots and disinclination to linger on the countenances of his actors will disappoint. Yakusho's face suggests the very depth and mystery that Imamura is aiming at, yet I don't think the camera lingers there enough. Also disappointing is how little we really see of Misa Shimizu's expressions. Chiho Terada, who plays the murdered wife, is also very pretty and completely convincing, but we see little of her. Her expression just before dying, a combination of shamelessness and resignation, funereal acceptance even, was unforgettable.

This is very much worth seeing, but expect to be irritated by the how slowly it unravels and by the central character's stubborn refusal to forgive both himself and his late wife, and his inability to embrace the life that is now his.

I've seen this and I give it____stars.
I want to see it___. I'll pass___.
The review was worth reading___. Not___.

Kadosh (1999) 7

What is "sacred"?

There are some thoughtful and well-written reviews both at Amazon and the IMDb and elsewhere in which it is claimed that the type of Jewish Orthodoxy presented here is not accurate. There are quibbles about the unnatural way that Meir puts on his garments. There is criticism of the selection of prayers recited, especially Meir giving thanks that he was not born a woman. Moreover, there is the assertion that orthodox Judaism does *not* require that a man repudiate his wife after ten years of marriage even though she may be barren. Furthermore, the character of Yossef is said not to be typical of orthodox Jewish men since he takes his wife sexually without love or tenderness, that he hits her when angry, and goes about the streets of Israel with a loudspeaker hawking his religious point of view.

First, it is a shame (if true) that the way Meir dressed and recited his morning prayers was inaccurate, because such details can easily be made accurate with some research. Certainly director Amos Gitai had access to many orthodox people who could have helped him. Putting that aside, the artistic point of the opening scene was to immerse the viewer into a world based on religious beliefs and practices that are strikingly different from the secular world of today. He also wanted to introduce his theme, which is that women in Orthodox Judaism, as in the other two great religions of the Middle East, in their fundamentalist interpretations—this bears repeating: in their fundamentalist interpretations—are not on an equal level with men. Certainly in a realistic sense, Meir, since he dearly loves his wife, would have chosen something else to recite. However, I think we can give Gitai some artistic license here. The fact that such a prayer exits in the Jewish canon is not to be denied.

Second, the film does *not* claim that Orthodox Judaism requires that a man repudiate his wife after ten years of childless marriage. Instead it makes the very strong point that, from the point of view of Orthodox Judaism, such a woman is not fulfilling her role in society, and that there will be people outside the marriage who will try to persuade him to abandon her. Gitai's screenplay contains several textual pronouncements to that effect. The fact that Meir is torn between his love for his wife and his love for his religion is really the point. How he resolves that dilemma is an individual choice, and that is what the film shows.

As for the unflattering character of Yossef, whom Rivka's sister Malka is persuaded to marry (not forced, mind you, but persuaded) he is a foil and a counterpoint for the loving and deeply religious Meir. The fact that he is not a poster boy for Orthodox Judaism is not a valid criticism of the film, since all religions have their black sheep.

I think a fairer criticism of the film can be made by addressing the question of, was it entertaining and/or a work of art?

Here I have mixed feelings. Certainly the acting was excellent, and the theme a worthy one. Gitai's desire to show the underlying similarities among the conservative expressions of all three Abrahamic religions, through their shared patriarchal attitudes toward women and their estrangement from the postmodern world, was very well taken and appropriate. Where I think Gitai failed as film maker is in his inability to be completely fair to the orthodox way of life—his failure to show the joys as well as the sorrows of its everyday life which would help outsiders to understand why people adhere to such a way of life.

I also think that the film could have been better edited. In the documentary about how the film was made we see scenes that were cut that I think should have been retained, especially the scene in which the omelette was made and the scene in which the mother critiques the life choices her three daughters have made. Instead we have some scenes that ran too long. It is a fine technique that Gitai sometimes employs of letting the silence speak for the characters, of holding the camera on the scene to allow the audience to reflect and then to reflect again. However, I think this can be overdone and was overdone, and that judicious cutting of some of the scenes would have strengthened the movie.

Bottom line: a slow polemic of a Hebrew language movie that nonetheless is worth seeing because of the importance and timeliness of its theme, the originality of some of the techniques, and the fine acting, especially by Yael Abecassis who played Rivka and Meital Barda who played Malka.

One more point: yellow subtitles, please!

I've seen this and I give it____stars.
I want to see it___. I'll pass___.
The review was worth reading___. Not___.

The Scent of Green Papaya *(Mui du du xanh)*

(1993) 7
Familiar, slow-moving story beautifully presented

This is a kind of Cinderella tale set in Saigon during the 1950s in which the yin and yang principles of the masculine element and the feminine are played out once again. We find ourselves in the airy, beautifully-appointed house of a well-to-do merchant family that has just hired a new servant. She is ten-year-old Mùi, played with grace and a kind of magical innocence by Man San Lu, who bestows her beatific little smile on all the little wonders of the world she sees around her. She learns her job quickly and works hard, always with a positive attitude. She loves all living things including insects and frogs. She tolerates the boorish behavior of the youngest son of the household who directs some indelicate gestures in her direction. Like a Taoist monk she just observes, judges not and says nothing.

Well, we know somebody is going to take notice of this splendid jeune fille, some wise young man, and when

she comes of age, marry her and elevate her station in life. Meanwhile the head of household squanders the family's funds and ten years pass. Now the family is almost broke and Mùi is sent to be the housekeeper and cook for Khuyen, played attractively by Hoa Hoi Vuong. She is now played by Tran Nu Yên-Khê who falls in love with the young man who is a classical pianist. Unfortunately he has a girl friend, a stylish woman of the city from a well-to-do family. Finally we have a bit of tension!

This, then, is an "art house" movie in which director Anh Hung Tran tells the story primarily with images and symbolism, and that he does very well. But the disjunction of the two very slight plots is never overcome, and the startling lack of any tension until near the end is disappointing. The central image of the film, the green papaya with the immature seeds inside representing the potential of the little girl is however not to be forgotten.

What carries this slow-moving extended vignette of antebellum Saigon, and saves us from abject boredom are the beautiful sets nestled in greenery with the Buddhist artwork, the wooden Venetian-slotted doors, the partitions, the lattice work, the vases, the statues, the arresting music, both eastern and western, the intensively focused cinematography, and the charm of ten-year-old Man San Lu. Many viewers, however charmed, will not stay for the finale, which will be too bad because it is in the later stages of the film that the fairy-tale quality of the film is fully realized. Mùi of course has come of age, and the developing love affair is revealed purely through camera work without any dialogue.

Incidentally, I was somewhat surprised to learn that this beautifully rendered film was shot not on locale in Saigon, Vietnam where the action takes place, but in a Paris studio! This makes me imagine that the trees, especially the papaya tree in the central courtyard, and the little animals, the frogs and geckos were shipped in. It also makes me realize that the ants that the one boy drips hot candle wax on, the ants that Mùi admires and her cricket in a cage are most likely Parisians.

I've seen this and I give it____stars.
I want to see it___. I'll pass___.
The review was worth reading___. Not___.

The Sea *(Hafið)*(2002) 9

Sharp, steamy, wild and funny

This Icelandic language film reminds me a bit of French family dramas with skeletons in the closet revealed amidst festive holiday get-togethers. But Director Baltasar Kormakur's Icelanders are decidedly on the wild side, corrupt, and often sloppy drunk. Their dialogue is sharp and rough, their language biting and crude, their behavior violent.

The story is a bit familiar with the head of a fishing family getting old and worrying about the business he has built. Currently running it is his elder son who does not inspire confidence. In fact, he frequently goes against the old man's wishes. But it soon becomes clear that the old man has lost his judgment and is living in the past, and it is he who is detrimental to the company's bottom line.

Plot point one is the return of the favorite son with his pregnant girl friend. This is the son who should be running the company, the patriarch believes. However the son has no interest in living out his life in the fishing village and neither does his girl friend. The girl friend is the objectifying element in the story, and we are compelled to see the story from her point of view.

Also returning are the daughter and her husband. Together she and the older son conspire to wrest control of the company from the father...and then all hell breaks loose.

Complicating matters is the fact that Kristin, the favorite son's old girl friend (and half-sibling), is still madly in love with him and won't let him go.

What makes this work is a steamy script with some laugh-out-loud moments, and a careful, atmospheric direction that shows a way of life that is familiar but distant. This is ultimately a story about the encroachment of the modern world on an Icelandic fishing village. It could be a fishing village anywhere.

See this for Baltasar Kormakur, a film maker of promise.

I've seen this and I give it___stars.
I want to see it___. I'll pass___.
The review was worth reading___. Not___.

A Short Film about Love (Krótki film o milosci)

(1988) 9
Is it obsession or love?

The only criticism I would have of this enthralling Polish language film by the great Polish-French director Krzysztof Kieslowski is his use of the "opened window" conceit. Magda (Grazyna Szapolowska) is a woman who lives alone in a high rise housing development. She is sexy and cynical to the point of not believing in love. To her it is all desire, and the fulfillment or frustration of desire. Across the way from her lives a virginal young man by the name of Tomek (Olaf Lubaszenko) who has been spying on her from his apartment window through a telescope.

He lives with a friend's mother (Stefania Iwinska) who looks after him as her own son. He works in the post office and obsesses about Magda's life. He watches her with her beaux. He even goes so far as to write a couple of phony money order slips for her and put them in her mailbox just so she will have to go to his window and ask about them. When she does he is able to examine her features closely. Is his an obsession or is it love? Kieslowski's answer is that it is love, love with the kind of depth and feeling that Magda cannot even imagine until she experiences it. And then she is amazed and dumbfounded.

The key scene in the movie occurs when Tomek is finally able to be together with the object of his love, in her apartment, with her telling him that "When a woman wants a man she gets wet inside." And she invites him to check it out, so to speak. But what happens does not lead to any kind of fulfillment. Instead Tomek is inadvertently humiliated.

And that's the story, more or less. As usual with Kieslowski, human feelings predominate and are stark and one might say conflicted—the conflict arising between humankind's baser instincts and the more civilized ones of society. What he does here is turn the stalker into the saint, in a sense, and the object of his love into something unworthy of that love.

The question might arise: is it realistic to believe that a woman would leave her windows open and her lights on for all to see inside while she goes about her private life? No, it isn't. But we have to accept this device. After that the film is fully realistic to the point of even being mundane in its depiction of middle class city life. The characters are ordinary and even a little boring except for Tomek's supreme obsession. It is this "jewel" in the heart of the Polish city that lifts his life and her life above the ordinary. Even though we know that she is too old and too world-weary for him and that he is too hopelessly young and inexperienced for her for lasting love to ever bloom between them, we cannot help but think how wonderful it would be if we could all feel as he does, or be the object of such love.

Usually when this theme is worked out it is the obsessed who suffer greatly, it is the obsessed who are to be pitied—and we do to some extent feel something close to that for Tomek. But here it is Magda who we end up pitying the more because of her inability to love. Compared to Tomek she is a deprived creature who will never find true happiness—unless she learns this lesson she has gotten from this young man whose passion for her was unlike anything she had ever experienced before.

And this is Kieslowski's point: it is not only better to have loved and lost than never to have loved at all. It is only through love that we can truly identify with another human being. We see this in the scene where Madga is looking through Tomek's telescope into her apartment window and recalling what he had seen one day, the day that she had come home and spilled the milk and sat at the table crying over that spilled milk (very typical of Kieslowski to use such an obvious, but telling and entirely apt cliché) after a breakup with one of her boy-friends. In memory she sees Tomek looking at her crying and running her finger through the spilled milk, and she realizes the depth of his commiseration with her and his love for her, and in her mind's eye she sees him beside her (as he truly was psychologically) with his hand on her shoulder and love in his heart.

We might think that at some other time she will look back on a relationship she had had in her life and real-ize that the failure was due to a lack of love on her part. Indeed she more or less reveals that to us when she tells Tomek's "Godmother" that no, she is not the right per-son for Tomek. We know that she is too cynical and would only use him temporarily for gratification, and that would be all.

But I was left with the sense that Magda would indeed learn from her experience and would be transformed. There is this sense of hope and the possibility of emo-tional and spiritual growth that is often seen in the films of Krzysztof Kieslowski.

I've seen this and I give it____stars.
I want to see it___. I'll pass___.
The review was worth reading___. Not___.

A Taxing Woman (*Marusa no onna*) (1987) 7

A sly, original comedy

She's rather memorable, this taxing woman. She has a face like a China doll all grown up with freckles around her eyes and a mat of thick dark hair on her head as though cut with the aid of a vegetable bowl. She is No-buko Miyamoto, wife of the late and lamented director Juzo Itami, and a comedic star worthy of "Saturday Night Live" in its better days. She plays Ryoke Hakura, tireless tax inspector hot on the trail of shady tax dodger Hideki Gondo, played with rakish self-indulgence by Tsutomi Yamazaki. Itami blends situation comedy with some soap opera angst (Japanese and American) to which he adds some ersatz action/adventure shtick (the chase scene near the end with Hakura legging it after Gondo's teenage son, comes to mind) seasoned with a touch of the traditional theater and a little zesty porn, well mixed. The result is interesting and a little jarring.

I was most affected by the atmosphere of this strange and original comedy. I found myself looking at the back-drops and the sets and into the faces of all those very neat Japanese bureaucrats as I followed Ryoko Hakura's tireless pursuit of the missing yen. All that paper work and all those numbers! Interesting were the attitudes and presumptions of the characters in terms of sexuality and social status. We can see that in the modern Japan a woman must navigate her way carefully through the sea of men, while a man must achieve financial success to command respect. And yet there lingers still the flavor and the swagger of the samurai as seen in the scene where Gondo cuts his finger to write a bank account number in blood.

Aside from getting a little soapy at the end, this is fine flick, sly and amusing.

I've seen this and I give it____stars.
I want to see it___. I'll pass___.
The review was worth reading___. Not___.

Chapter Twelve:

Celebrations

or

Wow, That Was Really Good!

These are reviews of nine and ten star movies not appearing elsewhere in the book. You might want to assign your own stars in the space provided after each review. You might even want to rate my review's worthiness at the same time. Charitably, of course.

21 Grams (2003) 9

Intense and stark

Intense performances by Sean Penn, Naomi Watts and Benicio Del Toro, not to mention some fine work by Charlotte Gainsbourg and Melissa Leo, make this almost too much to bear. Director Alejandro Gonzalez Inarritu throws out a line of tension and keeps it incredibly taunt from beginning to end while exploring the most fundamental human emotions: fear, love, lust, and tragic loss. He uses a technique being seen more and more in film, a technique in which the story is not told in chronological order, but temporally scattered. This technique is similar to that used by, for example, Christopher Nolan in *Memento* (2000) in which the story is told in reverse chronological order. Here there is a mixed pattern as the story unfolds, sometimes in sequence, sometimes out of sequence. At first it is disconcerting, then intriguing, and finally everything is abundantly clear. I don't think this technique is necessary, but it does have the virtue of forcing the viewer to become engaged in trying to figure out what is going on. And perhaps this heightens the cinematic experience.

There are three stories strung together on a single strand of fate. First there is the story of Jack Jordan (Del Toro) a petty macho criminal who has found Jesus. Second there is that of Paul Rivers (Penn), a college professor of mathematics who is dying because of a defective heart. And third there is that of Cristina Peck (Watts) who has found what she wants in life with a husband she loves and two young daughters. And then there is the tragic accident that seals their differing fates, and brings horror into their lives. The story is told in starkly realistic scenes spliced in jarring juxtapositions, skipping from one character's story to the other. The effect is to give us relief from the terrible events of one part of the story only to lead into another, and then to pull away from that story and into a third until the stories appear as one.

I cannot say enough about the performance of the three leads. Sean Penn is brilliant in an understated way as he projects (by turns) charm and tenderness, desperation and hope, and a kind of hopelessness headed for a flat line. Naomi Watts is electrifying in the intensity she brings to the most emotionally-wrought scenes. She is one of the most amazing actresses working today, and if you haven't seen her, see her here. You won't forget her. She was nominated for an Oscar for Best Actress (losing out to Charlize Theron in *Monster*). And much the same can be said of Benicio Del Toro who was also nominated for an Oscar for Best Supporting Actor (losing out to Tim Robbins in *Mystic River*). Del Toro's portrayal of a fated man who both found and lost his faith because of tragic events and his own failure of character was totally convincing and very sad.

If I had to nitpick I would say that Cristina's initial feeling that she couldn't be bothered to help prosecute Jack Jordan for killing her family did not square well with her later feeling that she wanted to kill him. Yet, I suppose, one's feelings can change. I also didn't think Jordan was the kind of character who would hit and run. He takes responsibility for his actions. He turns himself in and says that he has a responsibility to God.

As far as the ending goes, note that Cristina is dressed in bright, almost happy colors because of what was discovered when she donated her type O-positive blood to save Paul's life. Obviously I can't reveal what was discovered in a review, but I'm willing to bet some people found it redeeming and hopeful while others found it ironic while still others may have found it cheap and easy. Personally I thought it worked because everything in this movie revolves around very physical human events.

Bottom line: may be too intense for some viewers, and put the kiddies to bed.

I've seen this and I give it___stars.
I want to see it___. I'll pass___.
The review was worth reading___. Not___.

About Schmidt (2002) 9

Banality made into art

Warren Schmidt is 65 or 66. He is sitting in his office at Woodman Insurance in Omaha, Nebraska (that would be Mutual of Omaha, one imagines) waiting for the second hand and the minute hand to go straight up signaling that it is exactly five o'clock and he can go home. He is precise about this. It is also his last day at work. He is retiring. There is a retirement party. It is incredibly banal: the little speeches of appreciation about his loyalty and how much he did for the company, the lame jokes, the wooden chicken, etc. It's so bad that at one point Schmidt has to slip out for a vodka.

And now he is into the sheer terror of retirement itself. He is having trouble figuring out what to do with himself. Being around his wife all the time irritates him. Not having something worthwhile to do bores him. He grumbles. He flicks the remote on the TV. He sees an ad to be a foster parent of a child in Tanzania. Twenty-two bucks. And then his wife of 42 years drops dead. The even more banal funeral. Now he really doesn't know what to do with himself. He lets the house go to ruin: trash all over the place. He doesn't shave. He doesn't get out of his bathrobe. His only daughter is marrying a guy he considers a nincompoop. He writes letters to his six-year-old foster child telling him about his circumstances, but with the rose-colored glasses on. He has nobody to talk to.

Jack Nicholson stars as Schmidt and gives a very fine performance. He is still obviously Jack Nicholson, one of the great stars of our time, but he is also Schmidt and he portrays this hollow man as though he is filled with angry, repressed bile. Nicholson has the theatrical ability to overact without seeming to overact, to huff and puff and make hurt faces that seem so natural and in keeping with his character that we watch transfixed. Nicholson somehow makes this most commonplace man and his most ordinary life fascinating.

What I was wondering as I watched was, how does this play in Peoria? (BTW, that's Peoria, Illinois, which serves however reluctantly as the psychological and politically-correct heart of America—or at least it has since John Ehrlichman of the Nixon administration first used the term in 1970.) Will Peorians be offended? Will the stifling banality of Schmidt's life be seen as satire and criticism of the American way of life, the usual blue state effete snobbery inflicted on the heartland citizens of the red states? Or will heartlanders see no satire, no sarcasm,

and instead imagine that Schmidt is the embodiment of all that is right and proper (with a few understandable human peccadillos to round out his character)?

So I checked out some reader reviews. I couldn't find any reviewers that were offended. The ones who didn't like the movie said they were just bored to tears, or actually bored to anger. They wasted their time and money on this movie! Well, that doesn't mean much. Any movie without a constant stream of titillation is bound to bore some people.

But the movie is sad. Schmidt is a sad character. He calls himself a failure and asks if he has made any difference in anybody's life and he concludes that he hasn't. He is an empty shell of a man whose relationships with other people were invariably shallow including that with his daughter about whom he hasn't a clue.

Yet the movie is funny. Most of the humor comes from how perfectly director Alexander Payne got the insipid banalities of our culture and mentality: The knickknacks that Schmidt leaves on the roof of the Winnebago. The roadside museums with their self-important histories. The bromides and platitudes from the groom-to-be (Dermot Mulroney) and his Ponzi scheme dream of wealth. Schmidt's stupidity in mistaking a younger woman's pity for sexual desire. His stupefying inability to have the slightest clue about anybody but himself.

The supporting cast was very good, particularly Kathy Bates as Roberta the groom's earth mother with libido who fills the screen with her...uh, unmistakable presence, scaring Schmidt all the way back to Omaha. And Hope Davis is excellent as the daughter who no longer has any patience with her father's selfish obtuseness. The scene in which she tells him off in no uncertain terms is one of the best movie putdowns I've seen in years.

But see this for Alexander Payne whose directorial credits include *Election* (1999) and *Sideways* (2004). It is no coincidence that he was born in Omaha, Nebraska.

I've seen this and I give it___stars.
I want to see it___. I'll pass___.
The review was worth reading___. Not___.

The African Queen (1951) 10

One of John Huston's very best

There are three primary reasons you might want to see this old black and white classic.

First it is a beautiful and touching love story. Straitlaced teetotaler (and maiden sister of a preacher) Rose Sayer (Katharine Hepburn) meets a kind of ordinary joe who is a handyman deluxe sort of guy, Charlie Allnut (Humphrey Bogart) a man who is a bit crude and likes to swill his gin. They're in the middle of Africa during the Great War. Her brother has been killed, the Germans have the natives where they want them and, well, Charlie has an old river boat and offers to give the high-toned woman a ride.

There is nothing quite like the sparks that fly from opposite poles. And yes, opposites do attract, but of course it takes them awhile to feel the magnetic force. The beautiful thing about this love story is how Charlie proves his mettle and wins her heart—a heart never won before—by sheer gumption and by finding the courage he never knew he had—egged on and inspired by her relentless strength of character. The moment that she realizes, despite all the differences between them, that she loves him is beautifully and exactingly captured by John Huston's superb direction.

The second reason to see this cinematic masterwork is the performance by Katherine Hepburn. She has given many outstanding performances; there is hardly an actor anywhere held in higher esteem, nor one who has had a more lasting and admired career. I have seen many of her movies but never have I seen her better. She is just perfect for the part and delivers every line with style and a deep understanding of her character. She allows us to understand that Rose's crazy, naïve beliefs about what is possible infect Charlie to the extent that he becomes something more than himself, and it is that self that she falls madly in love with.

The third reason is the inspired performance by Humphrey Bogart. This is not the usual worldly-wise, tough guy that Bogart usually plays. Instead he is an ordinary, though pragmatic guy who knows his limitations. He didn't last this long as a self-styled river boat captain without taking certain precautions in what he would venture and what he would not. Yet, so taken with the relative status and the exquisite high-toned righteousness of Miss Rose Sayer, he is able to do things that ordinarily he wouldn't try. And when she falls in love with him, he is amply rewarded, and the audience loves it.

I should add that shots of the boat, the African Queen, and of the animals along the river and in the river seemed authentic and atmospherically perfect even though I've seen a couple hundred much more modern African nature videos.

By the way, this movie contains the famous quote, spoken by Miss Hepburn: "Human nature, Mr. Allnut, is what we were put on this earth to rise above."

One more thing to add: the movie was adapted by C.S. Forester and James Agee from Forester's novel. Those are two of the best writers to ever work a Hollywood screenplay, and it shows. The dialogue and the development of character and story are exquisitely done so

that one is lost in the events and only returns to the real world when the movie ends.

Truly, they don't make them like this anymore.

I've seen this and I give it___stars.
I want to see it___. I'll pass___.
The review was worth reading___. Not___.

Almost Famous (2000) 10

Warm, sweet and brilliant

Every time they do a writer story I get all choked up. This is like *Shakespeare in Love* only different. Like *Shakespeare in Love*? WHAT? Well, we have a writer as the hero. And...? And he's in love. And...? Okay the rest is different except that he's really working hard to be a success and he's around performers and... Anyway "it's all happening." By the way, that should be "It's all happening at the zoo" a lyric from the Simon and Garfunkel album in the opening scene.

Okay, okay. I'm having a little trouble with this one. I thought it was just so, so cute, and so touching and warm, even though I know it's only "[my] rock and roll fantasy." However I don't care. I watched practically the whole thing with tears in my eyes, partially from nostalgia from the music and the clothes and the hair styles done so perfectly, and partly because the story of "Penny Lane," sweet flower child groupie, "seamstress for the band" (to borrow a lyric) who has a "rock and roll record" to borrow another lyric (Great White, this time) who wears her sophistication on her sleeve to cover her heart that's also there. And for a slightly nerdish kid who grows up before our eyes and falls in love and is too young to really be loved in return, a nervous writer on his first assignment who overwrites and sees the best in people, even as they treat him like a little girl, a kid who is so, so unsure of himself. (Is writer and director Cameron Crowe again reprising his youth as he did so well in the script for the now classic coming of ager, *Fast Times at Ridgemont High* (1982)?)

Kate Hudson (Goldie Hawn's daughter) is unforgettable in a completely original creation dreamed up (or better yet, probably remembered) by Crowe, who here improves on his fine directorial work in *Jerry Maguire* (1996). I understand that Sarah Polley (*The Sweet Hereafter* 1997) was originally picked to play the part of Penny Lane, and she is a fine talent, but quite frankly Kate Hudson stole all the scenes she was in (she learned it from her mother!) and I don't think the movie would have been quite the beguiling, bittersweet experience it was without her.

Billy Crudup (a name to look at twice) manages to look exactly like all the wanna-be rock stars of the seventies wished they had while exuding the kind of charm that breaks hearts as Russell Hammond, guitarist for the band and Penny's true love. Patrick Fugit is William Miller the would-be teenaged writer as hero who is charming, boyish, vulnerable and well, heroic. Frances McDormand plays his mother with just the right combination of pigheaded earnestness and her unique sense of the comedic.

The entire cast was terrific and the characters were truly original. The Academy Award winning script was clever and at times profound, interspersed with sparkling lines. (My favorite, from Lester Bangs on William's school mates: "You'll meet them all again on their long journey to the middle.") Also, and this is important, Crowe paid close attention to detail throughout and never lost his concentration. Everything seemed amazingly authentic right down to the floral stitch on Russell's shirts and the bottles of Jack Daniels in his hands. And nothing was done in a routine manner. Every scene was carefully planned and even minor characters were roundly developed. I'm thinking in particular of Lester Bangs, mentor and cynical rock critic brought to life in a fine performance by Phillip Seymour Hoffman, and William's sweet and slightly dippy sister, vividly portrayed by Zooey Deschanel. Notice how Crowe even took the trouble to satirize flight attendants with a parody of the stewardess uniforms (day glow orange!).

Yes, I loved this film, and I predict that the Academy, whose members obviously did not really SEE this film, will be rewarding the producers sometime down the road for the oversight.

I've seen this and I give it___stars.
I want to see it___. I'll pass___.
The review was worth reading___. Not___.

Anatomy of a Murder (1959) 9

Wears surprisingly well

Otto Preminger, who produced and directed this fine courtroom drama starring James Stewart, Lee Remick, George C. Scott and Ben Gazzara, had a knack for translating best-selling mid-cult novels to the screen (*The Man with the Golden Arm* (1955); *Exodus* (1960); *Advise and Consent* (1962) and others) usually in a nervy manner, sometimes heavy-handed, sometimes pretentious, but always worth a look. Part of his secret was star power. Like Hitchcock, he liked to go with big names supported by fine character actors. And part of his secret was his long experience in both the theater and films going back to the silent film era. He knew how to put together a movie. But more than anything it was his near-dictatorial control over the production (something directors seldom have today, and never in big budget films—Preminger's were big budget for his day) that allowed him to successfully capture the movie-going audience at midcentury.

This and *Laura* (1944) are two of his films that go beyond the merely commercial and achieve something that can be called art. Seeing this for the first time forty-three years after it was released I was struck by the fine acting all around and the sturdy, well-constructed direction. James Stewart's performance as the Michigan north country lawyer Paul Biegler might shine even more luminously than it does except for a certain performance by Gregory Peck three years later as a southern country lawyer in the unforgettable *To Kill a Mockingbird* (1962). Lee Remick, in a frank, but imperfect imitation of Marilyn Monroe, co-stars as Laura Manion, the wife of army Lt. Frederick Manion (Gazzara) whom Bielger is defending on a murder charge. The defense is temporary insanity because the man he shot raped his wife. Bielger slyly gains sympathy for his client by deliberately allowing it to come out that Laura is sexy and flirtatious enough to drive any man crazy. Indeed, he tricks the prosecution into doing his work for him. George C. Scott plays Claude Dancer, a big city prosecutor, with snake-like precision while Gazzara manages to combine introspection and cockiness as the young lieutenant. Fine support comes from Eve Arden (best known as Our Miss Brooks on TV and in the movie of that name) as Biegler's loyal secretary and Arthur O'Connell as his alcoholic mentor. Kathryn Grant, who gave up a promising film career to marry Bing Crosby and have children, has a modest role as the murdered man's daughter.

I've seen many courtroom dramas, some real, some fictional, since this film first appeared, but I have to say it stands up well. The action (for the most part) feels realistic and the tension is nicely created and maintained. The resolution is satisfying and the ending is as sly and subtle as any country lawyer might want. Incidentally, if this movie had more total votes cast at IMDb, it would rank in their top 250, which is where it belongs.

See this for James Stewart whose easy, adroit style under Preminger's direction found full range. Although he gave many fine performances, I don't think Stewart was ever better than he was here.

I've seen this and I give it___stars.
I want to see it___. I'll pass___.
The review was worth reading___. Not___.

As Good As It Gets (1997) 10

With a nod to Charles Dickens's Scrooge

Brilliantly written, brilliantly acted and cleanly directed, this strange and wonderful tale is one of the best romantic comedies ever to hit the silver screen. Helen Hunt, as an unmarried thirtysomething waitress with an asthmatic five-year-old boy, is exquisite. Jack Nicholson, as a weird and mean obsessive/compulsive writer named Melvin Udall, is even better than he usually is, and he is one of the great actors of our time, and even Greg Kinnear in a supporting role as the sensitive gay guy next door is outstanding.

Of course I love impossible love, unrequited love, love that takes decades to culmination. This is a case of impossible love come true. Eat your heart out Nora Ephron! And you too Meg Ryan and Tom Hanks. But I couldn't help but think, considering the principals, how impossible it really is on another level. But never mind, in fact, all the better.

James L. Brooks, who directed and who, along with Mark Andrus (from his story) wrote the script, is to be highly commended. The concept of an obsessive/compulsive, self-centered (almost autistic) older guy, set in his ways beyond anything normal finding love is just wondrous strange. And a patient and caring, under-achieving, under-appreciated Manhattan waitress in a house dress, finding not just love but somebody who really knows who she is and what she's worth is also just wonderful.

Wonderful, yes. A wonderful movie to lift the spirit. But *As Good As It Gets* is more than that. The dialogue is sharp and witty and big-city sophisticated and sometimes laugh out loud funny. The underlying statements about relationships and love in urban America are subtle and thought-provoking. So much is said beside the point. Yes, off to the side we find some street hustlers juxtaposed with someone sensitive, and we see how irrelevant they are and how he overcomes them and this brutal thing they have done to him. And off to the side we see again how irrelevant is the homophobia of a man lost in prejudice and self-hatred, and how it changes when he becomes aware and when he learns to love.

The ancient rule in comedy, from the Greeks to Shakespeare to the musical comedy of the stage to the romantic comedies of the silver screen, has been young and attractive principals overcome obstacles and live happily ever after. Here we have obstacles of the most tiring sort, obstacles not of class or race or family, but of psychological problems, stuff straight out of the *Diagnostic and Statistical Manual of Mental Disorders*—although to be technical, the symptoms of Melvin Udall are a cornucopia of psychiatric delight. The bitter, cutting, hateful insults that he showers on everyone, even his most devoted admirers, seem more characteristic of Tourette's Syndrome than of an obsessive/compulsive disorder. But never mind. It works. In fact everything works in this movie, from the adorable little dog whom Melvin loves ("A dog...a blanky-blanky dog!" [who has captured his heart] he tells us in amazement), to Greg Kinnear's character's friend (Cuba Gooding) trying to act tough, to Shirley Knight in a bit part as Helen Hunt's character's mother, to the cute little boy with asthma.

However—and this is a big however—this movie is not for everybody, which accounts for some of the nasty reviews below. But ignore them. Trust me. This is a wonderful movie, although perhaps not for those who are homophobic or 13-years-old.

I've seen this and I give it___stars.
I want to see it___. I'll pass___.
The review was worth reading___. Not___.

The Assassination of Richard Nixon (2004) 10

Remarkable performance by Sean Penn

The movie is an intense focus on Sean Penn doing a sympathetic character study of a nut job named Samuel J. Bicke, a failed salesman who manages to lose at everything he does. He is a salesman who believes you shouldn't lie to make a sale. The only thing more ridiculous would be a lawyer who believes you shouldn't lie to win a case. I had a friend once who was a bit of a nut job like Bicke who said he never lied. To maintain this fiction he lied to himself. It was the only way he could continue to think he never lied. Such ideas ("a foolish consistency is the hobgoblin of little minds"—from Thoreau—is ironically similar) are the stuff of inflexible minds unable to adjust to the vagaries of humanity and to a world that is not rigidly set in black and white. Bicke lived surrounded by a cloud of his own making, a cloud that kept him from seeing the world in a realistic way, so that instead he saw things through the shroud of his personal delusions.

Sean Penn, in a virtuoso performance, makes us sympathize with Bicke's character. Bicke fails at his marriage and yet he has no idea why. It seems that his wife Marie (Naomi Watts) has cut him off from her and from his children (and even the dog) because she wants to move on to somebody better; yet we know he is unstable and unable to understand how he has failed her. And so she really does need to be rid of him. He also fails as a salesman, and then he fails as an entrepreneur. He is lost and desperate. And all the while there is Richard Milhous Nixon on the tube lying to the American people, the same Richard Nixon that Bicke's boss holds up as a shining example of a great salesman, the kind of man that Bicke could never be.

It is remarkable that Sean Penn was able to so convincingly portray such a character since he himself is nothing like the poor pathetic Bicke. Penn has a winning personality, is charismatic and attractive. Very few women would give up on him as Marie gives up on Bicke. I mention this because if you know people you know that people like Penn and arguably Mel Gibson who played a somewhat similar role in *Conspiracy Theory* (1997), could never be one of the Bickes of the world since the world loves them too much. It is only life's losers that become the crazies who do the things that Bicke does. They feel so much like failures and have such low self-esteem that they are desperate to do anything to gain some kind of emotional equilibrium. Penn worked hard on the role, and I thought he gave the kind of performance that would be the highlight of any actor's career. But again, it was just so hard to not notice that this guy in the move named Bicke was in fact Sean Penn.

The theme of the salesman as a tragic figure is an America staple. I am thinking of Arthur Miller's *Death of a Salesman*, and of David Mamet's *Glengarry Glen Ross* in which we see men who make a living by doing something they themselves respect only as an exploitive competition. Here we have Jack Thompson (in a nice supporting role) as Jack Jones, furniture salesman, handing motivational books by Dale Carnegie and Norman Vincent Peale to Bicke in an effort to get Bicke up to speed on how to sell by selling himself. I once knew a salesman who told me that the thing to remember is "you are always selling love. If you can do that, you will be a success."

I think director Niels Mueller did a good job of putting this story together. It is an offbeat vehicle for Sean Penn, but the movie goes beyond his performance to examine the shallow, cold and corrupt values of our society that prevailed during the Nixon administration and have led some years down the road to the George W. Bush administration (only two days left as it write this!). I hope that Mueller's gets another chance to do something as interesting with a similarly excellent cast.

I've seen this and I give it___stars.
I want to see it___. I'll pass___.
The review was worth reading___. Not___.

Atlantic City (1980) 10

A gem

Europeans have always delighted in introducing America to itself. (I am thinking of de Tocqueville and Nabokov.) There is something very valuable about seeing ourselves through the eyes of others. In *Atlantic City*, assumptions about the American way of life, the American dream and the America reality, circa 1978, are examined through the artistry of master French film director, Louis Malle (*Murmur of the Heart* (1971), *Pretty Baby* (1978), *Au Revoir Les Enfants* (1987), etc.)

The film begins with a shot of Sallie Matthews (Susan Sarandon at 34) at the kitchen sink of her apartment squeezing lemons and rubbing them on her arms, her neck, her face as Lou Pasco (Burt Lancaster at 68) watches unbeknownst to her from across the way, the window of his apartment looking into hers. She works at a clam bar in a casino on the boardwalk, which is why she smells like fish, which is why she is squeezing lemon on herself to get rid of the smell. She is taking classes to be a blackjack dealer. Her dream is to go to Monaco and deal blackjack in one of resort casinos and perhaps catch a glimpse of Princess Grace. She listens to French tapes and achieves...an amusing accent. He is a has-

been who never was, a pathetic old numbers runner well past any dream of his prime, pretending to be a "fancy man" as he picks up a few extra bucks waiting on an invalid woman.

Enter a hippy couple with all their belongings on their backs. It turns out that he is Sallie's estranged husband, a deceitful little guy who has found a bag of cocaine that he intends to cut and sell; and she is Sallie's not too bright sister, very pregnant. They need a place to stay and have the gall to impose on her.

Both Burt Lancaster and Susan Sarandon were nominated for Academy Awards for their performances, as was director Louis Malle and writer John Guare for his script. But none of them won. This was the year of *On Golden Pond* with Henry Fonda and Katharine Hepburn taking the Oscars while Warren Beatty won Best Director for *Reds*. (Best film was *Chariots of Fire* with Colin Welland winning the Oscar for his original screenplay.) Nonetheless, Lancaster and Sarandon are outstanding, and they are both beautifully directed by Malle. Lancaster in particular demonstrated that at age 68 he could still fill up the screen with his sometimes larger than life presence. The familiar flamboyance and sheer physical energy that he displayed in so many films, e.g., *Come Back, Little Sheba* (1952), *From Here to Eternity* (1953), *The Rose Tattoo* (1955), *Elmer Gantry* (1960), to name four of my favorites, are here properly subdued. He moves slowly and is easily winded. He is a sad, cowardly old man whom Malle, to our delight, will miraculously transform.

Sarandon's performance is also one of her best, on a par with, or even better than her work in *Thelma and Louise* (1991) for which she was also nominated for Best Actress and also did not win. She is an actress with "legs" (this is a pun and an allusion to an inside joke about her famous other attributes–nicely displayed in *Pretty Baby*—over which perhaps too much fuss has already been made!)—an actress with "legs," as in a fine wine that will only get better with age. She, like Goldie Hawn, Catherine Deneuve and a few others, have the gift of looking as good (or better) at fifty as they did at thirty.

Louis Malle films are characterized by a tolerance of human differences, a deep psychological understanding, a gentle touch and an overriding sense of humanity. *Atlantic City* is no exception. What Malle is aiming at here is redemption. He wants to show how this pathetic old man finds self-respect (in an ironic way) and how the clam bar waitress might be liberated. But he also wants to say something about America, and he uses Atlantic City, New Jersey—the "lungs of Philadelphia," the mafia's playground, the New Yorker's escape, a slum by the sea "saved" (actually further exploited) by the influx of legalized gambling in the seventies—as his symbol. He begins with decadence and ends with renewal and triumph, and as usual, somewhere along the way, achieves something akin to the quality of myth. Even though he emphasizes the tawdry and the commonplace: the un-talented trio singing off key, the slums semi-circling the casinos where Lou sells numbers, the boarded-up build-ings, the sad, tiny apartments about to be torn down, Robert Goulet as a cheap Vegas-style lounge act, etc., in the end we feel that it's not so bad after all.

I should also mention Kate Reid who played Grace, the invalid, ex-beauty queen widow of a mobster, who orders Lou about. She does a great job. Her character too will be transformed.

If the late, great Louis Malle were running the world the gross transgressors would surely get theirs and the rest of us would find forgiveness for our sins, and renewal.

I've seen this and I give it___stars.
I want to see it___. I'll pass___.
The review was worth reading___. Not___.

Atonement (2007) 10

Heart-wrenching, beautifully acted and directed

POSSIBLE SPOILERS.

There is little I can add to the myriad critics and viewers who have seen this beautifully rendered work of art from the novel by Ian McEwan. But I want to point to the commanding performance by Vanessa Redgrave at the end in which she tells us what has happened. She abso-lutely commands the screen and engages us in such a direct way that we are enthralled and touched. From an artistic point of view it is interesting that the words she speaks need no embellishment or any acting out. There are so perfect and her delivery is beyond professional. It is lived, as is the case with all great acting.

I also was very much taken with the performance of Romola Garai who played Briony at 18. Her face con-veyed more than words can tell. She felt so deeply not just her character's great sin, but the tragedy of the war and the dying she saw all around her and the sense that she could not be forgiven. Saoirse Ronan, who played Briony as a girl had a hard edge, almost an evil edge to her that was perfect for the part, a kind of "bad seed" depiction with her washed out face and small self-importance and her inability to not just understand what she saw and experienced, but her inability to un-derstand herself and to love instead of desiring only to be loved.

The way the story is presented with scenes out of chron-ological order but in psychological and emotional order was most effective. I was especially impressed with the idea of showing us the scene where Briony pretends to drown and is saved by Robbie after the fact of the great lie she tells. As presented we immediately understand why she lied. His anger and failure to understand her childish love for him perhaps worked like the Achilles

heel of his character. Had he been able to love her as one might love a child and help her to understand that he could not love her otherwise, everything might have been different. Or perhaps not. In a sense hers was an act of atonement, although not in a positive sense.

The epic scenes of the beginning of World War II with the British in retreat and all the bloodshed and waste of war magnified and accentuated, especially the scene with Briony and the dying French soldier Luc, made us un-derstand the how precious life was for those who wit-nessed this while serving as a dramatic and psychologi-cal foil for the love and life that Cecilia and Robbie could not experience.

I also like the economy with which the essential details of the story were presented. We see the dramatic scenes and then we understand with just a few words or even a look what actually happened. For example when Briony as a nurse attends the wedding of Lola and Paul and as the bride and groom walk away we see the shame in their faces, the same shame that Briony feels, only they are not going to own up to it, we know. And then there is the quick flashback to the scene that Briony as a girl had witnessed and this time her mind allows her to see the man's face. And then a bit later on in the scene that the author inside the author (Briony) makes up, we un-derstand that there will be no revelation of the truth because a spouse cannot testify against a spouse, or at least in this case would not.

And then there is the brilliant ending with Vanessa Red-grave summing it up and tying it all together—but more than that, showing us how Briony grew as she went from childhood to old age. In fact the emotional and human transformation that takes place in Briony's character is perhaps the central point of the story. I haven't read the novel by Ian McEwan but I am familiar with his work and know he must have been responsible for such a psychologically compelling development and ending—although it is obvious that the script by Chris-topher Hampton and the direction by Joe Wright are more than first rate.

I've seen this and I give it___stars.
I want to see it___. I'll pass___.
The review was worth reading___. Not___.

Babel (2006) 9

Less than six degrees of separation

There are some problems with this widely acclaimed film by Mexican director Alejandro Gonzalez Inarritu, who previously gave us *Amores perros* (2000) and *21 Grams* (2003), but they really don't matter because the film is so interesting and so very well acted and directed. The script by Guillermo Arriaga, who also wrote the script for *Amores perros* and *21 Grams*, weaves the lives of people from Mexico, the US, Morocco, and Japan into a single story held together tenuously by the delicate thread of a bullet from a rifle.

The rifle belonged to a Japanese businessman who gave it to a Moroccan guide after hunting in Morocco, who sold it to a goat herder, who gave it to his sons to shoot jackals. The younger son shot at a tour bus in which the very well-to-do American couple Richard and Susan (Brad Pitt and Cate Blanchett) are traveling, hitting Susan in the shoulder. Meanwhile, the two young children of Richard and Susan are being watched by their Mexican nanny Amelia (Adriana Barraza) who needs to attend her son's wedding. But she can find nobody to take care of the kids, so she takes them across the border with her to the wedding.

It really doesn't matter how contrived this plot is (actually I thought it was rather creative) because the point is to show how connected we are all in this world. A butterfly may flap its wings in the Sahara and it may rain in Florida and maybe there is some cause and effect, as they tell us is possible in chaos theory. And maybe these people are no closer that six degrees of separation, and maybe their voices are babel to one another. But what Inarritu is intent on showing us is that we are all human and share the same feelings, whether a lonely Japanese girl looking for love in all the wrong ways, or a privileged very white woman in the desert with a bullet hole in her shoulder looking for the love of a husband she thinks she has lost. Furthermore, the character and worth of a Mexican nanny is equal to that of a Japanese tycoon which is equal to that of a Moroccan goat herder which is equal to that of little white girl, and so on.

While most people admired this movie, and it received many awards and nominations for awards, some viewers did not like it; and some of those viewers vented. When a good movie is trashed because it has a few plot holes or because the logic is a bit off, you can be sure that that is not the problem. The problem is the person doing the trashing has been offended. Usually it is some kind of sexuality depicted that offends. Sometimes the source of the anger is political or even racial. Here it definitely could be sexual since we see some under age sexual activity (masturbation and exhibitionism) done in a somewhat kinky way. Or it could be that some viewers did not feel sympathetic toward the deaf and mute Chieko (Rinko Kikuchi) or were disgusted with a boy who spies on his sister and then gets sexually aroused. Or it could even be that some viewers really were offended by the stupid behavior of some of the characters.

Surely Amelia could have found somebody to watch the kids. Surely she knew it was dangerous to return to the US with her drunken nephew Santiago (Mexican heart throb, Gael Garcia Bernal) at the wheel. And of course the selfishness of Richard and Susan to put her in such a spot was wrong. And the pathetic desperation of Chieko acted out in such a blatant manner, as she throws herself at men must have offended many. To me,

though, the psychology projected by Inarritu and Arriaga was striking and largely compelling even while it was controversial. When a young girl presents her naked body to a man and is rejected, it could be psychologically devastating to the girl. She is offering her entire self to him and he doesn't want her. And perhaps the ambiguous question of why she appeared naked on the balcony as her father comes home and embraces her is troubling. We want to understand what is being asked and answered here. Something troubling to the ordinary human psyche perhaps.

Anyway, do not let the nay sayers dissuade you from watching this excellent movie. Regardless of how one might feel about the ideas of Inarritu and Arriaga, they are very much worth viewing in an artistic, a psychological, and a political sense. It may seem easy to construct a movie with a rising sense of tension and to develop characters that will interest the audience with just a few scenes and even fewer lines, but it isn't; and to do it with such a convoluted plot is even more remarkable.

So see this for Inarritu who got the most out of the actors, from top drawer professionals like Pitt and Blanchett to beginners like Boubker Ait El Caid who played the younger Moroccan boy, Yussef, and for Arriaga who wrote the excellent script.

I've seen this and I give it___stars.
I want to see it___. I'll pass___.
The review was worth reading___. Not___.

Bad Lieutenant (1992) 9

"Bad" is an understatement

Probably no cop ever sunk so low as Harvey Keitel's New York police lieutenant. He is the very personification of corruption and hypocrisy. Addicted to every street drug of note, heroin, cocaine, crack cocaine, which he both snorts and main lines. He chugalugs vodka. He neglects his family, his children. He consorts with prostitutes, two at a time. He goes to crime scenes to steal the drugs or the money. He takes bribes and stops young female drivers and shakes them down for sex.

He is a Catholic that considers the church a racket. He is a cop who solves no crimes, who lets the criminals go free if they pay him. He corrupts not only himself but the entire system of criminal justice. He is appetite incarnate.

But what does him in is his betting on baseball games. It is the year the Mets came from three games down to win the National League championship, and he bet against the Mets. With play by play in background in scene after scene we are reminded forcibly that the outcome of baseball games is one thing he cannot control, something that he cannot corrupt, and perhaps that is why he bets on the games.

Abel Ferarra's portrait of a man turbo'ed toward hell is one of the better films I have seen recently. It is uncompromising in its cynicism. Keitel's performance is strident and intense, all-consuming and depraved. He is a muscle, an artery that throbs. He is a man who will never be satisfied, who will never be fulfilled. His is the very antithesis of the nun who is raped and forgives those who rape her. She is fulfilled with the love of Jesus. But he cannot believe—or rather, what is worse, his belief is corrupted. In the end we see that he does believe in Jesus and the saints but while he cries out that he himself is weak, he blames Jesus.

He meets a fitting end, but I must warn you, this is a disturbing movie and one that will offend.

I've seen this and I give it___stars.
I want to see it___. I'll pass___.
The review was worth reading___. Not___.

The Barbarian Invasions (2003) 10

Great movie, but hits some hot buttons

A somewhat lovable epicurean womanizer (Rémy Girard as Rémy) is dying of cancer in the hallway of a crowded Quebec hospital. His accomplished millionaire son Sebastian (Stéphane Rousseau) decides that as a fitting last gesture of love for his partially estranged father he will make dad's last days as happy and comfortable as possible. To this end he gets him not just a private room, but a private floor in the basement of the hospital by bribing the right people. He recruits a handful of Rémy's old friends and ex-lovers to come and visit him amid sumptuous servings of food and wine. He pays some ex-students to come and remember their not exactly beloved teacher. And finally he gets a strayed family member Nathalie (Marie-Josee Croze who won the Best Actress award at Cannes for her performance) to procure and administer heroin to Rémy for his pain.

Girard is excellent in the part (although he carries a bit too much weight for a guy about to die of cancer); but what makes this an outstanding film is the award-winning script and direction by Denys Arcand. This is a movie that is witty, honest, funny, sentimental (but not too sentimental), deeply human, candid about life, love, sex, and death, and filled with the kind of sharp, satirical dialogue that all screenwriters wish they had the ability to write. However this movie will offend some people, which accounts for some of the nasty reviews.

First, there is the little matter of heroin. Arcand makes the experience seem like something wonderful and absolutely necessary in a medical sense. But a closer look reveals that this justified use is only for Rémy who is a terminal patient in excruciating pain. Note that Nathalie is a junkie who is ruining her life and knows it.

Second, there is the candor about Rémy's sex life and the many risque jokes including some from an old gay couple that may offend some mainstream viewers. And there is an elitist feel to the intellectual atmosphere of the gathered friends that will not set well in America's (or Canada's) Heartland. And some will be offended by the implication from Sebastian's arrogant and successful behavior that money can buy almost anything and that corruption is the order of the day. And finally there is the matter of euthanasia which some viewers find immoral.

However this is not primarily a political movie. The dialogue that refers to the evolution of some of the characters from socialists to deconstructionists, is kind of like somebody from say Texas recalling that "I used to be long-haired hippy but now I'm clean-shaven evangelical." It's appropriately atmospheric talk from Rémy's academic world. The real story here is about how to live and how to die. Arcand's prescription is to live life to the fullest and to die peacefully in your sleep. This is the civilized way, and that is part of the reason that the film is ironically called "The Barbarian Invasions" (from a line in the film). When it comes to civilization the barbarians are always at the gate.

Of course if we want to get symbolic, the barbarian invasions could include the cancer itself, especially when we consider that Rémy is a history professor who has spent a lifetime reading, writing and lecturing about barbarian invasions. (By the way, whether the 9/11 attacks on the US are barbarian invasions is again beside the point of the movie.)

Bottom line: this film won a slew of international awards including the Oscar for Best Foreign Language Film in 2004. It is one of the best films I've seen in a while. I would rate it in my top one hundred of all time.

I've seen this and I give it___stars.
I want to see it___. I'll pass___.
The review was worth reading___. Not___.

Barbershop (2002) 9

Hilarious and uplifting

From the Sisyphean (say what?) misadventures of a kind of black Laurel and Hardy duo (Anthony Anderson and Lahmard J. Tate) who steal an ATM machine with no money in it that they can't open, to the white dude who thinks he's black, to Cedric the Entertainer who thinks that Rosa Parks got too much credit for parking her butt on the bus, to sexy and saucy Eve who always loves the wrong guy, this is one fine piece of entertainment. And Ice Cube as Calvin who owns the shop ain't so bad himself, although he sure has to frown a lot.

Well, he's got troubles right here in the Windy City. He's always got an entrepreneurial scheme up his sleeve that just doesn't quite work out which causes him to fall behind in his property taxes. Now this might not be such a big deal but the barbershop has been in his family for three generations and it serves as a kind of neighborhood club where people can hang out and shoot the breeze. It's a beloved kind of place. Enter Lester Wallace the loan shark with muscle who makes Calvin an offer he can't refuse. Well, he does refuse it or at least he tries, but Wallace ain't the kind of dude to take a refusal.

Can Calvin save the barbershop? That's the question of the main plot line, but what really makes this movie such a treat are the barbershop mini-stories that are neatly tied together and the fine repartee. And what makes THAT work is that everything in the film is seen from a point of view inside the black community and not from somebody else looking in (which never works, but is often tried).

Add a warm and redemptive ending, and there ain't nobody cryin'.

But see this for Tim Story who directed and got it all right, and for Mark Brown, Don D. Scott and Marshall Todd who wrote the neat and very funny script.

I've seen this and I give it___stars.
I want to see it___. I'll pass___.
The review was worth reading___. Not___.

Barry Lyndon (1975) 10

Lavish, engrossing, picaresque

Stanley Kubrick's beautifully opulent production takes many liberties with William Makepeace Thackeray's picaresque romance, *The Memoirs of Barry Lyndon, Esq* (1843), narrated in the first person depicting events from the eighteenth century. In particular, Redmond Barry who becomes Barry Lyndon, is something of an admirable rake, whereas in Thackeray's novel he is a braggart, a bully and a scoundrel. No matter. Kubrick, in keeping with a long-standing film land tradition, certainly has license, and Thackeray won't mind.

Ryan O'Neal is the unlikely star, and he does a good job, rising from humble Irish origins to the decadence of titled wealth, employing a two-fisted competence in the manly arts, including some soldiering, some thievery at cards and a presumed consummate skill in the bedroom. Marisa Berenson plays Lady Lyndon, whom Barry has managed to seduce; and when her elderly husband dies, she marries Barry thus elevating his social and economic station in life. But Barry is rather clumsy at playing at peerage, and bit by bit manages to squander most of the Lyndon fortune until his stepson, Lord Bullingdon (Leon Vitali) grows old enough to do something about it.

This really is a gorgeous movie thanks to the exquisite sets and costumes and especially to John Alcott's dreamy cinematography and a fine score by Leonard Rosenman. The 184 minutes go by almost without notice as we are engrossed in the rise and fall of Barry's fortunes. There is fine acting support from Patrick Magee as the Chevalier de Balibari and Leonard Rossiter as Captain Quinn, and a number of lesser players, who through Kubrick's direction bring to life Europe around the time of the Seven Years War (1754-1763) when decadence and aristocratic privilege were still in full flower.

The script features two dueling scenes, the first showing the combatants firing at one another simultaneously at the drop of a white kerchief, the second has Barry and his stepson face each other ten paces apart, but due to the flip of a coin, the stepson fires first. Both scenes are engrossing as we see the loading of the pistols with powder, ball and ramrod, and we are able to note how heavy the pistols are and how difficult it must be to hit a silhouette at even a short distance. It is this kind of careful attention to directional detail that absorbs us in the action and makes veracious the story. Notice too the way the British soldiers march directly en mass toward the French guns. They actually used to fight battles that way! Also note the incredible pile of hair atop Lady Lyndon's head. Surely this is some kind of cinematic record.

Bottom line: one of Kubrick's best, certainly his most beautiful film.

I've seen this and I give it___stars.
I want to see it___. I'll pass___.
The review was worth reading___. Not___.

Batman Begins (2005) 9

Superior blend of realism and superhero fantasy

The idea here—and it is an admirable one—is to account for in a realistic way how the fictional character Bruce Wayne became Batman the superhero. Why did he become a crime fighter? How did he become so skilled, so tough and so motivated? How was he able to come up with such effective gadgetry including the super hi-tech Batmobile? And why did he choose the bat as his motif?

From what I can tell it was screenwriter David S. Goyer who asked himself these questions and saw that answering them could be made into a kind of blockbuster prequel to the Batman movie phenomenon. But it was director Christopher Nolan who made it work.

Nolan also directed the sensational *Memento* (2000) a story about a man who is only able to remember what has happened during the last minute or two and has no memory of anything before that up to the time he suffered a head injury. He has to write down where he parks his car so he can find it later, and he keeps pictures with notes on people he sees regularly because he can never remember them or any interaction he has with them. *Memento* is a stunningly brilliant film that sky-rocketed Nolan to fame.

Goyer wrote a number of screenplays before *Batman Begins*, none of them of much importance. I happened to have seen the film *Arcade* (1993), for which he wrote the script, a harmless, undistinguished scifi for teens but nothing else of his. Nonetheless, Goyer is a natural for something like *Batman Begins* because he is a writer of comics who attended the USC film school and (or was) a collector of comics. He cares about comics and comic book heroes and he knows enough about film to write a script that might work. He and Nolan share credit for the script.

The story begins in Tibet where a young Bruce Wayne learns how to fight like a ninja and gains insights into himself and who he is. There are flashbacks to his childhood in which he falls into a dry well and is terrified by the bats that fly out over his head as he lies trapped. He sees his parents murdered in a holdup. This moti-vates him to become a crime fighter.

The latter part of the movie shows Bruce Wayne discov-ering a cave under the Wayne Mansion, interacting with the loyal family butler Alfred (Michael Caine) and getting help with his crime-fighting inventions from tech and forensics expert Lucius Fox (Morgan Freeman). Katie Holmes plays Bruce's childhood friend who has become a prosecuting attorney fighting bravely against the crime and corruption that have become rampant in Gotham City.

There are a number of nice touches and the visuals are really arresting. The Batmobile itself is fascinating to watch in action, especial during one of the most spec-tacular chase scenes ever envisioned, as Batman directs the vehicle up a ramp to the top of a building and then leads the cops on a chase as the Batmobile leaps from one building to another!

Some of the early action is a bit beyond belief (although the intent is realism), most notably when Bruce Wayne manages to fight his way singlehandedly out of the ninja mountain training camp and has the strength in one arm to stop the fall of ninja leader Henri Ducard (Liam Neeson) and hold himself and Ducard at the precipice of a cliff and then pull Ducard up. Near the end of the film as Batman shoots up from the ground on wires and glides and springs from rooftop to rooftop with the great-est of ease, the action becomes clearly comic book like.

Regardless, this is without question the best superhero movie I've ever seen. It is not only a commercial triumph for Nolan and everybody connected with the picture but, given the genre, an artistic and creative one as well.

See this for Christopher Nolan who is quickly becoming one of Hollywood's most successful directors.

I've seen this and I give it___stars.
I want to see it___. I'll pass___.
The review was worth reading___. Not___.

Before the Devil Knows You're Dead (2007) 10

May you be in heaven half an hour...

This is a thoroughly diabolical tale of just how bad things can go wrong. A simple robbery. Pick up some serious change. Get our finances together and every-thing will be hunky-dory. But—mom and pop's jewelry store? No problem. Insurance pays for it all. No guns. Nobody gets hurt. Easy money.

Older, more successful (it would appear) brother Andy (Philip Seymour Hoffman) has a few minor problems. Heroin addiction, cocaine habituation. A wife (Marisa Tomei) that...well, he can't seem to perform for. His flat belly days long gone. Younger, sweet, slightly dim-witted younger brother, Hank (Ethan Hawke) with a few dinero problems of his own. Behind in child support payments for his daughter, in debt to friends and relatives, not exactly wowing them in the work of work, etc.

Sydney Lumet, in this performance at the age of 82 (!), directs and gets it 99.99 percent right, which is hard to do in a thriller. I have seen more thrillers than I can remember and most of the time the director gets the movie printed and lives with the plot holes, the improb-abilities, the cheesy scenes, and the hurry-up ending. Here Lumet makes a thriller like it's a work of art. Every detail is perfect. The acting is superb. The plot has no holes. The story rings true and clear and represents a tale about human frailty that would honor the greatest filmmakers and even the Bard himself.

Hoffman of course is excellent. When you don't have marquee, leading man presence, you have to get by on talent, workmanship and pure concentration. Ethan Hawke, who is no stranger to the sweet, little guy role, adds a layer of desperation and all too human incompe-tence to the part so that we don't know whether to pity him or trash him. Albert Finney plays the father of the wayward sons with a kind of steely intensity that belies his age. And Marisa Tomei, who has magical qualities of sexiness to go along with her unique creativity, manages to be both vulnerable and hard as nails as Andy's two timing wife. (But who could blame her?)

It's almost a movie reviewer's sacrilege to give a commer-cial thriller five or ten stars, but if you study this film, as all aspiring film makers would be well advised to do, you will notice the kind of excessive (according to most Hol-lywood producers) attention to detail that makes for real art—the sort of thing that only great artists can do, and indeed cannot help but do. (By the way, I think there were twenty producers on this film—well, maybe a dozen; check the credits.) All I can say in summation is, Way to go Sydney Lumet, author of a slew of excellent films, and to show such fidelity to your craft and your art at such an advanced age—kudos. May we all do half so well.

Okay, the 00.01 percent. It was unlikely that the father (Albert Finney) could have followed the cabs that Andy took around New York without somehow losing the tail. This is minor, and I wish all thrillers could have so small a blip. Also one wonders why Lumet decided not to tell us about the fate of Hank at the end. We can guess and guess. Perhaps his fate fell onto the cutting room floor. Perhaps Lumet was not satisfied with what was filmed and time ran out, and he just said, "Leave it like that. It really doesn't matter."

And I think it doesn't. What happens to Hank is not going to be good. He isn't the kind of guy who manages to run off to Mexico and is able to start a new life. He is the kind of guy who gets a "light" sentence of 10 to 20 and serves it and comes out a kind of shrunken human being who knows he wasn't really a man when he should have been.

See this for Sidney Lumet, one of Hollywood's best, director of *The Pawnbroker* (1964), *The Group* (1966), *Serpico* (1973), *Dog Day Afternoon* (1975), *Network* (1976), and many more.

I've seen this and I give it___stars.
I want to see it___. I'll pass___.
The review was worth reading___. Not___.

Blue Velvet (1986) 10

Stunning

That's "Blue Velvet" she's singing, and that's blue velvet he's got in his mouth.

Dennis Hopper combines pure evil with moral degeneracy in a style not to be forgotten in this original shocker from David Lynch. The juxtaposition of the sleepy logging town with the depraved Hopper and his sick crew really makes the evil stand out. Laura Dern, playing a fifties-style sweetheart, is likewise an apt foil for the compromised and befouled Isabella Rossellini (Ingrid Bergman's daughter, lest we forget) who plays a small town chanteuse with some very kinky sexual needs. Kyle MacLachlan stars as a Nancy Drew wanna-be who gets in a couple of fathoms over his head.

The plot is as clever as the devil, surprising us at several turns, yet at no time does it go beyond anything reasonable. The characters are vivid, memorable and entirely believable. This is very close to a great movie. To nit-pick I'd have to say that the feel good resolution could have used a touch of Tabasco, and I was a little annoyed at

being lead to believe that the father was a bad cop; in fact I have the feeling that Lynch had another ending in mind but gave us the old style Hollywood finale as a second thought.

Rossellini and her apartment—a simple, but exquisitely designed set—will probably stay with me through the next millennium. Also indelible is Hopper sucking on oxygen or nitrous to turbo himself up to do dirty deeds. The bit from Dean Stockwell as the clown-faced gay, lip syncing a Roy Orbison tune as we wait to see what he and Hopper are going to do to MacLachlan, made my skin crawl.

I've seen this and I give it___stars.
I want to see it___. I'll pass___.
The review was worth reading___. Not___.

Born on the Fourth of July (1989) 10

Haunting and disturbing, but ultimately redemptive

I avoided this when it came out in 1989 having seen *Coming Home* (1978) and not wanting to revisit the theme of paraplegic sexual dysfunction and frustration. I also didn't want to reprise the bloody horror of our involvement in the war in Vietnam that I knew Oliver Stone was going to serve up. And Tom Cruise as Ron Kovic? I just didn't think it would work.

Well, my preconceptions were wrong.

First of all, for those who think that Tom Cruise is just another pretty boy (which was basically my opinion), this movie sets that mistaken notion to rest. He is nothing short of brilliant in a role that is enormously demanding—physically, mentally, artistically, and emotionally. I don't see how anybody could play that role and still be the same person. Someday in his memoirs, Tom Cruise is going to talk about being Ron Kovic as directed by Oliver Stone.

And second, Stone's treatment of the sex life of Viet Vets in wheelchairs is absolutely without sentimentality or silver lining. There are no rose petals and no soft pedaling. There was no Jane Fonda, as in *Coming Home*, to play an angel of love. Instead the high school girl friend understandably went her own way, and love became something you bought if you could afford it.

And third, Stone's depiction of America—and this movie really is about America, from the 1950s to the 1970s—from the pseudo-innocence of childhood war games and 4th of July parades down Main street USA to having your guts spilled in a foreign land and your brothers-in-arms being sent home in body bags—was as indelible as black ink on white parchment. He takes us from proud moms and patriotic homilies to the shameful neglect in our Veteran's hospitals to the bloody clashes between anti-war demonstrators and the police outside convention halls where reveling conventioneers wave flags and mouth phony slogans.

I have seen most of Stone's work and as far as fidelity to authentic detail and sustained concentration, this is his best. There are a thousand details that Stone got exactly right, from Dalton Trumbo's paperback novel of a paraplegic from WW I, *Johnny Got His Gun*, that sat on a tray near Kovic's hospital bed, to the black medic telling him that there was a more important war going on at the same time as the Vietnam war, namely the civil rights movement, to a mother throwing her son out of the house when he no longer fulfilled her trophy case vision of what her son ought to be, to Willem DaFoe's remark about what you have to do sexually when nothing in the middle moves.

Also striking were some of the scenes. In particular, the confession scene at the home of the boy Kovic accidentally shot; the Mexican brothel scene of sex/love desperation, the drunken scene at the pool hall bar and the pretty girl's face he touches, and then the drunken, hate-filled rage against his mother, and of course the savage hospital scenes—these and some others were deeply moving and likely to haunt me for many years to come.

Of course, as usual, Oliver Stone's political message weighed heavily upon his artistic purpose. Straight-laced conservatives will find his portrait of America one-sided and offensive and something they'd rather forget. But I imagine that the guys who fought in Vietnam and managed to get back somehow and see this movie, will find it redemptive. Certainly to watch Ron Kovic, just an ordinary Joe who believed in his country and the sentiments of John Wayne movies and comic book heroics, go from a depressed, enraged, drug-addled waste of a human being to an enlightened, focused, articulate, and ultimately triumphant spokesman for the anti-war movement, for veterans, and the disabled was wonderful to see. As Stone reminds us, Kovic really did become the hero that his misguided mother dreamed he would be.

No other Vietnam war movie haunts me like this one. There is something about coming back less than whole that is worse than not coming back at all that eats away at our consciousness. And yet in the end there is here displayed the triumph of the human will and a story about how a man might find redemption in the most deplorable of circumstances.

Boys Don't Cry (1999) 9

Sometimes they do

This movie really made me think about sexual differences and what it means to have a sex change or to want one, or to be trapped in a gender you don't want. It was very effective to have us see Hilary Swank (who plays Brandon Teena/Teena Brandon) with short hair and male facial expressions and gestures without giving us a glimpse of her as Teena. (Actually we did get a brief glimpse in a photo.) Swank looks like a boy, acts like a boy, in fact works hard to be a boy; indeed that is (sadly) part of what this movie is about, what it means to be a boy in Middle America as opposed to being a girl. And then when we have the scene with the tampons and the breast wrapping and we see her legs, the effect is startling, an effect possibly lost on those who knew that the person playing Brandon was a woman. It was when I saw her legs and could tell at a glance that she was a woman with a woman's legs that I realized just how subtle, but unmistakable are the anatomical sexual differences, and how convincing Swank's portrayal was.

I was reminded as I watched this of being a young person, of being a teenager and going through all the rituals and rites, unspoken, unplanned, without social sanction, that we all go through to prove our identity, because that is what Brandon was so eager to do, to prove his identity as a boy. I thought, ah such an advantage he has with the girls because he knows what they like and what they want. He can be smooth, and how pretty he looks. It was strange. I actually knew some guys in my youth who had such talent, and the girls did love them.

The direction by Kimberly Peirce is nicely paced and the forebodings of horror to come are sprinkled lightly throughout so that we don't really think about the resolution perhaps until the campfire scene in which Tom Nissen shows his self-inflicted scars and tosses the knife to Brandon. Then we know for sure, something bad is going to happen.

Hilary Swank is very convincing. Her performance is stunning, and she deserved the Academy Award she won for Best Actress. She is the type of tomboy/girl so beloved of the French cinema, tomboyish, but obvious a girl like, for example, Zouzou as seen in *Chloe in the Afternoon* (1972) or Élodie Bouchez in the *The Dream Life of Angels* (1998), or many others. Indeed, one is even reminded of Juliette Binoche, who of course can play anything, or going way back, Leslie Caron in *Gigi* (1958). Chloe Signvey, who plays Lana Tisdel, the girl Brandon loves, whom I first saw in *Palmetto* (1998), where she stole a scene or two from Woody Allen and Elisabeth Shue, really comes off ironically as butch to Swank, yet manages a sexy, blue collar girl next door femininity. She also does a great job. Peter Sarsgaard is perfect as John Lotter, trailer trash car thief and homophobic redneck degenerate.

Very disturbing is the ending. If you know the story, you know the ending. Just how true this was to the real life story it is based on is really irrelevant. I knew nothing about the story, but I know that film makers always take license to tell it the way they think it will play best, and so it's best to just experience the film as the film, independent of the real story, which, like all real stories, can never be totally told.

Obviously this is not for the kiddies and comes as close to an "X" rating as any "R" movie you'll ever see. It will make most viewers uncomfortable, but it is the kind of story that needs to be told.

I've seen this and I give it___stars.
I want to see it___. I'll pass___.
The review was worth reading___. Not___.

Breaker Morant (1980) 10

Superb wartime courtroom drama

The question raised in this film is the same as that raised in the Nuremberg trials following World War II and at the trial of Lt. William Calley during the Vietnam War, namely should a soldier be punished for following orders?

The answer to that question depends not only on what the orders were—that is, were they legitimate orders consistent with the "rules of war"—but also on who is asking the question and why they are asking it. After WWII the Allies asked the question and they asked it because so many people were horrified by Nazi atrocities and wanted someone to punish. If the Axis powers had somehow won the war they might have tried US President Harry S Truman and others for the atomic bombings of the Japanese cities, or indeed for the fire bombings of Dresden. In Vietnam we asked the question of ourselves during the war because our government and military were being accused both at home and abroad of waging an unjustified war and going against our own value system.

Here the story goes back to the Boer War a hundred years ago in South Africa, as the British command for political reasons puts Lt. Breaker Morant, an Australian soldier fighting with the British forces, and two of his fellow Bushveldt Carbineers on trial for shooting Boer prisoners. Their defense is the same as the Nazi soldiers and that of Lt. Calley: they were just following orders.

The superb direction by Bruce Beresford (from the play by Kenneth Ross) makes us identify with Morant (Edward Woodward), Lt. Peter Handcock (Bryan Brown) and the third soldier because we can see that the horrors of war pervert the usual logic of right and wrong so completely that we can appreciate what drove them to do what they did. Jack Thompson, playing defense attorney Major J. F. Thomas, expresses this when he tells the court that war changes us and that therefore the usual rules of conduct no longer apply. Incidentally this film is based on actual events.

Regardless of which side of this very vexing question you come down on, I can promise you will enjoy this out-standing film, winner of 10 Australian Film Institute Awards. In the annuals of war films and courtroom dramas this ranks with the best of them.

I've seen this and I give it___stars.
I want to see it___. I'll pass___.
The review was worth reading___. Not___.

Bull Durham (1988) 10

A diamond in the rough

I thought I read the book, or at least I dreamed it, but this is NOT adapted from something by Larry McMurtry, although it sure seems like it oughta be. It is one hell of a funny, crafty, too real for life, kind of movie. The brilliant script, full of clever one-liners, was written by Ron Shelton (*White Men Can't Jump* (1992)), who actually played minor league ball in the Orioles' farm system. Shelton also directed and did a bang-up job. This is a funny movie that is really funny.

What I recalled (when I found out this wasn't from Larry McMurtry) was a baseball novel for juniors that I had read when I was a kid about a crafty, veteran minor league catcher who had once made it to the big leagues but got beaned and never got over it, always bailing out from an inside curve ball. (This was in the days before batting helmets.) He fell back to the minors and went from team to team and town to town, hitting a ton until somebody figured out that his knees would buckle if you brushed him back a bit, and then he'd have to move on. Kevin Costner's part reminds me of that guy (without the beaning phobia).

Susan Sarandon plays Annie Savoy, a baseball groupie in her sexual prime who likes to read poetry and give the players hitting advice. She is just wonderful as she plays sexy mom to the boys, a new one every summer, just so she can avoid any kind of real relationship or commitment. And so along comes Crash Davis (Kevin Costner, one of the more underrated and less flashy stars of our time), playing an itinerant catcher who has managed to hit nearly 300 minor league home runs. He is tough and savvy and once made it to The Show for 21 days. Tim Robbins plays Ebby Calvin "Nuke" "Meat" LaLoosh, a not too bright, wild-armed phenom who needs more than a little guidance. He gets a lot from both Crash and Annie, who are intent on schooling him in their differing expertise. Nuke is just the hunk Annie needs to keep her from falling in love with Crash, but...well, this is a romantic comedy, so you can be sure that love will find a way.

The baseball shtick and the interior dialogues of Robbins and Costner during the games ("*Why's he want the heat? I wanna throw the deuce...*" And, "Don't think, ... Get that...woman out of your head—Time out!") are really funny, and the bit where Robbins shakes him off and Costner, as an object lesson for his young pitcher, tells the batter what's coming next allowing the batter to hit it out of the park (or onto the Bull Durham sign to win a free steak dinner—is this genuine Americana or what?) are a crack up. But also great are the scenes with Sarandon as she philosophizes ("I believe in the Church of Baseball") and wise-cracks her way through the boys of summer, especially the scene where she ties Nuke up in bed and reads him some Walt Whitman. Now THAT really tires the boy out! Another great scene is on the bus when Crash lets the other players know that he once made it to the Bigs where "...you hit white balls for batting practice and the ballparks are like cathedrals." Beautiful.

Best dead-pan one-liner is when Crash catches Nuke in the locker room trying to adjust the panty hose girdle that Annie has talked him into wearing under his uniform: "The rose goes in the front, big guy."

By the way, the great rock and roll soundtrack includes the galvanizing baseball song, "Brown-Eyed Handsome Man" by John Fogerty of Creedence Clearwater Revival fame. (Or actually I think the title's "Center Field": "Put me in coach. I'm ready to play, today, in center field.")

It's a shame that Shelton did not win the Oscar for this script, it's really that good. (Ronald Bass won for *Rain Man*.) The characters are just fascinating and full of life, and not just the three leads. The bit players are funny too, including the hard-talking, middle-brained manager, the mindless pattering coaches, the sweet young groupie girl who makes it with all the players as fast as she can. Even the team clown is good.

The irreverent characterizations, the sweet story, the realistic atmosphere of baseball in small town America (only slightly burlesqued), and some fine acting all rolled together make this one highly diverting little film, actually one of the best baseball films ever made. See this with your best babe. She'll like it as much as you.

I've seen this and I give it___stars.
I want to see it___. I'll pass___.
The review was worth reading___. Not___.

The Cement Garden (1993) 9

It's a family affair

There's an almost heroic honesty to this urbanized, co-ed "Lord of the Flies"-ish love story. A square stone house serves as the isolated island while the jungle is the familiar setting of urban sprawl and other people. Director Andrew Birkin, in adapting Ian McEwan's novel (*The Comfort of Strangers*) to the screen, doesn't try to shock us. He just ignores our prejudices and lets fall away our preconceptions. What emerges is a sense of liberation from the usual hypocrisy.

The love story is an acting out of sister-brother incest, almost a celebration of it. "Seems natural to me" is what fifteen-year-old Jack (Andrew Robertson) says while in the naked embrace of his older sister Julie (Charlotte Gainsbourg). I could almost buy it, but I know of the "kibbutz effect" in which it was found that unrelated children growing up together virtually never married one another. If sister and brother grow up separately there can be sexual excitement between them, but if they grow up in the same household they tend to find each other sexually boring. Family members usually work out the sexual tension through play at an early age so that by the time they are sexually mature, they are looking elsewhere. That's how the incest taboo works. Its purpose is to channel the sexual drive outward, the better to mix the gene pool and to attract resources from afar. For the individual, incest is not an attractive option socially or economically because it is so much better to increase one's family and influence by joining with someone from another tribe or band. If you marry your sister, you don't gain any brothers. Consequently the average person recoils (or at least pretends to) at the mere suggestion of incest, and it is this mindless, knee jerk reaction that this film attacks.

Consider isolated families in the pre-history. What other reproductive choice would they have had? Certainly it is better to reproduce in the hope that the next generation might find partners. This evolutionary wisdom is what is captured here. The sexual drive is seen as stronger than society's ephemeral prejudices, and rightly so since our genes must survive even when the society is stupid and self-destructive in its mores.

Birkin's direction lacks focus in the beginning and the editing seems brilliant and disjointed by turns, but Birkin eschews even the hint of a cliché and ends up with a slightly flawed, but engrossing, strikingly original work of cinematic art.

I'm disappointed that the sound track did not include the seventies Motown tune, "It's a Family Affair."

I've seen this and I give it___stars.
I want to see it___. I'll pass___.
The review was worth reading___. Not___.

Closely Watched Trains (1966) 10

Oh, those randy Czechs!

The "Closely Watched Trains" are those that are carrying supplies to the German army in and through occupied Czechoslovakia during World War II. That is why they are closely watched—so that they run on time. But they are also closely watched by the people of Czechoslovakia, especially dispatcher Hubicka (Josef Somr) and his trainee Milos Hrma (Vaclav Neckar) for another reason, which will become apparent as the movie ends.

Not that Milos and Hubicka are especially diligent workers. On the contrary. What Hubicka is especially adept at is seduction of females while Milos is distracted by his worries about becoming a man. He has what must be seen as a problem demanding comic relief (if you will). He has trouble pleasing his girlfriend because of premature ejaculation. He is so consumed by this embarrassing failure that he seeks quietus in the warm bath of a bordello. Meanwhile Hubicka is able to please the pretty young telegraphist Virginia Svata (Jitka Zelenohorska) by playing a kind of strip poker with her and rubber stamping her pretty legs and butt much to her delight and to the consternation of her mother when she finds out. The German Councilor Zednicek (Vlastimil Brodsky) who tolerates no hanky-panky when it comes to keeping the trains moving conducts an investigation and comes to the conclusion that Hubicka is guilty of misuse and abuse of the great German language because he stamped German words onto Virginia's body!

This is the tone of the film, wryly ironic, irreverent and mildly comedic, employing in a sense a kind of off-center "theater of the absurd" treatment. Director Jiri Menzel, who appears briefly in the film as Dr. Brabec who diagnoses Milos's "affliction," spun this off from a novel by Bohumil Hrabal, but it could easily have come from a novel by Jaroslav Hasek, who wrote the celebrated Czech classic, *The Good Soldier Svejk*, so alike in treatment and tone are they, and so very characteristic of the Czech national mind-set vis-a-vis all the horrors of the European wars. Menzel concentrates on the petty affairs of day-to-day peasant life, sex, the raising of pigeons and geese, the boredom of bureaucratic jobs as he works toward the culminating scene in which the heroics seem almost light-hearted and to come about more from happenstance than from careful planning.

Some of the scenes in the movie are absolutely unique in the world of cinema and suggest a kind of cinematic genius. The creepy goose-stuffing (for *foie gras pate*) scene in which Milos seeks help with his "problem" from an older woman is riotous—or would be riotous if we were not so amazed as what she is doing while talking to him and what it LOOKS like she might be doing! The scene in which Stationmaster Lanska is torn between the prospect of seducing a voluptuous woman and the chance that he might miss supper reminded me of a little boy at play with his mother calling him home for dinner. The final scene in which it looks like Menzel may have employed a wind machine is just so perfectly presented, combining as it does the stark realism of the war and a delicious (but soon to be mixed) personal triumph of the resistance.

This is one of the classic films of all time. But prepare to put aside ordinary viewing habits and to concentrate with an alert mind. The subtleties of Menzel's little masterpiece will be obscured by inattention, preconceptions and faulty expectations. (Or at least that is what they'll tell you at film school.)

See this Oscar winner (Best Foreign Film, 1967) for Jiri Menzel who survived oppression and censorship by the Soviets and is still making movies.

I've seen this and I give it___stars.
I want to see it___. I'll pass___.
The review was worth reading___. Not___.

Closer to Home (1995) 9

A diamond in the rough

Much of the effectiveness of this deeply affecting and ultimately tragic film is due to what is not shown and what is not said.

Dalisay (Madeline Ortaliz) is a young and pretty Filipino girl who—perhaps among other strategies—puts herself up as a mail order bride in order to get to America to make money to help her family and get medical help for her younger sister who has a heart condition. Maybe that is her motivation. What makes this movie so beguiling and intriguing is the ambiguous nature of Dalisay's desire. She is a "good girl, a proper girl but...(I am reminded of an old song) one of the roving kind."

She tells her family that she will work in America and send them money. She doesn't tell them that she is a mail order bride. This is the essential duplicity that Dalisay enters into. She has a cousin in America who will help her with the details. Perhaps this is planned. We really don't know. Perhaps she is waiting until she sees her intended and will play it by ear from there. Again, the ambiguity of her desire—and indeed the ambiguity of anyone's desire, especially that of a young girl from a poor rural family in a poor country who has been making her living sewing clothes in a sweat shop—is what intrigues us. No one's motives are completely pristine. There is always an element of self-service involved, even in the most humanitarian ventures, even if it is only that of being the one who is doing good. Dalisay is being good, but one gets the sense as the film develops that she is being good partially for Dalisay. She has seen what it is like to work in a sweat shop and she has seen what happens to the girls who give their bodies away. She is wiser than that. She has a plan.

Director Joseph Nobile who co-wrote the script with Ruben Arthur Nicdao overplays the idyllic rural setting in the early scenes—the good father and family, their hard work, the happy, if poor, children, the bright and ambitious daughter in whom they believe. They are of course preyed upon by middle men and money lenders, but they hold their heads high. I think Nobile would have been wise to cut out about half of these opening sequences in the Philippines because they are too cloying, they too much recall the clichés of the good and noble peasants being used by the evil power structure.

However, there is something to be said for the buildup. We do see that although Dalisay brings gifts to her siblings when she visits, and she seems delighted to see the children run alongside the bus, there is some restraint in her affection, some slight distance from the little ones and from her father and mother. The family affection, although seemingly demonstrated, struck me as lukewarm. Perhaps that was the intent so as to account for Dalisay's leaving them.

The film begins slowly. I would have given up on it had I not known of the film's reputation. I stayed with it and I am glad I did because once Dalisay gets to America about halfway through, the story becomes riveting and develops into a powerful tragedy of conflicting desires, told in stark realism and beautifully acted by Ortaliz and John Michael Bolger who plays Dean.

He is one of live's pathetic losers who has a dream, an island girl of his own, to love him and to serve him and to be his wife and constitute the loving family that he doesn't have. Ah, but the intrusion of reality! We see that although Dalisay is good and non-exploitive herself, she has her own dreams and they are not likely to include an over-the-hill, broken-down and drunken cabbie, a guy with a dysfunctional family, a guy who can't keep a job and wears too much cologne. When he says he loves her we know there is no way she can say she loves him.

An important scene that foreshadows the end catches Dalisay and her cousin Tess at the kitchen table in the apartment. They are joking in Tagalog about Dean's physical attributes. We can see how cozy they are, the two women in their shared culture, and how alien Dean is as he comes upon them and doesn't understand what they are saying. Ultimately we feel sorry for Dean. We pity him. Yet we understand and appreciate Dalisay's decision. She does what she has to do, and she does it with dignity and honor.

A final point: When Dean is seen crying near the end, we the viewers know why he is crying, but his family does not. For the audience the tears are ambiguous and his tragedy is twofold, just as Dalisay's motivations are ambiguous and twofold.

This is very close to masterpiece. It is original and faithfully done without choosing sides or assigning blame one way or the other. Like a classical tragedy, the end is fated and due to human frailty rather than any conscious iniquity.

I've seen this and I give it___stars.
I want to see it___. I'll pass___.
The review was worth reading___. Not___.

Contact (1997) 9

"If it's just us, it seems like an awful waste of space"

The contact frequency is pi times hydrogen, and the first transmission is the prime numbers 2, 3, 5, 7.... This is what WE would transmit and do transmit because such signals cannot be mistaken for natural phenomena. It's obvious that what we have here is intelligent science fiction. The general public may be surprised to learn—I know I was—that a significant segment of the scientific community considers the Search for Extraterrestrial Intelligence (SETI) a pie in the sky waste of money and human energy. The prejudice is so great that until recently no self-respecting astrophysicist would dare specialize in it for fear of having no career. Well, there are a few brave souls. This is a movie about one of them.

I didn't read the book—shame on me, but works of fiction by scientists usually make me blush in embarrassment for their authors. But Carl Sagan was no ordinary scientist, nor was he an ordinary writer. Still I suspect that what made this an excellent movie was the script by James V. Hart and Michael Goldenberg. It is extraordinarily well thought out and carefully crafted with deft turns of plot and a satisfying conclusion, with no need for spaghetti code patches near the end, the bane of most sci-fi and action/adventure flicks. It is also emotionally moving.

There is, however, just the slightest "written by committee" feel to the movie. Everything is a little too neat and too well explained. It's a paradox of any art form that sometimes you can polish too much, you can overwrite and lose some spontaneity in the production. And yes, Palmer Joss (Matthew McConaughey) is a little too good to be true, and Arroway (Jodie Foster) really needs a serious fault or at least some kind of vice to round her out. Being a political innocent isn't enough. And the media and governmental reaction is a little too pat and cynical.

However all of that is insignificant compared with the most difficult thing about writing a futuristic or "superior civilization" story, namely coming up some unknown technology or information to make it seem real. The formula for cold fusion would work, or the cure to cancer. But how can you do THAT? You can't (otherwise what you come up with would probably be more important than your script). It is fascinating to see how Sagan, Hart, Goldenberg and Director Robert Zemeckis cleverly sidestep this pitfall. Only those who have tried it can know what a fine job was done here. And incidentally Zemeckis can be given credit for making *Contact* intelligible without any dumbing down, no mean feat in itself.

As far as star Jodie Foster goes, it's clear she inhaled and imbibed the persona of the modern woman of science in preparation for this role, so well does she play the part of astrophysicist Ellie Arroway. They have her come out looking androgynous, which is appropriate for two reasons, one, she lost her mother early and had to identify with her father more than most (an explanation, if one were needed, for how she became a scientist); and two, those little green beings aren't going to be men or women, having given up our sort of primitive sexuality long ago. She is never glamorized; even when she dresses up, she still looks like a normal woman in a gown. And she is appropriately unpolitical and naive and far too honest in front of the camera.

Second best line: "It's so beautiful. They should have sent a poet."

I've seen this and I give it___stars.
I want to see it___. I'll pass___.
The review was worth reading___. Not___.

The Conversation (1974) 9

Flawed brilliancy

In-between *The Godfather* (1972) and *The Godfather Part II* (1974), Francis Ford Coppola made this techno nerd favorite, a film he had wanted to make for years, but couldn't get the backing until *The Godfather* gave him the clout. Coppola has said this is the movie of his that he likes best, and Gene Hackman who stars as Harry Caul, the paranoid, nerdish surveillance snoop who suddenly develops a conscience, said it was his favorite role. In the case of Hackman, one can see why. He dominates the screen with a subtle touch and some serious acting skills. In the case of Coppola, well, I'm sure in his heart of hearts he knows he made at least three better films. And of course, "favorite" doesn't mean "best."

Because of some glaring plot holes and assorted implausibilities plus a slow pace, this film is not liked by some viewers. But it has a kind of haunting power, partly based on the studied camera work, and partly based on a chilling (and clever) story that explodes in Harry Caul's face and surprises the viewer. Also there is a nice underlying tension that Coppola develops and maintains that makes us want to know what is going on and to find out how it ends.

Cindy Williams of TV's "Laverne and Shirley" fame plays Ann, the wife of a Fortune 500 type exec who is being recorded as she has a conversation with a friend as they walk around Central Park. Harry Caul is doing the snooping. It isn't clear why the conversation is important, and even though we hear bits of it again and again, it seems innocent, although one notes, Cindy Williams isn't smiling. As the plot nears denouement, however, we and Harry Caul and the husband, who has hired Caul, realize something is being hidden behind the denotative meaning of the words that are spoken. Part of the intrigue is to catch the real meaning of what is said.

The plot holes? Well, it is unlikely that super-secret Harry Caul would invite rival snoopers to his studio for a party. He is so paranoid about people knowing his business that he loses his girlfriend Amy (Teri Garr) because he won't give her his phone number or tell her where he lives. And the way he tears up his apartment at the end looking for the hidden bug is silly (but psychologically correct of course since he has gone full blown obsessive). Rationally speaking, he would be better off just moving. I understand that in the original script penned by Coppola, Harry owned the apartment building and that would explain why he chose to tear up his apartment looking for the recording device rather than move somewhere else. And think of the professional challenge!

Frankly I didn't mind any of the inconsistencies that viewers have pointed out. Yes, he would suspect that the pen put in his pocket by rival snooper Bernie Moran (Allen Garfield) might be a microphone, and, no, the hidden bug was NOT in his saxophone, but may have been in his eyeglasses (and anyway it doesn't matter). What I didn't like were the dream sequences that you couldn't separate from reality. I also didn't like the pristine clean toilet in room 773 that overflowed with bright red blood when he flushes it. Not likely, when you think about it.

But none of this matters. This is an intriguing film with a significant theme, namely that the invasion of privacy has consequences, which is as relevant today as it was then. Look for a young Harrison Ford as Martin Stett, the exec's assistant, and for Elizabeth MacRae as a caloric-challenged seductress. But by all means see this for Francis Ford Coppola, one of the greats. *The Conversation* is rated #169 at the Internet Movie Database. It's a must see for Coppola fans.

I've seen this and I give it___stars.
I want to see it___. I'll pass___.
The review was worth reading___. Not___.

The Country Girl (1954) 9

Slow start but becomes fascinating

In the ranking of American playwrights Clifford Odets is usually placed in the second tier behind Eugene O'Neill, Arthur Miller, Lillian Hellman and Tennessee Williams. His output was something less than theirs and his two best-known plays, *Waiting for Lefty* and *The Country Girl*, never quite reached the artistic pinnacle of say, Miller's *Death of a Salesman* or Williams's *A Streetcar Named Desire*. Nonetheless as a movie *The Country Girl* is a brilliant piece of work thanks in part to a fine adaptation by director and screenwriter George Seaton (Oscar for best screen adaptation, 1954) and sterling performances by Grace Kelly, Bing Crosby and William Holden. Seeing this for the first time I was almost as much impressed by Holden, who played a part very much in keeping with his character and with other parts he has played, as I was by Kelly and Crosby who both did 180 degree turns in type-casting.

Grace Kelly won an Oscar as the faithful, strong-willed, bitter, dowdy co-dependent wife of crooner Crosby who played a whimpering, guilt-ridden alcoholic. You have to see Grace Kelly in the bags-under-her-eyes make-up and spinster get-ups to believe it. She looks at least ten years older than her 25 years with a sour puss of a face and an attitude to match. I think she won best actress (over Judy Garland in *A Star Is Born*) partly because her appearance was so stunningly...different. (While I'm musing, I wonder if this was the film of hers that was banned in Monaco.) It would seem to be the height of creative casting to put her into such a role, yet she is excellent, wonderful to watch as always, her timing exquisite, her expression indelible, and her sense of character perfect. When she says to Holden, "You kissed me—don't let that give you any ideas," and then when we see her face after he leaves, loving it, we believe her both times.

Bing Crosby too is a sight to behold in what must have been his finest 104 minutes as a dramatic actor. He too played way out of character and yet one had the sense that he knew the character well. He was absolutely pathetic as the spineless one. (In real life Der Bingo was reportedly a stern task master at home—ask his kids.) Clearly director Seaton should be given some of the credit for these fine performances. When your stars perform so well, it's clear you've done something right.

The production suffers—inevitably, I suppose—from the weakness of the play within the play. Crosby is to be the star of a Broadway musical called "The Land Around Us." (What we see of the musical assures us it's no *Oklahoma!*) He's a little too old and stationary for the part, but of course he sings beautifully. (Painful was the excruciatingly slow audition scene opening the movie with Crosby singing and walking through a thoroughly boring number.) Holden is the director and he is taking a chance on Crosby partly because he believes in him and partly because he has nobody else. Naturally if Crosby returns to the bottle, everything will fall apart.

What about the nature of alcoholism as depicted by Odets? Knowing what we now know of the disease, how accurate was his delineation? I think he got it surprising right except for the implied cause. Crosby's character goes downhill after the accidental death of his son, which he blames on himself. Odets reflects the belief, only finally dispelled in recent decades, that alcoholism was indicative of a character flaw, as he has Crosby say he used his son's death as an excuse to drink. Today we know that alcoholism is a disease, a chemical imbalance. Yet Odets knew this practical truth (from the words he puts into the mouth of William Holden's character): an alcoholic stops drinking when he dies or when he gives it up himself. It is interesting to note that as a play *The Country Girl* appeared in 1950, the same year as William Inge's *Come Back, Little Sheba*, which also dealt with alcoholism. The intuitive understanding of alcoholism by these two great playwrights might be compared with the present scientific understanding. (See for example, Milam, Dr. James R. and Katherine Ketcham. *Under the Influence: A Guide to the Myths and Realities of Alcoholism* [1981] or Ketcham, Katherine, et al. *Beyond the Influence: Understanding and Defeating Alcoholism* [2000].)

Here's a curiosity: the duet song (best number in the movie; Crosby sang it with Jacqueline Fontaine) has the lyric "What you learn is you haven't learned a thing," which is what the alcoholic learns every day.

And here's a familiar line, cribbed from somewhere in the long ago: Fontaine asks Crosby aren't you so-and-so, and he replies, "I used to be."

I've seen this and I give it___stars.
I want to see it___. I'll pass___.
The review was worth reading___. Not___.

Damage (1992) 10

Emotionally captivating with brilliant performances by Irons, Binoche and Richardson

I don't know whether I've ever watched a film in which I identified more with all the characters than I did in this emotionally wrenching masterwork from the late, great Louis Malle. It is part of the genius of Malle to, like Shakespeare, make every character real and to see and present the depth of even those only slightly on stage.

I could begin with the youngest, the daughter Sally (Gemma Clarke) who says little and is always at a slight distance, her serious face in the backseat of the car seemingly thinking dark thoughts, her face down the hallway at night, seemingly knowing that her father has committed adultery with her brother's fiancée—yet not knowing. Louis Malle wanted a certain expression on her face; he wanted the primeval depth of her character as a being that knows more than it knows to be etched upon the screen. And this is because what she knows and doesn't know is what we all know and don't tell ourselves, namely that there is a part of our nature that is not under our control, a part of our nature that can cause not just damage, but disaster. And we are helpless to even see it coming let alone stop it.

In the wife, played with precision and finesse by Miranda Richardson, we see a complex and open person who expresses herself with subtle incisiveness in little gestures and poignant pauses, but then when it all comes crashing down, she speaks with the passion of cold steel cutting into flesh.

Juliette Binoche's enigmatic Anna pulled me in the way she easily vacuumed in Jeremy Irons' high toned minister, Stephen Fleming. She was a low pressure area of enormous force that sucked Stephen to her like some bit of fluff and made him demand incredulously "Who are you?" while realizing that until now he never knew himself and what he could feel. For those who are more familiar with the Juliette Binoche of, say, *The English Patient* (1996) or *Cache* (2005), the pure sexual power that she can radiate on the screen may surprise you. Here her power is in what seems like pure surrender. But it is Stephen Fleming who is surrendering.

Anna's mother, played with a nuanced directness by Leslie Caron, is one of those women who say whatever is on her mind regardless of the circumstances, often to the great embarrassment of everyone present. Yet at the end we see in her an instinctive wisdom that in retrospect makes it right that she should speak so candidly and without guile. If only Stephen had listened to her! If only he had understood that what she said was to be taken literally and as a grave warning. Of course in such matters, warnings are of no avail.

Louis Malle remarked in the interview that is on the DVD that Jeremy Irons felt that his character had to be played in some sense "as himself." He would be not only naked to the audience in a physical sense (he was; beware prudes) but also as an emotional human being. He needed to project the fall from all that is proper and circumspect to become someone who would grovel before a passion he did not know existed within himself. He had to go from high dignity to abject humility. Anna was the siren's call and he her chosen sailor. He could not resist even though his passion for her would destroy everything he had, his career, his wife and family, his reputation, his personal homeostasis. He would think that, yes, I must leave my wife and go with Anna, and she would have to tell him that you can't do that, your son would hate you.

And then there is Anna's passion, not just in the physical, but in the deeply emotion sense of the irrational when she says "Do you think I would consent to marry Martyn if I could not have you?" As we see it is only the wife who knows and expresses, after it is all over, the obvious truth: "Did you think you could go on like this every day into the future?"

Well, when you think about it, of course not. Yet neither Anna nor Stephen, both blinded by the wild passion they felt for each other, knew the terrible state of danger they were creating. Anna's sin is that of arrogance to think she could satisfy both the father and the son and could manipulate them like toys on a string and nobody would be the wiser. And Stephen's failing is really that of a child-like surrender to this flood of emotion and passion that Anna evoked in him. He, even more than she, is irrational and blind.

Did she love him? Did he love her? And what is love? it might be asked. Long ago I once said to a young woman, "I love you," and she said what Anna says to Stephen, "I know." Such an answer should be an eye opener, but neither I nor Stephen noticed at the time.

Seldom have I felt so much emotion while watching a film. I have seen most of Malle's work, and he is always personal and deeply involved with his characters; but I think here he has created, if not a masterpiece, at least a most compelling story of what it is to be human and to fall from grace. I think it is only right that it took a combination of human error (the key left in the lock by Stephen) and the callous hand of fate that sends Martyn over the railing to bring about his modern tragedy. And, as in all great works of tragic art, the seeds of destruction are there in the psyches of the characters like the heel of Achilles.

Here's a quote from Anna that foreshadows the ending: "Damaged people are dangerous because they know they can survive."

I've seen this and I give it___stars.
I want to see it___. I'll pass___.
The review was worth reading___. Not___.

Dark Victory (1939) 10

If you are ever in need of a good cry...

Bette Davis gives a virtuoso performance here as Judith Traherne, a young, rich, headstrong woman who has a brain tumor. At first she denies her symptoms, the headaches, the blurred vision, the loss of sensitivity in her right arm, the fainting spells, but then she is taken to Dr. Frederick Steele (George Brent) who is about to quit his practice and devote himself to medical research. A wonderfully animated Bette Davis shows us how a young woman might react as she is won over by a man to whom she is becoming increasingly attracted. As he examines her she goes through the stages of reluctance, acquiescence, attraction, and then the headlong fall toward love.

Dark Victory is famously known as a "three-hankies tear-jerker" and it is that for sure. If you can keep a dry eye through the last reel, you need to have your pulse taken. This is a tragedy with a silver lining, a human victory over the darkness to come. It is melodramatic with the focus on the utter capriciousness of the tumor that medical science cannot arrest, and on what it is like to go from happiness to despair, to the depths of depression, and then to acceptance and even a since of triumph. Davis takes us on this bumpy ride in a most convincing manner.

Humphrey Bogart is the trainer of horses who loves Judith from afar. Geraldine Fitzgerald plays Judy's best friend Ann King. Ronald Reagan has a small part as Alec Hamm, a rich drunk. Edmund Goulding directed. He is the auteur of many fine movies from the studio days of Hollywood, most notably perhaps, *The Razor's Edge* (1946) and *Of Human Bondage* (1946). The movie was adapted from the stage play by George Emerson Bremer Jr. and Betram Bloch.

(Beware of possible spoilers to come.) I would like to see the script of that play because I think there is something in this movie that was handled so delicately as to be unrealistic and even unnatural. Although Dr. Steele and Judith declare their undying love for one another, we do not see them in a scene involving physical passion. The reason for this may have been because Goulding didn't know what to do about sex and the consequences of sex in a married woman who has but a few months to live. The implication is that their marriage may not have been consummated in the usual sense.

Also handled delicately—but very well, I think—is the relationship between Ann and Dr. Steele. At one point Judith has reason to believe that Ann and Dr. Steele have been intimate, but they have not, and she comes to realize that, although they have grown close because of their mutual love for Judith. Yet at the end Judy makes her friend swear that she will take care of Frederick after she is gone. We in the audience believe that she will and we also believe that that "care" is bound to blossom into something more.

If you want to know how Bette Davis became a great star, this movie is a great place to begin. She considered this her favorite role of a lifetime and it is not hard to see why. The part allows for a wide range of emotion. Vivacious, energetic Judith is a sympathetic character, yet there are places in the story where Davis is able to be the hard, mean Bette Davis that we know from other movies, and other places where she is as light and frivolous as an airy teen.

I've seen this and I give it___stars.
I want to see it___. I'll pass___.
The review was worth reading___. Not___.

Doubt (2008) 10

Starts slow but builds to a powerful climax

The doubt is on two levels. One, there is the doubt that Father Flynn (Philip Seymour Hoffman) molested the boy. The deeper doubt is that if he did, did he do anything wrong? Or on an even deeper level, did the wrong that he did outweigh the good that he did? This last question is at the very heart of the relationship between priests and boys in the near contemporary American society depicted in this film.

Personally I don't believe that the ephemeral culture in which we live can answer that question. Perhaps it is true that people like Father Flynn are compelled to do good in this world for just those boys who most need them because of their "nature" (as Meryl Streep's character Sister Aloysius puts it). Science has a lot of trouble accounting for homosexuality, and understandably most

scientists aren't interested in exploring why some men are sexually attracted to boys. The truth from an evolutionary point of view must be that in some sense that attraction leads to, paradoxically, a better fit for not only the boy, which is obvious in some circumstances, but also for the man. How can this be? Most theories about homosexuality invoke male bonding as the evolutionary force that makes the behavior adaptive. Homosexual males bond with other males (homosexual or not) and thereby increase their access to females. So great is the advantage that accrues to such males that even the homosexual males (who mate only to have offspring) have an adaptive advantage over outsider males. It is also believed by some that male homosexuals are in general more social and contribute to society to a greater extent than male straights thereby increasing the fitness of the tribe (society) which more than offsets their lower reproductive rate.

Be that as it may, what is the adaptive advantage to males who are sexually attracted only to boys?

In a way this film (and the direction by John Patrick Shanley based on his play) actually addresses this question. The answer comes from the scene in which Sister Aloysius and the boy's mother (Viola Davis as Mrs. Miller) talk and walk. The mother clearly sees that whether her boy is getting molested by the priest or not is secondary to the fact that the priest cares about him more than his father. In other words (and most specifically in other circumstances) the priest would become the ally of the mother and they would bond. In a world far removed from ours, in the prehistory, they might become as one. Or in a world removed from the celibacy of the priesthood he would love the boy and the mother and she would love him and sex would happen, although perhaps not as frequently as it would if the man were heterosexual. Certainly he is a better man for the boy and for any further boys than a father who would beat his son.

Meryl Streep who has given us so many brilliant performances gives yet another one here. And Hoffman ditto. I have said it before and I'll repeat it, Meryl Streep is nearly flawless in everything she does. Philip Seymour Hoffman ditto. To see two of the greatest actors of our time in the same film is quite a treat. To give them such indelible characters to work with and such a compelling story to act out is really wonderful. And I must say that Amy Adams who played Sister James was also excellent and was not noticeably overshadowed by Streep and Hoffman. Viola Davis who played the one scene as the boy's mother was also excellent.

The movie starts slowly as in a play, which it is. This is allowable since the play-going audience has an investment and won't get up even if the first act goes slowly. After a few minutes the story picks up and gathers power until, with a not entirely discernable suddenness, we are enthralled. In the end we realize how quickly the story was actually told.

Do not give up on this after the first ten or fifteen minutes. It is a story about an issue for our times not to be missed, told with dignity and compassion for all concerned, and with a deep appreciation for the subtleties and paradoxes of human nature and the complexities of our world.

I've seen this and I give it___stars.
I want to see it___. I'll pass___.
The review was worth reading___. Not___.

Election (1999) 9

Sharp, clever comedy

This is one of the funniest movies I've seen in years, featuring a fine comedic performance by Reese Witherspoon, who is a natural as goody-goody A-student Tracy Flick (watch the spelling of that last name: the second and third letters have a tendency to fuse, as they do in Tracy's campaign buttons and on some cupcakes she made, one of many sight jokes in the movie). She's a malevolent, scheming little monster who has her heart set on being elected Carver High School's student body president. Matthew Broderick (back in high school yet again, poor guy) plays Mr. McAllister, a somewhat hapless history and civics teacher who easily discerns her two-faced nature and would like to derail her campaign for the further good of humankind. So he convinces Paul Metzger (Chris Klein), a popular but dim-witted star athlete with a heart of gold, to run against Tracy. Unfortunately Mr. McAllister has a few problems of his own that distract him, not the least of which is a wandering libido and an inability to get his wife pregnant.

This is a nearly perfect satire of high school culture that does not pander to a teenaged audience, as does, e.g., *American Pie* (1999). The script by director Alexander Payne and Jim Taylor from the novel by Tom Perrotta sparkles with wit and keen observations of the way people really are, festooned with some very funny dialogue. It includes several clever subplots that all work together seamlessly. I particularly enjoyed the heartache, revenge and resolution of lesbian Tammy Metzger (Jessica Campbell) who maneuvers her way from counter-cultural dweeb to student body fav to the school of her heart's desire. The scene where she watches the Sacred Heart all-girls school soccer team perform and realizes that's where she REALLY wants to be is just a beautiful piece of movie making.

Payne's direction is smooth and sure-handed with an artist's attention to detail. The election denouement is well set up and the bee sting that McAllister gets that swells up his right eye is an inspired visual reminder of the "sting" planted on him by his friend's ex-wife. The ending which shows us with apt irony what happens to McAllister and Tracy and Tammy and Paul as they go their separate ways is a delight.

I've seen this and I give it___stars.
I want to see it___. I'll pass___.
The review was worth reading___. Not___.

Erin Brockovich (2000) 10

Everything she does is real

Julia Roberts stars as an unrelentingly tactless, thoroughly tasteless, charm-school dropout twice divorced, the mother of three who dresses like a Las Vegas whore. We love her. She is a woman who's been disappointed a time or two and generally expects the worst, and when she doesn't get it, she's surprised. She is her own worst enemy with a foul mouth and a skanky style and a chip on her shoulder. She is also very smart and incredibly strong and knows right from wrong (and that's the chip on her other shoulder). We love her.

Stir in Richard Gere or Tom Cruise (no, he's too short)... How about...no, no, NO. Give her someone near her equal. How about a real actor twice her age? How about Albert Finney (whom I first saw in the delightful *Tom Jones* (1963))? Together they play it like Katherine Hepburn and Spencer Tracy without the romance. Not only does it work, it's a triumph. Finney really is brilliant. His timing is exquisite as is his ability to round his character. Did you catch the shot of him with the one eye comically magnified through his glasses? For love interest give her a bandana-wearing biker whom she turns into a house husband to take care of her kids while she takes on Pacific Gas and Electric (market cap = $28-billion). For the first time in her life she is doing something important. For the first time in her life people respect her. There's something wonderful about this because even without an education people can see, and she can know, that she's their equal and maybe a bit more.

Aaron Eckhart, lately seen as the sociopathic Chad in the startlingly original *In the Company of Men* (1997) plays the biker house husband with fidelity and a kind of sappy warmth. She neglects him and her kids for her obsession. Susannah Grant, who penned the very clever script must have gotten a good laugh with this unusual household, the poor, stay at home neglected husband, the always on the road wife. Incidentally, don't miss the scene where he first kisses her. It was so real all I could think was this guy is kissing Julia Roberts! She is so powerfully expressive that everything she does is real. That's her gift.

A significant part of the success of *Erin Brockovich* of course is in the compelling (and substantially true) story of David versus Goliath ("and all his relatives," as Finney quips), of good versus evil, of the "little guy" versus the corporate behemoth. I won't be giving away anything by telling you that there's a happy ending. But this is also a triumph for Director Steven Soderbergh who can now add a box office success to critical acclaim. I haven't seen any of his latest movies, (I'm looking forward to seeing *Traffic*), but I recall with pleasure the very interesting *Sex, Lies, & Videotape* from 1989 for which he wrote the script. I am also looking forward to the Academy Awards presentations because I suspect the Academy is going to reward both Julia Roberts and Soderbergh by making *Erin Brockovich* the Best Picture of the year 2001. [I did see *Traffic* (2000) and reviewed it, but *Erin Brockovich* did not win the Oscar for Best Picture. *Gladiator* (2000) starring Russell Crowe did. By the way, *Traffic* was also nominated for Best Picture for the same year and also didn't win. Soderbergh had an embarrassment of riches that probably split the votes to his disadvantage.]

I've seen this and I give it___stars.
I want to see it___. I'll pass___.
The review was worth reading___. Not___.

Exotica (1994) 10

More of a woman's POV movie than might be expected

Atom Egoyan's *Exotica* is an outstanding movie. I have seen Egoyan's *The Sweet Hereafter* (1997) which is also very good. A father's (obsessive) love for his daughter(s) is featured in both movies, consequently the theme must mean something special to Egoyan. He is a most talented and original movie maker, a Canadian as are his players, Bruce Greenwood, (Francis Brown, the accountant whose daughter was murdered), Sarah Polley, (Tracey, the high school girl), and Mia Kirshner, (Christina, the exotic dancer). His wife, Arsinee Khanjian and Polley were also featured in *The Sweet Hereafter*.

What really makes the movie is Egoyan's use of time and action sequence. He cuts up the chronological order of events and then presents them in a dramatic way. This is not so easy to do. Christopher Nolan in *Memento* (2000) used the same technique to great advantage. I have come late to such a technique and would love to master it myself. I worked on it last year and a couple of years before. You can't just scissor it and then paste it back together. Something must be gained from reversing the order of events. When Eric and Christina are shown walking the fields in a long line of people I jumped to the conclusion that Tracey would be found dead. We don't learn that Francis lost his daughter until the film is nearly finished.

The psychology of Francis and the young girls is interesting. Christina says she gave something to him and he gave something to her. This vagueness with its unmistakable sexuality is something that always exists between young girls and older men. And, as Egoyan observes, there are rules and awkwardness, and confused emotions. However the girl wants it made unmistakably clear that she is desired physically and just talk is al-

most never sufficient. She often doesn't know whether she really wants to be "taken" fully, and of course that is usually, shall we say, problematic. Some great subtly is required in handling such a theme, and Egoyan realizes that. His character Francis Brown is content with fantasy and does not touch at all.

This film would have found a larger audience except for the title, the theme, and the milieu. The female audience for the most part didn't even consider watching the movie since, as one woman said, I thought it was just another movie with an older man lusting after a girl half his age. That theme bores women to death. But surprisingly at the IMDb.com a viewer asks how women feel about the film and several write in to say that they liked it. Another poster remarks that women over forty actually liked *Exotica* in higher percentages than males.

I thought the veracious and business-like depiction of the exotic dancer club was well done. The very nice side plot with the gay animal importer was just a perfect fit for the main plot. Egoyan wrote the script. It is a great script. So much surprises. It's almost too good. For me, since I have seen so many, many movies, something different, some surprises in plot, in character, in treatment are always welcome.

And the plot does surprise. Even when the protagonist Francis waits outside the club to shoot Eric, Egoyan turns the situation on its head by having Eric appear from the side and explain something that changes Francis's attitude toward him.

I am being vague because I don't want to spoil the story. Some movies—most movies I would say, since I go back to the generation that would go into the theatre and sit down during the middle of the movie; and then four or five hours later, realize, "This is where I came in"—in most movies to know the ending or the plot would not spoil the movie. We know so-and-so dies at the end. What is interesting is how he dies, how the actions develops. But in this movie to know the plot would take something away.

I think. I'm not sure. Anyway Francis is a tax auditor who lost his daughter when she was less than eight years old. She was murdered. The police initially thought he did it, but he was found innocent and the murderer was apprehended and convicted. But Francis is left hollow and tries to bring her back in a way by having teenage girls "babysit" his nonexistent daughter. Egoyan teases us near the beginning by showing Francis and Tracey in his car as he drops her off at her home giving her some money and asking, "Are you free Thursday?" Very near the end of the movie we find that Tracey had a precursor in that babysitting role. You might be able to guess who it was.

The sound track features "Everybody Knows" by Leonard Cohen.

I've seen this and I give it___stars.
I want to see it___. I'll pass___.
The review was worth reading___. Not___.

Eyes Wide Shut (1999) 9

Marriage is always under siege

Eyes Wide Shut is not the self-indulgent, opaque film that I had been led by some reviews to expect. It is clear and focused with an important and worthy theme. Kubrick is exploring the nature of human sexuality in light of recent conclusions derived from evolutionary biology. The theme can be stated simply: "marriage is a fortress continually under siege." To be able to use Tom Cruise and Nicole Kidman as his married couple, who not so incidentally were actually married to one another, was quite a coup since it lent accessibility and immediacy to his theme. We are able to catch glimpses of what their married life might be like and to see that marriage played out against the temptations of a cosmopolitan lifestyle.

Cruise plays Dr. Bill Harford, an attractive, high status, confident male who has always deceived himself about his sexual nature and the nature of women and especially the nature of his wife, Alice. They go to a party and act out some "teasing themselves" roles, as they have undoubtedly done before. Nothing comes of it since they are circumspect people. But the next night stoned on marijuana Alice decides to strip away her husband's smug confidence about her nature and expose to him the truth about feminine sexuality, and so tells him a little story about how she was moved to abandonment by just a glance from a man in uniform. Her expression is so vivid and powerful that Bill, stunned and shocked, begins to imagine this event that never took place, an event Alice has assured him, might well have taken place. As he visualizes, he begins to explore himself as various expressions of human sexuality are thrown his way, the prostitute, the gay-bashing young men, the teenage girl entertaining older men...etc. What he sees behind his mask watching the enactment of a secret medieval pagan ceremony tempts and enlightens him.

This film did not work well for a general audience for several reasons. One, many people did NOT identify with the privileged and glamorous couple. Two, the resolution of the theme was without the usual violence and/or sexual indulgence common in contemporary American cinema, a disappointment for some. Three, many young couples viewing the film together, or at least in light of their own marriages, were made uncomfortable and threatened by being reminded of their own temptations and frustrations. To have the truth of our duplicitous natures rubbed in our faces, as it were, is not something everybody wants to sit still for. Most people lie to themselves about sex and their sexual behavior and especially their hidden sexual desires most of the time. Kubrick

wanted us to see how compromised we really are. Finally, some were disappointed by an ending in which we see that we are human, all too human, and we have to accept that and live with it. Bill, realizing what he has done, not so much in action, as in his heart, cries out to Alice, what shall we do now? And she wisely says (because she has already figured this out) "Be grateful," that one day does not make an entire lifetime.

What is wonderful about a film like this is that, instead of going to the movies, fat and comfortable with the steak and wine in our bellies, expecting to be diverted from the irritations of our lives and to be massaged by the story upon the screen (as in say, *You've Got Mail* (1998) or *Titanic* (1998)) instead we are confronted with some uncomfortable truths about our own lives, and made to squirm. Our eyes are indeed wide shut, and we kid ourselves and tell ourselves lies about who we are sexually and what we really feel and want. Marriage is a compromise with the world and with our nature. Something is gained and something is lost, but this is no perfect world; and just as it is better to be respectable and a member of the establishment than to sleep in the streets, it is better to marry and maintain that marriage against our animal nature than it is to toss it away.

Kidman is mesmerizing and reinforces her reputation as great talent. As always she becomes the character she is playing. Cruise is clever, cute and has great timing. The sets are crisp and absolutely right for the story, and the dialogue is first class. The sometimes annoying score is appropriate. But this is not a great movie. Some of the scenes could have been sped up, and Kubrick did play the suspense card a little too slowly at times. I would rank it just below the best of Kubrick's work, somewhere between *Dr. Strangelove* (1964) and *The Shining* (1980), superior to *Spartacus* (1960) but not quite on the level of *2001: A Space Odyssey* (1968). Certainly we see the mark of the mature artist here in both theme and treatment.

For those interested in an academic discussion of the theme (and possibly where Kubrick got some of his ideas) I recommend the following books on human sexuality from the point of view of evolutionary psychology:

Baker, Robin. *Sperm Wars: The Science of Sex* (1996)
Diamond, Jared. *Why is Sex Fun? The Evolution of Human Sexuality* (1997)
Margulis, Lynn and Dorion Sagan. *Mystery Dance: On the Evolution of Human Sexuality* (1991).
Ridley, Matt. *The Red Queen: Sex and the Evolution of Human Nature* (1993)
Russell, Robert Jay. *The Lemur's Legacy: The Evolution of Power, Sex, and Love.* (1993)

I especially liked the latter two. No longer does a man have to ask, "What does a woman want?" It's pretty clear and understandable. (She wants to have her cake and eat it too.) And of course we always knew what a man wanted.

I've seen this and I give it___stars.
I want to see it___. I'll pass___.
The review was worth reading___. Not___.

Full Metal Jacket (1987) 9

Kubrick on Vietnam

Was this "the best war movie ever made" as the dust jacket proclaims, or just a contrived bit of entertainment, seductive, but ultimately paper thin? Or maybe this was anti-war propaganda with chuckles from a bleeding heart liberal? Looking back and seeing it again some fifteen years later (and about fifteen other years after the fact) one can say, "no" and "no" and "something like that, thank you." The sheer waste and stupidity of war is gotten across, and Kubrick is to be thanked for that. Comparing *Full Metal Jacket* to some other war movies, say, the pretentious *Saving Private Ryan* (1998), we note that it may be the *funniest* war movie ever made. (But then one recalls *Mister Roberts* (1955).)

Vietnam was a lovely war, as all wars are, kind of like America's loss of innocence. One would suppose we'd lost our cherry long ago at Gettysburg or somewhere thereabouts, but we proved in Vietnam it wasn't so. We helped to pile them high at Ypres and Verdun, but that was a limited engagement, and we learned jack-zero. And in World War II we really had no choice. But in Vietnam JFK and LBJ thought with a little use of force we could stem the tide of a feared ideology, not yet knowing it would start to die of its own accord, and so we sent off a few of our youngest and brightest as a small price to pay. Well, maybe not our brightest, just our unluckiest or perhaps just those stupid enough to go ("hell no, we won't go!" said some) or poor enough to have no choice. Those who went were mostly "young and dumb and full of come." But, what the hey, wars are always a good way to kill off superfluous males. By the time we figured out we weren't getting any kind of bang for our buck, meaning we could pile them high at Da Nang or anywhere in the Mekong Delta and it wouldn't make a rat's ass worth of difference, it was too late. The body bags were coming home and some of the bro's of conscription age clearly didn't like the fit. They staged a protest or two, and amazingly enough a lot of people saw the wisdom of their position, and we were forced to declare a victory and pull out, this in the heyday of Tricky Dick.

Kubrick recalls those balmy times with boot camp ditties and a whole lot of well-expressed jar head jargon to which he adds some amusing audio selections, e.g., Nancy Sinatra's "These Boots were Made for Walking," "Paint It Black" by the Rolling Stones, and most appropriately in the classic Kubrick ironic style, the Mickey Mouse Club's theme song, "Em-eye-cee, kay-ee-why, em-oh-you-ees-ee! Mickey Mouse! Mickey Mouse!"

Kubrick got the story from the novel *The Short Timers* by Gustav Hasford, the title referring to those lucky soldiers with only a short time left before rotating back to "the land of the big P.X.'s," the luckiest of whom were "so short" they could "crawl under a rattlesnake's belly with a high hat on."

Best poetic line: the lieutenant is telling Rafterman how to photograph Ann-Margaret, who is coming to entertain the troops, "Take some low shots, but don't make it too obvious. I want to see fur and early morning dew."

By the way, comparing this to Barry Levinson's fine *Good Morning Vietnam* from the same year, it's interesting to note that two directors independently came up with practically the same treatment of our experience in Vietnam, albeit with a different emphasis. I think they got it right.

I've seen this and I give it___stars.
I want to see it___. I'll pass___.
The review was worth reading___. Not___.

Garden State (2004) 9

Quirky love story with panache

This is a triumph for Zach Braff who directed, wrote, and also stars as Andrew Largeman who finds that love beats the holy heck out of lithium and assorted drugs bizarrely prescribed by his unfeeling father who just happens to be a shrink. Ladies and gentleman never let your father be your shrink.

I was quite taken with Natalie Portman who plays Sam who turns out to be Large's true love, and such a kinky, quirky, beautiful true love she is. Portman eschews beauty in every scene but manages to be cute and sweet and very emotionally evolved, which I liked. She is of course beautiful and brilliant as everybody knows, but here she tries something different. She strives to be ordinary and slight but with great emotive power. Nice performance.

The sound track which reminded this old guy of something from Simon and Garfunkel, and in fact there is a Simon and Garfunkel tune on it, was the sort of sweet, nostalgia-producing, alternative rock kind of sweet angst sound that lets you know that this is what youth is all about.

Largeman, wanna-be and somewhat successful/somewhat failed actor out on loan, comes home from the big city to rural New Jersey because his mother has died, unaccountable in a bathtub—which can happen if you are a paraplegic. He deals with a childhood tragedy and acquired guilt, meets his old buds, including Mark (Peter Sarsgaard) who is a full time slacker and part time dreamer and consummate doper. Largeman unveils his sidecar mobile—the only thing willed from his grandfather's estate—with its white star on combat green, and tools around town, parties a little and meets quirky Samantha who likes to tell lies as a kind of way to deal with the world. I knew a girl like that, only she knew when she was lying—if somebody caught her. Sam figures it's a tick like Tourette's, and anyway her lies are harmless.

The movie is sweet and mildly comedic with some original shtick, and at times a bit of a tear-jerker. More than anything it's a touching love story, which I can never resist. And, yes, it's very New Jersey like Bruce Springsteen and Bon Jovi, although no songs by them on the track—not to mention the absence of Elizabeth Shue who was a classmate of Braff's in high school.

See this for Zach Braff who put a lot of his emotional life into the film and deserves the accolades he's received.

I've seen this and I give it___stars.
I want to see it___. I'll pass___.
The review was worth reading___. Not___.

Gaslight (1944) 9

A classic and a great vehicle for Ingrid Bergman

Set in the 1870s when the lighting in English households was powered by gas—hence the title—this psychological mystery worked as a diversion from the constant presence of World War II when it was released in 1944. Starring the incomparable Ingrid Bergman (Paula) in an Oscar-winning role as a woman who marries a dark, handsome and mysterious man (Charles Boyer) only to fall prey to his desire to drive her mad and steal her jewels, *Gaslight* remains one of director George Cukor's many triumphs.

Joseph Cotton, Dame May Whitty, and Angela Lansbury (in her debut at seventeen as a saucy parlor maid) lent strong support. I was particularly delighted with the busybody Whitty, who was born in 1865 and had made her film debut at the age of 49. Here she is rapid-fire sure and feisty at age 78, and funny, both intentionally and unintentionally—or I should say that Whitty turned otherwise prosaic lines into little bits of delight. I also recall her in Hitchcock's Brit classic *The Lady Vanishes* (1938) in which she had the title role. The interesting thing is that in both movies Whitty meets the young star on a train (Margaret Lockwood there, and Bergman here) and they become friends—well, here their friendship is a bit difficult for Bergman's character for reasons that will become clear when you see the movie.

Some of this will seem familiar, especially the somewhat idiotic idea that a man may drive his wife crazy by playing nasty little tricks on her, such as taking down pictures and hiding them, or dimming the gaslights, or walking like a ghost above her bedroom. And the treat-

ment may be a bit leisurely for today's audiences. However this movie is very carefully constructed with plausible twists of plot and some fine foreshadowing. Boyer is almost comical in his machinations at times, mad with jewel lust and syrupy smooth by turns.

A good reason to see this black and white classic is to compare how past-master Cukor features his leading ladies. He also directed Audrey Hepburn in *My Fair Lady* (1964), Judy Garland in *A Star Is Born* (1954) and Katharine Hepburn in *Adam's Rib* (1950) and *Pat and Mike* (1952) to name a famous few. One thing is clear, for several decades if you were a leading actress, being in a George Cukor film was an opportunity not to be missed.

But see this for Ingrid Bergman. She dominates the movie with her exquisite beauty and her oh so expressive countenance in one of her more demanding roles. The famous, beguiling Bergman smile however is not much in evidence since her character is so long-suffering and passive—and this too may try the patience of today's audiences. You may find yourself wanting to say to Paula, "Get a backbone," "Live a little" and "Get rid of that rake!" But fear not. Paula does eventual get back at her oppressor culminating in a (somewhat implausible, but nonetheless agreeable) scene near the end where he is tied up and begging her to get a knife and cut him free.

I've seen this and I give it___stars.
I want to see it___. I'll pass___.
The review was worth reading___. Not___.

Ghost World (2001) 10

No ghosts, but funny in a sweet and melancholy way

The phone rings. Enid says, "Aren't you going to answer that?"
Seymour says, "I have no desire to talk to anyone who wants to talk to me."
He picks it up anyway and listens and then says, "That's my mother."

I just about cracked up.

Well, the whole movie cracked me up. It's a work of art from indie auteur Terry Zwigoff whom I recall as the director of the edgy documentary *Crumb* (1994). For some reason, as I was watching this, I thought it was directed by Todd Solondz who directed the amazingly real and funny *Welcome to the Doll House* (1995). I imagined this as a kind of high school/out of high school progression from the junior high school of *Welcome to the Doll House*. It could be, actually, with Thora Birch playing an older Dawn Weiner and having all those bad things happen to her, but still managing to survive it all. Both Enid Coleslaw and Dawn Weiner are amazingly true to life and also amazingly talented and unappreciated outsiders in this arbitrary and capricious world. Birch (whom I remember vividly from *American Beauty* 1999) in her glasses and all those campish outfits over her rather ample figure was just outstanding.

Scarlett Johansson who plays her friend Rebecca was as vivid as my high school date on prom night and actually prettier (I have to admit). She was also outstanding. Both Johansson and Birch are charismatic in a way that will glue your eyes to the screen. They play ultra-cynical slackers who love to satirize the world and their fellow creatures as they hide their vulnerability from themselves. They are so cute.

Steve Buscemi plays Seymour, a kind of autobiographical alter ego of cartoonist Daniel Clowes (thus Enid's last name, "Coleslaw") who wrote the comic from which he and Zwigoff adapted the movie. Buscemi manages a tricky part calling for old school dorkishness, vulnerability and self-consciousness portrayed in an ultimately winning and sympathetic way.

There are a lot of amusing insider "trivia" comments about this movie at IMDb.com, including the fact that Sophie Crumb, daughter of Robert Crumb, did the drawings in Enid's notebook. One of the most amusing is this: "The actor who plays the high school principal in the graduation scene also plays one of the customers in the porno shop. This was not intentional—Terry Zwigoff cast him as a porno shop customer forgetting that he also played the principal."

Right.

See this for Zwigoff who has the eye and the ear of a genius, a man who knows the hearts of his characters and the mass culture they live in, and how to satirize them both, but gently with affection.

I've seen this and I give it___stars.
I want to see it___. I'll pass___.
The review was worth reading___. Not___.

Girl, Interrupted (1999) 9

Heroic and redemptive

I tend to the sentimental, so the fact that I cried through most of the last twenty minutes of this touching and redemptive story of lost little women in the booby hatch doesn't mean much. This really isn't a tear-jerker as such, it's just that the material and the way it is handled made me feel such affection for those girls struggling so hard to be whole. Set in New England in the sixties with Vietnam in the background and free love in the streets, this is a fine film with an excellent cast that tells an original story without mawkish sentimentality or any pandering to the politically correct. The psychotherapeutic industry is not indicted, nor is society held over the coals. Everything is individual and the faults and fail-ures are individual faults and failures, and the ultimate redemption or lack thereof is also individual.

Winona Ryder gives a striking performance as 18-year-old Susanna Kaysen, writer to be who finds herself in a mental institution after a suicide attempt. Ryder, who has the expressive face of a silent film star, proves beyond any doubt that she is a gifted and tremendously hard working actress. Trickster Angelina Jolie is fascinating in her academy-award winning supporting role as a kind of femme bad boy. Whoopi Goldberg as a Nurse Ratched with a heart, anchors the film and brings strength and rationality to the lives of the girls. Vanessa Redgrave, elegant and wise as Dr. Wick, a shrink with compassion and intelligence, serves as a counterbalance to Jeffrey Tambor's incompetent Dr. Potts.

Some have compared this to *One Flew Over the Cuckoo's Nest* (1975) but this is an entirely different kind of movie. It has neither the range nor the outrageous humor of that great film. Director James Mangold, whose much admired *Heavy* (1995) showed what he can do, wisely attempts less here as he concentrates on the personal journey Susanna Kaysen takes to the brink of institutionalized insanity and back. He emphasizes how people can bond and show affection under dysfunctional circumstances, and how we can triumph over the darker aspects of our nature. In the final analysis, this is a heroic film and a tribute to those who rise above the demons in their souls.

I've seen this and I give it___stars.
I want to see it___. I'll pass___.
The review was worth reading___. Not___.

Glengarry Glen Ross (1992) 9

An intense emotional experience

It doesn't take a movie connoisseur to see that this is a stage play filmed. So what? The play is a work of genius—it won a Pulitzer Prize—and the cast is about as good as you can get. Jack Lemmon gives a performance that will tear your heart out...well, if you're like any of the characters in the play, you have no heart. And Al Pacino gets to put the pedal to the metal and fire on all cylinders. He is great when he's screaming, and he's even better when he's handing out buddy-buddy BS philosophy. Kevin Spacey as John Williamson, the boss of the boiler room crew, has the skin of a rhino and the heart of a baboon. Incidentally, the language is foul, fouler and foulest, and indeed, poor David Mamet, who wrote the play and adapted it for the screen, ran out of expletives. I mean how many ways can you suggest that someone perform impossible acts upon themselves? Yet, considering the moral fiber of the characters, the language seemed not inappropriate.

Indeed, Mamet is a master of inventive dialogue and some of the set pieces are just marvels. The exchange between Dave Moss (Ed Harris) and George Aaronow (Alan Arkin) as Moss leads up to his plan to steal the precious "leads" is like a ping pong match done as a *pas de deux*. And the harangue by Alec Baldwin as the brass-balled motivational speaker was a crack up.

This is an extraordinarily intense film, so intense if you watch carefully you can see first Jack Lemmon and then Al Pacino so fired up and wildly expressive that spit comes out of their mouths along with the words. (I've done that.) In fact, all the actors feed off of one another. Being on the set must have been just an amazing experience with everyone trying to outdo everyone else. The timing alone is worth the ticket.

Note that no women grace the screen. I mean zero. This is a war flick with con artists in the trenches. Note also how carefully plotted the story is. Mamet thought it out and worked and reworked it so that everything fits. For example when "The Machine" Levene makes his little slip revealing that he knew that the Roma contract had not been sent, we can immediately fill in the details realizing that Dave Moss had gotten to him with his cowardly scheme. And when Levene learns that his miraculous $82,000 sale is to crazies who have no money and just like to talk to salesmen, we see how perfectly ironic that is, and how tragic, like the life of Willy Loman in Arthur Miller's *Death of a Salesman*. We can also see, if we really want to look beyond the movie, that Jack Lemmon's interpretation of Levene owes something to Willy Loman as does Mamet's creation. I have seen Jack Lemmon in many things, beginning with *Mr. Roberts* (1955) through *Some Like It Hot* (1959) to *Grumpy Old Men* (1993) and he has been wonderful, one of the great stars of the silver screen, but I don't think I've ever seen him more convincing than here. All the other actors in this film also have done larger pieces and had more demanding roles, but I'll bet they seldom had more fun.

You don't want to miss this movie. It is one of a kind. The cynicism is palpable and the desperation so humanly demeaning that it's almost funny.

I've seen this and I give it___stars.
I want to see it___. I'll pass___.
The review was worth reading___. Not___.

Gloomy Sunday (*Ein Lied von Liebe und Tod*) (1999)

9

A triangle of love in the time of the Nazis

(Beware of spoilers.)

This is the kind of movie that brings to us a deep and abiding sadness that ultimately results in what tragedians call catharsis. Set in Budapest just before and during World War II we see the tragedy that engulfed Europe played out in a triangle of love involving a Jewish restaurateur, Laszlo (Joachim Krol), a brilliant young

pianist, Andras (Stefano Dionisi), and a beautiful waitress Ilone (Ericka Marozsan). That triangle is besieged by an outsider who is the antithesis of all that love should be. He is Hans Wieck (Ben Becker), a German Nazi.

Ericka Marozsan who plays the waitress Ilone is strikingly beautiful and sweetly and irresistibly charming as she must be since the two men agree to share her. They can't help themselves and in differing ways she loves them both. Whom she doesn't love is Hans Wieck.

Like so many movies set during this most shameful time for Europe and much of humankind in general, there is something close to an idyllic scene before the deluge, and then it all comes apart in the most horrific way, with the cattle cars and the mindless brutality of genocide and war. And yet there were those who endured, signified in the movie as Ilone puts it, "après le deluge, nous"(which is a play on the words of France's Louis XV who supposed said in the face of revolution, " après moi, le deluge," meaning after they kill me, the flood.

(This is an almost totally irrelevant aside, but as I looked up the Louis XV quote I ran across a surprising but strangely apt usage of the phrase by Roger Bannister, the first person to break the four minute barrier in the mile race. He is quoted as saying "après moi, le deluge," meaning in his case, "after I break four minute mile barrier, there will be many others." He was right.)

The plot revolves around a song "Gloomy Sunday," composed by the piano player. The song is sadly beautiful and for some people the effect is so intense that they kill themselves.

Now to a kind of explication of the story from the point of view of who got what and what the moral or existential lesson of the movie might be.

The film begins in the present. We see a maitre d' of a restaurant in Budapest—or perhaps he is also the owner—awaiting an important party that will dine at his restaurant. They arrive. They are German. They dine. The song is played and the important man who had been there many years before during the war falls dead. We don't know it but he is the last victim of the song, and he is the ex-Nazi Hans, now a very successful business man. The maitre d' is the son of the beautiful waitress. But we don't know that yet. This is the kind of film that, when it is over, you will want to go back and see the initial scene again. When you do you will realize that it wasn't the song that killed him. The only way most people will realize that is to see the opening scene again. If you missed it, don't feel bad. I didn't even get it completely until just few moments ago.

Who got what? The evil Nazi who betrayed a friend and forced himself upon a woman he supposedly loved and then betrayed her, became rich, successful and lived into his eighties. The brilliant composer died by his own hand ironically with the gun of the Nazi oppressor. The Jewish restaurateur, who is a wise and deeply loving man, is sent away on a cattle car and is never heard from again. Ilone is given the restaurant and bears a son. There is some ambiguity about who the father might be. He could be any of the three men. Since the way the scenes are ordered forcing us to see her pregnant at the grave of the young composer, yet only after she has been forced into intercourse by the Nazi, we are uncertain. The cinematic timing would suggest Hans, but what she says to the grave of the composer suggests the child is his. However when we see in retrospect (in the first scene of the movie) the man identified as her son (the maitre d') it is apparent that the restaurateur is the father.

So who triumphs? Nobody of course. The seduction of Europe by fascism was a great tragedy for Europe. Ilone survives and the restaurateur survives in the person of his son. Again what is the message? And I think the answer is, there is no message, there is no contrived or ordered moral to the story. There are only the blunt and mindless facts of what happened to these people and to Europe leading to a sense of the melancholy mystery of life for which we have no answer.

Ericka Marozsan is my new true love. She is talented, captivating, sensuous, smooth and very winning. She is a bit too beautiful for these old eyes to bear. It is funny that I had never seen her before, but she plays mostly in Hungarian productions.

I've seen this and I give it___stars.
I want to see it___. I'll pass___.
The review was worth reading___. Not___.

Hamlet (1996) 10

Not to be missed

Part of the genius of Kenneth Branagh's interpretation of Hamlet is in the use of the techniques of the cinema to enhance the production. Branagh has not condensed the acts like some mass market soup, as was done in Olivier's 1948 Oscar-winning production, or in, say, Zeffirelli's 1989 Hamlet lite starring Mel Gibson (both excellent, though, within their scope), but has kept every word while directing our understanding so that even those only casually familiar with the play might follow the intent and purpose with discernment. Recall that for Shakespeare—the ultimate actor's playwright who wrote with precious few stage directions—interpretation was left to the direction and the actors, an open invitation that Branagh rightly accepts.

The use of flashback scenes of things implied, such as the amorous union of Ophelia and her Lord Hamlet abed, or of a vast expanse of snow darkened with distant soldiers to represent the threat of Fortinbras' army from without, and especially the vivid remembrance in the mind's eye of the new king's dastardly deed of murder most foul, helps us all to more keenly appreciate just what it is that torments Hamlet's soul. I also liked the intense close-ups. How they would have bemused and delighted an Elizabethan audience.

Branagh's ambitious Hamlet is also one of the most accessible and entertaining, yet without the faintest hint of any dumbing down or abbreviation. A play is to divert, to entertain, to allow us to identify with others who trials and tribulations are so like our own. And so first the playwright seeks to engage his audience, and only then, by happenstance and indirection, to inspire and to inform. Shakespeare did this unconsciously, we might say. He wrote for the popular audience of his time, a broad audience, it should be noted, that included kings and queens as well as knaves and beggars, and he reached them, one and all. We are much removed from those times, and yet, this play, this singular achievement in theatre, still has the power to transcend mere entertainment, to fuse poetry and story, as well as the high and the low, and speak once again to a new audience twenty generations removed.

Branagh himself is a wonderful Hamlet, perhaps a bit of a ham at times (as I think was Shakespeare's intent), a prince who is the friend of itinerant players. He also lacks somewhat in statute (as we conceive our great heroes); nonetheless his interpretation of the great prince's torment and his singular obsession to avenge his father's murder speaks strongly to us all. Branagh, more than any other Hamlet, makes us understand the distracted, anguished and tortured prince, and guides us to not only an appreciation of his actions, wild and crazy as they sometimes are, but to an identification and an understanding of why (the eternal query) Hamlet is so long in assuming the name of action. In Branagh's production, this old quibble with Hamlet's character dissolves itself into a dew, and we realize that he was acting strongly, purposely all the while. He had to know the truth without doubt so that he might act in concert with it.

I was also very much impressed with Derek Jacobi's Claudius. One recalls that Jacobi played Hamlet in the only other full cinematic production of the play that I know of, produced in 1980 by the BBC with Claire Bloom as Gertrude; and he was an excellent Hamlet, although perhaps like Branagh something less than a massive presence. His Claudius combines second son ambition with a Machiavellian heart, whose words go up but whose thoughts remind below, as is the way of villains everywhere.

Kate Winslet is a remarkable Ophelia, lending an unusual strength to the role (strength of character is part of what Kate Winslet brings to any role), but with the poor, sweet girl's vulnerability intact. She does the mad scene with Claudius as well as I have seen it done, and of course her personal charisma and beauty embellishes the production.

Richard Briers as Polonius, proves that that officious fool is indeed that, and yet something more so that we can see why he was a counselor to the king. The famous speech he gives to Laertes as his son departs for France, is really ancient wisdom even though it comes from a fool.

Julie Christie was a delight as the besmirched and wretched queen. In the bedroom scene with Hamlet she becomes transparent to not only her son, but to us all, and we feel that the camera is reaching into her soul. She is outstanding.

The bit players had their time upon the stage and did middling well to very good. I liked Charlton Heston's player king (although I think he and John Gielgud might have switched roles to good effect) and Billy Crystal's gravedigger was finely etched. Only Jack Lemon's Marcellus really disappointed, but I think that was mainly because he was so poorly cast in such a role. Not once was he able to flash the Jack Lemon grin that we have come to know so well.

The idea of doing a Shakespearean play with nineteenth century dress in the late twentieth century worked wonderfully well, but I know not why. Perhaps the place and dress are just enough removed from our lives that they are somewhat strange but recognizable in a pleasing way. And perhaps it is just another tribute to the timeless nature of Shakespeare's play. The mirrors in the great hall added to the effect of a vast and indifferent castle environment, and in the scene with Ophelia and Laertes returned tended to magnify the focus.

There is so much more to say about this wonderful cinematic production. It is, all things considered, one of the best Hamlets ever done. Perhaps it is the best. See it, by all means, see it for yourself.

I've seen this and I give it___stars.
I want to see it___. I'll pass___.
The review was worth reading___. Not___.

Hamlet (2000) 9

Much better than might be expected

Some reviewers have complained about the acting and the casting for this modern dress Hamlet. Clearly Bill Murray as Polonius is something of a joke. He is competent in speaking his lines, but he might have achieved a better effect had he played the part for laughs. (Although The Bard certainly would not have liked that.) Polonius is paradoxically a figure of ridicule because of his pomposity while at the same time he is the repository of some ancient wisdom. It's a delicate part to play and I don't think Bill Murray got it right.

And then there is Julia Stiles as Ophelia. I thought she was competent, but failed to project the sort of distracted, suicidal imbalance that the part demands. And why didn't they let her sing the ditty instead of just pronouncing it before the king and queen in the mad scene? If Stiles can't sing a little (and it only requires the thinnest of voices) maybe she shouldn't have played Ophelia.

Kyle MacLachlan played Claudius as an Enron-type CEO, merciless in his greed and malevolent in his desire to secure his hold on the corporate reins of power. The prayerful scene (overheard by Hamlet) in which Claudius remarks aloud that his "words fly up," but his "thoughts remain below" is done in the backseat of a limo driven by Hamlet! In Shakespeare's play, Hamlet does not kill the king at that moment because Claudius's soul might very well go to heaven since he is in prayer. Recall that the ghost of Hamlet's father complains that *he* was murdered with "no reckoning made," but with all his "imperfections" (sins) still upon his head.

Most questionable to some is Ethan Hawke as the "sweet prince." But I thought he did an excellent job and was very like a 21st century, privileged American (a secular "prince") pretending to be going crazy. And I am sure that the Ophelias in the audience thought he was just wonderful.

Certainly there can be little criticism of Diane Venora who played Gertrude to a tee. Incidentally the queen's chamber scene worked wonderfully well with Hawke becoming the son disgusted with his mother, and she, seeing her tragic failings in her son's eyes, becoming the very embodiment of shame.

I also liked Karl Geary as Hamlet's loyal friend Horatio. I thought it was interesting that here he has a silent girlfriend who is almost always with him. (She's silent because Shakespeare wrote no lines for her!)

But putting all that aside, what I think is wonderful about this production is that it worked! Modern Hamlet in New York City, the "king" really the CEO of a Danish corporation, the kingdom, that corporation, the castle, its New York corporate headquarters. How simple. But would it play? And what adjustments and cuts and pastes would have to be performed on Shakespeare's immortal script? Well, practically none. A lot was cut out, but almost all productions of Hamlet leave out a lot, c.f., Olivier's Academy Award-winning film from 1948; Zeffirelli's 1989 Hamlet light starring Mel Gibson, etc. The most notable exception is Branagh's magnificent Hamlet from 1996 in which nary a word was cut from the text of the play. If you really want to experience Shakespeare's Hamlet at its best and fullest, see that Hamlet from 1996 starring Kenneth Branagh, Kate Winslet, Julie Christie and Derek Jacobi. You can read along as you watch it. (See my review.)

Here we have selected speeches played over a backdrop of modern life in the Big Apple. Every word is from Shakespeare with the exception of a couple of things seen on TV. A security guard plays Marcellus; Fortinbras' army in the background is a rival corporation seen in newspaper headlines; the drape behind which the ill-fated counselor hides only to be stabbed by Hamlet becomes here a hotel closet with mirror through which Hamlet fires a bullet so that Polonius becomes indeed "still."

There is a sword fight at the end as in the great play, between Laertes (Liev Schreiber, who brings some welcome subtlety to the role) and Hamlet. It seems natural in a sense because both privileged young men could have taken fencing at prep school and university. There is no bubbling brook across which Ophelia lies. Instead she finds her quietus in the hotel's fountain.

The graveyard scene in which the skull of "Yorick—I knew him well!" is unearthed is skipped over, probably because the tit-for-tat between Hamlet and the gravedigger would not make much sense to modern audiences. (Laertes still jumps into Ophelia's grave, but I must say without the full bravado that Shakespeare intended.)

I guess I liked this more than others because I expected a lot less and was pleasantly surprised. Part of the power of the production comes from the close camera work on the faces of the players—something that surely would have delighted Elizabethan audiences—particularly when listening to some of the longer speeches. The trick in all of this is to make the Shakespearean speeches sound natural and very like what people today might say. I thought that Michael Almereyda, who wrote the adaptation and directed, pulled this off very well.

For those of you who are high school teachers, I highly recommend that you show this to your classes. It will definitely help your students toward an appreciation of this great and timeless play. (And then show them the Branagh film.)

I've seen this and I give it___stars.
I want to see it___. I'll pass___.
The review was worth reading___. Not___.

The Handmaid's Tale (1990) 9

A Taliban-like Christian theocracy in the US

This is a haunting, psychologically compelling story about what the United States might be like under a right wing, fundamentalist theocracy. Adapted by acclaimed playwright Harold Pinter from the novel by Margaret Atwood, this is a tale of the suppression of women by a totalitarian state called the "Republic of Gilead." In some respects one is reminded of Orwell's *1984*: the endless war from without, designed to keep the populace preoccupied and beholden to the state; the paucity of basic

food stuffs and consumer goods expect for the ruling class, the general hopelessness, etc. There is horrendous pollution so that most women are not fertile, yet the state needs babies for the war effort and the economy. Consequently women's bodies are taken over by the state, and those women that are fertile are made to bear children for the sterile leaders. Those who are not fertile are reduced to servitude. All overt sexual expression and any kind of activity not in keeping with the strict dictates of the fundamentalist religion is forbidden, and transgressions are punishable by death, sometimes in public hangings. In one ugly scene the handmaids themselves are made to pull the rope that attaches to the noose that strangles a wayward handmaid. This is followed by a man accused of rape being thrown to the handmaids, who literally rip him apart with their bare hands.

Natasha Richardson has the starring role as a fertile handmaid for the Commander (Robert Duvall). She is not artificially inseminated (presumably since that would be against the dictates of the religion, which is, by the way, a kind of repressive fundamentalist Christianity), instead there is a "ceremony" in which the Commander's wife (Faye Dunaway) holds her hands (as they both wear veils) while the Commander with his clothes still on— Well, one can imagine.

I read the novel some years ago and was struck not by Atwood's attack on fundamentalist Christianity as much as I was by her attack on men, period. Harold Pinter's screenplay and Volker Schlondorff's direction emphasize the hypocrisy, willful ignorance and anti-human aspects of fundamentalism while attributing the sexism to the patriarchal religion. What is stunningly topical (viewing this in the year of Our Lord 2002) is the parallel between the repressive fundamentalist theocracy of Atwood's vision and that of the Taliban. The subjugation of women, using them strictly as servants or as reproductive machines, their bodies covered and their heads veiled (in bright red), is a striking bit of dead-on foresight by Atwood, Pinter and Schlondorff. This movie was perhaps made a decade ahead of its time.

Richardson is very good in her characteristic way. She has a quality unlike most movie stars in that she projects primarily not her looks or charisma or even her vitality, but instead her individual will, a quality that is exactly right for the part. Faye Dunaway as the commander's wife acts out (in contrasting blue) a kind of Daughters of the American Revolution club woman mentality to a tee. Duvall is wonderfully slimy as a warlord hypocrite always claiming to act in the name of God. (Seems familiar.) Elizabeth McGovern is believable as a sexy lesbian handmaid (a "gender criminal") while Victoria Tennant ("Aunt Lydia") is a kind of drill sergeant housemother to the handmaids. Aidan Quinn gets to be Richardson's heroic lover.

This may not be entirely faithful to the book, but it is a fine work in its own right. The direction is intelligent and focused and the script by Pinter excellent. The acting is superior all around and the story is true psychologically. This movie is also a warning that it *could* happen here.

I've seen this and I give it___stars.
I want to see it___. I'll pass___.
The review was worth reading___. Not___.

Happiness (1998) 10

A most original film sure to bemuse and offend almost everybody

This one will knock your socks off even if you aren't wearing any socks. I dare you to watch it. I double-dare you.

But first a few words. This is about sex. Not your Cinderella meets Prince Charming sex. Not your young man meets young woman sex at all, or not exactly. This is more like REAL sex, the kind you don't talk about. This is about several varieties of sex, most of them perverted or deviant and/or illegal in most states. And this is about "happiness" in only the most ironic sense of the word.

Yet, somehow this movie seems...well, not uplifting, heaven forbid, but somehow reassuring in a strange way. I guess what happens is that after all the perversions, the hang-ups, the unrequited desires, the bizarro fantasies, the unnatural desires, the depraved acts, the exploitation, the sheer desperation of the biological imperative, somehow with the family sitting around the dinner table at the end, somehow we are reassured that life not only goes on, but things could be worse.

It is interesting that director Todd Solondz—who previously gave us the captivating and totally original *Welcome to the Dollhouse* (1995), a strikingly truthful look at the middle child in junior high school—spun this out the way he did. The story is really about three sisters and their parents and the dysfunctional sex that they encounter and the pitiable/normal lives they live. Solondz could have begun with having us meet the sisters one by one like some kind of chick flick with the expectation that we will find out about their lives and their loves. Instead he starts from another angle, and only gradually does it develop that this really *is* about their lives and loves.

Well, their lives and loves are a bit beyond kinky or pathetic, and yet they are so very like the lives and loves so many people lead—if only we knew. By the way, at times the film is belly laugh funny.

Starring are Jane Adams (Joy), Lara Flynn Boyle (Helen), and Cynthia Stevenson (Trish) as the three sisters. Joy is the wallflower at the dance of life, Helen is the hard as a stiletto woman of fashion, accomplishment and beauty who can't find the right man, and Trish is the desperate housewife "happily" married to a man who is a homosexual pedophile and a psychiatrist. Dylan Baker plays the shrink who can't help himself in a way that makes it tough for the audience not to identify with his problem. He is so honest with his son and so clearly loves his son and his wife that we are almost won over. Almost. We do NOT see him with the boys he exploits, and in this way perhaps Solondz has stacked the deck. Still a movie that paints a pedophile in anything close to a positive light deserves credit for courage if nothing else.

The other characters who are anything but sympathetic in an objective assessment—one is a murderer—somehow come across as being vulnerable instead of monstrous. Perhaps Joy, who is so hopeful and so very, very vulnerable, is the one who most inspires our sympathy. The Russian who frankly admits he's a thief and exploits Joy seems more despicable than anyone in the film. Perhaps. I think it really depends on your point of view, your sexuality and perhaps your individual experience.

Ben Gazzara is the father who is just sick of his wife, and Louise Lasser (whom I haven't seen since she starred in the offbeat TV sit com "Mary Hartman, Mary Hartman" from the seventies) plays the wife. Philip Seymour Hoffman plays a guy who is terrified of performing with women, but gets his jollies dialing strangers on the phone and talking dirty. Camryn Manheim plays the large woman who wants intimacy but finds sex disgusting.

I think you've got the picture. This is sexual dysfunction as TV's Lifetime would never have it. Solondz's intent seems to be to demonstrate the truth of the adage "To know all is to forgive all." He also does a good job of showing that although we think we are the self that makes the decisions, maybe it is true that our biology overrides our intentions.

This is decidedly not for the straitlaced or the intolerant. This is the sort of movie that is so terrifying to social conservatives that they won't even attack it for fear that such an attack would only give it greater currency.

See this for Todd Solondz who is a film maker of verve and insight, a humanist who is not afraid to shock the bourgeoisie.

I've seen this and I give it___stars.
I want to see it___. I'll pass___.
The review was worth reading___. Not___.

High Noon (1952) 9

The tin star in the dust

This is the quintessential Hollywood western. It will continue to represent the genre for many decades to come.

It stars Gary Cooper, one of the most beloved of leading men who personified soft-spoken heroic courage in scores of important films, including *Beau Geste* (1939), *The Pride of the Yankees* (1942), *Along Came Jones* (1945), *The Court Martial of Billy Mitchell* (1955), etc., and Grace Kelly in her debut role. Directed by Fred Zinneman, whose credits include *From Here to Eternity* (1953), *A Man for All Seasons* (1966), *Julia* (1977) and a dozen more, *High Noon* tells the story of Will Kane, a small town marshal who, on his wedding day faces a man just let out of prison with three of his outlaw friends who are aiming to get revenge for his being sent up.

The enduring image of the film is Gary Cooper walking tall in the deserted streets of the town in a black Western hat, a black vest, long-sleeved white shirt, black string necktie, watch chain, boots, and low slung holster and two belts, while off to the side inside the wooden buildings we see "that big hand move along, nearin' high noon"—which is when the train arrives carrying the freed prisoner.

Will Kane has cleaned up the town, but now the gunslingers return and he is their target. His wife of less than an hour (Kelly) demands that he leave town. The town itself, in fear of the gunmen, also wants him to leave town, hoping to take the fight away from them. He tries to recruit deputies but everyone is afraid. Even his lone deputy (Lloyd Bridges) deserts him. In the background is Dimitri Tiomkin's haunting ballad, sung by Tex Ritter: "Do Not Forsake Me, Oh My Darling (On This Our Wedding Day)." Both Cooper and the song won Oscars. Noteworthy was the fine performance by Kay Jurado as Kane's ex, a shrewd barroom lady and proprietress.

What is interesting about the moral conflict (from the story, "The Tin Star" as interpreted for film by screenwriter Carl Foreman), that of facing your enemy rather than running, is that Kane's rationale is logical. If he runs they will only come after him again and again. Only two people get this, Kane and Ramirez. The larger moral issue of whether to fight to defend yourself (Grace Kelly is cast as a Quaker and does not believe in killing) is resolved during the climatic shootout by Grace Kelly's character herself in a manner that did not set well with Quakers.

How well does this black and white classic Western play today? The towns people seem clichés and the outlaws are quickly drawn, but Gary Cooper as Will Kane seems entirely believable, admirable, heroic in the best sense of the term as a man who knows the dangers, feels the fear, and yet must act, and he does. He is no shallow, two-fisted, machine-gun hero so often seen in Hollywood productions, but a man of maturity whose "grace under pressure" (a fine definition of courage) tells us and himself who he really is.

See this for Gary Cooper whose "slow-talking, slow-walking," (lyrics from the Coaster's hit song from the fifties, "And Along Came Jones"), and soft-spoken heroics delighted and enthralled a couple of generations of film-goers.

I've seen this and I give it___stars.
I want to see it___. I'll pass___.
The review was worth reading___. Not___.

Hotel Rwanda (2004) 10

Well-told story of genocide in our time

Paul Rusesabagina is Hutu. We see the word on his passport. His wife is Tutsi. She is in mortal danger. But Paul doesn't realize it yet. He believes that the violence threatened by the ruling Hutu against the once ruling Tutsi in Rwanda will not happen because the UN peacekeepers will not allow it, nor will the world stand by and watch the slaughter.

Paul manages a luxury hotel. He is a worldly-wise, efficient, suavely diplomatic man who dresses impeccably and who knows how to influence people with well-chosen gifts and flattery. His demeanor is calm and measured. He tells his driver that to give a government official or some other important person ten thousand francs is not as effective as giving him a rare Cuban cigar worth the same amount.

He visits a supplier to gain supplies for the hotel. While he is there a crate containing hundreds of machetes overturns. He is told they come from China at a cost of ten cents each and can be sold for many times that amount.

This is the first hint of the horror to come, and the way it is revealed is characteristic of director Terry George's calculated method. He has a story of genocide to tell, a story of criminal neglect by the West, especially by the United States under President Clinton who stood aside and allowed the slaughter of hundreds of thousands of people to take place, as did the rest of the world through the UN. The next hint comes from government radio in which the Tutsi people are referred to as "cockroaches." This is most chilling because when one tribe or nation sets out to kill the people of another tribe or nation the essential element is to turn those people into something less than human. The psychological trick is to make the killers believe they are killing vermin. One cannot help but recall the Nazi propaganda machine and its methods prior to and during the Holocaust.

Next we see in a scene at the hotel bar that it is really impossible to tell by appearance the difference between two young women, one Tutsi and the other Hutu. The Tutsi are said to be tall and to look down their noses at the Hutu who are said to be shorter and perhaps darker, but this may be a fiction. Even so, racial differences are invented and racism is inculcated into the mass mind. All of this is necessary because the slaughter is to take place using not bullets or gas chambers, but instead the cheap machetes from China. To get armies of young men to kill their neighbors and fellow countrymen, women and children with machetes requires the stirring up of a mass hatred of epic proportion and demonic intensity.

The personal story itself within this greater scenario is that of Paul and his family and how he was persuaded by a moral imperative that he himself felt to save hundreds of Tutsi by housing them in the luxury hotel he managed after the Europeans left. We see how he risked his life and family and how his courage and resourcefulness proved heroic. Terry George tells the story in a straightforward manner with vivid and deliberate detail. In particular there are scenes of carnage on a vast scale, including the chilling horror of the nighttime bumpy ride along the "river road" which was said by George Rutaganda, a sadistic man, to be "open" and the preferred route to take back to the hotel. The bumps in the road were the bodies of recently slaughtered Tutsi that the hotel van could not help but drive over.

The acting by Don Cheadle as Paul and by Sophie Okonedo who played his wife is outstanding. Nick Notle is effective in the role of a compromised and nearly helpless UN commander.

This is a message film. The message goes out to the whole world, and Terry George makes us understand that those people who were slaughtered could be people anywhere, in particular they could be middle class Americans or Europeans. He indicates that Western prejudice against black Africans in part allowed the slaughter to take place. By showing us the ordinary domestic life of Paul and his family at home, their love and affection for one another—their familiar humanity—we are made to share this horrific human tragedy and to realize that we could have prevented it had we only known or cared enough.

Will we care enough next time?—and there will be a next time, and a time after that and then another until such a day comes when the rule of law prevails internationally and people everywhere understand that we are all essentially the same and that the baser nature of our leaders must be controlled by law and justice.

I've seen this and I give it___stars.
I want to see it___. I'll pass___.
The review was worth reading___. Not___.

House of Sand and Fog (2003) 9
Affecting performances and an intriguing storyline

Behrani (Ben Kingsley in an Oscar-nominated performance) is working two jobs, one as a road construction worker and the other as a clerk/manager in a convenience store. He is a meticulous man, a man of dignity and pride. He has a wife Nadi (Shohreh Aghdashloo) and a teenaged son. They immigrated to the US from Iran where he was a colonel in the air force. They had a house in the days of the Shan on the Caspian Sea that they have no longer.

One day Behrani sees an ad for a repossessed house up for auction. This is the house of the title. It is owned by Kathy Nicolo (Jennifer Connelly) and her brother. We see her asleep in the house, which has gone to some disrepair, dirty dishes in the sink, unopened mail on the living room floor. She is awakened by a phone call from her mother on the east coast. It's 6 a.m. Kathy seems hung over. Her mother is coming to visit in a couple of weeks. Kathy says her husband will be out of down. She says he is lying next to her now, asleep. However he isn't.

Kathy is in a bad way. She is a recovering alcoholic. We can imagine her husband left her because of her drinking. She is trying to quit smoking. And worse yet, there comes a banging on the door and she learns that the house is being taken from her for back taxes. Signs are plastered on the doors. A county sheriff Lester (Ron Eldard) is there to make her exit the premises.

We can see the clash of cultures coming: the proud, hard-working immigrant who is going to buy the house dirt cheap and then sell it for a profit, the careless and self-indulgent American who is going to go live in her car.

Sheriff Lester is the joker in the deck. He is bored with his wife, whom he married young after growing up with her. He immediately takes a fancy to Kathy, and we can see that he will be instrumental in trying to get the house back.

So this is the premise of the movie. There are some problems with this premise, but they are minor. Behrani buys the house for forty-some thousand dollars and puts it up for sale for a hundred and seventy-some thousand. These numbers are pathetically low for the time, the 1990s, and the location, the San Francisco Bay area. Kathy is left with nothing. However after the taxes are paid she should be getting what's left of the forty-thousand. The direction by Vidim Perelman in his debut glosses over this. Furthermore, Kathy should be suing the county since they are the ones who wrongfully assessed her for a business tax.

What makes this movie work is the fine storyline, adapted by Perelman from the novel by Andre Dubus III, and superior performances by Ben Kingsley, Shohreh Aghdashloo, and Jennifer Connelly. Kingsley becomes the Iranian colonel in the most convincing manner. His motivations are clear and believable. His character is rounded and at once sympathetic and a bit off-putting. He is sexist and macho but at the same time civilized, compassionate and even admirable. Connelly, in her stringy hair and cheap cut offs becomes an injured and lost bird that has flown into this house that is no longer hers, this house that symbolizes both the American dream and the dream of the immigrant. I have seen her in a couple of other movies, most notably in *A Beautiful Mind* (2001). She is striking to look at, and here she proves she is a very talented actress. Her ability to turn her character from one that we are disposed to dislike to one for whom we feel great sympathy is part of what make this a superior film.

Aghdashloo, whose work got her a nomination for a Best Supporting Actress Oscar in 2004, also gives a fine performance in a delicate role requiring understanding and compassion. It is perhaps fitting that she was born in Tehran and speaks Farsi. (Excellent casting overall, by the way.) Also notable is the original score by James Horner, which also received an Oscar nomination.

This movie is not only a work of art, but is intriguingly plotted so that what develops and how it ends are not easily predicted. The ending for some may seem a bit stagy, but I believe that Kingsley sold it well, and considering his character, it is quite plausible.

I've seen this and I give it___stars.
I want to see it___. I'll pass___.
The review was worth reading___. Not___.

Imaginary Crimes (1994) 10

Willie Loman with daughters

This is a great movie. I'm amazed that it got made and done so well. First kudos go to Sheila Ballantyne who wrote the novel. A story like this cannot be made up in committee or by hiring the hottest screen writer in town. It has to be lived. There's no question that Ballantyne lived it. And then it has to be understood in the light of love before it can be shared with us. And she did that.

Second kudos go to Tony Drazan who directed and interpreted. It can be seen that he loved the story and he wanted it to be beautiful, and he made it so. He picked the dearest, sweetest girls to play the parts of Sonya and Greta at various ages. And he had to have the right man for their father, a flawed man, like all of us, a man doing the best he can, a man with values that don't really work, a man who lost his young wife to cancer and was left to raise his two daughters alone, a man like Arthur Miller's Willie Loman who had big dreams never realized, a man neither hero nor villain; in short a man who had to be played with delicacy and without maudlin senti-

ment. Harvey Keitel fit the part, that of a schemer and a dreamer and a self-deluded hustling con man, and did a fantastic, flawless job.

Fairuza Balk, who played Sonya was wonderful, and Elizabeth Moss as Greta was adorable beyond expression, and so beautifully directed. The girl who played the young Sonya was not only excellent, but looked enough like Fairuza Balk to be her younger sister: perfect casting. And Kelly Lynch who had a limited role as the mother was exquisite.

The interaction between the father and the daughters was painfully veracious, filled with real-life tension and heart-breaking disappointments, but done without abuse and without any of the dysfunctional family sicknesses so often expressed. We see his failure as a father on one level, and yet in the end we see through the eyes and the voice of Sonya a greater truth: in spite of his weaknesses he actually succeeded as a father. In fact we see that whether he knew it or not, the one thing that he did right in his life, although he wavered plenty, was bringing up his girls against the great odds of his defective character. And the love shown him by his daughters, so beautifully projected by both Balk and Moss, was wonderful to experience since it is so seldom seen these days when the usual style is to trash men and their part in the family. And the non-exploitive, nurturing and loving role of Sonya's English teacher, played with a fine delicacy by Vincent D'Onfrio, was a much-needed change from the usual cinematic use of teachers as sexual lechers. In this movie we can see that men are people too.

I should mention that the screenplay by Kristine Johnson and Davia Nelson was carefully crafted to showcase the story dramatically, and to warn you that this is a tear jerker. It starts a little slow, and seems a touch old fashioned, but stay with it: it's a beautiful movie, one the best I've seen in a long time.

I've seen this and I give it___stars.
I want to see it___. I'll pass___.
The review was worth reading___. Not___.

I Shot Andy Warhol (1996) 9

Totally degenerate, but very well done

Director Mary Harron invades the sixties tinfoil castle of Andy Warhol and spins a kind of art deco loser romance with the very talented Lili Taylor playing the very butch Valerie Solanas, who actually did shoot Andy Warhol. I have been driving myself crazy trying to recall who Taylor is taking off on, some little guy, ghetto denizen from a forgotten flick of my mind. If anybody recognizes the style, please let me know. Anyway, she manages to be surprisingly sympathetic as the authoress of the SCUM manifesto (that's "Society for the Cutting Up of Men") and a play entitled "Up Your ...," which I suppose is appropriate considering the decadence depicted. Taylor's Valerie Solanas is strangely winning as a victim of a desperate, mad integrity. (I suspect the real Valerie was anything but sympathetic.) She won't take a job but will beg, panhandle, turn tricks and steal. She's a true believer whose main tenet is that men are something akin to a disease. Because she is bright and witty and courageous she wins us over even though she hates us. We forgive her because we know she hurts a lot and can't help herself. (To which she would say, "...")

Harron decorates this sixties cum nineties version of New York chic/flophouse reality with the kind of degenerate personalities for which the Big Apple is justly famous. Jared Harris plays Andy Warhol brilliantly with something like a truer than true characterization, combining a sympathetic, eccentric and gentle exterior with an exploitive mercantile heart. One gets the sense that he had it coming. Stephen Dorff is Candy Darling, a transvestite so fetching that he makes a guy like me wish he had a sister. Lothaire Bluteau as Olympia Press publisher Maurice Girodias seems a little young, but otherwise fits the bill, and Martha Plimpton as Stevie does a nice job in a modest part. The sound track might catch your ear with Blue Cheer performing the Coasters' "Summertime Blues" and Bettie Serveert doing a fine interpretation of Dylan's "I'll Keep It with Mine." Jewel (yes, the very same) sings "Sunshine Superman," and completing the nineties accent on the sixties, REM does "Love Is All Around." Probably outright anachronistic is the use of an aluminum soda can to smoke grass. I don't think that came into practice until later when the skunkweed got so strong you could smoke it like hash.

Some other sights: the Andy Warhol hanger-ons doing a faux sand-painting mandala with pills as they party, and then one of them rolling her naked torso into the pills so that they stick to her body. Or the guy coming out of—an encounter, we'll call it—with a jar of Vaseline in hand in time to greet some slumming French aristocratic ladies whose hands (one gloved) he kisses. In a bit of haute culture ridicule, another of the hangers-on asks poor Candy Darling, "We've been wondering, how often do you get your period?" To which s/he replies, "Every day. I'm all woman."

If you're the kind of person who watches the Disney Channel, I would recommend you skip this. Otherwise you might want to check it out. I found it surprisingly smart and witty. The print is finely cut, the acting is superior, and there's an underlying sense of something close to the heroic in a clearly quixotic way.

I've seen this and I give it___stars.
I want to see it___. I'll pass___.
The review was worth reading___. Not___.

The Insider (1999) 9

Al Pacino is the real John Wayne...

Or the Ronnie Reagan of the left. I mean this in both the positive sense that he is a cultural hero, and in the negative sense that he is a celluloid hero. I have seen so many Al Pacino movies that I feel not only that I know him, but that he is actually a character from my own life. I like him here as Lowell Bergman, a radical ex-Ramparts Magazine editor grown into middle age but still fighting the good fight from within the establishment of CBS and 60 Minutes. His hair still flies about, showing that he is a free soul who cares more about substance than appearance. (We realize that the dye job is a necessary concession to the media world in which he lives.) And the passion still burns bright in his dark eyes, and he's still as wiry as a teenager.

But is this history? Is this the truth about what happened with Jeffrey Wigand, big tobacco and CBS? Or is this "revisionist history" dressed up dramatically to make the good guys look good and the bad guys look bad? I wish I could say this is how big time journalism really works, and that we have been afforded a true view inside the system. But it's hard to tell where the truth leaves off and dramatic license takes over. We learned in journalism long ago that there is no real objectivity; that all is to some extent interpretive. In fact I recall a college text we used in the sixties with the (then) arresting title, "Interpretive Journalism." Today's text might be called "Subjective Journalism" and tomorrow's "The Age of Tabloid Journalism."

Nonetheless, this is a very good movie. The script by Michael Mann and Eric Roth sparkles with the immediacy of today's headlines, and Mann's direction is clean, crisp and dramatically very sharp. Russell Crowe as Wigand, the biochemist who blew the whistle on big tobacco and lost his wife and children to divorce in the process, is excellent. His subtle and restrained interpretation of Wigand reminds me so much of those guys from my generation who opted for the security of the corporate structure, only in his case the misgivings got to him. Diane Venova is chilling in a small role as his wife, a house and home centered woman who leaves him because she doesn't think it's fair to subject her and the children to the dangers and financial uncertainties of his whistle-blowing activities. Wigand is the reluctant hero and she is the woman who did not stand by her man.

Christopher Plummer does a good job of playing 60 Minutes's Mike Wallace, who gets plenty of egg on his face here. He looks pathetic in the scene where he talks about what he will be remembered for. I'm sure Wallace is mad as hell about the portrayal, but I don't think anybody is going to sue the producers of this movie, since it is so popular and so much in tune with what most of us believe to be true. Gina Gershon appears briefly as a greedy bottom line lawyer who cares nothing about journalism or the ethics of journalism.

John Wayne fought the enemies of our culture on celluloid with true grit and an unwavering, if sometimes moronic, sense of what's right. Al Pacino does the same here, except our enemies have changed and what's right isn't so clear anymore and the war room has become the board room. The really melancholy thing is I guess I wanted to believe in John Wayne when I was a kid, and now as a middle aged man, I want to believe in Al Pacino and 60 Minutes. This movie helps.

I've seen this and I give it___stars.
I want to see it___. I'll pass___.
The review was worth reading___. Not___.

In the Company of Men (1997) 9

Uncomfortable, but worth it

This is a deceptive tale from the corporate jungle. Chad (Aaron Eckhart) is a virile, handsome middle level manager capable of some charm. However he doesn't relate to other people the way most people do. He has some superficial tricks for getting close. He tells women he likes the way they smell. He knows they love that. He bonds with men by appealing to their prejudices. He tells sexist jokes: "What's the difference between a golf ball and a G-spot?" Answer: "I can spend twenty minutes looking for a golf ball." He likes to get close to people to use and exploit them. But he goes further than that. He likes to hurt them. Why? "Because I can," he says.

In other words, Chad's a sociopath who specializes in humiliating people. He gets a black worker to pull down his pants and show him his balls. He says he needs to see if he really has the stuff to be recommended for a promotion. He tells him, the guy who wins is the guy who has "the nastiest sack of venom." In case the guy doesn't know he's been humiliated, as he pulls up his pants, Chad tells him to get him a cup of coffee, black.

Christine (Stacy Edwards) is a pretty girl in her twenties, a lightning fast typist in the secretarial pool. She's very nice and caring. Problem is she's deaf and talks funny. Chad spots her and decides she is perfect for this little game of broken hearts he wants to play with Howard (Matt Malloy), his slightly nerdy friend, co-worker and sometime boss. We'll both date her, he says, and then dump her. That way we'll get back at all the women who have done us dirt. He has an ulterior motive as well. He wants to destroy Howard, just to prove he can.

What makes this film work is the sheer brutality of Chad's bloodless methods, and Director Neil LaBute's suffocating depiction of predatory life in the corporate structure. LaBute, who also wrote the script, is uncompromising in his desire to make us see that people are animals. He succeeds.

I've seen this and I give it___stars.

I want to see it___. I'll pass___.
The review was worth reading___. Not___.

Into the Wild (2007) 10

Call everything by its proper name.

But don't make a mistake.

The theme of this emotionally wrenching drama (script and direction from Sean Penn, from a best-selling non-fiction book by Jon Krakauer) is not man versus wild, as it was in the works of one of the protagonist's heroes, Jack London. Instead the conflict is between man and society. Chris McCandless has just graduated from college. His parents are proud. His grades are good enough for a top grad school. He's bright, personable. It seems he has everything going for him.

But he's bitter and disappointed. He disrespects his parents and believes that the last thing he wants to do is act out their idea of success. So he gives the $24,000 he has in the bank for grad school to charity and just ups and leaves home. He has some Kerouac-like adventures on the road where as a "leather tramp" he meets some ordinary people, some good people, some retro hippies, some Middle American farm workers, some derelicts and a social worker in L.A., a pretty girl, an old man, etc., and then, believing "you don't need human relationships to be happy," it's north to Alaska to live out a dream that might have been dreamt by Thoreau or Jack London.

But we know from the very beginning of the film that Chris McCandless AKA "Alexander Supertramp" will die in the Alaskan wilderness at a tender age in 1992. Was his death the result of stupidity regarding the dangers of going "into the wild" or was it a result of bad luck or accident? Or was it the indirect result of the hypocritical and mercantile values of his parents and his society to which he overreacted? Or even, was it the indirect result of a kind of youthful bravado that could overtake many a young man?

What Chris does is what a renunciant in an Eastern religion might do: he leaves society to live alone in the woods. He renounces society's shallow values and lives as simply as possible. But Chris is not practicing an Eastern religion. He is not an old man near the end of his life looking for *moksha*. He is under the influence of Thoreau and Jack London, whose books he has read and loved. He wants to test himself against the wild without help from anyone. He wants to prove his manhood to himself without the help of society or society's culture

But he is a greenhorn in the Alaskan wilderness whose fate is sealed.

The way that Jon Krakauer and Sean Penn have reconstructed this story (partly from notes and even from some carvings that Chris made, and partly from interviews with people who knew Chris) we see that at one point after some weeks in the wilderness Chris suddenly realizes something profound and moving. He says, referring to the great beauty of life and the world that he is able to see: "Happiness is only real when it's shared." At that point he has learned what he needed to learn from the wilderness and from the people he met in his trek across the country.

The great tragedy of this movie is what then befalls Chris.

The ending is emotionally gut-retching and yet somehow cathartic. To watch such a likeable, honest and spiritually advanced young man with such potential seem to throw it all away, carelessly, foolishly, or accidently, is a human tragedy brilliantly brought to the printed page and to the screen for all of us to share. And in this sharing Chris's life gains new meaning and he becomes a guide and a teacher for all of us.

I know it must have been very difficult for his parents to cooperate in the telling of Chris's story since the story does not show them in a favorable light. Yet the very fact that they helped bring Chris's story to us shows perhaps where Chris got his moral courage. I have no doubt that it was their deep love for their son that moved them to find that emotional courage. This movie gives meaning to Chris's life and shows their love for him, and allows a wide audience to see that he did not die in vain.

I want to congratulate not only Krakauer and Penn but also Emile Hirsch who played the part of Chris McCandless. The role was enormously demanding, the sort of role that an actor may only get once in a lifetime, if he's lucky. And Hirsch played it well. He was charming and witty and very strong of character. What a splendid tribute to the real Chris. And kudos to Hal Holbrook who played Ron Krantz to an emotional tee, deeply sympathetic to both his character and to Chris's, and to the significance of the film itself.

And the rest of the cast was also very good, although Kristen Stewart was a little too pretty for the part of the 16-year-old trailer troubadour, and of course William Hurt could have used a larger role.

The lesson of this story, it seems to me is this: Young people of courage and honor, even though they may make mistakes, even though they may be mistaken at a fundamental level, can, through their valor, teach us all something important. As Chris told Ron Krantz, "Get off your butt, old man. The core of a man's spirit comes from new experiences." What he is also saying is: live every moment in a genuine way. And we can see that is what Chris did. A life so lived, although short, may well be the equal of a much longer life lived not so authentically.

I've seen this and I give it___stars.
I want to see it___. I'll pass___.
The review was worth reading___. Not___.

The King of Hearts (*Le roi de coeur*) (1967) 9

The madness and madcap-ness of war

The madness of war makes the members of the asylum seem sane. Such is the theme of this anti-war comedy directed by France's Philippe de Broca, starring the English actor Alan Bates wearing a jaunty crown, and featuring a young and delectable Genevieve Bujold in a yellow tutu.

She's insane. A virgin who believes she's a prostitute. Her madame is also insane, or so the townsmen of Marville believe. But theirs is such a pleasant insanity that we in the audience are persuaded to ask what is sanity and who needs it? Can nerve gas and rat-infested trenches with bloated, rotting bodies be sane?

But hold on there, that last sentence better describes some other anti-war movies from the time of The Great War, perhaps *All Quiet on the Western Front* (1930) or Kubrick's *Paths of Glory* (1957). Here the tone is light, the treatment burlesque, and the plot absurdly amusing.

Bates plays Private Charles Plumpick (in Scottish kilt) a keeper of messenger pigeons who has "volunteered" to find and defuse a bomb left in Marville by the retreating Jerrys. It's set to go off at the stroke of midnight. The townspeople learn of the bomb and desert the town, leaving the inmates at the sanitarium and the circus animals to fend for themselves. So when Plumpick arrives he finds only a detachment of Germans who spot him and chase him into the asylum. Inside as cover he joins a game of cards with two of the inmates. The Jerrys confront the inmates who identify themselves in absurd ways. Plumpick, with some on the spot inspiration, calls himself "the king of hearts."

And so we have our premise. When the Jerrys retreat to the countryside to await the explosion, and while the English watch for the return of one of Plumpick's pigeons with news that the bomb has been defused, the inmates stream out of the asylum. They take over the town, dressing up in various costumes: this one becomes the mayor, another the priest, and little Mademoiselle "Poppy" (Bujold) awaits her first trick.

This the kind of movie that Monty Python fans would adore, and I suspect it had some effect on the directorial style of Terry Gilliam.

Anyway I wrote a little ditty to anticipate the ending:

I'll have no more of war
Such a craven whore!
To the asylum I will go

To be my true love's beau.

By the way, this movie is mostly in French with subtitles, but some of it is in English without.

I've seen this and I give it___stars.
I want to see it___. I'll pass___.
The review was worth reading___. Not___.

Lantana (2001) 9

Something close to a masterpiece

In this starkly realistic examination of love and infidelity among the thirtysomething crowd from down under we learn that you may desire to cheat on your spouse, but it's better if you don't.

Leon Zat, a police detective played with an original and striking demeanor by Anthony LaPaglia, cheats on his wife and finds that his adultery compromises not only his marriage but his performance on the job. He becomes irritable and flies off the handle at things of little importance, and becomes consumed with guilt.

He is not alone. The marriage of John Knox (Geoffrey Rush) and psychiatrist Valerie Somers (Barbara Hershey) is falling apart as Knox seeks something from the outside and Somers is torn apart with the suspicion that he is having a homosexual affair, perhaps with one of her clients. Meanwhile Jane O'May (Zat's adulteress played by Rachael Blake) finds that she needs a man, or maybe two, other than her estranged husband. Even Sonja Zat (Kerry Armstrong) feels the pressure and yearns to feel attractive, perhaps with younger men.

More than halfway through we have an apparent murder and an investigation during the course of which some of the adulteries come to light and cause the participants to examine themselves and their lives closely.

Andrew Dovell wrote the subtle, richly attired script, full of penetrating dialogue and an uncompromising veracity, adapting it from his play *Speaking in Tongues*. Ray Lawrence directed in an unusual but compelling manner in which the scenes are sharply focused and cut to linger in our minds. Again and again I was startled with just how exactly right was something a character said or did. Lawrence's exacting attention to detail gives the film a textured and deeply layered feel so that one has the sense of real life fully lived. The cast is uniformly excellent although LaPaglia stands out because of his most demanding role. His performance is one of the best I have seen in recent years. The only weakness in the film is a somewhat lethargic start, partially caused by Lawrence's *cinéma vérité* scene construction and editing. What he likes to do is lead us to a realization along with the characters and then punctuate the experience by lingering on the scene, or in other cases by cutting quickly away. Often what other directors might show, he leaves to our imagination, and at other times he shows something seemingly trivial which nonetheless stays in our mind. John Knox's affair, for example, is not shown. Jane O'May and her husband's reconciliation is left to our mind's eye. Yet the scene with Valerie Somers in the lighted telephone booth (with graffiti) is shown at length and then what happens next is not. These are interesting directorial choices.

The ending comes upon us, as it sometimes should, unexpectedly, but then resonates so that we can see and feel the resolution. Not everything is tied up. Again we are left in some cases to use our own imagination.

This original film, one of the best of the new millennium I have seen, stayed with me long after they ran the closing credits. It is well worth the two hours.

I've seen this and I give it___stars.
I want to see it___. I'll pass___.
The review was worth reading___. Not___.

L.I.E. (2001) 10

A movie you won't soon forget

Big John is a retired marine homosexual pedophile whose Long Island doorbell plays "From the Halls of Montezuma..." when rung. He is a guy who has lived a James Bond kind of life who likes to... Well, I can't say, but it should be obvious what he likes to do.

Howie is a 15-year-old boy who has lost his beloved mother and has a father who is too busy for him and hasn't a clue about what is going on in his son's life. Howie and his friends are into breaking into the minimansions on Long Island for fun and profit. One night they break into the cellar of Big John's house and steal his prized set of handguns. Big John goes looking for the perps and what he finds is true paternal love.

What makes this an outstanding movie is director Michael Cuesta's relentless and uncompromisingly realistic treatment of what is essentially a taboo coming of age story. I can tell you that if the theme appeals to you, you will be completely captivated by this movie. And even if such a tale is not your cup of tea, you might want to see this anyway because it is so very, very well done without a hint of contrivance or pandering. It is beautifully acted (Paul Dano playing Howie is outstanding, as is Brian Cox as Big John) and beautifully directed and cut. The script by Stephen M. Ryder, Michael Cuesta and Gerald Cuesta is replete with precise and totally authentic dialogue. The characters are nuanced and faithfully realized. The theme of love over predatory sexuality is convincing and worthy. Furthermore, the sexuality depicted is just vivid enough to make sure we understand what is going on without resorting to anything graphic.

(I saw the R-rated version. I understand there is an NC-17, but I don't think it matters. For those who are going to be offended, I think a PG-13 version of this movie—were it possible—would offend them.)

I think the resolution of the film, both in terms of what happens to Big John and to Howie was exactly right, but some may find it a little too neat. Certainly the ending as done does not leave any ambiguities lying around, although I suspect there is a scene where Howie's dad accuses him of stealing his hundred dollar bills somewhere on the cutting room floor, and really that's okay, since it wasn't needed. Or maybe I missed it.

Bottom line: something close to a small masterpiece: the kind of movie that tells us some truths about life that cannot be expressed in so many words—in other words, a work of art.

By the way, L.I.E. stands for Long Island Expressway.

I've seen this and I give it___stars.
I want to see it___. I'll pass___.
The review was worth reading___. Not___.

The Life and Death of Colonel Blimp (1943) 9

A delightful Brit historical romance

Beware spoilers.

"Jolly good show, old chap," is what directors Michael Powell and Emeric Pressburger might have said to one another as they watched the final cut of their movie in a private showing in 1943. Because Winston Churchill did not like the movie, feeling that it was too generous to the Germans in its positive depiction of the German army officer Theo Kretschmar-Schuldorff (Anton Walbrook), it was banned from public showing in Britain until 1945.

The Life and Death of Colonel Blimp is a jolly good show and then some, a remarkable movie in several ways. However it is not about "Colonel Blimp" who I understand was a popular cartoon character in the British press at the time. Instead it is about a fictional character named Clive Candy (Roger Livesey) who actually rose to the rank of general. It begins with his experience in the Boer War and ends with him working as a retired general on the home front during World War II. It is a movie about friendship across international boundaries and cultures, about Brit spunk and fair play, and includes a long-running love story that might have had the title "The Portrait of Deborah Kerr" since she first appears near the beginning of the film and then during World War I and then again during World War II, but never ages!

She is the true love of both Candy and Kretschmar-Schuldorff, and here is how it plays out: Candy loses her to Kretschmar-Schuldorff in her first incarnation, but with stiff Brit upper lip never lets on or breathes a sigh of regret. He wins her in her next incarnation and they are happily married. In the third incarnation, both Candy and Kretschmar-Schuldorff, now widowers, realize that they are too old for the new her and admire her from afar, her previous incarnations long deceased. I liked this conceit very much since it allowed us to see a lot of Deborah Kerr.

Most of the movie depicts Candy's life as a historical romance, full of adventure and high purpose. The last part of the movie, dovetailed back into after the long flashback of Candy's life, plays a bit like a patriotic wartime film, showing the pluck and readiness of the British people to fight the Nazis. This part Churchill would have approved of. However I doubt that he had the time to watch that far into the film, which runs for two hours and forty-three minutes.

All in all the film is a delightful entertainment, carefully scripted and directed, the sort of uplifting show, full of wit and sparkle and honor among men that makes the viewer feel good about humanity, in short the sort of film that is seldom done these days.

I've seen this and I give it___stars.
I want to see it___. I'll pass___.
The review was worth reading___. Not___.

Little Children (2006) 9

Sexual realism?

The way director Todd Field handles human sexuality in this movie reminds me a bit of the way Todd Solondz handled it in *Happiness* (1998). There are the same starkly realistic depictions of a variety of human desires, lusts and cravings with perhaps an emphasis on what devotees of the missionary position might call "perversions." Although not quite as wild as Solondz's film, *Little Children* is equally challenging to politically correct notions of sexuality.

Kate Winslet stars as Sarah Pierce, a suburban mom who has a Master's in English lit and a husband who finds sex in cyber space more satisfying than sex with her. She joins (at a slight distance) some other more conventional suburban moms at the local playground where they sit around and talk while watching their children play. One of the things the women talk about is Brad Adamson (Patrick Wilson), who is a handsome stay at home dad who has twice fluked the bar exam. He takes care of his son while his high powered wife Kathy (Jennifer Connelly) is busy bringing home the bacon. The women don't talk to him. They watch him warily but with keen interest and call him "the prom king." When Sarah catches her husband having sex with his computer (so to speak) she resolves to gain the Prom King for herself, partly out of sheer romantic lust and partly out of revenge.

While we watch the adulterous union unfold, we are given some perspective in the form of Ronnie J. McGorvey (played with appropriate creepiness by Jackie Earle Haley) who has just been released from prison after serving a term for exposing himself to children. A side complication arrives in the form of Larry Hedges (Noah Emmerich), who is a "retired" cop with a temper management problem and a tendency to find objects of hate onto which to direct his anger. Ronnie the pervert becomes his target.

All this seems...well, unremarkable and even tiresome except for the fact that everybody in the movie is flawed in some very serious and interesting way, and director Field's interpretation of the characters comes down resolutely on the side of the nonconventional. In some respects what Field and Tom Perrotta, who wrote the novel from which he and Field adapted the screenplay, are saying is that the characters are all little children (hence the title). And not only that, but we're all a bit perverse. It just depends on your point of view. Sarah's parenting skills are less than optimal and it's obvious that she is bored with being a stay at home mom. Her "perversion" is similar to Gustav Flaubert's Madame Bovary in that she wants more out of life than being a wife and mother. She wants, as she explains to the woman's book club, what Madame Bovary wanted, to satisfy "the hunger, the hunger for an alternative and the refusal to accept a life of unhappiness."

Brad wants to remain a child, being taken care of by his wife, while he pretends to study for the bar exam but instead plays touch football and watches the boys at the skateboard park as though a boy himself, or allows himself to be seduced by Sarah.

Ronnie wants to have sex with little girls, and Sarah's husband wants to have sex with a porn star—or perhaps they just want to masturbate to fantasies of same...and so on.

What makes this an excellent movie is first of all Kate Winslet who continues to prove she can play a wide variety of characters and get into their skin and become them as she has done in so many films. She brings the nuances of Sarah Pierce's character, her strengths and weaknesses, to life in a vivid and compelling way that forces us to identify with her, much the same way we identify with Madame Bovary.

Also first rate is the unflinching way human sexuality is presented and the refusal to accept conventionality that is the heart of this story. I think that directors Todd Field and Todd Solondz may be working in a new genre for the 21st century that might be called "sexual realism." Perhaps it is just a coincidence but both directors had Jane Adams play a kind of forlorn wallflower at the game of life in both movies. Perhaps she symbolizes in some strange way the confused, frustrated and deeply masked phenomenon that is human sexuality.

The real essence of the film is contained in the scene in which Ronnie enters the pool with all the children playing in it and the moms in the lounge chairs watching. Suddenly Sarah becomes aware that Ronnie the pervert is in the pool and then all the other moms become aware. There is a mass hysteria and a mass exit from the pool by the children. The moms are horrified and are desperate to know, "Did he touch you?" Ronnie is seen as some kind of bug-like creature who somehow will bring a contagion upon them through his touch. The point here and indeed throughout the film (and also in Solondz's film) is that we overreact to sex that offends us. We find the touch of a creepy pedophile worse than some kind of physical violence.

This is a thesis that will not find acceptance in America for many years to come if ever because sexual perversity is more threatening to most Americans than extreme violence. Why this should be so is not really a mystery. But to explain it here is beyond the scope of this review, and anyway explaining it would hardly change it. However the fact that Field and Solandz are bringing it to our attention is something new and is perhaps the beginning of a challenge to conventional morality.

I've seen this and I give it___stars.
I want to see it___. I'll pass___.
The review was worth reading___. Not___.

Little Miss Sunshine (2006) 9

Heartwarming madcap dysfunctional family caper

Albuquerque homemaker Sheryl (Toni Collette) has a few problems, causing her some stress, leading to nicotine addiction. ("I am NOT smoking!")

First, there is Richard (Greg Kinnear) her husband, who is an annoying and uninspired motivation speaker who thinks he's going to get rich hustling his nine-step pyramid to success. *Loser!*

Then there is her brother Frank (Steve Carell) who has bandages on his wrists after trying to kill himself because his homosexual lover (one of his grad students) dumped him, the number one American authority on Marcel Proust, for his academic rival, the number two authority. *Pathetic!*

Next there is Grandpa (Alan Arkin) a randy nursing home reject who snorts heroin, has a potty mouth and complains a lot. (Maybe he'll overdose!)

Then there is her teenaged son Dwayne (Paul Dano) an antisocial loner who reads Nietzsche, hates everyone, and is on a vow of silence until he gets into flight training in the Air Force. (Our children always disappoint us. Sometimes we forgive them.)

And finally there is Miss Sunshine herself, her daughter Olive (Abigail Breslin) a little overweight, a little nerdy, not exactly a looker, who has entered the Little Miss Sunshine beauty pageant for little girls and is honing her dance routine following the pornographic advice of Grandpa. *Oh, boy!*

Credit Michael Arndt whose script won the Academy Award for Best Original Screenplay for this lineup and for a wonderful and strikingly original comedic and satirical romp through dysfunctional land. For reasons too complex to relate, the whole family piles into the Volkswagen bus and heads for Redondo Beach, California where the beauty pageant is being held. Along the madcap way, the bus's clutch goes out, Grandpa suffers, shall we say, a major setback, Richard learns that the family finances are not going to work out, Frank gets the heartbreak rubbed in his face, and Dwayne finds out that his dream is not going to come true. But can Olive win the pageant?

The pageant itself is pretty funny with the girls in their plastic hairdos and their Tammy Faye makeup and their fake smiles pitted against the decidedly unglamorous but ever hopeful Olive Hoover. Who will win?

Alan Arkin won the Oscar for Best Supporting Actor, and Abigail Breslin and the picture itself garnered Oscar nominations. But see this for the writer. Michael Arndt's warm, funny and highly original script has me (and half the screenwriters in Hollywood and New York) Kermit green with envy.

I've seen this and I give it___stars.
I want to see it___. I'll pass___.
The review was worth reading___. Not___.

Lost in Translation (2003) 9

A Platonic May-September affair

I don't know why I had trouble with this movie. Old guy gets young, beautiful girl ought to work for me, being an old guy myself. Maybe I was jealous. I couldn't do karaoke the way Bill Murray does it. And after a night on the Tokyo town, I couldn't carry Scarlett Johansson home in my arms and tuck her into bed and turn out the light. Well, I couldn't carry her. And she does have pretty eyes and nice legs and beautiful skin. And she's a good actress, although this part did not stretch her or even challenge her. And after a fashion one gets used to the slightly arrogant Bill Murray style. His character is, after all, an action hero who gets paid $2-million to make a whiskey commercial.

Whiskey. I think that is what it is. I don't like whiskey or cigarettes and I usually don't like people who like ciga-

rettes and whiskey, although I recall a song from my parents' time: "Cigarettes and whiskey, and wild, wild women/They'll drive you crazy, they'll drive you insane." (I'll take the wild, wild women.) Such might conquer the boredom felt by out-of-towners in a high rise hotel in downtown Tokyo that director Sofia Coppola (Francis Ford's daughter) was at great pains to get across to us in the opening scenes. I also don't like bars and I think that people who spend their time hanging out in bars are mostly lonely alcoholics. Ditto for gratuitous smoking in movies and obvious product placements.

So I almost gave up on this, but the DVD jacket does say, "OVER 80 FOUR-STAR REVIEWS." (That would be five stars on Amazon.) Something must be wrong with me. Or maybe there is a big contrast coming in the second half of the film, and all this 21st century, big city, international First World ennui is necessary to set that up. But isn't it a little heavy how Scarlett hangs around in her panties waiting for her husband to return, and when he does he either goes to sleep or off to doing something else. Wow, one would think he would NOTICE. The camera surely does.

Okay, I saw the rest of the film and ...

There is a lot of artistic shtick in this movie. In fact it would be an art movie if it weren't aimed so directly at the mass mind—well, the mass mind over thirty. The long pauses and the way the camera lingers to SHOUT: notice this scene! how excellent it is, or to punctuate a point, how profound or how prosaic.

But I like the clumsiness of their relationship and the way it is drawn out.

The shots of Japan are wonderful, like a travel log. Mount Fujiyama in gray in the background; Mount Fujisan in the background in full color and snow cap. The games arcade in Tokyo, the game machines like Vegas slot machines all in a row. The clean, straight lines of the bars and the exercise rooms, black and whites; the square wooden bowls out of which they drink the wine; the lights at night on the boulevard, outdoing Times Square in their gaudy neon-ness. The touristy feel to the movie. The Japanese untranslated. The sleeplessness as though they were near the Arctic Circle with twenty hours of daylight. The easy Hollywood feel to the psychology: our hero's pix on the side of trucks drinking Japanese whiskey, suavely; the need for the hero to hide from his public; his obviously dyed hair; the "satire" of the blonde mediocre starlet who affects anorexia; the sense that Sofia Coppola lived something like this. One can imagine her boredom, and then the interested older man.

I also liked the bit with the semi-talented lounge singer, again like Las Vegas—her picking him up, so to speak, he too drunk to protest or to remember. Again the Hollywood idea of the pecking order. The banality of the glamorous life.

It is also to Sofia Coppola's credit that she got the relationship exactly right: she knew how the old guy felt and she knew how the young girl felt, and she knew what was right and what would be the right ending.

I guess I should say why this movie affects me and brings out the impatience in me and calls forth my sardonic nature. It is that I have been there where Bill Murray's character was and I played it the same way. I am not so sure I did the right thing. I tell myself I did, but I am not so sure.

See this for Sofia Coppola who made her father proud.

I've seen this and I give it___stars.
I want to see it___. I'll pass___.
The review was worth reading___. Not___.

Love Serenade (1996) 10

A delightfully diabolic comedic tale from down under

Ken Sherry (George Shevtsov), a tall, divorced, sleazy, and a bit in love with himself disc jockey from Brisbane, Australia comes to the tiny berg of Sunray to take over disc jockeying duties at the local radio station. He likes to spin platters with deep vocals from seductive male voices like Barry White's while spewing out tidbits of philosophy and poetry designed to enthrall the ladies. In the house next door to the one he has acquired, live two unmarried sisters, Dimity (Miranda Otto) and Vicki-Ann (Rebecca Frith) who toss out the lures in the hope of landing such a catch.

(The fishing metaphor here and those to follow are appropriate because at one point Dimity notices that Ken has a kind of scar on his neck making her think he has gills. Additionally he has a marlin on one of his walls, although he won't eat fish. Furthermore, in the opening scene of the movie, Dimity and Vicki-Ann are actually fishing.)

Anyway, for the girls the lesson here is be careful what you fish for since the catch of your dreams might turn out to be the tomcod of your nightmares. Dimity is younger, virginal and a bit odd. She's a waitress at the local Chinese restaurant. Older sister Rebecca is slightly desperate and on the make. She runs the town's beauty parlor. As the competition for Ken heats up they decide they hate each other. At first the younger sister Dimity seems to have him hooked, but then Rebecca seems to be hauling him in and headed for matrimonial bliss, so much so that she opens her trousseau and takes out her wedding gown to try it on and show him..., and then....

Well, the key here is that the script and direction by Shirley Barrett is just so diabolically clever and so full of

keen insights into the psychology of men and women, especially women, that it is just a riot. Otto manages the sweet innocence and naiveté of a 14-year-old, although she is supposed to be twenty. The expressions she gets on her face are just so, so funny. I loved the scene where she is on Ken's couch and he is sitting arrogantly on the other end and at length asks her if she wants to be kissed. Yes, she does; and the way she slides over to him, bit by anxious bit, was just too funny. I also loved the scene where Ken is on top of her and she is lying on her back looking up at ceiling (at the camera of course) with an somewhat puzzled, pleased and expectant expression on her face, as if she is searching for what she is supposed to be feeling while Ken mechanically continues to do what he is doing.

Also good is the scene near the end, high in the silo, where Ken is explaining something to Rebecca. The camera is on him, but directly behind him we see Dimity's face smiling in some delight as if she knows how this is going to end. (And she does.)

I thought it was interesting that the small town of Sunray, Australia could have easily been Sunray, Kansas or Sunray, Ohio, so much was it like a typical small American town. I also found apt how the soundtrack of seductive hits from the seventies, "Love Serenade" itself, and two others by Barry White, but also "Me and Mrs. Jones" by Billy Paul, mirrored Ken Sherry's "philosophy" of love and meshed well with his deep, sonorous voice. The song "My Coo Ca Choo" by Alvin Stardust played near the end was apparently a hit in Australia, but this was the first time I'd heard it. Good song.

See this for Shirley Barrett who simultaneously satirizes both male and female sexuality in a manner that would have delighted Oscar Wilde and any number of comedy writers, and for Miranda Otto who was both funny and charming.

Masked and Anonymous (2003) 9

Dylan self-analyzes in public—but cryptically

The "mask" could be Bob Dylan's face so stoically does he hold his expression. And the "anonymous" could be any tin horn banana republic dictator. As The Who phrased it years ago: "The new boss, just like the old boss."

The surprising thing about this film is how good it is. Clearly experimental in form (which often equals boring) *Masked and Anonymous* is instead a fascinating work of art with outstanding performances amid a meandering chaos replete with cunning little speeches that defy analysis. I was not really surprised to learn that credited screenwriter "Sergei Petrov" is really Bob Dylan. Kudos to him and to "Rene Fontaine" (actually Larry Charles of "Seinfeld" fame) for coming up with this little gem.

However I have to say that without Dylan's music and the fine cast this could have been an unmitigated disaster.

One of the things I love about Bob Dylan is the intensity. It's always there. He never stops. It's as though the next lyric will be the line to end all lines (pun intended) or that the next musical hook will exhaust the music.

Like Emily Dickinson he invented a new kind of poetry that confounded the poetic establishment and confused academia. When I first heard Dylan's lyrics in the sixties referred to as poetry, I was an undergraduate at UCLA and thought (apparently along with Carl Sandburg): this isn't poetry. It's a string of clichés. And it is. But what Bob Dylan did was to use the phrases and the clichés and the rhythms of our world as the poet uses words. The clichés became the building blocks of his poems. And of course they filled his head to overflowing, echoing and ricocheting around in his mind like the wares of Quinn the Eskimo running all around his brain. And they had to get out, and he tossed them out with tune after tune and a lyric to string them together, and he ended up writing some of the best poetry of the latter half of the 20th century. But of course his poetry, like that of all song writers does not stand entirely alone without its music. Still his phrases that look into our soul and chronicle our times are as indelible as the color of our eyes. It is no coincidence that in the age of the sound bite, Dylan wrote his poems in sound bites.

Like the 19th century academics who wanted to edit Emily Dickinson's poetry and improve her meter and adjust her "imperfect" (slant) rhymes and normalize her punctuation, the academic world of the 20th century wanted to get Dylan to eschew cliché. But what they missed is the poet knows the language better than they and his clichés are in the modules of our minds. They are the wings of the zeitgeist and the linguist's meme.

Goodman was perfect as Uncle Sweetheart who might be a deeply buried persona of Dylan with his cryptic one-liners and his desolation soul, his corrupted heart and his huge appetite for life. And Jessica Lange was also excellent as were the cameos by all sorts of name actors appearing on stage to confront a stoic Dylan. In a way they were intriguing and perhaps nothing more than that. Like Shakespearean players they came and had their time upon the stage and were heard no more.

Yes, this film seems to signify in the final analysis not much, but, isn't that the point of life: there is no point. Life *is* that tale by an idiot signifying nothing.

Here's a nice string of quotes from the cynic, Jack Fate, Dylan's alter ego: "I was always a singer and maybe no more than that. Sometimes it's not enough to know the meaning of things, sometimes we have to know what things don't mean as well...Things fall apart...The way we look at the world is what we really are. See it from a fair garden and everything looks cheerful. Climb to a higher plateau and you'll see plunder and murder. Truth and beauty are in the eye of the beholder...I don't pay much attention to my dreams...I stopped trying to figure everything out a long time ago..."

I have only one criticism of this film: I wish there had been a lot more of the hauntingly beautiful Penélope Cruz.

I've seen this and I give it___stars.
I want to see it___. I'll pass___.
The review was worth reading___. Not___.

Match Point (2005) 9

Clever, very clever, with a nice surprise ending

This has one of the neatest bits of stage business you are likely to ever see in a movie. Keep your eye the ball (or ring) as it hits the net, or perhaps a railing. Whether it falls forward or backward can make all the difference in the world.

I can't believe that tennis players say the same thing that poker players say: "I'd rather be lucky than good." Poker players say that because there is a significant element of chance involved in any given hand; and besides they already think they're good. It is the other guy who is lucky.

Jonathan Rhys-Meyers stars as Chris Wilton, a poor Irish boy on the make. He is handsome, charming, smart, and a very good tennis player who is candid about not quite being good enough against the very best. He gets a job teaching tennis at an exclusive English club and quickly meets and charms a very rich student (Matthew Goode as Tom Hewitt) who has a sister (Chloe, played by Emily Mortimer) who finds him irresistible.

Well, how lucky can you get? Complication: Scarlett (the sexiest woman on earth, at one time, anyway, according to some magazine) Johansson playing Nola Rice, who is seriously dating the very eligible Tom Hewitt. (You could say she's on the make as well.) She's an American would-be actress who can't quite wow them at the auditions in London. She is sitting pretty however because if she marries Tom she will be set for life.

I could go on, but the plot is so delicious that I don't want to spoil it for you. It's a variation on the venerable theme of rake's progress, employing in an interesting way the old adage, "The man who marries for money, earns it." I have only one criticism of this especially well directed effort from the redoubtable Mr. Allen: you could have done without that cheesy ghost or hallucination scene near the end, involving sweet lips Scarlett and her neighbor.

See this for Woody Allen, who is just as smooth with this upscale noir/Hitchcockian thriller as he is with his renowned comedic and satirical efforts.

I've seen this and I give it___stars.
I want to see it___. I'll pass___.
The review was worth reading___. Not___.

Metropolis (1927) 10

The city as nightmare

Fritz Lang's futuristic *Metropolis* is set in as it happens something like the then current era. Most of the population are workers who slave underground to keep the massive machine that is the city going while the privileged stay above ground and live hedonistic lives. It is impossible not to see this in Marxian terms, the prols exploited by the capitalist class. At the time of the film's production in Germany, there was indeed a specter haunting Europe and it was indeed the specter of communism. Curiously Lang ends the film with a blatant political statement. He has labor and capital reluctantly shake hands. I find this curious because there is little doubt that for the previous two and a half hours the film depicts the capitalist class in the person of Joh Fredersen (Alfred Abel) as seeing the workers as mere automations to be exploited. I think Lang wanted to dodge the political implications of his film. I think he was less interested in ideology than in showing striking visuals of man in the world of machines, of humans as machines themselves, and other humans more like brains without bodies, "wet wear" blind to anything but production and keeping the hive buzzing.

Metropolis is like a hive or an ant colony except that the workers never get to go out and forage. Their world is dark and steamy; they are for the most part without hope as they come and go with their heads bowed in submission.

In another sense (and this metaphor is directly from the film) the workers are the hands of the body and the capitalists the mind. Maria says, "Between the mind that plans and the hands that build there must be a Mediator, and this must be the heart." Maria is a prophet who predicts the coming of this Mediator, who one might, in all innocence, believe to be a nice stand-in for, say, Jesus Christ. Politically speaking, then, perhaps what Lang is saying is that the war between communism and capitalism will eventually be mediated by the Second Coming. Expressing this commonplace idea with striking visuals rather than speaking it in so many words, exemplified the power of the relatively new medium of the "picture show."

This is the first silent film I've seen in many years. It's a bit over the top in terms of acting, which of course was deliberate since facial expressions and body language were used to replace words that would have to be read.

Modern audiences may find this convention comical or just weird. I found the scenes showing the characters running at something like one and a half times real human speed a bit amusing. I don't know enough about silent films to know whether that was deliberate or something Lang thought effective. Gustav Frohlich, who has the male lead, in particular is a frenzy of action and contorted facial expressions. Brigitte Helm, who plays Maria and her deadly clone (and the robot and the dancing woman as well) is even more over the top in her physical gyrations, but her performance stands out because there is nothing quite like it in filmdom, at least nothing that I have ever seen. It is both the heavy makeup and her wild, demonic (and seductive) expressions that allow us to clearly see when she is the evil clone and not the demur, heroic Maria. For me she was the most memorable part of the film.

There is quite a bit of trivia and film history associated with this landmark film. The film seen today is a 2001 reconstruction of the original, part of which has been lost. The missing action is explained in text before going on to the next scene. *Metropolis* was said to be Hitler's favorite film, which doesn't surprise me, and it was the most expensive film made up until that time, and employed a huge cast.

But see this for Fritz Lang's stunning and haunting visuals, which remain even to this day as striking works of art.

I've seen this and I give it___stars.
I want to see it___. I'll pass___.
The review was worth reading___. Not___.

Mystic River (2003) 10

Outstanding

Clint Eastwood does a great job of getting the best out of some very fine actors in this urban working class instant classic. Sean Penn, reminding me of some of the best work by such stars as Al Pacino and Robert De Niro, is absolutely authentic as Jimmy Markum from the mean streets of Boston, a guy who brushed with the law, went straight, and then, when his beloved daughter comes up murdered, is tested and found to be...all too human.

He is supported by Tim Robbins as his boyhood chum Dave Boyle, a man tottering on the edge of sanity, a man haunted by a childhood abduction by pedophiles, one of whom flashes a priest's ring. Penn won an academy award in 2004 as Best Actor, and Robbins won as Best Supporting Actor. Best film that year went to *Lord of the Rings*, but *Mystic River* couldn't have been far behind in the voting.

Kevin Bacon, the third of the boyhood pals who have gone their separate ways in adulthood, plays Sean Devine, a homicide detective with the Boston police. He also does a great job. His sidekick is played by Laurence Fishburne who brings the very familiar black police detective role to a new level of excellence with his balanced and realistic portrayal. Also excellent is Marcia Gay Harden as Celeste Boyle, Dave's wife, who through stupidity, fear, and a misreading of human grief, makes a fatal mistake in judgment, a mistake that leads to a needless murder.

The story itself is riveting. Eastwood's direction is tight, focused, always believable, and atmospheric. The script by Brian Helgeland, adapted from the novel by Dennis Lehane, is nothing short of mesmerizing. This movie is that good. It reminds me a little of some great mafia classics like *The Godfather* in the way it depicts east coast urban America: the family ties and betrayals, fateful acts born of anger and frustration, stupidity and human frailty, and most notably in the high quality of all aspects of the production, especially the most important ones, story, character and veracious setting and atmosphere.

A couple of other things set this film apart. One is the interesting and deep psychological situations that some of the characters find themselves in. Detective Sean Devine has an estranged wife who calls him but doesn't speak; Jimmy has dark secrets in his past known only to himself; Dave Boyle does something that nobody knows about until the end, something totally in keeping with his character; and finally, the boyfriend of Jimmy's daughter, Brendan Harris (Tom Guiry) knows something that solves the murder in his mind, but he doesn't want to tell it just yet.

The second is, even as Brendan runs home to confirm what he knows, you'll never guess who murdered Jimmy's daughter. Only in the next scene as the film nears its climax, is it clear what happened and why. And the difficulty isn't anything artificial as is so often the case in movie thrillers. The difficulty results from a beautifully constructed story based on a realistic and believable plot that makes us feel when the truth finally comes out, that it is right and understandable although almost impossible to guess beforehand.

See this for Clint Eastwood who, with this film, can take his place alongside Hollywood's great directors, and for Sean Penn who gives a splendid performance.

I've seen this and I give it___stars.
I want to see it___. I'll pass___.
The review was worth reading___. Not___.

The Night of the Iguana (1964) 9

Much better than I had been led to believe

Although *The Night of the Iguana* is not considered one of Tennessee Williams's best plays it is nonetheless an interesting piece of work. John Huston's interpretation, starring Richard Burton as the Rev. Dr. T. Lawrence Shannon, Williams's defrocked, alcoholic clergyman, is also not considered one of Huston's best films, but is nonetheless an interesting venture.

Burton gives a steady performance while Ava Gardner is excellent in a limited role as Maxine Faulk, a woman of a certain age: too old for boy toys and too young to toss in the towel. What she would like now that her old hubby is dead is for Shannon to fall in love with her. Shannon has come to her Mexican hotel and restaurant with a busload of unhappy Baptist College faculty tourists. He has failed as a clergyman and is now failing as a tour guide. Sue Lyon, not far removed from the title role in Kubrick's *Lolita* (1962) plays Charlotte Goodall, a teen-aged tease trying to further debauch the compromised Rev. Shannon. Deborah Kerr has an interesting part as the chaste daughter of a free-spirit traveling grandfather/granddaughter team of street artists who happens to arrive at the hotel as her elderly grandfather is near collapse. Grayson Hall plays Judith Fellowes, a hard-nosed Baptist lady about whom Shannon says: "Miss Fellowes is a highly moral person. If she ever recognized the truth about herself it would destroy her"—that truth being...well, let's just say she likes Charlotte more than she knows.

The film was shot on locale in Puerta Vallarta, Mexico before the tourist build-up during an era in which Mexico was Hollywood's safe and idyllic playground. A sense of the laidback attitude prevailing then can be recalled in the popular song from the forties "Manana, Manana is good enough for me." It was a playground in which anything could be had for pennies on the peso including things immoral, illegal and even downright unhealthy—come to think of it, pretty much as now, except the price has gone up quite a bit and it's not so safe anymore.

The Night of the Iguana comes in the middle of John Huston's long career as one of filmland's greatest directors, 23 years after *The Maltese Falcon* (1941) and 23 years before *The Dead* (1987). It is a film characterized by an authentic locale, atmospheric shots and the sharp, witty dialogue of one of America's pre-eminent playwrights in Tennessee Williams. It is a film at once satirical with clearly etched characters, deeply understood as only Williams, Chekov, Shakespeare and a few other playwrights are capable of creating. Huston stays faithful to Williams's underlying critique of human sexuality and the hypocrisy surrounding it while getting the best out of a very good cast.

The only disappointment is Miss Lyon who played her part without finesse. She complained at some point in her career that she had been typecast out of good parts because she had played Lolita. However one can see here that Lyon, as pretty as she was, was not talented or charismatic enough to become a star.

Ava Gardner on the other hand had already been a star and was in fine form, relishing playing Maxine Faulk, the in-charge, earthy woman of the world. She gets to take a shot at the prissy but slightly butch Judith Fellowes when Fellowes allows that she teaches "voice" at the college. Maxine counters with, "Well, geography is my specialty. Did you know that if it wasn't for the dikes, the plains of Texas would be engulfed by the gulf?"

Burton seemed entirely at home playing a character who was not far removed from his own persona, as was the case with Deborah Kerr whose character here was not too far removed from that of Anna Leonowens whom she played so beautifully in *The King and I* (1956).

See this for John Huston, one of cinema's greatest directors.

I've seen this and I give it___stars.
I want to see it___. I'll pass___.
The review was worth reading___. Not___.

Nixon (1995) 10

Flawed, yes, but a great film nonetheless

This may indeed be Oliver Stone's masterpiece, although as one would expect from Oliver Stone, it is a flawed and disjointed masterpiece, a monumental tragedy in the cathartic mode of the ancient Greeks. There is an Orson Welles/Citizen Kane quality about the film that is fascinating, including a journalistic/newsreel-ish feel that is unmistakably derivative. But it isn't really about Richard Nixon. Rather what Oliver Stone has constructed here is a mythology about a certain political persona that resembles Nixon in a milieu that resembles American politics and some things that happened once upon a time some forty years ago.

Anthony Hopkins is brilliant and compelling in the title role, but in no way would I mistake him for Richard Milhous Nixon. He is both too depraved and all too human in his intense portrayal of the only president to resign under the pressure of impeachment. The Richard Nixon that I recall played his cards much closer to his vest (he was a terrific poker player, according to his naval buddies who lost a lot of their mustering out money to him aboard ship) and was not nearly as sympathetic as Hopkins and Stone make him. Nixon was cold and unfeeling except when it came to something that touched on his self-interest, and then he became pathological.

One sees in this film traces of Oliver Stone's *JFK* (1991) in that he hints of a Cuban plot to kill John F. Kennedy while imagining that Lee Harvey Oswald was Cuban-inspired. Indeed, Stone intimates that J. Edgar Hoover was somehow involved in the assassination of Robert Kennedy in 1968 partly because he wanted to insure Nixon's victory by eliminating the one person who could beat him, and partly because his experience with Robert Kennedy as Attorney General was not a pleasant one for Hoover.

But Oliver Stone is not really interested in actual history as much as he is in his vision of the tortured Nixon himself and his fall from grace. It is strange but although Hopkins did not really look like Nixon or behave like Nixon (although he had some of the mannerisms down pat) it didn't matter because somehow he became a Nixon-like personage, a kind of ghost of Nixon, perhaps, a Nixon truer than true in some ways with his ever present worry about his image and his obsession with the Kennedy glamour that he could never have, his "Republican cloth-coat" middle-class heritage, and his gift for political infighting.

One of the best scenes occurs under the Lincoln memorial as Nixon is confronted by some Vietnam War protestors and especially one 19-year-old girl who challenges his view of his responsibility and ultimately of himself. What Stone is able to do through such scenes is to make Anthony Hopkins's Nixon more sympathetic than the real Nixon ever was. We see Hopkins as a tortured Shakespearean protagonist, King Lear or Othello or Hamlet, souls tormented with the contrast between the grandeur of their station, and the weakness of their flesh.

Another great scene is when the Texas power broker threatens Nixon by reminding him "who made him" and "who can destroy him." Nixon is unperturbed as he counter-threatens the power broker with the holy terror of the IRS, and then smiles as though it is just another day at the office.

A third great scene is late in the film as a drunken Pat Nixon confronts Nixon, who is falling apart under the pressure of the Watergate investigation, her eyes the eyes of woman looking at a worm, her manner accusatory and venomous.

In the end we come to identify with Nixon as we did with Lear and Hamlet, although of course Nixon properly seen is more like Claudius.

The cast is eclectic and you really need a program to keep track of them. Although I recall the players from the Nixon years, Haldeman, Erhlichman, Henry Kissinger, John Dean, Al Haig, Attorney General John Mitchell and his bimbo wife Martha (burlesqued in a fine cameo by Madeline Kahn), and the rest of them, I couldn't form distinct persons in my mind. The actors themselves are top notch for the most part, James Woods, J. T. Walsh, Paul Sorvino, Ed Harris, E.G. Marshall, etc., but the real world contrast between their countenances and those of the historical figures was so glaring as to be almost comical at times.

Of course there was no getting around this. Stone had to either hire unknown actors or to just live with the unreality of the actors not really resembling the people they were portraying. There were some striking exceptions, however. Joan Allen as Pat Nixon, the president's strait-laced and ever loyal (in public) wife was something close to a dead-ringer, and Allen did a brilliant job of bringing the historical first lady to life. Sorvino did not look all that much like Henry Kissinger, but his voice and manner were absolutely perfect. David Barry Gray who played Nixon as a young man did indeed look a lot like the young Nixon. Corey Carrier who played him as a boy was much like I would imagine Nixon as a boy.

Also worth noting are Mary Steenburgen who played Nixon's mother, and Bob Hoskins who played J. Edgar Hoover. Steenburgen seemed the very embodiment of the wise and hardtack Quaker mother while Hoskins's sleazy lampoon of Hoover was creepy enough to make your skin crawl.

I've seen this and I give it___stars.
I want to see it___. I'll pass___.
The review was worth reading___. Not___.

Notes on a Scandal (2006) 10

Enthralling clash of hidden desires

I watched this transfixed. I've never had any doubt about the acting ability of Judi Dench, or Cate Blanchett for that matter. They are both at the very top of their profession. But their work here just blew me away.

However it was not just their superlative acting that carried this film well beyond anything one might expect. It was the superb direction by Richard Eyre who spun out a riveting and emotionally moving experience from something that could have been ordinary: An unfulfilled wife of an older man is seduced by one of her 15-year-old students—or, properly speaking, we should say that she *allowed* herself to be seduced by one of her students. If it ever comes out, it will be a scandal to be sure since not only is she a teacher but she is a wife and mother. But the boy (Andrew Simpson) is mature for his age and rather clever and very persistent. And so she gives in and finds that she likes it very much, very much indeed.

Such banality, really, this might be. But all along this tale is being narrated by another teacher, a woman in her sixties, an old battle ax, as she calls herself (Judi Dench as Barbara Covett, spinster). Like the others she is interested in this new art teacher (Cate Blanchett as Sheba Hart), who is deeper than anyone realizes. From a distance Barbara watches her and takes notes for her diary. She is sharp and candid in her expression with a Shakespearean eye for the foibles of the people around her, whom she watches with consummate cynicism.

We are surprised at what happens next. There is a row in Sheba's classroom. Barbara appears and stills the row, and puts the boys in their place. One of the boys is THE boy. But we don't know that yet. Neither does Barbara. Now Sheba is thankful and now a friendship may develop between the mentor teacher, Barbara, and the ingenue, Sheba. And something to that effect is written in Barbara's diary, and it is here that we realize that she too has eyes for the new teacher.

And now comes the revelation of the affair between the boy and the woman, and it is Barbara who by chance spies them. Now the interesting dynamics of the personalities of the two women begin to show themselves. Barbara immediately calls Sheba upon the carpet, so to speak, and dresses her down. How dare you! I mean he is 15-years-old! Etc. Sheba who needs a confessor tells all, and begs Barbara to keep it a secret until after Christmas for the sake of her family. And now we find out that of course Barbara is certainly going to keep it a secret. This is in fact a wonderful development because now Sheba will be indebted to her. I will not tell, she says. Instead I will help you. But you must end it now. Yes, yes, thank you, thank you, Sheba says. And she does mean to end it, but...well the boy is persistent and she wants him.

The next development is very interesting, but I am afraid that I may have revealed too much already...

The denouement and then the finish are just so very well spun out. The scenes and the revelations come flying out in lickety split fashion, and everything is just so dramatically perfect. I have to hand it to not only the director but the writers—Zoe Heller, who wrote the novel, and Patrick Marber, who wrote the screenplay. The story, the splendid characterizations, and the sharp dialogue enthrall us. How delectable it must have been for Judi Dench to pronounce some of the lines. One is reminded of Nabokov's first person narrator in *Lolita* in the way that Barbara reveals her flawed and ultimately pathetic character through her own words. This is one of those scripts that make scriptwriters say spontaneously, "I could never, but never, have written it as well." Everything is set up so perfectly, and it comes spinning out in a most delicious way. Well, delicious for the audience. Not so for the protagonists.

Judi Dench has never been better and Cate Blanchett is as good as she was in *Elizabeth* (1998), which is very good indeed.

I've seen this and I give it___stars.
I want to see it___. I'll pass___.
The review was worth reading___. Not___.

Nurse Betty (2000) 9

Cute, edgy and very funny

This is an adorable, if somewhat edgy, comedy from a clever and witty script by John C. Richards, crisply directed by the very talented Neil LaBute, proving that he can handle comedy just as adroitly as he can the art house movie.

Renée Zellweger stars as Betty Sizemore, a sort of Doris Day of the 21st century, a waitress from Kansas whose fantasy life centers around Dr. David Ravell (Greg Kinnear), star of a TV soap opera called, "A Reason to Live," to such a fanatical degree that she has memorized lines from the show after watching the tapes over and over again. (This will come in handy later on.)

Morgan Freeman and Chris Rock play a father-son team of cocaine-dealing hit men who ignite the premise of the movie by murdering Betty's slimy used car salesman husband, played by Aaron Eckhart, who starred in *In the Company of Men* (1997), also directed by Neil LaBute. Chris Rock is a comedic psychopath, and Freeman a fatherly murderer whose favorite dictum is "three in the head, you know they're dead." One of the amazing and characteristic things about Morgan Freeman is that even while playing a professional criminal, he manages to sound like the wisest, gentlest man you ever knew.

True, the plot relies heavily on co-incidence (Betty copping the keys to the Buick that just happens to have the goods in the trunk), precise timing (meeting Dr. David and entourage at exactly the right moment), and some questionable psychology (Betty's partial and convenient amnesia). But such contrivances should be written off as poetic license and ignored. After all, who would criticize Shakespeare for the tortured plots of his comedies? More significantly, what makes this work is the cleverness of the plot melded well with the personalities of the characters (while gently satirizing them), and some very funny dialogue. My favorite line is when Freeman, looking gravely at a picture of the disappeared little miss Nurse Betty, soberly remarks to Rock, "We may be dealing with a cunning, ruthless woman here." I wonder, could it be that some of the pseudonymous (and humorless) reviewers who trashed this movie here and at IMDb are jealous, out-of-work screen writers?

An observation and a question: Renée Zellweger has the kind of on-screen presence to delight the most jagged heart. And who really is the reigning queen of contemporary film land comedy, Zellweger or Reese Witherspoon? They are both brilliant. Witherspoon is a little more over the top while Zellweger is more impish. It would be interesting to see them trade roles, say, Zellweger as goody-goody A-student Tracy Flick in *Election* (1999) and Witherspoon as Nurse Betty. Too bad something like that can't be done.

Incidentally, the song, "Ca Sera, Sera" heard in the background won an academy award for best song in the Hitchcock thriller, *The Man Who Knew Too Much* (1956), starring James Stewart and Doris Day. The reason it reappears here is not entirely clear, but the resemblance of the wonderfully naive Nurse Betty to the on- and off-screen Doris Day (who also had a hit recording of "Ca Sera, Sera,") goes beyond the strawberry blond hair to a kind of irrepressible innocence. In *Nurse Betty*, however, the Doris Day world of white picket fences and monogamy is given a contemporary spin. Although this is to some extent a romantic comedy, it is one in which the answer to the question, Who gets the girl? is one never seen in a Doris Day flick.

Bottom line: if you can watch this without laughing old loud and crying some real tears, you need to get your hard drive fixed.

I've seen this and I give it___stars.
I want to see it___. I'll pass___.
The review was worth reading___. Not___.

O, Brother, Where Art Thou? (2000) 9

You're gonna love this movie

This depression era period piece is simply a delight. The music is wonderful; the fanciful, on the road story of lovable escaped convict country bumpkins, who pratfall their way through numerous scrapes invites hilarity; and the beautifully dove-tailed script by the Coen brothers is marvelous.

That script was nominated for the Oscar for Best Screenplay based on material from another medium for 2001, but didn't win. (Stephen Gaghan won for *Traffic*.) But never mind. The writing is just so clever and that is part of what makes this movie so much fun to watch.

That won't surprise viewers who are familiar with the work of Ethan and Joel Coen. Those guys are strikingly original talents who can write comedy and noir with the best of them as in, e.g., *Raising Arizona* (1987), *Blood Simple* (1984)—their first, and in some ways, their best—and of course *Fargo* (1996). Their work is characterized by irony, satirical intent, and sly plotting in which later events are foreshadowed by previous events. *O, Brother, Where Art Thou?* is especially replete with clever foreshadowing. Characters appear, as they are wont to do in road movies or epic wanderings, and then they are left behind as our heroes move on. Here however, the first appearance of a character is probably not the last appearance. When John Goodman first appears as a morally and ethnically-challenged Bible salesman who welds a mean stick, we may think he is gone, but (I'll keep this vague) when he reappears we are not surprised; in fact his reappearance is just right.

One of the highlights is George Clooney as Ulysses Everett McGill whose sweet-smelling Dapper Dan hair pomade plays a bit of a role in the plot. He is perfect as a slick-talking, hairnet-wearing country wordsmith who could charm the birds out of the trees. With the slicked-back hair and the thin moustache, he reminded me a bit of Clark Gable, which is only right since Gable was a thirties film star whose style was much imitated.

Clooney is supported by John Turturro, who has played in at least two other Coen and Coen movies that I have seen. He is one of those non-glamorous actors who is at the top of the profession. It may seem a bit of a casting stretch to play him as a Mississippi bumpkin, but he pulls it off. This is the same guy who was just perfect as a New York Jewish writer gone to Hollywood in Coen and Coen's *Barton Fink* (1991).

This is the first time I've seen Tim Blake Nelson, but he was also very good as the third country musketeer. As usual the alluring Holly Hunter gives a solid performance as Everett's estranged wife about to marry another man, the mother of his six daughters. But make no mistake about it, Clooney clearly steals the show, and I am surprised he wasn't nominated for Best Actor. He was really that good. (He did win a Golden Globe award.)

And the music: country, bluegrass, hillbilly, gospel, traditional—and I know not what else—is really at the heart of the flick. When the "Soggy Bottom Boys" come on with their "I Am a Man of Constant Sorrow" it really brings the house down. The Coens know this, and so later in the movie when the boys appear on stage, looking a little like ZZTop on a budget, they reprise it to the delight of the Mississippi folk at a political rally and really get the joint to jumping—and of course it all figures in the plot. And how appropriate is that lyric for a depression era song: "I Am a Man of Constant Sorrow"!

See this for both the Coen Brothers who know how to have fun with a movie, and for George Clooney, who puts on a mighty good show.

I've seen this and I give it___stars.
I want to see it___. I'll pass___.
The review was worth reading___. Not___.

The Player (1992) 10

"Joe Gillis calling..."

"Players only love you when they're playing." —Stevie Nicks

Griffin Mill, whose name has a kind of ersatz Hollywood feel to it (cf., D. W. Griffith/Cecil B. De Mille), is not a player with hearts so much as a player with dreams. He is a young and powerful film exec who hears thousands of movie pitches a year, but can only buy twelve. So he must do a lot of dissembling, not to mention outright lying, along with saying "We'll get back to you," etc. This is what he especially must say to writers. And sometimes they hold a grudge. In this case one of the rejected writers begins to stalk Griffin Mill and send him threatening postcards. And so the plot begins.

Tim Robbins, in a creative tour de force, plays Griffin Mill with such a delightful, ironic charm that we cannot help but identify with him even as he violates several layers of human trust. The script by Michael Tolkin smoothly combines the best elements of a thriller with a kind of Terry Southern satirical intent that keeps us totally engrossed throughout. The direction by Robert Altman is full of inside Hollywood jokes and remembrances, including cameos by dozens of Hollywood stars, some of whom get to say nasty things about producers. The scenes are well-planned and then infused with witty asides. The tampon scene at police headquarters with Whoopi Goldberg is a hilarious case in point, while the sequence of scenes from Greta Scacchi's character's house to the manslaughter scene outside the Pasadena Rialto, is wonderfully conceived and nicely cut. Also memorable is the all black and white dress dinner scene in which Cher is the only person in red, a kind of mean or silly joke, depending on your perspective. During the same scene Mill gives a little speech in which he avers that "movies are art," a statement that amounts to sardonic irony since, as a greedy producer, he cares nothing at all about art, but only about box office success. His words also form a kind of dramatic irony when one realizes that this movie itself really is a work of art. As Altman observes in a trailing clip, the movie "becomes itself." The Machiavellian ending illustrates this with an almost miraculous dovetailing. This is the kind of script that turns most screen writers Kermit-green with envy.

Incidentally, Joe Gillis, the Hollywood writer played by William Holden in *Sunset Boulevard*—personifying all unsuccessful screen writers—actually does call during the movie, but Mill doesn't recognize the name and has to be told he is being put on, further revealing the narrow confines of his character.

In short, this is a wonderfully clever, diabolically cynical satire of Hollywood and the movie industry. This is one of those movies that, if you care anything at all about film, you must see. Period. It is especially delicious if you hate Hollywood. It is also one of the best movies ever made about Hollywood, to be ranked up there with *A Star is Born* (1937) (Janet Gaynor, Fredric March); *Sunset Boulevard* (1950); *A Star is Born* (1954) (Judy Garland, James Mason); and *Postcards from the Edge* (1990).

I must add that in the annals of film, this has to go down as one of the best Hollywood movies not to win a single Academy Award, although it was nominated for three: Best Director, Best Adapted Screenplay and Best Editing. I suspect the Academy felt that the satire hit a little too close to home for comfort.

I've seen this and I give it___stars.
I want to see it___. I'll pass___.
The review was worth reading___. Not___.

The Pledge (2001) 9

Unpredictable thriller, beautifully realized

The ending of this movie, of which we see glimpses in the beginning, is an example of the sort of cosmic irony that some world-renown writers apply to human affairs. It is not the sort of thing usually seen in a movie of course, since the mass mind at which most movies are directed will find it dissatisfying, even irritating.

The world-renowned author responsible for the ending of this tale of a retired cop on the trail of a serial killer of blond little girls in red dresses is none other than Swiss novelist and playwright Friedrich Dürrenmatt who wrote the novel from which the screen play was adapted.

The "pledge" in the title is that of just-retiring Reno, Nevada cop Jerry Black (Jack Nicholson) who is not convinced that a confession by a mentally-disturbed Native American, played convincingly by Benicio Del Toro, is genuine. Jerry Black gives his word to the mother of the murdered little girl that he will find the killer. However, he is no longer on the force and gets only intermittent help from his colleagues who think he has gone a little daffy. Nicholson, as usual, totally becomes the character he is playing and gives an outstanding performance. He is assisted by Aaron Eckhart who plays the detective who got the "confession," and by Robin Wright Penn who plays Lori, the mother of another little girl.

The direction by Sean Penn is uncluttered, focused and visually astute. For example, note the way the little girl playing in the swings between the highway and the gas station affects our expectation of what is to come. Penn also captures well the high country atmosphere around Reno, Nevada and attendant lifestyles, and for the most part keeps his *auteur* ambitions secondary to the telling of the story. The script by Jerzy Kromolowski and Mary Olson-Kromolowski is artistically true with crisp, direct dialogue and a fine dramatic structure. The film is also nicely cut so that everything is clear without any belaboring of the obvious. Some of the set scenes as Jerry Black interviews the grandmother of the slain little girl (Vanessa Redgrave in a cameo) and then a psychiatrist are very well done. Most importantly though, Penn did not give in to those who would demand a commercial ending over an artistic one. And for this he paid the price, since this film was not well-received by the mass audience.

Of course it is impossible to discuss the ending without giving away too much, but I think we can safely say that in real life sometimes chance and fate (if you will) step in and change things dramatically which makes us see our limitations and realize that some of what happens to us is beyond our control. I think that is what happened to Jerry Black and Lori; yet notice, too, that it is integral to Jerry Black's character and all that he has been all his life for him to make the insensitive mistake that he does.

Incidentally the ending can be fixed in a sequel... Well, that is not likely to happen since this was NOT a box office success. Only box office successes get to be sequels—which somehow (bizarrely) reminds me of the line from the old Charlie the Tuna TV commercial: "Only good-tasting tunas get to be Starkist."

For those who are wondering who really did kill the little girls, I will give you a hint: he got his just deserts in a symbolically appropriate manner.

Bottom line: a fine artistic achievement, an excellent diversion, and a treat for those who are fed up with films that play out in a tiresome, predictable manner.

I've seen this and I give it___stars.
I want to see it___. I'll pass___.
The review was worth reading___. Not___.

Ponette (1996) 10

A deeply spiritual film

Victoire Thivisol is very good, extraordinary really. The breadth and depth of the part she plays would challenge the greatest actresses. She is also very beautiful. She has beautiful eyes and thick, luxurious hair. She was named best actress at the Venice Film Festival in 1996 for her work in this film. She was then four-years-old. Amazing.

But this is also a tour de force for Director Jacques Doillon who, one can see, guided the children to be actors, while they in turn taught him about their world. The magic on the screen is the magic in the world of the children and what they feel. We see them cope with the existence they have been thrust into. We watch as they struggle to make sense of it through experience, fantasy and play. We see how they learn to distinguish between what adults think is real and what they themselves discover is real.

Her father is a rationalist and feels that his daughter's prolonged sadness about her mother's accidental death is "crazy." He tells her he will not yell at her if she stops acting crazy. She wisely tells him she will. Already she is learning to placate the world and its madness; already we see that she is working out what is "crazy" and what is not, and right now she is not sure which is which. Her father does not believe in a personal god, but the women taking care of her do, and so do the other children. She does not know what to believe but she wants to believe in anything that will bring her mother back or allow her to talk to her mother.

One may wonder how Doillon was able to get the children to be so good. It's clear he had to immerse himself in their world and win their respect. He had to listen to them and remember what it was like to be a child. These children are creating their world, as all children are, right before our eyes, and usually we do not see because we are so filled with our own lives and with our preconceptions. The children must learn the world and experience it all for themselves, regardless of what we think. Doillon shows us that process through the eyes of the children and especially through the extraordinary eyes of Victoire Thivisol, who will steal your heart, I promise.

There is something of the spirit of the lives of the saints in this film of and about a child. We see this in Ponette's struggle to believe in a God who took her mother away and would not answer her. She is a saint as a little girl, and she is her very own doubting Thomas. But she does not give in to despair. She talks to God and when God does not answer, her rationalist streak takes hold and she demands to know why He doesn't answer her. When she is blamed by a mean little boy for causing her mother's death, she doubts herself and wants to die. Pretending is not enough for her.

Unlike some others I thought the ending was good. I think the problem was the way the latter part of the scene in the graveyard was filmed with the false color, too hurriedly, and (especially) the unconvincing performance of Marie Trintignant who played her mother.

The final words of the film, "She told me to learn to be happy" are at once great words of wisdom that we all might heed; but at the same time these words are her first compromise with a profane world, in a sense her first lie, her first "sin." It is fitting that they were spoken to her father with the underlying understanding that men will want you to be happy and will be dissatisfied with you if you are not. Her pleasing little half smile from the car seat for him shows us that she has learned she will have to put on a face for the world, and she will. Nonetheless one feels there will be a part of her that will remain hers alone.

This is a beautiful, touching, and spiritually moving film, an original work of art.

I've seen this and I give it___stars.
I want to see it___. I'll pass___.
The review was worth reading___. Not___.

Presumed Innocent (1990) 9

Excellent criminal law thriller

As a thriller this is top notch; as any kind of a movie it is also top notch. Based on Scott Turow's best-selling novel of the same name (his first), it relies on a well-coordinated directorial effort by Alan J. Pakula (*Sophie's Choice* 1982, *All the President's Men* 1976, *Klute* 1971, etc.), a fine script by Frank Pierson (whose credits include *Cool Hand Luke* 1967, *Dog Day Afternoon* 1975, *A Star Is Born* 1976, etc.), and an experienced, talented and well-directed cast headed by Harrison Ford, Brian Dennehy, Raul Julia, Bonnie Bedelia, Greta Scacchi and Paul Winfield.

Ford plays Rusty Sabich, a prosecutor compromised by his sexual obsession with a fellow prosecutor, Caroline Polhemus (Scacchi) who is found murdered as the film opens. We see her in flashback as a conniving mantrap who uses her wiles to further her career. Sabich is assigned to the case by his boss, Raymond Horgan (Dennehy) who is up for reelection. Sabich would like to recuse himself but Horgan demands that he take the case and get the perp "yesterday" otherwise they will all be out a job because he will lose the election. Bedelia, looking particularly beguiling, plays Sabich's sexually frustrated and deeply hurt wife, Barbara.

When the election is lost the new prosecutors arrest Sabich and charge him with murder. He is defended by the very smooth Raul Julia who plays defense attorney Sandy Stern. Paul Winfield, in a somewhat flamboyant style, plays Judge Larren Lyttle.

Because Scott Turow knows the way the law works in practice as well as in theory, he having been a lawyer before he became a best-selling writer, we are treated to wood paneled intrigues and courtroom theatrics that have the unmistakable feel of authenticity. The dialogue is veracious and the character cross-currents vividly real. Ford gives what I think is one of his best performances as a man tormented by his infidelity and caught in a vise of circumstance largely stemming from that infidelity. Dennehy is a big-mouthed and big-headed politician in the familiar Windy City style. Raul Julia's Sandy Stern is cosmopolitan and brilliant, cynical and slick, a kind of Latin Johnny Cochran. Bedelia, whom I recall best as Shirley Muldowney in *Heart Like a Wheel* (1983) manages a delicate (and slightly unbelievable) persona with just the right amount of forbearance so that when the surprise ending comes we almost believe it.

I say "almost," but you might want to judge for yourself.

See this for Harrison Ford who plays a foolish and morally compromised man with just the sort of right stuff and disarming vulnerability we've come to expect from one of Hollywood's most popular leading men.

I've seen this and I give it___stars.
I want to see it___. I'll pass___.
The review was worth reading___. Not___.

Pride and Prejudice (1940) 10

A classic and a delight

As it has been many years, I dare say, very many years, since I have read *Pride and Prejudice*, my opinion here is tentative until such time as I have reread it (which may be never, considering how the calendar advances); nonetheless, it seems to me that this production has captured entirely the spirit and intent of Miss Austen's satirical novel. Seeing *Pride and Prejudice* as a movie, and therefore experiencing it as a screenplay rather than a novel, I am led to believe that Jane Austen, in a sense, bridged the theatrical gap in English letters between Shakespeare and Oscar Wilde. I could almost say that Oscar Wilde achieved his great success with the otherwise incomparable *The Importance of Being Earnest* principally by stealing Jane Austen's characters and her lines—if not the exact expression thereof—certainly the comedic, satiric spirit therein. But then, perhaps I exaggerate.

Greer Garson is an excellent actress; but if I may be so bold, not nearly so pretty as I had been led to believe. It would be boorish of me to point out that she was at the time entirely too old for the role, so I won't. However she *is* quite handsome in a slightly overbearing way. She has such excellent lines to deliver and the character she plays is so admirable, it would be hard to fail, and indeed she gives a fine performance.

Aldous Huxley, who wrote the screen play, does a nice job of translating Jane Austen's justly celebrated comedic novel of manners to the screen. Huxley was never known for his ability to write dialogue or to create character; his talent lay in ideas and the eloquent expression of same; yet here we have a cinematic triumph, somewhat surprising from the staid author of *Brave New World*, *Ape and Essence*, etc., as he effectively molds Jane Austen's nineteenth century witticisms into language designed for the twentieth century screen, sometimes, I must say, without the slightest improvisation.

Darcy, played impeccably by Olivier has a surfeit of pride while Garson's Elizabeth, a spirited and forthright country girl, is understandably prejudiced against such a man. Therefore we have our title, and of course the basis for true love, or at least a lively match. Edna May Oliver as Lady Catherine displays such a wonderful condescension that we are all charmed, I'm sure, or at least subdued. She manages to remind me of both Lady Bracknell from *The Importance of Being Earnest* and the red queen in *Alice in Wonderland*, whom of course she played in the indelible production of 1933 that I saw as a child on TV, many years later, of course.

The costumes were quite amusing. The outfit that Lady Catherine wore at the Bennet's—and I say outfit because dress and bonnet and petticoats would hardly do it justice—perhaps I should say, the livery she wore, allowed her to be surrounded, as it were, by her garments so that her long and sour face seemed shrined right in the middle!

Mary Boland as Mrs. Bennet, who had the exciting, yet daunting task of marrying off five daughters, is a treat and obviously enjoyed herself immensely. Edmund Gwenn as Mr. Bennet is quite winning, and much more sophisticated and clever than I had imagined him in the novel (but of course there was the limitation of my youthful discernment). Melville Cooper as Mr. Collins is just perfect, full of well-timed wit and inoffensive bumbling.

This is one of the great classics of the Hollywood cinema, the kind of movie that can be seen again and again with pleasure.

I've seen this and I give it___stars.
I want to see it___. I'll pass___.
The review was worth reading___. Not___.

Proof (1991) 10

People can fool you

If you're blind people can fool you. They can lie to you. And if you're a photographer and you are blind, who will believe you? You need proof, and this is what Martin (Hugo Weaving) seeks. He is a man who projects onto others the lovelessness of his own soul. He believed as a child that his mother died to get away from the shame of having a son who was blind. Even as an adult he believed she lied to him. He goes to the mortuary and is led to her grave where he reads the head stone with his fingers. He asks the mortician if a coffin is sometimes buried empty. The mortician asks why anyone would do that. Martin suggests a prank. The mortician replies, "Seems like a pretty expensive prank." Martin spends his whole life obsessively seeking proof because he can trust no one. Until he meets Andy. He trusts Andy.

It hardly need be said that Andy, played with boyish charm and just the right amount of discovery by Russell Crowe, will both disappoint Martin and teach him a lesson. Martin certainly needs some kind of lesson. He exploits his housekeeper Celia's obsessive love for him, tormenting her by keeping her on, while denying her love as he inflicts little humiliations. For her part Celia, played with a penetrating and desperate sexuality by Geneviève Picot, mothers him and seeks to dominate. She wants to keep Martin dependent on her in the hope that someday he will seek her love. She controls his life, teaching the dog to prefer her and to come to her when signaled. In her frustration she plays little tricks on Martin, such as putting objects in his path so he will run into them. When Andy threatens to become important to Martin, predictably she seduces him. Thus we have our triangle. Andy also serves as an objectifying device to underscore the obsessions of Martin and Celia.

Jocelyn Moorhouse wrote and directed this original little masterpiece of dark humor from down under. She carefully worked out the character-driven story so that humor and tragedy are in balance and we experience the revelations from the perspective of all three characters. Nothing is fake or hackneyed and no one point of view is preferred. She has the gift of seeing more than one side of the human condition, and it is this gift that makes her scenes so effective. Note that the drive-in theater scene depends on our knowing what Martin is doing and why, while seeing his actions from the point of view of the bikers. He faces the bikers from the driver's seat in the next car and holds up a packet of prophylactics. The biker guy looks over and thinks that he is being taunted by a "fag."

I have seen Moorhouse's *How to Make an American Quilt* (1995), which also explored the underlying psychological motives of human beings, but this is a better film. It will be interesting to see what she does next.

I've seen this and I give it___stars.
I want to see it___. I'll pass___.
The review was worth reading___. Not___.

Proof (2005) 10

Affecting performance by Paltrow

John Madden, who directed *Shakespeare in Love* (1998), and David Auburn, who wrote the script for *Proof* (adapted from his play), have put together a moving story about mathematical genius admixed with mental instability much in the manner of the life of John Nash who was the subject of *A Beautiful Mind* (2001).

Nash was a paranoid schizophrenic who was tormented by voices in his head warning him of dangers and conspiracies that didn't exist. Like Nash, Robert (Anthony Hopkins) is a brilliant mathematician who, having done spectacular work in his early twenties, goes crazy. Unlike Nash he is never able to regain control of "the machinery," as he calls his mind, and is never able to do any worthwhile work again.

Or is he? As he is taken care of by his mathematically astute daughter, Catherine (Gwyneth Paltrow in a most affecting and beguiling performance) he fills scores of notebooks with intense writings. At one point he seems in remission and at another point Catherine rushes home to find him in out in the backyard in the middle of a snowy night fired with enthusiasm about his latest work. At another point, he and Catherine work together on a project. And herein lies the crux of the matter. As we discover, this project turns out to be a proof of a difficult mathematical theorem or conjecture that will be internationally celebrated if it is correct.

Jake Gyllenhaal plays Hal, one of Robert's students who is going through his mentor's papers in the hope of discovering something wonderful. Catherine tells him that among the 103 notebooks that her father filled during his days of mental instability there is not a single one that has anything of value in it. But when Hal wins her heart she produces a notebook that was locked away in a drawer. It turns out that this notebook contains that most amazing proof mentioned above. And it is here that Catherine says—in line that is so very well set up that her expression fairly takes your breath away—"I wrote it."

Well, did she or didn't she? Because the work seems to be in her father's handwriting and seems to be well beyond her abilities, her sister Claire, played in that clever but somewhat annoying style that Hope Davis has so perfected (*About Schmidt; American Splendor),* claims that Catherine is deluded and couldn't have written it. To Catherine's grievous disappointment Hal reluctantly agrees, and this seeming lack of faith in her sends Catherine toward the precipice of insanity. This is the key question of the plot. Who wrote the proof? Its resolution will be the denouement of the story.

Clearly Claire believes that Catherine is so like her father that she is about to go crazy herself. So she tells Catherine she wants to sell the house now that their father is dead and bring Catherine to New York where she lives so that she can take care of her.

Will Catherine go or will she trust her heart and begin a life with Hal?

This movie does not play well with some audiences I think because the wonderment that some of the characters feel—the absolute awe that transfigures them when they behold a great mathematical proof, is not entirely appreciated by the average person. Madden makes sure that Catherine, Hal and one of the mathematicians form on their faces an expression something akin to a religious enthrallment when they understand the thrilling logic of the proof. I suspect that for many viewers something was lost in the translation. Consequently, although many others, including myself, believe this to be one of the outstanding movies of 2005 it only rates a 7.0 at IMDb.com and was not nominated for any Academy Awards. Paltrow won the Best Actress Oscar for her performance in *Shakespeare in Love*, also directed by Madden (he seems to bring out the best in her), and that award was richly deserved. But here in *Proof* I believe she was every bit as good (in a different way) although she was only nominated for a Golden Globe award and did not win.

Another thing about this movie is that it is strangely affecting emotionally. You might find yourself misting up a bit as you watch. I know I did.

See this for Gwyneth Paltrow, a gifted actress giving one of her best performances, and for John Madden, a director who makes beautiful movies with style and finesse.

I've seen this and I give it___stars.
I want to see it___. I'll pass___.
The review was worth reading___. Not___.

The Reader (2008) 10

Exquisitely done, deep and emotionally draining

BEWARE OF SPOILERS.

There is a certain segment of the German mentality that is Hanna Schmidt. English Kate Winslet captures the intent of novelist Bernhard Schlink in her interpretation of the character. Hanna was an ordinary but proud woman of discipline who always did her duty, a woman without the ability to separate herself from what she knew was right and what was wrong, but a woman who was able to hide from herself what she did that was wrong.

She seduces fifteen-year-old Michael Berg. She finds him doubly useful as a reader of great literature. She knows it will not work. Of course how could it? She indulges herself but, being strong and proud, is able to divorce herself from him emotionally when the time comes, as it must. When he reads D.H. Lawrence's *Lady Chatterley's Lover* to her, she is genuinely offended at the open sexuality, but we viewers are taken back since what she is doing with 15-year-old Michael Berg is on the screen and naked before our eyes.

In a sense this is the somewhat familiar story of the young man of station and potential had briefly in his youth by the older woman who has neither station nor potential. They take advantage of one another for the time being, both knowing that they will move on. But young Michael is not fully aware of this old story because his station in life is, although above hers, still rather modest, and being fifteen and knowing a woman for the first time, he is in love as much as—or even more than—a fifteen-year-old can be.

She is short with him and selfish because she knows she will be tossed aside and so instinctively knows she needs to get something now. She calls him "kid" and consumes him, as would be the case in such a relationship. Yet there is his "reading." He has a talent for it and he enjoys reading to her. At one point she instructs him, reading first and then making love.

What is love? Hanna Schmidt does not know. And so her character is triply flawed. She has low self-esteem, hiding her illiteracy from all. She is removed from her feelings because of the past. That is how she has coped. What she has done she knows on one level was something horrendous; but on another level she only took the

job at Siemens. What else was she to do? She was a guard. She had to guard the prisoners, otherwise there would be chaos. This is her defense. This is her belief. And finally, she cares for young Michael as she cares for herself, as one might care for valuable livestock, but she neither loves him nor herself. For again "What is love," as Tina Turner once had it, "but a second-hand emotion"?

At the end we see her, an old woman in prison being visited by the adult Michael Berg. She has put out her hand to him, and he, being human, has touched it. But he has withdrawn his hand. And now they stand and she leans, ever so slightly toward him to be hugged perhaps, to be touched for perhaps the first time in decades. But he does not respond. He cannot.

This echoes back to an earlier scene when he, as a young law student suddenly finds himself observing her trial. He realizes that she is taking the blame for the deaths of the Jewish "prisoners" because she would rather do that then reveal that she cannot read or write. It is interesting that young Berg realizes the truth of why she liked to be read to only then. And so he thinks to save her by letting the court know that she could not have written the order that condemned the prisoners to death. And so he makes an appointment to go to the prison and see her. But as she waits for her unknown visitor to arrive, he suddenly turns away. What he realizes, one speculates, is that there is nothing he can say to her or to the court that will change anything. Whether she wrote the actual order or not really doesn't matter. The others get off with lighter sentences, but all of them are equally guilty of whatever it was that was that allowed the German psyche to allow the holocaust. And too Berg is not clear about how he feels. Here is a woman he once loved who now is revealed as a monster. Yes, she is a monster, but strange to say almost an innocent monster.

It is curious that Berg so deeply loved her that he acquires her trait of emotional distance. He learns he can only sleep alone. His marriage fails. He is not as close to his daughter as he would like. And finally he is not able to help Hanna when she is alone in prison. He cannot bring himself to respond to her letters. And yet he reads to her. Hour after hour after hour he reads the classics into a microphone and sends the tapes to her to listen to in prison.

I wonder how this was received in Germany. There is such a guilt that hangs over the generations after the war. I wonder what they think of the humanization of a certain familiar mentality. And I must add that this mentality that follows orders and does its duty to the exclusive of its humanity is not something special with the Germans of that era. It is a human trait that is expressive of a human type that can be found in any society.

This is a deeply moving film, exquisitely written and directed and wondrously acted by especially the great Kate Winslet, and Ralph Fiennes who plays the older Michael Berg, and David Kross who plays the younger Michael Berg. *The Reader* is easily the best film I've seen during the past year.

I've seen this and I give it___stars.
I want to see it___. I'll pass___.
The review was worth reading___. Not___.

Repulsion (1965) 10

An absolutely brilliant film, deeply disturbing

It would not be a good idea to try to psychoanalyze Catherine Deneuve's character in this film. What director Roman Polanski has done is make a composite of a number of disorders and give them to Carole. She is a bit autistic in that she stares at cracks in the ground or at the shape of objects and is basically unsocial. She has a bit of a tic as might be found in say Tourette's syndrome as she rubs the right side of her nose sharply several times when perhaps she is nervous or unsure. She is catatonic at times and violently psychopathic. The repulsion she feels most strongly is toward men. They make her physically ill. She has nightmares and/or delusions or fantasies about being raped. She is reticent to an extreme. I doubt whether such a combination of behaviors actually exists in the DSM-IV, which of course was not yet in print when Polanski made this film.

I was tempted to title this review, "Catherine Deneuve as a slasher: a dyke thriller," which is accurate to some extent, but it would be unfair to the movie to narrow it so. Carole (Deneuve at 21 or 22) is strikingly appealing despite the weirdly overdone blonde hair, and she is in nightgown for most of the last part of the film. But don't look for any nudity. Polanski concentrates on the horror angle throughout.

But this is a horror movie with artistic power. Instead of the woman alone in her apartment with tinkling music in the background as we wait for the monster who is to rape and murder her, we have Carole alone in her apartment with the madness in her mind and people wanting to get in to show her their love or to collect the overdue rent. Instead of us fearing for her safety, we fear for those who come into contact with her.

Polanski's direction is taunt, focused and filled with tension because we have no idea what is going to happen until the film is over. I liked the touch of having us hear the water drip. Somehow that sound, which we would only hear when everything is quiet and we (or she) are listening intently, heightened the tension and the sense of madness. I also liked the ending with all the neighbors nosily pouring into the apartment.

Deneuve's performance in this English language film set in London is one of her best without any doubt, and she has a very long line of credits. Everything is about her face and her body language. She even walks a bit awkwardly, and her continence is anything but becoming and she seldom smiles. She does laugh once when a coworker tells her about a Charlie Chaplin movie—in fact she laughs uproariously—but Polanski does not give us a frontal shot of her face at that time. Mostly hers is a face filled with fear and apprehension. Her eyes dart about and her lips remain shut. She looks longingly out the window at the nuns and children in the church's playground next door. Perhaps she should have entered a convent. Perhaps, barring what really happens, she might have.

Of course the setup is not perfect. The very fact that Carole could be in her twenties and have gone so long without her symptoms leading to her incarceration is surprising. That she could have kept a job is also surprising. And how such a beautiful girl could have kept the boys and lechers at bay for so long is also a mystery. On the other hand it can be argued that the fact that she is left alone by her sister for a few days combined with the overly earnest advances of an insensitive man brought her to a crisis.

This is a deeply disturbing film done in a sparse and focused manner that will put you and keep you on the edge of your seat until "The End" appears on the screen, which it does.

I've seen this and I give it___stars.
I want to see it___. I'll pass___.
The review was worth reading___. Not___.

Sense and Sensibility (1995) 9

Although it rained, we saw no mud

This would appear to be the sort of production the Academy votes as best picture, and indeed *Sense and Sensibility* was duly nominated in 1996, but lost out to *Braveheart*. I'm not sure why, but my guess is that *Sense and Sensibility* lacked something in the minds of the members of the Academy, call it...dirt.

Everything is a little too pretty, a little too clean and well behaved in this charming adaptation of Jane Austen's first novel. Director Ang Lee might have provided some insight into late18th and early 19th century England by showing the poverty and squalor of the London streets instead of just having the girls step around a little horse manure. Lee might also have shown that the servants had it worse than the gentry by expanding the scene where they are let go by showing just where some of them did go. Lee's direction hints at a wider world of poverty and real pain, but rejects having it intrude. Although the full force of the industrial revolution and attendant horrors were yet to come, they might have been presaged so that Austen's world is given perspective for the modern audience. Soon the skies of England would be blackened with smoke from coal and many of its citizens turned into proletarian cogs.

But Austen knew and/or cared about that not at all, and instead wrote with singular attention about the gentry and their acquisitive aspirations and genteel manners, and this is the novel that Emma Thompson captured so well in her Academy Award winning screenplay. The fact that the Dashwoods lost their estate and had to live in a cottage and practice thrift within a budget was a very real tragedy to Austen, although not to us. She was obsessed with the injustice of being a young woman without means living within a society that allowed upward mobility by women only through marriage. So she showed women playing that game to perfection, and winning.

Emma Thompson as the sensible Elinor Dashwood was flawless, as usual; and Kate Winslet as her sister, the sensual Marianne who wears her heart on her sleeve, proved once again that she is a gifted and charismatic actress second to none. The supporting cast, especially Elizabeth Spriggs as Mrs. Jennings, and Harriet Walter as Fanny Dashwood, was superb. The cinematography was gorgeous, even arresting at times.

Most uncomfortable scene: Marianne being bled. This reminds us that sometimes one has to overcome both the disease and the physician.

I've seen this and I give it___stars.
I want to see it___. I'll pass___.
The review was worth reading___. Not___.

Seven (1995) 9

The preeminent serial killer movie

We plummet the depths of depravity here. Arrogance never got such a cinematic comeuppance (not to mention gluttony, pride, greed and the rest of the seven deadly sins), nor was innocence ever made such an alien as in this masterpiece of monstrous intent. Morgan Freeman stars as William Somerset, a wise and modest big city homicide detective ready to retire who finds himself partnered with David Mills, an arrogant young detective effortlessly depicted by Brad Pitt. As they try to find the killer there develops between them a nice chemistry that helps to make this an engrossing movie. Kevin Spacey arrives after a bit as "John Doe," a 20th century version of a medieval scribe obsessed with sin morphed into a monster from hell. He sees himself as the personal judge, executioner and torturer *extraordinaire* of a vengeful god gone amuck.

Momma, lock the doors and bar the windows. Don't let this video into your home. You'll watch it, every last minute, and your kids will watch it, several times, their eyes between their fingers, and the end result will be a cynicism about humanity so deep that it'll take the blood of the lamb to wash it clean.

Well, that, or the realization that this is just Hollywood up to its old tricks. After all it's only a movie—or is there something more to this extraordinary commercialization of evil? One of the penetrating things about *Seven* is the implication that, through the Christian concept of sin and by our very nature, we ourselves create the serial killer and give him a justification to turn upon us and do his wretched deeds. The ending slyly suggests the triumph of evil; and indeed this cagey movie would be depressing beyond redemption were it not for the three things: One, the modest wisdom projected by Morgan Freeman; two, the essential innocence of Brad Pitt's character; and three, the fact that the horrible deeds are the work of only one man. Whether he is just an insane "nut-bag" as Pitt's character exclaims, or part of our nature as the film implies, is an interesting question.

Serial killer film makers of the future will try to top this one, but I doubt if it will happen any time soon. This is already a classic. Incidentally, I do wonder about these guys (Walker and Fincher) who lie awake nights dreaming up this stuff. I hope they're only doing it for the money.

By the way, perfect font for the credits.

I've seen this and I give it___stars.
I want to see it___. I'll pass___.
The review was worth reading___. Not___.

The Shawshank Redemption (1994) 10

Great story, wondrously told and acted

At the heart of this extraordinary movie is a brilliant and indelible performance by Morgan Freeman as Red, the man who knows how to get things, the "only" guilty man at Shawshank prison. He was nominated by the Academy for Best Actor in 1995 but didn't win. (Tom Hanks won for Forrest Gump.) What Freeman does so beautifully is to slightly underplay the part so that the eternal boredom and cynicism of the lifer comes through, and yet we can see how very much alive with the warmth of life the man is despite his confinement. Someday Morgan Freeman is going to win an Academy Award and it will be in belated recognition for this performance, which I think was a little too subtle for some Academy members to fully appreciate at the time.

But Freeman is not alone. Tim Robbins plays the hero of the story, banker Andy Dufresne, who has been falsely convicted of murdering his wife and her lover. Robbins has a unique quality as an actor in that he lends ever so slightly a bemused irony to the characters he plays. It is as though part of him is amused at what he is doing. I believe this is the best performance of his career, but it might be compared with his work in *The Player* (1992), another excellent movie, and in *Mystic River* (2003) for which he won an Oscar as Best Supporting Actor.

It is said that every good story needs a villain, and in the Bible-quoting, Bible-thumping, massively hypocritical, sadistic Warden Samuel Norton, played perfectly by Bob Gunton, we have a doozy. I want to tell you that Norton is so evil that some fundamentalist Christians actually hate this movie because of how precisely his vile character is revealed. They also hate the movie because of its depiction of violent, predatory homosexual behavior (which is the reason the movie is rated R). On the wall of his office (hiding his safe with its ill-gotten contents and duplicitous accounts) is a framed plaque of the words "His judgment cometh and that right soon." The irony of these words as they apply to the men in the prison and ultimately to the warden himself is just perfect. You will take delight, I promise.

Here is some other information about the movie that may interest you. As aficionados know, it was adapted from a novella by Stephen King entitled "Rita Hayworth and the Shawshank Redemption." Rita Hayworth figures in the story because Red procures a poster of her for Andy that he pins up on the wall of his cell. The poster is a still from the film *Gilda* (1946) starring her and Glenn Ford. We see a clip from the black and white film as the prisoners watch, cheering and hollering when Rita Hayworth appears. If you haven't seen her, check out that old movie. She really is gorgeous and a forerunner of Marilyn Monroe, who next appears on Andy's wall in a still from *The Seven Year Itch* (1955). It's the famous shot of her in which her skirt is blown up to reveal her shapely legs. Following her on Andy's wall (and, by the way, these pinups figure prominently in the plot) is Rachel Welsh from *One Million Years B.C.* (1966). In a simple and effective device these pinups show us graphically how long Andy and Red have been pining away.

Frank Darabont's direction is full of similar devices that clearly and naturally tell the story. There is Brooks (James Whitmore) who gets out after fifty years but is so institutionalized that he can't cope with life on the outside and hangs himself. Playing off of this is Red's periodic appearance before the parole board where his parole is summarily REJECTED. Watch how this plays out at the end.

The cinematography by Roger Deakins is excellent. The editing superb: there's not a single dead spot in the whole movie. The difference between the good guys (Red, Andy, Brooks, etc.) and the bad guys (the warden, the guards, the "sisters," etc.) is perhaps too starkly drawn, and perhaps Andy is a bit too heroic and determined beyond what might be realistic, and perhaps the "redemption" is a bit too miraculous in how beautifully it works out. But never mind. We love it.

All in all this is a great story vividly told that will leave you with a true sense of redemption in your soul. It is not a chick flick, and that is an understatement. It is a male bonding movie about friendship and the strength of character, about going up against what is wrong and unfair and coming out on top through pure true grit and a little luck.

Bottom line: one of the best ever made, currently rated #2 (behind *The Godfather*) at the IMDb.com. Don't miss it.

I've seen this and I give it___stars.
I want to see it___. I'll pass___.
The review was worth reading___. Not___.

Sherrybaby (2006) 10

Uncompromisingly realistic, beautifully realized

She is what she is. She is not able to restrain herself. She needs gratification. She can't postpone it. She succumbs to whatever it is, sex, heroin, alcohol, nicotine...love. She is impulsive and she flies off the handle easily. She doesn't know that she behaves badly. She doesn't know *that* is not the way to dress. Or perhaps she does. She needs to be gratified, and so probably that is why she dresses that way.

She was sexually abused by her father who loved her. But who does she love? She desperately wants her daughter to love her. Do you love me? she asks. Say, "I love you, Mommie." The child does, but suddenly—and this is the denouement of the movie—Sherry realizes that there is some question about whether the child should love her. Yes, she has the stretch marks, but really does she deserve the title of "mother"? And does she love herself? Probably not, and maybe that is her biggest problem. It is said that women who are always seeking sex are really seeking a love that they cannot find. One always feels that if only they would pick the right man. But this is an illusion. There is no right man until she is the right woman.

Maggie Gyllenhaal does an outstanding job of becoming this woman who is lost in this world without a compass as to how she should behave and why, who is lost to everything but her immediate feelings. She is a child emotionally and she cannot understand why it is that life is so hard for her and why the world is so cruel.

This is a masterful portrait of a kind of person that is part of humanity. A good person at heart, not someone who would do others deliberate harm, but a person who is blind to who she is and to how others see her. Into what world does she belong? is a question I kept asking myself. I don't know the answer.

Laurie Collyer's direction is exquisite. The players and especially the little girl are wonderfully directed. Everything is like the people next door without a hint of anything phony. The contemporary Garden State setting is real and the details and the atmosphere are as genuine as the New Jersey Turnpike. And the ending surprises. It is perfect but in a way that I suspect most viewers will not be able to predict. I know it surprised me.

My hat is off to Laurie Collyer and Maggie Gyllenhaal. Thank you for this modest little masterpiece and for not compromising reality or putting in any unnecessary fig leaves or giving in to any notions of political correctness. This is just a pure slice of life movie with a beginning, a middle and an end, beautifully realized. And yes it is rated R.

I've seen this and I give it___stars.
I want to see it___. I'll pass___.
The review was worth reading___. Not___.

Sideways (2004) 10

Clever, very clever

I was a little surprised to see this billed as a comedy. Not that I didn't experience many wry grins, tickling chuckles, and some outright belly laughs as I watched it. I did. And it is a whole lot funnier than most movies that are supposed to be comedies. But this is not a comedy, per se. It is a relationship movie. It is a buddy movie. It is a brilliant tour de force by Alexander Payne, who along with Jim Taylor wrote the script, and who directed, based on the novel by Rex Pickett. On the basis of seeing two of his movies, this and *Election* (1999) I can say without the slightest doubt, Payne is one very talented man who has Hollywood by the proverbials.

Both the script and the direction were superb. One might say Payne spent a little too much time developing character, but when you see the result, you have to say, it was worth it. Yes, the movie begins a little slowly, just a little. Everything seems a little on the ordinary side. There is not much happening. We can see that Miles is one of life's losers and that his best bud Jack is one of life's lucky guys. They are off to the wine country for one last buddy time together before Jack gets married.

Jack is a sometime, somewhat talented actor. God, I knew a few of those guys. And Miles is a talented but somehow failed writer, a school teacher who has penned a 750-page novel. Oh, Lord let me buy you a Mercedes Benz. (Sorry that lyric just slipped in.) He also reminds me of someone.

Miles recently (two years ago actually) got dumped by the true love of his life, his now ex-wife Victoria. And Jack, bless his heart, is about to marry a very well appointed and very nice looking young woman who lives in a grand house in Palos Verdes (in the script; in the movie it's more like Bel Air or thereabouts—which amount to about the same thing). And so off the two go for wine and golf and the open road. But be back by Friday night for the rehearsal. (I'll say no more about that, but keep the word "rehearsal" in mind. Those who have seen the movie know what I mean.)

All right I confess. This movie hit home with me. I have been there and done that in a number of ways. In fact, the familiarity kind of put me off at the beginning. I mean, I have been to France and I have drunk Chateau Cheval Blanc, and to be honest I have also drunk great burgundies with (God help us) fast food, although unlike Miles I took the food home; I wouldn't de-sanctify the wine by drinking it on the sly at a diner. By the way, Cheval Blanc is NOT a burgundy and it not made with Pinot Noir grapes. It is a red wine from Bordeaux made with Merlot and Cabernet Franc grapes.

And I and a buddy dated two young women many years ago and almost the same thing happened. But never mind.

In other words, the movie is realistic, so much so that I suspect a lot of viewers will find something in it that relates directly and even spookily to their own lives. Watch it and see.

Can you be too realistic? Can a movie be so absolutely true to life that it...what? Loses something? Is too painful? Is too prosaic? Well, I almost thought that in the beginning. But the movie is so well planned, so well contrived (if you will) so aggressively true to life and honest about human nature that I came within a hair breath of turning it off.

Don't you do that! Don't give up on this movie! It is craftily planned to reward the viewer with a most interesting and enjoyable movie experience. This is not to say it is perfect. Some of the wine dialogue is compromised because what is said must make sense to the general viewer while at the same time remain true (almost) to what aficionados of wine would actually say. And yes, Payne could have cut to the chase a little quicker. But sometimes the appetite is whetted when the meal is delayed.

In addition to a brilliant script and some very fine direction from Payne, the movie is blessed with some excellent casting. Paul Giamatti is perfect as Miles, who really is not a loser. Thomas Haden Church is exactly right as the attractive and confident, every-hustling, womanizing, marginal actor who will get his comeuppance in the next life, not in this one. Sandra Oh provides a perfect fit as the Asian-American who falls heavily for American men who are not necessarily of Asian descent; and Virginia Madsen keeps just enough of her beauty hidden to be believable as the waitress with a head on her shoulders.

I guess I could give Hollywood the ultimate compliment and say that this movie is so slick that it doesn't seem in the slightest bit slick. That it is so realistic that one never thinks for a moment that it is contrived. To paraphrase somebody, the essence of the art of story, whether it be a novel, a short story or a movie, is in believable characters in believable situations doing the things we all do, but in a way that goes beyond realism to artistry. If you can fake that you can make it big not only in Hollywood but anywhere there is an audience, a viewer, a reader, anybody who seeks to be enlightened and entertained and experience the catharsis that art can bring.

See this for director Alexander Payne who knows what he is doing at all times.

I've seen this and I give it___stars.
I want to see it___. I'll pass___.
The review was worth reading___. Not___.

Stalag 17 (1953) 10

Quasi-realism and burlesque: a comedic drama

There was surprisingly enough a lot of humor in the American attitude toward the Nazis and the Germans during World War II. Life goes on even under the conditions of being prisoners of war, and people need to laugh. In such circumstances, they especially need to laugh. We can see that in some of the songs from that time and in this play from Donald Bevant and Edmund Trzcinski that Billy Wilder made into an unusually good movie. It should be realized that the full extent of the horror that the Nazis had visited upon Europe was not known until after the war was over and we saw the films of the concentration camps.

William Holden stars as Sgt J.J. Sefton whose amoral cynicism and gift for the cheap hustle allow him to feather his nest even while a prisoner of war. He's the guy who always had a storehouse of cigarettes, booze, silk stockings, candy, etc. under his bunk, the guy who always won at cards, whose proposition bets always gave him the edge. We had a guy like that when I was in the army. We called him "Slick."

But William Holden's Sefton is more than Slick. He is outrageously cynical and uncommonly brave. He takes chances because he doesn't have the same kind of fear that others have. Most people would feel self-conscious (and nervous) eating a fried egg while everybody else in the barracks had watery-thin potato soup. Others might feel uncomfortable with bribing German guards for bottles of Riesling or tins of sardines. Not Sefton. He flaunts his store of goodies.

Perhaps that is overdone. Perhaps the real hardships that prisoners went through are glossed over in this comedic drama—a comedy, incidentally, that plays very much like a Broadway musical without the music. Perhaps it is the case that from the distance of 1953 the deprivations of *Stalag 17* have faded from memory and it is the "good times" that are recalled.

At any rate, I think it is this kind of psychology that accounts for the success of this unusual blend of quasi-realism and burlesque. Certainly *Stalag 17* has been widely imitated, most familiarly in the TV sit-com "Hogan's Heroes" and to some extent on Rowan and Martin's "Laugh-In." Roberto Benigni's *Life Is Beautiful*, on the other hand, which also finds humor in the horrific, is of a different genre. Like Ionesco's *Rhinoceros*, Benigni's movie is from the theater of the absurd, not the Broadway stage.

Holden won an Oscar for his performance and Robert Strauss who played Animal was nominated in a supporting role. Otto Preminger, the legendary director and producer, was excellent as the two-faced Col Von Scherbach, the ex-calvary commander and camp commandant who can only take a phone call from the high command with his boots on so he can click his heels. I also liked Sig Rumann as Sgt Johann Sebastian Schulz ("always making with the jokes, you Americans") whose previous career as a wrestler in the US accounts for his English-language skills. Gil Stratton, who for years did the sports for CBS Channel 2 in Los Angeles, is interesting as Sefton's sidekick and funky. Indeed, what is responsible for the success of this movie as much as anything is this fine cast playing well-defined character roles. By the way, Strauss and Harvey Lembeck ("Sugar Lips" Shapiro) were reprising their roles from Broadway.

Important is the plot line in which Sefton is accused of being a spy for the Nazis while the real spy is exposed step by step. At first we don't know who it is, and then we do, and then the prisoners find out.

This should be compared with *Sunset Boulevard* (1950). While very different movies they have similar elements which reveal part of the psyche and methods of director Billy Wilder. First there is the anti-hero as the protagonist, in both cases played by William Holden. Then there is a lot of the old Hollywood crowd appearing in both films including directors appearing as actors, Erich von Stroheim (not to mention Cecil B. DeMille in his memorable cameo as himself) in *Sunset Boulevard,* and Otto Preminger here. Sig Rumann has over a 100 credits going back to at least the early thirties. Finally there is the discordant mix of comedic and dramatic elements, a mix that works on our psyches because life is to some very real extent filled with tragedy in close congruence with the laughable.

But see this for William Holden who was the kind of actor who was best playing a compromised character as here and as the failed writer/reluctant gigolo in *Sunset Boulevard,* an actor who drank too much and tended to be undistinguished, but when carefully directed could rise above his intentions and give a sterling performance.

I've seen this and I give it___stars.

I want to see it___. I'll pass___.
The review was worth reading___. Not___.

The Sweet Hereafter (1997) 9

Poetic, beautiful and bittersweet

This is innocence lost, but it isn't just the children who lose their innocence: it's the whole town and all the adults. Nicole (Sarah Polley) dreams of being a rock star, and her father lovingly fosters the dream. He does everything for her including being her first lover. And then there is a bus accident and she ends up in a wheel chair and is told she is lucky, since many of the other children died. But she doesn't feel lucky. She turns her bitterness toward her father. She has read Robert Browning's "The Pied Piper of Hamelin" to two of the children who died, and now sees her father as a piper who has failed her. The love they had, now in the light of the loss of her innocence, is seen as a fraud. And she hates him.

Meanwhile, big city lawyer Mitchell Stephens (Ian Holms) comes to town with the promise of getting a big settlement for the parents of the dead and injured children. He has an axe to grind and that axe is all that is left of his life. His sadness is a daughter who is a drug addict who calls him only for money. He can never say no, and she can never stop using him.

Billy Ansell lost his wife to cancer and is left with two young children. He finds sexual gratification from another man's wife. When his children are killed he loses his love for her. The lie that Nicole finally tells to hurt her father is for him, and symbolizes her turning from her father outward to another man.

Director Atom Egoyan seems to be saying that people stop loving one another sometimes with reason, and sometimes without; and that the sadness of life is a failure of love, that the brutality of life can kill our love. This is the tragedy of innocence lost, of our expulsion from the Garden of Eden, forcing us to see ourselves as naked and morally corrupt. The cold white mountain slopes that surround the little northern town remind us of how cold it is in the world away from childhood.

I have always objected to "the loss of innocence" as a falsification of who we are. We were never innocent: it only seems so in retrospect. It is not the fathers who corrupt their daughters nor the daughters who betray their fathers: it is rather the species mechanism that drives them apart, sometimes with such brutal force that all are hurt. Our expulsion from the Garden of Eden symbolizes our loss of *ignorance*, the growth of our neocortex, and our assumption of consciousness. Again we were never innocent: we just didn't know what the hell we were doing or why. Now we know, except we kid ourselves a lot.

Sarah Polley's performance is so natural, vivid and balanced that I felt that I knew her as someone in my own life. The entire cast does a good job, especially Ian Holm. Atom Egoyan has a deft touch that is focused and realistic, never extreme. He doesn't preach to us and he works hard to be fair to his characters. Ultimately, he's a cinematic artist, and a good one.

I've seen this and I give it___stars.
I want to see it___. I'll pass___.
The review was worth reading___. Not___.

Taxi Driver (1976) 9

After all the flowers are gone in post-sixties America

This is one of those milestone films in America cinema about which millions of words have been written, and everybody who's anybody in filmdom has seen. It received a mixed reception when it appeared twenty-five years ago, and of course the Academy did not reward it.

Taxi Driver remains a difficult movie to evaluate. On the one hand there can be no doubt about the brilliance of Martin Scorsese's direction in which he makes excruciatingly real the street level life of a taxicab driver in the big city. Harsh, multi-hued lighting of predatory street scenes, the cheap, bleak interior of the taxi driver's apartment, the vacuous phrases and promises of the politician, the brutality of guns and knives, the sordidness of things left in the backseat of cabs, and the gritty litter of the streets have the effect of immersing us into the cabby's world. Nor can there be any doubt about the brilliance of Robert De Niro in the title role. He portrays the alienated, psychotic mentality of Vietnam vet Joshua Bickle poignantly, compellingly, and with a larger than life lividness. Jodie Foster is the very essence of a post-sixties flower child morphed into a twelve and a half year old prostitute. Her childlike ability to find sustenance amid the objective horror of her life compelled our sympathy. Foster's flawless projection of the little girl's pathetic street-wise facade rightfully catapulted her to national attention. Cybill Shepherd was also excellent as a post-Kennedy era political strawberry, and Harvey Keitel was very good as the sleazy pimp, as was Peter Boyle as a cabby philosopher.

On the other hand, the stagy blood splashing toward the end, and the lingering thereon, seemed a little cheap, as though Scorsese did not have complete faith in his production and thought a violence fix was needed to satisfy his audience. Also the fantasy ending in which the unlikely happens like a cartoon joke seemed a contrivance from someone not sure about the import of his movie. The scene in which Cybill Shepherd enters De Niro's empty cab, seemingly to entice him, plays at first like a fantasy, but after he deposits her on the curb, we know it is supposed to be real. Incidentally, the fact that he doesn't notice her until he sees her in his rearview mirror, although he walked up to the cab with her in it, suggests something hurriedly dreamed up during production as a quick commentary on what has gone before.

Nonetheless the ending is transcended because Scorsese had a great movie all along, with outstanding acting and a compelling story artfully shot, leading to a socially-conscience experience vividly reflecting the disillusionment of post sixties America.

I've seen this and I give it___stars.
I want to see it___. I'll pass___.
The review was worth reading___. Not___.

A Thousand Acres (1997) 9

Underrated family drama with sizzling work by Pfeiffer and Lange

One of the Message Boards threads at IMDb had two women talking about Colin Firth, how they watched the movie only because of him. Obviously these were two young women; but what struck me is how little this movie has been appreciated by audiences generally. The brilliant, and I mean brilliant, performances by Michelle Pfeiffer and Jessica Lange were hardly noticed, not only by audiences, but by the Academy and by most of the critics.

I think I know why. First, the plot—or actually just the setup—is a kind of bastardization of Shakespeare's King Lear with the dying, crazy patriarch and the three scheming daughters who will inherit. Their names even begin with the same letters, Regan, Goneril, and Cordelia—Rose, Ginny, and Caroline. And I guess "Larry" (Jason Robards) works for "Lear." The apparent idea envisioned by Jane Smiley in her Pulitzer Prize winning novel was to tell a Lear-like story from the point of view of the daughters, and to tell it in a sort of late twentieth century realistic way not considered by the Bard. The problem is, in Smiley and Moorhouse's story, the two older daughters are very human with strengths and weaknesses while the father is a most despicable character without much in the way of redeeming qualities. His only strength was his ability to make a financial success of the farm; however, we can even discount that since his father and grandfather before him built the farm and he inherited it.

The second problem—and this is one I cannot personally attest to, not having read Smiley's novel—is that the movie is only a limited and partial interpretation of that novel. Still, it is almost always the case that an excellent novel, especially a long and ambitious one with many psychological nuances, cannot be faithfully transferred to the screen. The vision and audio demands of film drown out the subtleties of a narration while the time constraints don't allow for the full development of character and motivation achieved by the novelist. Given five

or six hours, perhaps Moorhouse could have made a movie more in keeping with Smiley's novel.

A third problem is one that is perhaps Moorhouse's alone. She began her directing career with the very well done Aussie film *Proof* (1991) starring Russell Crowe. She followed it up with *How to Make an American Quilt* (1995) which celebrated women, especially women of a certain age. However it was a bit heavy-handed and clearly and determinedly a chick flick. In a sense *A Thousand Acres* takes off from there, showing us not only the point of view of women, but does so in a way that may seem politically motivated to some. Larry Cook is clearly a bad, bad daddy. He beat his daughters and he had carnal knowledge of them. He ran the household with an iron fist. Jess (Colin Firth's character) seduces the inexperienced Ginny and breaks her heart for nothing more than a bit of fun it would appear. And then he goes to Rose, who clearly is going to be the power behind the new ownership, and hooks up with her, while incidentally inducing her husband to end his life in a drunken accident. The rest of the men are one-dimensional characters without nuance, the way they often appear in romance novels. I think most audiences were put off by the heavy-handed incest, adultery and sexual betrayal that was woven into the story.

Having said all this, I think the critics and the public are wrong. I think the direction was biased against men, but in this story it needed to be. I think Moorhouse did a fine job of making an emotional and engaging film about family dynamics that were none too pretty. And the acting by Pfeiffer and Lange was nothing short of sensational. They seemed to feed off of one another in a way that I found absolutely authentic and deeply moving. In particular Pfeiffer was riveting as she projected her bent-up anger and hatred. The way Moorhouse allowed her character to be revealed to us gradually is a tribute to her ability as a director as well as to Pfeiffer's outstanding performance. And the skill with which Moorhouse guided the change in Ginny's character as she went from a "ninny," as she called herself, to someone with self-awareness and some understandable bitterness, was also excellent. The fact that she left her husband was as much out of shame as anything else. He needed to go get her and forgive her and bring her back. And Robards in his intensity and madness was also very good.

I predict that this film, which bombed in theaters, will be better appreciated in the years to come as people see it on DVD. My question is, whatever happened to Moorhouse? Her talent is obvious, but she has yet to director her fourth feature film. When she does I hope she remembers to go with what she believes but to be fair as well. I think, actually she was fair to the two lead character in this film, but didn't pay enough attention to the others. In addition to the unnuanced father, Jennifer Jason Leigh's Caroline was unfinished, leaving us to wonder about why she did some of the things she did.

And the husbands needed to be something more than mannequins. They needed to be engaged and involved.

I've seen this and I give it___stars.
I want to see it___. I'll pass___.
The review was worth reading___. Not___.

Towelhead *(Nothing Is Private)* (2007) 10

An Arab-American "American Beauty" sort of tale

BEWARE SPOILERS

The story begins as Jasira (Summer Bishil) is about to get a bikini line shave from her mother's boyfriend. Oops. Mom finds out and sends Jasira to live with her overbearing Lebanese father (Peter Macdissi) who, although much Americanized, still sees some things, especially things to do with his daughter, in a more conservative, Middle Eastern way. Naturally we know that her budding sexuality is going to collide with his prohibitions. It could get ugly. Throw in a black boyfriend (Eugene Jones III), some noisy neighbors, an army reservist Travis (Aaron Eckhart, who gets to play yet another jerk; c.f., his roles in *Thank You for Smoking* (2005) *and In the Company of Men* (1997)) who is smitten with her but doesn't know what to do about it (and what he does do, he does badly), and Jasira begins to live, shall we say, in interesting times.

I think we can understand the relationship depicted between Travis and Jasira by realizing that a point is being made: even though Jasira comes on to him, he has a societal responsibility to deflect her school girl advances regardless of how he feels. Her coming on to him is portrayed as girlish and equivocal. Again his responsibility is to keep his hands off of her. The overarching point is that no matter what happens between them since she is 13-years-old and he is an adult, it is entirely his fault.

On the other hand, her experience with the ultra-clean cut Thomas Bradley who is black is seemingly okay. They took precautions and he was gentle and they were more or less equals. All of this is carefully thought out to appeal to the mentality of a general audience. Of course the mentality of the Arab-American counsel (if there is such a thing) as well as conservative religious groups in general, will find this outrageous. In Islam countries you can be sure that this film is banned.

What I liked about the movie was the light comedic intent from director Alan Ball, reminiscent of his work in the Academy Award winning *American Beauty* (1999) especially in the true-to-life (in a satirical way) the action is depicted, and in the way the men are a bit clueless. Some of it was strange. The "competing" flag poles, the business with the little white cat, Jasira's orgasms at the drop of...well at seeing pictures of naked women or rocking herself with her legs crossed—but perhaps there is a

lesson here for someone: some people are polymorphous perverse (especially as children) as it was once said (by Freud, I think); that is, they have a generalized sense of sexuality. And some people are auto erotic.

I also liked the implicit forgiveness of the characters. And I liked the way Ball didn't try to resolve the moral issues. Certainly racism is wrong. Certainly grown men cannot have sex with 13-year-olds. But beyond that, Ball did not go in a prescriptive way. Instead, through different characters he showed different points of view, all related to Jasira's awakening sexuality. Finally I liked the character of Jasira, who was brave, assertive at times, passive at other times, and fair and honest with herself in the face of some demanding adolescent challenges. And I liked the young actress who played her. She was pretty, and very winning. And, by the way, Summer Bishil was born in 1988 and therefore was 18 or 19 years old when this movie came out. She did a terrific job of acting 13.

Note that the title of this movie, for politically correct reasons, one supposes, has been changed to "Nothing Is Private." At least that is how it is listed at IMDb.com.

I've seen this and I give it___stars.
I want to see it___. I'll pass___.
The review was worth reading___. Not___.

Training Day (2001) 9

Outstanding corrupt cop drama

The ending was a bit of overkill. That could be said. And the mano-a-mano fight après the ending was a bit drawn out. That too could be said. But the rest of the film was more than excellent.

Training Day is the best of the bad cop dramas that I have seen, and I've seen a few. Both Denzel Washington as the psychopathic bad cop, Alonzo, and Ethan Hawke as the idealistic rookie, Jake, were full out. Denzel Washington won the Best Actor Oscar for his performance, and Ethan Hawke was nominated for Best Supporting Actor. The direction by Antoine Fuqua was superb. The LA street scenes and milieu were as real and vivid as my old buddy Taco Bender. (And trust me, Taco Bender was very real.) The extras in the crowd scenes should get some kind of prize for macho scary. I've been there, and I still have a few nightmares. There are some streets in LA you don't want to walk down unless you are a homey, or a brother, and some other streets you don't want to walk down, period.

Unlike some cop dramas and shoot 'em up thrillers, this one was carefully planned, so that the scene in the barrio at the card table, the rook all alone set up for the kill, came across as real because what had happened before was just about the only thing in the world that could have saved him. The LA atmosphere was like a rush, as stunningly authentic in a different way as, say, that in *Chinatown* (1974) or *LA Confidential* (1997), but more contemporary.

I wonder how many guys starting in say the sixties or maybe a little before have experienced the kind of initiation that Jake experiences in terms of being fed some dope never before tasted and then "led" on the "trip" by someone wanting to exploit them. Most of the time, for most guys it was an initiation into something other worldly, scary, but something that was only psychological and would be gone the next day. For Jake it was a matter of, first, his livelihood as an idealistic cop, and second a matter of groking to a paranoid view of the world in which the good guys are the bad guys and everything is hopelessly corrupt and there is no good, only evil—and you just found out. And third, a matter of life and death with either acid and grass running all around your brain or maybe PCP and speed, and some suddenly obviously evil person (as Washington so well depicted) giving you the kind of "guidance" you can't refuse. And then finally it is beyond life and death and only a matter of primeval justice and a revenge you must perform.

Look for Snoop Dogg in a wheelchair and Dr. Dre as one of Alonzo's posse cops.

Don't miss this one. You will stay until they run the closing credits.

I've seen this and I give it___stars.
I want to see it___. I'll pass___.
The review was worth reading___. Not___.

Twelve Monkeys (1995) 9

Visually and intellectually complex

Properly speaking this should be called "The Army of the Twelve Monkeys." It only takes twelve, strategically placed throughout the world, to kill five billion people with a mutant virus. (Actually glass canisters are used.)

The central character, James Cole, played with heavyweight restraint by Bruce Willis, is a convict from the future where the survivors live underground, leaving the surface to the animals. He and other nonconformists live in cages and are made to "volunteer" to go back in time to search for the original virus before it mutated in 1996. Problem is they keep getting the destination year screwed up. Once they send him to 1917 and land him naked in the middle of a battle from World War I, where he gets shot in the leg. Another time they send him to 1990 where he ends up in a mental institution and meets attractive co-star Madeleine Stowe, who plays psychiatrist Dr. Kathryn Railly, leading to an interesting subplot: shrink falls in love with her mentally disturbed patient. Brad Pitt entertains as Jeffrey Goines, a hyperactive nut case, son of a sick virologist, and leader of an animal rights activist group. He is crazy/wise.

The film is heavily populated by unfeeling, semi-competent scientists, mental patients and their caretakers. There are all sorts of apocalyptic fools ranting and raving about the end of the world, etc. Most of human society as we know it is in shadow, off camera. There's an understandable terror of psychoactive drugs among the patients. Thorazine in particular is mentioned. Cole's body is continually being assaulted by hypodermics, electrodes, the fists and boots of the guards and other hard objects. His face is continually smeared with blood. One gets the idea that director Terry Gilliam had a bad dream and wanted to share.

Regardless, this brooding, atmospheric yarn is the best cinematic sci-fi I have seen since *Blade Runner* (1982); and it is no co-incidence that it was scripted in part by the gifted David Peoples who helped write the screen play for *Blade Runner*. Never mind that time travel to the past is an absurdity. We're forced to rise above that because Gilliam presents time similar to the way Kurt Vonnegut did in his novel *Slaughterhouse-Five* (1969), namely that all time is happening "simultaneously" and especially right now, forever.

We are reminded that time is an illusion. Our experience and perception of time is, as it were, linear, allowing us a comprehension of "time" similar to what two-dimensional creatures might have of three dimensional space. "Time" does not exist. It is a construct from the way we compare events. Notice that when James Cole dies Dr. Railly is not sad because Cole lives on in the person of his younger self, the child at the airport watching his death. This will be the case for eternity.

There are some funny bits in the script. After Cole beats up the pimp to save Dr. Railly, and forces a trade of teeth (to evade the trackers implanted in his teeth), and the cops come, the pimp says, all hurt, "I was attacked by a coked-up whore and a crazy dentist." Another nice touch is to have the virologist father of crazy/visionary Jeffrey Goines sound like a southern politician instead of your usual mad scientist. I also liked it when psychiatrist Dr. Kathryn Railly said, "Psychiatry is the latest religion...I'm in trouble. I'm losing my faith." She's right: psychiatry and clinical psychology in general is a secular religion less than two hundred years old that we as a society ought to regard with suspicion.

In short this is not your usual Bruce Willis outing. The action/adventure stuff is secondary to story and character development and to the social and political statements of the film, the more important of which is to protest the suppression of the individual by the larger society. The forces of evil really are those who dictate what is normal and those who enforce conformity. This film is commercially successful because many young people, corporate cogs, and the underclass feel oppressed by the constraints of society and can readily identify with Cole's struggle. What is worse, Thorazine and Prozac or marijuana and beer? Anyone who identified even in the slightest with this film can answer that question.

The second statement is that humans are ruining the planet and should be killed to save the animals. This melancholy idea is not so far-fetched. That some cult of nuts (or visionaries, as you like) might someday infect humanity with a deadly virus so that the flora and fauna of the planet might resume their natural state is at least plausible.

I've seen this and I give it___stars.
I want to see it___. I'll pass___.
The review was worth reading___. Not___.

Twelve O'Clock High (1949) 10

Still unsurpassed

Those who think that *Saving Private Ryan* was a great movie ought to watch this old black and white classic. In virtually every aspect except photography *Twelve O'Clock High* is superior. The script by Sy Bartlett in particular is vastly superior.

Spielberg's film focused on some of the command problems faced by Capt. John Miller (Tom Hanks) in fulfilling his combat mission, but the treatment and development were almost high schoolish (if I may) compared to the enthralling delineation in *Twelve O'Clock High*. The problems encountered by Gregory Peck as the bomber group commander were complex, subtle and psychologically demanding, while the resolution was filled with the kind of male social and political dynamics not much explored at the movies these days. (We have female dynamics aplenty.)

Director Henry King's clean, crisp, "invisible" direction was also superior to the uneven and far too showy pandering from Spielberg. Furthermore the acting, with Gary Merrill and Hugh Marlowe supporting Peck, was also better. Ted Danson in his cameo and Matt Damon at times in *Saving Private Ryan* were almost laughable.

Comparing the two movies makes one wonder how much movies really have improved. Technically they have in every respect, but too often today's film-makers think they can get by with special effects and splashy sets. Pour a lot of blood, show a lot of skin, get people at each other's throat, and it will play, seems to be the attitude. What is often forgotten are the two most important aspects of film, namely, story and character development. In this respect I don't think today's films have improved on the great classics of the past.

I've seen this and I give it___stars.
I want to see it___. I'll pass___.
The review was worth reading___. Not___.

What's Eating Gilbert Grape? (1993) 10

You want to know what's eating him...?

He's got a mother that weighs 400 pounds, or maybe it's 600. There's a married woman who can't keep her hands off of him whose husband would like to kill him. He's got a younger brother that is cuckoo, and he's responsible for him. He's got to take care of him. He works in a grocery store. His life is about groceries. Honk if you've got groceries...

He's trapped in Endora, somewhere, probably Kansas or Nebraska or Iowa (actually filmed in Texas), somewhere in the heart of the Heartland—by the way this is the sort of American film that plays as a foreign film in, say, France or Sweden. Along comes Juliette Lewis who's a bit of a short-haired punk to his long-haired country ("Get in the car, longhair"). He is wallowing in self-pity and she sees it. "What about you?" she asks. "What do you want?"

She attracts him and frightens him. She may make him upset his predictable life as Job. And then one day, he loses it and hits Arnie, and hits him again. Who can blame him? But you don't hurt Arnie. He is just a boy who will always be a boy.

Johnny Depp is Gilbert Grape, Leonardo DiCaprio is Arnie, Mary Steenburgen is the married woman, Juliette Lewis is Becky and Darlene Cates is Mama. They all give sterling performances. The script and direction are flawless. You've probably seen bits and pieces of this movie on TV. See the whole thing. It is an outstanding flick. Gilbert is an America hero. He knows the good and the bad, and he always tries to do the good. But it's tough. Life is an embarrassment and a boredom, and when it isn't boring, it's scary emotionally. Depp is perfectly cast as a man whose loyalty to his family and his love for them has trapped him. And they are using him, and they don't appreciate him. His father disappeared. His older brother is gone. Gilbert has the responsibility. And he knows it. And he can't escape it.

But it's hard, and when Becky comes along, she is something different. She is something he's never seen before. She isn't predictable, and she is striking. And she is smart and sensitive, like him.

Don't answer the phone. Don't answer the door. This is a heartland masterpiece about real people living real lives, and director Lasse Halstrom (*The Cider House Rules* (1999) *Chocolat* (2000) after many Swedish films) doesn't flinch and he doesn't do clichés, and he gets it right. You will be moved.

But see this for Johnny Depp and see why women love him.

I've seen this and I give it___stars.

I want to see it___. I'll pass___.
The review was worth reading___. Not___.

Witness (1985) 9

The thriller as a passionate love story

As a connoisseur of the thriller genre I can tell you this is one of the best ever made. Harrison Ford is better than I have ever seen him; the scenes with eight-year-old Lukas Haas are magical, and Kelly McGillis projects the primeval power of a woman like few you'll ever see. Peter Weir's direction is practically flawless. The evil cops are as evil as evil can be, and the Amish are treated kindly, with respect and admiration. Quite simply though, the reason this is a great thriller is that it is a powerful love story.

The passionate love that is felt and built upon, but not consummated, envelops the audience in anticipation. What makes this happen is some real—not contrived—obstacle to the expression of that love, such as the lovers being from different and warring families, as in "Romeo and Juliet," or from different cultures, as here in "Witness." She is Amish, and he is a big city cop who "whacks" people. For their love to work, a gulf as wide as the Pacific Ocean has to be bridged. I think the carefully constructed script by William Kelley gives us an ending we can live with. Watch it and see if you agree.

I've seen this and I give it___stars.
I want to see it___. I'll pass___.
The review was worth reading___. Not___.

Chapter Thirteen:

Indulgences

or

Yeah, I Wasted an Hour and a Half, So What?

Some of these are just indulgences, maybe because the movie is about a favorite subject or stars a favorite actor or (more likely!) a favorite actress. And some of these are very good indeed.

2 Days in the Valley (1996) 8

THIS is a romantic comedy?

Yes. You've seen "grunge on the run" romantic comedies—*Wild at Heart* (1990), *Natural Born Killers* (1994) come to mind, and poor waitress/crazy old man romantic comedies, e.g., *As Good As It Gets* (1997)—well, this is a mousy secretary/aging hit man romantic comedy.

Somewhat. It's also a tongue-in-the cheek satire on all things that Hollywood thinks movie-goers crave: cute dogs, sexy women, good-hearted underdogs winning out, dumb cops, the ugly rich (Greg Cruttwell's wormy Allan Hopper fits the bill), shoot-outs, blood, dead bodies (enough to grace a Shakespearean stage) and that favorite of testosterone males everywhere: a good old-fashioned cat fight.

Charlize Theron and Teri Hatcher provide the eye appeal as they slap and toss each other around; and to be honest I have to say they are definitely worth watching. Excellent support comes from James Spader, as an amazingly clean-shaven (what does he use—Nair?) psycho-sickie with a stopwatch.

But Danny Aiello is the real star. He plays Dosmo Pizzo, the over-the-hill hit man (currently moonlighting in embarrassment at the local pizzeria). He loses his hairpiece, finds redemption, true love, thirty thousand Big Ones, and presumably lives happily ever after on the lam with his unlikely moll (Glenne Headly) in this clever plot by coincidence from director and scriptwriter John Herzfeld.

(By the way, what's with Hollywood and its perverse love affair with sympathetic hit men? A new genre? The hit man as the underclass hero? I just saw *Grosse Pointe Blank* (1997) which stars John Cusack as a "cute" amoral murder artist. What next? The lovable terrorist? Knowing Hollywood, I think we can count on it.)

Anyway, Spader's character is not so lovable. He kills without the slightest qualm and takes a great delight in blowing people away. Charlize is his girlfriend and they have lots of you-know-what together. Teri Hatcher is an Olympic class skier with a loser boyfriend. And the Valley of course is the San Fernando Valley just north of L.A., onetime home of the Valley girls, now best known as the porn capital of America.

Jeff Daniels and Eric Stoltz play Valley cops (who are not as smart as L.A. cops—one of the jokes in the movie, ha, ha, ha). Both do a great job. Daniels is street wise and quick on the trigger and a bit of a prude while Stoltz is naive and a wanna-be homicide inspector. There are half a dozen cameos by not so well-known but talented people like veteran Austin Pendleton who does a killer sarcastic monologue on the directorial failures of suicidal Teddy Peppers (Paul Mazursky). One-time "Goodbye Girl" Marsha Mason has a modest part as a sweet and realistic nurse, and she is excellent. And there are dogs. You gotta have dogs.

319

However what makes this work is some clever dialogue and some satirical plot ideas, but mainly it is a tour de force of acting by a talented and highly professional cast. This is one of those movies in which every actor is a threat to steal the show at any time one way or the other. In a way it's a parade of cameos cleverly stitched together and then nicely edited.

But see this for James Spader whose skill playing nerdish weirdos is on fine display.

I've seen this and I give it___stars.
I want to see it___. I'll pass___.
The review was worth reading___. Not___.

9 1/2 Weeks (1986) 7

Kim Basinger makes this worth seeing

What one realizes while watching this is how limited and ultimately unsatisfactory is a relationship based purely on sex.

I imagine that the familiar dominance/submissive psychology at the heart of this visually stunning movie—and it really is beautifully shot—comes from the novel by Elizabeth MacNeil. I say that, not having read the novel, because the seduction of Manhattan art dealer Elizabeth (Kim Basinger) by the smooth and supremely confident financier John (Mickey Rourke) is so very well done with the expensive presents, the well-timed flower deliveries, little endearments, etc., that it amounts to a woman's fantasy. The partial debasement of Elizabeth and her eventual triumph over her darker instincts and her realization that there is a difference between love and submission is also something that one might expect to find in a woman's point-of-view novel.

However when we get to the actual sexuality and how it is acted out, it is unclear who dreamed up the scenes, MacNeil or director Adrian Lyne or the scriptwriters. I say this because the scenes were so predictable and so ordinary, and when not ordinary and predictable, were bordering on the just plain dumb. Making love in the rain, at the top of a tall building (inside the clock tower), blindfolding the woman, making her crawl, feeding her strawberries, etc., bring nothing new to eroticism. And the scene requiring some imagination—baiting the gay bashers—was not realistically done. Why directors insist on allowing a man holding onto the hand of woman to outrun the men chasing them never ceases to amaze me. And then to have Elizabeth and John stop in the middle of the street to allow the bashers they have outrun to catch up was just plain stupid, not to mention the phony fight that followed.

Not only were the sexual scenes predictable but clearly Lyne was in harness (and I am glad of that) since he

stops well short of what might happen if this sort of theme were fully played out.

Putting all that aside what makes this movie worth seeing is Kim Basinger. She is absolutely stunning, and it is clear that Lyne and his camera adored her. More than that Basinger does a fine job of acting in a demanding role. I was impressed. Before seeing this film I thought she was a rather ordinary actress, but her ability to combine grown-up New York chic with little-girl vulnerability and to make absolutely clear the psychological dilemma her character's heart faced really held the movie together.

Lyne's insistence on whispered dialogue difficult to hear was consistent with the theme of the movie but not kind to these ears. But that was okay because much of the dialogue was secondary to the visual exploration of the woman's sexuality. The peek-a-boo and off center and shadowed shots of Basinger's face and her silhouette, and the studied smile from Rourke combined with the stark black and whites of their clothes and the furnishings served to highlight and emphasis the flesh tones of Basinger's skin while lending an appropriate artistic and fashionable atmosphere to the movie, which after all has an art dealer at its center. The many scenes that were began and suggested, and then cut away from, allowed a richer texture of experience for the viewer than would have been possible had the scenes been played out. And that was doubly good because again it is the visuals that make this movie worth seeing, not the originality of the story and its development.

To those viewers who thought that this was some sort of high class pornography, I can only say you missed the point entirely, and indeed, you may be projecting your own sorry mentality. For those others who were not, shall we say, sufficiently stimulated, I can point you to a more graphic novel with a similar theme (written by a man) entitled *The Story of O* which will NOT be coming to a theater near you anytime soon.

See this for Kim Basinger whose sensitive and robust beauty dominated the screen.

I've seen this and I give it___stars.
I want to see it___. I'll pass___.
The review was worth reading___. Not___.

About Last Night (1986) 7

David Mamet turned into "thirtysomething"

This is a pretty good movie, although the initial effect is disconcerting, like watching a sit-com that is painfully real and not just escapist fare. The players, Demi Moore and Rob Lowe as the lovers, and Jim Belushi and Elizabeth Perkins as their jealous friends, are very good, and Director Edward Zwick is to be complimented on getting so much out of all of them. The script, loosely based on

David Mamet's play *Sexual Perversions in Chicago* is filled with sharp, clever and sometimes insightful lines worth quoting.

One is when Moore breaks off the relationship with her boss to be exclusively with Lowe. Taken back, he says, "But I thought we had something special." She replies, "No. It was sleazy. And now it's over."

Another is when Moore's sensitive and brutally sarcastic (and jealous) friend Perkins arrives for Thanksgiving and says to Lowe about cloddish, working-class Jim Belushi, who hasn't arrived yet, "Your vulgarian friend is downstairs denting innocent people's fenders."

After the two lovers move in together, and she has more than a drawer in his apartment and doesn't have to carry an extra pair of panties in her purse, they begin with "I love..." (awkward pause) "making love with you" (pure Mamet). But when he doesn't share his feelings with her, she says, "I don't want to be your roommate anymore. I had a roommate."

What she wants is emotional intimacy. A woman needs emotional intimacy because then she knows where she stands and she has some control. They move closer and she (caught unaware) says, "I love you." He (on the spot, camera close) replies, "I love you too." She sheds a tear, just one, as they hug, perhaps in joy, or perhaps because she doesn't know whether he really loves her or not, and it's so very, very important. The next day Belushi asks who said it first and cavalier Lowe says he did. Belushi, who boorishly fancies himself a lady's man, lectures his friend on just how very poor studly style that is.

About Last Night is really about forming and securing the bond between a man and a woman. It's trial by fire. Their emotions are on edge and their individuality is threatened. And all around them are people and circumstances, and their very own animal natures, testing and probing the strength of the bond. When it breaks the pain is enormous.

Lowe says: "I didn't fool around. Not once!" Moore rejoins: "Give the boy a medal. I didn't realize it was such a sacrifice."

Then comes her awkward and sad double date with the nerdy card trick artist with the British accent. Perkins says, "Couldn't you just listen to him all night?" and we're thinking, "NOT EVEN for one minute."

Meanwhile we have Lowe's casual pickups. Meaningless sex and then not even that. But when he saves his friend's cafe, he grows up.

Belushi and Perkins are wonderful as "opposites attract." They fight the magnetism to the very end—

speaking of which, the best part of the movie is the ending. It is perfect.

It should be noted that the movie is larger than Mamet's one-act play and covers ground not even considered in the play. The play was an insightful but somewhat crude comedy about sex. The movie is a popular drama about relationships.

I've seen this and I give it___stars.
I want to see it___. I'll pass___.
The review was worth reading___. Not___.

Adam's Rib (1949) 8

Pleasant midcentury skirmish in the sexual wars

Two New York lawyers, husband Adam Bonner (Spencer Tracy) and wife Amanda Bonner (Katharine Hepburn), work out the marital tension and fight the sexual wars in the courtroom on opposite sides of a wife (Judy Holliday) shoots cheating husband (Tom Ewell) case. Adam's masculinity is seemingly challenged and his sense of justice offended by his wife's insistence on showing how smart she is while furthering her feminist agenda at the expense of the law. Will their public confrontation destroy their marriage, or will it ultimately make the bond stronger?

This still plays mainly because of the charisma of Hepburn and Tracy and the fine chemistry they create together. The script by Garson Kanin and Ruth Gordon is profound and shallow by turns, yet ultimately witty and pleasing. Judy Holliday as the lower middle-class Doris Attinger (on her way to her signature role in *Born Yesterday* (1950)) and David Wayne, as the song-writing neighbor who adores Amanda, shine in supporting roles. George Cukor's direction is clear, crisp and always focused. In the end we can see that Adam can be as feminine as Amanda can be masculine. The bit where Tracy cries real tears to win her back and then tells her, "We all have our tricks" is classic. It's his clever answer to her outrageous courtroom theatrics. Memorable as it illuminates their contrasting personalities is the early scene where the unsophisticated Doris is interviewed by Yale law school grad Amanda.

As a political movie, was *Adam's Rib* ahead of its time as a vehicle for feminist expression, or was it just another apology for male chauvinism, or was it balanced and fair? I'll give you a hint: the title is ironic. One of the things that made the Tracy/Hepburn romance work so well for so long was the creative balance they maintained in the battle of the sexes. The script by Kanin and Gordon carefully continues that profoundly true equilibrium.

I've seen this and I give it___stars.
I want to see it___. I'll pass___.
The review was worth reading___. Not___.

All the President's Men (1976) 8

The Watergate scandal from the reporters' perspective

This dramatization of how it was discovered that the burglary of the Democratic Party headquarters at the Watergate Hotel in Washington, D. C. was funded and directed by the Nixon White House is a lot better than it has any right to be. Given the tedious, non-glamorous and frankly boring leg- and phone-work that is often the lot of the investigative reporter, it is surprising that this is a very interesting movie even if you don't care two beans about the Watergate scandal. In fact, this is really more about how the story was put together than it is about the scandal itself. It is also a lot less political than might be expected.

It stars Robert Redford and Dustin Hoffman as Washington *Post* reporters, Bob Woodward and Carl Bernstein, and they are good, with excellent support from Jason Robards (Oscar as Best Supporting Actor) playing *Post* Executive Editor Ben Bradlee, and Jane Alexander as an innocent caught up in the machinations. But what makes the movie work is the Oscar-winning script adapted from the Woodward and Bernstein best seller by that old Hollywood pro, William Goldman (*Butch Cassidy and the Sundance Kid* 1969, *Misery* 1990, etc.). What he does so very well, even though we know the outcome, is to establish and maintain the tension as Woodward and Bernstein run all over town chasing leads and misdirections. He accomplishes this by putting just enough varied obstacles in the path of our intrepid reporters, notably the Washington bureaucracy and the understandably cautious senior editors at the *Post*.

The direction by Alan J. Pakula (*Comes a Horseman* 1978, *Sophie's Choice* 1982, etc.) focuses the scenes nicely, keeps the camera where it belongs, and highlights the story with a shadowy Deep Throat (Hal Holbrook), skitterish sources, and a vivid recreation of a top American newspaper at work. I was especially enthralled to see the interactions among the reporters, the editors and the sources. I thought they all looked and sounded authentic, Redford's good looks having nothing to do with the story, which was right, and Hoffman's flair for the intense reigned in, which was necessary. The diffidence of Alexander's character and the soft pushiness of Woodward and Bernstein were tempered just right. Bradlee's stewardship of the story and his ability to take a calculated risk seemed true to life.

Some details that stood out: Redford's hunt and peck typing contrasted with Hoffman's all fingers flying; the talking heads on the strategically placed TVs, reacting (via actual video footage) to the developing story—deny, deny, deny! of course. The thin reporter's spiral notebooks being pulled out and then later flipped through to find a quote. The bright lights of the newsroom looking expansive with all those desks as though there were mirrors on the walls extending an illusion. The seemingly silly tricks to get a source to confirm: just nod your head; I'll count to ten and if you're still on the line... And you know what I liked best? No annoying subplot!

The rather abrupt resolution with the teletype banging out the leads to a sequence of stories that led to President Nixon's resignation had just the right feel to it, especially for those of us who have actually experienced the goosepimply sensation that comes with watching a breaking story come in over the teletype. The quick wrap-up surprised me, but delighted me at the same time.

Bottom line: an excellent movie that wears well, a fine example of some of Hollywood's top professionals at work some thirty years ago. #30

I've seen this and I give it___stars.
I want to see it___. I'll pass___.
The review was worth reading___. Not___.

Amazon Women on the Moon (1987) 7

A lot funnier than might be expected

The opening skit "Apartment Victim" with Arsenio Hall is pure slapstick—not my favorite comedy type but for some reason I found it hilarious. I just cracked up on all the mishaps and the great timing by Arsenio and the cameras. The way the video cassette shoots back out of the player and hits him and knocks him over was just so funny; and the way the TV blows up when he hits the remote was a crack up. Which reminds me, Confucius says "Woman who flies upside down has hairy..." [I censored these last two words for the benefit of sensitive readers. Discerning readers will be able to figure out the last two words by re-reading the previous sentence.]

(Sorry about that.)

Anyway, I also liked David Alan Grier as Don (No Soul) Simmons in the segment "Blacks without Soul." The Laurence Welk way he sang the Broadway show type tunes was just a riot. I also liked the skit featuring Rosanna Arquette, "Two I.D.'s" in which she takes the prospective date's credit cards and two forms of ID to investigate what kind of guy he is on a date.

I also kind of liked the comedic roast at the wake in "Roast your loved one." Kind of. The jokes ranged from funny but old to lame-o.

The overall shtick of this being a TV late night movie show was also good—the idea, anyway. The featured movie "Amazon Women on the Moon" (actually this was a skit too; no such movie exists although one wonders why), which spoofs 1950s cheapo sci-fi flicks was so, so very bad as to almost be campy—but not quite. It was frankly just bad bad, and a little on the very cognitively challenged side, that is to say, dumb.

Overall this was a lot funnier than might be expected, at least for me, but then again I have actually watched most of the episodes of "Married with Children" although I would never admit it.

I've seen this and I give it___stars.
I want to see it___. I'll pass___.
The review was worth reading___. Not___.

Apollo 13 (1995) 8

Gripping story professionally rendered

I don't think it matters whether you remember the story of the Apollo 13 space mission or not. Whether you know the ending or whether you were otherwise occupied at the time in 1970, the tension created and maintained by the fine script (by William Broyles Jr. and Al Reinert with uncredited help from John Sayles) and the direction of Ron Howard will compel your interest. And when the resolution comes it will command your emotions.

Part of the success of this movie goes to the fine acting by Tom Hanks, who is, in a professional and psychological sense, very much like those fly boys with the Right Stuff who fearlessly left our comfort cocoon here on earth and ventured into the cold, dark airlessness of space for glory and honor and maybe for proof of their manhood. Like the astronauts depicted, Tom Hanks is always on task and always delivers an arresting and believable performance.

Ed Harris, who played the flight director in Houston was also excellent as was Kevin Bacon as the replacement astronaut who had to fly the ship. In fact the entire cast, especially a whole lot of people with small roles as part of the nearly anonymous support techno nerds at NASA, gave believable and compelling performances. A lot of the credit for that has to go to Ron Howard, who made sure that they all looked the way they were supposed to look. After all, they were engaged in the success or failure of the mission in the most immediate sense.

I also was very much moved by the musical score by James Horner. When you have an extraterrestrial epic, you need the music of the spheres, and Horner provided that. The music was so triumphantly married to the events and to the cosmic adventure that it inspired without drawing undue attention to itself. It is one of the most beautiful film scores I have ever heard.

Although this was nominated for nine Academy Awards, including Best Picture, it won only two, for Best Film Editing and Best Sound. Perhaps the movie was considered too much of a purely commercial venture at the time (and because of the budget it was largely that of course), and perhaps Howard's direction and intention seemed very much by the book. However I think the final result turned out to be more than some thought when it was released in 1995. It is a heroic epic, with a worthy theme, professionally done. Everybody worked hard for veracity and they certainly convinced me. Nonetheless there is perhaps something missing here. Although the sheer horror of dying in the cold vacuum of space or being burned up by a too rapid descent into the atmosphere is kept very much on our minds, there is a level of psychological reality that lives within the heart and soul of the astronaut and within the astronaut's family that was attempted here but not entirely achieved.

See this for Ron Howard who did a great job as director and for Tom Hanks, one of the most charismatic actors of our time, and especially for astronaut Jim Lovell who lived it and (with help from Jeffrey Kluger) wrote the book *Lost Moon* (1994) upon which the film was based.

I've seen this and I give it___stars.
I want to see it___. I'll pass___.
The review was worth reading___. Not___.

Artificial Intelligence (2001) 8

Best Sci Fi since Blade Runner?

I understand that Steven Spielberg took over this project started by the late Stanley Kubrick, which would explain the uneasy edge to the usual Spielbergian treatment. The remnants of Kubrick's message, namely that humans are soon-to-be obsolete beasts, contend with the usual Spielberg formula of corn syrup, tears and awe, so that the result is unsettling and more than a bit curious.

First of all, be aware that, despite the fact that there is a full serving of the Spielberg recipe here (cute kids, dazzling special effects, a beautiful score by John Williams, social consciousness seen largely from a kid's POV, etc.), this is not a "feel good" movie that will appeal to the mass audience at which Spielberg usually aims. The heartland of America will find this film disturbing and will tell their neighbors to stay away. Sci fi aficionados of the hard science variety (like me) will have mixed feelings since some of the science is, shall we say, unlikely. The fantasy/sorcery crowd will probably be disenchanted for other reasons, although there is a glorious ending that might mist up one's eyes (it did mine). Overall, however, this is an unsettling look at humanity and where we're headin' ("Is that Lincoln County Road or Armageddon?"), and the treatment is definitely NOT something for the kiddies. It's liable to give them nightmares.

The central hook of the film is that we are made to identify with the robotic mechas, especially Haley Joel Osment's David and Jack Angel's Teddy and Jude Law's Gigolo Joe, while being reminded that they are not human, or more properly, that they are more admirable than human. In a way the robots resemble the have-nots of the current society, the handicapped and the poor, while the humans in the persons of Monica Swinton (Frances O'Connor), her son Martin (Jake Thomas) and the Flesh Fair entrepreneur (Brendan Gleeson) represent respectively the privileged, the cruel, and the exploitive. Monica's compromised morality is made clear in the scene in the woods (which I won't describe for fear of giving away too much). One also gets the sense that she and her husband (who portray the usual kid-show parental mentality) are not actually bright enough to figure out what has happened when siblings and friends have conflicts. Monica simply sides with her biological child and throws David to the wolves, as it were.

On another level this is a movie about a child's undying love for his mother, a love that lasts for two thousand years and a day and is never compromised. It is about believing in fairy tales and the miraculous, a modern day Pinocchio in Wonderland as might be dreamed up by admirers of *Blade Runner* (1982). In the Spielberg canon, echoes from his cinematic predecessors mesh with echoes from his own movies in a sometimes all too obvious way. Note the return of the moon (in sinister splendor) from E.T. with Teddy (who could have been retrieved from the set of *Blade Runner*—as could Prof. Hobby, AKA Geppetto) trudging across the top of a rise in front of it.

The sets and the animations are sumptuous and beautiful. The robots and the aliens are ingeniously crafted. I very much liked the vision of a drowned Manhattan with the upper stories of the skyscrapers rising above the level of the sea (presumably from global warming), giving us a very quiet and almost contemplative Manhattan, and then the skyscrapers immersed in ice as the earth falls into a prolonged ice age. The sense of the rapid passage of awesome time reminded me a bit of Kubrick's *2001: A Space Odyssey* (1968), while Dr. Know (voice of Robin Williams) recalled *The Wizard of Oz* (1939), and the Blue Fairy (voice of Meryl Streep) something from Disney.

This is a substantially compromised masterpiece, as it certainly had to be coming from the ghost of Kubrick as fashioned by Hollywood's most powerful and most commercially successful director, but an engaging, ambitious spiral into the future, one well worth watching, one that will linger in the mind awhile.

See this to encourage Spielberg to emphasize creativity over formula, to encourage him to make more movies that dare to offend the mass mind while intriguing the rest of us.

I've seen this and I give it___stars.
I want to see it___. I'll pass___.
The review was worth reading___. Not___.

Bad Day at Black Rock (1954) 8

Fine faux western with a "film noir" touch

Spencer Tracy rides into town on the Southern Pacific. The engine is diesel. He's carrying a suitcase and wearing a black fedora. The town is smack in the middle of the Mojave Desert, just a handful of wooden buildings, like the back lot at Paramount during the days when they made a lot of cowboy movies.

This is, and is not, a cowboy movie. It's the late forties, just after World War II. Tracy has the left sleeve of his suit coat tucked into the pocket. He lost an arm somewhere. He's slow to anger. He has a mission. What it is, is mysterious. In fact part of the effectiveness of this unusual movie is in how mysterious everything is. Why this godforsaken town? Why are the people so uptight about his arrival? Who is he and what does he want?

Robert Ryan plays the villain, the leader of the gang, so to speak. Lee Marvin plays a tough gunslinger. Ernest Borgnine plays a bully who gets the tar kicked out of him in a barroom fight—well, the place is like a saloon, only there's a soda fountain/café counter and no swinging doors.

There's a one-cell jail in which the alcoholic sheriff can be found sleeping it off. There a telegraph station at the train station where telegrams might or might not be sent. Walter Brennan co-stars as the obligatory town "Doc" a washed-up man ashamed of himself. So much like an old-style western is this slightly "noir" film from 1954 that at some point I actually expected to see Gabby Hayes come running up to gum a line or two. There's a gal (Anne Francis) looking as neat and cute as Dale Evans in her prime, but she doesn't amount to much. This is a guy kind of flick, a faux western in which manhood is tested, in which men find out what they're made of, in which the good guys win and the old movieland code is rigorously upheld.

Some of the scenes were probably shot out in Simi Valley where they used to shoot the old Tom Mix and Johnny Mack Brown westerns with large granite boulders adorning dirt trails. You can almost hear the horses gallop and see the chips fly off the boulders as the bullets sing out. Instead of horses however there are Ford coupes and a Jeep. The gunfight scene at night has Robert Ryan rifling down at Tracy using the headlights of his car to see, while Tracy is without firearms, but of course not without resources.

The plot concerns a certain Japanese man who had a homestead farm out among the boulders who ended up missing after his farm was burned to the ground. Seems that Robert Ryan's character doesn't like the Nipponese and is still fighting the war in his mind. Somehow even before it is revealed we know how Tracy lost his arm, but we don't exactly know why he's here. I won't reveal that for those who haven't seen this, but you might guess. He served in the infantry in Italy. Robert Ryan for mysterious reasons was not allowed to enlist—he says.

Aside from the nicely developed and held tension and the beautiful score by Andre Previn, the effectiveness of this movie lies in the interesting performances by the talented cast. One of the first Cinemascope movies, *Bad Day at Black Rock* (great title!) is also wondrously filmed so that the empty feel of the desert and loneliness of the isolated town surrounded by stark mountains and a high blue sky will stay with you long after you see the old style "The End" as the film fades to black for the last time.

See this for Spencer Tracy (a little past his prime), one of Hollywood's greatest who had a long and distinguished career.

I've seen this and I give it___stars.
I want to see it___. I'll pass___.
The review was worth reading___. Not___.

Barton Fink (1991) 8

A writer's life under the studio system, 1941

This won some international awards and was nominated for Oscars for Art/Set Decoration, Costume Design, and Best Supporting Actor (Michael Lerner), all nominations well-deserved. It is a fine period piece movie, a little slow in spots, but original and ultimately engaging.

Barton Fink, played with fidelity and deep concentration by John Turturro, is an idealistic New York playwright experiencing his first success. He is called to Hollywood to write screenplays under the old studio system. Lerner, in a burlesque performance that is strikingly and hilariously over the top (you've got to love the shot of him in open robe and bathing trunks by the pool, his ample, hairy belly vividly displayed, perhaps as a symbol of a devouring cauldron), plays the movie mogul who instructs Fink to write the script for a "B" wrestling picture starring Wallace Beery. This is a kind of Coen and Coen joke, part of the satirical intent of the movie since what Wallace Beery did star in were boxing pictures. Same difference, one might say. (Actually, Beery did star in at least one wrestling movie, *Flesh* (1932), I discovered by checking at IMDb.com.)

Anyway, Fink of course knows nothing about wrestling, and finding himself in an old Los Angeles hotel (where one may stay a day, or ominously, a lifetime), begins to unravel since he can't get beyond the first couple of lines of the screenplay. We are treated to close ups of all that white space on the paper as it sits rolled up in the old manual typewriter. The satirical idea here is to measure the great gulf between literary art and writing film scripts for a mass audience, an audience further dumbed down by the expectations of studio execs.

Next door to Fink is Charlie Meadows (John Goodman) ostensibly a life insurance salesman. Goodman works hard to portray a monstrous (in more ways than one) sort of guy. He huffs and puffs his way into friendship with Fink, showing him a wrestling move or two. At this point it is impossible to tell where the movie is headed. Are they going to become more than friends? Enter Judy Davis as Audrey Taylor the "secretary" of an alcoholic novelist working in the "Writer's Building" at the studio (reminding me of a similar set from Billy Wilder's *Sunset Boulevard*). Fink gets an undisguised yen for her and manages to get her to help him with his script. And then comes a characteristic Coen and Coen twist, and all heck breaks loose.

Memorable in a small role as the desk clerk and bellhop is Steve Buscemi who is first revealed to us coming enigmatically out of the hotel's cellar where God only knows what he was doing.

They loved this at Cannes because just about every aspect of the Hollywood industry is made fun of, except the actors, who interestingly enough, make nary an appearance. Clever those Coen brothers.

This is a dark, nasty but somewhat redemptive writer's movie, an art film about Hollywood that aficionados will not want to miss.

I've seen this and I give it___stars.
I want to see it___. I'll pass___.
The review was worth reading___. Not___.

Beat the Devil (1953) 7

Quirky, campy, cultish, and somewhat flawed

This is a quirky kind of movie with an excellent cast who are not necessarily at their best, with a screenplay by a famed novelist, Truman Capote, directed by a Hollywood legend, John Huston, also perhaps not at their best. Adapted from the novel by James Helvick, *Beat the Devil* is morphed into something of a self-conscious comedic spoof by Huston of his classic *The Maltese Falcon* (1941). Here we have Robert Morley instead of Sidney Greenstreet as the greedy ring leader and Ivor Barnard as the bodyguard with a knife instead of Elisha Cook Jr. the bodyguard with a gun. There is no Mary Astor, but Gina Lollibrigida, the Italian brunette bombshell and a blonde Jennifer Jones appear as the female leads. Humphrey Bogart again is the star. Peter Lorre returns as a German named O'Hara (part of a running joke about Argentina where so many ex-Nazis became "Irish" settlers after World War II). But Bogey is now 55-years-old, "a middle-aged roustabout"—to quote (twice) from the script, apparently a good-natured Capote dig at the legendary actor—whose tar-stained teeth do so detract from his leading man role. (Gina, his on-screen wife, was 26.) And Peter Lorre has gone from a bug-eyed skinny little perfumed dandy to a fully rounded, tired, middle aged man. Alas, how cruel the camera!

Nonetheless, this is interesting and diverting, full of double entendres and clever put-downs of all sorts, including jabs at marriage, English puffery and neo-Nazis. I understand the movie has overcome the disappointment of its original audience and has become something of a cult classic. I think those fifties matinee viewers probably missed most of the comedy and were offended by the easy adultery of the principals and the improper use of Humphrey Bogart. A year later he was wonderfully cast as Captain Queeg in *The Caine Mutiny*, where he gave one of his greatest performances.

This is the kind of movie that Old Hollywood likes to watch nostalgically while satirically dissecting the performances, the script, etc., while nonetheless finding nuggets of humor, both intentional and inadvertent. It is, for example, possible to find some hidden meaning in the fact that the rogues, once aboard ship, break out into a lusty rendition of the anonymous chantey, "Blow the Man Down." And it is possible to observe that during the scene in which Jennifer Jones easily beats her husband at chess with her back mostly to the board (afterwards she quips, "Harry's been all out of sorts today. Usually he is a wonderful loser."), that what Bogart really wanted to do was get the scene over with and get back to his cigarettes and the chess games he so loved to play on location. One might also observe that had Peter Lorre been a little younger, and had they made a life of Truman Capote, the former could have played the latter with consummate ease.

Speaking of location, this was filmed in Italy in black and white, clearly on a budget, and as such might be seen as a spaghetti comedy.

I've seen this and I give it___stars.
I want to see it___. I'll pass___.
The review was worth reading___. Not___.

Being John Malkovich (1999) 8

One of a kind

This is a strikingly original film that is part science fiction, part love triangle romance, and part comedy with an undercurrent of psychological insight into human relationships, marred slightly by some familiar elements in the resolution. Charlie Kaufman, who wrote the script, and Spike Jonze who directed, are to be commended for being so daring and free with the usual notions of reality while callously demonstrating just how selfish human relationships can be. To analyze this film is very much beside the point, but I'm going to do a little bit of that anyway.

John Cusack stars as an out of work puppeteer with a cheating heart. Cameron Diaz is his hard-working mousey little wife who supports him and a menagerie of animals including a chimpanzee ensconced in their New York apartment. An early scene shows her going off to work while Cusack rolls over and goes back to sleep. Catherine Keener enters the scene with her big smile and long legs as a supremely confident amoral user of people and quickly becomes the focus of the triangle as both Cusack and Diaz fall madly in love with her. She, however, is not so enamored. She is not attracted to Cusack at all and tells him so, and finds Diaz interesting but only after seeing her adoring eyes inside the eyes of John Malkovich, who plays himself.

Offbeat enough? Not yet. Cusack has met Keener through his new job as a fast-fingered file clerk at a data storage firm with offices on the seventh and a half floor in a New York high rise. The floor is just about four and a half feet high (low overhead!) so that everybody has to bend over whenever they stand up. Orson Bean plays the head of the firm who is 110 years old or so with Mary Kay Place as his annoying secretary. While filing Cusack drops a folder behind a filing cabinet. He pulls out the cabinet and lo and behold discovers a little Alice in Wonderland door. He opens it and crawls forward in the dark and swoosh! is drawn into the person of actor John Malkovich, who is going about his daily life. Cusack looks out and sees what John is seeing, hears what John is hearing, experiences what John is experiencing. He is BEING John Malkovich!

Okay, we have our strikingly original premise. Where the film goes from here is the tough part. It includes some funny shtick and some intriguing ideas about identity, a prospect for immortality, Malkovich being turned into a puppet, some unusual sex games, a couple of appearances by Charlie Sheen as his contemporary self and later as a balding middle aged man, ending with the resolution of the triangle and a hint of a possible sequel. I was entertained mainly because of the strong performances by Keener, Cusack, Malkovich and Diaz. I was somewhat disappointed that the last part of the film did not live up to the beginning in terms of originality. The old people waiting for rebirth reminded me of something out of *Cocoons* (1985). But Cusack's prospective life as a little girl was a chuckle to contemplate, and I couldn't help but applaud Keener's sly triumph. But enough of these beguiling hints about what happens. See it for yourself.

I've seen this and I give it___stars.
I want to see it___. I'll pass___.
The review was worth reading___. Not___.

The Belly of an Architect (1987) 8

Longing for his flat belly days?

Perhaps it is a mid-life crisis and a fear of death that simultaneously hits Chicago architect Stourley Kracklite (Brian Dennehy). He has traveled to Rome to present an elaborate tribute to the French architect Louis Boullee. Kracklite is fifty-four years old, uncertain that he has fulfilled the promise of his youth. He is married to a woman (Chloe Webb) young enough to be his daughter. So when he begins to develop stomach pains (perhaps due to a growing stomach tumor) while working in Rome and gets no satisfaction from doctors, he begins to believe his wife is poisoning him. Furthermore it appears that she is having an affair with an Italian architect named Caspasian (Lambert Wilson) who also desires to take over Kracklite's Boullee project. I think a lot of men in their fifties can identify with these sorts of threats to their well-being and perhaps be unable to tell the real from the unreal.

So the human belly is a big deal in this film. At one point Kracklite prints out scores of photocopies of the belly of a Roman statue as if in scrutinizing mass copies of a flat belly he might somehow explain why he is in pain. Or perhaps the flat belly symbolizes his lost youth and the insecure feeling he has about the affection and faithfulness of Louisa, his young wife. Maybe it is even the case that the belly is a euphemistic symbol of something else that is no longer as vital as it once was. When men in their fifties worry about such things they also worry about their ability not just to cut the mustard but the quality of their work. In short, they worry about being superseded. One cannot help but feel in this case that Kracklite's growing paranoia is in part responsible for his declining power. Fear of something may give it strength.

As for the way cinematic *auteur* Peter Greenaway directs this film, I think his intent is to let the film reflect the subject matter in the sense that both are of artistic intent rather than the movie being a commercial enterprise. (That is perhaps an understatement.) He shows the beauty of the architectural ruins of Rome. He thinks in terms of tableaux in wide shots. He picks a backdrop and sets the camera at some distance from the backdrop: Italian ruins, a spacious lobby, expansive steps in front of an impressive building. And then he plays the scene. Unlike most modern directors he mostly eschews close-ups. I'd rather he didn't. The effect is like being in a theater watching a play. There is a certain appropriateness I suppose about this technique since it creates in the viewer a feeling of spying, which is exactly what Kracklite finds himself doing in one scene, looking through a keyhole to see what his wife and Capasian are doing; and Greenaway has us see too, at the same distance.

In another sense, there is a studied feel to this movie that suggests something a bit cold like marble which again is appropriate. Yet Brian Dennehy, in an intense, engaging performance, makes us feel for him and his predicament. We understand that he is realizing his mortality and we appreciate that his reaction is understandably confused and frightened. As for his wife, she seems distant not only because of the camera work but

perhaps because she is psychologically estranged from her husband and from what he is going through.

I've seen this and I give it___stars.
I want to see it___. I'll pass___.
The review was worth reading___. Not___.

The Border (1982) 8

Underrated and overlooked, but definitely worthwhile

Although this is not a great film it is a lot better than its reputation. Jack Nicholson is excellent and Harvey Keitel is very good. The beautiful and beguiling Mexican actress, Elpidia Carrillo, handles a limited role with enough artistry to make me wonder why I never heard of her before. Turns out she does have a healthy list of credits both internationally and in the US.

The direction by Tony Richardson, who had his heyday in the sixties with films as varied as *The Loneliness of the Long Distance Runner* (1962), *Tom Jones* (1963), and *The Loved One* (1965), all adapted from novels, is at times inspired and artistic, and at other times as ordinary as dishwater. I don't think he was able to make up his mind while directing this film about whether he wanted win an award at Cannes or Venice or to just sell some tickets. As it turns out he did neither as well as he might have. Nonetheless as a snapshot of poor Mexican immigrants (and would-be immigrants) as they clash with the border patrol culture some thirty years ago *The Border* is definitely worth a look. Particularly vivid is the depiction of the absurdities and hypocrisies among the coyotes, the "wets," the border patrol rank-and-file, the law and the realities of life along both sides of the thin strip separating the promised land from the third world.

Nicholson plays Charlie Smith, a border patrol cop with a trailer trash wife (Valerie Perrine) who yearns to move up to the luxury of duplex living. In particular she wants to move in next door to her high school girlfriend Savannah (Shannon Wilcox) who is married to the "Cat" (Harvey Keitel). Charlie Smith is a bit of an innocent who was satisfied with his trailer home and his sexy, loving, but not overly sharp, wife Mary. When they do pick up and move to Texas he runs headlong into the corrupt lifestyle of the Cat and the cruel realities of his job which consists of arresting illegal immigrants and sending them back to Mexico. Meanwhile Mary isn't just sitting home twiddling her thumbs. Instead she is out buying water beds and dinette sets, overstuffed chairs and sofas, and other knickknacks that put a strain on the couple's budget which leads Charlie into temptation. But when taking kickbacks turns to murder, Charlie draws the line in the sand (literally as it happens) and he and the Cat have a rather rude falling out. Meanwhile Charles spots Carrillo as the lovely Maria with babe in arms and a little brother at her side. Predictably the system cruelly exploits her, bringing Charlie to her rescue.

I think the striking contrast between Charlie's air-headed Mary and the desperate and needy Maria needed to be further explored. As it was played Charlie is just a good joe doing a good deed or two when in fact we know he is much more involved than that. I think the movie would have been improved by making him choose between the two women as he had to make the moral choice between going with the Cat's corruption or going against him.

See this for Jack Nicholson, one of the great actors of our time, who brings subtlety and veracity to a role that could have been ordinary, while giving us only a hint of the commanding and irreverent style that he would adopt in later years.

I've seen this and I give it___stars.
I want to see it___. I'll pass___.
The review was worth reading___. Not___.

Cast Away (2000) 8

Engrossing story with good psychological depth

The theme of the cast away goes back long before *Robinson Crusoe* by Daniel Defoe (1660-1731) or *The Swiss Family Robinson* by Johann Wyss (1781-1830); indeed it probably goes back to a time when people first set out on the open sea in boats. It is a wonderfully romantic genre, employing the classic "man versus nature" theme while allowing us to indulge in the fantasy of escape from the confines and restrictions of civilization.

Here we have Tom Hanks as Chuck Nolan, a Fed Ex executive whose plane ditches into the South Pacific. He washes up on a tiny, deserted island as the sole survivor of the plane crash. His four-year stay on the island forms the bulk of the movie, but perhaps the most engaging part for most movie-goers is what happens afterwards.

Tom Hanks was excellent throughout, as usual, and the direction by Robert Zemeckis from a script by William Broyles Jr. was compelling. Especially good was the irony about what happens to Chuck's beloved (Helen Hunt) while he is gone. This has been done before (but I forget where), and is the kind of heart-wrenching development that could have been pure saccharin but instead came across as thought-provoking, veracious and very affecting.

Zemeckis also directed the excellent film, *Contact* (1997), made from the novel by Carl Sagan. We can see here (and there) that Zemeckis's work owes a lot to the influence of Steven Spielberg in both a positive and a negative sense. Zemeckis, like Spielberg, can be cloying at times in his effort to secure the audience's identification. We can see this in the beginning with Chuck cutely trying to sell efficiency to the Russians with the help of a little boy. But splendid was the plane crash sequence,

the kind of thing Spielberg would want to be intensely vivid, and it was. And later the startling sight of the huge cargo ship, like a sea-going skyscraper, recalled to mind the first shot of the spaceship from Spielberg's *Close Encounters of the Third Kind* (1977). The Fed Ex packages flying out all over the world engendering a kind of corporate "we're all one world" feeling like something from a Coca-Cola commercial was pure Spielberg.

But what I like to do when I look at a movie like this is to lean forward and scrutinize it for authenticity. Did the cast away lose weight? Yes, as a matter of fact, Tom Hanks must have dropped about ten pounds, or perhaps he fattened up for the first part of the film (or was that body cosmetology?) and then fasted for the scenes showing him four years later. But did he lose enough weight? For those who have been watching TV's "Survivor," we know he didn't. And was he tan enough? His hair was little lighter after his ordeal, but he really needed to be baked a dark brown, which he wasn't.

I also look at how he ate. What was his source of vitamin C? Do coconuts contain Vitamin C? I don't know. But showing him eating seaweed, which does contain vitamin C, would have worked. Using the coconuts to hold water was a nice touch. Learning to spear fish with a wooden spear is plausible, but spearing a fish with a wooden spear in the open ocean is unlikely. Notice there were no birds or bird eggs or bird guano on the island. An uninhabited island in the middle of the ocean is always a nesting place for birds.

This last observation reveals that the setting was not in fact a tiny island but part of a larger body of land. Notice there was no clear, encircling shot of the island (as from the air). In fact we never see the other side of the island.

It was interesting to see how he got the fire going (again "Survivor" fans—and boy scouts—know how hard that is to do), but I was thinking that maybe he could have used the glass on the watch face or from the flashlight as a way to concentrate sunlight to make a fire.

I also watched to see whether he did what I would have done. Of course what I would have done doesn't mean that much, but I would not have left the island for the open ocean (which seemed almost suicidal), unless there was out there on that ocean a ship's corridor, so to speak, which is possible. Of course, who can say what a man might do after being four years entirely alone on a tiny island? I also would not have tried to cure my toothache, regardless of how bad it hurt, by breaking the tooth off with the ice skates. After all, that might make things worse. Trying to *pull* the tooth would have been my strategy—but how?

I liked the irony of finding the ice skates in a washed up Fed Ex package, and then Chuck's use of the blades as mirror and knife. I know why he didn't take the dead man's clothes, but I think he should have plugged his

328

nose and peeled them off anyway. The washed up metal "sail" was a nice inspiration, and there were many others: the "discovery" of tool-making by striking the volcanic rock at the right angle; burning the base of the trees to make wood for the raft; the petroglyphs he made in the cave; sleeping on the floor in the hotel room, etc.

Best no comment scene: Chuck looking at the Alaskan king crab legs at the buffet.

I've seen this and I give it___stars.
I want to see it___. I'll pass___.
The review was worth reading___. Not___.

Charade (1963) 7

A bit of a farce, but enjoyable

This is a distinctly Stanley Donen film (some others: *Singin' in the Rain* 1952, *Seven Brides for Seven Brothers* 1954, *Funny Face* 1957, *Damn Yankees* 1958, *Indiscreet* 1958) characterized by light comedy prepared expressly for the middle American palate a little past mid-century, professionally done with offense to no one. There is just the barest hint of satire with a few laugh-at-the-genre jokes but nothing so blatant as to detract from the woman's fantasy, wish-fulfillment that is the essential point.

One of the jokes in the film is that Audrey Hepburn always kisses Cary Grant first. This is entirely appropriate, I suppose, considering that he was at the time 59-years-old and she was 34. Both were (and are) two of Hollywood's enduring stars, Miss Hepburn perhaps at or near the pinnacle of her career when this movie was made, and Cary Grant in his last significant role. The chemistry is nice, creative and there are some funny lines. She chases him and he catches her, is the way it is played, when of course it is usually the other way around: HE chases her and SHE catches him!

The stars are given fine support from Walter Matthau, James Colburn, George Kennedy and Ned Glass in quasi-comedic roles as a quartet of sinister bad guys. The music (and the memorable "Charade" theme) are by Henry Mancini whose musical scores adorned nearly a hundred Hollywood movies beginning in the fifties. I particularly remember his music from the Pink Panther flicks in the sixties and seventies.

Director Stanley Donen, despite being a paragon of commercial success, has a quality of making sardonic fun of the audience or of his stars in a way that is barely discernable. I think it's the cynicism of the Hollywood product that he became so adept at making, and his subconscious realization of what he was doing, that sometimes seeps through. Here he begins with "Boy Meets Girl, Cute" in the Alps with Hepburn in a costume reminiscent of something out of the middle ages, covering almost as much of her as a burka, her beautiful eyes masked by big dark glasses. It's a joke and perhaps a

setup for contrast. When Audrey Hepburn smiles and her eyes light up in delight, she is most arresting. Imagine the whole film without seeing her eyes. (In *Blame It on Rio* 1984, Donen deliberately had Michael Caine in those hideous square plastic frames big enough for Mrs.Doubtfire.) And what I mean by Donen's attitude toward his audience, that he believes they only want familiar escapism, is the touristy feel of the Parisian scenes in which most of the action takes place. They are mostly spots frequented by American tourists seeing Europe for the first time, the Seine, the Metro, the Arc d'Triumph, Notre Dame cathedral, the Louis XVI apartment sans furnishing, the Paris opera house, etc. The fact that we can't be sure who-done-it until the very end when it becomes obvious by the process of elimination, didn't sit well with me. I also did not like the chase scenes in the Metro because it seemed abundantly silly to imagine that Hepburn in her long skirt and dress shoes could outrun Cary Grant, who had, in a previous scene, engaged in fisticuffs a bigger man (Kennedy with a steel claw for one of his hands).

Nonetheless, Cary Grant and Audrey Hepburn together for the first (and only) time is a treat not to be missed. Cary Grant is particularly good as he maintains a wry stoicism against the power of Miss Hepburn's charms. Noteworthy is the excellent camera work exemplified in the two shots of Hepburn's face caught in light and shadow in the Paris opera house.

For those of you thinking of seeing Jonathan Demme's remake of this film, *The Truth About Charlie* (2002), I would caution against it since the unreality of the story borders on the ridiculous and must be played as comedy. Without the star power and some of the clever dialogue of Donen's film I am afraid the plot contrivances would be embarrassingly exposed, although the idea of getting a quarter of a million dollars past customs in the form of very expensive (hint: small) art objects that appear to be ordinary objects, is a nice device that would probably work.

See this for Cary Grant whose rugged good looks and smooth and effortless delivery made him a Hollywood legend and the epitome of a suave leading man.

I've seen this and I give it___stars.
I want to see it___. I'll pass___.
The review was worth reading___. Not___.

Charlie Wilson's War (2007) 8

How an east Texas congressman made Afghanistan safe for the Taliban

Director Mike Nichols is a past master of women's point of view films that go beyond the narrow confines of the "chick flick." *Silkwood* (1983); *Heartburn* (1986); *Working Girl* (1988); and the very fine *Postcards from the Edge* (1990) come to mind. His first feature was an adaptation of Edward Albee's play *Who's Afraid of Virginia Woolf* with Richard Burton and Elizabeth Taylor back in 1966. He followed the next year with the generation-defining *The Graduate* with Dustin Hoffman. His films feature fine satire played along the cutting edge of the popular culture.

Here he deviates slightly to celebrate Texas congressman Charlie Wilson who managed to persuade Congress to support the Northern Alliance in Afghanistan against the Soviet Union in the 1980s. In particular Wilson was able to get American shoulder-launched Stinger missiles for the locals to shoot down Soviet aircraft. In the film we see some nice graphics of just how effective those missiles were. It is no exaggeration to say that Charlie Wilson's intervention turned the tide against the Soviets and eventually persuaded them to withdraw. A few years later, as we all know, the Soviet Union came to its sputtering end.

Nichols's "celebration" of Congressman Wilson is however mitigated by the revelation that Good Time Charlie was no angel. Tom Hanks plays the alcoholic and cocaine snorting congressman with a genial—almost innocent—duplicity that only hints at the Machiavellian personality required to properly grace the hallowed halls of Congress. Hanks is just too sweet, a nice guy playing at being a practiced power broker. What is missing is the edge of obsession and single-minded egoism. Perhaps we needed John Malkovich with an east Texas twang.

Julia Roberts plays Wilson's long-time girlfriend whose interest in defeating the godless communists stems not from any sympathy for the out-gunned Afghans but from religious sensibilities of the sort usually associated with evangelical members of the Daughters of the American Revolution. I found her white wig and high-toned manner a step in the wrong direction for Miss Roberts. I fear that the transition she is making from starlet to star to character actor is an embarrassment that she might want to avoid.

The real star of this film is Phillip Seymour Hoffman who plays the international operative and sometime American spy, Gust Avrakotos, a sneaky, blunt and very smart guy who also wants to defeat the Soviets. Hoffman brings to the part the kind of rough edge and frankly Machiavellian intent missing in Tom Hanks' character.

The film is marred slightly by a depiction of people in power and their environs that conforms to something like television's mass culture with lots of sleeping around and sharp-edged wise-cracking on the spot, and a somewhat simplistic story line. None of this is to be helped since a living must be made and producers must be assured that the mass audience will attend. Mike Nichols is used to this, and it is remarkable how many fine films he has made that simultaneously seduced not only the money men and the audience, but the critics as well.

The message of the film is contained in a Zen master story that goes like this (I am paraphrasing from the quotations page at the Internet Movie Database site):

There's a little boy who on his 14th birthday gets a horse, and everybody in the village says, "How wonderful. The boy got a horse." And the Zen master says, "we'll see." Two years later the boy falls off the horse, breaks his leg, and everyone in the village says, "how terrible." And the Zen master says, "we'll see." Then, a war breaks out and all the young men have to go off and fight except the boy who can't because his legs are all messed up. And everybody in the village says, "How wonderful." And again the Zen master says, "we'll see."

This captures the spirit of our continuing military involvement in the Middle East. Today's results may look good or bad but can only be really defined by the unintended consequences to come. We armed the Afghans. Unfortunately their triumph against the Soviet Union led to the rise of the Taliban, and that to their harboring of Al Qaeda which led to 9/11, which led to... and so on. How Charlie Wilson's War ultimately ends may not be known for generations.

See this for Mike Nichols whose clear direction and sharp eye for satire is undiminished as he approaches his ninth decade of life. (He was 76 when this film came out.)

I've seen this and I give it___stars.
I want to see it___. I'll pass___.
The review was worth reading___. Not___.

Children of Men (2006) 7

Mostly a routine action film set in a childless future

Science fiction is always about the present. This has been true since the beginning of science fiction. It has to be true since we can only extrapolate from the present to the future. Only rarely, once in a million tries perhaps, does somebody come up with something truly original, or something unpredictable. Leonard Da Vinci foresaw submarines, but if you think about it, he had the example of turtles, whales and dolphins. Who foresaw nuclear energy? Who foresaw electricity and all that it can do?

So this is about the present. The refugee camp could be in Palestine. The roundup of immigrants is what many people in Europe and the US want. It may happen tomorrow; in fact it is happening to some extent. The irony and perhaps the illogic of this film is that with no babies being born, now for eighteen years, there is no labor force coming on to do the grunt work of society. So why are the Brits in a frenzy of anti-immigration? Apparently because a fascist government has come to power.

The way this is done reminds me a bit of something from Terry Gilliam who directed *12 Monkeys* (1995) and *Brazil* (1985). There is something about the decadent and bombed-out feel of the scenes that is the same.

This is a film for the underdog, for the oppressed. It is in a symbolic sense a statement about aging Europe with its declining birth rates needing the fertility of people from southern climes, people of color to save the world from extinction. In Europe today there are countries with birth rates so low that their populations are declining. In both Europe and the US it is immigrants who are supporting the declining populations which are increasingly old. In the US we have winked at the influx of illegal immigrants for decades because those in power know two things: (1) cheap labor is good for their bottom line; and (2) without young people paying into social security, the system will go bankrupt.

The sets were exquisite, the battle scenes in the refugee camp seemed as authentic as the nightly news, well focused and involving. The camera work was outstanding and carefully set up. Michael Caine as the aging hippy was perfect. I saw him recently in *The Prestige* (2006) and I have to say, he is like a man with a new career in his mid-seventies. Claire-Hope Ashitey, who played Kee with her big eyes and her fresh face and her reserved style was also very good. Clive Owen looked as heroic as the part demanded, and Julianne Moore in a limited role was good.

There was some corniness in the movie and some politically correct stuff, like Kee braiding the old woman's hair and our hero being sensitive enough to be a midwife (today's men are above and beyond the purely macho). There is also a root for the underdog feel throughout with the good guys (relatively speaking) being outsiders. The scene where the government troops stand in awe of a baby's cry was striking (imagine how Spielberg would have milked this!), but I suspect that somebody, at hearing of the first human birth in over eighteen years, would have ignored the resumption of fire and stayed with the only woman on earth who was fertile. I think everyone would have wanted to protect her and her baby.

A nice touch that director Alfonso Cuaron could have brought to the film was to show us people doing extreme things in their desperation to have children, worshipping icons of fertility maybe, acting out weird rituals while imbibing strange concoctions. Instead of just showing some religious demonstrators blaming the lack of human fertility on sinfulness, we might have gotten a glimpse of fertility cults drinking the essence of goat eggs or rhino horns as they danced around some fertility symbol. Maybe there could have been a national health crisis as myriads of people, especially women, went crazy or committed suicide because of depression brought on by infertility. Actually there was a hint of this in the movie but it was greatly underdeveloped.

Another problem with this film (from my POV; for others this might be a plus) is that the direction relies heavily on action sequences. There are chase scenes (and a nice car door opening gimmick used twice, once to knock the bad guys off their motorcycles, and once to knock down one of the fishes holding a gun). But there was little subtlety in the story. Most of the subtlety in the movie is in the scenes themselves and in the camera work. And the characters are rather one-dimensional. Theo (Clive Owen) is merely heroic. He fights through the bullets and the other obstacles to help Kee and her baby. Kee herself is hardly developed at all. Michael Caine's character Jasper is the only one with any real depth.

Two final points: I don't think this film is nearly as interesting as Cuaron's *Y tu mama tambien* (2001), and I would not dream of watching this film without subtitles since a lot of the dialogue is almost inaudible to these ancient ears.

By the way, a discussion of why women were infertile and how the movie differs from the book can be found at the IMDb.com.

I've seen this and I give it___stars.
I want to see it___. I'll pass___.
The review was worth reading___. Not___.

Chocolat (2000) 8

Chocolate reforms the church!

This is an American movie directed by Swedish born director Lasse Hallstrom (*The Cider House Rules*, 1999; *Something to Talk About*, 1995), set in France with a distinct French flavor. The cast, headed by the very talented Juliette Binoche as Vianne Rocher, a wandering proprietress of chocolate, is highly accomplished and very much worth watching. Judi Dench has a substantial role as the cranky Armande, and Johnny Depp makes a belated appearance as Binoche's love interest, Roux, the River Rat. Alfred Molina plays the small town's semi-fascist Catholic mayor, Comte Paul de Reynaud. With his slicked-back, straight black hair and the precise black mustache and his imposing countenance, one is somehow reminded of Count Dracula. Leslie Caron (*An American in Paris*, 1951; *The L-Shaped Room*, 1963), now in her seventies, has a small part as the widow Madame Audel. Carrie Anne-Moss of Matrix fame (but I recall her most memorably in *Memento*, 2000) plays Armande's straitlaced and estranged daughter. Noteworthy is the captivating Victoire Thivisol as Anouk Rocher, Vianne's nine-year-old daughter. Thivisol won the best actress award at the Venice Film Festival in 1996 for her work as a four-year-old (!) in *Ponette* (1996). She is surely the youngest actor ever to win such an award.

Chocolat is also a kind of modern Dionysian morality tale in reverse with the Catholic Church and small town

331

narrow-mindedness as the bad guys. It gets more than a bit sappy at times, and the unrelenting celebration of outsiders and non-conformists is wearisome and sorely tried my patience throughout. However, just as is the case with chocolate with its uplifting qualities amidst the lure to overindulgence, the good surely outweighs the bad. Hallstrom is an ambitious director who is comfortable playing to an adult feminist audience. He attempts the complex and the unlikely. Here, there is more than the usual Hollywood seduction of the intended audience. There is underneath the surface a strong symbolic presence, giving the story a kind of resonating, fairy tale existence.

Chocolate of course serves as the Dionysian wine, but it is also a semi-addictive substance from a tropical American plant, the cacao, rich in sumptuous oils and theobromine, a heart and general nervous system stimulant similar to caffeine. Cocoa was the first stimulant drink to break the unrelenting hold of beer and wine on the European palate. It was quickly followed by coffee and tea. Prior to the rise of these cerebral drinks, it was commonplace for Europeans to drink beer for breakfast, and indeed to drink beer and wine throughout the day. Many believe that caffeine was a handmaiden of the Renaissance, which of course led to the eventual weakening of the hold of the Roman Catholic Church. Vianne, who is the daughter of a Central American mother and a European father, represents the shamanism of the New World, leading the populace away from the narrow confines of the medieval mentality with her irresistible confections made with the seed of *Theoboma cacao*.

The problem with the movie, and the reason it did not achieve a more wide-spread acclaim, lay not only with its cloyingly unbalanced feminist viewpoint and its anti-Catholicism, but with the difficulty Binoche (and Hallstrom) had with her complex role. Her character is a woman who wants desperately to find a place in society and to be accepted by the petite bourgeoisie while maintaining her personal sense of value (and her red shoes!). She is, in a sense, a gypsy fortune teller (recall the spinning plates) who longs to be a pillar of the community. She is worldly wise, kind and forgiving, but partly a shopkeeper with a shopkeeper's need to set down roots. She is also a Mayan princess born to wander with the sly wind that ushers her about. So, underneath all else, this is a story about finding a home. Because Vianne is frequently attacked for her lifestyle while being the sort of person who does not return insult with insult, Binoche is reduced in many scenes to a kind of tolerant, slightly superior, patient smile that becomes wearying. It is only when Johnny Depp appears that we see the real Juliette Binoche and a true indication of her ability. Incidentally Depp is excellent as a gypsy musician who understands himself and his place as a counter balance to a conservative society. He is an inspiration to Vianne because he alone is not transparent to her; she only discovers his "favorite" chocolate by happenstance after two wrong guesses. Depp also serves to save this film

from the near monotony of inadequate males and dissatisfied females. When he appears I can almost hear the audience sigh.

Incidentally, you might want to compare this to *Babette's Feast* (1987) in which the narrow-minded and in need of liberation are northern Protestants, while the woman with the tempting goodies is an exiled Catholic chef from France. If Hallstrom had taken a clue from Gabriel Axel, who directed *Babette's Feast*, and followed a more objective and balanced treatment, *Chocolat* might have been a great movie. As it is, it is a very interesting one, and one you're not likely to forget or to feel neutral about.

I've seen this and I give it___stars.
I want to see it___. I'll pass___.
The review was worth reading___. Not___.

Clerks (1994) 8

Original, crude, and funny

This is an indie film (VideoHound gives a $27,575 budget) filmed in not so glorious black and white that is strikingly original, and I mean strikingly, and funny. Depicting the early twenties slacker set in suburban New Jersey a couple of decades ago, it focuses on convenience store clerk Dante Hicks (Brian O'Halloran), who is adrift in that never-never land between high school and Making Something of Himself. He still pines for his high school hottie Caitlin Bree (Lisa Spoonhauer), especially when he learns that his current girlfriend Veronica (Marilyn Ghigliotti) has had, shall we say, intimate rocket knowledge of thirty-seven different guys, although she had sex with only three of them, including him. Ah, well, what's a snowball or two between friends?

Next door to the convenience store is a video rental store clerked by Dante's best bud, Randal Graves (Jeff Anderson). Randal scares off the customers, rents his videos elsewhere and just generally slacks off and offends at all times, except when giving career and sexual advice to Dante. Hanging around outside and dealing are Jay (Jason Mewes) and Silent Bob (Kevin Smith). Kevin Smith also directed and wrote the script and probably did the catering and clean up as well. He is one very clever and talented dude who told it like it almost was while mildly satirizing the New Jersey denizens and the slacker mentality, but with affection and a kind of light-hearted aplomb.

There's some absurdity, Caitlin making love to a dead man and not realizing he's dead, the guys playing stick ball hockey on the roof of the convenience store, Randal selling cigs to a four-year-old who lights up, etc., mixed with the pathos of making minimum wage and going nowhere, and some sight gags and a whole lot of spiffy, crude dead-panned one-liners. Nothing is taken too seriously, including Kevin Smith and his film, so that when they run the final credits we are pleased with this slice of indeterminate life in the Garden State.

I was reminded of some other low budget films made about the same time including *Bang* (1995), *Floundering* (1994) and *The Unbelievable Truth* (1990), especially the latter, but none are as outrageously funny as *Clerks*. Incidentally, this actually made IMDb's Top 250.

I've seen this and I give it___stars.
I want to see it___. I'll pass___.
The review was worth reading___. Not___.

Closer (2004) 8

Quadrangles are more fun

Okay, let's get something straight right away. If you cheat on your partner, you do NOT tell. In fact, if you are asked about who you slept with in the past, you do not tell. Even in junior high school you learned, you do not kiss and tell.

Cheating is the big lie. This movie is about cheating and lying. People cheat. They get tempted. They want excitement. People are animals. But it is worse than adding insult to injury if you cheat and tell. Don't cheat. But if you do, don't tell.

This is a clever—although I wouldn't call it slick—film about how attractive people of a certain age and milieu are always hitting on and being hit upon. It is about the shallowness of love and the urgency of sex. It is about pretty people on the screen fulfilling fantasies. The dialogue is hip, sharp, although sometimes too cute and superficial.

It is stylish and ephemeral. It has the facade of realism. Note that none of the characters have children and none of them are trying to save the world. They are sexual and emotional hedonists, and maybe they are saying something about our times, in the big cities of the Western world at the dawn of the new millennium. On the other hand, they are urban professionals, skillfully navigating their way through the urban jungle toward a life of fulfillment and meaning... Well, maybe not.

But the emotions that the characters experience are very real. When you love someone and that someone sleeps with your rival, it is very painful. And when you love someone and you find that that someone doesn't love you, it is very painful. But the psychological pain that is visited upon us at such times is also ephemeral and will pass.

If you live on a farm in the middle of Nebraska, Jude Law is not going to kiss you and tempt you into cheating on your husband even if you are as pretty as Julia Roberts. If you really are a plain Jane without style or looks, Clive Owen is going to pass you by as you sit in the aquarium. He'll study the fish. So this is really about Hollywood itself (although set in London) and the usual musical beds. This is TV's "Friends" in the raw. This is Mike Nichols updating *Carnal Knowledge*, his very sixties-ish quadrangle film released in 1971 starring Jack Nicholson, Art Garfunkel, Ann-Margret and Candice Bergen. As in *Carnal Knowledge*—and, by the way, in Milan Kundera's novel *The Unbearable Lightness of Being* (made into a film starring Juliette Binoche)—there are four attractive, sexually active people who can't keep their hands off of one another. If you liked triangles, you randy geometricians, you'll really love quads, seems to be the thinking here.

Well, I did kind of like this film. What's not to like about Natalie Portman, Julia Roberts, Jude Law and Clive Owen? They are attractive and they are talented. The script from Patrick Marber adapting his play of the same name (with some very real influence from Milan Kundera's novel: note that in both cases there is a doctor and one of the women is in the sexual professions and the other is either a photographer or a painter) is witty and, yes, sexy. The direction by Mike Nichols (now in his seventies) is a little uneven and sometimes cryptic, especially as regards the ending and the beginning. (Never mind. I would like to discuss the ending, but, alas, that might spoil the film for somebody. As for the "Boy Meets Girl, Cute" beginning...well, it was VERY familiar.) But the film is crisply edited and there are no dead spots. You will be entertained, even if you later feel that you got seduced yourself and feel like you just ate a whole box of sugary bon-bons.

Irony: while Natalie Portman plays the lower-class stripper, in real life she is (or was) working toward a medical degree at Harvard.

And yes, Alice always lies and Larry always tells the truth...well, almost. Alice's character is very complex, but not entirely realized in the film. We are too much distracted by the sexcapades and the other personalities to see her as clearly as we might. Portman does a good job in a challenging role. There is something almost pathological about Alice that Portman conveys with modulated swings in mood and expression. Larry, the doc, is, as he tells us, the caveman, while Dan is the emotional pretty boy. And Anna...well, Anna is smart and has a deeper appreciation than the other characters of who she is and what she wants. And she does manage to get what she wants.

See this for Mike Nichols whose credits include *Who's Afraid of Virginia Woolf* (1966), *The Graduate* (1967), *Silkwood* (1983), *Postcards from the Edge* (1990), and a number of other very successful films. In *Closer*, he shows once again that he stills knows what interests the current generation.

I've seen this and I give it___stars.
I want to see it___. I'll pass___.

Collateral (2004) 8

Whiz-bang thriller with some substance

And some fine acting by Jamie Foxx and Tom Cruise.

This stylish, atmospheric thriller is yet another Hollywood ode to the hit man. I mean, what is with this subgenre? Consider these engaging hit man movies from the 90s:

2 Days in the Valley (1996) Danny Aiello as an over the hill hit man turned pizza baker.
Grosse Pointe Blank (1997) John Cusack as a cute whimsical amoral murder artist with Dan Aykroyd giving some comedic support in an over-the-top portrayal of a rival hit man always making with the jokes.
The Professional (1994) Jean Reno stars as Leon, a cold-blooded professional hit man sans people skills who doesn't know how to read (but has a heart).
La Femme Nikita (1990) Anne Parillaud plays a bitter, drug-dependent, unsocialized child of the streets who becomes a highly skilled hit woman.
Point of No Return (1993) starring Bridget Fonda, is a kind of Americanized *La Femme Nikita*.

And there are more I'm sure that I've missed. In fact Morgan Freeman and Chris Rock in *Nurse Betty* (2000) could be added to the list.

I think this sub-genre came about when film makers got desperate to do something besides "on the lam" movies and mafia glorifications. I also think this sub-genre has something in common with "the whore with the heart of gold" flick. It would appear that these days an actress doesn't really feel fulfilled and accomplished unless she has played a prostitute. Can it be that actors in general will feel unfulfilled until they have played a hit man/woman?

Surprisingly enough *Collateral* is also a buddy movie of sorts, or at least Tom Cruise's Vincent thinks he is making a friend, in as much as he is capable of making a friend. Jamie Foxx doesn't think so since he clearly divines that Vincent is one very sick psychopath.

But what makes this movie stand out, aside from Foxx and Cruise doing such a great job, is how stylish is the development, how worldly wise the dialogue, and how crisp the direction. The fact that Jamie Foxx could have and should have gotten away from Cruise half a dozen times is really the only flaw in the movie.

Another good film directed by Michael Mann is *The Insider* (1999) starring Al Pacino and Russell Crowe.

I've seen this and I give it___stars.
I want to see it___. I'll pass___.

Conspiracy Theory (1997) 7

A romantic comedy for the 90's

Forgive me, but I liked this movie. I was seduced, I guess, because objectively speaking this is just your usual phony thriller, with chase scenes beginning in the first reel and continuing throughout, with the little guy as hero, and a convoluted plot worthy of a wanna-be thriller writer retired from the CIA.

Mel Gibson plays a New York City cabby addicted to conspiracy theories, but (of course) it turns out that "just because you're paranoid doesn't mean they're not out to get you." And boy are they ever! I felt every second that this was a stretch for Gibson, yet I think he almost made it. I admire his ability and his supreme confidence that he can play anybody. (He didn't do a bad job as Hamlet.) But here I think he is just too handsome and balanced and just too, too normal looking to make us believe he is a paranoid stalker. I mean, how many women would be worried if Mel Gibson was stalking them? (Note: recent revelations about Gibson put my point in some serious doubt!) Still the plot, properly understood, allows for a normal man to end up in his situation since he was brainwashed and drugged.

Julia Roberts as a justice department lawyer is beautiful beyond any telling of it, and she does have a face for the silver screen like few others. Hollywood, as Norma Desmond told us, is about faces, and director Richard Donner had the very good sense to put the camera tight, very tight, on Julia Roberts' face as often as possible and keep it there. She is especially good at projecting a wide range of emotions, including love, without saying a word, and I would say that is what has made her the great star that she is. Her face is so sexy that the five-second scene where she hops out of bed in her loose-fitting pajamas was pure eroticism.

There are a number of clever bits in the movie, including our paranoid hero keeping his food locked in canisters in a locked refrigerator. I also liked the part where Roberts gains entrance by telling the hospital orderly that she is with the Treasury Department, and for ID hands him a hundred-dollar bill, allowing him to quip, "This IS from the Treasury Department." Good too was Gibson caught by a network hook-up to a price scanner at the book store compulsively buying a copy of J. D. Salinger's *Catcher in the Rye*. (Shades of a future—actually present—when, through the Web, our every purchase will be known to whoever cares.)

With Mel Gibson and Julia Roberts as the stars, the subplot has got to be romantic, and it is. In this sense the movie is as silly as Spencer Tracy and Katharine Hepburn ever got, and just as satisfying.

The Cooler (2003) 7

Be prepared to suspend disbelief

In the most important sense this is a "premise" movie, the premise being that Bernie Lootz (William H. Macy) is a magical personage who can bring bad luck to others just by his presence. In a premise movie, the suspension of disbelief that is required in all works of fiction (this movie is a fiction), is mandatory. Personally, I don't for a moment believe that anybody can influence the roll of the dice or the fall of the roulette wheel just by their presence or by buying somebody a drink, or even, as Bernie does at the blackjack table, by taking a hand himself and thereby making the house dealer lucky and the players and himself unlucky.

For this movie to work the premise must be accepted. If it isn't, the movie is semi-ridiculous. But this is not a full-blown fantasy like *The Wizard of Oz* or *Mary Poppins*. Aside from the premise, most of the rest of the movie is an attempt at realism.

Unfortunately some of the assumptions following the premise are themselves articles of faith and indeed amount to further premises that the viewer must accept for the movie to work. The problem with *The Cooler* is that it isn't long before many viewers are no longer able to suspend their disbelief and begin to find the movie preposterous. What struck me as most unlikely following the initial premise is to suppose that a Las Vegas casino, even one run by people from the old school of casino management, would believe that some unlucky schmuck could actually influence the fall of the dice and their gambling apparatus. How unlikely is it that a casino would actually hire such a guy and pay him money? The Las Vegas "cooler" is an urban legend.

Furthermore, since Bernie almost always loses and causes the players at the table to lose, someone could make a small fortune by betting against him. If he takes the dice, bet that he will crap out. If he bets on black at roulette, bet on red. To get really ridiculous have him bet on sports events. You like the New York Yankees? Have him bet on the team playing the Yankees.

In a sense then what this movie is really all about is magic versus mathematics and cold logic with the winner predictably being magic (and the power of true love, by the way), which is what the mass public wants. They want something beyond mathematics and logic and they want humans with the ability (through love) to rise above the empirical world and triumph over the forces of power and privilege, especially if that power and privilege is as corrupt and sadistic as Shelly Kaplow (Alex Baldwin in a fine, Oscar-nominated supporting role). The fact that Harvard-educated bean counters might also triumph is just a sop to realism.

All that aside I think this movie rises or falls mostly based on the viewer's appreciation of the acting of Macy. He is one of the most original actors of our time, whose style is truly his own, a striking cinema personage because he is so unlike anyone else on screen. He is a thinking person's actor, an auteur's choice to star in an independent film; but he is not a charismatic presence in the same sense that say Al Pacino or Tom Hanks or Tom Cruise are. It is unlikely that he could convincingly and consistently play the sort of leading roles required of box-office buffos. To some he is just plain boring. But I always like to say that "boredom is in the mind of the boree."

This is the first time I've seen Maria Bello. She too is not a top drawer charismatic star. She is a good actress and really fits well the role of a cocktail waitress with a past. Would the movie had been better if say Reese Witherspoon or Julia Roberts had played her part? Hard to say, but I don't think so—although a more mainstream audience would have watched the film.

The movie is also about corporate power versus the individual. Bernie and Natalie are low functioning cogs in the casino corporate machinery. The way they are brutally used and disposed of by management is just a burlesque of what happens at Wal-Mart or Enron. Alex Baldwin's Shelley is in a sense a violent caricature of Ken Lay. Instead of just ripping people off, Shelley also physically brutalizes them.

As for the ending, which some have criticized, I want to say that given our acceptance of the magical premise of the movie in the first place, it was nicely done.

Cop Land (1997) 7

Sorta like Wild Animal Park in bloody blue

Director James Mangold makes good use of Sylvester Stallone in this cop corruption saga while capturing the mentality of a small New Jersey town atmospherically named "Garrison" (Fort Lee?), a town that serves as an inbred bedroom community for the NYPD blue. I could tell by the foliage that most of this was filmed during an eastern seaboard summer: I could feel the humidity and it made me want to wring out my shirt and slap some mosquitoes.

Stallone is very good as Sheriff Freddy Heflin, who was rejected for the NYPD because of a bum ear suffered saving a beloved girl's life. He's the simple sap who's not so simple, slow to anger, but once aroused, look out!

(Compare to the ingredients of the Stallone Formula.) De Niro plays an Internal Affairs investigator while Harvey Keitel is his mortal enemy, a corrupt sleaze-ball cop. What I want to know is, was the choice of the name Figgis for Ray Liotta's part a director's inside joke? Incidentally, Liotta is entirely believable as a testosterone/coke-hyped cop wanting OUT.

The story is reasonable as these things go, and the old style Western shoot 'em up near the end tolerable. I found some of the plot devices, such as Figgis finding Freddy in the burnt out house, and one of the corrupt cops popping up in the back seat of Freddy's patrol car, a little too convenient. (But a contrivance is better than lollygagging the plot.) I also thought the rationale for the cops' violent turning on their own a little underdeveloped and especially difficult to appreciate near the beginning of the film. The ensemble of corruption and degeneracy fully revealed however made sense. The sound track is excellent and the cinematography and backdrops make New Jersey along the Hudson almost picturesque.

What Mangold proves here is he can conjure up an action/adventure ditty with the best of them. He's already made an excellent art film, *Heavy* (1995), and a superior and original coming of ager, *Girl, Interrupted* (1999). I believe that the romantic comedy and the epic cannot be far behind. For a young director with his talent, the only question (aside from money, chance and the availability of the box office buffos) is does he want to be a cinematic artist or a commercial artist? I hope he can be both.

Best joke: "I didn't know they allowed classical music in New Jersey."

One more thing: this phenomenon of a concentration of cops—comprising a virtual "Cop Land"—living in a certain suburban community outside a great urban area also occurs in Simi Valley near Los Angeles. A significant number of the cops working for the LAPD actually live in Simi Valley, or at least did twenty years ago. They all know each other and go to the same little league games, etc. Maybe they even have "Desperate Housewives of Simi Valley." :-)

I've seen this and I give it___stars.
I want to see it___. I'll pass___.
The review was worth reading___. Not___.

CQ (2001) 6

Modest debut for Francis Ford Coppola's son Roman

There are two films within a film in this campy debut from Roman Coppola. There is the introspective black and white, experimental, "student" sort of film that the young director Paul (Jeremy Davies) is making in his Paris apartment, and there is "Dragonfly," a kind of *Barbarella* (1968) sci-fi space shoot 'em up that he ends up directing. These might be seen as the twin realities of the

young film maker: on the one hand there are those short films you made at USC or UCLA film school to get your degree; on the other, there are those mindless commercial entertainments that Hollywood needs to crank out for the masses. These represent the bookends of the young director's reality.

The third film, the film that exists over and above these two, is the film that Roman/Paul would like to make, a film about what it is like to be a young film maker amid the crass commercialism of the producers, the seductive lure of the glamor that is the film maker's world, and the daily often tedious work of the actual film making. In other words, Roman Coppola is self-exploring in public. He is the novelist as a film maker.

"Dragonfly" itself is indeed *Barbarella* without the benefit of Terry Southern's contributions to the script or the services of Jane Fonda. It is unconsciously campy and a satire on such films. Model Angela Lindvall, five feet ten and three-quarters inches tall, anorexically thin, and sporting some very serious hair, plays Dragonfly with a kind of Barbie doll intensity. It is immediately obvious that she has the muscle tone of the languid and the gymnastic athletic ability of a teen/twentysomething. Yet her character is a "for hire" secret agent skilled in the martial arts and the use of weapons. Playing opposite her is Billy Zane as "Mr. E" a kind of Che Guevara revolutionary who is absurdly stationed on the far side of the moon where he is training revolutionaries.

In the introspective black and white film, Paul sits on the commode and talks to the camera much to the disdain of his live-in girlfriend Marlene (French actress Elodie Bouchez, best known for her work in the outstanding *The Dream Life of Angels* (1998)) who would like him to pay more attention to her.

This might be compared (distantly) with Francois Truffaut's *La Nuit Américaine* (Day for Night) from 1973 in which the great French director plays himself making a film—in other words a film within a film. Jeremy Davies reminds me somewhat of the sensitive, boyish actor Jean-Pierre Leaud, who played in that film after gaining prominence in Truffaut's *Les Quatre cents coup* (1959). It is easy to see Truffaut's influence on Roman Coppola, as indeed Truffaut has influenced many directors.

I don't think CQ ("Seek You") was entirely successful mainly because I don't think Roman made the transition from the self-indulgence and showiness characteristic of the very films he is satirizing to the mature project that addresses itself more directly to the needs of the audience. There is some fancy camera work with mirrors and characters seen from interesting angles, and some beautifully constructed sets, and some witty dialogue amid some telling satire of film land people and their world (especially producer Enzo played by Giancarlo Giannini and Dragonfly's idiot second director), but we are never made to care about what happens to any of the characters, this despite the fact that Davies is a very sympathetic actor.

Some of the jokes in the film include the three-day five o'clock shadows on the faces of the young actors. (That style is almost contemporary—*not* sixties-ish.) The hairstyles of the women with the beehives and such hinted of 1969, the year of the main film, but the eye makeup again was more contemporary than sixties-ish since it lacked the very heavy black eyelashes and eye liner that one recalls. To get it right, Roman should have reviewed, e.g., *Blow-Up* (1966) or *Elvira Madigan* (1967), films I am sure he has seen. Another is the view of Paris in the year 2001 as seen from 1970. It is futuristic in a silly way, and recalls some science fiction that exaggerated the technological changes that would take place. Orwell's *1984* (from 1948) has not yet arrived, nor has the overpopulated, polluted world from *Blade Runner* (1982).

Appearing in small roles are Dean Stockwell as Paul's father, and veteran French film star Gerard Depardieu as Dragonfly's original director.

Bottom line: worth seeing if only because it is the first film of the son of Francis Ford Coppola who may yet do something to rival the great works of his father. By the way, this might also be compared to *The Virgin Suicides* (2000), his sister Sofia Coppola's first film, just to see who is more likely to best please Dad. I'm taking no bets.

I've seen this and I give it___stars.
I want to see it___. I'll pass___.
The review was worth reading___. Not___.

Dead Calm (1989) 8

Nicole Kidman will fetch your eyes

The first few minutes suggest Polanski's *Knife in the Water* (1962) with harbingers of the Coleridge poem, "The Rime of the Ancient Mariner." But this is a film with its intent squarely on the box office; and, aside from the riveting Nicole Kidman, whose sensual vitality dominates the film, nothing so interesting materializes. Nonetheless the tension is nearly unbearable even though it's all predictable: the idyllic couple aboard their yacht alone on the open ocean take on a psychopath whose ship is sinking. Well, we can see he's a nut case from the first grin, and our only thought is, keep him away from your wife! So naturally the husband, played with leading man true grit by Sam Neill, leaves her alone with him while he pokes around in the other vessel with anticipated horrific consequences.

The close ups on Nicole Kidman's face are so intense you can feel her skin and almost smell her breath. She proves to be quite an actress as she wrestles with the psycho, played with such fidelity by Billy Zane that I found myself repeatedly urging her to shoot the sickie.

As the situation rapidly becomes impossible for our heroic couple, we realize that it's all very stagy, and upon further thought, fake; yet the intense photography, the seemingly veracious nautical business, and the fine acting by all, plus all that water, make it almost real. Very far out from reality however is the final scene where psycho-boy comes back to life, so to speak, and then—well, watch it and see.

Incidentally, it is interesting to compare this Nicole Kidman with the one seen nowadays. Clearly she has matured and become more shapely; but I wonder, has she lost some intensity? Regardless, she is a charismatic, hard-working, very serious actress who may eventually have a career to match, say, Jane Fonda or even Shirley MacLaine. (Note: now I would say that Nicole Kidman has surpassed those fine actresses and is going after the really greats like Meryl Streep...)

I've seen this and I give it___stars.
I want to see it___. I'll pass___.
The review was worth reading___. Not___.

Digging to China (1998) 7

Flawed, but still touching

"You're going to grow up and I'm not."

This is what Ricky Schroth (Kevin Bacon) says to Harriet Frankovitz (Evan Rachel Wood) near the end of the film, expressing both the promise of her life, and the tragedy of his. It is precisely because of the potential of this sharp spoken, sharp witted, beautiful little girl with a mind of her own that we are mesmerized by her, as we are by our own children, and why we are so deeply saddened by the young man who is not a man and never will be.

This is a film that discovers itself after a clumsy start and develops until at the end we see the beauty and the tragedy of its story as an affirmation of life. Kevin Bacon starts awkwardly and has to work hard to conquer a demanding role. But so does Wood, who in the beginning at times seemed unsure of who she is and how she should feel and react. But both actors grow into their characters and become stronger and stronger as the film progresses. However, I think Director Timothy Hutton (Best Supporting Actor for *Ordinary People* in 1980) might have profited by re-shooting some of the earlier scenes. (It has been pointed out to me that the scenes were not necessarily shot in chronological order, so take my comment with a grain of salt.)

It is interesting to compare Bacon's performance with that of other actors who have attempted to play mentally retarded or mentally challenged characters—I'm thinking here of Dustin Hoffman in *The Rain Man* (1988) and Billy Bob Thornton in *Sling Blade* (1996). Dustin Hoffman was of course something close to brilliant in his

Academy Award winning role. He had a charming script, and because he played alongside Tom Cruise he benefitted from not having to carry the picture by himself. This was not the case for Billy Bob Thornton in *Sling Blade*, where too much was attempted without enough help so that Thornton ended up too much in front of the camera, and that was not always to his benefit. Here Bacon is wonderfully supported not only by Miss Wood, but by Mary Stuart Masterson who plays Harriet's "sister" Gwen. Some people have criticized Masterson's performance, but I think they are reacting to her non-sympathetic character, a woman, who, as Harriet says, "should have been a nurse. She's always making some guy feel better." I think Masterson was very subtle in an unrefined role, and touching as a woman who had a lot to learn. Also excellent and completely believable in a limited role was Marian Seldes as Ricky's mother.

I was surprised that such an original and deeply lived script was not adapted from a novel. No writer could have just dreamed up this story. It had to have been lived in some sense. (Part of it *was* dreamed up of course.) So I guess, Karen Janszen, who wrote the script must have lived it. At any rate, she is to be commended for such an original conception. The setting in North Carolina at a rural motel ("Mom won it in a divorce"), and the three who ran "Mac's Indian Cabins" was perfect for the tale. Her celebration of the spirit of a ten-year-old who thinks she can dig to China was precious and warm. Some of the lines were so perfect. I am thinking of Harriet's voice over after it is revealed that she and Ricky "got married" (baptized is more like it!). The ten-year-old says, "Gwen was mostly upset cause I got married before her."

There were some pretty sets and scenes as well. The last classroom scene with Harriet's proud smile was nicely conceived and very winning; and the finale in which we see Gwen at dusk sitting in front of the motel office with Harriet upstairs and then out on the roof, was like a painting.

I've seen this and I give it___stars.
I want to see it___. I'll pass___.
The review was worth reading___. Not___.

Enigma (2001) 8

Interesting fictionalization of the Bletchley Park story

This is a story loosely, very loosely, based on British intelligence's efforts to crack the Nazi encryption codes used during World War II. The screenplay was adapted from the novel by Robert Harris by playwright Tom Stoppard whose cinematic credits include *Brazil* (1985) and *Shakespeare in Love* (1998). Dougray Scott stars as Tom Jericho who is decidedly not Alan Turing, the troubled genius who spearheaded the amazingly successful effort that allowed the Allies to know in advance what

the Nazis were up to. The true story is one of the most fascinating to come out of WWII.

This fictionalization is also a very good story. Michael Apted's direction gives us a nice feel for the era and for the type of people involved, intellectual and somewhat nerdish, creative people who were as valuable to the war effort, or even more so, than the soldiers in the field. Dougray Scott does a nice job of depicting a mathematician who has gone a little crazy because of an abortive love affair with a beautiful intelligence clerk, Claire Romilly (Saffron Burrows). He is sent away after cracking the Nazi code, but when the Nazis institute a new code he is returned from the nut house and pressed back into service. Still haunted by the memory of Claire, it is not clear that he is of any use. When he discovers that Claire is missing, the subplot begins with Jericho and Hester Wallace (Kate Winslet), once Claire's roommate, sleuthing through top secret intelligence files looking for clues to determine what happened to Claire and whether she was a spy or not. What they discover along the way predictably is each other. Watching them is Wigram, a rakish secret service agent with a heart of pure darkness, played with mystery and an arrogant ruthlessness by Jeremy Northam.

Billed as a thinking man's thriller, it is that. However, the plot suffers from two main problems: Claire can only be seen in flashback (I would like to have seen more of the woman who said, "Poor you. I really got under your skin, didn't I?"), and the action of the film must take place within a few days' time, which means that Jericho must simultaneously crack the new code, find out what happened to Claire, and romance Hester. I don't think Apted's direction successfully solved these problems. His concentration on a realistic "feel" to the movie merely masked them.

Nonetheless, one can appreciate the action and remain fully immersed even while not following all of the plot's intricacies. The juxtaposition of the tall, blonde player of men in the person of the beautiful Saffron Burrows with the short, full-figured, Nancy Drew-like Hester in the person of the beautiful and gifted Kate Winslet was a stroke of casting genius. They are fascinating to watch. The contrast between the sensitive and vulnerable Jericho and the worldly and immoral Wigram provided an interesting balance. All four of the leads were excellent.

But see this for Tom Stoppard, who might be called "a thinking man's" screenwriter. His gift for writing witty and authentic dialogue based on research and a finely trained ear is part of what makes this an interesting film well worth seeing.

I've seen this and I give it___stars.
I want to see it___. I'll pass___.
The review was worth reading___. Not___.

Eternal Sunshine of the Spotless Mind (2004)

7

But now I really do have spots on my mind

I'm sure watching this a few times will have the effect of erasing any confusion you might have. I am sure. But...well, I can't recall if I ever saw this film. Yet, yet... There's Jim Carrey in my mind playing a straight role. Sorta straight. Actually Kate Winslet has most of the good comedic lines. I can't tell whether she was once a girl friend of mine or if I watched her in a movie. She says she's high maintenance and she has to have a different color for her hair every week. Yeah, I remember her. My god she was nice. Quirky, but nice.

And then she erased all memory of me. I saw her in this book store and she pretended she didn't know me. Didn't know me! Wow, after all we had been through. I mean she's an emotional roller coaster. And that really dissed me off so I had my memory of her erased. And then we began to see each other in strange places, on the beach—but that was right. I met her on the beach. But then I was a child and she was there under the kitchen table, and my mom washed me in the sink and I felt so secure and Clementine oh my darling you are lost and gone forward, dreadful sorry Clementine was so, so sweet and so so pretty and just a nut case.

And then there's Kirsten Dunst, she of the incredibly agreeable figure, dancing over my body as I lay electronically stoned. Mary, her name is. She and the doc had this fling. He would get her to somehow seduce him and then erase the memory and then get her to do it again. Really bummed his wife out.

Oh, but Clem and I are here as on a darkling plain where ignorant armies clash by night and I think something's missing, the ground or the sky or some wall or maybe something is fused together that shouldn't be fused together, like this old house on the beach that Clem broke into, I mean she has balls, and I was just a fraidy cat, and wait, wait, I am gaining control. She and I together are chasing down the missing parts of our memories erased by the evil Lacuna Inc. people. All these memory movies going through my head—Memento (2000) especially, by Christopher Nolan. There's something going on here with these memory movies. I think Oliver Sacks has something to do with it. Are we just our memories, and who would we be without our memories? Would life be worth living? If we just lived in the here and the now would we be animals?

Anyway, this is a love story, the love story of my life. But is it possible to selectively erase memories? I mean creating lacunar infarcts on purpose? Is that legal? It is safe? Lacunar infarcts come from strokes that leave little blank spaces in your brain so that you're missing something like the memory of your first kiss or the time you saw Wayne's World.

Okay, this is science fiction like Vanilla Sky (2001) with Tom Cruise and Penélope Cruz. The dialogue is really sharp with all sorts of witticism written mostly by screenwriter Charlie Kaufman who also wrote the script for Being John Malkovich (1999). Need I say more? I mean clever with a capital K. By the way, idle thought: Clementine's last name is Kruczynski. Isn't that the Unibomber's last name, good old Ted? No, that was Kaczynski. Okay, never mind. Anyway, here's a clever line: "Are we like couples you see in restaurants? Are we the dining dead?" I think I said that, or wish I had. Or, "Drink up young man. It'll make the whole seduction part less repugnant." She said that, and I guess she oughta know, heaven help us, from firsthand experience.

Look, if I ever, but ever, get a chance to fall in love with Kate Winslet, please, please, do NOT erase the memory. Thank you.

Bottom line: bizarro and entertaining, witty and cute, with a nice cast. And Jim Carrey as a straight up kinda guy is a terrific actor, and Kate, well I'll tell you a secret, gentlemen. You can see a full frontal sans clothes shot of her in the movie Jude (1996). Yes. Also worth watching is her debut film Heavenly Creatures (1994) shot when she was 18 and still living in Australia.

One last line, as Joel says, "Constantly talking isn't necessarily communicating."

I've seen this and I give it___stars.
I want to see it___. I'll pass___.
The review was worth reading___. Not___.

Evita (1996) 8

Wonderful to watch but unfulfilling

One of the interesting sidelights to this movie is the fact that Oliver Stone wrote part of the screenplay. While watching it I kept wondering which part? Stone, whose edgy, over the top indictments of oppression, corruption and especially military stupidity, wouldn't seem to be one to celebrate the elevation of Eva Peron to something close to sainthood, which is what this movie does. Maybe all his work ended up on the cutting room floor. Or maybe it was obscured by Andrew Lloyd Webber's music. Certainly we do not see the decamisados (Peron's version of his friend Mussolini's Blackshirts) torturing anyone, and although the "disappeared" are mentioned in passing, there is no retrospective that allows us to see just how widespread and horrific were the murders committed by the Peronists.

Anyway, Madonna, who certainly fits the part like a glove, stars as Evita, and she gives the performance of her life. Yet somehow it is unconvincing, or I should say, somehow the film doesn't really get to the essence of the woman who rose from poverty to the pinnacle of power in Argentina, a woman extravagantly loved by the common people of Argentina even while she was a party to the fascist oppression. I don't think this is Madonna's fault. Her voice is good, not great, of course, but her dramatic skills are very much in evidence, skills that have always been underrated, although I'm not sure why. If you watch her in this and in *Desperately Seeking Susan* (1985) you can see that she has a range easily exceeding that of most actresses. I think that ironically it is the very quality of common origin and common appeal that the Argentines so loved in Evita that the critics hold against Madonna.

Antonio Banderas plays Che, who narrates and attempts to objectify the events while symbolizing both Evita's alter-ego and the man who would really be her proper mate were it not for her rapacious political appetite. Che's character and his dramatic role (from the play by Tim Rice) is perhaps the most important artistic achievement of the musical after Webber's beautiful and inspiring music. Banderas is winning and enormously vivid in the part, and he sings well and expressively.

Jonathan Pryce plays Peron with more dignity and humanity than history might allow. His sensitivity as an actor combined with a modest demeanor seemed to me so unrealistic as to be almost a miscasting. Yet he is perhaps as compelling as anyone on the screen and he certainly looked the part. Interesting is Jimmy Nail as the cabaret singer Magaldi. He combines sleazy good looks with a kind of vulnerable persona that seems exactly right.

Well, what can be said about the music except that it is one of Webber's great triumphs and so very typical of his work. It is beautiful, stirring, moving, enchanting and memorable. Who can forget the haunting, plaintive refrain of "Don't Cry for Me, Argentina" or the gorgeous simplicity of "You Must Love Me"? While Madonna's voice would not fill up a concert hall or take her by itself to the Broadway stage, she does an outstanding job with Webber's songs. A natural performer (Madonna's key talent), her expressive interpretations range from the ordinary to the transfixing. I very much enjoyed her efforts and predict that critics in the future will be kinder to her than today's critics.

The ending seemed too drawn out and then when the screen faded to black and the credits began to run it seemed almost abrupt and without resolution. I also did not like the way that Madonna (38 at the time) seemed no younger in the earlier scenes with her hair dyed pitch black. I think director Alan Parker should have given us more of an illusion of youth, perhaps spared her some of the close-ups and fuzzed out the lines under her eyes. Strange how the golden blonde hair and exquisitely applied makeup in the remainder of the film made her look younger. All directors should know what Madonna learned many years ago: blonde hair usually makes a woman look younger because those with naturally light-colored hair are their blondest as children. Like big eyes and relatively big heads, blonde hair is a signal of youth that arrests our eyes.

Despite the flaws this is an engrossing cinematic experience, and for Madonna fans, Banderas fans, and in particular fans of Andrew Lloyd Webber, it is a film not to be missed.

I've seen this and I give it___stars.
I want to see it___. I'll pass___.
The review was worth reading___. Not___.

Fargo (1996) 8

Satirical thriller with atmosphere

Fargo is a totally original thriller with sharp turns and pop-up surprises, but be forewarned that it contains graphic, and to some extent, gratuitous violence, and some unsavory sex. Put the kiddies to bed.

Frances McDormand stars as the local sheriff, and she's pregnant. The perps are psychos of course; there are three of them and each is a different breed of psycho. William H. Macy is a car salesman who dreams up a scheme to cheat his rich father-in-law out of a million dollars by getting some degenerates to kidnap his wife. He's a white collar sociopath who always lies whenever his lips are moving unless there is some very good reason to tell the truth. One of the degenerates is a big silent guy (Peter Stormare) who kills people as one squishes bugs. The other (Steve Buscemi) is an ugly little bantam who lies and cheats and kills and steals and whines until finally somebody puts him out of his misery.

This is Fargo, North Dakota, where people are country and it's cold and not very sophisticated. The movie makes gentle fun of the locals while guiding us to identify with them. McDormand eats at Hardee's and Arby's a whole lot and likes greasy dishes from the cafeteria piled high on her plate. She's eating for two. She loves her husband and he loves her. They lie in bed at night and watch TV. She's the police chief, affecting a self-effacing, aw-sucks, I'm not too bright (but I really am) style reminiscent of Tyne Daly in TV's "Cagey and Lacy" from some years back. Her husband Norm is a big guy who cooks for her and is an artist who paints wildlife. One of his duck paintings becomes a postage stamp. They all say "yaw" a lot.

The forlorn cold and desolate landscape of North Dakota is an Americana locale not used cinematically since perhaps Clint Eastwood's *High Plains Drifter* (1973). The script and direction are tidy without being too flashy. Everything is designed to surprise or bemuse the audience, even the accents. There is the requisite quota of bright red blood; plenty of bullets puncture flesh and split bone. There's some gutter sex and a few shocking sights (one of the perps stuffs an unfortunate into a wood chip machine). All in all it's a carefully crafted thriller with an artistic veneer, nicely photographed. It's clear that Coen and Coen have watched the movies of Atom Egoyan, Gus Van Sant, David Lynch, Oliver Stone, etc., and here pay them the sincere compliment of imitation with variation—or is it the other way around?

Another excellent Coen and Coen film is the less well-known *Blood Simple* (1984). It was their first film and—although uneven and sometimes a bit contrived—in some ways is still their best.

I've seen this and I give it___stars.
I want to see it___. I'll pass___.
The review was worth reading___. Not___.

Fear and Loathing in Las Vegas (1998) 7

Don't see this straight

This is a funny, garish version of the Hunter S. Thompson novel directed by Terry Gilliam with the usual Gilliam brush strokes: cluttered sets, Monty Python remembrances, funky camera angles, relentless energy and a satirical eye. His "shoot me if you find a plot," and "torture me first if you find a subplot" style is regressed to after the agreeable hiatus of *12 Monkeys* (1995). Of course such a chaotic style goes well with gonzo journalism on a bad acid trip—a *very* bad acid trip.

Johnny Depp plays Hunter S. Thompson as Doonesbury's Duke with the FDR cigarette holder and pastel shades. Benicio Del Toro is offensively loutish as Dr. Gonzo, a fake Samoan from East L.A. or thereabouts. Most of this is pretty "bad," but Depp got the cartoon character down pat. The psychedelic and day-glow sets, populated with lizards and ugly Americans, splashed with glaring reds and pinks, etc., captured well not only the "fear and loathing" but the seventies Las Vegas milieu as well. The voice overs from the novel seemed a bit miraculous in the movie since at no time is Duke ever coherent or sober enough to write. Piping Debbie Reynolds's "Tammy's in Love" into the Duke/Gonzo hotel room amid the brain cell mayhem was an inspired cultural juxtaposition. Ditto for the Barbra Streisand portraits.

Best scene: Gonzo and Duke watching a clip from "Reefer Madness" at the narc's convention. Second best scene: Duke being admired by the highway patrolman who wants a kiss. Most fun: trash driving those two big Caddy convertibles.

One of the amazing things about Gilliam is how he can make fun of people without their seeming to notice. Hunter S. Thompson looks like an idiot here, and Gilliam is really satirizing the sixties/early seventies drug culture just as surely as he trashes the cops. His rapier is razor sharp, so sharp you don't feel it until you look down and see the blood on your hand.

I've seen this and I give it___stars.
I want to see it___. I'll pass___.
The review was worth reading___. Not___.

Fight Club (1999) 8

Shocking the burghers; energizing the proles

Director David Fincher, who brought us into the extraordinarily depraved serial-killer world of *Se7en* (1995), fires up the shock cauldron again with this high testosterone examination of our primal need to seek adrenaline highs through physical violence. Indeed, the message is we are not really alive unless we are involved in something extreme.

Ed Norton plays the Narrator, a corporate structure clog with insomnia who gets off (and finds the arms of Morpheus) by going to therapy groups for people with cancer, disfigurement, drug addiction, etc. The idea is that seeing the acute and terrible misery of others affords him a catharsis that clears the neuro-emotional blockage and allows him to relax enough to get some sleep.

But after a while he begins to notice Marla Singer (Helena Bonham Carter—no relation to Hillary Rodham Clinton, ha, ha) hanging out at some of the meetings. Her hair and eyes are black widow black, all the better to set off her pasty white skin, giving her a witchy/sexy allure that really in itself ought to excite Norton's deadened neurons. (I know she excited mine.) But instead what her presence at the talk-therapy sessions does is remind him that he isn't really suffering like the others, and once again he has insomnia.

Meanwhile he meets Tyler Durden (Brad Pitt) a handsome and virile beauty soap salesman who is quick with the banter and has the confidence of a demi-god, something Norton's character lacks. They become best buds (and a bit more) after Durden introduces him to the full-out adrenaline rush of getting your face pounded in. As the fight club scenes unfold, getting more and more ridiculous with each bone-crunching punch and each darkening pool of blood, more and more young men join the club allowing Tyler Durden to become an underground hero and charismatic leader of human sheep dressed in black. By the way, the real truth of the postmodern cowboy fisticuffs is that the participants couldn't even stand the injury to their hands from one punch, let alone the repeated blows to face, head and body.

But never mind. There's a lot more to this movie than phony fight scenes. The strange thing is a lot of the scenes are funny! Somehow an aura of humor adheres to Fincher's street mayhem, rock-the-house sex, and body-slamming/bone-cracking absurdities. Not only that but the acting by the principals and Meat Loaf's massively-breasted Bob Paulson is excellent. Norton's confused and determined whimsy is nicely off-set by Pitt's brazen pathology. The story plays out well with some nice surprises and some good tension. You will not be bored.

Philosophically speaking too there is more than a grain of truth in the thesis: we really are divorced to some extent from our primal nature. We are animals who have domesticated ourselves. A return to the jungle (for example, by watching this film) energizes us and reminds us that part of our nature is largely incompatible with civilization.

Be forewarned however that this is a grossly violent movie that is difficult to watch at times. Fincher's primary intent is to shock, and he works hard at that. The scene at the back alley of a liposuction clinic as our boys are dumpster-diving for soap ingredients is particularly grossitating. When one of the bags holding human fat gets snagged on a barbed wire fence, it bursts, dripping it contents onto the Narrator.

If you can stand this sort of thing, watch and be beguiled or revolted, but first, please send the kiddies to bed.

I've seen this and I give it___stars.
I want to see it___. I'll pass___.
The review was worth reading___. Not___.

Flirting (1991) 8

Superior coming of ager from down under

Don't let the title fool you. Although this is one of the sweetest movies you'll ever see, it is no beach blanket bingo for bimbos. This is an Aussie story of teen love set in 1965, heroic as only teens can play it. It is fun to watch, authentic and original at the same time, a coming of age flick in the English boarding school tradition of *Dead Poet's Society* (1989) and *A Separate Peace* (the novel, not the so-so movie). Noah Taylor stars as Danny Embling, an outsider who reads Sartre and Camus while satirizing the school's empty traditions. Across the lake is the girl's school where Thandiwe Adjewa (Thandie Newton), daughter of the Ugandan ambassador, is learning to meld with the Aussie pale faces, including a gifted pre-Hollywood Nicole Kidman.

Thandie Newton and Noah Taylor, as beautifully directed by John Duigan, are the reasons this film is so good. She has a fearless integrity about her that overcomes the prejudices of her school mates. He is wise and brave at a hundred and twenty pounds. She too is ultra-sophisticated. She even *met* Sartre. This is a story about the love between two outsiders who, with their strength of character win over not only their classmates, but the audience as well. Imagine teenagers as witty and poised as say Eartha Kitt and Gore Vidal, and you get a hint of how it's played.

Nicole Kidman as the snobby Nicola Radcliffe (the name says it all) manages a subtle supporting role with a diamond-in-the-rough kind of charm and just the right touch of on-screen growth. The scene where she shares her stash of vodka (or perhaps a clear fruit liquor) with Thandiwe Adjewa is beautifully turned by Director John Duigan. Also excellent is the hotel scene where the adults are revealed as intrusive in the extreme. I like Danny Embling's line as he deadpans to a re-robing Thandiwe, "They're all funny, aren't they?" Yes, those adults are a little peculiar.

This is not unflawed, however. The ending, despite the rousing music, seemed a bland washout, leaving us with a sense of disappointment. And I thought the first love scene with the two "touching" was a little unreal. I mean he might have kissed her! There's a limit to how great a coming of age, boarding school movie can be, especially when the adults have only scarecrow parts. Nonetheless *Flirting* is a confectioner's delight, and one of the best coming of age movies I've ever seen.

I've seen this and I give it___stars.
I want to see it___. I'll pass___.
The review was worth reading___. Not___.

Floundering (1994) 7

Better than its reputation

This sixties time-warped retro kind of "power to the people" nineties flick is mostly a procession of set pieces, some of which are not bad. The bit at the gun store with Billy Bob Thornton was superb. The crack philosopher's scene was also very good. And the way "What's So Funny 'Bout Peace, Love and Understanding?" was sung so badly was just perfectola. (Actually that's "What's So Bad about Peace, Love and Understanding?" but whatever...) And the way that big silver fish popped those gold fish...gulp!

I think some of the negative comments about this movie ought to be greeted with a "Whoa, dudes—get a sense of humor." Or, "Don't be offended, man, it's only a movie." Or maybe, "Uh, the soundtrack is awesome, dude." (Oh, god, people really did talk like that!) The dream sequences fooled me at least twice. They were funny. Funniest line: when the trash lady pulls her rifle out of her cart and says "Vive la Revolution!" Second funniest line: "What kind of music do you want to hear?" "The farm report."

Okay, this was no masterpiece, and any episodic movie sans plot is not going to rival *The Godfather* at IMDb.com. And James LeGros ain't no Marlon Brando. And if you've ever been to Venice Beach...well, you know it's a freak show. But I think director and screen writer Peter McCarthy did a nice job of bringing that slacker street scene to life. I think the big mistake was to headline actors like Steve Buscemi, John Cusack, Ethan

Hawke, and Billy Bob Thornton when they only had cameos. That should have been made clear up front. And there was more than a touch of the kind of sixties moral pretension that we've all grown a little tired of. But bottom line for me, this was a funny movie.

I've seen this and I give it___stars.
I want to see it___. I'll pass___.
The review was worth reading___. Not___.

Following (1998) 8

Stalking as a hobby; burglary as a thrill

In this intriguing noir thriller (looking like the Forties, but with a psychology befitting the Nineties), Director Christopher Nolan employs a number of techniques he would perfect in his internationally acclaimed *Memento* (2000), most notably scenes presented out of time sequence for effect, and a naive protagonist taken advantage of by others.

The film opens with "Bill, the Innocent" (as I might dub him), played by Jeremy Theobald, trying to explain to someone, perhaps a social worker, perhaps even a police inspector (John Nolan), why he took up following people just for the fun of it. He doesn't just follow women, he points out. He's not a stalker, as such. He's just curious. He's an intriguing and sympathetic character, a Brit writer with a lot of time on his hands who seems something of a throwback to an earlier age with his clanking manual typewriter and the photo of a pursed-lips Marilyn Monroe on the wall of his shabby apartment.

Things began to go wrong for him, he further explains, when he broke some of his "following rules" and got too close to his prey. What he doesn't know and what we don't know yet, is that his clumsy following technique has allowed him to unwittingly become the followed himself.

Enter a juicy blonde (Lucy Russell) walking down some steps from her apartment. (This scene is out of sequence as far as chronological time goes, but psychologically speaking, her appearance signals his entanglement). Enter now a scheming, sophisticated psychopathic thrill-seeker named Cobb (Alex Haw) who entices Bill with his (apparent) practice of burglary just for the powerful feeling one gets from invading the sanctity of another's life.

Although justification for the temporal inversions here is not as clearly established as in *Memento*, nonetheless the technique works well, and Nolan provides us with a clever ending that sneaks up on us and makes in a few seconds all that went before clear. Or mostly clear. You might want to rewind and view the first few minutes of the film, and then everything should be clarity.

This low-budget, black and white, deliciously ironic little film (71 minutes) marked the auspicious debut of a film maker who has made quite a name for himself, not only with the aforementioned *Memento*, but with *Insomnia* (2002). It will be interesting to see what Nolan does next.

I've seen this and I give it___stars.
I want to see it___. I'll pass___.
The review was worth reading___. Not___.

Freeway (1996) 7

Through the woods to grandmother's house we go

There are any number of very sick jokes in this, not the least of which is the poor john is still in the trunk (ha!), and the sight of that girl with the...ah, legs from the sixth grade. Director Matthew Bright, you are one sick puppy. And the plot is at times a farcical burlesque of contrivance (Wolverton as the wolf in grandmother's bed; his resurrection). But no matter. Reese Witherspoon is very funny as Vanessa Lutz, a semi-literate teen who's got a whore for a mother and a lecherous junkie for a stepfather. By the way, Vanessa was faking that she couldn't read "The cat drinks the milk" in the opening scene just to make fun of the not entirely bright teacher. She's a home girl who can kick Major Buttski along with any celluloid hero, doing here a nice variation of a Bridget Fonda-like La Femme Nikita. She also has some admirable integrity and she's cute.

Kiefer Sutherland got way into his role as a child psychologist turned serial killer. The satanic leers and psychopathic drooling on his face as he contemplates his necromantic encounter with Witherspoon was enough to curdle sweet cream. Later when he gets the appliance to hold up half his mouth, displaying buck teeth, Witherspoon calls him a "chipmunk," but I thought he looked a little like Stephen Hawking after an injection of protoplasm. And Brooke Shields as his grieving, empty-headed wife was a scream. (And I did like that white skirt!) We are talking *creative casting* here!

Director Matthew Bright takes dead satirical aim at shrinks, prison guards, cops, social workers, judges, teachers, and any other societal cogs he can find and lets Vanessa, representing the underclass, choke 'em, gouge 'em, cuff 'em, shot 'em, outsmart 'em, and slap 'em across the face. One gets the impression that he was getting even with some people from his early years, which is good, since there's no revenge more satisfying than to trash your tormentors up there on the silver screen for all the world to see.

What I didn't like about this comedic romp through the barrios and the freeways and the institutions of SoCal Land was all that blood and nary a bit of skin. What IS it with you, Matthew Bright? You've got nubile Reese Witherspoon and a whole bunch of home girls, and

Brooke Shields in that white dress, and you can't score some flesh tones? Are you some kind of prude?

I've seen this and I give it___stars.
I want to see it___. I'll pass___.
The review was worth reading___. Not___.

Friday Night Lights (2004) 8

High school football as a glorious religion

For an appreciation of this excellent film see the beautifully written review by D. Mikels at Amazon.com. What I want to do here is present a counterpoint. I played high school football too and might have sat on the bench a little less except that I was a slow-footed T-quarterback at a school that ran the single wing. Yes, it was that long ago.

The football presented in this film by director Peter Berg is a little different. In fact it is a whole lot different. Here high school football is the most important thing in the world, not just for the players and coaches, but for the entire town. If you drive through a west Texas town or an Oklahoma or even an Indiana town on a Friday night in the fall, the town will be deserted (as in the movie) while the stadium at the high school will be lit up like a gigantic Christian revival meeting in which it might be fully expected that Christ will appear to perform the Second Coming.

It is no exaggeration to say that in the heartland of America the rites and rituals of football, joined into by almost the entire populous, take on all the trappings of a most zealous and evangelical religion. What Peter Berg has done here is capture that maniacal devotion and idolatry—that oh, so American way of life in a quasi-realistic way.

I say "quasi" because there is some license taken with reality by the film makers. First of all, and most importantly, the players are too old. Derek Luke, who plays star running back Boobie Miles (and does an outstanding job), was 29 when the movie was filmed. Jay Hernandez who played Chavez was 25. Anybody who really plays football or coaches it can tell you there is a world of difference between a young man of seventeen or eighteen and one of twenty-five or thirty.

And the scenes filmed especially for the movie with the flying tackles and the rolling flips and the bone-crunching open field tackles—forget it. Those are staged tackles, like kung fu fights in Chinese movies. Everything looks fantastic, only it's about as realistic as a barroom fight in an old cowboy movie from the forties.

What is realistic? When sexy, saucy blonde Melissa goes looking for her trophy seduction of the MoJo quarterback—that's real. She knows that the highest status in town belongs to the star of the high school football team, and the highest status of any girl is to get that guy. Also realistic is the pressure put on coaches and administrators to win football games. Winning isn't a matter of life and death. As some coaches will tell you, it's more important than that. And they mean it. Die and you're only dead. But lose at football and you are disgraced for life. Typifying this mentality is Don Billingsley, father of running back Charles, who wants to beat the life out of his son for fumbling the football. Can't the kid see that you let down your teammates, your school, your town, your friends, your relatives and God Almighty if you fumble the f-ing football?

Also real is Boobie Miles's answer to what subject he gets all A's in: "There's only one subject. That's football." Or this line from a disappointed fan calling in to the local radio jock show after the team loses a game: "There's too much learning going on at that school." He's not kidding. He means it. Too much time in the classroom. Too little on the field.

So is this film—as its devoted fans believe and know to be true—an ode to the glory and beauty of football? Think again, jockstrap. It's a glorification. It represents a mentality in which the greatest events of life occur when you're eighteen years old. After that it's all over. What you got left is beer, the wife, TV, and Bruce Springsteen's "Glory Days." Or to choose another lyric, what you've got are "Veterans of the fight/Fast asleep at the traffic light." (Jackson Browne)

There are a number of goofs and anachronisms in the movie. IMDb.com lists a dozen or so including cars in the parking lots that weren't even made in 1988, the year of the film, and football gear used that didn't exist then. But that doesn't matter, and nobody who loves this film cares in the slightest about that because what really counts is the fantasy, the imagined and recalled glory of a time when everything was new and astonishingly vivid, when events made indelible marks on our hearts and souls. When we were all 17. This then is mythology in the making and in the living.

The question begs itself: is this good or is this bad? Is football as a religion something to be treasured or condemned? Personally I have mixed feelings. Young men have aggressive tendencies that need to be channeled and middle-aged men need to play war games. Football allows an acting out of these needs without undue harm to anyone. Certainly football is better than gang-banging.

When, some many years down the road, the history of cinema is brought up to date, this film will be remembered because it is a very good film, and Billy Bob Thornton's fine performance as Coach Gary Grimes will be appreciated. But instead of the film being seen as a realistic portrayal of what it's like to play and be involved in high school football, it will be seen as a commentary on the sociology of middle America in the late

20th century, a time when the nation was very rich and football was not only king but something close to a way of life, something indistinguishable from a national religion.

I've seen this and I give it___stars.
I want to see it___. I'll pass___.
The review was worth reading___. Not___.

Gattaca (1997) 8

Superior, thought-provoking sci-fi thriller

Andrew Niccol, who wrote the screenplay for *The Truman Show* (1998), directs this superior sci-fi from his own script. The result is a well-plotted, character-driven science fiction thriller for intelligent viewers, a pleasing combination of worthiness not always associated with the genre. This is science fiction that will play with mainstream audiences as well as with aficionados. From Michael Nyman's beautiful and complementary musical score to the clever opening credits in which the letter codes, "g, a, t, c" (for the chemical bases of DNA—thus the movie's title) shimmer and glow in the names of those credited, everything in the movie is professionally done. There is little violence and virtually no sex. I would say this is a perfect flick for the kids except for the embedded "ads" for cigarettes and booze that mar some of the early scenes.

Ethan Hawke stars as the genetically-challenged Vincent Freeman, an "In-Valid" conceived in the back seat of a Buick Riviera instead of through the fine art of the genetic engineers who now dominate society. His dream is to go into space, but his genes, in this meritocracy based on genetic endowment, fit him only for cleaning the bathrooms. Yet he has a monstrous drive to succeed, and when he strikes a deal with the genetically superior Jerome Morrow, a "valid" who is in a wheel chair with paralyzed legs, to use his identity, body fluids, hair samples and urine to fool the genetic screening devices of the Gattaca Aerospace Corporation, he is ready to fulfill his dream.

Uma Thurman plays his love interest. Her statuesque beauty and her exotic features are perfect for the part of a futuristic babe in a retro fifties landscape of gray flannelled over achievers. (Actually they aren't gray in dress, but in their uniform adherence to the corporate mentality.) Jude Law as Jerome, the wheel-chair bound "Valid," is perhaps the star performer, bringing subtlety and a bitter, but somehow uplifting verisimilitude to the role. A puffed up Gore Vidal (who incidentally once wrote, "after forty the death watch") is Director Josef, and Alan Arkin is a street wise homicide investigator from another era.

The interesting question asked by this movie is, could a caste system based on genetic endowment be our future? My vision of the future is that of a "brown society" in which everyone strives to be the same, but in which small subtle differences of appearance are increasingly appreciated. If every movie star looked like, say Jennifer Lopez, however beautiful she is, I would nonetheless find particular delight in a Penélope Cruz or an occasional Reese Witherspoon. This sort of pressure would keep some variety in the gene pool. I also think that a society in which the genetic endowment of its members is too widely separated can only lead to class hatreds resulting in violent conflict and ultimately genocide, most likely by fiat, so that the survivors will be genetically rather similar. Possibly humanoid types will be genetically engineered to do the baser work of society. These creatures may be thought of as organic robots, not as bona fide members of society, thereby raising another question, what is it to be human? A society greatly stratified in terms of wealth can exist, as the present society shows, but a society in which the difference between haves and the have-nots is too great is not stable and eventually leads to revolution (there being a limit to the number of people that can be put in prison). Furthermore, as this movie suggests, just which qualities of character, appearance and/or ability are the most valuable? And when such qualities become abundant, might we then have a need for other qualities now made scarce? Finally, as is asked of the notion of I.Q: "intelligence for what?" Is it more powerful in an evolutionary sense to be "intelligent" or to be healthy? Is it more adaptive to have a powerful drive to succeed, or a powerful urge to procreate? Tough questions that the very talented Andrew Niccol might consider when making his next movie.

I've seen this and I give it___stars.
I want to see it___. I'll pass___.
The review was worth reading___. Not___.

Gilda (1946) 8

She makes you want her

Some of this reminds me of *Casablanca* (1942) with the "philosopher of the washroom" (Steve Geray) sporting a Peter Lorrie accent and Glenn Ford playing tough like Humphrey Bogart running a night spot in a foreign land, this time Argentina. Rita Hayworth is Gilda, of course, and the forties Marilyn Monroe. I'm sure MM studied this film. The way Monroe does her shoulders and flashes her arms as she sings and removes her long-sleeved black gloves in *Gentleman Prefer Blondes* (1953) is virtually copied from Hayworth's performance here. You could check it out.

Ford is your confident, two-fisted bad boy that women love, circa 1945, kind of like an old-fashioned John Travolta from *Pulp Fiction* (1994). But notice how benign those bad boys used to be. The worst thing he does is cheat at dice. And while he's fast and street wise about most things, he's like a little boy with women. That used to pass for charm. Maybe it still does.

The plot is a little too precious in places and Charles Vidor's attention to detail hit and miss, mostly hit; yet there's a nice mysterious forties Hollywood atmosphere created (even though it's supposed to be Buenos Aires). There's a night life, night time feel to the movie with passwords at the door and evening gowns and dark cars caught in street lamps that helps to recall the forties.

You can see the influence of *Gilda* in movies coming many years after, *Chinatown* (1974) and *L.A. Confidential* (1997) come to mind, the former in the night scenes and the latter because Kim Basinger really looks and behaves more like Rita Hayworth than the Veronica Lake look-alike she portrayed.

Memorable is George Macready as the casino owner, he of the pinched face and the long, curved scar on his right cheek, giving him the sinister, devil-may-care air of a man who has fought and won many duels. I recall he always played villains and made us believe.

I liked the resolution which showed that Gilda was more a tease than anything else and kind of sweet even though she said, "If I had been a ranch, they'd have named me the Bar-Nothing." Quaint and curious is the old Hollywood code which forbade showing her belly button even in a mid-drift and skirt. They tease us with her globes always sheltered and her little belly and the line of her butt just hinted at. She has a mouth as big as Julia Roberts' and sexy eyes. The scene where she really sells it is when her face comes out of shadow and she puckers up to Ford and tells him, "I hate you so much that I think I am going to die for it." She seems to be begging him, if that's what it takes. He holds a light for her cigarette down near his waist (everything had to be subtle in those days), and then some scenes later, she does get down on the floor with her arm around his legs.

Hayworth has a sultry and low feminine voice like Laurel Bacall (that's the way we liked 'em then!) which is nicely displayed as she sings "Put the Blame on Mame, Boys."

I've seen this and I give it___stars.
I want to see it___. I'll pass___.
The review was worth reading___. Not___.

Good Morning, Night (2003) 8

Christians 1, Commies 0

Not to be flippant, but the Christian Democrats outshine the Red Brigade by quite a bit in this political dramatization of the kidnapping and murder of Italy's former prime minister in 1978. Highlight of the movie is the performance by Maya Sansa as Chiara, one of the kidnappers. She is a Red because of what happened to her father at the hands of the government. Consequently Chiara is an emotional communist, not an ideological one; and so the up close and personal kidnapping, "trial," and eventual murder of the gentle and truly Christian Aldo Moro (played with strength and grace by Roberto Herlitzka) began to wear on her spirit, making her question what she is a part of—not, however, enough for her to do anything about it except in her dreams.

The reason the Christians outshine the communists here (and elsewhere by the way) is that the communist ideology requires murders in the name of ideology whereas Christianity does not condone murder for any reason, although some Christians seem unaware of that fact. The movie includes the communist rationale for the murder, which Chiara, with tears in her eyes, cannot accept even though she hates the bourgeois who have run Italy since World War II. Incidentally the mini speech that one of the kidnappers gives to Chiara to justify the murder sounded a bit like something one might hear from Al Qaeda.

Maya Sansa is brilliant and her countenance captured my eyes, but I question whether she was the right person to play this role. Although strong and charismatic, she seems anything but the rabid revolutionary.

Director Marco Bellocchio's use of fantasy scenes was effective in that it highlighted the torn and nearly (nearly!) impossible desire of Chiara to free Moro. However the unlikely device of a co-worker at the library writing a screenplay called "Good Morning, Night" which depicts the events of the movie and the fictionalized kidnapping seemed a bit much. That he could divine these events just by knowing Chiara, as though channeling her, seemed almost mawkish in the face of the historical reality. But Bellocchio and Anna Laura Braghetti, who wrote the novel from which the movie was adapted, were perhaps inspired by an actual séance attended by some government officials who used a psychic medium in an effort to locate the kidnapper's hideout.

Clearly a plus was to see Christian values triumph over communist ones, and to see in retrospect a triumph for the good over the not so good. Moro died, but he died a hero and a respected man. His killers were disgraced and given (by American standards anyway) relatively lenient sentences, perhaps because they were so young. This is in keeping with the forgiveness that is at the heart of Christianity, allowing the Italian people to maintain the moral high road over what was then called the Red Menace.

But I have to be honest. I would have found this movie almost boring were it not for the presence of Maya Sansa. Bellocchio wisely focused the camera on her as often as possible. Her emotional experience, as revealed by her features and her voice, went a long way toward carrying the movie.

I've seen this and I give it___stars.
I want to see it___. I'll pass___.
The review was worth reading___. Not___.

Good Night, and Good Luck (2005) 8

Lacks somewhat in focus and tension, but still worthwhile

I won't join the chorus of accolades for George Clooney for his direction of this movie, but I will give him credit for making it. The way the press has been pushed around (and especially let itself be pushed around) during the George W. Bush years is a disgrace, and it is good that Clooney is here to remind us of a journalist who had the guts to go after a power-hungry demagogue whose agenda included finding traitors among those who disagreed with him. Sound familiar?

So, just as Arthur Miller's celebrated play *The Crucible* was timely in that it symbolically chastised those who would conduct witch hunts in the name of patriotism, Clooney's film is timely in that it reminds the Fourth Estate of its responsibility, a responsibility sorely neglected in the buildup to the war in Iraq.

As far as the film itself goes, a black and white fusion of documentary footage and an acted-out story line, it was good, but not great. David Strathairn, playing Edward R. Murrow, certainly had Murrow's voice, cadences and mannerisms down pat. However, because there would be a viewer's eye conflict with the actor's appearance and the way the real Edward R. Murrow looked, we were unfortunately not shown footage of Murrow himself. Which is a shame. Even though I was a child at the time, seeing Murrow's dark, penetrating presence on the old Muntz TV was indelible. He had a way of talking straight to the viewer and doing so in a manner that was clear, fair and to the point. Strathairn does a good job of reenacting that presence.

And it was good to see some footage of the demagogic junior Republican senator from Minnesota, Joseph McCarthy, in all his drunken, bullying vainglory. And I was fascinated to see President Eisenhower giving a spirited speech. Indeed the film managed to atmospherically recall the era of the early fifties when TV was all in black and white and everybody smoked to excess, especially Murrow. (But softening accusations of receiving Big Tobacco money, Clooney was wise to include an old TV commercial for Kent cigarettes in which the hyping of their new "safe" filters sounds cruelly ironic today.)

Frank Langella was excellent as Murrow's careful, yet supportive boss, media legend William Paley. And Clooney himself played a nicely understated Fred Friendly. I have to say however that the film lacked a certain tension and that the focus was not as clearly defined as it might have been. A film without much tension and with a fuzzy focus can be boring (as some viewers have had the temerity to point out). Yet would it have been better to have simplified the issues for the sake of an easier understanding and accessibility for the average viewer? I don't know, but if I had been Clooney I would

have more directly tied the issue of the responsibility and independence of a free press (the central issue in the film) in with what is happening today and what has happened in recent years.

Almost stopping the show by herself was jazz vocalist Dianne Reeves singing some of the standards of the era, including "How High the Moon," "One for My Baby," etc., and the very catchy and ironic, "TV is the Thing This Year." Her easy but intense concentration, her beautiful voice, and her exquisite timing were for me one of the highlights of the movie.

Bottom line: After seeing this on a return flight from Hawaii I can now say that not *every* film that I have seen on an airline has been unwatchable. However flawed, *Good Night, and Good Luck* is definitely worth the time and effort, especially for those who care about the history of broadcast journalism and governmental attempts to control the media.

I've seen this and I give it___stars.
I want to see it___. I'll pass___.
The review was worth reading___. Not___.

Grosse Pointe Blank (1997) 7

Yeah, it's point blank gross in parts

The main feature of this movie—depending on your point of view—is John Cusack, who looks like he's having a lot of fun in a quirky story quirkily done. Fans will probably find his portrayal of a whimsical professional hit man a nice departure for the accomplished and sensitive actor.

I would too except I just couldn't get over the disconnect between the sweet personality and the amoral nature of his character. Of course this is a comedy, indeed a satire and burlesque of hit man films with shootouts (two guns a-blazing) and car chases aplenty.

There is also a romance between ex-high school sweethearts Martin Q. Blank (Cusack) and Debi Newberry (Minnie Driver), and they seem nicely paired. The story is framed around Blank's disappearance on prom night ten years previous and his sudden and unexpected return on the eve of his ten-year class reunion at Grosse Pointe (Michigan) High School. His "profession" is so unlikely that he can be candid about it and nobody will believe him. "I'm a professional killer." "Nice. I'm glad that's working out for you." (Okay, I made up that dialogue, but it's close to what's really said.)

Dan Aykroyd gives comedic support in an over-the-top portrayal of a rival hit man always making with the jokes even as the bullets fly. Funny too with a lot of original shtick is John Cusack's sister, Joan Cusack, as the hit man's strange but conscientious secretary, Marcella. Alan Arkin has a modest part as Dr. Oatman, Blank's frightened shrink—frightened because he knows what Blank does for a living.

Bottom line: a bona fide cult classic with repeat viewing appeal that may not work for all audiences.

I've seen this and I give it___stars.
I want to see it___. I'll pass___.
The review was worth reading___. Not___.

Hard Eight (1996) 7

Off-beat casino drama

This is also known as "Sydney" (director Paul Thomas Anderson's original title) after the name of the movie's central character, a somewhat mysterious casino gambler (and murderer, by the way) played by veteran Philip Baker Hall. The new and more commercially-viable title comes from the game of craps in which the dice player can roll an eight with a six and a two or with a five and a three or with two fours. Since probabilistically it's harder to roll an eight with two fours than otherwise, it's called a "hard eight." Such a choice occurs twice in the movie, and symbolically a "hard eight" may represent the gambler's psychology.

Co-starring as Sydney's protégé is John C. Reilly as John Finnegan, a kind of loveable schmuck who falls in love with a Reno waitress/prostitute named Clementine, played quirkily by Gwyneth Paltrow. Samuel L. Jackson has a modest but very convincing part as a casino security sleaze.

Anderson's direction of these very talented actors was excellent. I wish I could say the same for his script. Most viewers I suspect will find this a bit dull; and, as it unfolds and we find out why Sydney is playing guardian angel to John, viewers may even be disappointed. I know I was. I had expected something original as Sydney's motivation, but what we learn in the last reel is quite ordinary (as movie motivations go).

What kept me watching was trying to figure out what makes Sydney tick and why and how he can spend his time so aimlessly gambling (and almost always losing), and where his money comes from. I also was intrigued by the originality of Anderson's treatment as opposed to his story per se. The stylized, slightly "off" dialogue, especially well-suited to Reilly's studied interpretation and Philip Baker Hall's inscrutability, reminded me of something that might have been written by David Mamet or even Quentin Tarantino. Finally I was interested in seeing how Paltrow would play a role seemingly quite removed from her screen persona. I thought the delicate and very winning star of *Shakespeare in Love* (1998), etc., worked hard to create the sort of lower-class, uneducated, "victim" of the Las Vegas/ Reno casino culture that Anderson had in mind, and I thought she did it well. However, hers was not a sympathetic role and it

did not test Paltrow's range as an actress, although playing a prostitute is something many actresses find interesting. I am thinking of Julia Roberts in *Pretty Woman* (1990) and Elisabeth Shue in *Leaving Las Vegas* (1995) or even Catherine Deneuve in *Belle de Jour* (1967).

Bottom line here is that this is a studied, "arty" movie well worth seeing because of the performances and as an example of Anderson's unique style, but not something for a mass audience or for those viewers looking for a diverting thriller.

But see this for Philip Baker Hall, one of those rare actors to actually find his best roles and do his best work in his sixties. Indeed, his performance here revitalized a career that had long languished. In this regard I am reminded of the Swedish actor Victor Sjostrom who gave perhaps his greatest performance in Ingmar Bergman's *Wild Strawberries* (1957) when he was 80 years old. Although I have seen little of Hall's work, I am willing to bet that this was one of his greatest performances.

I've seen this and I give it___stars.
I want to see it___. I'll pass___.
The review was worth reading___. Not___.

Heat (1995) 7

Superior thriller with some depth

How can a film starring Al Pacino and Robert De Niro be bad? It really can't because they would never approve the script or director. By that I mean, they would pass. The fact that neither of them passed says something. At the very least, this is a pretty good film.

And it is. In fact I think this will be one of the defining films of the nineties. I suspect it will be viewed in distant eras and scrutinized for clues about the American psyche, circa 1995. Some will see a fantasy glorifying professional criminals and the men who fight them. This will be true. Others will see a morality tale about good and evil played out with women in the background, but actually in the forefront of our consciousness. I wish this part had been more fully developed.

Eady, played by Amy Brenneman, chooses the man who excites her (De Niro) and ends up with nothing (but she had an exhilarating ride). Charlene, played by Ashley Judd, swaps her men around, searching for the best deal, the one who will best provide for her and the one she can best manipulate. Justine, played by Diane Venova, cannot help but choose the workaholic super cop (Pacino) because he is so superior to any other man she's ever met, particularly to her first husband, the uncaring father of her adolescent girl. But her life will never be secure because he is always leaving her alone so he can chase criminals because that is what he really loves.

Some of this is a mafia-style film without the mafia. We have the same worshipful attitude toward those who thumb their noses at society and give orders that must be obeyed, super macho guys who bond together and follow the code, guys who can out shoot and out fight mere mortals. This is part of the fantasy. We see the expensive cars and the dinners with the beautiful women and the adorable children at fancy restaurants as part of the booty of being men who aren't afraid to take what they want regardless of risk. These men will always have the pick of the herd because, if successful, their mates know they will get a lot of the goodies of this world, and if unsuccessful, there's always the next risk taker who might succeed.

This is a complex film and I would have to view it twice to make sure it all fits. Being a thriller, I know off hand that it won't. Thrillers unravel. But life is too short to view this twice, so I will say I wasn't offended by the unlikely events: the fact that the touted bank robbery scene was like a war scene filmed with surround sound effects and jittery camera immersions and bullets flying everywhere—semi-plausible even if nobody seemed to run out of ammunition. The robbery of the armored truck was nicely done except that the tire-puncturing chain strewn across the street for the pursuing cop cars seemed a bit stagy, and the whole thing required the most exquisite timing. In the uncompleted break-in there was a familiar "Mission Impossible" tension-filled race against the clock that seemed authentic, but probably wasn't. The Los Angeles environs, especially the final scene at LAX, provided atmospheric locales that made everything seem real and immediate.

Where I think director Michael Mann went astray was his insistence on giving the audience the expected confrontation between the two big stars, a subplot that reached its low point with the phony bonding scene with De Niro the bad guy and Pacino the good guy having coffee together and exchanging dreams like blood brothers. This mutual admiration society was right out of some WWII film in which the American general admires the courage and cunning of his Nazi counterpart and vice versa. De Niro's final line was a little corny, but Pacino's squeezing his hand reminded me of the way a big cat lovingly licks its prey after killing it. Bottom line though, Pacino and De Niro made us believe, or at least suspend judgment for a while, and that is one of the things that Hollywood is all about.

I've seen this and I give it___stars.
I want to see it___. I'll pass___.
The review was worth reading___. Not___.

Heavenly Creatures (1994) 8

Kate Winslet at 18

Christchurch, New Zealand, 1952: two school girls become friends and swoon over Mario Lanza, "world's greatest tenor," as they create a fantasy world of royalty and intense emotional attachment to one another. This is teen escapism carried to the nth degree. Innocence and wholesome fun do NOT prevail. As the parents grow increasingly concerned about their daughters' obsessive relationship, the girls begin to hate the parents... Based on a rather shocking (for its time) true story.

Kate Winslet made her film debut in this modest *comédie noire* from way down under. It is amazing to realize that three years later she starred in the Academy Award winning *Titanic* (1997), on her way to establishing herself as one of the most charismatic and talented stars of the past decade. In retrospect, her budding talent is apparent here as the spinning, laughing, crazy teen who went off the deep end emotionally. There is no mistaking the sharp, confident and commanding Winslet style. Despite the part, Kate looks as wholesome and delicious as apple pie with cherry vanilla ice cream, yet manages to convey the demented edge necessary to the role.

Full-figured and brooding Melanie Lynskey is intriguing and not easily forgotten as Kate's manic/depressive friend.

Director Peter Jackson is to be commended for getting the most out of the girls, and for making their fantasy world believable. We can imagine how they fell into it.

I've seen this and I give it___stars.
I want to see it___. I'll pass___.
The review was worth reading___. Not___.

Heavy (1995) 8

Depressing and uplifting at the same time

You might find yourself tapping your fingers with impatience with this slow motion character study, but if you stay with it you might find it indelible. Director and writer James Mangold is uncompromising in his determination that we live, breathe, feel and taste this man's loneliness, his isolation from others and his pitiful desire to find some beauty in his dreary life.

Pruitt Taylor Vince stars as a fat thirty-something who still lives with his mother and is the fry cook at her cafe/bar. I think he over acts at times, but perhaps that's what makes him so effective. He is painful to watch. Deborah Harry is entirely believable as the trampy waitress who's seen better days, and Shelley Winters is her natural self as the mother. Liv Tyler, daughter of Aerosmith rocker Steve Tyler, and seen a few years back with Alicia Silverstone in the "Crazy" music video, proves there's more to her than a beautiful figure.

The images, like still pieces from an art gallery, will stay with you: the breakfast left on the table for two weeks, the orange juice turning brown; the ugly little black and white dog: the Pete & Dolly's neon sign in red letters; the dirty dishes in the sink with the water dripping. They won't need subtitles for this one in foreign lands because not much is said. Mangold eschews dialogue for the camera.

Memorable are the breathe mints at the end of the runway and the visit to the Culinary Institute of America. The best line is Deborah Harry's sarcastic question (when Vince rejects her blatant seduction attempt): "Saving yourself for somebody special?"

I've seen this and I give it___stars.
I want to see it___. I'll pass___.
The review was worth reading___. Not___.

Hideous Kinky (1998) 6

Warm, charming and honest but lacks tension

Kate Winslet (Julia) eschews the glamour here in favor of depicting a 25-year-old mother of two seeking adventure and enlightenment with the Sufis in Morocco (instead of with the yogis in India, as was once the fashion). The year is 1972 and Julia might be a welfare mother except that there's no dole and the locale is rather exotic. Having left her poet husband behind in London, rather than "share him," Julia seeks the annihilation of the ego, and the god within. What she finds (aside from the fact that she's a little too young for that) is Bilal (Said Taghmaoui), a Marrakech street performer of questionable character who speaks English and charms her and her daughters.

Beautiful cinematography combined with a steady effort by Kate and winning performances from Bella Riza (Bea) and Carrie Mullan (Lucy) as her pre-adolescent daughters, however, cannot quite save this slightly plotted, although always realistic tale, from the bargain video bin.

Too bad because there is something wonderfully charming and honest about this film. "Wow! Hideous! Kinky!" is what the girls like to exclaim (in their London accents) in reaction to their experiences in the world. When Bea, wise as only a nine-year-old can be, describes the women on the balcony as "prostitutes," so thick is her accent that only the context allowed this old Yankee's ears to comprehend. There is a little peek-a-boo nudity that might offend some, and yes Marrakech and environs look as clean and sparkling as an upscale suburban mall, and true the editing is jumpy and a little chaotic; but in the land of the whirling dervishes perhaps this is as it should be. Bea is the daughter who disapproves of mum's adventurous spirit and wants to be "normal" and go to school every day (reminding me of Cher and Winona Ryder in *Mermaids* (1990)), while younger daughter Lucy finds love in her heart for all, especially for mum's new boyfriend, Bilal. Somehow she actually teaches him the beginnings of responsibility, while he shares with them the delight of being alive.

I think what carries this story (from the novel by Esther Freud–yes, a relation) and made it an attractive part for Kate Winslet is the fair and honest character of Julia who struggles to find herself while caring for two little girls, which is what it is like for all women. A woman cannot find herself alone. She cannot throw off the constraints and responsibility of being a mother, because those are HER children. So she must take them along where ever she goes and find with them whatever it is she seeks, and this is a burden and a delight, as this film, despite its shortcomings, clearly shows.

I've seen this and I give it___stars.
I want to see it___. I'll pass___.
The review was worth reading___. Not___.

High Plains Drifter (1973) 7

Not a chick flick

Obviously this was produced before the age of feminist political correctness. The anti-hero with no name—Clint Eastwood, of course, a throwback to his days making spaghetti westerns in Italy with Sergio Leone—comes riding tall in the saddle down into a valley with a mining town by a lake. (The movie was shot around the Mono Lake area of California.) Particularly effective in this unforgettable opening scene is the music sounding like the high whine of the wind off of the desert. This town would be "Lago," later to be renamed "Hell" by Eastwood's character who is identified in the titles as "The Stranger."

The stranger really just wants a shave and a bath and something to drink and eat and place to lay his head for the night. What he gets is a bad time from some roughnecks and a woman (Callie Travers, played by Marianna Hill) who has attraction/avoidance feelings for him. He shoots the three guys and rapes the woman before the movie is twenty minutes old. What I mean by this not being politically correct is that, despite herself, she likes it! That sort of thing is not done in cinema these days. The idea that a woman might be turned on by being raped would not play before today's audiences, nor would a Hollywood producer make such a film.

I won't go any further into the plot but suffice it to say that Eastwood is just beginning to kick tail. It seems that everybody in town is cowardly and without the will to protect themselves from the bad guys, especially the three who just got out of jail and are headed their way. How Eastwood, who directed from a script by Ernest Tidyman (*The French Connection* (1971); *Shaft* (1971), etc.), handles the familiar revenge theme is interesting.

First it is no accident that Eastwood's protagonist is named "the Stranger." That is the English title of a famous novel by Albert Camus that surely influenced Eastwood. Camus's stranger is an existential anti-hero, a kind of benign sociopath who really doesn't feel anything for others except as they affect his life. But he is not particularly violent and just lives from one day to the next without any direction or goal. He just "exists."

But Eastwood's stranger does more than just exist. He takes action, and he is very good at it. Indeed, I can't recall a western movie in which a gunman could draw faster or shot straighter, or any movie hero who was less afraid of putting his life on the line. So, in a sense what Eastwood has added to Camus's stranger is Nietzsche's superman. And herein lies, I think, the underpinning of Eastwood's philosophy and his "message." Note that the people in the town to a man are cowardly. The only exception is Sarah Belding (Verna Bloom) who, like the aforementioned Callie Travers, can't resist the stranger's forceful charm, and falls in love with him. This somehow inspires her to leave the corrupt town.

Yes, the town, like most of human society is corrupt. And yes the average man in the street is cowardly and without the will to defend himself. It is only the *ubermensch*, that rare breed celebrated in the works of the German philosopher, who has the skill, the strength and the will to bend events to his liking and to take on those who would use violence to achieve their ends.

So what Eastwood does here in his second directorial effort (following *Play Misty for Me* (1971)) is to diverge from Leone's formula. While there is some very funny and intentionally ridiculous dialogue in such films as, for example, *The Good, the Bad, and the Ugly* (1966), *or For a Few Dollars More* (1965) or *A Fistful of Dollars* (1964), there is little that is funny, intentionally or otherwise in *High Plains Drifter*. Furthermore, whereas Leone just wanted to make a buck and saw that tough-minded heroes or anti-heroes involved in action-filled revenge plots was a good way to do it, Eastwood is interested in also making a philosophic (and perhaps political) statement. We are degenerate, we humans, he is saying, except for those rare individuals who take the law into their own hands, make their own rules, and through superior skill and bravery, make their own luck and create their own reality, as does his stranger.

In this film there is also an element of the supernatural, or so it would appear. The stranger "sees" in his head the whipping of a past sheriff of the town. Perhaps it comes from the mind of the dwarf Mordecai (very well played by Billy Curtis, by the way) who witnessed the tortured death while hiding under the saloon. At any rate, the stranger shows that he is just as handy with the whip himself as he is with his six-gun.

By all means see this for an early look at the work of Clint Eastwood as both an actor and a director. You will not be bored I can assure you. But don't invite the girl friend over. If there was ever an anti-"chick flick," this is it.

I've seen this and I give it___stars.
I want to see it___. I'll pass___.
The review was worth reading___. Not___.

The Human Stain (2003) 7

Interesting plot-driven character study

Classics Professor Coleman Silk (Anthony Hopkins), exasperated that two students have yet to show up for his class points to their empty seats and ask rhetorically, "Do they exist or are they spooks?" He should have chosen his words more carefully because the two absent students are black and Silk is subsequently charged with using racial slurs by the college.

Yes, this could definitely happen, although one would expect it to be cleared up once there was an investigation. However, Coleman Silk gets more than a little uptight. Something has hit a nerve. He has enemies. He doesn't cooperate and in fact resigns in face of the charge. His wife drops dead, and at the age of 71 Coleman gets involved in a Viagra-hyped love affair with Faunia Farley (Nicole Kidman), a 34-year-old cleaning woman and high school dropout with a past.

Turns out that Coleman too has a past, and that past partially explains why he got so uptight about the racial slur charge. Seems that Coleman has "passed." Seems that he was "colored" and didn't want to be colored and so forsook his family and passed into the white world and never looked back.

This is from the novel by Philip Roth, who has written many splendid novels. The adaptation is by Nicholas Meyer who did most of the scripts for the Star Trek movies. Robert Benton's direction is professional and clear. Anthony Hopkins is very good as one would expect and Nicole Kidman as a hardtack brunette with worry lines on her face is vividly real as the bitter, but vulnerable Faunia Farley. Ed Harris plays her also bitter, spaced-out, estranged husband, a twisted Viet Vet with malevolence on his mind.

The story is told in a straight-forward way with flashbacks to Coleman's past where we see that he was a welterweight prize fighter for a while and had his heart broken because his very blonde bride-to-be just couldn't stomach the thought of marrying into a Negro family. Wentworth Miller plays young Coleman and definitely looks and acts the part. Anna Deavere Smith plays his mother with the kind of dignity you would expect from a woman who raised the son of a Pullman porter to become a classics professor at a small New England private college. Gary Sinise as Coleman's neighbor, Nathan Zuckerman (and Philip Roth perennial), narrates the story from the novel he eventually writes.

All in all an interesting movie that recalls an age gone by while at the same time reminding us that the politically correct postmodern world is upon us.

See this for Nicole Kidman who is on her way to becoming one of the great stars of the cinema as yet again she shows that she cannot be typecast, and for Anthony Hopkins, one of the more accomplished actors of our time.

I've seen this and I give it___stars.
I want to see it___. I'll pass___.
The review was worth reading___. Not___.

Indictment: The McMartin Trial (1995) 7

Vivid and compelling

This account of the most celebrated trial arising out of the child molestation and satanic abuse hysteria of the eighties and nineties—a witch hunt far worse than that of the McCarthy era in terms of lives destroyed and innocent people thrown in jail, and even worse than the Salem witch trials of the 17th century in extent, except that nobody was actually stoned or hanged, was only the tip of the iceberg. Hundreds of innocent people went to jail and some are still there. Nobody can give them back their lives, ruined by immoral prosecutors bent on career-building at any cost and by guilt-ridden latch key parents out to excite their blood lust. Yes, children do lie and more important, as this film demonstrates, they can be brainwashed and coerced into telling the most outrageous and horrific tales (and believing them) to escape the Gestapo tactics of their interrogators.

Oliver Stone produced, and Abby Mann, who wrote the celebrated Stanley Kramer film, *Judgement at Nuremberg* (1961) and Myra Mann penned the compelling script. James Woods is excellent as Ray Buckey's attorney, but Lolita Davidovich who plays the evil and sick Kee MacFarlane (who led the indoctrination of the children) is both too pretty and too sane to be truly effective. Mercedes Ruehl plays incompetent L.A. County prosecutor Lael Rubin with enough vile to drip. Sada Thompson brings warmth and charm to the part of Virginia McMartin, and Henry Thomas plays Ray Buckey to a perfect fit.

But this movie was made too soon. In the years since its production, the full extent of the hysteria has come to light. When a significant portion of a society is taken in by something like this, it takes the passage of time before the full truth can be accepted. Had director Mick Jackson known of the near pandemic extent of the sickness he might have made a larger film. As it is, this is a vivid and compelling film.

I've seen this and I give it___stars.
I want to see it___. I'll pass___.
The review was worth reading___. Not___.

The Interpreter (2005) 8

Sophisticated political thriller

The premise in this tightly wrought thriller directed by the very accomplished Sydney Pollack is that Zuwanie (Earl Cameron) the old dictator (once "freedom fighter") of an African nation called "Matobo" is coming to New York to make a speech in front of the General Assembly of the United Nations. Silvia Broome (Nicole Kidman), an interpreter at the UN, overhears part of a conversation after-hours that leads her to believe that there will be an assassination attempt on the leader's life. She tells security. Federal agent Tobin Keller (Sean Penn) is called in to investigate and help prevent an assassination.

Keller quickly discovers that Silvia is from Matobo where her parents were murdered by some of Zuwanie's henchmen and where she was subsequently involved in some political/paramilitary activities. Two questions that Keller must answer are, does she have some sort of motive to lie and how is she involved?

The problem with the film (aside from some of the usual improbabilities and contortions found in Hollywood thrillers—and to be honest there weren't that many in this one) is the ending. Without giving anything away, the probability of Zumanie being left alone after what had happened is something like zero. But the real problem is what happens between Tobin and Silvia at the end. They are both very available and after they have had the opportunity to bond under very difficult circumstances, can you guess how their relationship is resolved? I understand there was an alternative ending. Maybe Pollack should have employed it.

Pollack's films going back several decades are characterized by diversity of subject matter, excellent scripts, and star power. Four of his best are *They Shoot Horses Don't They?* (1969) (depression ear dance marathon drama starring Jane Fonda); *Tootsie* (1982) (romantic comedy starring Dustin Hoffman); *Out of Africa* (1985) (adapted from the famous book by Karen Blixen under her pen name "Isak Dinesen," starring Meryl Streep and Robert Redford); and *Sabrina* (1995) (splendid remake of the Audrey Hepburn film this time starring Julie Ormond and Harrison Ford). But he tends to like action/adventure as much as comedy or drama. He is one of filmdom's most versatile directors, and this film, while not his best, is very representative of his work.

But what carries the film is the charisma of the stars, Sean Penn and Nicole Kidman, especially Kidman who seems the very impersonation of what an interpreter at the UN might be. She manages to be delicate but tough, thoroughly professional and beautiful. I have seen her in seven or eight films and can say that she is as talented as any actress currently working. In her ability to concentrate and to completely immerse herself in a role she is comparable to Meryl Streep. Some early films of hers that display her youthful vitality and the natural sophistication and nuanced manner of her style are *Dead Calm* (1989), *Flirting* (1991), and *To Die For* (1995).

By the way, "Matobo" is not an actual nation but is the name of a national park in Zimbabwe and as far as I can tell "Ku" is not an actual language. (I have no idea what they were speaking.)

Bottom line: Can a film directed by Sydney Pollack starring Nicole Kidman and Sean Penn be anything but worth seeing?

I've seen this and I give it___stars.
I want to see it___. I'll pass___.
The review was worth reading___. Not___.

In the Loop (2009) 8

Over the top political satire

I don't know how funny this would be the second or third time around, but it was pretty funny the first. What we have is the run-up to an invasion of an unnamed Middle Eastern country with the focus on American and Brit governmental operatives as some advance the program and others try to stop it. It's an over-the-top satirical comedy, a kind of burlesque version of the real run-up prior to the invasion of Iraq.

Tom Hollander stars as a nice boy minister who wants to stop the war train. Peter Capaldi plays some kind of Brit gov attack dog with a bad case of coprolalia who enjoys nothing more than humiliating subordinates and the occasional Yank as he salivates about the marvelous maiming and killing to come. David Rasche plays Linton Barwick the American Secretary of...well they don't say, but it would be Defense. Rasche has the voice and mannerisms of the real Secretary of Defense during the Iraq War (Donald Rumsfeld) down pat. Rasche's parody of the ultimate micromanaging war-nit was for me the highlight of the movie.

There's a nice comedic take on the relationship between Karen Clarke, who plays an American assistant secretary and her intern played by Anna Chlumsky resulting in a lampoon of polticos running helter-skelter as they go about managing the ship of state.

Everything is lickety-split. The dialogue comes at you like water from a fire hose, and everybody is just drunk with nerd-gov power. There is a certain truth behind the sexually demeaning expletives coming out of just about everybody's mouth, revealing a kind of repressed macho that is the dream of persons in positions of petty power. The script and the improvs by the actors set a new high water mark in the creative use of not only the f-word but in the expression of the myriad ways one can get really hosed in various orifices.

Anyway, *In the Loop* is good for a one-time viewing with many laughs and some insight into the stupidities of our glorious leaders and their staffs.

I've seen this and I give it___stars.
I want to see it___. I'll pass___.
The review was worth reading___. Not___.

Jude (1996) 8

Don't let the kids see this

This pessimistic and rather brutal cinematic production is based on the nineteenth century novel *Jude the Obscure* by Thomas Hardy. A bowdlerized and altered version of that novel first appeared in *Harper's New Monthly Magazine* as a serial beginning in December 1894. Its original title was "The Simpletons," a title modern viewers of this movie might find appropriate considering how Jude and Sue round out their lives.

It need hardly be said that any motion picture, and certainly not one running only about two hours, can hope to do justice to Hardy's novel (his last, incidentally) which is about 180,000 words long (about 400 pages of dense text). An earlier TV miniseries version made by the BBC that I have not seen, *Jude the Obscure* (1971), ran for almost four and a half hours in six episodes. But this is a pretty good movie anyway, highlighted by an enthralling performance by Kate Winslet.

The movie starts rather slowly, if picturesquely, until Kate appears and then the movie comes to life. I have seen Winslet in several films, including her first feature film when she was 18-years-old, *Heavenly Creatures* (1994), an interesting film made in New Zealand based on a sensational matricide from the 1950s. She was very good in that film, her budding talent immediately obvious as the spinning, laughing, crazy teen who went off the deep end emotionally. In *Jude*, Winslet's sharp, confident and commanding style is given greater range and she comes across with a performance that is full of life, effervescent, delightful, witty, sly, clever, and very expressive, and she looks beautiful doing it.

The story itself, a naturalistic tragedy that in some respects anticipates Theodore Dreiser, et al., was considered immoral in its time. "The Bishop of Wakefield, disgusted with the novel's 'insolence and indecency,' threw it in the fire," according to Terry Eagleton who wrote the Introduction for the New Wessex Edition of the book. Modern film goers will hardly notice the implied critique of marriage that offended Victorian readers, but they might find the scene where Arabella throws the pig's "part" at Jude indelicate. Victorian readers found that scene most offensive. As a public service I want to warn any modern viewer who might be offended at seeing Kate Winslet naked to avoid this film. (Just Joking: Kate is quite fetching in the Rubenesque shot.) To be honest, though, this really is a tragedy that still has the power to offend some sensibilities. Certainly you don't want the kids to see it.

Christopher Eccleston plays Jude and does a good job, and Rachel Griffiths in a modest part plays Jude's first wife Arabella. Director Michael Winterbottom stayed spiritually true to Hardy's dark vision while tailoring the tale for modern audiences. There's a nice period piece feel and some charming cinematography. The denouement is well set up and so realistically done that we don't know whether to be horrified or outraged. I think I was both.

I've seen this and I give it___stars.
I want to see it___. I'll pass___.
The review was worth reading___. Not___.

The Juror (1996) 8

Underrated thriller

Alec Baldwin comes on quoting from the *Tao Te Ching*, making me think he's my kind of antihero. He's urban, sophisticated and seemingly very safe since he's an art curator, or seems to be. Demi Moore as Annie Laird, a gifted and original sculptor (she sculpts works of art that you feel with your hands by reaching up into them: it's all tactile), is thrilled when he offers to buy her work and sell it to the Japanese. Wow. She has arrived as an artist.

Thus we have an intriguing and original premise for a thriller. One almost wishes that there weren't this little matter of her agreeing to serve on the jury in the case of a Mafia boss on trial for murder.

I will gloss over the excellent, if unlikely, plot since it would be preemptive to reveal any of it, and concentrate on Demi Moore who is gorgeous, strange and riveting.

It might seem impossible to give a "heroic" performance in a thriller, since the point of a thriller is pure entertainment, but this movie manages to look into the nature of good and evil a bit more than most, and Moore plays her part like our dream of a true heroine. Her character has strength and cunning; she's sharp without pretension. I always thought Moore was better than her reputation, but somehow she always seemed a little on the not entirely bright side, the kind of actress who would never presume to play Shakespeare. But now I think she's a "natural," like a gifted athlete—I'd almost say an "animal"—as an actress, which is probably why some people don't like her. She can project the beautiful woman, an ordinary woman, or herself as a matronly woman with just a turn of her head. She can display a wide range of emotions and be, by turns, both a masculine and a feminine entity; but she is not androgynous. The role she plays here is, in a sense, the feminine counterpart of many Harrison Ford roles, the ordinary person elevated to heroic action by compelling circumstances. I

would not say that Demi Moore is a great actress, but she is close, and I could be wrong.

Alec Baldwin combines megalomania with a seductive cynicism. He fills the screen with his presence like something you can't get rid of. He is so compelling you want to push him away or just give up. And he is charming—evil, but charming.

Brian Gibson's direction is unobtrusive and clever, and he pays attention to detail. The script is relatively free of the implausibilities that usually mar the genre, and the editing is crisp without jarring. The story practically transcends the genre by making us feel the evil of violent crime and how it perverts society, the sort of revelation not usually attempted in a thriller. I was especially delighted to see the Mafia demeaned and defeated, even if it's only by a new breed of international criminal. This is a superior thriller.

I've seen this and I give it___stars.
I want to see it___. I'll pass___.
The review was worth reading___. Not___.

The Lady Vanishes (1938) 8

Early, British Hitchcock

This is a British film directed by Hitchcock before he went to Hollywood in which we see the basic Hitchcock recipe taking shape.

First there is star power in the romantic leads, the beautiful and very interesting Margaret Lockwood (if you've never seen her, you're in for a treat), who plays an ingénue about to marry the wrong man, and the accomplished Sir Michael Redgrave, who plays the right man. Next there is the so-called "Boy Meets Girl, Cute" formula—in this case it's more of a clash than a meeting. Then there's a romantic setting, first the alpine resort and then the train. (European train holidays were romantic in those days; perhaps they still are.) Then there is mystery and danger. This is accomplished by the inexplicable disappearance on the train of the lady Lockwood met at the resort, a disappearance that nobody but her seems to notice. When she tries to bring it to everyone's attention there is a kind of sinister cover up and some deliberate lying by third parties (with their own agendas) so that at first nobody believes her. Indeed, there is a psychiatrist aboard who casts doubt on her mental state. Add to this mix some interesting character play by a fine supporting cast, including Dame May Whitty, Paul Lukas, Basil Radford and Naunton Wayne; stir in some romantic indirections and mystery plot red herrings, and you have a delightful repast.

It is interesting to compare this to some later Hitchcock films. It is more of an old fashioned "who done it" than it is a psychological thriller, more like, say, *Dial M for Murder* (1954) than, *Spellbound* (1945) or *The Birds* (1963).

It is not as polished as those productions, but in some ways it is the better for it in that we never know where an individual scene is going. The whimsical business with Radford and Wayne and the Swiss maid, for example, is really extraneous to the story. Note the *Grand Hotel* (1932) feel to the opening scene with the desk clerk trying to find rooms for everyone at the inn. I don't know when Agatha Christie wrote her *Murder on the Orient Express* (the movie version came out in 1972) but she may have been influenced by *The Lady Vanishes*, or it may have been the other way around. At any rate, both stories take place in the thirties abroad trains.

Redgrave, who is the father of Lynn and Vanessa Redgrave, was thirty years old when this film was released and already a star on the London stage. Lockwood was only twenty-two, despite being a veteran of fourteen or fifteen previous films. Their performance here is an early example of the romantic comedy pair set amidst a field of danger, one of most enduring traditions in the movies.

See this for Margaret Lockwood whose strength of character and pretty features are still fresh and most appealing despite the intervening years. Such is part of the magic of film.

I've seen this and I give it____stars.
I want to see it___. I'll pass___.
The review was worth reading___. Not___.

A League of Their Own (1992) 8

Stylish, warm and fun to watch

This movie is about ten times better than it has any right to be considering how sappy director Penny Marshall could have been tempted to make it, and how phony is the actual baseball played by the young women. (More on this below.)

What makes it work are fine performances by Geena Davis as catcher Dottie Hinson, "the best player in the league," and Lori Petty as her younger sister, Kit Keller. Geena Davis absolutely looks the part with her cool confidence and stately figure while Lori Petty is scrappy and believable as the little sister whose puck and determination set the stage for a sister-rivalry climax at the end.

Jon Lovitz as Ernie Capadino, the baseball talent scout, is a crackup as he delivers just about all the best one liners. (Example: he's watching Dottie and Kit milk the cows and asks, "Doesn't that hurt them?" Geena shrugs for the city slicker, "They don't seem to mind." Ernie thinks about it and then says, "Well, it would bruise the heck out of me," which was doubly funny since he may have his anatomy confused.) But the guy who really holds the whole thing together is Tom Hanks as onetime home run king Jimmy Dugan, who is now the Rockford Peaches' alcoholic manager. I have seen Tom Hanks in a number of films, but I don't think he was ever any better than he is here. His transformation from a crude, uncaring drunk to the team's hard-nosed but soft-hearted leader is very well and believably done. And Hanks was never more charming and seldom funnier.

Just as good as the work of the fine cast is Marshall's clear, old-fashioned direction. In many ways this film is a throwback to an earlier time when films set out to warm the hearts of the audience and uplift their spirits. Sure, there is evil in the world and you can't win them all, but you can try, is what this film makes us feel, and if you do try, something good will happen. There is of course a somewhat self-conscious retrospective look at the sorry political and social state of women sixty years ago, but Marshall does not wallow in the politics. Instead she emphasizes a fun-to-watch tale with real human characters. The unpredictable, but believable ending was very agreeable.

Okay now to some of the problems with the "baseball." Notice that we first see Kit as a softball pitcher. How she made the transition from throwing underhanded to being one of the best overhand hardball throwers in the league in just a few months is...well, doubtful. And the outfits they wore! Ever try to slide into second trying to break up the double play without sliding pads or even jersey pants? I don't think so. The girls were bare-legged. To Marshall's credit she does show one girl with a huge strawberry bruise on her thigh. Furthermore for those viewers who have actually played baseball, the way many of the young women threw and caught the ball was again, shall we say, doubtful. Marshall employed as extras some young ladies who could actually play a little and we see some shots of their style and grace, but the only star who could even pretend to play at that level would be Rosie O'Donnell. Madonna has some athletic ability, but to imagine her patrolling center field and hauling down long drives strains credibility.

Okay, so what? If we put Tom Hanks at bat against even the most mediocre of Class A pitchers, it would be obvious that he is no home run king. In fact, I think Penny Marshall did a great job of creating and maintaining the illusion of Big League skills for the players so that we were not distracted from the story itself. Skillful editing helped.

By the way, if they gave Academy Awards for a performance in a role short of a supporting role but longer than a cameo (and maybe they should), Megan Cavanagh would have won it for her touching impersonation of Marla Hooch, a painfully shy and vulnerable, less than pretty girl from the farm who finds herself as a baseball player in the city as she steals some guy's heart with an unselfconscious, boozy, off-key torch song. I also loved the scene where she is rocketing line drives off the walls and through the windows of the high school gymnasium.

Note the appearance of David L. Lander as the radio play-by-play guy. He's best known as the wacky/creepy "Squiggy" Squiggman from the old "Laverne and Shirley" TV sit-com. Here he plays it mostly straight but does get to wear his hat with the bill up as Leo Gorcey did in the East Side Kids (AKA The Bowery Boys) movies from the early forties.

Bottom line here: Uplifting, fun, and even worth seeing again.

I've seen this and I give it___stars.
I want to see it___. I'll pass___.
The review was worth reading___. Not___.

Liar Liar (1997) 7

Pants on fire

Jim Carrey puts so much energy and pure comedic brilliance into this movie that we hardly noticed how corny and hackneyed was the plot or how wearily didactic was the moral lesson for all fathers who neglect their children for the goddess of success. And really we didn't care. What we loved almost as much as Carrey's rubber mouth and oral blockage (like an overheated boiler fighting not to explode) was the premise: a lawyer that can't lie. Now there's an oxymoron! As Carrey tries to explain to his son Max, lawyers need to lie. Actually he says grownups need to lie, which is a truth that we really do not need to exam too closely here. To laugh at something deeply troubling in our nature is a way of dealing with it.

So the genius of this movie is first the talent of Jim Carrey, but second, for kids who come to the realization of adult mendacity for the first time, it is the discovery of comedy as a way to cope. Why do adults need to lie? is a question that a kid can never figure out, and then by the time he is an adult himself (or actually a teenager), he can no longer comprehend how important the question once was. Call it innocence lost, or the socialization process.

My favorite part of the movie is the courtroom scene with Jennifer Tilly dressed oh so sluttily and her adulterous beaux looking like a model for the cover of a romance novel and Carrey in tatters in his $900 suit. Second would be the bathroom scene in which Carrey tries to tear himself apart (and seems to almost succeed). His flapping mouth between the toilet seat and the bowl was inspired. Give some credit to director Tom Shadyac, who managed to steer the vehicle with Carrey at the controls, and to writers, Paul Guay and Stephen Mazur, who wrote some funny lines.

The great comedians totally let themselves go. They are totally *on*. They go to extremes and beyond. It's like transcending not just the ordinary, but even the imagined. See this obviously for Jim Carrey, one of the great comedic talents of our time, an original who would have delighted Charlie Chaplin with his extraordinary muggings, his blatant audacity and his suburb timing.

I've seen this and I give it___stars.
I want to see it___. I'll pass___.
The review was worth reading___. Not___.

Lost in America (1985) 8

Yuppie love gets the road test

Los Angeles ad agency exec David Howard (Albert Brooks, who also directed and with Monica Johnson co-wrote the script) doesn't get the promotion he expected. In fact he's being sent to New York. He blows his stack, does a "you can take this job and shove it" routine and is out the door. He tells his wife Linda (Julie Hagerty, whom I recall as the flight attendant in the very funny *Airplane!*(1980)) that this is all for the best because, like his hero from the movie *Easy Rider* (1969), he wants to quit the rat race, drop out of society and just get on the road and see America.

She too quits her job. They sell the house, consolidate their cash, buy a Winnebago and hit the road. How wonderful this is going to be!

Well, no. Of course things go haywire. I'll leave the details for you to observe while noting that this is a funny and ultimately charming movie, a romantic comedy for the already married done in a low-key manner ending in yuppie irony.

See this for Albert Brooks whose modest career includes roles in some fine flicks most notably, *Broadcast News* (1987), and *Taxi Driver* (1976).

I've seen this and I give it___stars.
I want to see it___. I'll pass___.
The review was worth reading___. Not___.

Macao (1952) 7

Interesting exotic film noir featuring a sultry Jane Russell

This begins with a chase scene: a man in a white suit and white hat running, being chased by some thugs and a sinister Chinese guy with a knife. The man stops and looks back, forgetting Satchel Paige's dictum: "Don't look back, something might be gaining on you." They are in fact only a dozen yards or so behind. But he starts running again and miraculously they are now further behind! (Typical chase scene camera work resulting in illogic. But never mind.) He ducks around a corner and hides. One of the thugs pauses, turns and sees him, which gives the man in the white suit a chance to knock him off his feet with a swift uppercut. Then he runs off in the direction he had turned. I was thinking how much he would be ahead of everybody by now if he had just kept running.

Chase scene ends with a knife thrown at him landing in the middle of his back. He's a cop from New York. Dead. Somehow this scene reminded me of something from Bud Abbott and Lou Costello.

Next scene is much better. Jane Russell as Julie Benson is in a cabin room on a passenger ship with a touristy kind of guy who's dancing, if you can call it that. He wants more than dancing. Julie pushes him away. He won't take no for an answer. She takes off a high heel and throws it at him. He ducks and the high heel flies out the window and hits Robert Mitchum who's playing an adventurer named Nick Cochran who just happened to be walking by. Boy meets girl, cute.

After a fashion he rescues the lady in distress. She's a hard talking, sultry babe with attitude. He wants to continue the party after knocking the masher out, but Julie isn't interested. So he takes her and kisses her. Very manly. She still isn't interested and tells him to beat it.

He does, but some time later he notices that his wallet is missing. We see her take out the dough and toss the wallet overboard. A few minutes later she meets up with William Bendix playing a global traveling salesman named Lawrence C. Trumble. Of course we know this is an elaborate disguise and he is somebody other than who he pretends to be. The "C" stands for Cicero, he later tells Nick, "but don't tell anybody." Trumble makes with the pleasantries, but Julie brushes him off. He tells her what he's selling. One thing she likes is nylons. He gives her a free pair, "no strings attached." She takes off her old nylons right there on the deck, tossing them overboard, one by one. Nick manages to be passing on the deck beneath and catches one of them as she puts on the new nylons. Later she asks, "Did you get a nice view?"

It's Macao, 36 miles from Hong Kong. It's hot. People are smoking and smuggling and gambling, and ex-pats who are stranded tend to make friends quickly. Naturally there's romance with Julie falling for Nick and vice versa, but some misunderstandings come between them. One has to do with Margie, played by the always intriguing Gloria Grahame, who, unlike Jane Russell, actually has an Oscar statue for her work in *The Bad and the Beautiful* from 1952, which, alas, I haven't seen. Seems that Margie would like to get her mitts on Nick and so manages at the urging of her boss, who owns a gambling nightclub, to make it seem like Nick bedded her down, or vice-versa, as you like.

This reminded me a bit of *Casablanca* (1942) and *To Have and Have Not* (1944) in that we have an American in an exotic locale with a dame in a joint amid some nefarious goings-on. As in *To Have and Have Not*, Jane Russell, like Lauren Bacall, does some singing. One of

the numbers is "Make It One for My Baby and One More for the Road," which she does very well. Russell hails from a time when movies featured full-figured babes, and she was one of the best. Sexy, shapely and not a bad actress, Russell melted a few hearts in her time.

In a way "Macao" is almost a parody of Far Eastern intrigue films, which might account for the slight Abbott and Costello feel. I think this may come from the fact that Josef von Sternberg began as director, but Howard Hughes fired him and had Nicholas Ray finish up. Anyway, this moves right along and there is some nice chemistry between the two stars. Personally I got a kick out of seeing them both again after all these years.

Bottom line: a kind of film noir done with atmosphere and a lot of snappy one-liners. Definitely worth seeing.

I've seen this and I give it___stars.
I want to see it___. I'll pass___.
The review was worth reading___. Not___.

Marnie (1964) 8

Haunting performance by Tippi Hedren

The cheesy backdrops offend the contemporary eye. The score is obtrusive, even, at times, dictatorial. Miss Hedren on horseback for the most part isn't, both in the sense that the stunt person is clearly not her, and in the sense that sometimes we can't help but notice that she is in studio with the background moving behind her. And, as others have pointed out, the red of bloody remembrance that offends Marnie's eyes is a trite and obvious device, not worthy of Hitchcock at his best. Furthermore, some of the scenes are stagy almost to the point of naïveté (but Hitchcock never worried about that as long as his effect was clear). The scene with the children outside the Baltimore apartment—done twice, actually to set up a third scene in which the children are quiet and stare—comes to mind, as does the scene in front of the Rutland residence as the newlyweds are about to depart for their bizarre honeymoon. Perhaps "artificial" is a better word than "stagy." The overall psychology is strictly "Freudian for the Millions," but with a certain plausibility, while the story itself is far from convincing, regardless of whether you see it from Marnie's viewpoint or from that of Mark Rutland.

Nonetheless this uneven psychodrama is an interesting and enjoyable movie, clearly within the hallowed Hitchcock canon, mainly due to a haunting performance by Tippi Hedren that will not soon leave my mind. It is clear that Hitchcock could not take his eyes off of her and neither could I. This is not to say Miss Hedren was brilliant. She was not. But in a sense, because her performance was striking and ordinary by turns, somehow it became—at least for me—indelibly real and entirely believable. It is to Hedren's credit that, in a movie in which the plot strains credibility at times, she is strikingly real.

She plays the sociopathic office girl from the wrong side of the tracks with intelligence and vulnerability. Add her great beauty and one can almost believe that the rich, ultra-eligible Mark Rutland would actually be moved to marry her out of obsession and a desire to save her.

Alfred Hitchcock's signature technique, in which the plot elements are made childishly clear to even the most inexperienced viewer through audio and visual repetition, camera focus, silence and/or a surging score, is perhaps a bit too much on display here. Yet, once in motion, the plot plays out very well and we are comfortably ensconced in the world of small business America at mid-century. Sean Connery, who plays Mark Rutland, gives a fairly convincing performance in an unlikely role. I was thinking how much more tension might have been created had Rutland been played by somebody less attractive and more menacing. But Hitchcock rightly insisted on glamour and box office appeal in his leading characters, and sought to win the feminine side of the audience at all costs (therefore only *attractive* leading men!). And he was right in following this formula. One can imagine a remake of *Marnie* with, say, Nicole Kidman and John Malkovich, both excellent actors; but what would be lost? And would the movie be as interesting? We would lose some glamour and charisma—mainstays of the Hitchcock oeuvre—and the result would probably not be as engaging. Incidentally, Nicole Kidman did play a sociopathic little sickie in *To Die For* (1995), an underrated film that I recommend. Comparing performances I have to say that while Nicole was good, Tippi was mesmerizing.

The sharp and convincing response of Marnie to the forced marriage in which her frigidity is made manifest owes a lot to Hitchcock's passionate direction. I have to say though, that this is, in part, a little Hitchcockian joke on his audience. After all, how many poor little office girls would not delight in being "forced" to marry such a rich and handsome man whose wedding presents include a six and a half caret diamond ring? In other words, the staples of women's romance—the big house with servants, wealth, and a strong, handsome man who adores the central character and proves it—are very much in evidence amidst the psycho dynamics. All those who would imitate Hitchcock should keep this point in mind.

The script (adapting the novel by Winston Graham) by Jay Presson Allen, who has *The Prime of Miss Jean Brodie* (1969) and *Cabaret* (1972) among his credits, contains some attractive dialogue, especially in some of the exchanges between the stars. An example is Sean Connery's reassuring line to Marnie, "Dad goes by scent. If you smell anything like a horse, you're in."

Initially, I didn't care for the character of Marnie's mother, played strangely by Louise Latham, but upon reflection she is off beat enough to be real. The scene (with a cameo of Bruce Dern as a sailor) revealing why Marnie

became a pathological liar, a thief and frigid was plausible but not entirely convincing. The frigidity was understandable given her mother's hatred of men and what happened to her as a little girl, but why she became a sociopath fixated on trying to win her mother's love above all else seemed inconsistent. The ending is nicely ambiguous, allowing one to draw his or her own conclusion about the effect that such insights will have on Marnie's character.

It was nice to see Diane Baker as the girl who doesn't get the guy, and Mariette Hartley as a gossipy secretary.

I've seen this and I give it___stars.
I want to see it___. I'll pass___.
The review was worth reading___. Not___.

Mean Girls (2004) 7

Familiar but with some good laughs

This is partially a rip off of *Heathers* (1989) in that there are three mean girls ("The Plastics"—in Heathers they were all named "Heather") who control the high school social scene until along comes a new girl who changes the dynamics. In Heathers, a kind of darker comedy with some uneasy belly laughs, Winona Ryder is the new girl. Here we have perky Lindsay Lohan starring as Cady Heron, a previously home-schooled girl whose parents decide she might need some socializing American-style before embarking on college. Lohan is wholesome and cute, and does a fine job of getting us to identify with her character.

Rachel McAdams (ten years older than 17-year-old Lohan, by the way) plays Regina George, the leader of the plastic pack. She is voluptuous, spoiled, vain, and as mean behind her smile as a junkyard dog. She gives perhaps the best performance. The other two girls are Lacy Chabert as Gretchen Wieners and Amanda Seyfried as Karen Smith, who tends to play dumb. Lizzy Caplan is noticeable as the goth girl who, along with her sidekick Damien played by Daniel Franzese, attempt to thwart the power of the plastics. The teen heartthrob is Jonathan Bennett playing Aaron Samuels.

The screenplay is by Tina Fey who also plays teacher Ms. Norbury. She adapted the script from the nonfiction book, *Queen Bees and Wannabes: Helping Your Daughter Survive Cliques, Gossip, Boyfriends and Other Realities of Adolescence* by Rosalind Wiseman. What I think happened (since the book was hardly needed as a starting point for Fey) is that the producers credited Wiseman with some inspiration to detract from the fact that the premise and some of the treatment are taken directly from *Heathers*. Oh, well, in Hollywood whatever works once will surely return in some kind of sequel or remake or as cinematic plagiarism—if such a thing exists.

Note well the PG-13 rating here. The "f" word is phased out and replaced with some clever euphemisms (and that is good since the "f" word really needs a long Hollywood rest) and (I understand) some of the raunchier jokes were cut.

This may be a little too simplistic for some high school students and a bit too familiar for experienced movie goers, but a good fit for a thirtysomething mother to watch with her teenaged daughter and share some laughs since the social dynamics haven't changed much over the years.

I've seen this and I give it___stars.
I want to see it___. I'll pass___.
The review was worth reading___. Not___.

Meet the Fockers (2004) 7

Fockerizing the CIA?

So as I left the theater I was thinking, how funny you think this film is depends a lot on how old you are, and who you are, and who you identify with in the stratified society. If you are a couple of New Aging hippies nostalgic for the summer of love and your lost libido, you gotta love it. But if you are Oliver North or Dick Cheney, welding loose cannons or loose nukes—whatever—this has got to be some kind of insult to American manhood.

Anyway, there was this carnival guy in the lobby with a pink top hat and a big red nose and a microphone getting comments—for publicity I guess. "DID YA MEET THE FOCKERS? he says, eyes wide. Most people ignore him but some guy in a NASCAR baseball cap says:

"Yeah, I met 'em and the Byrnes too. I wasn't too impressed. They're kinda gay and touchie-feelie. So fock off, would you?"

He and his bud crack up.

An older woman says in passing, "Bobbie De Niro used to be such a fine actor. And so handsome. Now look what they've done to him. Oy ve! But Bah-bra. Wasn't *she* divine! She is sooo good at comedy. So funny, so natural."

"Perfect casting," her friend says.

One teenaged boy says, "Yeah, dude, just like Frankie's parents. You know Frankie Rigotelli...I mean crack me up like wow it was so, so identical, I mean *identical.* Dude, like when he f..in' kisses him on the neck like he wants blood or something. I mean, dude, it was bogus."

His buddy says, "Teri Polo is hot."

"Yeah, I'd like to—."

Never mind.

A pregnant woman with her husband, beaming: "We loved it. So funny and the little boy was just adorable, wasn't he, honey?"

"Adorable."

An old guy in a World War II red hat with gold scrambled egg on the bill, snarls, "No retired CIA operative would stand for that. It's just not natural. That's not the way he would act. He'd, he'd...take *control* of the situation. Dustin Hoffman's a pussy. He can't knock Robert De Niro down. That's as phony as a three-dollar bill."

"'Meet the Parents' was better," a woman says to the guy she's with.

"Yeah, but the kid was adorable."

"Adorable."

So I thought, what did *I* think of the movie? Well, you have two of the most outstanding actors of our time, De Niro and Dustin Hoffman in it (totally miscast, of course). But they do a good job anyway. You have a really fine performance by Barbra Streisand. She is just perfect as a sex therapist for seniors. Seems like she was born for the part. And yes, Bradley Pickren as the boy whose first spoken word is "asshole" is as cute as cute can be. And what is more, they did a great job of getting all those expressions out of him on film and then splicing them in at exactly the right spot.

But I wonder if this is director Jay Roach's best work. My laugh-o-meter says no. I understand the prequel *Meet the Parents* (2000) which also starred De Niro and Ben Stiller (but no Dustin Hoffman or Barbra Steisand) was funnier, but I haven't seen it so I can't say. I did see one of the Austin Powers movies that Roach directed and it was very funny.

A warning: some straight-laced types might find this movie a bit creepy. After all, the Fockers are parents who have a trophy wall for their son showing off his ninth or tenth place ribbons for whatever along with his jock strap, framed. On the other hand, I think young people might get some chuckles laughing at people who remind them of their parents. And, for some aging hippies this might come off as a very warm movie. There's a happy ending in which the uptight learn to loosen up a bit, and they did, as Barbra Streisand's character says, "Fockerize" De Niro's Jack Byrnes, who is a retired CIA agent.

So bottom line is chill out. This is a comedy and if you don't feel Fockerized, well, then you can just—

Never mind. But remember, as Dustin Hoffman says, trying to keep it quiet at night and maybe save a little on the water bill:"If it's yellow, let it mellow, and if it's brown, flush it down."

I've seen this and I give it___stars.
I want to see it___. I'll pass___.
The review was worth reading___. Not___.

Miami Blues (1990) 7

Better than the title might suggest

I caught this out of KTLA Channel 5 in Los Angeles flipping channels. I do not like to watch movies on TV because they cut a lot and stack the commercials so heavily at the end that you can never stand to see how they turn out—although missing the inevitable chase scene is good.

But here we have some surprising stuff amidst the usual corrupt cops and big city decadence. Jennifer Jason Leigh, when she was still as sweet as Tupolo honey—before *Single White Female*—plays a Mississippi girl working her way through the local college by hooking. (If I had read the plot summary I'd have passed: just the title is enough to make me want to burn a leisure suit). She meets Alec Baldwin, who plays a buff psychopathic killer just out of jail. He latches on to her naiveté, discovers that she can cook and has a heart of gold; so he makes love to her like he means it, rents her a furnished house and tells her they're married. She only wants white picket fences and being a mommie... He only wants to crash and burn. You can guess who gets what.

Fred Ward plays a crusty detective whose gun, badge and dentures (!) are stolen by Baldwin. Sight joke: as Ward closes in, we see him through the window of his grit mobile peeling a banana to gum.

There's enough clever play here to divert the mind once upon a rainy afternoon. Look for vinegar pie used as a lie detector and a pawn-brokering momma with a mean machete.

I've seen this and I give it___stars.
I want to see it___. I'll pass___.
The review was worth reading___. Not___.

Monster (2003) 8

Riveting, sensational, and horrific

As advertised (and Academy-awarded) this movie contains a brilliant, startling and sensational performance by Charlize Theron as the true-life prostitute/serial killer Aileen Wuornos. Theron is over the top yet at the same time so totally controlled that her character is beautifully—if horrifically—realized. Opening as a much-abused street hooker who is treated like trash by almost everybody, Theron morphs "Lee" into a swaggering, macho murderess in a manner sure to chill many viewers straight to the bone. Yet all the while Theron conveys the vulnerability of a tragically twisted person who was never loved, only beaten, raped and tossed aside. The sordidness of her life and the hopelessness of her future are indelibly etched upon our memory.

Much of the credit for this once in a lifetime performance must go to director Patty Jenkins who also wrote the script, which is itself quite a sensation. Jenkins books no compromise with propriety or with the audience's sensitivities. She rubs our face in Aileen's dehumanized life as a street hooker picked up by strangers who treat her like filth and abuse her in ways that are unspeakable. Central to the irony of the film is the fact that her life is that of a likely serial killer victim herself, since women who ply their trade in such a way are most vulnerable to sadistic attacks. But "Lee," inspired by her passionate and first-in-a-lifetime love for Selby, her mousy lesbian girlfriend, played with sly and sneaky sparkle by Christina Ricci, turns the tables on the sickies who pick her up and finds a measure of short-lived empowerment by blowing the johns away with a large revolver.

Jenkins uses quick and deft strokes to establish who and what Aileen is, and just as deftly establishes Selby as the church-going wallflower at the local same-sex bar. Jenkins's technique thrusts the viewer headlong into the story as Aileen drags herself out of the rain and into the bar to meet Selby who immediately latches onto her. Quickly they become friends, and then in a compelling and entirely convincing scene, fall in love while roller skating. This is followed by a steamy alley engagement in which both "Lee" and Selby discover their wild passion for one another. Both scenes are among the best of their type that I have ever seen.

Although Theron got the major share of the glory for the success of this movie, and Jenkins most of the credit, Ricci was not far behind. Her character too is etched in my mind. How wonderfully cast were the two, the one physical and manlike, the other weak, naive and femme. And how lifelike the chemistry and how tragic the conjoining.

Yes, this is an American tragedy thurbo'ed up for sensation-seeking audiences, presented with relentless views of violence and sensuality, featuring humanity at its most debased. So over-the-top were some of the scenes that I found myself unaccountably laughing in surprise at the sheer hutzpah of Jenkins's savage treatment.

Be forewarned that this movie leaves little to the imagination, and when it does, it makes sure you know exactly what depravity you are to imagine. As such I would not recommend that anyone with delicate sensibilities view it. It is a study of the character of two women who find first love and first real passion together, but it is so thoroughly laced with violence and depravity that for many that love will become nothing more than ignoble animal lust.

See this for both Charlize Theron and Christina Ricci, two of cinema's most gifted young actresses.

I've seen this and I give it___stars.
I want to see it___. I'll pass___.
The review was worth reading___. Not___.

Mortal Thoughts (1991) 7

Better than its reputation

First of all I have no idea why this was named "Mortal Thoughts." More appropriate would be, "Fatal Lies" or "An Inadvertent Confession," or maybe "Desperate Friends."

Be that as it may, this is a superior thriller mainly because the story is compelling and the acting is first rate. Demi Moore who plays Cynthia is just outstanding. She commands the screen with her beautiful and expressive features and her great natural skill. If you don't like her, I guarantee you will not like this movie because she dominates the film. She is as vivid and unforgettable as an Al Pacino or a Betty Davis.

As an aside on the career of Demi Moore, I want to say that it's a shame for her that her off-screen personality is not well liked, which in large part accounts for the fact that she is one of the most underrated, although one of the most often seen and hardest-working stars of the last fifteen years or so. This movie is an example of how she is ignored. The plain fact is her performance here is better than many who have won Oscars, and she wasn't even nominated. Another problem for her is that this movie (and others she has made) are not the sort of films that the Academy pays much attention to. *Mortal Thoughts* (which she co-produced, by the way) is too low-budget, too "common" one might say, for any part in it to be taken seriously in an artistic sense. Too bad.

Glenne Headly (Joyce) is also outstanding while Bruce Willis is excellent as Joyce's drug-addled, boozing, wife-beating loser of a husband. The dialogue is right on, realistically depicting the lives of New Jersey beauty shop people while the plot told in ersatz flashbacks unfolds nicely with a fine tension.

The story is that of two friends, Joyce and Cynthia who find they have to cover up a killing (NOT a murder, but at worst a manslaughter, or better yet, a case of self-defense), but fall apart as the investigation closes in on them. In a sense they are both like Lady Macbeth with blood on their hands and no effective way to wash it off. They are both appropriately naive as young working-class women, and both act foolishly, as many of us might in their predicament.

Here's a nice bit of ironic dialogue. Joyce is questioning her ability to convince people about what happened. She tells Cynthia that she isn't a very good liar. But Cynthia reassures her: "Joyce, you're a terrific liar. You just lost confidence in yourself."

This is all to the good as far as film-making goes. It is the ending that is the problem.

One might ask, what happened to the ending? Maybe I need to watch this again to be sure I didn't miss anything. But better yet, YOU watch it and you be the judge. What I think happened is director Alan Rudolph truncated it. Either that or he decided to try something artistic, which I don't recommend in a commercial thriller flick. Maybe they just ran out of money and had to wrap it up. At any rate, we are left wondering what is going to happen and who actually did what to whom. Presumably, the last flashback from Cynthia tells us how Bruce Willis's character met his end, but that doesn't solve the problem of how or why (somebody else) was shot full of holes. Maybe the producers thought they would wrap it all up in a sequel. Actually, there's enough there for one, easily.

I would also like to complain about a movie that acts out a false story told by one of the characters as though the story were true. That can be done, but it must be done in such a way that there is some kind of hint or "coloring" of the story that allows the viewer to suspect that something is amiss. True, Det. John Woods (Harvey Keitel) makes some compelling arguments along the way to suggest that Cynthia is not telling the truth, but we are misled by the actions that our eyes see and the sounds that our ears hear. In movies, since anything can be contrived, it is the usual rule to have the camera show the truth while letting the characters do the lying.

What might have saved this (and what I was expecting all the way through) is Joyce's side of the story acted out on screen so that we could compare the stories and make our choice about who was telling the truth.

Bottom line: better than one might expect with a realistic edge clearly a notch or two above the usual thriller fare.

I've seen this and I give it___stars.
I want to see it___. I'll pass___.
The review was worth reading___. Not___.

Murder by Death (1976) 7

Grade B+ Neil Simon

Despite the (mostly) excellent cast this movie production of Neil Simon's play leaves a little to be desired. In particular I think that director Robert Moore needed to work harder toward getting the timing of his players down pat and focusing the jokes. I also think it was a mistake to cast Truman Capote in the role of Lionel Twain, the eccentric millionaire who invites the five world famous detectives to his estate with the idea of matching murderous wits with them and fooling them. Although he looks the part, Capote stands out like a sore thumb amidst the much more experienced and talented cast, so much so that I almost felt sorry for him. He pronounces his lines competently but with neither flair nor finesse.

The premise of the play reveals Neil Simon's satirical intent: the characters are all caricatures of famous fictional detectives: Inspector Sidney Wang (Peter Sellers) as a Charlie Chan type; Sam Diamond (Peter Falk) as a Sam Spade type; Inspector Milo Perrier (James Coco) as a famous Belgique detective of similar name who could also be Georges Simenon's famous French detective (except that he cries out, "Not Frenchie—Belgie!"). The absurd plot begins as the detectives motor toward Twain's haunted, fog-shrouded castle in northern California for a dinner that is never served. Everything is played as a farce ("farce —n. 1. a comedy based on unlikely situations and exaggerated effects." —Random House College Dictionary) and everybody tries to ham it up. I particularly liked Peter Sellers as the Chinese Wang with his #3 adopted Japanese son in tow. Alec Guinness plays the blind butler ("The butler did it?") while Nancy Walker has a small part as the blind and deaf cook. David Niven is mildly amusing as the debonair Dick Charleston who, unbeknownst to his wife (Maggie Smith), has only a buck-seventy-some in his tuxedo pocket (and some stamps) after going through some of her millions.

Representative joke: When asked by his #3 adopted Japanese son why *he* has to clean up the dead body, Inspector Wang tells him, "Because your mother isn't here." By the way, the makeup on Peter Sellers ("Inspector Slanty," according to Sam Diamond) is especially well done. As usual Peter Sellers manages to look more like the character he is playing than himself, so much so that one needs to do a double take to realize it is Peter Sellers at work.

One of the problems with a movie like this is that all the actors are trying to upstage one another and every line and pratfall is played as *my* moment in the spotlight so there is little contrast around which to frame the best bits. Still, aficionados, especially those viewing this repeatedly, will find plenty to crack up about.

See this for Neil Simon, one of America's most popular playwrights, whose semi-sophisticated, upbeat comedies delighted theater and movie audiences for several decades beginning in the Sixties. I particularly loved *The Out-of-Towners* (1970) with Jack Lemmon and Sandy Dennis; *The Good-bye Girl* (1977) with Richard Dreyfuss and Marsha Mason; and the unforgettable *The Odd Couple* (1968) starring Jack Lemmon and Walter Matthau. Simon and Peter Falk followed this up with *The Cheap Detective* (1978). Incidentally, Falk's work here and in *The Cheap Detective* and in a couple of earlier Columbo movies served as a proving ground for his long-running TV hit *Columbo*.

I've seen this and I give it___stars.
I want to see it___. I'll pass___.
The review was worth reading___. Not___.

Nadine (1987) 7

Entertaining eye candy

This is the kind of movie that starts out with strikingly real characterizations—Nadine is herself quite a piece of work, Texas country simple but shrewd with a strong will—and an interesting premise, but doesn't maintain the excellence.

Kim Basinger is gorgeous in the title role and natural. Jeff Brides plays her estranged husband Vernon Hightower who owns a bar in Austin, Texas circa 1954 that is not doing much in the way of business. He is one of those guys who dream of making it big financially in business as a proof of his manhood, a guy who has always just gotten by on his good looks, a guy who often lies and cuts corners and can't be trusted, but a guy with a smile to charm a rattlesnake. These two really love each other but are currently in the process of getting divorced and Vernon has a girlfriend (Renée, played with eager finesse by Glenne Headly) that he wants to marry, he thinks.

The plot begins with Nadine going to a photographer's studio and demanding to get back some "art studio" shots of her that were taken under the guise of being shown to Hugh Hefner at Playboy. The photographer is murdered and Nadine mistakenly ends up with some photos of the plans for the new Interstate that will be built nearby, plans that Buford Pope (Rip Torn) and his thugs want for themselves because, if you know where the highway will be built you can buy up the property near it on the cheap and then sell it later for a big profit. Vernon knows this too and when he finds the photos in Nadine's purse, he takes off with them.

The questions that the plot will answer are (1) Will Vernon and Nadine escape from Buford Pope and his strongmen with the photos and their lives? and (2) Will Vernon and Nadine realize they really love each other and find true love and happiness together?

There is a shoot-out in a junkyard near the end that's...different, and there's a neat car chase and...well, the movie that started out so well deteriorates into something ordinary, but not all that bad.

Robert Benton, who wrote the script for *Bonnie and Clyde* (1967) and both wrote and directed *Kramer vs. Kramer* (1979) directed. He has a fine feel for character and can write authentic and witty dialogue. He is not at his best here; nonetheless this is definitely worth seeing mainly because Bridges and Basinger do such a great job of filling up the screen. Basinger in particular is wonderful. See it for her.

I've seen this and I give it___stars.
I want to see it___. I'll pass___.
The review was worth reading___. Not___.

Never Cry Wolf (1983) 8

Fine fictionalized documentary ahead of its time

This fictionalization of the Farley Mowat book about his Arctic adventures studying wolves is amazingly enough perhaps the most controversial film Disney studios ever made. How sad is that? The reasons for the controversy would seem minor: first, the movie is not entirely true to Mowat's book; two, it's lightly plotted; and three, a man is seen running around naked in the tundra. To which I say, so what? so what? and gee, how offensive. (Maybe they should have clothed the wolves.)

The latter complaint is the major reason for all the ranting by some "reviewers." To them a Disney film showing human nakedness seems a sacrilege and they want their bowdlerized world returned to them, and they want Disney censured and made to promise never to do anything like that again! The complaint that there wasn't enough tension in the film is also off base since this is a contemplative, even spiritual film, not a slick thriller. People with sound-bite attention spans who need to mainline exploding cars and ripped flesh to keep them interested need not apply.

The criticism that Director Carroll Ballard's film is not entirely true to the book is legitimate, but I would point out that movies are seldom if ever entirely true to their source material. A film is one kind of media with its particular demands while a book is another. It is impossible to completely translate a book into a movie. Something is always inevitably lost, but something is often gained. Here the cinematography and the beautiful musical score by Mark Isham are fine compensations.

The acting by Charles Martin Smith as "Tyler" (Farley Mowat) and Brian Dennehy as Rosie, the exploitive redneck bush pilot, and Samason Jorah as Mike the compromised Inuit (who sells wolf skins for dentures) and especially Zachary Ittimangnaq as Ootek, the quiet, wise man of the north are also pluses. Note how compactly the main issues of the film are exemplified in these four characters. Indeed, what this film is about is the dying of a way of life, not just that of the wolves, but of the Inuit people themselves who are losing their land and their resources while their young people are being seduced away from what is real and true and time-honored for the glittering trinkets of the postmodern world. This is a story of impending loss and it is as melancholy as the cold autumn wind that blows across the tundra.

What I think elevates this above most nature films is first the intense sense of what it would be like for a lower forty-eight kind of guy to survive in a most inhospitable wilderness, and second the witty presentation of some of the scenes. Ballard works hard to make sure we understand that it is cold, very cold and desolate and that there are dangers of exposure and weather and just plain loss of perspective that have killed many a would-be adventurer and might very well kill Tyler. I think it was entirely right that near the end of the film we get the sense that Tyler is going off the deep end emotionally, that the majestic and profoundly melancholy experience has been too much for him.

Tyler begins as a greenhorn biologist dropped alone onto a frozen lake amid snow covered mountains rising in the distance so that we can see immediately how puny he is within this incredibly harsh vastness. The following scene when Ootek finds him and leaves him and he chases Ootek until he drops, and then Ootek saves him, gives him shelter, and leaves again without a word, was just beautiful. And the scenes with the "mice" and running naked among the caribou and teaching Ootek to juggle were delightful. The territorial marking scene was apt and witty and tastefully done. (At least, I don't think the wolves were offended.)

This movie was not perfect, however. The "interior" of Tyler's tent was way too big to fit into the tent as displayed. Also it would be important from a nutritional point of view for Tyler to eat the "mice" raw as the wolves did! (The actual creatures that Mowat ate I assume were mice.) If Tyler had to exist purely on roasted and boiled rodent for many months, he would encounter some nutritional deficiencies. Still, eating a diet of the whole, uncooked mouse would be sustaining whereas a diet of lean meat only would not. (Add blubber and internal organs for an all-meat diet to work.) Incidentally, the Inuit people get their vitamin C from blubber and the contents of the stomachs of the animals they kill.

Where were the mosquitos and the biting flies that the tundra is infamous for?

Since this movie appeared almost twenty years ago, the public image of the wolf has greatly improved and wolves have been reintroduced to Yellowstone Park. I think everybody in this fine production can take some credit for that.

I've seen this and I give it___stars.
I want to see it___. I'll pass___.
The review was worth reading___. Not___.

Night and the City (1992) 7

Fine performance by De Niro

This is a remake of *Night and the City* (1950) directed by Jules Dissan, who was blacklisted by Hollywood because of actions by the House Un-American Activities Committee, and for that reason is dedicated to Dissan who had to continue his career in Europe. The original film starred Richard Widmark, Gene Tierney, Francis L. Sullivan and Herbert Lom. I haven't seen that film, but I understand that it is very good.

This film from 1992 is not bad; however for some reason its reputation isn't much. The voters at IMDb give it a rather tepid 5.7 stars out of 10 while giving the original 8 out of 10. I'm not sure why, but I think it has to do with:

(1) Robert De Niro playing a non-heroic character. It certainly doesn't have anything to do with his acting. He is outstanding as Harry Fabian, flimflam low life lawyer and cheap BS artist who tries desperately to make a big splash as a fight promoter. I think most De Niro fans would prefer to see him in a more two-fisted role. At any rate, those who didn't like the movie almost certainly didn't care for De Niro's performance since his character dominates the action.

(2) The ending, which some might see as unfinished and others as disagreeable since, regardless of what transpires, Fabian is still a loser, perhaps bigger than ever.

(3) Some rather cheesy plot play. Near the end Fabian and Helen (Jessica Lange looking as fetching as ever) hide in a dead end alley among dumpsters and trash cans. Well, they should have continued running since the guys after them were only walking. Also when Fabian and Helen run out the side door of the restaurant they go the wrong way so that the heavies can see them running across the street. Had they turned left instead of right (as anybody in their situation would have done) they would not even have been seen. Furthermore, Fabian in a flamboyant gesture throws $12,000 into the air that flutters to the ground in the dead end alley. Nobody bothers to pick it up. That could happen.

What cannot be faulted is the authentic New York atmosphere created by director Irvin Winkler, who is better known as a producer, most notably of the Sylvester Stallone "Rocky" films, and the fine work by the rest of the cast, especially Alan King (Ira "Boom Boom" Grossman), Eli Wallach (Peck), Cliff Gorman (Phil Nasseros), and Jack Warden (Al Grossman). The story itself, from a novel by Gerald Kersh (script by Richard Price), is a variation on the "lovable, colorful loser makes good" theme, only in this case, like an inept noir anti-hero, he falls on his face—more than once, by the way.

No real De Niro fan should miss this. Personally I thought it was one of his best performances. The rapid fire dialogue, the fawning, pathetic, yet somehow uplifting personality were not something most actors could pull off, at least not nearly as well. De Niro became the character he portrayed.

Bottom line: definitely worth seeing. You will not be bored.

I've seen this and I give it___stars.
I want to see it___. I'll pass___.
The review was worth reading___. Not___.

Night on Earth (1991) 6

"At least I can still smoke in my own cab."

No, this is not a posted sign in the film. The tobacco companies tried to include it, but Director Jim Jarmusch had too much integrity to allow it.

But what could be a more natural setting for sucking on the killer weed than the inside of a taxi cab? Here we've got five of them, cabs that is. The tobacco companies saw the script and fronted mass bucks, or actually in this case, for a small Indie episodic venture by a director without a commercial hit to his credit, they fronted small bucks and sent an accountant.

Anyway, this is a collection of five short stories filmed at night in five cities, Los Angeles, New York, Paris, Rome, and Helsinki. In the first, Winona Ryder is an L.A. cabby looking like a ninth-grade grunge girl with her own sweet dreams who picks up Hollywood casting director Gena Rowlands at LAX and takes her to Beverly Hills. It's a cute idea, their bonding, but Ryder is without subtlety and clichéd to the hilt in dark glasses, bubble gum, baseball cap on backwards, and the endless puffing, talking sarcastically out of the side of her mouth: "All right, MOM." I actually expected some Joan Jett and the Blackhearts in the background. Rowland is very good however and overcomes a cloying script.

In New York, veteran German character actor Armin Mueller-Stahl, looking for all the world like a dead ringer for Albert Einstein, is the cabby, Helmut, and Giancarlo Esposito is Yoyo, his fare. Problem is Helmut drives with one foot on the gas pedal and the other on the brake so that the cab starts and stops every two seconds. So they switch positions. Meanwhile Rosie Perez arrives for a cameo.

In Paris, Isaach De Bankolé is the cabby and blind Béatrice Dalle, in white zombie contact lenses, is his fare. This is perhaps the best piece. Bankolé, who is a black dude from the Ivory Coast, asks her kindly, "Don't blind people usually wear dark glasses?" She has the great rejoinder, "Do they? I've never seen a blind person."

Roberto Benigni is the cabby in Rome. He picks up a priest and to the priest's great discomfort confesses in vivid detail his rather revolting sexual experiences.

Finally in Helsinki we have Matti Pellonpää as the "taksi" driver. The stark lighting on the snow and the empty streets captures well the cold northern night. Incidentally, the European stories are done in the local language with subtitles.

This is obviously an art film and requires a relatively sophisticated audience. The editing isn't sharp (some of that's deliberate) and the dialogue is uneven, but some of the camera work is excellent. See it for the acting, which is mostly very good.

I've seen this and I give it___stars.
I want to see it___. I'll pass___.
The review was worth reading___. Not___.

Nothing But the Truth (2008) 8

Sharp, engaging take on a journalist protecting her sources

The men are real scum in this one. David Schwimmer gets to play a guy who basically gives up on his heroic wife while Matt Dillon gets to play a blood-thirsty prosecutor bent on furthering his career whatever the human cost. Even Alan Alda (minus a fine little speech before the Supreme Court) gets to basically fail in defending his client.

His client is Rachel Armstrong (Kate Beckinsale) a journalist who finds herself in contempt of court for not revealing her source for a story on the outing of a CIA agent. (Shades of the Judith Miller/Valerie Plame Wilson case.) Here instead of the Iraq war we have an assignation attempt on the President supposedly by somebody in Venezuela after which the US takes some military action. Rachel ends up in jail and we get to see her suffer all the deprivations of being in jail, getting beaten up, estranged from her son and her husband, who betrays her. She is doing all this to protect a source, and a kind of journalistic honor code. David Swimmer's character isn't interested in journalist honor codes. He is displeased that she cares more about protecting her source than in being with him and her son.

Clearly this is a Belt Way story told as a woman's POV flick. It is engaging and it moves right along. It is sharp, just a tad short of slick. We cannot help but identify with Kate Beckinsale's character. And when we find out at the very, very end whom she is protecting we understand. It is a nice twist, one of the cleverest I've seen in movies in quite a while. The ending is just perfect.

I was about to write that "every soccer mom and indeed every mom will identify with Kate Beckinsale's character" but actually not all of them will. But when they see the ending they might change their mind.

See this for the clever twist, for the sharp direction and editing and for a fine performance by Kate Beckinsale.

I've seen this and I give it___stars.
I want to see it___. I'll pass___.
The review was worth reading___. Not___.

The Ogre (*Der Unhold*) (1996) 8

Original, featuring a fine performance by Malkovich

This strange and original work is a French film about Nazi Germany done in English. Director Volker Schlondorff is German, the screenplay is by veteran French writer Jean-Claude-Carriere, who has scores of films to his credit including *Bell de Jour* (1967) and *Valmont* (1989), and the star is the American, John Malkovich, who plays a French simpleton named Abel Tiffauges who ends up as a servant in Field Marshall Herman Goering's hunting estate during World War II, and then later in a Hitler youth academy for boys.

Malkovich's Abel is enormously sympathetic because he has suffered but harbors no bitterness, because he genuinely loves children, and because he has a certain magic about him based on his childish belief that somehow he will survive any catastrophe. In a boy's home as a child he survives the brutality of a proto Goering-like fat boy, and then later as an auto mechanic he overcomes a false accusation of child molestation. Both of these little stories are vividly rendered and seem entirely realistic. Then begins Abel's war time adventures, and it is here that the story becomes, as some have observed, something of a fairy tale. Abel is able to leave his barracks at the prison to wander about where he meets a blind moose and then a German army officer at a deserted cabin in the woods. This leads to his being established at Goering's hunting estate, and from there to the Hitler youth academy where he is treated as a privileged servant. We see the Nazis as just another part of the bizarre personages of his world.

The depiction of Goering as a kind of self-indulgent Nero, living in opulence as the world burns, seemed entirely believable. The overall portrait of the Germans in an objective and balanced manner was refreshing and thought-provoking and one of the strengths of the film. The Nazi eugenicist is contrasted with the officer who was part of a failed plot against Hitler, both men enormously sincere and dedicated, the one unbalanced, the other unlucky.

This is not a film for those looking primarily to be entertained. This is a work of art, dark, uneven, and a bit curious.

I've seen this and I give it___stars.

I want to see it___. I'll pass___.
The review was worth reading___. Not___.

Oleanna (1994) 8

Classic Mamet

David Mamet, the Tony and Pulitzer Prize winning author of the Broadway and later cinematic masterpiece, *Glengarry Glen Ross*, and other works, wrote and directed this artistic and quasi-realistic look at the gender wars. It starts out so slow that I almost gave up on it in the middle of the second reel (or actually in the middle of what would be the second act—it's adapted from his play) but I am surely glad I held on as it gathered momentum and power. It's about a college professor and a student who accuses him of sexual harassment. He's weak willed and likes his position and she's a ball-breaker who projects her desire for him by attacking him. He doesn't see the danger until it's too late.

William H. Macy, who played the fifties TV husband in *Pleasantville* (1998) and before that was the murderous car salesman in *Fargo* (1996), plays the pompous professor while Debra Eisenstadt is the unpleasant student looking to hurt. The dialogue is repetitious and purposely banal in an attempt to imitate actual speech. If you've never seen or read a Mamet play, his unique and highly characteristic style may startle you. What he tries to do with the repetition and the indirection is to imitate and burlesque the manner of normal speech. His effort is less successful here, in fact annoying at times, partly because Macy's unique acting style is almost a natural parody of misdirection and obtuseness. Taken together perhaps we have overkill. Nonetheless, this is fascinating to watch. People do talk at cross purposes and practice miss-communication. The tension, once developed, is maintained throughout because we can't decide whose side we're on. Both characters are purposely unsympathetic, and both compromised because of their personality weaknesses.

Mamet is a master at exposing human hypocrisy and ulterior motivation. We can see that the professor is in fact innocent of sexual harassment, but entirely guilty in his heart, while the unattractive girl although lying and out to hurt has been devalued by our society to the point of self-hatred. They are unsympathetic, yet we can, through them, if we are honest with ourselves, catch a glimpse of our own compromised nature. They are out to abuse or hurt one another because of established character defects. The lecher leches to control and to prove his masculinity, while the harassed "victim" seeks some attention to spice up her dreary life.

I've seen this and I give it___stars.
I want to see it___. I'll pass___.
The review was worth reading___. Not___.

One False Move (1991) 7

And you're dead

This cult favorite degenerate cocaine crime caper starts out in what looks like South Central L.A and ends up in rural Arkansas. Directed by Carl Franklin from a script by Billy Bob Thornton, and starring Thornton, Bill Paxton, Cynda Williams, and Michael Beach, it begins with bloody bodies on the floor and ends with bloody bodies on the ground. There is some sprightly dialogue en route, some sharp editing, fine acting all around, and the dramatic tension is well maintained. We are intrigued by the clash of personalities and the degenerate hijinks. However, after a while I began to feel that if they light up one more cigarette I will be forced to rip the pack from their hands, tear the stogies into shreds, and feed the debris to them with a large spoon. Also the standard quota of one thousand improvisations on the f-word was exceeded here. I am therefore condemning director Carl Franklin to an absurdist nightmare in which he dreams of getting scripts in the mail in which the dialogue for all characters consists of just that one word in its various grammatical forms, repeated for one hundred and twenty-six pages.

Paxton plays a small town sheriff in awe of the cops from the big city who is nonetheless intent on proving his manhood. (One of the cops, by the way, in a bit of prescient genius, looks a whole lot like former L.A. cop Mark Fuhrman before he got all those bags under his eyes.) Thornton is a kind of murderous cocaine-addled urban animal in a long greasy pigtail whose life has neither direction, purpose nor insight. Williams, whose primal sexiness will keep your eyes open even if it's two a.m., plays a chocolate strawberry who can kill when she has to. Beach is an icy cold-blooded knife murderer who spends his off-duty hours worshiping his well-muscled body and practicing squeaky-clean living. The familiar Billy Bob Thornton fascination with things country contrasted with things city is explored here and reminds us a little of *A Simple Plan* (1998) in which he also teamed up with Bill Paxton. This genre, which I might call "Grunge City gore," was morphed into an art form during the eighties and nineties in films from, e.g., Coen and Coen, *Blood Simple* (1984), David Lynch, *Wild at Heart* (1990), Quentin Tarantino, *Reservoir Dogs* (1992), Oliver Stone, *Natural Born Killers* (1994), and others. This is actually one of the better ones, but I think I need a break. Maybe a nice Disney favorite or something with Meg Ryan and Tom Hanks...or even something with Bette Midler and Whoopie Goldberg.

Then again, maybe NOT.

Incidentally, the reason all these films made especially during the late eighties and early nineties contain some much blood and guts and cigarette smoke is (1) Sex had become somewhat taboo because of the rise of AIDS, and so Hollywood switched to violence, and (2) The tobacco companies fronted money for films that promised to have a whole lot of puffing going on. Hopefully we are living in more enlightened times.

I've seen this and I give it___stars.
I want to see it___. I'll pass___.
The review was worth reading___. Not___.

Pacific Heights (1990) 7

Tenants are the curse of the propertied class

This is a carefully programmed yuppie nightmare, something to titillate the emotions betwixt the sushi and the creme de mint, something to remind the upwardly mobile that you have to keep your guard up at all times because there are animals out there waiting to take it all away from you.

Clever plot premise: Yuppie couple, stylishly unmarried, possibly for tax purposes, buy a painted lady in the Pacific Heights district of San Francisco, a Victorian fixer upper for $750,000. It's the 1980's and everybody is getting rich in California real estate. They are now in yuppie heaven since there are two rentals on the property which take care of $2300 of the $3700 monthly mortgage, which leaves them responsible for only $1400, which is less than they were paying before, and now they have a huge tax write-off and hopefully an appreciating property. Of course they are margined to the gills, but what can go wrong?

How about the tenant from hell? Forget about your wild parties and your late-with-the-rent dead beats. This guy (Michael Keaton as a slimy, upper crust psycho genius) doesn't even pay the deposit. He just moves in, squats, and our yuppie couple is helpless to get rid of him since by law he now has possession. He changes the locks, cultivates big ugly cockroaches, and pounds away at all hours of the night, and chases off the other tenant. Seems he has done this before. Seems it is an elaborate scam to gain total possession of the entire property. Next to go are the owners. Naturally the cops and the law seem to work for him, not our adorable couple. (This is a little fiction to further excite the passions of the audience, call it poetic license, since we all know that the tenant/landlord laws in California are written by and for the propertied class, as they are anywhere else, as is only right.)

But this is a morality play. Could it be that our yuppies are undeserving of their wealth and are easy prey in the econ jungle because of their naiveté? Could be. But as this is a modern morality tale, you can be sure that the woman, played with worrisome lines under her eyes by the ever adorable Melanie Griffith, will turn the tables and kick some male butt despite the handicap of having a not too bright boyfriend, who is easily manipulated by our villain into some rather stupid male behavior that makes things worse for our heroine. Incidentally, he is

played with such annoying exactitude by Matthew Modine that I can hear the rednecks in the audience screaming: "Die yuppie scum!"

It should be noticed that the adversary of the yuppies is not your standard ghetto dweller, but a wayward member of the upper class, a fitting adversary in this yuppie trial by fire.

I'll let you guess who wins.

I've seen this and I give it___stars.
I want to see it___. I'll pass___.
The review was worth reading___. Not___.

The People Versus Larry Flynt (1996) 8

Ugly but worth the viewing

Strange bedfellows, those two, Jerry Falwell and Larry Flynt. I never liked either one of them, which is why it has taken me so long to get around to watching this movie. Make no mistake about it, the central point here is that Falwell and Flynt are two sides of the same coin: pick your pig.

Milos Forman's direction starts slow and is almost without distinction nearly three-quarters through, yet the entire movie is saved by that last quarter after Flynt is shot. I think there is something to be said for boring your audience a little in the beginning, showing them only the tired and ordinary just so they will better appreciate it when the going gets good. And it does. I think this strategy worked on me: after rot gut even vin ordinaire can seem like the ambrosia of the gods.

Turning Larry Flynt into an American hero, as this movie does, may seem a bit of a stretch, yet consider the obverse: Jerry Falwell as our hero. Now THAT is a bit scary.

Courtney Love proves herself to be a wonderful exhibitionist (but we knew that) as well as a natural and talented actress (we didn't know that) who knows how to have a good time in front of the camera; and I think that is half the task for an actor: love the red light; love the audience looking at you. Woody Harrelson, in keeping with Foreman's direction seems to be walking through the part in the beginning, looking almost like a clone of himself from *Natural Born Killers* (1994) with a fey hair style; but he picks up steam, and as the paralyzed Flynt really comes to life and gives a fine performance. Ed Norton is also excellent and so believable and winning as Flynt's lawyer, especially in the scene before the Supreme Court. Think about it: in this movie the lawyer is the good guy!

Politically speaking this is a no brainer, a shoot the fish in the barrel exercise: First Amendment wins out over public figures wanting to manage their images. Thank you. And what IS more obscene, sex or war? Strange that that should be a question, but it is and has been for at least a couple of millennia. When I was young I used to wonder why. Wasn't it obvious that sex was good and war was bad? However, it is not so simple. It turns out that sex (which leads to the creation of new karmas) is really just the obverse side of the coin of war. You make 'em, and in some circumstances you have to kill 'em. That's why the other guy's sexuality is offensive, and why we have prudes. Sex really is war by other means. I always think of the example of Easter Island where initially they practiced a fertility religion until the island's protein resources ran out, and then came the repression of reproduction and sex. Christianity is a religion one step removed from the old fertility religions in this sense. It is paranoid (in its more conservative forms) about sexuality because it has evolved to fear unbridled reproduction. Of course its practitioners, like Jerry Falwell, have no understanding of this: they are just social and political animals acting out their social and political roles.

In short, like most things in life, this film is a flawed but interesting venture. Incidentally, the so-called "unusual" marriage between Flynt and Althea Leasure is one of the things that makes this movie good: their marriage is a lot more like real life than ninety percent of what we see in the movies.

I've seen this and I give it___stars.
I want to see it___. I'll pass___.
The review was worth reading___. Not___.

Pi (1998) 7

Not really about 3.14159... per se

Pi, I understand, has now been factored to over a billion places. My question: are the digits random? Anybody out there know?* This film does not answer that question (nor does it address it). What it asks is, are numbers the language of life? Max Cohen, mathematical genius, believes they are. There is a pattern, and he would like to find it, partly because it's there and partly for use in the stock market. So would some other people. He is thus tormented both within and without.

One of the things that made this a successful commercial film (for an indie venture, of course) is the fine acting by Sean Gullette who plays Max Cohen. He was entirely convincing as a reclusive and paranoid mathematical genius; but he is also a man like Einstein who emanates charisma and something perhaps beyond charm. Also effective was the story by Director Darren Aronofsky, which, unlike some indie films, actually had a plot with clear conflicts. The choice of Pamela Hart, a strong black woman as a kind of hit woman from Wall Street was excellent. Also very good was Mark Margolis as Cohen's mentor, Sol Robeson. Aimed at a popular audience were, alas, some chase scenes; but they were not badly done, and even seemed appropriate, although I think there should be a moratorium placed on subway chase scenes in movies, at least for the next decade or so. Also aimed at a popular audience was some of the violent images, in particular the scene where Cohen places the power drill to his temple, like the barrel of an executioner's handgun, turns it on and presses. Kids love that shtick. (I could hardly watch.)

Much of the detail was completely veracious, the spiral as an example of complexity in nature, or the wonderful re-enactment of the programmer's moment of truth just before he hits the return key and finds out if his creation will run, crash or go into infinite loop; or a group of fundamental religious people (in this case Hasidic Jews) believing that some sort of numerology will miraculously reveal some major truth of their religion; or even the fact that Max Cohen still used five and one-quarter inch floppies for his data. Also wondrously right was the spider/moth sticky cocoon that gummed up his computer, or the little girl who multiplies on her calculator and then asks Max for the answer, delighted when he gets it right. That a stock market bonanza served as the El Dorado of number crunchers was also right on target. And an especially good fit was the techno rock in the background.

But some of this was definitely wrong. The idea that Sol Robeson would think Max's computer had become or was becoming "conscious" was too much of a leap. Or the notion that the human brain, or any brain for that matter, could predict stock prices as they come out of the ticker is absurd. Complexity theory would argue strongly that such specific data, like the number of rain drops in a storm tomorrow, is in principle impossible to predict. I also didn't like the resolution which allows us to treat whichever of the foregone scenes we like as dream-fantasies. I don't like plots that are resolved by "it was a dream" mechanisms, even, or especially, retrospective ones.

But movies are about images and the image of Cohen's head and his brain and of what hard, metallic things can do to it, is something that lingers long after the lights have come up. Indeed what makes this an engrossing movie is its psychological and visual content. The stark, grainy black and white cinematography actually enhanced our appreciation. Indeed, light and dark and other dichotomies are part of the expression of Aronofsky's vision. He juxtaposes contrasting elements of our culture, of the mind and of nature to tease us into seeing that the world is vastly more mysterious than we can imagine. There is order and there is chaos. There is number and there is the organism that is an expression of number. There is rationality and there is insanity. There is the soft, fragile brain and the hard electrodes. There is the game of go, more complex than chess, the wooden board with the simple lines and the black and white pebbles that spring open the door to chaos (the mathematical kind). And there is life, fragile, uncertain, teetering on the edge, and in the fuzzy distance there is the shimmering certainly of a fundamental religion. Aronsky catches all of this and ends up with an electronic poem camouflaged as a movie.

*I got a couple of answers to this question. Obviously the digits can't be random in the strict sense of a definition of randomness because they can be expressed in a non-exhaustive way simply by supplying the formula. However it appears that the distribution of the digits does not significantly differ from what one would expect of a random distribution with each digit appearing about ten percent of the time. (I think I got this right.)

I've seen this and I give it___stars.
I want to see it___. I'll pass___.
The review was worth reading___. Not___.

The Plot Against Harry (1969) 7

Deep sleeper worth a look

This little indie sleeper—made in the sixties, died immediately, was resurrected in the 1989, and is now part of the New Yorker Video series—is distinguished by an original satiric story and a fine, sympathetic performance by Martin Priest who plays the title character Harry Plotnick, a middle-aged New York Jewish racketeer.

The film begins as Harry is being released from prison after a nine-month stay. His chauffeur immediately tells him some of his numbers runners have jumped ship and his gambling flotilla is in danger of sinking. They pick up a couple of his lieutenants who speak Spanish (which Harry doesn't understand) and they more or less ignore him. Harry quickly learns that they and his other runners think of him as washed up. Meanwhile he runs into a couple of his ex-wives and discovers that he has grandchildren. Now a rather unusual mid-life crisis ensues for Harry. He wants to give up the rackets and become an upstanding member of the community, to attend weddings and bar mitzvahs. Just how difficult that is and what transpires form the comedic story of the film.

Director Michael Roemer who also wrote the script uses authentic New York/New Jersey lifestyle details from the sixties (contemporary to him and therefore without the strained or flashy, obtrusive effect we often encounter in period piece movies) to spin his tale. There is a documentary feel to the film overlaid with light-hearted irony. The camera work is amateurish at times and the abrupt cuts lend a kind of jumpy, somehow authentic feel to the story. This can be seen as a satire of gangster films with the warm-hearted and gentle Harry as a kind of anti-Al Capone.

Bottom line: wryly original.

I've seen this and I give it___stars.
I want to see it___. I'll pass___.
The review was worth reading___. Not___.

The Prestige (2006) 8

Dueling magicians in London a century ago

The Prestige is a period piece fantasy made into something resembling reality. At its heart it relies on a device from science fiction, a machine that transports people and objects by replicating them. How such a device might work is beside the intent of the movie. And that's okay. Movie goers accept premises and then follow the action without any need to examine the premise further. However I think that director Christopher Nolan might have looked more closely at the consequences of his premise. Replicating objects with electricity (pretty far-fetched of course) and moving them some distance from the replicating point is quite a feat even in the imagination. But what to do with the replications? Nolan's solution: kill them off. In fact kill off the original and keep the replication.

Now if you are magician Robert Angier (Hugh Jackson) and you know that you are about to die, and in fact in a most unpleasant way by drowning, I think you might be a little hesitant to perform the trick, even though a replication of you will come to life and live on. Note that both the replication and the original Angier would want to live and prefer that the other be the one to die.

Nolan thought about this and that is why one is forced to die. Nolan probably would have himself preferred to keep the original and do away with the duplicate, but then the trick wouldn't work properly since the original would still be in place and not moved at all.

This is an old theme in science fiction and Nolan does not attempt to improve on it. And again that's okay. But another problem with the way the premise is handled is that, although surely Angier would want to go one up on his nemesis, fellow magician Alfred Borden (Christian Bale) and dazzle the world with this amazing trick, he might have at some point just replicated some pound notes or some bullion. If Borden had gotten hold of the machine, maybe he could have replicated Scarlett Johansson so that he and Fallon could have one each for themselves. (And one for me would be nice as well.) Or he could have replicated his beloved daughter.

What I am pointing to is the irony in the way the machine was used as a vehicle for a magic trick. The trick as performed is so much less amazing than the real magic that could have been displayed, that of replicating enormously complex objects like human beings. Nobody in the film seems to realize this. This is perhaps the major—shall we say—plot cheesiness. Another, as pointed out elsewhere, is that the question Angier asks of Borden, "Which knot did you use?" The question is bogus as is his answer, "I don't know," since Julia was still tied and the knot could be seen. Also there is the question of what to do with all those bodies being created? We see them near the end of the film in the water boxes. Seems a bit of a stretch to make all those new boxes and just leave the bodies there. Somebody might call the bobbies, don't you think?

For these reasons I am beginning to wonder if Nolan is getting a little careless or if he has been corrupted by success to the point where he no longer cares about logical consistency and artistic rigor. Perhaps we'll see in his next opus. However scheduled for release next year is *The Dark Knight* another Batman caper starring Christian Bale.

Putting all this aside, the movie is entertaining and thought provoking. Nolan's time-stirred delineation of the plot is done well and kept this viewer interested. I also liked the razor sharp psychological tension created between Borden and Angier as they compete against each other. And the many surprising plot twists and turns—something that Nolan does very well—were nice.

And the cast was excellent. Michael Caine who plays the old magician and front man Cutter was perfect, and the glimpse or two we get of Scarlett Johansson was more than agreeable. Bale and Jackson were very good as well. But I especially liked Rebecca Hall who played Borden's wife Sarah. I thought she was outstanding.

Now that Christopher Nolan has had back to back commercial successes with *Batman Begins* (2005), and *The Prestige* (2006), maybe it's time to think about where his career is going. Is he going to become a film maker known for his artistry like Stanley Kubrick or a film maker who knows how to appeal to the marketplace like Steven Spielberg? On the one hand there are Nolan's artistic films, *Memento* (2000) and *Insomnia* (2002) and on the other hand there are his big screen commercial successes, this film and *Batman Begins.* Knowing the constraints placed on film makers by the need to get funding and to turn a profit, it may be that he is trying to be both. In fact perhaps the best way to look at *The Prestige* and *Batman Begins* is to recognize that they are artistic films made within industry constraints that require mass market appeal.

I've seen this and I give it___stars.
I want to see it___. I'll pass___.
The review was worth reading___. Not___.

Pretty Woman (1990) 7

New spin on an old theme

Pretty Woman is a popular and very familiar movie meant for a popular audience, the main attraction being the charisma of its two box-office buffos, Julia Roberts and Richard Gere.

I always feel a certain sense of interest when anticipating a Richard Gere film. I know that in some way he will be slick and sleazy (e.g., *Breathless* (1983), *Internal Affairs* (1990), etc.) and I can get involved in his contrary nature. In other words, he won't bore me with a one-dimensional persona. Here however he is thoughtful, kind, considerate, intelligent—a non-sleazy, gray-suited business man with a wise and fatherly manner. Perhaps this is Gere's persona for his middle years.

In the case of Julia Roberts, not only is she nice to look at, she is *interesting* to look at. It is no accident that her face is one of the silver screen's dominate images from the nineties. She has a powerfully expression nature and can assume a role as easily as one puts on a coat. She is striking physically, the huge mouth, the delicate nose, the long limbs... She is also the quintessence of a woman who can appear ordinary or beautiful according to circumstances. I have seen her in two PBS productions of *Nature.* (Yes, she is a Hollywood star with compassion, or at least one who loves animals.) In one she is in Borneo with orangutans, and in the other in Mongolia with the descendants of Genghis Khan and the wild horses. In both cases she throws herself into the dirt and discomfort like a trooper without a hint of the glamour she left thousands of miles behind. She charms both the children of the nomads and the orangutans. In fact, one randy orangutan becomes so smitten with her that he starts to put the moves on, and has to be restrained! In other words she has an equalitarian, democratic, down-to-earth nature which sits well with a popular audience. She has made so many movies lately (hurriedly as her youth is expiring: she is now over thirty, the age of death for most Hollywood actresses) that I cannot keep up with them, so many that her ranking among the great stars of the screen is still up for grabs as we evaluate her many performances.

Will her role in *Pretty Woman* help? Although I found it difficult to swallow her fake bad grammar, the phony lack of sophistication, and the predictability of her golden heart, I thought it marginally plausible that such a striking woman COULD in some strange parallel universe be reduced to hooking in Hollywood. And I thought she did a creditable job by bringing some originality to a well-worn role. Certainly I believed in Julia Roberts, the whore, as much as I did in Elisabeth Shue, the whore (from *Leaving Las Vegas* (1995)). Had Roberts been portrayed as a drug addict—which of course Hollywood made a stringent point of NOT doing, since they needed Middle America to identify with her in order to sell tickets—I might have bought it. Most American prostitutes are drug addicts. That's how most of them they got enslaved into the business in the first place.

So what we have here is a variation on an old Hollywood fantasy: poor, underclass girl, through her natural beauty, lovable nature and good common sense wins the heart of a man of considerable means, thus upgrading her social and economic status, etc. In others words, this is a woman's fantasy-fulfillment movie all the way. The real question to be asked, though, is how did the chemistry between the two stars work? Do Spencer Tracy and Katharine Hepburn or Tom Hanks and Meg Ryan have anything to be jealous about? I think not, but judging from the box office success and the fact that they were paired again in *Runaway Bride* (1999), I am probably wrong. But see it and judge for yourself. Despite the cliché situation, this is more than a confectioner's diversion because of what it implies, and what we can learn, about the American psyche, circa 1990.

I've seen this and I give it___stars.
I want to see it___. I'll pass___.
The review was worth reading___. Not___.

Pulp Fiction (1995) 8

We can really explore ourselves only as bad guys

Well, it rocks, I guess. It jumps. It moves. It's flashy and clever. The acting is excellent. The direction is interesting... I could write a book, but what I kept thinking was how much the audience worships not just the violence, but the power. How much they love the Fascist criminal, the mob boss who must be obeyed and shown loyalty to. Uma Thurman is just decadently sexy. John Travolta is amazingly lovable as a "low-rent" hood and Bruce Willis is believable as a prize fighter who turns the tables and wins the fight instead of throwing it (and, in an up-to-date spin, bets on himself—seems right! How come they never did that before? They probably did, I just missed it.). Samuel Jackson is interesting as the Bible-quoting black hit man.

Naturally they make us root for the bad guys; indeed the bad guys are almost always the heroes in the modern Hollywood. We can really explore ourselves only as bad guys. The pro-mo's for cigarettes, heroin, cocaine, booze and decadence are getting a little thin, however. A Hollywood movie, a commercial flick, is always a cliché. The art part comes from doing spins on the cliché, in putting a new twist on the old BS, on the old standards. Ironically interesting was the sensuous indulgence of dinner for Travolta and Thurman. He's shot heroin, she's done a few lines, they smoke some pot, they smoke some cigarettes, but they really get off on milk shakes and vanilla cokes, steaks and hamburgers. Poor Hollywood. They've done it all and now must find real indulgence in fat, salt, sugar and meat, which for the stars really is an indulgence. If your life span is only sixteen to about thirty-five, then the forbidden things really are fat, salt, meat and anything else that puts on the weight. Cocaine and cigarettes can't hurt you because by the time the ill effects kick in, your career is over anyway.

I've seen this and I give it___stars.
I want to see it___. I'll pass___.
The review was worth reading___. Not___.

Punchline (1988) 7

Underrated, almost brilliant, but flawed

Punchline begins with an engaging premise. Steven Gold (Tom Hanks at age 31) is a med student driven by his physician father to become a doctor. But Steven hates medical school, can't stand the sight of blood, etc. Instead of going to class, he goes to the local comedy club (The Gas Station). Instead of doing his homework, he does standup. He's very good. Lilah Krytsick (Sally Field at 42) is a frumpy Jersey housewife with three kids and a husband (John Goodman) who sells insurance. He wants her to stay home nights, but she has a passion for wanting to make people laugh. So she too moonlights at The Gas Station. She is not funny. In desperation she spends five hundred dollars of household funds to buy jokes to use on the audience. Everything bombs.

Meanwhile, Steven is a little behind in his rent and thinks that, what the hey, he can sell Lilah some jokes. But it never comes to that. Instead he becomes enchanted with her and helps her break free of her inhibitions and perform naturally and effectively on stage. Can true love be far behind? (Rhetorical question, but the answer is not pat.)

If you are a Tom Hanks fan, see this movie. You will be delighted. He puts on a versatile performance depicting a guy who needed to be, in the very fiber of his being, a comedian. The role shows off his talent, and makes us understand why he is now, at the relatively young age of 45, one of America's premiere screen idols.

The rest of the movie, however, is a mix of strengths and weaknesses. Sally Field, in a difficult role, gives an uneven performance which I think is partly the fault of director David Seltzer, who also wrote the script. His direction is brilliant and awful by turns. In particular the schmaltzy, unnecessarily unrealistic ending is very disappointing. He also dug himself a hole because the top comedic performance had to be the last, yet it wasn't. All the expectations of the audience fell, and perhaps that is why Seltzer stuck himself with an ending that played like something devised by a committee of filmland execs intent on political correctness above all else. Also, any difference between the John Goodman who played Rosanne Arnold's husband on TV and the John Goodman here was not immediately discernable.

However some of the scenes were just perfect I especially liked it when Steven's overbearing father (instead of a network producer) shows up at the club. Steven Gold's anguished, self-revelatory on stage reaction is excellent. —Or when Lilah rushes to prepare dinner slapstick style for company; or when night is done and it's four or five am and Steven has helped her discover herself and he asks how she will explain being out all night to her husband and she says she will crawl into bed with one of the kids and he will think she slept there all night. Also good was the singing in the rain scene and the scene in which the daughter, showing the wisdom of children, says to Lilah, after her husband asks to see her perform, "Say yes, mom." Also good were the motley troupe of semi-pro comedians, including a fine performance by Mark Rydell as Romeo, the manager of the club.

This rates a five point something at IMDb, but that's a little unfair. It's a better movie than that. See it for Tom Hanks, and for David Seltzer, who just missed making a great movie.

I've seen this and I give it___stars.
I want to see it___. I'll pass___.
The review was worth reading___. Not___.

Rear Window (1954) 8

Midcentury voyeurism

This is the quintessential Hitchcock flick, easy to understand, addictively interesting, featuring great stars (Grace Kelly and James Stewart), familiar bit players (Thelma Ritter in one of her best roles as Stewart's talkative nurse), and a kind of almost imperceptible satire on the human animal. In this case, Hitchcock has glorious fun displaying a whole range of human behaviors through the device of watching them through a Greenwich Village rear window before the age of air conditioners when everyone had to leave their windows open (and some even slept on the fire escape–I've done something like that) to cope with the appalling heat and humidity during an eastern seaboard heat wave.

James Stewart stars as L.B. Jeffries, an adventurous photographer who has a broken leg and is confined to his apartment in a cast while it heals. Bored beyond belief, he becomes a voyeur of his neighbors. Meanwhile there is his girlfriend, none other than Grace Kelly playing a "too perfect" socialite intent on winning his heart and soul. Trouble is Jeff worries that it won't work out, that they are essentially incompatible, she a socialite, who always goes first class, he a roughing it man of the world comfortable with second class accommodations. Naturally the audience (me!) finds it incredible that he isn't madly in love with her.

Raymond Burr (long TV's Perry Mason of long ago) in gray hair and specks has an interesting role as Lars Thorwald, seen almost entirely from a distance across the courtyard doing very suspicious things with knives and suitcases and mysterious comings and goings in the middle of the night. Bored voyeurs wonder what is going on. There is some light romantic play between Stewart and Kelly, but it is decidedly secondary to the voyeuristic adventures seen through the rear window: the saga of Miss Lonelyhearts, the ardor of the newlyweds, the angst of the songwriter, the exhibitionism of the dancing beauty, the pampered dog in a basket, and Thorwald and his

invalid and then missing wife. Hitchcock's America at midcentury. Each of the little stories within the story has a plot and a resolution: Miss Lonelyhearts finds her man. The songwriter finds somebody who appreciates his work. Dancing beauty's man (looking from a distance a little like Woody Allen in an army uniform) returns. The groom seeks a break from his exhaustive marital duties, etc. Hitchcock's sense of satire has the softest touch, which is why, I think, he is so beloved. In the final scene Grace Kelly, finding her man asleep, puts down the adventure book she is reading (for his benefit) and picks up Harper's Bazaar to check the fashions. One gets the sense of future marital bliss and especially, marital reality.

There is some tension and some mystery, but nothing too strenuous for little old ladies from Pasadena, and nothing to offend anybody and nothing too graphic. You can see this with the kids and your maiden aunt and all will find it interesting. See it for Thelma Ritter, the sardonic character actress of many films, most notably this and *All About Eve* (1950).

I've seen this and I give it___stars.
I want to see it___. I'll pass___.
The review was worth reading___. Not___.

Repo Man (1984) 8

"This is intense."

I put this eighties cult classic right up there on a level just below *Blazing Saddles* (1974) and *Dr. Stranglove* (1964) as one of the best satires ever to hit the silver screen. No exaggeration: this is one bizarre and one very funny flick. Seeing it again after almost twenty years, I gotta say, it didn't lose much.

Emilio Estevez stars as Otto Maddox, a head-strong and slightly naive ex-supermarket stock clerk and sometime punk rocker. He's kicking a can down the street when up pulls Bud, "a repo man," played with a fine degeneracy by Harry Dean Stanton, who asks him if he wants to make ten bucks. (Otto's reply is memorable but not printable here.) When he learns that Bud just wants him to drive a car and not...uh, never mind, he bargains it to twenty-five bucks. When he finds out that Bud repossesses cars for the "Helping Hand Acceptance Corporation," he is sorely offended. But when he realizes how intense the life is (and how bleak his other employment opportunities), he becomes a repo man himself.

Meanwhile there's J. Frank Parnell (Fox Harris wearing a demonic grin and weird black and empty frame glasses) driving a "hot" '64 Chevy Malibu. "You don't want to look in the trunk, Officer," he tells a cop who pulls him over on a desert highway. By the way, the map under the opening credits shows the action of this film beginning somewhere on old Route 66 in New Mexico, suggesting alien mecca Roswell territory perhaps, but most of scenes were clearly shot in LA, and the desert scene just mentioned was also probably shot in California as evidenced by the Joshua trees in the background.

What director and scriptster Alex Cox does is combine urban ghetto realism with bizarro sci-fi shtick. He adds a fine punk soundtrack including the title song from Iggy Pop with a brief appearance by the Circle Jerks, and wow are they appropriate, but you have be a punker or a 15-year-old to really visualize their moniker. The supporting players, Sy Richardson as Lite, a black cat repo ace, and Tracey Walter as Miller, a demented street philosopher, really stand out. I also liked the black girl repo person with attitude (Vonetta McGee).

The real strength of the movie, aside from probably the best performance of Estevez's career, is in the street scene hijinks, the funny and raunchy dialogue, and all those sight gags. My favorite scene has Otto coming home to find his parents smoking weed on the couch zombie-like in front of the TV listening to a Christian evangelist while he scarfs down "Food" out of a blue and white can from the refrigerator. I mean "Food" is on the label, period. The Ralphs plain wrap (remember them) are all over the sets, in the convenience store, at the supermarket, bottles of plain wrap whiskey and plain wrap "Tasteetos," plain wrap beer and plain wrap cigarettes.

Some other good shtick: the dead rat thrown in the car with the woman that doesn't accomplish its purpose; the money in the presents that Otto throws out the window busted open by the tires of another car for us to see and drool over; the "I left a book of matches" line that diverts Otto's idiot friend pumping gas; the pepper spray; Miller by the ashcan fire contemplating the disappeared from the future and "the lattice of coincidence that lays on top of everything" (trippy, man); and the punk criminal act of "Let's go get sushi and not pay." And Otto's clean pressed white dress shirt and the tie—I love the tie—as Lite tells him, "Doing my job, white boy."

See this for the authentic eighties street scenes and for my UCLA Bruin buddy (by way of Oxford) director Alex Cox who dreamed the whole thing up. Only an Englishman could really see America authentically.

I've seen this and I give it___stars.
I want to see it___. I'll pass___.
The review was worth reading___. Not___.

Reservoir Dogs (1992) 7

The delineation of violence

Future historians may well look back at the cinema of the nineties in the United States and wonder why it spawned so many movies that seemed to celebrate gratuitous violence while catering to an audience fascinated with gore. (I have some ideas on this, but I'll skip them here.) Some may say this is nothing new, that there has always been gore in the movies, that the horror flick is a standard genre, and that, at any rate, human beings are quite naturally interested in violence because even if it is rare in their suburban experience, when it does occur it is of overriding significance.

When historians do look back they will surely take a gander at this film, director Quentin Tarantino's celebrated breakout cult classic. Anyone reading this has already seen the movie or certainly knows about its content. It contains one of the most unredeeming scenes of sadistic violence ever to strike the silver screen. It depicts a world in which men stick their guns out at each other the way little boys play with themselves. It is a world in which women exist only on the periphery (like an old war movie there are virtually no women in the film), a world in which men are constantly preoccupied with macho notions and the phenomena of male bonding to the exclusion of anything else. The behavior of the men while superficially realistic is actually stylized in the extreme. Anything and everything may set a man off. His ego is under continual fire, his manhood is constantly being tested. Life is short, brutal and bestial.

Question: where did this vision come from, and why did it resonate so strongly with an audience, and what is that audience? It can be said that *Reservoir Dogs* appeals primarily to young men and teenaged boys, who are preoccupied with coming to grips with violence because it represents an important part of their lives, and how they might relate to violence is an essential part of their self-discovery. This is true, but it is not the whole story. After all, as I write this, *Reservoir Dogs* is the 58th most popular movie of all time according to votes tabulated at the International Movie Database web site, IMDb.com. Even given that there is still a male bias on the web, this is an extraordinarily high rating for the first film of any director and for such a low budget enterprise.

Part of the explanation for the near reverence shown this film lies not in the blood-letting and the macho posturing, but in a story well told, well-plotted and of characters well-drawn and especially the indelible acting performances from most of the cast. Harvey Kietel as a hardened criminal with a soft heart, and Steve Buscemi as the amoral Mr. Pink, and Michael Madsen as the sadistic Mr. Blonde and Chris Penn as the slightly soft and slightly spoiled son of a criminal father and Tim Roth as the high wire acting Mr. Orange, really rivet us to the screen. The professional cadre of criminals depicted here, the cheap thugs and psychopathic killers, are well realized and their life styles and preoccupations well delineated. Tarantino begins with a scene in which the boys around some tables in a cafe "analyze" Madonna's "Like a Virgin" in manner that might be described as Oxford Don crude. They continually espouse the racist, sexist macho values of the criminal underclass, in which loyalty to the band and bravery under fire are the highest values, while cowardice and "turning rat" are the lowest. Furthermore the script is punctuated with sick little jokes (e.g., about the imagined nature of black women), and wryly obscene juxtapositions, notably the macabre dance of Mr. Blonde to the radio playing "Stuck in the Middle with You" as he tortures the cop. Finally there is the structure of the film itself in which time is splintered and events are recalled and presented not chronologically, but according to the logic of the film itself. This technique allows Tarantino great freedom of expression and emphasis.

Okay, so why am I only giving this seven stars? Mainly because, while the treatment was striking and original, the story and the milieu presented were not. And some of this was unrealistic to the point of annoyance. That Mr. Orange did not bleed to death or at least go into shock and faint dead away with a gaping hole in his stomach is beyond me. And the "neat" karmic ending was more than a little far-fetched. And all those stylized speeches! You'd think part of this was written for the Shakespearean stage. Indeed, although Tarantino may not realize it, he owes something to the Bard. Didn't Hamlet end much the same way with dead bodies all over the stage? Additionally, while Tarantino's vision appeals strongly to his targeted audience (and his own psyche), it does not relate well with a larger audience. The last thing a man of my age is concerned about is how macho he might be. Such concerns seem childish. And the nature and phenomenon of human violence is very far from a mystery to me; furthermore I know very well exactly how I feel about violence and how I might react in the face of it. I think if I had seen this movie when I was seventeen, I might have been stunned and thrilled with its power. Seeing it in my middle years leaves me a little cold.

Incidentally I agree with those who say that this is a greater artistic achievement than the "Hollywoodized" *Pulp Fiction* (1995), also directed by Tarantino.

I've seen this and I give it___stars.
I want to see it___. I'll pass___.
The review was worth reading___. Not___.

Reversal of Fortune (1990) 8

Fascinating character studies

Striking, if sometimes creepy, performances by Glenn Close and Jeremy Irons highlight this unevenly directed take on the Claus Von Bulow story of the degenerate rich adapted from the book by Harvard Law School Professor Alan Dershowitz. Dershowitz, who loves being in the limelight almost as much as he loves the law, took on the task of saving Claus Von Bulow from prison for the attempted murder of his rich wife initially as a means of raising money to help him in his pro bono cases. The rather heavy-handed manner in which we are advised of this should not detract from Dershowitz's

work. The irony is that as the case developed Dershowitz became persuaded that Claus was innocent.

Whether Dershowitz convinced himself of Von Bulow's innocence to assuage a possibly guilty conscience is a good question. Remember Dershowitz is the guy who said after the O.J. Simpson trial (he was one of Simpson's lawyers) that he didn't know whether Simpson was guilty or not. While that may be a good stance for a defense attorney, it is an insincere one for the public figure that Dershowitz has become.

Starring as Dershowitz is Ron Silver in an uneven performance that at times made me think of Gabe Kaplan doing a young and uncomedic Groucho Marx. I wonder if Dershowitz was entirely flattered.

Director Barbet Schroeder (*Barfly* 1987; *Single White Female* 1992) uses several points of view to tell the story, including a voice-over from Glenn Close's Sunny Von Bulow as she lies comatose, but also from recollections by Jeremy Irons' Claus Von Bulow. We see some scenes twice, colored by the differing points of view. This technique is entirely appropriate since what really happened is far from clear to this day. It is Claus Von Bulow's fortune that was reversed. Whether the first two juries or the third were right is something Schroeder leaves for the audience to determine.

But make no mistake about it: the heart of the movie is Jeremy Irons' Oscar-winning performance. His subtle artistry based on a deep conception (true to life or not) of the aristocratic and Germanic Claus allowed him to create a persona that is cold and aloft, yet somehow sympathetic. The contrast with Silver's Brooklyn-born hyperenergetic Dershowitz made for some good cinematic chemistry, although sometimes it came across like nice Jewish boy defends a vampire.

Glenn Close's flawless rendition of the idle, drug-befouled Sunny reminds us once again that she is a great actress. Unfortunately I don't think Schroeder spent as much time and energy as he should have with the people who played Dershowitz's law students. They seemed amateurish and unconvincing in just about every scene. And there were too many of them. Some distillation of intent, and more directorial guidance might have helped.

Nicholas Kazan's script has a number of good lines in it, not the least of which is this: Dershowitz: "You are a very strange man." Claus Von Bulow: "You have no idea." Also nice was Von Bulow's observation after they are seated in the restaurant and after the waiter has called him "Doctor" Von Bulow: "When I was married to Sunny, we never got this table. Now, two injections of insulin and I'm a doctor." Indeed it is partly Kazan's snappy, comedic and self-revelatory lines that humanize Claus Von Bulow's character and persuade us that he could very well be innocent.

While I like Dershowitz's self-serving style and his confidence, what I admire most about the man is his realistic conception of the defense attorney's role in our society and his idea of what makes a good lawyer; that is, a good lawyer is one who recognizes not only that every person deserves the best defense their resources allow, but that he himself deserves to defend those with the best resources.

I've seen this and I give it___stars.
I want to see it___. I'll pass___.
The review was worth reading___. Not___.

Rounders (1998) 7

Why do you think they make them round?

The chips, that is.

As poker movies go, this is actually pretty good. It is the only movie about poker that is authentic both technically and psychologically. The only real competition at the time was *Cincinnati Kid* (1965); however that film is greatly marred by the improbability of Steve McQueen being dealt a royal flush in five-card stud to win (or was it to lose?) the key hand. The odds against being dealt a royal on any given hand are 649,739 to 1. Multiply that by the odds against getting it just when you need it, and we are in Fantasyland.

Part of the power of the script comes from the technical help of Mike Caro and other professional poker players. I know the triptych themes of (1) buddy for buddy (until it becomes ridiculous—as Matt Damon was for Ed Norton), and (2) honestly among poker players, and (3) The Game and male-bonding before women (as when Damon gives up the very fetching Gretchen Mol for cards and "feeling alive") are macho poker-guy bonding themes espoused by Mike Caro and others in the profession.

Matt Damon is very winning in the starring role, and Norton is properly despicable as one of life's losers, and John Malkovich is riveting as Teddy KGB in spite of what some might say about his accent.

The fact that the players play Hold'em, which is the most widely-played game in the poker clubs and the Vegas casinos today, and the one played for the world championship, lends to the overall authenticity of the film. Again, this contrasts with the Cincinnati Kid where five-card stud was played. However, even in 1965 that game was seldom if ever spread in most clubs, the dominate games at the time being low-ball, draw, and seven-card stud. Five-card stud is too simplistic for the modern player.

Much of the plot of Rounders is familiar and could be (and has been) wrapped around other themes and sleazy backdrops. The ending, which I will skip here, is howev-

er original as far as I know, and psychologically true, just ask any rounder. The key bit of authenticity that I think Director John Dahl and company got exactly right is that it takes courage and a devil-may-care sort of aggressiveness to win at high-stakes poker, and Mike McDermott had that.

Incidentally, the derivation of the word "rounder" is unclear as far as I know. It was used in England two hundred years ago to refer to a vagabond. It appeared in the clubs in Gardena, California at least as early as the 1960's to identify a regular player who went from club to club looking for a game he could beat. The term has sticking power because the chips really are round and roll from player to player, just as the fortunes of the rounders fluctuate from day to day as they make their rounds from club to club.

I've seen this and I give it___stars.
I want to see it___. I'll pass___.
The review was worth reading___. Not___.

Saving Private Ryan (1998) 8

Frank Capra updated

Tom Hanks is excellent and his character is nicely developed, while the action sequences are second to none. But ultimately *Saving Private Ryan* is like so many war movies I saw as a kid, regardless of how well rendered. The opening scene (after the shlocky frame) as they storm the beach at Normandy is pretty awful. You get the sense that a nation shows its resolve by how many of its young men it is willing to sacrifice. Just throw the bodies out there. In Kosovo we held that number to zero. Such a lovely way to fight a war. In WW II the number was, however many it took. Says something. Spielberg makes this point with the wide-angled shot of the channel filled with Allied landing craft and support vessels for as far as the eye can see—a scene incidentally right out of Frank Capra's seminal series "Why We Fight" to which this film is indebted whether Spielberg acknowledges it or not.

World War II was a war so horrible and so all-encompassing that to this day we really don't understand it or comprehend it. Spielberg thought he was being "objective" in showing war "as it really was," with Americans murdering prisoners and vomiting from fear and dying like cattle without a chance (something Capra of course was not able to do). Yes, but to show the "saving grace" of individual valor is to perpetuate the war system, because that valor is a fraud. It was not the bravery of our soldiers that won the war. Just as it didn't matter how brave or how cowardly the soldiers were in the landing craft, it was the sheer volume of them that prevailed.

I think as long as one believes that individual heroics amount to something we will have war. Spielberg no doubt thinks he has shown us the horror and waste of war, but while plying the trade he knows so well (seducing the audience) he has trumpeted the glory of war, that old fraud, and so he is just like the rest of the proselytizers, only more skillful.

Still it is impossible to say what is right. If we had not won WW II the world today would be vastly different. Totalitarian, imperial, repressive, racist regimes in which the state tortures and enslaves the people would have prevailed. They may have nuked one another by now and we could be living in the rubble of a bestial existence. Who knows? Thank God for the United States and its incredible industrial capacity, because that is what won the war, not individual heroics, much as our tribal minds, along with Spielberg's, would like to believe such fairy tales.

I've seen this and I give it___stars.
I want to see it___. I'll pass___.
The review was worth reading___. Not___.

Scarface (1983) 8

Compelling

I missed this intentionally when it came out in 1983 believing it to be another version of the Al Capone story. Of course Al Pacino would be brilliant as Al Capone and demand every square inch of the screen and get it. And he was and he did. And director Brian DePalma would spray the screen in scarlet, and he did. However this updated and revised version set in Miami from a script by Oliver Stone is very much worth watching even though it's almost three hours long.

First of all, Al Pacino is riveting as Tony Montana, a Cuban refugee released from prison by Fidel Castro in 1980 who arrives in Florida with a yearning to rule the world and a huge chip on his shoulder. His character is an extreme version of the "live fast, die young" species, the kind of guy who takes extreme chances and fears nothing. It is a shame that it is not obvious that for every one of the Tony Montanas in the world who actually made it to the top of the cocaine pile, there are thousands who weren't able to dodge the bullets and died not just young, but very young.

Second, there is not a dead spot in the whole movie. Stone's action-driven script and DePalma's focused direction compel our attention. If you can stand the bestial mentality and the animalistic flash culture of the drug lords and their sleazy world, you might even want to see this twice.

What I found myself watching closely was Michelle Pfeiffer at twenty-something, strikingly beautiful and totally degenerate as the cocaine-addled moll. Also very much worth watching was Mary Elizabeth Mastrantonio as Tony Montana's sister Gina. The big brother/little

sister incestuous theme (from the original *Scarface* of 1931 starring Paul Muni and directed by Howard Hawks) was craftily prepared and reached a striking climax (if you will) in the scene in which Gina tells Montana that he must "have her" (that's not exactly the words she used) since he won't let anybody else have her. The touch of necrophilia that followed was perhaps gratuitous.

What I loved was the way DePalma reminded us again and again of how trapped the characters were by their desperate indulgences, the expensive liquor, the cigars, the cocaine, the stacks of money that took hours to count by machine. The scene in which Pfeiffer takes a snort of cocaine, a puff of a cigarette and a swallow of booze one after the other as the only thing she knows how to do in this world (with the white powder still on her nostrils) was wonderful in its piteous effect. I also liked the scene in which Montana, seated in his black leather chair with his initials in gold lettering, surrounded by his security video screens, dives into a pile of cocaine and comes up with it on his nose. Reminds me of the old doper saying, "Too much is never enough."

The shoot 'em up finale of course was much, much overdone and about as realistic as a John Wayne barroom fight, but I loved the way Pacino played Montana near the end as a kind of paranoid Napoleon, the little guy who wanted to rule the world now finished and insane. Note, by the way, in how many scenes Pacino played a very vigorous persona sitting down.

In the final analysis this is a morality tale, a kind of very flashy "crime does not pay" saga not because the cops will get you (they don't) but because the life itself will corrupt you beyond anything human. Those who live by the gun will die by the gun, and there is no security among murders and thieves.

I've seen this and I give it___stars.
I want to see it___. I'll pass___.
The review was worth reading___. Not___.

Seduction of a Small Town (1997) 6

Not a work of art, but...

This is a political movie in reaction to the child-abuse hysteria that swept this country during the eighties and early nineties, only this time the good guys are the parents and the bad guys are the social workers and the accusers. You don't have to guess who's who when Melissa Gilbert plays the mother, nor when Dennis Weaver plays the grandfather. This is Little House on the Prairie circa 1997 versus Big Brother (as played by the social welfare system). We can depend on TV MOW's to reflect the current PC position, even if they have to make a 180 degree turn from what they were spouting just a few years before.

Joely Fisher does an excellent job as the evil woman who makes the false accusations and tries to frame the mother out of jealousy. Brian McNamara gives a not-so-strangely Michael Landon-ish portrayal of the father despite the scraggly beard, while Dennis Weaver is something close to wonderful in a bit part as the grand-father. Gilbert, looking solid and healthy, is steady but without finesse in a part big enough for a great actress.

When we see the cop cars and the social welfare people drive up and haul off the family's two children, we know this is about war in America, the family against the larg-er community. Unfortunately there are few shades of gray in the script: the family is clearly innocent and vic-timized. Nonetheless, since MOWs always reflect the zeitgeist and of course pander to their audiences, telling them what they want to hear, this movie is clear and welcome evidence that the public has finally seen that the social welfare industry has been given too much power: the crucial point being that it is horribly wrong to allow children to be taken from their parents without due process of law. With this movie it might be said that the tide has turned and the justice system and the pub-lic have awaken from their long, self-induced nightmare of hysteria. One hopes so.

I've seen this and I give it___stars.
I want to see it___. I'll pass___.
The review was worth reading___. Not___.

Shampoo (1975) 8

Casanova as a harried Hollywood hairdresser

Robert Towne, who has written a number of popular movies and at least one critically acclaimed one—*Chinatown* (1974)—and Warren Beatty wrote this satire of Hollywood. Beatty plays George Roundy, a not entirely bright but nimble hairdresser on a motorcycle who is much beloved and desired by women. The women doing most of the desiring are Lee Grant (Felicia), Julie Chris-tie (Jackie), and Goldie Hawn (Jill). Jack Warden plays Lester a successful investor who, to his chagrin and ultimate amusement, learns that his wife, his mistress, and his daughter Lorna (Carrie Fisher) are being bedded by the guy he thinks is gay. (Shades of the sham eunuch in the harem!)

This is a premise that many in the Hollywood Hills could not resist, the irony cutting so beautifully through the canyons and swimming pools and the lavish parties. Most of the action takes place on that November day in 1968 when Nixon and Agnew were swept into the White House by the "silent majority." Lester and his friends are quite pleased and are celebrating as the election returns come in. Meanwhile George is trying to raise money so he can open his own shop since he's got the "heads." Keeping the heads though turns out to be more than he can handle—and to be honest jumping from bed to bed

several times a day with several different women might be too much for any man.

Will Georgie-Porgie, puddin' pie (who kissed the girls and made them cry) get the money for his shop and the girl he loves—and which girl is it, that he loves? Goldie Hawn wears a micro-mini (but there's no peeking!) and Julie Christie sports a short pony skirt with boots while Lee Grant has to play the eldest woman. Now, who gets George and would she really want him?

Some nice sixties/seventies Hollywood decadence graces the screen along with free love and don't bogart that number. In the background there are a lot of mug shots of Nixon and Agnew in juxtaposition as a kind of joke since the movie was made in 1975 not long after Wa-tergate.

Beatty, playing a role said to be patterned after makeup artist Jay Sebring, is competent and wins our sympathy, maybe because we know he's never going to amount to much. Or does he? Lee Grant won an Oscar as Best Supporting Actress, but to be honest I thought Julie Christie was better, although they both were good. Ac-tors carried this with Warden and Hawn also putting in strong performances.

Shampoo is not so much funny as it is amusing. It's like a superior sit-com without the laugh track, but in no way is it a "defining" Hollywood film.

See this for Warren Beatty, one of the Hollywood royalty, brother of Shirley MacLaine and husband of Annette Bening.

I've seen this and I give it___stars.
I want to see it___. I'll pass___.
The review was worth reading___. Not___.

A Simple Plan (1998) 8

Did you ever feel evil?

This is a diabolical tale about the wages of greed. Alt-hough it is played straight without intentional humor, the irony is so delicious at times that you might find yourself laughing.

Jacob Mitchell (Billy Bob Thornton) is the one who be-gins to feel evil, and rightly so as the bodies begin to pile up. His presumably smarter brother Hank (Bill Paxton) feels mostly fear as he struggles to cover up one mishap after another. Their problems begin when they and Jacob's buddy Lou Chambers (Brent Briscoe) stumble onto a downed airplane in the woods covered with snow in which they find one dead person being feasted on by crows and a duffle bag full of hundred dollar bills. Lou, who might represent the common man, says, let's keep it. Hank, who could be rational man, says, whoa, this money belongs to somebody and besides we could get into trouble. We better turn it in. And Jacob, who is the natural man, sides with his buddy Lou. Afterall they're country poor and this is probably drug money that nobody is going to miss. And anyway, what can go wrong?

Well, as Ben Franklin observed a long time ago, "Three can keep a secret, if two of them are dead." As they wait for spring to come and the plane to be discovered before they risk spending the money, the "simple plan" begins to unravel with horrific consequences.

Thornton and Briscoe play country boys to perfection, and Paxton does a great job as a small town golden boy majorly compromised. Bridget Fonda plays Hank's pregnant wife, who turns out to be the brains (as it were) of the group. There are some very nice plot twists as the all too human emotions of the characters begin to crash into one another. Inevitably we have a morality tale in which the wages of sin are fully realized.

Sam Raimi's direction captures well the atmosphere of north country America without any obvious straining for effect. He gets great mileage out of a few crows (or maybe they're ravens) and a whole lot of snow. Scott B. Smith's script (from his novel) is clever and morally astute. The characterizations are excellent and the story psychologically satisfying. Particularly agreeable was the very sad, ironic end for Hank and his wife, who find that all the self-created hell they went through led them back to where they began, but without their souls.

I've seen this and I give it___stars.
I want to see it___. I'll pass___.
The review was worth reading___. Not___.

The Snapper (1993) 7

Warm and funny, but only superficially realistic

Fine acting by Colm Meaney (Dessie Curley) and Tina Kellegher (Sharon Curley) carry this offbeat tragi-comedy about the perils of out of wedlock pregnancy in a working class Irish family. I think the Pope would approve of how this subject was handled, if he approved of the subject being handled in the first place.

What do I mean? Well, here's an unwanted pregnancy that in the apprehension of some people could arguably be seen as a result of something about as close to a rape as it gets without technically being rape, depending upon how you define your "technically." (She was drunk and an older man took advantage of her in the parking lot of the pub.) I won't say more for fear of spoiling the plot for you, but be forewarned that some viewers will find the whole thing uncomfortable.

Roddy Doyle, the gifted fictionalist (*Paddy Clarke, Ha, Ha, Ha, The Woman Who Walked into Doors*, etc) wrote the novel and the screenplay. Stephen Frears (*My Beautiful Laundrette* 1985, *Dangerous Liaisons* 1988, etc.) directed. Doyle is a master of dialogue and has a warm sense of people that he imposes on his readers. Known as a realistic writer, he is actually a sentimentalist with a keen feel for the foibles of his characters.

There is a kind of TV sit-com feeling to Frears's direction in that nothing really depressing occurs. There's a neighborhood feel to the taunting, some windows are broken, and there's a fistfight, but none of the kids are on heroin or planting bombs. There's little violence and the sex depicted is minimalist. There's a sense that nothing is really wrong in the world, just some slips of behavior and some misunderstandings. You realize, for example, that despite Sharon's continued drinking the baby is not going to be born suffering from any kind of alcoholic syndrome. Furthermore, although Dessie has six kids to support, we never see him working overtime or worrying about money.

Doyle is also a political writer and has a message. His message here is that the gift of life is precious over and above how it is conceived and that narrow-minded men (grandfather-to-be Dessie Curley) can, through love, understanding and a little effort, rise above their prejudices and do the right thing and feel the right way. Politically speaking, the film walks softly and carries no banner between the two sides of the abortion question, clearly identifying with the pro-lifers without overtly offending the pro-choice side.

Perhaps it is best to leave the politics behind and, like many viewers, simply enjoy the laughs, the realistic dialogue and the warm, chaotic family atmosphere presented and save the moralizing for another day. By the way, you might have to watch this twice to catch some of the humor. Either that or have a good ear for the Irish brogue. For myself, I could have used subtitles.

I've seen this and I give it___stars.
I want to see it___. I'll pass___.
The review was worth reading___. Not___.

Soapdish (1991) 8

Very funny

This is a romantic comedy with the emphasis on comedy for a change. As usual the lovers—Sally Field as almost-over-the-hill soap opera queen, Celeste Talbert; and Kevin Kline as marginally employed and marginally talented actor, Jeffrey Anderson—are working at cross purposes, seemingly unaware that they are madly in love, etc. Owing a little to Bette Davis's Margo Channing in *All About Eve* (1950) and a whole lot to the slapstick theatrical tradition, Sally Field goes over the top towards hilarity as she malaprops her way to love and happiness. Kevin Kline, one of the more underrated leading men of recent years, is also very good and very winning as he manages to be handsome, vulnerable, egotistical and lovable all at the same time.

The misadventures center around Celeste's fear of losing her audience as she has entered her forties, and reach the crisis point with the arrival of her niece, aspiring actress Cori Craven (Elisabeth Shue) who turns out NOT to be her niece, with ensuing plot complications. Cori manages to get a small part in the soap opera as a homeless deaf mute before discovering her true relationship to Celeste (and to Jeffrey Anderson as well)—but never mind.

As a romantic counterpoint or foil to the leads are Robert Downey Jr. (soap opera director, David Barnes) and Cathy Moriarty (Montana and Nurse Nan). David Barnes is oh so hot for her, but she cares only about one thing: getting rid of Celeste so that she might shine more brightly on the set. To this end she gets Barnes to do all sorts of things to wreck Celeste's career, but through happenstance and/or a perverse logic, all his attempts go awry, much to the delight of the viewer.

Whoopie Goldberg plays Rose Schwartz, the show's chief writer and Celeste's alter-ego and confidant while Carrie Fisher has a modest part as the hard-as-nails producer of the show.

I thought this was funnier than the only other spoof of the soap opera world that I have seen (*Young Doctors in Love* 1982 which burlesqued TV's General Hospital and was pretty good). Soapdish is funnier with a daffy script and plenty of laugh-out-loud one-liners and terrific performances by Field, Kline and Downy, Jr. But see this for Sally Field who is outstanding.

I've seen this and I give it___stars.
I want to see it___. I'll pass___.
The review was worth reading___. Not___.

Suspicion (1941) 7

Slight thriller with star power

Cary Grant (Johnnie Aysgarth) was 37 when this was released and perhaps at the pinnacle of his sexual charm (but not at the pinnacle of his career by a long shot); and Joan Fontaine (Lina Aysgarth—not "Linda," as the video jacket mistakenly has it), 24, was fresh from her very fine performance in *Rebecca* (1940) alongside Laurence Olivier, also directed by Alfred Hitchcock, for which he garnered his only Best Picture Oscar. I don't think this film is nearly as good. It is saved from being something close to annoying at times only by the star power of the leads and a fine supporting cast, especially Nigel Bruce (best known perhaps as Dr. Watson in a number of Sherlock Holmes films) as Cary Grant's friend "Beaky."

The problem with the film lies partly with the casting of Cary Grant, although not in his performance as such. He was seen as such a valuable property by the studio

that the proper ending of the film was considered inappropriate and so it was changed. Along the way we see a lot of mixed foreshadowing so it is impossible to tell whether his character is that of a loving husband who is a bit of a rogue or a cold-blooded murderer who married Lina for her inheritance and intends to kill her. We can see how the latter possibility might not work so well since she was only getting a subsistence allowance from the will of her father who disapproved of the marriage. And there are all those dark scowls that Grant manufactures, somewhat awkwardly I must say, to keep us in doubt. What is apparent is that Hitchcock had one ending in mind and then had to change it and wasn't able to redo some of the earlier scenes that worked better with the old ending.

At any rate, Joan Fontaine is very good, lovely, graceful and focused. With this performance she went one up on her older sister Olivia de Havilland by winning the Best Actress Oscar. And it is a bit of a spicy treat to see Cary Grant as something of a heavy, at least part of the time. For most of us, who have seen him in many films, his character has always been sterling.

I must also note that some of the production seems a bit unnatural. Grant wears his suit and tie all buttoned up even when visiting Fontaine in their bedroom (carrying the infamous glass of milk, which I understand was backlighted with a bulb inside the glass to make it almost glow). Fontaine's Lina appears mousey and bookish at the beginning (it is suggested that she was in danger of being an old maid!) but later develops a more sophisticated style. And I don't think Hitchcock or Grant really gave her enough cause for the sort of fear she experienced. The final scene with its quick about-face was not entirely convincing or conclusive either.

Contemporary audiences might wince at the plodding direction by Hitchcock. They might even wonder why he decided to make a movie from such a familiar and lightly plotted tale not far removed psychologically from a romance novel. But Hitchcock always erred on the side of giving the mass audience what he thought they wanted. What they wanted here was Cary Grant and Joan Fontaine together romantically with some mystery and doubt along the way.

I've seen this and I give it___stars.
I want to see it___. I'll pass___.
The review was worth reading___. Not___.

Thank You for Smoking (2007) 8

Clever satire

One of the many ironies in this blatant satire (which is *not* a documentary) is that at no time is anybody seen smoking! No Hollywood cinematic light ups. Even Nick Naylor, who is vice president of the smoking PR conglomerate, does not actually light up on screen. We see him once look into an empty pack of cigarettes wishing he had one, that's it.

The joke on the square is that although this movie is about smoking nobody associated with the movie wants to be accused of supporting smoking in any way. Now you might think that, well, a movie that puts smoking in a bad light as this movie does, certainly is not what the tobacco companies want to see. However, if the movie producers also threw in a few scenes with the stars puffing happily away, the message would surely be mixed.

No mixed messages here. Aaron Eckhart who stars as Nick Naylor is a sort of charming sociopath. He describes himself as the kind of guy who could get any woman into bed. In a relentlessly ironic follow up to that we have Katie Holmes playing an intrepid reporter for the "Washington Probe" newspaper who gets him into bed, all the better to get him to reveal all his dirty secrets and dirty tricks. He was owned, so to speak, and taken advantage of sexually.

Eckhart is perfect for the part with his handsome winning ways. You may recall that he played a corporate sexist pig sociopath in the critically acclaimed film *In the Company of Men* (1997), which I highly recommend. Here he is a little sweeter, a little more charming, and amazingly enough a good role model for his son Joey (Cameron Bright), who, by the way, has a lot of sharp lines and delivers them well. How this is pulled off is something to behold, for sure. But basically the rationale is that Nick is doing it all "to pay the mortgage" ("the yuppie Nuremberg defense") and that is the lesson that Joey learns, and presumably he will be able to adapt to more socially correct employment when he grows up.

Some satirical bits include the Marlboro Man (Sam Elliott) with cancer getting a bribe; a senator from Vermont (William H. Macy) holding a senate hearing about getting a skull and crossbones logo put on cigarette packages while Nick tells him that the Vermont cows and their cheese are causing clogged arteries and heart attacks; Nick hanging out with a RP person representing the interests of alcohol (Maria Bello), and another (David Koechner) whoring for the gun industry. They like to sit around over dinner and compare the number of people their products have killed.

Robert Duvall has a modest part as the "Captain" of tobacco and Rob Lowe gets to play Jeff Megall, a big time, Machiavellian Hollywood money man, who is lining up Catherine Zeta-Jones and I forget who else, to play a "naked in a space" movie with some serious smoking scenes—for a price to be paid for by Big Tobacco. The joke here is that this practice has long been a source of Hollywood film production up-front revenue. There's a scene showing old Hollywood stars with PC touch ups of their movies, showing them with lollypops or pencils hanging out of their mouths instead of cigarettes.

The script (adapted from a novel by Christopher Buckley, son of conservative pundit William F. Buckley) and direction by Jason Reitman deserve some kind of award for originality. The film is definitely a put down of industry PR people, yet somehow it makes them look human.

I've seen this and I give it___stars.
I want to see it___. I'll pass___.
The review was worth reading___. Not___.

They Drive by Night (1940) 8
Before Bogey was a legend

It was a pleasure seeing Ida Lupino in this, her first significant role at age 22. She is sexy, pretty and more than a bit nasty. Sometimes dubbed "the poor man's Bette Davis" she shows here that she could have handled some of Davis's roles very well.

The story itself is a tale about truck drivers that pits them against the loan sharks and emphasizes the danger of driving without much sleep on roads not yet of Interstate quality. It takes place in California in the late thirties. Lupino plays Lana Carlsen, the bored wife of the head of a trucking company who only has eyes for Joe Fabrini (George Raft), who only has eyes for Cassie Hartley (Ann Sheridan). Humphrey Bogart plays his brother Paul Fabrini and really takes a backseat. That would change beginning the next year when Bogey would star with Ida Lupino in *High Sierra* (1941).

It is interesting to contrast the two films both directed by long time Hollywood legend Raoul Walsh. *They Drive by Night* has a distinct thirties feel to it and not just because George Raft stars. The sense of the Depression is still with the characters in *They Drive by Night* as the truck drivers and waitress Cassie worry about their jobs. There is a sense of identification with the working man that is absent *from High Sierra*, which really began Bogart's tough guy movie persona.

Alan Hale (235 acting credits at IMDb.com!) plays Lana's fun-loving and clueless husband, Ed Carlsen. Roscoe Karns provides some wise-cracking relief as Irish McGurn, truck-driving pinball wizard. The script by Jerry Wald is full of snappy one liners like this between Joe and Cassie. He asks, "Do you believe in love at first sight?" She counters with, "It saves a lot of time." Wald later became a producer of some of Hollywood's most memorable flicks including *Pride of the Yankees* (1945), *Mildred Pierce* (1945), *Key Largo* (1948), *The Glass Menagerie* (1950), etc.

By all means see this for Ida Lupino, who to escape from the typecasting that began with this movie later went on to become one of Hollywood's first woman directors.

I've seen this and I give it___stars.

I want to see it___. I'll pass___.
The review was worth reading___. Not___.

The Thin Red Line (1998) 7

War as nihilism

I rented this back in the days of the VCR and noticed that the previous viewer had given up after about a tenth of an inch of tape, not having rewound it. I could see why. This begins as an arty war movie that is not doing either the arty or the war part right. I would have given up on it myself except that it had been nominated for a number of awards, and I knew there had to be something I was missing. So I rewound the tape and listened and watched carefully. Gradually something began to build. The impressionistic and stream of consciousness techniques began to pull me in and to mesh with the flashbacks and poetic voice-overs to make a meaningful contrast with the jungle and carnage. The studied camera work with the long takes on the faces of the soldiers, interspersed with panoramic vistas of jungle and mountain and naturalistic shots of tropical island animals, lead me to believe that in making this, Director Terrence Malick had taken Shakespeare as his muse, in particular the celebrated words from MacBeth: "...[Life] is a tale/Told by an idiot, full of sound and fury,/Signifying nothing."

As other critics have pointed out, Malick's movie does indeed signify nothing, and perhaps that is the point. But I am somewhat troubled by such an interpretation of our involvement in World War II. I would feel more comfortable had such a point of view and attendant techniques been employed in depicting our involvement in Vietnam or even in World War I. But to imply that the sacrifices made by our soldiers at Guadalcanal and elsewhere in the South Pacific were for nothing is entirely off base. Almost any war fought anywhere is a monumental waste; but if there is one exception is it without doubt World War II. We had no choice but to oppose European fascism and the expansionist policies of Imperial Japan. I shudder to think what the world would be like now, had we not. Imagine being surrounded by totalitarian regimes with their gas ovens and their slave labor, their policies of racial and cultural genocide. By comparison, such a reality would make George Orwell's *1984* nightmare a benign fantasy.

I am also wondering how James Jones himself would feel about this impressionistic interpretation of his realistic novel. He was one of a generation of writers, including Norman Mailer and James Michener, who found their inspiration in the war in the Pacific. He is also the author of *From Here To Eternity* (1951), made a couple of years later into an academy-award winning movie starring Burt Lancaster (an excellent movie, by the way). I suspect that Jones would have to feel some ambiguity toward Director Terrence Malick's production of this sequel. Jones certainly did not feel that our participation

and experience in World War II was meaningless. Nor was his personal experience meaningless. Furthermore to make his novel into a revisionist impression of war as nihilistic hell misses not only the spirit of his novel but the entire point of our involvement in World War II. I wonder how those who survived the horrific experience of Guadalcanal and similar battles feel about this movie. I wonder if they think it was accurate and fair and expressed their sense of experience.

The performances by James Caviezel as Pvt. Witt and Sean Penn as First Sergeant Welsh were excellent. Nick Nolte as Col. Gordon Tall was also good, although he occasionally reminded me of George C. Scott doing General Patton. Perhaps the best sequence in the movie was the recollection in flashback by Pvt. Jack Bell (Ben Chaplin) of his sensual wife back in the states and the agony of being separated from her, and then the brutal knife of her letter telling him she had fallen in love with another man. The inclusion of a third element, that of the Pacific Islanders themselves amid the strife as innocents watching the gladiators, was valuable as perspective. However what might have been added was the brutality and enslavement they experienced at the hands of the Japanese military. Malick gave us none of that perhaps because such a view might have detracted from his purpose, that of depicting war as an expression of our nihilistic nature. Incidentally some have said that this treatment owes something to Tim O'Brien's short story, "The Things They Carried," or even to the spirit of the Thomas Hardy poem, "The Man He Killed." Certainly there is an intentional allusion to Carl Sandberg's poem "Grass" when one of the soldiers holds up some grass and says something like, "This is us." O'Brien's short story was an intense focus on the artifacts carried by soldiers and what the bare artifacts implied. Yes, I believe Malick was influenced by O'Brien, certainly in the sense that this is a strongly visual film. It's what our eyes see that counts, and not so much the story or what is said.

I've seen this and I give it___stars.
I want to see it___. I'll pass___.
The review was worth reading___. Not___.

To Catch a Thief (1955) 8

Languid but beautiful romantic thriller

This is probably Hitchcock's most beautiful movie. Grace Kelly is well (but of course decorously) displayed in delicate and perfectly fitted summer dresses and evening gowns (designed by Edith Head) that show off her exquisite arms and shoulders while accentuating her elegant neck and jaw line—and, as she turns for the camera, the graceful line of her back. Opposite her is one of Hollywood's most dashing leading men, the incomparable Cary Grant.

The cinematography by long-time Hitchcock collaborator Robert Burks was shot on location in the French Riviera. The style is daylight clear and sparkling, bright as the dream of a princess to be, always focused without a hint of darkness anywhere. Even the scenes shot at night on the rooftops seem to glow. The houses on the hills overlooking Princess Grace's future home and the narrow cobble stone roads with the low-lying stone walls suggest a refined and elegant lifestyle to come. Even though she drives too fast, one is not worried that she might crash...

Cary Grant is John Robie who fought with the French resistance during WWII and then became a jewel thief, dubbed "The Cat" for his ability to slink quietly in the night over roof tops and to steal into the bedrooms of the rich and take their jewels without waking them. As the movie opens he is retired from his life of crime and living comfortably in a villa in the hills above Nice. The complications begin immediately as the police arrive at his villa to question him about some recent cat-like jewel robberies. Robie is innocent of course (we are led to believe) and to prove his innocence he is motivated to find the real thief.

Grace Kelly plays Frances Stevens, the slightly naughty nouveau riche daughter of the widow of a Texas-style oil millionaire. She is used to having men fall all over themselves trying to court her, but Robie seems uninterested, and this excites her fancy and she goes after him. It is interesting to note that by this time Cary Grant (51 when the film was released) had become such a heart throb that directors liked to have the women (who were always noticeably younger; Kelly was 26) chase after him. Audrey Hepburn does as much in *Charade* (1963). One notes that here, as in *Charade*, the women kiss Cary Grant first, not the other way around. Here it is nicely done as the previously demure Frances takes a surprising initiative at the door of her hotel suite.

The story itself is rather bland and predictable, reminding me of a James Bond flick from, say, the sixties as though toned down for an audience of old maids. Notable in supporting roles are Brigitte Auber as the athletic Danielle Foussard, John Williams as the British insurance agent, and Jessie Royce Landis as Frances Stevens' mother. Hitch makes his *de rigueur* appearance as a passenger on the mini-bus that Robie takes to get away from the gendarmes early in the film.

See this for Grace Kelly whose cool and playful demeanor and statuesque beauty form the heart of this somewhat languid romantic thriller.

I've seen this and I give it___stars.
I want to see it___. I'll pass___.
The review was worth reading___. Not___.

To Have and Have Not (1944) 8

Bogie and Bacall at their best together

This was billed as "Hemingway's To Have and Have Not," but if there is one thing it isn't, it isn't Hemingway's novel. It is a fine quasi-remake of *Casablanca* (1942) with Humphrey Bogart playing essentially the same kind of character he played in *Casablanca*, a worldly wise, cynical America ex-pat who doesn't want to get involved in politics as the storm clouds of World War II gather. Instead of a saloon in Casablanca Bogie has a fishing boat in Martinique. Instead of Ingrid Bergman he has Lauren Bacall. Instead of Claude Rains as perfect of police, he has Dan Seymour as Capt. Renard working for the Germans. Instead of Dooley Wilson to play the piano and sing, he has Hoagy Carmichael. Instead of Peter Lorre as a sniveling lowlife, he has Walter Brennan as an alcoholic friend. In either case, Bogie ends up helping the Free French even though he'd rather not get involved.

This was Lauren Bacall's debut. She was 22-years-old and legend has it that she and Bogart, who was in his forties, fell in love during the filming. She plays a sultry babe with a hard edge, and she does it very well. Her famous line, "You know how to whistle, don't you Steve? You just put your lips together and blow" more or less defined her character.

I found Walter Brennan's Eddie annoying, but then I never liked lushes. Dan Seymour is memorable as the portly man with a scar who speaks with weighty precision as he works for the Vichy government. Hoagy Carmichael warbles a tune or two and Dolores Moran looks good enough to eat. Howard Hawks' direction is sharp and focused, although supposedly he was eating his heart out because Bacall preferred Bogart over him.

Clearly this is all about Bogart and Bacall, probably their best work together. They seem delighted with one another. And they were.

I've seen this and I give it___stars.
I want to see it___. I'll pass___.
The review was worth reading___. Not___.

Traffic (2000) 8

Very well done

Obviously this is first and foremost an entertainment. We don't want to be confused about that. But director Steven Soderbergh does have a didactic point, and it's one I agree with. The "war" on drugs will never be won with guns or law enforcement. We can see this in the extraordinary sequence in which Michael Douglas, playing the newly appointed drug czar of the United States, steps away from his job and returns to his family. He stops his speech and simply asks how can we fight a war in which the enemies are members of our own family?

Better yet, he might have asked, how can we fight a war when the enemy is ourself?

Soderbergh carefully avoids the appearance of taking sides, but the ending makes it clear that the "war" will go on; indeed the war has become institutionalized, a way of life for us and those involved in it. In some sense the war on drugs has become an entertainment for couch potatoes napping in front of the TV, as well as a patriotic rallying point for others.

I thought Michael Douglas gave one of his finest performances, and Benicio Del Toro as the Tijuana cop torn between what he believes is right and the reality of his situation, was excellent. The hauntingly beautiful Catherine Zeta-Jones was chillingly effective as a woman without morality, a sociopath with the survival instincts of a hyena. Dennis Quaid, hardly recognizable without the grin, was competent as a sleazy lawyer who gambled big time and lost. Don Cheadle as the "solider" in the war who loves the battle, the "war lover," so to speak, was intriguing. Erika Christensen deserves special praise for her compellingly true portrayal of an insecure teen who finds escape in the little death of heroin.

But I wonder if the average person seeing this movie realizes what the message is, that the war on drugs is a fraud. Like the war in Vietnam it is a war that is, without changing the very nature of our society, unwinnable. It is a bureaucratic monstrosity that we have created because we need an evil we can hate.

There is no "solution" to the "drug problem" because there is no solution to human nature. A better approach to keeping the problem at a manageable level would be decriminalization and a massive program of education. Why doesn't this happen? First, because the entrenched bureaucracy that has a vested interest in maintaining its position. Second, because the old "moral majority" in this country, people who imagine that they know the truth, and have the right to regulate the morality of others, will not allow it to end. They need a target for their hate. Note well that Douglas came home and renewed his efforts as a father because he realized that that is where he failed, as a father, and that is where we as a nation are failing. Education begins at home. If you don't know what kind of drugs your children are doing, then, as a parent, you don't know anything.

Soderbergh tells this tragic story in a somewhat simplistic, but ultimately, very effective way. The use of tinted filters to lend atmosphere and perhaps to help orient the viewer did not bother me, but I agree with those who found them unnecessary and not particularly effective. On the other hand I thought the use of hand held cameras lend an intensity and immediacy to the action. Note that one of Soderbergh's techniques is to show just a partial view of the action, such as just the guns and the hands and arms of the killers as Dennis Quiad puts down the phone. We know what is going to happen from seeing only that much, and so does Quiad. In fact, this is the way we sometimes view the world, the salient objects in our view register and we act. Soderbergh's technique of showing the "war" at various levels and in differing environments and from differing points of view was obvious but nonetheless very effective.

But Soderbergh did not go far enough. Instead of showing the vulnerability of a judge with a junkie for a daughter, he might have had the local police catch her trafficking out of her house and had them unconstitutionally seize his property. Maybe then the message would get home to the American people that the war on drugs has the potential to become a threat to our democracy and our republican form of government.

I've seen this and I give it___stars.
I want to see it___. I'll pass___.
The review was worth reading___. Not___.

Trainspotting (1996) 8

Money is the power god of heroin

Of course *Trainspotting* is a disturbing film. It is also gross and disgusting, as though Larry Flynt had gotten his hands on something like *A Clockwork Orange*. But this Brit production with the heavy Scottish brogue is fortunately more than that; it is original and clever and moves right along. This is partly a cult film with all sorts of indie shibboleths and counter-cultural references; and partly an art film, with splashy sets and studied camera work; but mostly this is a full-blown commercial seduction of contemporary youth, worthy of the talent of somebody at, say, Sony or Pepsi or even the WB.

The opening theme (actually voiced over) is the idea that heroin or any really demanding addiction is preferable to ordinary life, an intriguing but stale notion designed to shock the bourgeoisie. The central theme proclaims that a heroin addict is just another kind of junkie, along with your cigarette, cola, beer, sex, grease, etc. junkies. (Bingo!) Yet at the end we see, as one might discover by watching all the commercials now on PBS, that money will out. Kinda reminds me of what Omar Khayyam asked about wine nine hundred years ago: "I wonder...what the Vintners buy/One half so precious as the stuff they sell." Here the answer is clear: money itself. Closing theme: money triumphs over heroin; money is the power god of heroin.

I guess something like that is the commercially correct "message" of this film.

Ewan McGregor is excellent in the leading role as a junkie who is as cute as your brother, with fine support by Robert Carlyle, who plays a bantam who likes to cut people. The script by John Hodge is partly unintelligible, which is good; and the direction by Danny Boyle combines cartoon fantasy with stark realism, slick horror with black comedy, in a manner sure to be imitated. The sound track, "available on Capitol Records," (I rest my case) sold well. Some might say that this is a penetrating critique of modern urban society, but the only thing being penetrated is your pocket book.

I've seen this and I give it___stars.
I want to see it___. I'll pass___.
The review was worth reading___. Not___.

The Truman Show (1998) 8

Can all of life be fake?

This movie is spooky, profound and perhaps prophetic. Could the world we live in be Truman's world? Instead of Christof (or his predecessor, the Wizard of Oz) could there be aliens Out There running their TV show of us?

We can't get out of this solar system. The sun is rigged Out There. Just as Truman could never sail to Fiji, no human can live long enough to transverse interstellar space to Alpha Centuri Proxima, the nearest star. Before the gods we must have demigods in the form of those looking over us, real or imagined. Does it make any difference? And as Christof says, we accept the reality that is given us, so we could be fooled.

Anyway, *The Truman Show* begins with a startling premise marvelously presented. The script by Andrew Niccol is a work of art and the direction by Peter Weir surehanded and seamless. He allows the story to unfold at a convincing pace and the fifties cum nineties TV Americana feel to the "Seahaven" sets is delightful. Jim Carrey is perfect as Truman Burbank, the poor sap in a fishbowl. Everything about his life, including his wife and best friend are totally fake (try that on for size). Ed Harris as the megalomaniac TV artist Christof is creepy enough, although the scenes with him are ironically less convincing than those in Truman's world. I thought he came across a little too much like a mad scientist. Laura Linny as Carrey's TV wife/product spokesperson with the ever present TV smile is wonderful, and good too is his estranged girlfriend, Natascha McElhone with the big eyes.

Some unanswered questions. We know there is a camera in the bathroom. Do they switch to another shot when he is using it or does the world-wide audience watch him move his bowels? And is his wife a "whore" as well as a TV actress or is their relationship purely Platonic? Does the audience see them together in the bedroom? Does she have a life away from him? Weir chose not to address these questions.

Although the premise looks a little messy when examined closely, the inspired and completely apropos ending

is as crisp and clean as the dot at the end of this sentence.

I've seen this and I give it___stars.
I want to see it___. I'll pass___.
The review was worth reading___. Not___.

The Unbelievable Truth (1990) 8

A cute and quirky, offbeat romantic comedy

What we have here is an indie romantic comedy, adorably done. Adrienne Shelly, who is petite and cute and pale as winter snow, stars as Audrey Hugo, a mechanic's daughter who has been accepted at Harvard (or so she says) but has no intention of going. She is obsessed with what she sees as the inevitability of nuclear war and attendant horrors, which she reads about aloud to herself and anyone who will listen.

It is 1988 and this is Long Island, New York, although it looks a lot like Jersey to me. Certainly this is not the high rent district of Long Island. Her boyfriend is shallow and doesn't listen to her. Her father thinks she ought to go to the local community college which he notes is a whole lot cheaper than Harvard. She is bored with her senior year at high school and usually cuts.

Enter tall, handsome, dressed all in black Robert Burke as Josh Hutton just released from prison. People who meet him ask, "Are you a priest?" He answers, "I'm a mechanic." And indeed he is an especially wondrous one who, of course, goes to work for Audrey's father, Vic Hugo (Chris Cooke) and becomes invaluable. Although it seems that Josh killed a girl and then the girl's father some years ago, we of course know from the title and from Josh's obviously sterling character that the "unbelievable truth" must be otherwise. And of course so does Audrey who is immediately smitten with him. But Josh is apparently practicing something like celibacy ("Are you a priest?") and rebuffs Audrey's advances, thereby initiating a whole slew of romantic misunderstandings wittily tossed about by director Hal Hartley along with some spiffy Mamet-like dialogue.

Now enter a photographer who makes Audrey into a fashion model, first her feet, but eventually the entire petite torso. Physically she moves to New York City, but her heart is still with Josh at her dad's auto repair shop. She even carries Josh's wrench in her handbag, with which she threatens the photo guy when he tries to get too close.

What makes this film a delight in spite of all the obvious elements and the predictable complications is the original, independent and sparkling character of Audrey, the true blue integrity of Josh, some clever and funny dialogue, and a kind of warm puppy feel usually the signature property of a Nora Ephron film starring Meg Ryan.

I've seen this and I give it___stars.
I want to see it___. I'll pass___.
The review was worth reading___. Not___.

The Usual Suspects (1995) 8

Testosterone thriller cleverly done

The title might suggest a comedic takeoff on a crime thriller employing some sophisticated shtick or maybe we're in for something like Danny DeVito in *Throw Mama from the Train*. But this is not a comedy. It is not exactly your usual crime thriller either. It is an unconscious parody of crime thrillers with some curious depth replete with corrupt cops, shadowy off screen sinister villains and pathetic low lifes.

Although I don't think director Bryan Singer and his high school pal and collaborator, scriptwriter Christopher McQuarrie, had the slightest intention toward burlesque, I was again and again struck by an unconscious underlying tone of parody. The title is the tip off.

"Round up the usual suspects" is a line from *Casablanca* (1942), as most movie buffs know. Claude Rains, as Captain Renault, head of the police in Casablanca, says "round up the usual suspects" more as an indication of local Moroccan justice than as a real order. It is just the sort of cynically ironic line that would inspire Singer and McQuarrie to dream up this exceedingly cynical, but bordering on the funny, flick.

While Casablanca was a bittersweet love story, *The Usual Suspects* is anything but. The cast is decidedly and deliberately all male with only Suzy Amis in a minor role as Edie Finneran to interfere with the macho lineup of crooks, cops and shady sinister types. The movie features Stephen Baldwin (Mike McManus), Gabriel Bryne (Dean Keaton), Benicio Del Toro (Fred Fenster), Chazz Palminteri (Dave Kujan), Kevin Pollak (Todd Hockney), and stars Kevin Spacey as Verbal Kint. These guys are all excellent actors who together create a kind mass energy that propels the film. In more ways than one I am reminded of Quentin Tarantino's *Reservoir Dogs* (1992) and David Mamet's *Glengarry Glen Ross* (1992) (movie directed by James Foley). Consider these similarities:

In both *Glengarry Glen Ross* and *The Usual Suspects* you have a virtually all male cast who sling expletives at one another in an "at your throat" style. In both *Reservoir Dogs* and *The Usual Suspects* you have five crooks thrown together to do a job, and again everything is exceedingly macho with threats and expletives flying around like water in a hurricane. In all three films the cast is outstanding, with Al Pacino, Jack Lemon, Ed Harris, Alex Baldwin, Kevin Spacey and Alan Arkin leading the cast in Glengarry, and Harvey Keitel, Tim Roth, Steve Buscemi doing the same in Reservoir Dogs. These guys are not your run of the mill actors. They are the kind of guys that star in kick butt movies. They know how to look and act authentic.

But an even more startling way to compare *The Usual Suspects* with *Glengarry Glen Ross* and *Reservoir Dogs* is in the dialogue. In all three movies the dialogue is preciously wrought with an emphasis on sounding just a little different. In *Reservoir Dogs* Tarantino sometimes makes the characters sound like they are spouting Shakespeare, and in *Glengarry Glen Ross* Mamet has them playing verbal hijinks like machine gun chatter in an experimental stage play. Here Singer and McQuarrie (his script won the Oscar for Best Original Screenplay) employ a lot of the same rapid fire, seemingly authentic vernacular interspersed with theatrical sounding speech especially in the case of Kobayashi (Pete Postlethwaite) who calmly calls everybody "Mister" like an English butler. And of course Verbal is very verbal and able to spout lines like, "The greatest trick the devil ever pulled was convincing the world that he didn't exist."

Keep that line in mind as you watch, and ask yourself who plays Keyser Soze, the devil incarnate, so to speak. And pay attention to references to Skokie, Illinois. That will help to unravel the plot. The ending contains a nicely set up surprise.

The Usual Suspects is the sort of cult favorite beloved by young males fascinated with testosterone-hyped action, macho-inspired dialogue and devil man care anti-heroics. But it's a little better than that. And clearly this is not a chick flick, and therein lies a problem. While most males will at least find this interesting, many females will just shake their heads at how obvious is the seduction of the targeted audience. Personally I thought the movie was a laugh. I actually laughed out loud at some of the theatrics and grinned with appreciation at how surely Singer had captured the mentality of the targeted audience while bonding with it. But I have to say (for those directors, writers and producers who would like to do half as well), you can't fake it. Tarantino and Singer and others have been able to pull this sort of thing off because they really believe in the psychology. They really believe there are tough guys who say "f-you" even with a gun shoved in their face, and there really are guys who see the world in a kind of cops/robbers, good guy/bad guy, buddy/rat persona world. And there's some truth to it.

Spacey won a supporting actor Oscar playing Verbal Kint, a kind of crippled loser, it would seem. He should have won Best Actor, he was that good and he was the heart of the film and the guy with whom the audience most identified. He is the seeming loser, the little guy, the underdog who turns out to be smarter and tougher than anybody else. I think that is what the targeted audience really loves about this movie.

Bottom line: a must see for anybody interested in the history of the American cinema and in the evolution of the mystery/thriller/noir genre. A few academic dissertations have been and will be written on how the cinematic hero has evolved from, say, Tom Mix to Verbal Kint. You might want to write one yourself.

I've seen this and I give it___stars.
I want to see it___. I'll pass___.
The review was worth reading___. Not___.

U Turn (1997) 8

A feast for vultures

Small time hood, played with fidelity by Sean Penn, blows a hole in the water hose of his 1964 and a half red Mustang out in the desert and has to limp into Superior, Arizona, pop. about 100, temp 100-plus. He shoulda made a u turn. He's already lost two fingers because he wasn't able to pay some dudes the $13,000 he owned them, but now he has the cash in his backpack. Next problem (number two) getting his car fixed by Darrell's other brother Darrell, an inbred hick mechanic from hell, played chillingly by Billy Bob Thornton. This guy you won't forget. Problem number three, a *muy caliente* Apache babe (Jennifer Lopez) who starts to play with more than his mind. Problem number four, her husband, (a lecherous and morally corrupt Nick Nolte) who wants him to kill her. Problem number four and a half is a blind Indian shaman (Jon Voight, believe it or not) who plays with his soul.

All this is tolerable, but as he's getting a soda in the local groceria, it's robbed and they take his backpack with all the money in it. The senora who is robbed recovers in time to shot the robber with the backpack in the back with a shotgun. Only problem is number five, the buckshot blows Penn's money to smithereens (nice touch), and he is now flat broke and can't pay the $150 to get his Mustang back on the road. Problem number six, a small town tart (Claire Danes) cozies up to him to get her macho boyfriend jealous enough to want to beat our boy to a pulp. Problem number seven, in his desperation to get enough money to blow town, our hero calls his main creditor and tells him where he is (seems dumb). His creditor wants more than the other three fingers. Problem number eight...

Well, I didn't take notes, so I'm losing track. But trust me, he's got more troubles to come.

This is in some ways an amazing film. It's part Clint Eastwood western, where there are no good guys, and part urban thriller, where you never know who is double crossing whom (but take a hint, they all are) or what is going to happen next. The atmosphere is compelling, all hangs together well, and we have something close to a film noir masterpiece until the scene on the cliff where our hero is supposed to push her off. Juggling the psychology in the film with the psychology he's working on the audience, Oliver Stone loses his grip and everything goes to ill-logic and blood and bodies. Hey, it's tough to concentrate through a whole stinkin' movie, even if you are Oliver Stone! Nonetheless there are so many striking images and clever scenes and so much original movie shtick here that I give you a Kmart guarantee you'll be entertained.

I've seen this and I give it___stars.
I want to see it___. I'll pass___.
The review was worth reading___. Not___.

Vertigo (1958) 8

THIS is a masterpiece? (Beware spoilers)

Vertigo is considered one of the greatest films ever made and celebrated as Hitchcock's masterpiece. Perhaps it is. But I found myself bored as I watched it even though I had to admire the artistic intent. There are so many holes in the film it could qualify as cheesy. However, try telling that to those who love it. I think they love it as much for its flaws as for its perfections.

Perfections: the feel of the San Francisco Bay area, the sense of historical California, the great beauty of the ocean framed by Monterey cypresses, the redwoods, the Golden Gate Bridge as seen from below and off to the side, the Bautista Mission, the fifties interior decor, Madeleine's costumes, the angle of Scottie's fedora, the acting by the three stars, James Stewart, Kim Novak, and Barbara Bel Geddes. The musical score by Bernard Herrmann is also celebrated, but I found it a bit overbearing at times, and of course Hitchcock loved using music to direct our sensitivities, and one can tire of that.

Flaws:

Scottie hanging from the drainpipe railing, watching the cop trying to save him fly over to land several stories down, dead. What is not explained is how the cop was expected to pull him up with nothing to hold onto or how Scottie managed to survive. Apparently he fell but only broke his back because in the next scene he is in surgical corset unable to scratch certain itches. (Yes, Stewart had a similar problem in Hitchcock's *Rear Window(1954)*.)

The ersatz psychology. It was the fifties and psychoanalytic psychology was all the rage. One of the bestsellers of the day was *The Fifty-Minute Hour: A Collection of True Psychoanalytic Tales* by Robert Lindner in which a shrink relates tales told by his patients. Hitchcock loved this sort of thing (cf., *Spellbound* (1945) with Gregory Peck and Ingrid Bergman). Audiences also loved it. But the psychology is strictly bananas.

Driving on the wrong side of the road (about which Hitchcock is reported to have said when it was pointed out to him, "You drive your way. I'll drive mine.")

The plot. Oh, the plot. Never but never has there been a more elaborate and unlikely murder-your-rich-wife scheme. Judy Barton is hired, persuaded or, gee, maybe hypnotized into playing Gavin Elster's wife who is to commit suicide by jumping off the bell tower at the mission. First Gavin (Tom Helmore) has to establish that she's crazy and suicidal. This is done by having her drive dreamily around the Frisco Bay area looking for the haunts of her great grandmother who committed suicide. The key is to get Scottie to believe it so he can testify that she was suicidal. For this to work, (1) Madeleine has to fool a police detective—one might say mesmerize him, which she does, (2) Get him to the bell tower at the right time where he is afraid to go to the top—that works, but you have to buy the psychology, (3) Time it so that Madeleine appears to jump off, but in reality you throw the dead body of your wife off after having broken her neck (body kept warm perhaps in your car with the heater on?), (4) Hide with Madeleine at the top of the tower until the coast is clear (whenever that might be).

Although Kim Novak's performance is interesting it is unlikely that she could fool ex-detective Scottie into believing she was somebody else. When she reappears as Judy Barton in the brown hair and the different makeup, it really makes the audience do a double take before realizing that she and Madeleine are the same. But Scottie's take seems to be that she (and some other women at first glance) look like Madeleine—after all, he just got out of the nut house. It is only when he sees the necklace that he comes to his senses.

Another thing aficionados love about this movie is the way Hitchcock was able to subtly strip his stars of their glamour and make them look more or less human. James Stewart never played a part anything like this before. All the funny faces he has to make, perplexed while driving, terrified on the way up the bell tower, insane and terrified in the dream sequence, etc. It is said that Hitchcock blamed the lack of popular success of this movie (when it was belatedly released, not now) on Stewart looking too old, and therefore Hitchcock never worked with him again. But I think Stewart, after seeing the way he looked in this movie—so unheroic, so lost as a real human being—decided he was never going to let Hitchcock do *that* to him again, and that's probably why they never worked together again.

Kim Novak's curvy body and flopping you-know-whats are revealed in outfits that Grace Kelly would never wear. And poor Barbara Bel Geddes with those most unattractive glasses! How she pines for Scottie. One of the best scenes occurs when she shows Scottie her self-portrait as the mysterious Carlotta with the glasses on (!) followed by her "Stupid, stupid, stupid!" self-flagellation after Scottie, who was offended at the grotesque sight, walks out.

But why is Scottie always hanging out at her place? And how they talk the plot in the beginning so that we might know that they were once a couple! But Hitchcock never worried about anything but the effect his movie might have on the audience. Improbabilities, clumsy plot devices, etc., were secondary. And you know what, he was right, as P.T. Barnum was right. Hitchcock never overestimated the sophistication of his audience and that was one of his strengths. The audience just wants to be entertained, to be diverted, to live the fantasy for a while.

Somebody said that the real entertainment in watching this movie is in watching it again after you know the story. I think they're right. It's definitely a film buff's movie.

I've seen this and I give it___stars.
I want to see it___. I'll pass___.
The review was worth reading___. Not___.

The Virgin Suicides (2000) 8

A strange and original teen angst film

This was Sofia Coppola's first film, and it is an interesting one. Superficially it's a teen angst story featuring the usual dysfunctional parents, idiot school teachers, prom night hijinks, first love, and the inevitable loss of innocence. But on a deeper level this film is a variation on such films, done in an artistic manner and told from an unlikely point of view.

Consider that the story focuses on five teenaged girls who committed suicide. Yet their story is seen from the point of view of the high school boys who adored the girls, boys who seem curiously younger than the girls (as in reality most boys are relative to girls of the same age). There is one exception and that is Trip Fontaine played by Josh Hartnett. He is big and handsome and worldly wise (for his age). He is charming and adored by just about everyone, especially by all the girls in the school. But his desire is directed toward Lux Lisbon, the oldest of the ill-fated Lisbon sisters. Initially she doesn't seem interested in him, but that only serves to whet his appetite, and then... Well, let's just say that players only love you when they're playing—or something like that.

The tragedy seems a bit effete in the telling. The suicides seem excessive and monstrously headstrong. Mom and Dad, you WILL pay for this! There's the overbearing and dictatorial mother who cares only about appearances, played menacingly by Kathleen Turner. James Woods serves as both the father of the girls and as a somewhat spacey math teacher who seems to have no idea that he and his wife are suffocating their children. Kirsten Dunst is the enigmatic Lux who dies more from a broken heart than from the fumes of exhaust.

In the end the boys are left wondering what happened and why and what they could have done differently. But life in the upper middle class suburban town goes on. An older Trip Fontaine is interviewed as in a documentary. He more or less shrugs his shoulders. TV reporters mouth clichés. Neighbors play golf and flirt and drink excessively. The boys grow older but no wiser. The elms are cut down, the house is sold, and again life goes on and on and yet there is no answer, no justification, no meaning to the tragedy of five girls who snuffed out their lives for...what?

Bottom line: interesting and original but strangely artificial as though the girls were Barbie dolls briefly brought to life and then put back into their boxes.

I've seen this and I give it___stars.
I want to see it___. I'll pass___.
The review was worth reading___. Not___.

W. (2008) 6

A vain little man

Vain because he thought he was the decider and that God had chosen his ear in which to whisper. Little as measured by his talent compared to others who have held the office. But more than that, the tragedy of George W. Bush, the 43rd president of the United States, is a direct result of a sociopathic personality that this film was not able to fully capture.

That personality belonged and belongs to Dick Cheney, Bush's prince of darkness-like vice president, a man who was able to manipulate W. as a puppeteer might manipulate a puppet by playing on W.'s vanity and insecurities, and on his vainglorious lust to outdo his father and to shine brighter than his brother Jed.

Or is it George W. himself who has the sociopathic personality? How can you approve the torture of people to find a justification to invade another country knowing full well that thousands of people will die because of your actions? Can you tell yourself you are bringing democracy to another land when in your heart of hearts you know that your motive is to be able to run for reelection as a wartime president or one who has just won a war and thereby upstage your father who was not reelected? I think the question of whether George W. was the more manipulated or more the manipulator has not yet been answered.

This film is curious in what it shows and where it would not go. We do not see W. as a boy blowing up frogs with firecrackers. There is no snorting of cocaine. We see him as a fraternity pledge at Yale ticking off the names and nicknames of his fellows, but what is missed is the significance of the nicknaming for George W., which is to control others through the threat of demeaning them with an embarrassing tag. We do see how nicknaming allows him to simplistically regard others, as he calls Cheney "Vice" (yes!) and slaps derogatory names on foreign leaders who fail to come into his war coalition. But

the psychological essence of calling other people names is to boast a personality suffering from a poor self-image.

So the 43rd president was simultaneously a vain and self-conscious man acutely aware of his limitations, always working to boast himself up. He went to all the best private schools, knowing of course that only his father's money and prestige got him in, and of course as a C-student felt his miss-measure against the others. Yet he is that C-student who became the most powerful man in the world, and yet he had no idea how to use his power. He became isolated and controlled by the office of the presidency and by those in his inner circle.

There is always the danger when making a film focused on a putatively despicable character that you will by showing his all too human attributes and behaviors make him into an anti-hero with whom the audience cannot help but identify. I'm sure Oliver Stone was aware of this trap, but nevertheless he fell into it. We see George W. on the John, watching ballgames on TV, in domestic embrace with his wife. We see his father favoring the other son. We see George W. fail and fail again, and then we see him give up drinking and become a rousing political success as he helps guide his father's winning campaign for the presidency, as he wins the governorship of Texas and as he becomes president of the United States. In some ways—at least as far as intelligence and compromised morality goes—he rose from greater depths than perhaps any other American president.

But of course without the intervention of his father and being the son of a powerful man, George W. would probably have amounted to little. And so his triumph in becoming the 43rd president is tainted by the full knowledge that, as this film makes clear, he couldn't have done it without his father's influence and his father's name.

The real truth of the phenomenon that is George W. Bush lies not in him or the political dynasty he derailed or the shame he brought on America, but in the fact that so many Americans actually voted for him. He is the product of his times, and these were the times of great moral corruption in America, times in which preemptive war and torture became accepted practice, times in which the Republican Party became the property of people like Karl Rove and Rush Limbaugh, Pat Robertson and Jerry Falwell, Dick Cheney and the neocons, until in 2008 it became a parody of itself with Sarah Palin and Joe the Plumber.

Josh Brolin is convincing in capturing the contradictions in W.'s personality while Richard Dreyfuss makes for a surprisingly apt Dick Cheney. Elizabeth Banks as Laura Bush is as pretty as pretty can be, and James Cromwell as the senior Bush is very true to type. Thandie Newton captured well Condoleezza Rice's quality of quiet, submissive loyalty while being able to keep her hands clean.

The unavoidable weakness of the casting however is that the characters unfortunately do not look enough like the characters we have seen on TV to fool our eyes.

The script by Stanley Weiser, who also co-scripted Oliver Stone's *Wall Street* (1987), and Stone's direction are competent but undistinguished and a bit shallow. The right way to make this film in my not so humble opinion is to really show us the evil of George W. Bush, the evil that was tragically the man, and the harm that he did to this country and to the people of Iraq, and to show us how America itself, from the Congress to the media to the pulpit and pew, was manipulated and complaisance in bringing about the tragedy. Instead Stone and Weiser emphasized George W.'s little guy vain personality and the irony of his rise to power.

I've seen this and I give it___stars.
I want to see it___. I'll pass___.
The review was worth reading___. Not___.

White Men Can't Jump (1992) 7

Entertaining? Yes. Realistic? No.

This is not a comedy. This is a Basketball Jones fantasy. It's gritty and full of low rent district locales in SoCal: Watts, Venice Beach, South Central L.A., maybe East L.A.. There's a lot of trash talk and mother talk, some of it funny. This is about a white dude who is black even though he is as white as Gomer Pyle. And about as smart. This is about being white in a black world. It's about being a loser as far as women are concerned. This is about being a loser period.

Woody Harrelson as Billy Hoyle is the loser. Wesley Snipes as Sidney Dean is the hotshot, hotdog, streetwise hoops hustler who sees some value in an undersized white guy who plays better than he looks, although he can't jump. In a sense this is a buddy movie, 1990s style. They team up and hustle two-on-two pickup basketball for cash on outdoor courts with metal nets. They're good and they usually win.

This is also about their relationship with their women. Rosie Perez plays Gloria Clemente who is a bit too smart for Billy. She spends her time imbibing endless trivia in prep for being on TV's "Jeopardy." Tyra Ferrell plays Sidney's wife. She's also smarter than her man but long suffering in the ghetto. Some real life hoopsters make an appearance. I spotted Marques Johnson and Nigel Miguel, both of whom played for UCLA. Ron Shelton, who wrote and directed the excellent baseball movie *Bull Durham* (1988) wrote and directed here. He does a good job although I do have some points to make.

One, you can't hustle hoops in the manner depicted. The main problem is the officiating. There is no way to settle disputes about fouls and who touched the ball last when going out of bounds. I played pickup basketball all over the South Bay area of Los Angeles for decades and I can tell you that when the games were close every missed shot was a foul, and the only way it got settled was to "shoot for it"; that is, the guy who claimed he was fouled when he missed the shot had to "do or die" from the free throw line or (more often in the bigger games) from the top of the key. If he makes it, his team gets the ball out of bounds. If he misses, the other team gets the ball. If you're playing for some serious money, these disputes would go on forever, not to mention the fact that somebody might just lay some hard fouls on somebody and what you would end up with is the bigger, tougher guys winning. In fact, if one team is about to win against a bigger, badder team they might NEVER get a shot off.

A secondary problem is the white ringer deal only works once.

In reality there is enough ego involvement in these pickup games that you don't need to put any money on the line. Your self-identity as a basketball player is already on the line. Additionally, most guys who play pickup basketball play it for recreation, for staying in shape, for camaraderie. And yes there are some VERY serious pickup games with some very good players all over the Los Angeles area, although the best of them are played in high school, JC or college gyms indoors. Incidentally, by the time this movie was produced (it came out in 1992) most of the games in the L.A. area were played full court, not two on two; and before that, going back to the sixties, the default half court game was three on three.

Well, in a Hollywood movie a realistic depiction of a milieu usually isn't the point. The point is entertainment, and in this sense *White Men Can't Jump* does alright. Snipes and Harrelson, by the way, can play a little, although it's mostly the camera work and the slow-mo that makes them look good.

I've seen this and I give it___stars.
I want to see it___. I'll pass___.
The review was worth reading___. Not___.

The Wild Bunch (1969) 8

Bloody eye candy

This bloody extravaganza made Sam Peckinpah's reputation. A kind of fantasy of machismo set along the Texas-Mexico border around 1913—yes, very late for a Western—*The Wild Bunch* has thrilled adolescent boys and twentysomethings for almost four decades. The slow-mo shots of horses falling awkwardly, of bodies squirting blood as they fall off of roof tops or cliffs, of tough hombres talking tough while they grab loose women and bottles of booze replete with numerous other bits of acrobatic mayhem amid some fantastic scenery makes this a non-cerebral feast for the eyes. The stars, William Holden (Pike Bishop), Ernest Borgnine (Dutch

Engstrom), Robert Ryan (Deke Thornton), Edmund O'Brien (Freddie Sykes), etc. are first rate and on form. The plot is a variant of the old "one last job" story which begins with Pike's not-quite over-the-hill gang doing one last bank robbery.

Needless to say something goes wrong. Interspersed between the opening credits we see Pike's gang ride into town dressed as members of the US Army Calvary. On roof tops are some rascals and scallywags with rifles, missing teeth, and murderous gleams in their eyes. They are led by Deke Thornton, who it turns out is working for the railroad. What follows is a good old fashioned shoot 'em up of rather unlikely proportions as Pike's gang exits the bank with bags of loot, dodging and slinging bullets with abandon.

Turns out...well, no I won't say because I don't want to spoil the surprise. Suffice it to say, they need to do another job, this one a good-old-fashioned train robbery with a few tricks and extras, like blowing up a bridge and running a locomotive at full throttle backwards. And then across the border into Mexico and some fun and games with Mexican generals, senoritas, banditos and such.

Been there, done that. But Peckinpah's colorful yarn has a few things you might not have seen before, and some of those things that you have seen, he did first and better. The Mexican color with a lot of authentic-looking extras doing authentic-looking Mexican activities was good. The fact that the Spanish spoken was not translated (and didn't need to be translated) was good. General Mapache (Emilio Fernandez) as the drunken, power-

Okay, that's one level. On another level this should be compared to *Rebel without a Cause* (1955) as a mid-century testament to teen angst. Or to *Blackboard Jungle* (1955) with the fake juvenile delinquency and the phony slang. Marlon Brando as Johnny Strabler, whose claim to fame (aside from being the leader of the pack) is that he stole a second-place biker trophy, stars in a role that helped to launch his career, not that his acting in this film was so great. (He was better in half a dozen other roles, for example, as Stanley Kowalski in *A Streetcar Named Desire* 1951, or as Terry Malloy in *On the Waterfront* 1954). What stands out here is his tough-guy vulnerability with women: the irresistible little boy playing big. In one sense, this is, despite all the men running around and the macho delirium, something very close to ladies night out. It's a period piece love story, as delicate as a teenager's heart.

Mary Murphy, who in my opinion really steals the show, is at the very center of the drama and the psychology (not to mention that she looks downright yummy in her cashmere sweater and close fitting skirt). She plays Kathie Bleeker, a small town girl whose heart yearns for something—anything—to break the tedium. Along comes Johnny to sweep her off her feet. Only he isn't sure how.

hungry warlord bandito was good. The kids feeding scorpions to the ants and then burning them was good. Edmund O'Brien as a degenerate Gabby Hayes kind of character was a hoot and a holler. But mostly this was about grim-faced men, toughened by long hours in saddle under the hot sun who, after decades of outlawing, finally ride gloriously into that last battle. Next stop: boot hill.

I watched the "original director's cut" that runs 145 minutes. At no time was my brain involved, but my eyes couldn't stop watching.

I've seen this and I give it___stars.
I want to see it___. I'll pass___.
The review was worth reading___. Not___.

The Wild One (1954) 7

He's really just a pussy cat

The "bikers" are like Broadway show extras. The dialogue is embarrassingly unauthentic. Believe me, nobody outside of 42nd Street ever talked like that, daddy-o. The story plays out like some kind of "B" Western with a horse shortage. The "town" even looks like a Western set made over for what somebody in Hollywood thought might be a new genre. There's a café and a saloon rolled into one and a gal working there to catch the eye, and a town posse and a jail and a sheriff (father of the gal) and some "decent citizens" turning into vigilantes, and instead of outlaws we have "hooligans." The bikers do everything but tie their bikes up to the hitching post after roaring into town as though to take over.

Furthermore, she has a problem: although she falls in love with the wild one, she sees right through him. The scene that makes the movie begins with her jumping onto the back of his motorcycle (of course) and, after roaring down the night highway, they retire to what looks like a park. She is about a breath away from what used to be called swooning, but despite her fluttering heart, she sets him straight on who he is and how she feels and why. It's like a woman talking to a wild boy. Then she falls to the ground and just about caresses his motorcycle. It really hits home because she sees through all his pretense and exposes his vulnerability, but is vulnerable herself.

Lee Marvin plays the rival gang leader with a lot of showmanship and Robert Keith plays the ineffectual father. Just about everybody else (including longtime LA sports anchor, Gil Stratton) amounts to an extra.

See this for a glimpse at mid-century psychology as seen through the eyes of Hollywood's seduction machine, and especially for Mary Murphy (running in those heels) who, for whatever reason, never became a star.

I've seen this and I give it___stars.
I want to see it___. I'll pass___.

The review was worth reading___. Not___.

A Woman is a Woman (*Une femme est une femme*)
(1961) 8
New wave romantic comedy: cute, playful

Godard is beginning to grow on me. Maybe it's because I'm watching his films from the sixties, made when I was a teenager in France, and the nostalgia appeals to me. Maybe it's because his work seems free and easy, uncontrived, almost amateurish compared to some other famous film makers. Or maybe it's just that I like this particular pretty girl he features.

She is pretty, gangly Anna Karina starring as Angela, an exotic dancer who is madly in love and wants to have a baby. Godard has a lot of fun with her, encouraging her to mug for the camera, getting her to do movements that cause her to trip and look not just gangly and very young like a pre-adolescent, but even clumsy—and then to leave the shots in the film, probably telling her, "This is a comedy. You need to be not just beautiful, but funny, warm, vulnerable."

Karina does manage a lot of vulnerability. Her exotic act including her singing is...well, there are usually only a handful of customers in the joint and so her skills are probably appropriately remunerated. Again this is intentional since Godard wants her to be just an ordinary girl without any great talent, someone with whom the girls in the audience can identify. But the irony is that the girl must needs be at least pretty. Karina is more than pretty. She is exquisite with her long shapely limbs and her gorgeous countenance.

One of the compelling nostalgic elements is the way women did their eyes in the sixties: so, so overdone! Although I thought that look was oh so sexy then, today I would like to clean the blue, blue—or is it purple?—eye shadow and the black, black mascara off of Karina's face and see her au naturel!

But it is the sixties in Paris—Gay Paree, Paris in the Spring, the City of Light! Well, 1960 to be exact, which really is more like the fifties than the sixties if you know what I mean. Everything is so innocent, Ike still in the American White House, De Gaulle the triumphant hero of France. Algeria and Vietnam completely offstage of course—this is a romantic comedy. The German occupation, the horrific world war and its aftermath are distant memories for Angela and her friends who were only children then. Life is young, the girls are pretty, the boys are cute, prosperity is upon them. It's Godard's Paris. Life is playful. Life is fun. You tease and you have no real worries. The Cold War is of no concern. The 100,000 or so American troops still stationed in France to support the troops in Germany are not seen. But Godard's love affair with the mass American culture is there in little asides and jokes. Emile or Alfred (I forget which) asks Angela what she would like to hear on the jukebox. "Istsy-bitsy bikini," he offers. No. She wants Charles Aznavour. She wants romance and an adult love that leads to marriage and maternity.

Angela's beloved is Emile played with a studied forbearance by an eternally youthful Jean-Claude Brialy. He doesn't want to father a baby, at least not yet. She pouts, she makes faces, she threatens, she burns the roast and drops the eggs, she crosses her arms, and she gives him the silent treatment. It doesn't work. He prefers to read the Worker's Daily. Ah, but will Alfred (Jean-Paul Belmondo, who seems intent on out boyish-ing Brialy) pull himself away from TV reruns of "Breathless" to do the job? Will she let him? Is Emile really so indifferent as to allow his friend carnal knowledge of his girlfriend? Is this a kind of threesome, a prelude to a menage a trois?

Watch for a shot of Jeanne Moreau being asked how Truffaut's film Jules et Jim (1962) which she was working on at the time, is coming along, a kind of cinematic insider jest that Godard liked to include in his films. She gives a one word reply, "Moderato."

See this for Anna Karina, and see her also in Godard's *Band of Outsiders* (1964) in which she looks even more teenager-ish than she does here. She is not a great actress, but she is wondrously directed by Godard who was then her husband.

Chapter Fourteen

Lists

I

Twenty-four favorite directors and five representative films

I would need another twenty years' experience in film criticism to presume to name the top twenty directors. Instead these are personal favorites and the films mentioned are not necessarily their best films or their most popular. They are films that I have seen and enjoyed.

Some directors were tough to leave off. In the case of Orson Welles, frankly I haven't seen enough of his work to credit him in my top twenty, but of course on the basis of reputation he probably belongs there. In the case of David Lynch, I didn't think he has the range of those on this list. Robert Altman almost made it, but the number of really outstanding films he made is a little short. The same can be said for Bernardo Bertolucci. Their top two films, M*A*S*H (1970) and The Player *(1992) for Altman, and* The Conformist *(1970) and* Last Tango in Paris *(1972) for Bertolucci, are very good indeed, but the rest of their work is not up to that level. Quentin Tarantino is good, but relies too much on shock and flash to make my top twenty.*

Some others that almost made my list: Stephen Frears, Claude Berri, Howard Hawks, Martin Scorsese, Steven Soderbergh, Gus Van Sant, and Sydney Pollack.

Length of career and number of films was a criterion as was creativity. I also considered artistry, mastery of story and character, and something indefinable, which I probably should just call personal preference based on having seen perhaps two thousand movies. Alphabetically.

Woody Allen

Take the Money and Run (1969)
Annie Hall (1977)
Crimes and Misdemeanors (1989)
Everybody Says I Love You (1996)
Match Point (2005)

Ingmar Bergman

Smiles of a Summer Night (1955)
Wild Strawberries (1957)
Persona (1966)
Cries and Whispers (1972)
Scenes from a Marriage (1973)

Luis Buñuel

L'âge d'or (The Age of Gold) (1930)
Le journal d'une femme de chambre (Diary of a Chambermaid) (1964)
Belle de jour (1967)
The Discreet Charm of the Bourgeoisie (1972)
That Obscure Object of Desire (1977)

Claude Chabrol

Les Biches (Bad Girls) (1968)
Une affaire de femmes (1988)
La Cérémonie (1995)
Merci pour le chocolat (2000)
La fleur du mal (2003)

Joel Coen and Ethan Coen

Blood Simple (1984)
Raising Arizona (1987)
Barton Fink (1991)
Fargo (1996)
Oh Brother, Where Are Thou? (2000)

Francis Ford Coppola

The Godfather (1972)
The Conversation (1974)
The Godfather Part II (1974)
Apocalypse Now (1979)
Peggy Sue Got Married (1986)

George Cukor

Little Women (1933)
Gaslight (1944)
Born Yesterday (1950)
A Star is Born (1954)
My Fair Lady (1964)

Clint Eastwood

Play Misty for Me (1971)
High Plains Drifter (1973)
Unforgiven (1992)
Mystic River (2003)
Million Dollar Baby (2004)

Alfred Hitchcock

The Lady Vanishes (1938)
Spellbound (1945)
Rear Window (1954)
The Birds (1963)
Marnie (1964)

John Huston

The Maltese Falcon (1941)
The Treasure of the Sierra Madre (1948)
The African Queen (1951)
The Misfits (1961)
Fat City (1972)

Krysztof Kieslowski

The Decalogue (1990)
The Double Life of Veronique (1991)
Trois couleurs: Bleu (1993)
Trzy kolory: Bialy (1994)
Trois couleurs: Rouge (1994)

Stanley Kubrick

Lolita (1962)
Dr. Strangelove, or How I Learned to Stop Worrying and Love the Bomb (1964)
2001: A Space Odyssey (1968)
Full Metal Jacket (1987)
Eyes Wide Shut (1999)

Sydney Lumet

12 Angry Men (1957)
Serpico (1973)
Dog Day Afternoon (1975)
Network (1976)
Before the Devil Knows You're Dead (2007)

Louis Malle

Elevator to the Gallows (1958)
Murmur of the Heart (1971)
Pretty Baby (1978)
Atlantic City (1980)
Au revoir, les enfants (1987)

Christopher Nolan

Following (1998)
Memento (2000)
Insomnia (2002)
Batman Begins (2005)
The Prestige (2006)

Mike Nichols

Who's Afraid of Virginia Woolf? (1966)
The Graduate (1967)
Postcards from the Edge (1990)
Closer (2004)
Charlie Wilson's War (2007)

Roman Polanski

A Knife in the Water (1962)
Repulsion (1965)
Rosemary's Baby (1968)
Chinatown (1974)
The Pianist (2002)

Eric Rohmer

Ma nuit chez Maud (1969)
Le Genou de Claire (Claire's Knee) (1970)
L'amour l'après-midi (Chloe in the Afternoon) (1972)
La femme de l'aviateur (The Aviator's Wife) (1981)
Conte d'automne (Autumn Tale) (1998)

Steven Spielberg

Duel (1971)
Close Encounters of the Third Kind (1977)
E.T. (1982)
Jurassic Park (1993)
Schindler's List (1993)

Oliver Stone

Platoon (1986)
Born on the Fourth of July (1989)
Natural Born Killers (1994)
Nixon (1995)
U Turn (1997)

André Téchiné

Rendez-vous (1985)
Le lieu du crime (Scene of the Crime) (1986)
Ma saison préférée (My Favorite Season) (1993)
Les roseaux sauvages (Wild Reeds) (1994)
Les voleurs (Thieves) (1996)

Francois Truffaut

Les quatre cents coups (The 400 Blows) (1959)
Baisers volés (Stolen Kisses) (1968)
La sirène du Mississipi (Mississippi Mermaid) (1969)
La nuit américaine (Day for Night) (1973)
L'histoire d'Adèle H. (The Story of Adele H.) (1975)

Billy Wilder

Double Indemity (1944)
Sunset Boulevard (1950)
Stalag 17 (1953)
Some Like It Hot (1959)
The Apartment (1960)

Zhang Yimou

Red Sorghum (1987)
Ju Dou (1990)
Raise the Red Lantern (1991)
Not One Less (1999)
Hero (2002)

Okay, if I had to name my top three favorite directors, I would go with Stanley Kubrick, Zhang Yimou, and Billy Wilder. The greatest director of all time? I don't think there is a clear choice.

II

Thirty-one favorite actresses and three of their memorable films

Again these are my favorites and the films are just representative of the actress's work, not necessarily films in which she did her best work. Alphabetically.

Lauren Bacall

To Have and Have Not (1944)
The Big Sleep (1946)
Key Largo (1948)

Emmanuelle Béart

Manon des sources (1986)
Un coeur en hiver (A Heart in Winter) (1992)
Nelly & Monsieur Arnaud (1995)

Annette Bening

Valmont (1989)
The Grifters (1990)
American Beauty (1999)

Ingrid Bergman

Casablanca (1942)
Gaslight (1944)
Spellbound (1945)

Juliette Binoche

Rendez-vous (1985)
The English Patient (1996)
Chocolat (2000)

Julie Christie

Darling (1965)
Doctor Zhivago (1965)
Hamlet (1996)

Penélope Cruz

Belle epoque (1992)
Abre los ojos (Open Your Eyes) (1997)
Don't Move (2004)

Bette Davis

Of Human Bondage (1934)
Dark Victory (1939)
All About Eve (1950)

Catherine Deneuve

Les parapluies de Cherbourg (The Umbrellas of Cherbourg) (1964)
Repulsion (1965)
La sirène du Mississipi (Mississippi Mermaid) (1969)

Audrey Hepburn

Roman Holiday (1953)
Breakfast at Tiffany's (1961)
My Fair Lady (1964)

Katharine Hepburn

The Philadelphia Story (1940)
The African Queen (1951)
On Golden Pond (1981)

Isabelle Huppert

La dentellière (The Lacemaker) (1977)
Une affaire de femmes (1988)
Merci pour le chocolat (2000)

Nicole Kidman

Dead Calm (1989)
To Die For (1995)
The Human Stain (2003)

Jessica Lange

The Postman Always Rings Twice (1981)
A Streetcar Named Desire (1995)
A Thousand Acres (1997)

Vivien Leigh

Gone with the Wind (1939)
A Streetcar Named Desire (1951)
The Roman Spring of Mrs. Stone (1961)

Gong Li

Ju Dou (1990)
Raise the Red Lantern (1991)
Memoirs of a Geisha (2005)

Shirley MacLaine

The Apartment (1960)
Terms of Endearment (1983)
Postcards from the Edge (1990)

Marilyn Monroe

Niagara (1953)
The Seven Year Itch (1955)
Some Like It Hot (1959)

Gwyneth Paltrow

Sliding Doors (1998)
Shakespeare in Love (1998)
Proof (2005)

Michelle Pfeiffer

Scarface (1983)
The Witches of Eastwick (1987)
Dangerous Liaisons (1988)

Natalie Portman

The Professional (1994)
Anywhere But Here (1999)
Garden State (2004)

Julia Roberts

Pretty Woman (1990)
Conspiracy Theory (1997)
Erin Brockovich (2000)

Meg Ryan

Prelude to a Kiss (1992)
French Kiss (1995)
You've Got Mail (1998)

Susan Sarandon

Atlantic City (1980)
Bull Durham (1988)
Thelma & Louise (1991)

Meryl Streep

Kramer vs. Kramer (1979)
Sophie's Choice (1982)
Postcards from the Edge (1990)

Hilary Swank

Boys Don't Cry (1999)
Insomnia (2002)
Million Dollar Baby (2004)

Elizabeth Taylor

Cat on a Hot Tin Roof (1958)
BUtterfield 8 (1960)
Who's Afraid of Virginia Woolf? (1966)

Liv Ullmann

Persona (1966)
Viskningar och rop (Cries and Whispers) (1972)
Scener ur ett äktenskap (Scenes from a Marriage) (1973)

Kate Winslet

Heavenly Creatures (1994)
Jude (1996)
Eternal Sunshine of the Spotless Mind (2004)

Reese Witherspoon

Freeway (1996)
Election (1999)
Walk the Line (2005)

Natalie Wood

Rebel without a Cause (1955)
West Side Story (1961)
Gypsy (1962)

The three I love the most? Oh boy, is this hard. Okay, but I reserve the right to change my mind at any time: Audrey Hepburn, Isabelle Huppert, and Kate Winslet. No, make that, Ingrid Bergman, Gwyneth Paltrow, and Penélope Cruz. On third thought...
Never mind.
Less subjectively speaking, the actress with the greatest range and the most accomplishments is Meryl Streep. She is the greatest actress of our time.

III

Thirty-one favorite actors and three of their memorable films

Again these are my favorites and the films are just representative of the actor's work, not necessarily films in which he did his best work.

Humphrey Bogart

The Maltese Falcon (1941)
The Treasure of the Sierra Madre (1948)
The Caine Munity (1954)

Marlon Brando

A Streetcar Named Desire (1951)
The Wild One (1953)
Last Tango in Paris (1972)

Gary Cooper

Sergeant York (1941)
The Pride of the Yankees (1942)
High Noon (1952)

Kevin Costner

The Untouchables (1987)
Bull Durham (1988)
Dances with Wolves (1990)

Tom Cruise

Born on the Fourth of July (1989)
Jerry Maguire (1996)
Vanilla Sky (2001)

Robert De Niro

Taxi Driver (1976)
Raging Bull (1980)
Meet the Fockers (2004)

Johnny Depp

What's Eating Gilbert Grape (1993)
Fear and Loathing in Las Vegas (1998)
The Pirates of the Caribbean: The Curse of the Black Pearl (2003)

Henry Fonda

The Grapes of Wrath (1940)
Mister Roberts (1955)
12 Angry Men (1957)

Harrison Ford

Raiders of the Lost Ark (1981)
Blade Runner (1982)
Witness (1985)

Morgan Freeman

Driving Miss Daisy (1989)
The Shawshank Redemption (1994)
Million Dollar Baby (2004)

Cary Grant

Suspicion (1941)
Arsenic and Old Lace (1944)
North by Northwest (1959)

Tom Hanks

Punchline (1988)
A League of Their Own (1992)
Castaway (2000)

Dustin Hoffman

The Graduate (1967)
Tootsie (1982)
Rain Man (1988)

William Holden

Sunset Boulevard (1950)
Stalag 17 (1953)
The Bridge on the River Kwai (1957)

ny Irons

)ead Ringers (1988)
versal of Fortune (1990)
ta (1997)

Harvey Keitel

Bad Lieutenant (1992)
Imaginary Crimes (1994)
Holy Smoke (1999)

Burt Lancaster

From Here to Eternity (1953)
Elmer Gantry (1960)
Atlantic City (1980)

Jack Lemmon

Mister Roberts (1955)
Some Like It Hot (1959)
The Apartment (1960)

John Malkovich

Dangerous Liaisons (1988)
Rounders (1998)
The Unhold (The Ogre) (1996)

Marcello Mastroianni

La dolce vita (1960)
Il bell'Antonio (1960)
Divorzio all'italiana (1961)

Paul Newman

Cat on a Hot Tin Roof (1958)
Butch Cassidy and the Sundance Kid (1969)
The Sting (1973)

Jack Nicholson

Chinatown (1974)
One Flew Over the Cuckoo's Nest (1975)
As Good as It Gets (1997)

Al Pacino

The Godfather (1972)
Dog Day Afternoon (1975)
Scarface (1983)

Gregory Peck

Twelve O'Clock High (1949)
Roman Holiday (1953)
To Kill a Mockingbird (1962)

Sean Penn

Fast Times at Ridgemont High (1982)
U Turn (1997)
Mystic River (2003)

Brad Pitt

Thelma & Louise (1991)
Kalifornia (1993)
Fight Club (1999)

George C. Scott

Dr. Strangelove or: How I Learned to Stop Worrying and Love the Bomb (1964)
Patton (1970)
The Hospital (1971)

Peter Sellers

Lolita (1962)
The Pink Panther (1963)
Dr. Strangelove or: How I Learned to Stop Worrying and Love the Bomb (1964)

Kevin Spacey

Glengarry Glen Ross (1992)
The Usual Suspects (1995)
American Beauty (1999)

James Stewart

Mr. Smith Goes to Washington (1939)
Rear Window (1954)
Anatomy of a Murder (1959)

Robin Williams

Good Morning, Vietnam (1987)
Dead Poets Society (1989)
Mrs. Doubtfire (1993)

For what it's worth, I believe that Jack Nicholson is the greatest actor of our time followed by Marlon Brando and Humphrey Bogart.

IV

Greatest Movie Writer Ever?

I want to make special mention of the man I think is the greatest movie writer ever. No, it's not Woody Allen. He comes in third, and it's not Billy Wilder, he comes in second. It's the French writer Jean-Claude Carrière.

Consider this: Carrière has 134 credits listed at the Internet Movie Database. He has written original screenplays, adaptations, stories, scenarios and dialogue. His credits include work on some very impressive films in several different languages. For example:

Diary of a Chambermaid (1964)
Hotel Paradiso (1966)
Belle de Jour (1967)
The Discreet Charm of the Bourgeoisie (1972)
That Obscure Object of Desire (1977)
The Unbearable Lightness of Being (1988)
Valmont (1989)
Der Unhold (1996)

V

Seven very good recent nature documentaries

The Blue Planet (2001)

A kind of precursor to "Planet Earth," in eight parts limited to water environments, e.g., open oceans, the coasts, the deep, etc. Narrated by Attenborough. Excellent.

Life (2009)

Like Planet Earth this is in eleven parts but the focus of each part is on a different life form, e.g., fish, birds, insects. I've seen the version shaped for TV in the US and it's marred by a kind of simplistic script and the voice of Oprah Winfrey. Beautiful nonetheless in High Definition.

Life in the Undergrowth (2005)

Five part series on the lives of invertebrates. Some sequences are in high definition. Fascinating.

Miracle Planet (2005)

A kind of history of the Earth in five parts: The Violent Past; Snowball Earth; New Frontiers Extinction and Rebirth; Survival of the Fittest. Nice narration by Christopher Plummer.

Planet Earth (2006)

The original BBC version in 11 parts by habitat (e.g., mountains, freshwater, deserts, etc.) is narrated by Sir David Attenborough. The Discovery channel version is narrated by Sigourney Weaver. Both do a good job but I prefer Attenborough. "PlanetEarth" is perhaps the greatest nature documentary ever made. It will dazzle you in high definition.

Wild Russia (2008)

I loved this series mainly because of the wild animals seen nowhere else, especially the beautiful Amur tiger and the Amur leopard. The narration by Jason Hidlebrandt is a bit annoying, but the series is an eye-opener about places most people have never seen or even heard of.

Winged Migration (*Le peuple migrateur*) (2001)

The lives of birds with an emphasis on insights into how, why and where they fly. 89 minutes, in either French or English.

I also recommend "Nature" on public television.

142 nature documentaries are rated at thefullwiki.org. "Planet Earth" is ranked number one.

VI

My most popular movie reviews

Here are the top 20 in terms of "helpful" or not so helpful votes garnered at Amazon.com and at IMDb.com (combined as of January 4, 2011):

Movie Title	Positive Votes	Total Votes
1 Hamlet (1996)	440	474
2 Twelve O'Clock High (1949)	229	258
3 Wild Strawberries (1957)	200	213
4 American Beauty (1999)	189	294
5 2001: A Space Odyssey (1968)	160	220
6 Boys Don't Cry (1999)	152	185
7 Black Orpheus (1959)	141	145
8 Forbidden Games (1952)	138	146
9 Born on the Fourth of July (1989)	130	150
10 Thelma & Louise (1991)	114	155
11 Super Size Me (2004)	111	132

Movie Title	Positive Votes	Total Votes
12 Roman Holiday (1953)	110	113
13 Raise the Red Lantern (1991)	103	115
14 Mister Roberts (1955)	101	106
15 The Importance of Being Earnest (2002)	101	132
16 Sabrina (1995)	96	110
17 The Importance of Being Earnest (1952)	95	104
18 Barry Lyndon (1975)	92	98
19 Welcome to the Doll House (1995)	90	95
20 Never Cry Wolf (1983)	90	98

Whether a review is voted "helpful" or "not helpful" at Amazon and the Internet Movie Database depends heavily on how exposed it is to readers. If the movie you are reviewing has over a thousand reviews, as some like The Matrix *do have, and your review gets "buried" by subsequent reviews before people get a chance to read it, then your review is likely to get few or no votes regardless of how helpful the review may be. This point is emphasized when you consider that two of my top vote getters,* American Beauty *and* 2001: A Space Odyssey *received zero votes on IMDb.com! Both reviews were always buried under so many reviews that it would require several minutes of deliberate searching just to find the reviews. So nobody bothered—which by the way, is one of the reasons I wrote this book: to give readers easy access to my reviews. However on Amazon, both reviews spent substantial time on the first page which made it easy for people to read the reviews and vote on them.*

Incidentally, "helpful" usually ends up indicating whether the voter agreed with the reviewer's sentiments or not. On the Amazon pages three reviews are selected by Amazon (according to some formula unknown to me) to be displayed on the first page. Those reviews have a much better chance of gaining votes since they are right in front of the reader. At the IMDB.com the first review to appear on the movie page is rotated according to some other formula (also unknown to me).

However it is no coincidence that my top vote-getting review for Kenneth Branagh's Hamlet *(1996) is one of the best reviews I have ever written. So it can be said that not all voters vote their sentiments; many voters do in fact reward a good review. It must be said however in the vote-getting game it helps to lavish praise on movies that the public adores. Pan a beloved movie and you will get ignored or catch a lot of negative votes regardless of how well expressed your review is. Illustrating this point is the fact that the only negative review of my mine to get more than a hundred positive votes is for the 2002 version of* The Importance of Being Earnest. *It might be asked why that particular review beat the odds. I think it's because I was able to effectively point out where the director went wrong.*

Anyway, the twenty reviews mentioned above are some of the best reviews I ever wrote. I hope you enjoy reading them.

Chapter Fifteen

Some Quick Movie Categories
(with page numbers)

Gay/Lesbian/Kinky

Scifi/Fantasy

Impossible or unrequited love

The Lacemaker (La Dentellière) (1977), 242
Nelly and Monsieur Arnaud (1995), 260
Roman Holiday (1953), 31
The Story of Adele H. (L'histoire d'Adèle H.) (1975), 263
Three Colors: Red (Trois Couleurs: Rouge) (1994), 182

Two especially wet tear jerkers

Or why is the remote in the tissue box?

Antonia's Line (1995), 161
Dark Victory (1939), 340

Especially beautiful

Barry Lyndon (1975), 328
The Conformist (1970), 122
The Dream Life of Angels (La vie rêvée des anges) (1998), 235
Elvira Madigan (1967), 303
The English Patient (1996), 132
Farewell, My Concubine (Ba wang bie ji) (1993), 269
The Garden of the Finzi-Continis (1971), 283
Girl with a Pearl Earring (2003), 134
Hamlet (1996), 351
Hero (Ying xiong) (2002), 270
Memoirs of a Geisha (2005), 138
Raise the Red Lantern (Da hong deng long gao gao gua) (1991), 159
The Scent of Green Papaya (Mui du du xanh) (1993), 313
Shakespeare in Love (1998), 33
The Umbrellas of Cherbourg, (Les parapluies de Cherbourg) (1963), 250

Grunge love

Or, yes this IS a romantic comedy, butthead.

2 Days in the Valley (1996), 397
Band of Outsiders (Bande à part) (1964), 229
Garden State (2004), 347
Kiss or Kill (1997), 101
Nadine (1987), 449
Natural Born Killers (1994), 103
Read My Lips (Sur mes lèvres) (2001), 246
The Unbelievable Truth (1990), 476
Wild at Heart (1990), 117

Romantic comedies

Or "boy meets girl, cute," but for 1,001 wacky reasons true love is delayed until the last reel.

A Lot Like Love (2005) Amanda Peet and Ashton Kutcher, 160
As Good As It Gets (1997) Helen Hunt and Jack Nicholson, 321
Bridget Jones's Diary (2001) Renée Zellweger, Colin Firth and Hugh Grant, 161
Charade (1963) Audrey Hepburn and Cary Grant, 409
Conspiracy Theory (1997) Julia Roberts and Mel Gibson, 415
French Kiss (1995) Meg Ryan and Kevin Kline, 98
Garden State (2004) Natalie Portman and Zach Braff, 347
The Girl on the Bridge (La fille sur la pont) (1999) Vanessa Paradis and Daniel Auteuil, 238
Prelude to a Kiss (1992) Meg Ryan and Alec Baldwin, 108
Sabrina (1954) Audrey Hepburn, William Holden and Humphrey Bogart, 63
Sabrina (1995) Julie Ormond, Harrison Ford and Greg Kinnear, 64
Sliding Doors (1998) Gwyneth Paltrow, John Lynch and John Hannah, 111
Speechless (1994) Geena Davis and Michael Keaton, 114
Stolen Kisses (Baisers volés) (1968) Claude Jade and Jean-Pierre Leaud, 248
You've Got Mail (1998) Meg Ryan and Tom Hanks, 118

Comedies

Amazon Women on the Moon (1987), 401
Austin Powers: International Man of Mystery (1997), 85
Barbershop (2002), 327
Borat (2006), 88
Importance of Being Earnest, The (1952), 60
Importance of Being Earnest, The (2002), 61
Joe's Apartment (1996), 100
Little Miss Sunshine (2006), 366
Lost in America (1985), 442
Meet the Fockers (2004), 445
Mister Roberts (1955), 27
Punchline (1988), 460
Shampoo (1975), 467
Shower (Xizao) (1999), 276
Soapdish (1991), 469
Tampopo (1985), 310
A Taxing Woman, (Marusa no onna) (1987), 315

Satires

Borat (2006), 88
Dr. Strangelove, or: How I Learned to Stop Worrying and Love the Bomb (1964), 18
Election (1999), 342

Glengarry Glen Ross (1992), 349
Importance of Being Earnest, The (1952), 60
Importance of Being Earnest, The (2002), 61
Legally Blonde (2001), 101
Liar Liar (1997), 442
Young Doctors in Love (1982), 118

Sixteen Significant War Movies

Or "I love the smell of naplam in the morning."

All Quiet on the Western Front (1930)
Apocalypse Now (1979), 13
Born on the Fourth of July (1989), 331
Breaker Morant (1980), 332
The Bridge on the River Kwai (1957)
The Bridges at Toko-Ri (1955)
Das Boot (1981), 288
Dr. Strangelove, or: How I Learned to Stop Worrying and Love the Bomb (1964), 18
Full Metal Jacket (1987), 346
Mister Roberts (1955), 27
Paths of Glory (1957)
Platoon (1986), 30
Saving Private Ryan (1998), 465
Stalag 17 (1953), 388
The Thin Red Line, (1998), 472
Twelve O'Clock High (1949), 394

Musicals

Chicago (2002), 16
Evita (1996), 422
Jesus Christ, Superstar (1973), 71
Jesus Christ, Superstar (2000), 72
My Fair Lady (1964), 28
The Umbrellas of Cherbourg, (Les parapluies de Cherbourg) (1963), 250

Mysteries palatable for Little Old Ladies from Pasadena or Russell Square

8 Women (8 femmes) (2002), 154
The Lady Vanishes (1938), 440
Laura (1944), 194
Murder by Death (1976), 449
Rear Window (1954), 461
The Thin Man (1934), 34

Chapter Sixteen

Quizzes

or

Test Your Movie IQ

Here are twelve movie lore questions. Most questions are worth 20 points, but you get partial credit for partial answers, and for questions 8, 9 and 11 there are bonus points possible for correctly naming the films in which the Academy Awards were given. Total possible score is 210. Average score for a movie buff is about the same as average IQ, that is 100 points.
Answers and scoring on page 427.

1.

Which of these actresses is the daughter of Ingrid Bergman? Which is the daughter of Goldie Hawn?

Isabella Rossolini
Meg Ryan
Reese Witherspoon
Kate Hudson
Naomi Watts

2.

By drawing lines, fit the following actresses to their starring title roles:

Julie Andrews   Citizen Ruth
Renée Zellweger   Erin Brockovich
Laura Dern   Gilda
Rita Hayworth   Mary Poppins
Julia Roberts   Nurse Betty

3.

In which movie did which actress play a prostitute?

Pretty Woman   Charlize Theron
Belle de Jour   Elisabeth Shue
Leaving Las Vegas   Catherine Deneuve
Hard Eight   Gwyneth Paltrow
Monster   Julia Roberts

Quizzes

4.

Match the following quotes with the movies in which they appeared.

A) "Round up the usual suspects." _____

B) "Badges? We ain't got no badges. We don't need no badges. I don't have to show you any stinkin' badges!" _____

C) "What we've got here is a failure to communicate." _____

D) "It's so beautiful, they should have sent a poet." _____

E) "The greatest trick the devil ever pulled was convincing the world that he didn't exist."
_____

Contact
Casablanca
The Usual Suspects
Cool Hand Luke
The Treasure of the Sierra Madre

5.

Surprisingly Alfred Hitchcock won only one Best Picture Academy Award. The movie that garnered the Oscar was (circle the winner):

Rebecca (1940)
Rear Window (1954)
Vertigo (1958)
The Birds (1963)
Marnie (1964)

6.

Which of these actresses won four Best Actress Oscars? Which won none? How many did the others win?

Bette Davis _____
Luise Rainer _____
Vivian Leigh _____
Ingrid Bergman _____
Elizabeth Taylor _____
Katharine Hepburn _____
Jane Fonda _____
Jodie Foster _____
Hilary Swank _____
Marilyn Monroe _____

7.

Who is the only African-American actress to win a Best Actress Academy Award?

8.

Who is the most often nominated *actress* for any kind of Oscar? (Bonus points possible for naming the movies in which she won Oscars.)

9.

Who is the most often nominated *actor* for any kind of Oscar? (Bonus points possible for naming the movies in which he won Oscars.)

10.

What is the highest grossing film of all time?

11.

Which of these actors won two Oscars for best actor? (Bonus points possible for naming the movies in which the actors won Oscars.)

Marlon Brando
Michael Caine
Gary Cooper
Cary Grant
Tom Hanks
Dustin Hoffman
Sean Penn
James Stewart

(Note: nobody has yet won three Oscars for best actor.)

12.

Fit the following actors to their starring title roles:

Tom Hanks   Mister Roberts
Gary Cooper   Nixon
Peter Sellers   Sergeant York
Henry Fonda   Dr. Strangelove
Anthony Hopkins   Forrest Gump

Index of Movies Reviewed

Quiz answers

1.

Isabella Rossellini is the daughter of Ingrid Bergman. Kate Hudson is the daughter of Goldie Hawn.

(Score ten points for each right answer.)

Score: _____

2.

Julie Andrews	Mary Poppins
Renée Zellweger	Nurse Betty
Laura Dern	Citizen Ruth
Rita Hayworth	Gilda
Julia Roberts	Erin Brockovich

(Score four points for each right answer.)

Score: _____ Total so far: _____

3.

Pretty Woman	Julia Roberts
Belle de Jour	Catherine Deneuve
Leaving Las Vegas	Elisabeth Shue
Hard Eight	Gwyneth Paltrow
Monster	Charlize Theron

(Score four points for each right answer.)

Score: _____ Total so far: _____

4.

A) Casablanca
B) The Treasure of the Sierra Madre
C) Cool Hand Luke
D) Contact
E) The Usual Suspects

(Score four points for each right answer.)

Score: _____ Total so far: _____

5.

Rebecca (1940)

(Score ten points for the right answer.)

Score: _____ Total so far: _____

6.

All of the actresses won two Academy Awards for Best Actress except Katharine Hepburn who won four and Marilyn Monroe who won none.

(Score two points for each right answer, for a possible total of 20.)

Score: _____ Total so far: _____

7.

Halle Berry in 2001 for Monster's Ball.

(Score ten for the right answer.)

Score: _____ Total so far: _____

8.

Meryl Streep 16 times. She won twice, as best actress in Sophie's Choice (1982) and as best supporting actress in Kramer vs. Kramer (1979).

(Score ten for the right answer. Add two bonus points for correcting identifying the films.)

Score: _____ Total so far: _____

9.

Jack Nicholson 12 times. He won three times, twice for best actor: in 1975 for his role in One Flew Over the Cuckoo's Nest and in 1997 for As Good as It Gets; and once for best actor in a supporting role in 1983 for Terms of Endearment.

(Score ten for the right answer. Add two bonus points for correcting identifying the films.)

Score: _____ Total so far: _____

10.

Avatar (2009) with nearly $3-billion last time I checked is the highest grossing film of all time. By comparison, The Godfather from 1972 grossed a relatively paltry $245-million.

(Score ten for the right answer.)

Score: _____ Total so far: _____

11.

Marlon Brando for On the Waterfront (1954) and The Godfather (1972)
Gary Cooper for Sergeant York (1941) and High Noon (1952)
Tom Hanks for Philadelphia (1993) and Forrest Gump (1994)
Dustin Hoffman for Kramer vs. Kramer (1979) and Rain Man (1988)
Sean Penn for Mystic River (2003) and Milk (2008)

(Score four points for each right answer. Add two bonus points for any correct film identification.)

Score: _____ *Total so far:* _____

12.

Tom Hanks	Forrest Gump
Gary Cooper	Sergeant York
Peter Sellers	Dr. Strangelove
Henry Fonda	Mister Roberts
Anthony Hopkins	Nixon

(Score four points for each right answer.)

Score: _____ *Final score (your movie buff IQ):* _____